Switching *to the* Mac

THE MISSING MANUAL

*The book that
should have been
in the box*

Switching *to the* Mac
THE MISSING MANUAL

David Pogue and Adam Goldstein

POGUE PRESS™
O'REILLY®

Beijing • Cambridge • Farnham • Köln • Paris • Sebastopol • Taipei • Tokyo

Switching to the Mac: The Missing Manual, Tiger Edition

by David Pogue and Adam Goldstein

Copyright © 2005 David Pogue. All rights reserved.
Printed in the United States of America.

Published by O'Reilly Media, Inc., 1005 Gravenstein Highway North, Sebastopol, CA 95472.

O'Reilly Media books may be purchased for educational, business, or sales promotional use. Online editions are also available for most titles: *safari.oreilly. com*. For more information, contract our corporate/institutional sales department: (800) 998-9938 or *corporate@oreilly.com*.

September 2005:   First Edition.
March 2006:   Second Printing.
July 2006:   Third Printing.

RepKover.™ This book uses RepKover™, a durable and flexible lay-flat binding.

ISBN: 0-596-00660-8

Table of Contents

The Missing Credits

About the Author

David **Pogue** is the weekly tech columnist for the *New York Times*, an Emmy-winning correspondent for *CBS News Sunday Morning*, and the creator of the Missing Manual series. He's the author or co-author of 39 books, including 17 in this series and six in the "For Dummies" line (including *Macs, Magic, Opera,* and *Classical Music*). In his other life, David is a former Broadway show conductor, a magician, and a pianist. News, photos, links to his columns and weekly videos await at *www.davidpogue.com.* He welcomes feedback about his books by email at *david@pogueman.com.*

Adam **Goldstein** is the author of *AppleScript: The Missing Manual,* and has contributed to a number of other titles, including *Mac OS X: The Missing Manual, Mac OS X Power Hound,* and *Google: The Missing Manual.* In his ample free time, Adam attends M.I.T. Email: *mail@goldfishsoft.com.* Web: *www.goldfishsoft.com.*

About the Creative Team

Nan Barber (copy editor, previous edition) co-authored *Office X for the Macintosh: The Missing Manual* and *Office 2001 for Macintosh: The Missing Manual.* As the principal copy editor for this series, she has edited the titles on iPhoto, Mac OS 9, AppleWorks 6, iMovie, Dreamweaver, Windows XP, and many others.

Phil Simpson (design and layout) works out of his office in Southbury, Connecticut, where he has had his graphic design business since 1982. He is experienced in many facets of graphic design, including corporate identity, publication design, and corporate and medical communications. Email: *pmsimpson@earthlink.net.*

Winn Schwartau (technical editor) is one of the country's leading experts on information security and electronic privacy. He's the author of numerous books and novels, a sought-after speaker and consultant, and a contributor to *Wired,* the *New York Times, Information Week, Network World, ComputerWorld,* and dozens of other publications. Email: *winn@thesecurityawarenesscompany.com.*

Acknowledgments

The Missing Manual series is a joint venture between the dream team introduced on these pages and O'Reilly Media: Tim O'Reilly, Mark Brokering, and company. I'm grateful to all of them, and also to a few people who did massive favors for this book. They include Joseph Schorr, who wrote the original version of Chapter 6; John

Rizzo, technical editor for the first edition; Brook Stein, Apple's "Switch" guru; John Cacciatore for his proofreading smarts; and Lesa Snider, beta-reader extraordinaire. Thanks to David Rogelberg for believing in the idea, and above all, to Jennifer, Kelly, Tia, and Jeffrey, who make these books—and everything else—possible.

—David Pogue

I would like to acknowledge, as always, my parents and sister. During the work on this book, their tolerance for my hours writing and editing was within a few percentage points of perfect. Without that (and without the complimentary food and shelter), this book never would have been possible.

In particular, I would like to thank David Pogue, who gave me the amazing opportunity to work on a real Missing Manual once again—and who was responsible for most of the writing, editing, and screen photography in this book. And I'll never forget: It was David's example that inspired me to start writing books in the first place.

—Adam Goldstein

The Missing Manual Series

Missing Manual books are superbly written guides to computer products that don't come with printed manuals (which is just about all of them). Each book features a handcrafted index; cross-references to specific page numbers (not just "See Chapter 14"); and RepKover, a detached-spine binding that lets the book lie perfectly flat without the assistance of weights or cinder blocks. Recent and upcoming titles include:

- *Mac OS X: The Missing Manual,* Tiger Edition by David Pogue
- *iPhoto 6: The Missing Manual* by David Pogue and Derrick Story
- *iMovie 6 & iDVD: The Missing Manual* by David Pogue and Derrick Story
- *iPod & iTunes: The Missing Manual,* Fourth Edition by J.D. Biersdorfer
- *AppleScript: The Missing Manual* by Adam Goldstein
- *Office 2004 for Macintosh: The Missing Manual* by Mark H. Walker, Franklin Tessler, and Paul Berkowitz
- *FileMaker Pro 8: The Missing Manual* by Geoff Coffey and Susan Prosser
- *Google: The Missing Manual* by Sarah Milstein and Rael Dornfest
- *eBay: The Missing Manual* by Nancy Conner
- *Dreamweaver 8: The Missing Manual* by David Sawyer McFarland
- *Flash 8: The Missing Manual* by Emily Moore
- *CSS: The Missing Manual* by David Sawyer McFarland
- *Windows XP Home Edition: The Missing Manual,* 2nd Edition by David Pogue
- *Windows Vista: The Missing Manual,* by David Pogue

Introduction

Why are Windows PC people getting Macs all of a sudden?

Maybe the iPod's coolness factor is rubbing off onto the rest of Apple's product line. Maybe people have grown weary of their boring beige and black boxes. Or maybe they've just spent one Saturday too many dealing with viruses, worms, spyware, excessive startup processes, questionable firewalls, inefficient permissions, and all the other land mines strewn across the Windows world.

In any case, there's never been a better time to make the switch. Mac OS X version 10.4 has been hailed as the best operating system on earth; it's gorgeous, easy to understand, and virus-free. Apple's computers are in top form, too, complete with features like built-in Ethernet, DVD burners, and two different kinds of wireless connections. Among laptops, the story is even better: Most of Apple's laptops cost less than similarly outfitted Windows laptops, yet weigh less. Plus, they look a lot cooler.

And then there's that Intel processor that sizzles away inside all 2006 Mac models. It not only gives you delicious speed, but it also lets you *run Windows XP*—and Windows XP programs—at blazing speed, right there on your Macintosh. (Hell has really frozen over this time.) Because you were smart enough to wait until now to pick up this book, you can enjoy Appendix B, "Running Windows on the Mac," which makes its debut in this printing.

That's not to say, however, that switching to the Mac is all sunshine and bunnies. The Macintosh is a different machine, running a different operating system, and built by a company with a different philosophy—a fanatical perfectionist/artistic zeal. When it comes to their missions and ideals, Apple and Microsoft have about as much in common as a melon and a shoehorn.

In any case, you have three challenges before you. First, you'll probably want to copy your Windows stuff over to the new Mac. Some of that is easy to transfer (photos, MP3s, Microsoft Office documents) and some is trickier to extract (email messages, address books, buddy lists).

Second, you have to assemble a suite of Macintosh programs that do what you're used to doing in Windows. Most programs from Microsoft, Adobe, Macromedia, and other major players are available in nearly identical Mac and Windows formats. But occasionally, it's more difficult: Many second-tier programs are available only for Windows, and it takes some research (or Chapter 7 of this book) to help you find Macintosh replacements.

Finally, you have to learn Mac OS X itself. In some respects, it resembles the latest versions of Windows: There's a taskbar-like thing, a Control Panel–like thing, and, of course, a Trash can. At the same time, hundreds of features you thought you knew have been removed, replaced, or relocated. (If you ever find yourself groping for an old favorite feature, see Appendix A, the "Where'd It Go?" dictionary.)

Note: In Mac OS X, the X is meant to be a Roman numeral, pronounced "ten." Unfortunately, many people see "Mac OS X" and say "Mac Oh Ess Sex." That's a sure way to get made fun of by Mac nerds.

What Mac OS X Gives You

These days, a key attraction of the Mac—at least as far as switchers are concerned—is its security features. There isn't yet a single widespread Mac OS X virus. (Even Microsoft Word macro viruses don't run "correctly" in Mac OS X.) For many people, that's a good enough reason to move to Mac OS X right there.

Along the same lines, there have been no reported sightings of *adware* (software that displays annoying ads when you use your Web browser) or *spyware* (malicious software that tracks your computer use and reports it back to a shady company) for Mac

---

FREQUENTLY ASKED QUESTION

All About "Tiger"

What's this business about Tiger?

Like Microsoft, Apple develops its wares in secret, giving new products code names to throw outsiders off the scent. Apple's code names for Mac OS X and its descendants all refer to big cats: Mac OS X was Cheetah, 10.1 was Puma, 10.2 was Jaguar, 10.3 was Panther, and 10.4 is Tiger. Apple has even announced that 10.5 (available in late 2006 or early 2007) will be called Leopard.

Usually, software code names are dropped as soon as the

products are complete, at which time the marketing department provides the real names. In Mac OS X's case, though, Apple thinks that its cat names are cool enough to retain for the finished product.

It makes you wonder what Apple plans to call future versions. Since Apple only increases the decimal point with each major upgrade, it's got five big cats to go before it hits Mac OS XI.

Let's see: Bobcat, Cougar...um...Ocelot?

OS X. Mail, Mac OS X's built-in email program, deals surprisingly well with *spam*—the unsolicited junk email that's become the scourge of the Internet.

If you ask the average person why the Mac isn't overrun by viruses and spyware, as Windows is, they'll probably tell you, "Because the Mac's market share is too small for the bad guys to write for."

That may be true (although 25 million machines isn't too shabby, as targets go). But there's another reason, too: Mac OS X is a very young operating system, written only a few years ago, with security in mind. (Contrast with Windows, whose original versions were written before the Internet even existed.) Mac OS X is simply designed better. Its built-in firewall makes it virtually impossible for hackers to break into your Mac, and the system insists on getting your permission before *anything* gets installed on your Mac. Nothing can get installed behind your back, as it can in Windows.

But freedom from gunkware and viruses is only one big-ticket item. Here are a few other joys of becoming a Mac fan:

- **Stability.** You and your Mac may go for years without ever witnessing a system crash. Sure, it's technically possible for Mac OS X to crash—but few have actually witnessed such an event. Rumors of such crashes circulate on the Internet like Bigfoot sightings. (If it ever happens to you, turn promptly to the Appendix.)

  Underneath the shimmering, translucent desktop of Mac OS X is Unix, the industrial strength, rock-solid OS that drives many a Web site and university. It's not new by any means; in fact, it's decades old, and has been polished by generations of programmers. That's precisely why Apple CEO Steve Jobs and his team chose it as the basis for the NeXT operating system, which Jobs worked on during his 12 years away from Apple and which Apple bought in 1997 to turn into Mac OS X.

- **No nagging.** Unlike Windows XP, Mac OS X isn't copy-protected. You can install the same copy on your desktop and laptop Macs, if you have a permissive conscience. When you buy a new Mac, you're never, ever asked to type in a code off a sticker. Nor must you "register," "activate," sign up for ".NET Passport," or endure any other friendly suggestions unrelated to your work. In short, Mac OS X leaves you alone.

- **Sensational software.** Mac OS X comes with several dozen useful programs, from Mail (for email) to a 3-D, voice-activated Chess program. The most famous programs, though, are the famous Apple "i-Apps": iTunes for working with audio files, iMovie for editing video, iPhoto for managing your digital photos, and so on. You also get iChat, an AOL-compatible instant messaging program that also offers videoconferencing, and iCal, a calendar program. (This book covers the basics of all of them.)

- **Simpler everything.** Most applications in Mac OS X show up as a single icon. All of the support files are hidden away inside, where you don't have to look at them. In general, you can remove a program from your Mac just by dragging that one application icon to the Trash, without having to worry that you're leaving scraps behind; there is no Add/Remove Programs program on the Macintosh.

- **Desktop features.** Microsoft is a neat freak. Windows XP, for example, is so opposed to your using the desktop as a parking lot for icons, it actually interrupts you every 60 days to sweep all your infrequently used icons into an "Unused" folder.

  The Mac approach is different. Mac people often leave their desktops absolutely littered with icons. As a result, Mac OS X offers a long list of useful desktop features that will be new to you, the Windows refugee.

  For example, *spring-loaded* folders let you drag an icon into a folder within a folder within a folder with a single drag, without leaving a wake of open windows. An optional second line under an icon's name tells you how many items are in a folder, what the dimensions are of a graphic, and so on. And there's a useful column view, which lets you view the contents of many nested folders at a glance. (You can think of it as a horizontal version of Windows Explorer.)

  When your screen gets cluttered with windows, you can temporarily hide all of them with a single keystroke. If you want to see *all* the windows on your screen without any of them overlapping, Mac OS X's Exposé feature is your best friend (page 104).

  Apple didn't combine Web searching and disk searching functions into a single, sluggish Search program. Instead, a speedy, system-wide Find command called Spotlight, new in Tiger, is accessible from the menu bar of any program. It searches not just the names of your files and folders, but also the words *inside* your documents, and can even search your email, calendar, address book, Web bookmarks, and about 100 other kinds of data, all at once.

  Finally, in Tiger, Apple added one of the coolest features ever to grace a computer screen. It's called Dashboard, and it lets you summon dozens of mini-programs—a calculator, weather forecaster, dictionary, and so on—with a single keystroke, and dismiss them just as easily. You can download more of these so-called widgets from the Internet, making it even easier to find TV listings, Google search results, and more, no matter what program you're using at the moment.

- **Advanced graphics.** What Mac programmers get excited about is the set of advanced graphics technologies called *Quartz* (for two-dimensional graphics) and *OpenGL* (for three-dimensional graphics). For the rest of us, these technologies translate into a beautiful, translucent look for the desktop (a design scheme Apple calls Aqua); smooth-looking (*antialiased*) onscreen lettering; and the ability to turn any document on the screen into an Adobe Acrobat (PDF) file. And then there are the slick animations that permeate every aspect of Mac OS X: the rotating-cube effect when you switch from one logged-in user to another, the "Genie" effect when you minimize a window to the Dock, and so on.

- **Advanced networking.** When it comes to hooking up your computer to others, including those on the Internet, few operating systems can touch Mac OS X. It offers advanced features like *multihoming,* which lets your laptop switch automatically from its cable modem settings to its wireless or dial-up modem settings when you take it on the road.

If you're not so much a switcher as an *adder* (you're getting a Mac but keeping the PC around), you'll be happy to hear that Macs and Windows PCs can "see" each other on a network automatically, too. As a result, you can open, copy, and work on files on each other's machines as though the religious war between Macs and PCs had never even existed.

- **Voice control, keyboard control.** You can operate almost every aspect of every program entirely from the keyboard—or even by voice. These are terrific timesavers for efficiency freaks. In fact, the Mac can also read aloud *any text in any program*, including Web pages, email, your novel, you name it. You can even turn the Mac's spoken performance into an MP3 file, ready to transfer to a CD or a music player to enjoy on the road.

- **Full buzzword compliance.** You can't read an article about Mac OS X without hearing certain technical buzzwords that were once exclusively the domain of computer engineers: *preemptive multitasking, multithreading, symmetrical multiprocessing, dynamic memory allocation,* and *memory protection,* for example.

  What it all adds up to is that Mac OS X is very stable; that a crashy program can't crash the whole machine; that the Macintosh can exploit multiple processors; and that the Mac can easily do more than one thing at once—downloading files, playing music, and opening a program, for example—all simultaneously.

- **A command-line interface.** In general, Apple has completely hidden from you every trace of the Unix operating system that lurks beneath Mac OS X's beautiful skin. For the benefit of programmers and other technically oriented fans, however, Apple left uncovered a tiny passageway into that far more complex realm: Terminal, a program in your Applications→Utilities folder.

  This isn't a Unix book, so you won't find much instruction in using Terminal here. Still, if the idea of an all-text operating system gets you going, you can capitalize on the *command-line interface* of Mac OS X by typing out cryptic commands in the Terminal window, which the Mac executes instantly and efficiently (think DOS prompt, just faster and more useful).

What Mac OS X Takes Away

Besides quirks like viruses, spyware, and the Start menu, there are some substantial things on a PC that you lose when you switch to the Mac:

- **Programs.** As mentioned above, there are certain programs that are stubbornly Windows-only. You can always search for replacements—using Chapter 7 of this book as a guide, for example—but you may end up having to pay for them. And, of course, there are *certain* programs—like some proprietary accounting and laboratory software—where the Windows versions are simply irreplaceable. For those, you have to keep a PC around, use the Virtual PC emulation program (page 202), or restart your Intel-based Mac in Windows (page 6).

• **Peripherals.** Most add-on devices nowadays work equally well on both Windows PCs and Macs. That includes printers, scanners, digital cameras (still- and video-varieties), and "multifunction" devices that incorporate several of those attributes into one machine.

Unfortunately, not every company is that enlightened. If you have a device made by an obscure manufacturer—especially if the device is more than a few years old—it may not work with your Mac at all. That's especially true if the peripheral uses an old kind of connection (like SCSI) that isn't included on modern Macs.

Still, all hope is not lost. Chapter 8 can get you out of any hardware ruts you may find yourself in while making the Big Switch.

The Dual-Platform Option

Now that you can get a Mac for less than the cost of a washing machine, a once-radical proposition suddenly makes a lot more sense: *supplementing* your old PC with a Mac, rather than buying the Mac as a wholesale replacement. You get the ease-of-use and virus immunity of a Mac for your everyday use, but if you ever need to run an old program on your PC, it's there for you too.

It's never been easier to get a Mac and PC to coexist peacefully. With a little know-how, you can get the two talking over a network, sharing an Internet connection, and working with each other's files, as described on page 140.

About This Book

Switching to the Mac: The Missing Manual is divided into five parts, each containing several chapters:

• Part 1, **Welcome to Macintosh,** covers the essentials of the Macintosh. It's a crash course in everything you see on the screen when you turn on the machine: the Dock, Sidebar, icons, windows, menus, scroll bars, Trash, aliases,  menu, and so on.

• Part 2, **Moving In,** is dedicated to the actual process of hauling your software, settings, and even peripherals (like printers and monitors) across the chasm from the PC to the Mac. It covers both the easy parts (copying over your documents, pictures, and music files) and the harder ones (transferring your email, address books, buddy lists, and so on).

• Part 3, **Making Connections,** lets you know where to find your Internet settings on the old Windows machine—and where to plug them in on the Macintosh. In doing so, it covers Apple's Internet software suite: Mail, Address Book, Safari, and iChat.

• Part 4, **Putting Down Roots,** treads in more advanced topics—and aims to turn you into a Macintosh power user. It teaches you how to set up private accounts for people who share a single Mac, navigate the System Preferences program (the Mac equivalent of the Windows Control Panel), and operate the 50 freebie bonus programs that come with Mac OS X.

FUTURE SHOCK

Intel Inside

In the Windows world, those "Intel Inside" stickers are everyday sights. It came as a surprise to millions, though, when Apple announced that, starting in 2006, Macs would come with Intel chips inside.

Yes, *that* Intel. The company that Mac partisans had derided for years as part of the Dark Side. The company that Steve Jobs routinely belittled in his demonstrations of PowerPC chips (which IBM and Motorola supplied to Apple for more than a decade). The company whose marketing mascot Apple lit on fire in a 1996 attack ad on TV.

Why the change? Apple's computers can only be as fast as the chips inside them, and the chips that IBM had in the works just weren't keeping up with the industry. As one editorial put it, "Apple's doing a U-turn out of a dead-end road."

But behind the scenes, Apple had to execute two massive software transitions:

Operating Systems. Apple has already *recompiled* (rejiggered) Mac OS X to run on Intel chips, beginning with Mac OS X 10.4.4. The new Macs start up and run much faster than the old Macs, thanks to the endless march of speed improvements in the chip-making world.

The mind-blowing part, though, is that the new Macs are capable of running Microsoft Windows, too. That's right, the unthinkable has happened: you can now run thousands of Windows-only programs for business, accounting, gaming, and more, right on your Intel-based Mac—and dive right back into Mac OS X when you're finished.

You can take either of two avenues, both of which are described in Appendix B. First, you can install Apple's free Boot Camp utility, which lets you restart your Intel-based Mac in Windows. Alternatively (or additionally), you can install an $80 program called Parallels Workstation, whose huge advantage is that it doesn't require a restart; you can have Windows in a window while still remaining in Mac OS X.

The opposite, by the way, is *not* true: You can't run Mac OS X on, say, Dell and HP boxes. Hackers have attempted to jerry-rig such a system, but Apple has done everything in its legal and technical power to stop them.

Programs. The other half of the Mac experience, of course, is the library of programs: TextEdit, Photoshop, Word, and so on. Luckily, Intel-based Macs run today's versions of most programs seamlessly, thanks to an invisible translation program code-named Rosetta. You'll have only two indications that you're using a program originally designed for PowerPC-based Macs: first, you'll see a notation in the program's Get Info window (saying *Application: PowerPC* instead of *Application: Universal*). Second, you'll probably discover that the program isn't as fast as it used to be.

To make their programs perform at *full speed* on Intel-based Macs, programmers have to update their wares. All the big software companies have promised to make their programs into *universal binaries*—programs that run equally well on PowerPC- *and* Intel-based Macs with a double-click on the very same Finder icon. You can expect to have to pay an upgrade fee to get the new, universal software versions.

(Disk-intensive programs like video and audio editors are among those that won't run successfully, if at all, in Rosetta. If your job involves these apps, you should not upgrade to an Intel Mac until they've been issued as universal binaries.)

Back in the real world, the chip inside a computer is like the engine in a car. It determines how fast the thing can go, but most people do just fine without knowing the details what's going on inside. So if all this talk about architectures and chips makes your brain hurt, you can at least take comfort in one fact: No matter which kind of Mac you've got Tiger installed on, every feature, tip, and trick you've learned from this book will work exactly the same.

Note: Some of the material in this book is adapted from the bestselling *Mac OS X: The Missing Manual*, Tiger Edition. That book is a much fatter, more in-depth guide to Mac OS X (and a worthy investment if you grow into a true Macoholic).

At the end of the book, you'll find two appendixes. The first covers Mac OS X troubleshooting and installation. The second is the "Where'd It Go?" Dictionary—an essential reference for anyone who occasionally (or frequently) flounders to find some familiar control in the new, alien Macintosh environment.

About→These→Arrows

Throughout this book—and throughout the Missing Manual series—you'll find sentences like this one: "Open the System→Libraries→Fonts folder." That's shorthand for a much longer instruction that directs you to open three nested folders in sequence, like this: "On your hard drive, you'll find a folder called System. Open that. Inside the System folder window is a folder called Libraries; double-click it to open it. Inside *that* folder is yet another one called Fonts. Double-click to open it, too."

Similarly, this kind of arrow shorthand helps to simplify the business of choosing commands in menus, as shown in Figure I-1.

Figure I-1:
In this book, arrow notations help to simplify folder and menu instructions. For example, "Choose **&**→Dock →Position on Left" *is a more compact way of saying, "From the* **&** *menu, choose Dock; from the submenu that then appears, choose Position on Left," as shown here.*

About MissingManuals.com

If you visit *www.missingmanuals.com* and click the "Missing CD-ROM" link, you'll find a neat, organized, chapter-by-chapter list of the shareware and freeware mentioned in this book. (As noted on the inside back cover, having the software online instead of on a CD-ROM saved you $5 on the cost of the book.)

The Web site also offers corrections and updates to the book (to see them, click the book's title, then click Errata). In fact, you're encouraged to submit such corrections and updates yourself. In an effort to keep the book as up-to-date and accurate as possible, each time we print more copies of this book, we'll make any confirmed corrections you've suggested. We'll also note such changes on the Web site, so that you can mark important corrections into your own copy of the book, if you like.

In the meantime, we'd love to hear your own suggestions for books in the Missing Manual line. There's a place for that on the Web site, too, as well as a place to sign up for free email notification of new titles in the series.

The Very Basics

To use this book, and indeed to use any kind of computer, you need to know a few basics. This book assumes that, as somebody who's used Windows, you're already familiar with a few terms and concepts:

- **Clicking.** To *click* means to point the arrow cursor at something on the screen and then— without moving the cursor at all—to press and release the button on the mouse (or your laptop trackpad). To *double-click*, of course, means to click twice in rapid succession, again without moving the cursor at all. And to *drag* means to move the cursor while pressing the button.

    When you're told to ⌘-*click* something, you click while pressing the ⌘ key (which is next to the Space bar). Such related procedures as *Shift-clicking, Option-clicking*, and *Control-clicking* work the same way—just click while pressing the corresponding key at the bottom of your keyboard.

- **Menus.** The *menus* are the words at the top of your screen: File, Edit, and so on. (The at the top left corner of your screen is a menu, too.) Click any of these to make a list of commands appear, as though they're written on a window shade you've just pulled down.

    Some people click to open a menu and then release the mouse button. After reading the menu command choices, they click again on the one they want. Other people like to press the mouse button continuously after the initial click on the menu title, drag down the list to the desired command, and only then release the mouse button. Either method works fine.

- **Keyboard shortcuts.** If you're typing along in a burst of creative energy, it's sometimes disruptive to have to take your hand off the keyboard, grab the mouse, and then use a menu (for example, to use the Bold command). That's why many experienced Mac fans prefer to trigger menu commands by pressing certain combinations on the keyboard. For example, in most word processors, you can press ⌘-B to produce a **boldface** word. When you read an instruction like "press ⌘-B," start by pressing the ⌘ key; while it's down, type the letter B, and then release both keys.

- **Icons.** The colorful inch-tall pictures that appear in your various desktop folders are the *icons*—graphic symbols that represent each program, disk, and document on your computer. If you click an icon one time, it darkens; you've just *highlighted* or *selected* it, in readiness to manipulate it by using, for example, a menu command.

If you've mastered this much information, you have all the technical background you need to enjoy *Switching to the Mac: The Missing Manual.*

Part One:
Welcome to Macintosh

1

How the Mac Is Different

When you get right down to it, the job description of every operating system is pretty much the same. Whether it's Mac OS X, Windows XP, or Billy Bob's System-Software Special, any OS must serve as the ambassador between the computer and you, its human operator. It must somehow represent your files and programs on the screen so that you can open them; offer some method of organizing your files; present onscreen controls that affect your speaker volume, mouse speed, and so on; and communicate with your external gadgets, like disks, printers, and digital cameras.

In other words, Mac OS X offers roughly the same features as recent versions of Windows. That's the good news.

The bad news is that these features are called different things and parked in different spots. As you could have predicted, this rearrangement of features can mean a good deal of confusion for you, the Macintosh foreigner. For the first few days or weeks, you may instinctively reach for certain familiar features that simply aren't where you expect to find them, the way your tongue keeps sticking itself into the socket of the newly extracted tooth.

To minimize the frustration, therefore, read this chapter first. It makes plain the most important and dramatic differences between the Windows method and the Macintosh way.

Power On, Dude

As a critic might say, Apple is always consistent with its placement of the power button: It's different on every model.

On iMacs and Mac Minis, the power button is on the back panel. On Power Macs, it's on the front panel. And on laptop Macs, the button is near the upper-right corner of the keyboard. (Then again, if you have a laptop, you should get into the habit of just closing the lid when you're done working, and opening it to resume; the power button rarely plays a role in your life.)

In every case, though, the power button looks the same (Figure 1-1): it bears the ⏻ logo.

Figure 1-1:
Every Mac's power button looks like this, although it might be hard to find. The good news: Once you find it, it'll pretty much stay in the same place.

That One-Button Mouse

Every Windows mouse ever made has at least two mouse buttons. You use the left one for selecting things, and the right one for making shortcut menus appear (Figure 1-2). If you have a newer mouse, it might even have a scroll wheel in the middle for efficiently scrolling long documents and Web pages.

The mouse that came with your Mac, however, has only one mouse button—the equivalent of the Windows left mouse button. You use it exclusively for selecting and clicking things.

That's not to say that you can't "right-click" things with your one-button mouse—you can, as shown in Figure 1-2. On the Mac, though, you're supposed to produce shortcut menus by holding down the Control key as you click things on the screen.

Furthermore, if this Control-clicking business bothers you, you'll be happy to hear that two-button mice work just fine on the Mac, too; they let you go back to right-clicking things, and the little scroll wheel works, too.

You can connect the two-button USB mouse from an old PC, for example, or buy one for $10 or $15 to use with your Mac. (Heck, even Apple sells something called the Mighty Mouse. It *looks* like it has no buttons at all, but its single, unified shell has left-side and right-side sensors that let you left- and right-click.)

Note: You generally don't need to install driver software for USB mice, even if they're designed for use with Windows. Still, it's worth checking the manufacturer's Web site for Mac OS X drivers, since such software may give your two-button mouse even *more* features than it has by default. For example, the driver software may make a mouse's *third* and *fourth* buttons trigger special functions.

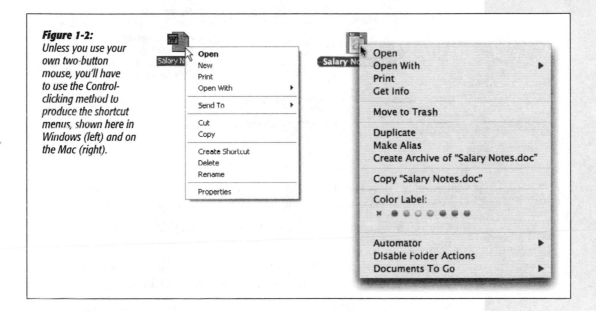

Figure 1-2:
Unless you use your own two-button mouse, you'll have to use the Control-clicking method to produce the shortcut menus, shown here in Windows (left) and on the Mac (right).

On, Off, and Sleep

If you're the only person who uses your Mac, finishing up a work session is simple. You can either turn off the machine or simply let it go to sleep, in any of several ways.

Sleep Mode

It's clear that Apple expects its customers *not* to shut down their machines between sessions, because the company has gone to great lengths to make doing so inconvenient. (For example, you have to save your work in all open programs before you can shut down.)

That's OK. *Sleep mode* (called Standby on the PC) consumes very little power, keeps everything you were doing open and in memory, and wakes the Mac up almost immediately when you press a key or click the mouse. To make your machine sleep, use any of these techniques:

- Choose ●→Sleep. (The ● menu, available no matter what program you're using, is at the upper-left corner of your screen.)

- Press the Power button on your machine—or, if you don't have one easily accessible, press Control-Eject key. On some models, doing so makes the Mac sleep immediately; on others, you have to click Sleep in the dialog box that appears (Figure 1-3).

- Just walk away, confident that the Energy Saver control panel described on page 365 will send the machine off to dreamland automatically at the specified time.

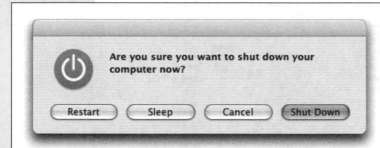

Figure 1-3:
Once the Shut Down dialog box appears, you can press the S key instead of clicking Sleep, R for Restart, Esc for Cancel, or Enter for Shut Down.

Restart

You shouldn't have to restart the Mac very often. But on those rare occasions, including severe troubleshooting mystification, here are a few ways to do it:

- Choose ●→Restart. Click Restart (or press Enter) in the confirmation dialog box.

- Press the Power button or Control-Eject to summon the dialog box shown in Figure 1-3, if your Mac doesn't automatically go to sleep. Click Restart (or type R).

- If all else fails, press Control-⌘-Power key. (On newer keyboards that lack a power key, use Control-⌘-Eject instead.) That restarts the Mac instantly, but you lose any chance to save changes in your open documents.

Shut Down

To shut down your machine completely (when you don't plan to use it for more than a couple of days or when you plan to transport it, for example), do one of the following:

- Choose ●→Shut Down. A simple confirmation dialog box appears; click Shut Down (or press Enter).

- Press Control-Option-⌘-Eject. (It's not as complex as it looks—the first three keys are all in a tidy row to the left of the Space bar.)

- Press the Power key or Control-Eject to summon the dialog box shown in Figure 1-3; click Shut Down (or press Enter).

- As a last resort, hold down the Power key for about five seconds. The Mac will shut down in a snap, but you'll lose any unsaved work.

Note: The Macintosh has no equivalent of the modern PC's Hibernate mode.

Log Out

If you share your Mac with other people, you should *log out* when you're done. Doing so ensures that your stuff is safe from the evil and the clueless when you're out of the room. To do it, choose →Log Out (or press Shift-⌘-Q). When the confirmation dialog box appears, click Log Out (or press Enter), or just wait for two minutes. The Mac hides your world from view and displays the login dialog box, ready for the next victim.

Another option is to use *fast user switching*—a feature that lets you switch from one user to another without actually logging out, just as in Windows XP. With fast user switching turned on, your Mac can have several people logged in at once, although only one person at a time actually sees his own desktop.

In either case, this whole accounts system is described in much more detail in Chapter 12.

Tip: If you press the Option key as you release the mouse when choosing the Restart, Shut Down, or Log Out commands, you eliminate the "Are you sure?" confirmation dialog box. The mouse clicks you save each time can really add up.

The Menu Bar

It won't take you long to discover that on the Macintosh, there's only one menu bar. It's always at the top of the screen. The names of these menus, and the commands inside them, change to suit the window you're currently using. That's different from Windows, where a separate menu bar appears at the top of *every* window.

Mac and Windows devotees can argue the relative merits of these two approaches until they're blue in the face. All that matters, though, is that you know where to look when you want to reach for a menu command. On the Mac, you always look upward.

Finder = Windows Explorer

In Mac OS X, the "home base" program—the one that appears when you first turn on the machine and shows you the icons of all your folders and files—is called the Finder. This is where you manage your folders and files, throw things away, manipulate disks, and so on. (You may also hear it called the *desktop,* since the items you find there mirror the files and folders you might find on a real-life desktop.)

Getting used to the term Finder is worthwhile right up front, because it comes up so often. For example, the first icon on your Dock is labeled Finder, and clicking it always takes you back to your desktop.

Dock = Taskbar

At the bottom of almost every Mac OS X screen sits a tiny row of photorealistic icons. This is the Dock, a close parallel to the Windows taskbar. (As in Windows, it may be hidden or placed on the left or right edge of the screen instead—but those are options primarily preferred by power users and eccentrics.)

The Dock displays the icons of all your open windows and programs, which are denoted by small black triangles beneath their icons. Clicking these icons opens the corresponding files, folders, disks, documents, and programs. If you click and hold (or right-click, or Control-click) an open program's icon, you'll see a pop-up list of the open windows in that program, along with Quit and a few other commands.

When you close a program, its icon disappears from the Dock (unless you've secured it there for easy access, as described on page 86).

Tip: You can cycle through the various open programs on your Mac by holding down the ⌘ key and pressing Tab repeatedly. (Sound familiar? It's just like Alt-Tabbing in Windows.) And each time you just *tap* ⌘-Tab, you bounce back and forth between the two programs you've used most recently.

What you may find confusing at first, though, is that the Dock also performs one function of the Windows Start menu: It provides a "short list" of programs and files that you use often, for easy access. To add a new icon to the Dock, just drag it there (put programs to the left of the divider line; everything else goes on the right). To remove an icon from the Dock, just drag the icon away from the Dock. As long as that item isn't actually open at the moment, it disappears from the Dock with a little animated puff of smoke when you release the mouse button.

The bottom line: On the Mac, a single interface element—the Dock—exhibits characteristics of *both* the Start menu (it lists frequently used programs) and the taskbar (it lists currently open programs and files).

If you're still confused, Chapter 3 should help clear things up.

Menulets = Tray

Most Windows fans refer to the row of tiny status icons at the lower-right corner of the screen as the *tray,* even though Microsoft's official term is the notification area. (Why use one syllable when eight will do?)

Macintosh fans wage a similar battle of terminology when it comes to the little menubar icons shown in Figure 1-4. Apple calls them Menu Extras, but Mac fans prefer to call them *menulets.*

In any case, these menu-bar icons are cousins of the Windows tray—that is, each is both an indicator and a menu that provides direct access to certain settings in System Preferences. One menulet lets you adjust your Mac's speaker volume, another lets you change the screen resolution, another shows you the remaining power in your laptop battery, and so on.

Figure 1-4:
The little icons at the upper-right corner of the Mac OS X screen are called Menu Extras or menulets. Almost every one is both a status indicator and a pop-up menu.

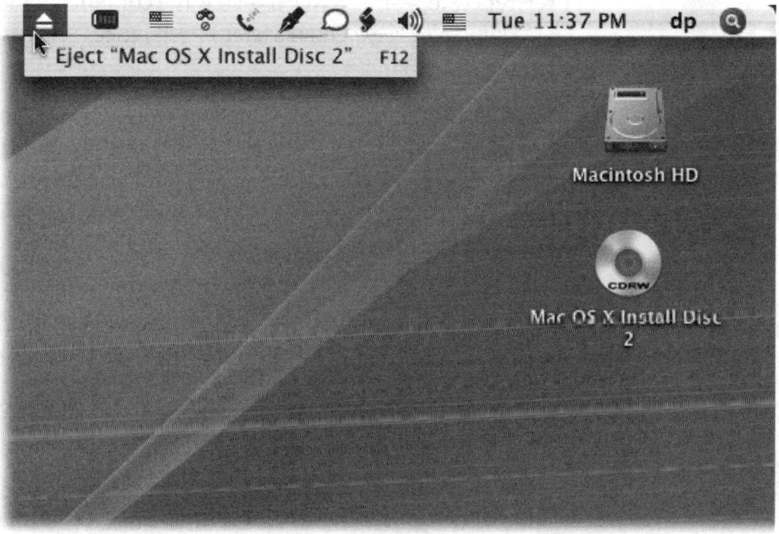

Making a menulet appear usually involves turning on a certain checkbox. These checkboxes lurk on the various panes of *System Preferences* (Chapter 13), which is the Mac equivalent of the Control Panel. (To open System Preferences, choose its name from the menu, or click the light-switch icon on the Dock.)

Here's a rundown of the various Apple menulets that you may encounter, complete with instructions on where to find this magic on/off checkbox for each.

Tip: The following descriptions indicate the official, authorized steps for installing a menulet. There is, however, a single folder on your hard drive that contains *all 23 of them* in a single window, so that you can install one with a quick double-click. To find them, open your hard drive→System→Library→CoreServices→Menu Extras folder.

- **AirPort status** lets you turn your wireless networking card on or off, join existing wireless networks, and create your own private ones. *To find the "Show" checkbox:* Open System Preferences→Network. From the "Show:" pop-up menu, choose AirPort.

- **Battery** shows how much power remains in your laptop's battery (laptops only). *To find the "Show" checkbox:* Open System Preferences→Energy Saver, and click the Options tab.

- **Bluetooth** (for connecting to Bluetooth devices, "pairing" your Mac with a cellphone, and so on). *To find the "Show" checkbox:* Open System Preferences→ Bluetooth. The "Show Bluetooth status in the menu bar" checkbox appears at the bottom of the Settings tab.

- **Classic.** Using this menulet, you can start or stop Classic (which is Mac OS X's "Mac OS 9 simulator," as described on page 123), open the Classic pane of System Preferences, or—this is weird—view the contents of the Mac OS 9 🍎 menu. *To find the "Show" checkbox:* Open System Preferences→Classic. Look near the middle of the Start/Stop pane.

- **Clock.** This is the standard menu-bar clock that's probably been sitting at the upper-right corner of your screen from Day 1. Click it to open a menu where you can check today's date, convert the menu-bar display to a tiny analog clock, and so on. *To find the "Show" checkbox:* Open System Preferences→Date & Time. On the Clock tab, turn on "Show the date and time."

- **Displays** adjusts screen resolution; on laptops with a projector or external monitor attached, it lets you turn screen mirroring on or off. *To find the "Show" checkbox:* Open System Preferences→Displays, and click the Display tab.

- **Eject disc.** This one's the oddball: There's no checkbox in System Preferences to make it appear. The fact that it even exists is something of a secret.

  To make it appear, open your System→Library→CoreServices→Menu Extras folder as described above, and double-click the Eject.menu icon. That's it! The Eject menulet appears.

  You'll discover that the menulet's wording changes. It might say "Open Combo Drive," "Close DVD-RAM Drive," "Eject [Name of Disc]," or whatever, to reflect your particular drive type and what's in it at the moment.

- **Fax.** This menulet reveals the current status of a fax you're sending or receiving, so you're not kept in suspense. *To find the "Show" checkbox:* Open System Preferences→Print & Fax, and click Faxing.

- **iChat.** Here's a quick way to let the world know, via iChat and the Internet, that you're away from your keyboard, or available and ready to chat. Choosing the Buddy List command is also a quick way to open iChat itself. *To find the "Show" checkbox:* Open iChat (in your Applications folder). Choose iChat→Preferences, click the General button, and turn on "Show status in menu bar."

- **PC Card.** You can use this item to eject a PC card that you've inserted into the slot in your PowerBook, if it has such a slot. To make it appear, open your System→Library→CoreServices→Menu Extras folder, and double-click the PCCard.menu icon.

- **PPPoE** (PPP over Ethernet) lets you control certain kinds of DSL connections. *To find the "Show" checkbox:* Open System Preferences→Network. From the "Show:" pop-up menu, choose Built-in Ethernet. Click the PPoE tab button.

- **PPP** lets you connect or disconnect from the Internet. *To find the "Show" checkbox:* Open System Preferences→Network. From the "Show:" pop-up menu, choose Internal Modem. Click the Modem tab button.

- **Remote Desktop** is a program, sold separately, that lets teachers or system administrators tap into your Mac from across the network. In fact, they can actually see what's on your screen and move the cursor around. The menulet lets you turn remote control on and off, send a message to the administrator, and so on. *To find the "Show" checkbox:* Open System Preferences→Sharing, and click Apple Remote Desktop.

- **Script menu** lists a variety of useful, ready-to-run *AppleScript* programs. (AppleScript is a fairly easy programming language that lets Mac programs share information with each other and act on it appropriately. These scripts—one searches and replaces text in a folder full of file names, one prepares a handsome sampler poster of the fonts you have installed, and so on—are intended to show off AppleScript's flexibility. *To find the "Show" checkbox:* Open your Applications folder, and open the program called AppleScript Utility.

- **Sync** is useful only if you have a .Mac account (page 147)—but in that case, it's *very* handy. It lets you start and stop the synchronization of your Mac's Web bookmarks, calendar, address book, keychains, and email with another Mac across the Internet, and it always lets you know the date of your last sync. *To find the "Show" checkbox:* Open System Preferences→.Mac, and click Sync.

- **Text Input** makes it easy for you to switch among different *text input modes*. You're probably most familiar with the normal keyboard. But what if your language, like Japanese Kanji, has hundreds of symbols in it? How will a 26-letter keyboard help you then? You'll need a floating palette of all of these symbols, and this menulet summons and dismisses such palettes. Details on page 369. *To find the "Show" checkbox:* Open System Preferences→International. Click the Input Menu tab.

- **User** identifies the account holder (page 321) who's logged in at the moment. To make this menulet appear (in bold, at the far right end of the menu bar), turn on *fast user switching,* which is described on page 338.

- **Volume,** of course, adjusts your Mac's speaker or headphones volume. *To find the "Show" checkbox:* Open System Preferences→Sound.

- **VPN** stands for virtual private networking, which is a system of letting you tap into a corporation's network so you can, for example, check your email from home. You can use the menulet to connect and disconnect, for example. *To find the "Show" checkbox:* Open the program called Internet Connect (in your Applications folder). Click the VPN button.

To remove a menulet, turn off the corresponding checkbox described above (or just drag the menulet off of your menu bar while pressing the ⌘ key). You can also rearrange menulets by ⌘-dragging them horizontally.

Keyboard Differences

Mac and PC keyboards are subtly different, too. Making the switch involves two big adjustments: Figuring out where the special Windows keys went (like Alt and Ctrl)—and figuring out what to do with the special Macintosh keys (like ⌘ and Option).

Where the Windows Keys Went

Here's how to find the Macintosh equivalents of familiar PC keyboard keys:

- **Ctrl key.** The Macintosh offers a key labeled Control (or, on laptops, "ctrl"), but it isn't the equivalent of the PC's Ctrl key. The Mac's Control key is primarily for helping you "right-click" things, as described above.

  Instead, the Macintosh equivalent of the *Windows* Ctrl key is the ⌘ key. It's right next to the Space bar, bearing both the cloverleaf symbol and the Apple logo. It's pronounced "command," although novices can often be heard calling it the "pretzel key," "Apple key," or "clover key."

  Most Windows Ctrl-key combos correspond perfectly to ⌘ key sequences on the Mac. The Save command is now ⌘-S instead of Ctrl-S, Open is ⌘-O instead of Ctrl-O, and so on.

Note: Mac keyboard shortcuts are listed at the right side of each open menu, just as in Windows. Unfortunately, they're represented in the menu with goofy symbols instead of their true key names. Here's your cheat sheet to the menu keyboard symbols: ⇧ represents the Shift key, ⌥ means the Option key, and ⌃ refers to the Control key.

- **Alt key.** On most Mac keyboards, a key on the bottom row of the Macintosh keyboard is labeled both Alt and Option (at least on Macs sold in the U.S.). This is the closest thing the Mac offers to the old Alt key.

  In many situations, keyboard shortcuts that involve the Alt key in Windows use the Option key on the Mac. For example, in Microsoft Word, the keyboard shortcut for the Split Document Window command is *Alt*-Ctrl-S in Windows, but *Option*-⌘-T on the Macintosh.

  Still, these two keys aren't exactly the same. Whereas the Alt key's most popular function is to control the menus in Windows programs, the Option key on the Mac is a "miscellaneous" key that triggers secret functions and secret characters.

  For example, when you hold down the Option key as you click the Close or Minimize button on a Macintosh window, you close or minimize *all* open desktop windows. And if you press the Option key while you type R, G, or 2, you get the ®, ©, and ™ symbols in your document, respectively. (See page 369 to find out how you can see which letters turn into which symbols when you press Option.)

- **⊞ key.** As you probably could have guessed, there is no Windows-logo key on the Macintosh. Then again, there's no Start menu to open by pressing it, either.

Tip: Just about any USB keyboard works on the Mac, even if the keyboard was originally designed to work with a PC. Depending on the manufacturer of the keyboard, the Windows-logo key may work just like the Mac's ⌘ key.

- **Backspace and Delete.** On the Mac, the backspace key is labeled Delete, although it's in exactly the same place as the Windows Backspace key.

  The Delete key in Windows (technically, the *forward delete* key, because it deletes the character to the right of the insertion point) is a different story. On a desktop Macintosh, it's labeled with the word *Del* and the ⌦ symbol.

  On laptop Macs, this key is missing. You can still perform a forward delete, however, by pressing the regular Delete key while pressing the Fn key in the lower-left corner of the laptop keyboard.

- **Enter.** Most full-size Windows keyboards have *two* Enter keys: one at the right side of the alphabet keyboard, and one at the lower-right corner of the number pad. They're identical in function; pressing either one serves to "click" the OK button in a dialog box, for example.

  On the Mac, the big key on the number pad still says Enter, but the key on the alphabet keyboard is labeled Return. Most of the time, their function is identical—once again, either can "click" the OK button of a dialog box. Every now and then, though, you'll run across a Mac program where Return and Enter do different things. In Microsoft Word for Mac OS X, for example, Shift-*Return* inserts a line break, but Shift-*Enter* creates a page break.

Note: See page 236 for a summary of the Mac's text-navigation keystrokes.

What the Special Mac Keys Do

So much for finding Windows keys you're used to. There's another category of keys worth discussing, however: keys on the modern Macintosh keyboard that you've never seen before. For example:

- ◀, ◀)), ◀. These keys give you one-touch control of your Mac's volume—a great feature when, for example, you intend to use your laptop in a library or in church. (Yes, every Macintosh has built-in speakers. You're welcome to attach external ones or a pair of headphones, but you don't have to.) The three symbols here mean Quieter, Louder, and Mute, respectively. (Press Mute a second time to turn the speakers back on.)

- ⏏. This key, in the upper-right corner of the keyboard, means Eject. When you press it, your Mac's CD or DVD drawer opens so that you can insert or remove a disc. Or, if your Mac has a *slot-loading* CD or DVD drive (one that slurps in the disc rather than providing a tray for it), pressing the Eject key spits out whatever disc is in the machine.

contained in a single icon, too (rather than being composed of hundreds of little support files), which makes copying or deleting them extremely easy.

Home Folder

Your documents, files, and preferences, meanwhile, sit in an important folder called your *Home folder*. Inside are folders that closely resemble the My Documents, My Pictures, and My Music folders on Windows—except that on the Mac, they don't say "My."

One way to find it is to open the Macintosh HD (hard drive) window, double-click the Users folder inside it, and then double-click the folder inside *it* that bears your name and looks like a house (see Figure 1-7). Here, at last, is the window that you'll eventually fill with new folders to organize, back up, and so on.

Mac OS X is rife with shortcuts for opening this all-important folder, however.

- Choose Go→Home.

- Press Shift-⌘-H.

- Click the Home icon in the Sidebar (page 88).

- Click the Home icon on the Dock. (If you don't see one, consult page 88 for instructions on how to put one there.)

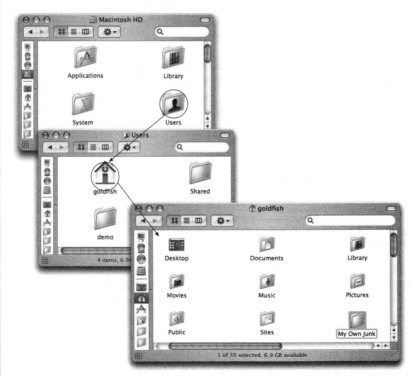

Figure 1-7:
For the most part, the folders you care about on the Mac are the Applications folder in the main hard drive window (top) and your own Home folder (middle and bottom). You're welcome to save your documents and park your icons almost anywhere on your Mac (except inside the System folder or other people's Home folders).

But keeping your work in your Home folder makes backing up and file sharing a heck of a lot easier.

The rationale for forcing you to keep all of your stuff in a single folder is described in Chapter 12. (Windows 2000 and Windows XP work very similarly.) For now, it's enough to note that the approach has some major advantages. Most notably, by keeping such tight control over which files go where, Mac OS X keeps itself pure—and very, very stable.

Furthermore, keeping all of your stuff in a single folder makes it very easy for you to back up your work. It also makes life easier when you try to connect to your machine from elsewhere in the office (over the network) or elsewhere in the world (over the Internet).

System Folder

This folder is the same idea as the Windows or WINNT folder on a PC, in that it contains hundreds of files that are critical to the functioning of the operating system. These files are so important that moving or renaming them could render the computer useless, as it would in Windows. And although there are thousands of files within, many are hidden for your protection.

For maximum safety and stability, you should ignore Mac OS X's System folder just as thoroughly as you ignored the old Windows folder.

Window Controls

As in Windows, a window on the Mac is framed by an assortment of doodads and gizmos (Figure 1-8). You'll need these to move a window, close it, resize it, scroll it, and so on. But once you get to know the ones on a Macintosh, you're likely to be pleased by the amount of thought those fussy perfectionists at Apple have put into their design.

Here's an overview of the various Mac OS X window-edge gizmos and what they do.

Title Bar

When several windows are open, the darkened window name and colorful upper-left controls tell you which window is *active* (in front). Windows in the background have gray, dimmed lettering and gray upper-left control buttons. As in Windows, the title bar also acts as a *handle* that lets you move the entire window around on the screen.

Tip: Here's a nifty keyboard shortcut with no Windows equivalent: You can cycle through the different open windows in one program without using the mouse. Just press ⌘-` (that's the tilde key, to the left of the number 1 key). With each press, you bring a different window forward within the current program. It works both in the Finder and in your programs.

Perhaps more usefully, you can use Control-F4 to cycle through the open windows in *all* programs.

After you've opened one folder inside another, the title bar's secret *folder hierarchy menu* is an efficient way to backtrack—to return to the enclosing window. Figure 1-9 reveals everything about the process after this key move: pressing the ⌘ key as you click the name of the window. (You can release the ⌘ key immediately after clicking.)

Tip: Instead of using this title bar menu, you can also jump to the enclosing window by pressing ⌘-up arrow. Pressing ⌘-down arrow takes you back into the folder you started in. (This makes more sense when you try it than when you read it.)

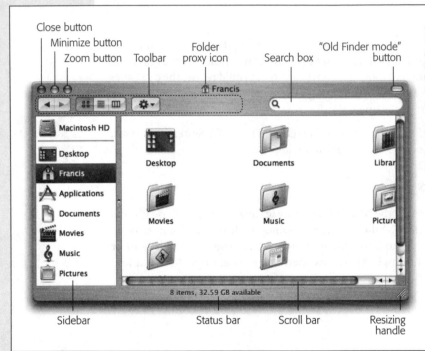

Close button
Minimize button
Zoom button   Toolbar   Folder proxy icon   Search box   "Old Finder mode" button

Sidebar   Status bar   Scroll bar   Resizing handle

Figure 1-8:
When Steve Jobs unveiled Mac OS X at a Macworld Expo in 1999, he said that his goal was to oversee the creation of an interface so attractive, "you just want to lick it." Desktop windows, with their juicy, fruit-flavored controls, are a good starting point.

One more title bar trick: By double-clicking the title bar, you *minimize* the window (see the facing page).

Tip: The Option key means "apply this action to all windows." For example, Option-double-clicking any title bar minimizes *all* desktop windows, sending them flying to the Dock. Option-clicking the Close button closes all open desktop windows, and so on. (The Option-key trick doesn't close all windows in every program, however—only those in the current program. Option-closing a Safari window closes *Safari* windows, but your desktop windows remain open. Moreover, Option-closing doesn't work at all in Microsoft Office programs.)

Close Button

As the tip of your cursor crosses the three buttons at the upper-left corner of a window, tiny symbols appear inside them: x, –, and +. The most important window gadget is the close button, the red, droplet-like button in the upper-left corner (see Figure 1-8). It closes the window, exactly like the X button at the upper-*right* corner in Windows. Learning to reach for the upper-left corner instead of the upper-right will probably confound your muscle memory for the first week of using the Macintosh.

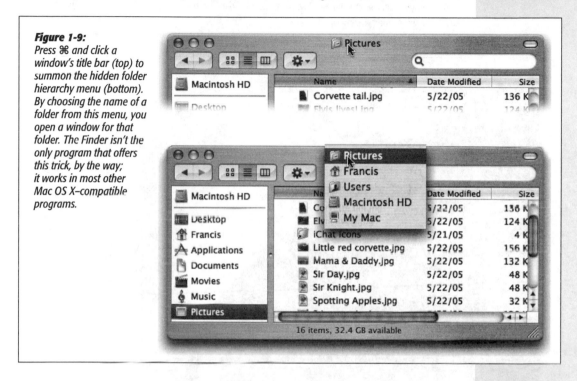

Figure 1-9:
Press ⌘ and click a window's title bar (top) to summon the hidden folder hierarchy menu (bottom). By choosing the name of a folder from this menu, you open a window for that folder. The Finder isn't the only program that offers this trick, by the way; it works in most other Mac OS X–compatible programs.

If you can't break the old habit, you can avoid the frustration entirely by learning the keyboard shortcut: ⌘-W (for *window*)—an easier keystroke to type than the Windows version (Alt-F4), which for most people is a two-handed operation. If you get into the habit of dismissing windows with that deft flex of your left hand, you'll find it far easier to close several windows in a row, because you don't have to aim for successive close buttons.

Tip: If, while working on a document, you see a tiny dot in the center of the Close button, Mac OS X is trying to tell you that you haven't yet saved your work. The dot goes away when you save the document.

Minimize Button

Click this yellow drop of gel to minimize any Mac window, sending it shrinking, with a genie-like animated effect, into the right end of the Dock, where it now appears as an icon. It's exactly like minimizing a window in Windows, except that the window is now represented by a Dock icon rather than a taskbar button (Figure 1-10). To bring the window back to full size, click the newly created Dock icon. See Chapter 3 for more on the Dock.

Tip: If you enjoy the ability to roll up your windows in this way, remember that you actually have a bigger target than the tiny minimize button. The entire striped title bar becomes a giant minimize button when you double-click anywhere on it.

Better yet, you can minimize a window from the keyboard (in most programs) by pressing ⌘-M. That's a keystroke worth memorizing on Day One.

Figure 1-10:
Clicking the Minimize button sends a window scurrying down to the Dock, collapsing in on itself as though being forced through a tiny, invisible funnel. If you collapse a window in this way, a tiny icon appears on the corner of its minimized image to identify the program it's running in.

Zoom Button

A click on this green geltab (see Figure 1-8) makes a desktop window just large enough to show you all of the icons inside it. If your monitor isn't big enough to show all the icons in a window, the zoom box resizes the window to show as many as possible. In either case, a second click on the zoom button restores the window to its original size. (The Window→Zoom Window command does the same thing.)

This should sound familiar: It's a lot like the Maximize button at the top right of a Windows window. On the Macintosh, however, the window rarely springs so big that it fills the *entire* screen, leaving a lot of empty space around the window contents; it only grows enough to show you as much of the contents as possible.

The Folder Proxy Icon

Virtually every Macintosh title bar features a small icon next to the window's name (Figure 1-11), representing the open window's actual folder or disk icon. In the Finder, dragging this tiny icon (technically called the *folder proxy icon*) lets you move or copy the folder to a different folder or disk, to the Trash, or into the Dock, without having to close the window first. (When clicking this proxy icon, hold down the mouse button for a half second, or until the icon darkens. Only then are you allowed to drag it.) It's a handy little function with no Windows equivalent.

Tip: In some programs, including Microsoft Word, dragging this proxy icon lets you move the *actual file* to a different disk or folder—without even leaving the program. It's a great way to make a backup of the document that you're working on without interrupting your work.

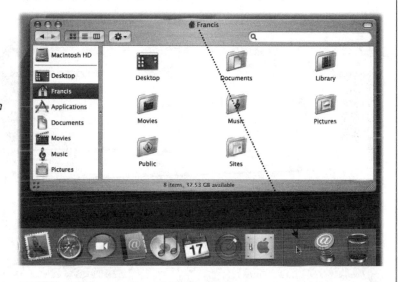

Figure 1-11:
When you find yourself confronting a Finder window that contains useful stuff, consider dragging its proxy icon to the Dock. You wind up installing its folder or disk icon there for future use. That's different from minimizing the window, which only puts an icon for the window itself into the Dock, and even then only temporarily.

The Finder Sidebar and Toolbar

Chapter 3 describes these fascinating desktop-window elements in great detail.

Toolbar Button

Mac OS X prefers to keep only one Finder window open at a time. That is, if a window called United States is filled with folders for the individual states, double-clicking the New York folder doesn't open a second window. Instead, the New York window replaces the United States window (Figure 1-12). Modern versions of Windows work exactly the same way.

So what if you've now opened inner folder B, and you want to backtrack to outer folder A? In that case, just click the tiny left-arrow button labeled Back, shown in Figure 1-11, or use one of these alternatives:

- Choose Go →Back.
- Press ⌘-[(left bracket).

• Press ⌘-up arrow.

None of that helps you, however, if you want to copy a file from one folder into another, or compare the contents of two windows. In such cases, you'll probably want to see both windows open at the same time.

You can open a second window using any of these techniques:

• Choose File→New Finder Window (⌘-N).

Tip: *The window that appears when you do this is your Home folder by default, but you can change that setting in Finder→Preferences→General.*

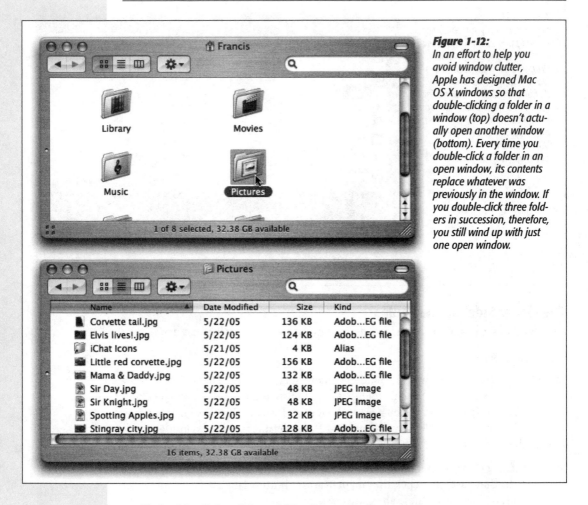

Figure 1-12:
In an effort to help you avoid window clutter, Apple has designed Mac OS X windows so that double-clicking a folder in a window (top) doesn't actually open another window (bottom). Every time you double-click a folder in an open window, its contents replace whatever was previously in the window. If you double-click three folders in succession, therefore, you still wind up with just one open window.

• ⌘-double-click a disk or folder icon.

• Double-click a folder or disk icon on your desktop.

- Choose File→Preferences, and turn on "Always open folders in a new window." Now when you double-click a folder, it always opens into a new window of its own.

Another alternative is to switch to "bare-bones window mode" (not the official Apple terminology). The upper-right corner of every Finder window contains a little button that looks like a half-inch squirt of Crest toothpaste. When you click it, you enter a hidden-toolbar, hidden-Sidebar mode. (You can also enter this mode by pressing Option-⌘-T, the equivalent for the View→Hide Toolbar command.)

In this mode, two things happen. First, the Finder window toolbar, identified in Figure 1-7, slides out of sight, along with the Sidebar on the left. Second, double-clicking a folder now opens a new corresponding window.

You can return to regular Mac OS X mode by clicking the toolbar button again, by pressing Option-⌘-T again, or by choosing View→Show Toolbar.

Note: You'll find this little white toolbar-control nubbin in a number of toolbar-endowed programs, including Mail, Preview, and others. Clicking it always makes the toolbar go away.

Scroll Bars

In general, scroll bars work on the Mac just as they do in Windows.

Tip: One key difference: Out of the box, the Mac's scroll-up arrow and scroll-down arrow are nestled together, at the same end of the scroll bar. To "fix" them so that they sit at opposite ends as in Windows, choose ⌘→System Preferences. Click Appearance. Where it says "Place scroll arrows," click "At top and bottom."

Mac OS X, however, introduces a new scroll bar option called "Scroll to here." Ordinarily, when you click into the scroll-bar track above or below the gelatinous handle, the window scrolls by one screenful. But your other option is to turn on "Scroll to here" mode in the Appearance panel of your System Preferences (see page 352). Now when you click in the scroll-bar track, the Mac considers the entire scroll bar a proportional map of the document and scrolls directly to the spot you clicked. That is, if you click at the very bottom of the scroll-bar track, you see the very last page.

It's worth noting, however, that the true speed expert eschews scroll bars altogether. The Mac has the usual complement of navigation keys: Page Up, Page Down, Home, and End (although these don't always work the way you're used to; see page 235). And if you bought a mouse that has a scroll wheel on the top, you can use it to scroll windows, too, without pressing any keys at all.

Resize Box

The lower-right corner of every standard Mac OS X window is ribbed, a design that's meant to imply that you can grip it by dragging. Doing so lets you resize and reshape the window, just as on the PC.

Unfortunately, you can't also change the shape of a Macintosh window by dragging its *edges*, as you can in Windows.

Status Bar

If you're using the "bare-bones" window view described above, you can choose View→Show Status Bar to get a handy information strip just beneath the title bar in every Finder window. It tells you how many icons are in the window ("14 items," for example) and the amount of free space remaining on the disk.

Otherwise, in normal Finder mode, those statistics show up at the *bottom* of each window.

Terminology Differences

There are enough other differences between Mac and Windows to fill 15 pages. Indeed, that's what you'll find the end of this book: an alphabetical listing of every familiar Windows feature and where to find its equivalent on the Mac.

As you read both that section of the book and the chapters that precede it, however, you'll discover that some functions are almost identical in Mac OS X and Windows, but have different names. Here's a quick-reference summary:

Windows term	Macintosh term
Control Panel	System Preferences
Drop-down menu	Pop-up menu
Program	Application
Properties	Get Info
Recycle Bin	Trash
Search command	Spotlight
Shortcuts	Aliases
Taskbar	Dock
Tray (notification area)	Menulets
Windows Explorer	Finder
Windows folder	System folder

With that much under your belt, you're well on your way to learning the ways of Mac OS X.

Windows and Icons

When you turn on a Mac, you hear a startup chime from the Mac's built-in speakers. You see the Apple logo as the machine warms up, followed by an animated, liquidy blue progress bar.

Logging In

What happens next depends on whether you are the Mac's sole proprietor or have to share it with other people in an office, school, or household.

- If it's your own Mac, and you've already been through the Mac OS X setup wizard (the "What's your time zone? What's your name?" screens that appear the first time you turn on a new Mac), no big deal. You arrive at the Mac OS X desktop.

- If it's a shared Mac, you may encounter the Login dialog box, shown in Figure 2-1. Click your name in the list, type your password, and then click Log In (or press Return). You arrive at the desktop. Chapter 12 covers much more of this business of user accounts and logging in.

The Elements of the Mac OS X Desktop

Most of the objects on your screen should seem familiar. They are, in fact, cousins of elements you already know from Windows. Here's a quick tour (see Figure 2-2).

Note: If your desktop looks absolutely nothing like this—no menus, no icons, almost nothing on the Dock—then somebody in charge of your Mac has turned on *Simple Finder mode* for you. Details on page 330.

Disk Icons

In the Mac world, the icons of your hard drive and any other disks attached to your Mac generally appear on your desktop for quick access.

Figure 2-1:
Left: On Macs that have been configured to accommodate different people at different times, one of the first things you see upon turning on the computer is this dialog box. Click your name. (If the list is long, you may have to scroll to find your name—or just type the first couple of letters of it.)

Right: Then type in your password and then click Log In (or press Return or Enter). If you've typed the wrong password, the entire dialog box vibrates, in effect shaking its little head, suggesting that you mistyped your password.

The Dock

This ribbon of translucent, almost photographic icons is a launcher for programs, files, folders, and disks you use often.

In principle, the Dock is very simple:

- Programs go on the left side. Everything else goes on the right, including documents, folders, disks, and minimized windows. (Figure 2-2 shows the dividing line.)

- You can add a new icon to the Dock by dragging it there. Rearrange Dock icons by dragging them like tiles on a puzzle. Remove a Dock icon by dragging it away from the Dock, and enjoy the animated puff of smoke that appears when you release the mouse button. (You can't remove the icon of a program that's currently open, however.)

- Click something *once* to open it. A tiny triangle underneath a program's icon lets you know that it's open.

- Each Dock icon sprouts a pop-up menu, similar to a shortcut menu. A folder can show you a list of what's inside, for example, while a program's pop-up menu gives you options to quit, hide the program, and so on. To see the menu, hold the mouse button down on a Dock icon, or Control-click it, or (if you have a two-button mouse) right-click it.

Figure 2-2:
The Mac OS X landscape looks like a futuristic version of a Windows desktop. This is just a starting point, however. You can dress it up with a different background picture, adjust your windows in a million ways, and fill the Dock with only the programs, disks, folders, and files you care about.

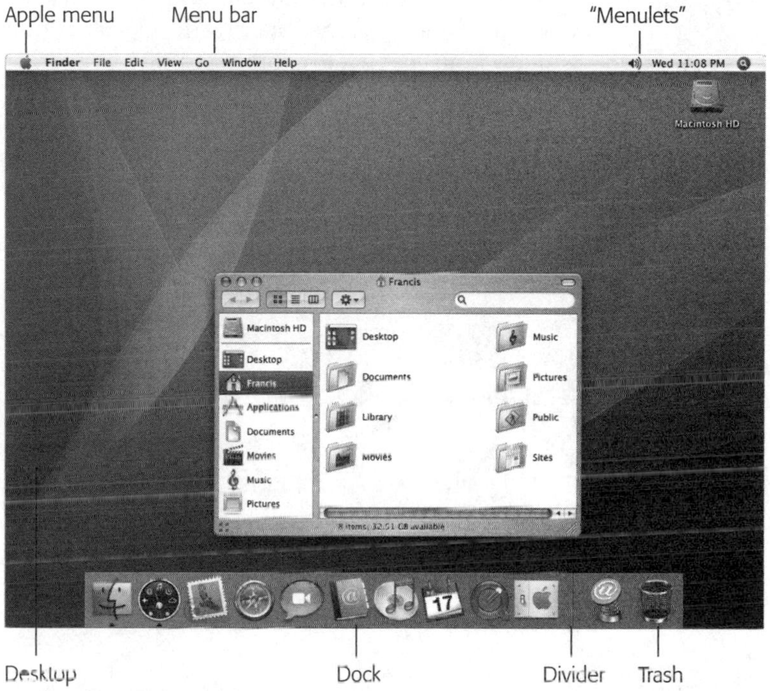

You can change the Dock's size, move it to the sides of your screen, or hide it entirely. Chapter 3 contains complete instructions for using and understanding the Dock.

The Menu

The menu at the top left of the screen houses important Mac-wide commands like Sleep, Restart, and Shut Down. In a sense, it's like the Start menu on a diet: It lists recent programs, system-wide functions, and includes a quick way to jump to System Preferences.

The Menu Bar

The first menu in every program, in boldface, tells you at a glance what program you're in. The commands in this Application menu include About (which tells you what version of the program you're using), Preferences, Quit, and others like Hide Others and Show All (which help you control window clutter, as described on page 100).

The File and Edit menus come next, exactly as in Windows. The last menu is almost always Help. It opens a miniature Web browser that lets you search the online Mac Help files for explanatory text.

Icon View

Chapter 1 provides a guided tour of the various gizmos around the *edges* of a window (the Close button, Resize box, and so on)—but what about what's *inside* a window?

As it turns out, you can view the files and folders in a desktop window in any of three ways: as icons, as a single list, or in a series of neat columns (see Figure 2-3). To switch a window from one view to another, just click one of the three corresponding icons in

Icon/List/Column view buttons

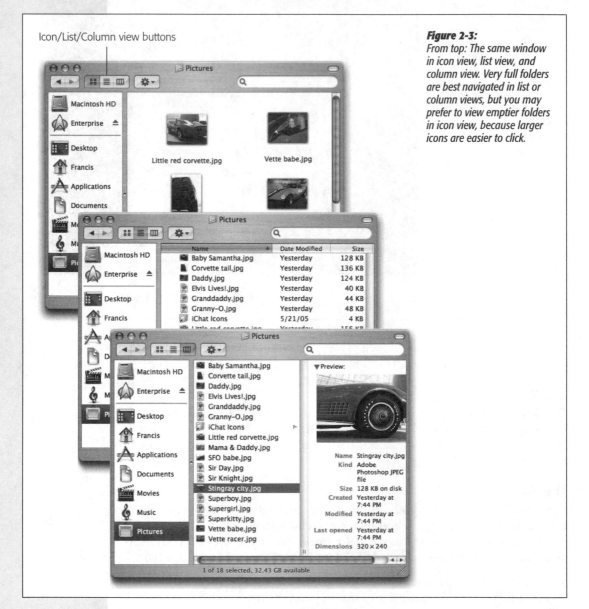

Figure 2-3:
From top: The same window in icon view, list view, and column view. Very full folders are best navigated in list or column views, but you may prefer to view emptier folders in icon view, because larger icons are easier to click.

the window's toolbar, as shown in Figure 2-3, or choose View→as Icons (or View→as Columns, or View→as List). The keystrokes ⌘-1, ⌘-2, and ⌘-3 achieve the same results, but save you time since you don't have to use the mouse.

In icon view, each file, folder, and disk is represented by a small picture—an *icon*. This humble image, a visual representation of electronic bits and bytes, is the cornerstone of the entire Macintosh religion. (Maybe that's why it's called an icon.)

If you then choose View→Show View Options (or press ⌘-J), you'll discover a wealth of interesting display options for this view.

Icon Sizes

Mac OS X can scale your icons to almost any size without losing any quality or smoothness. In the View→Show View Options window (Figure 2-4), click one of the buttons at the top of the window—either "This window only" or "All windows"—to indicate whether you want to change the icon sizes in just the frontmost window or everywhere on the Mac. Then drag the Icon Size slider back and forth until you find an icon size you like. (For added fun, make little cartoon sounds with your mouth.)

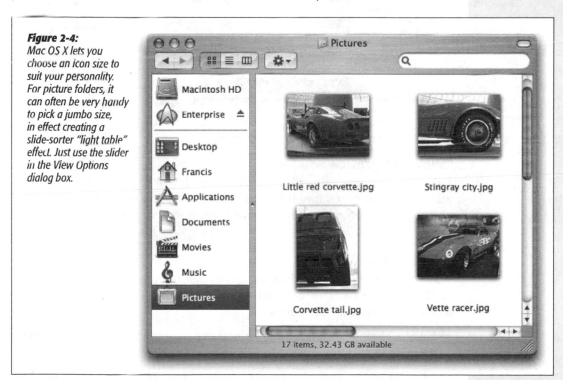

Figure 2-4:
Mac OS X lets you choose an icon size to suit your personality. For picture folders, it can often be very handy to pick a jumbo size, in effect creating a slide-sorter "light table" effect. Just use the slider in the View Options dialog box.

Text Size

You can control the type size of icon names on the Mac. In fact, if you choose "This window only" at the top of the dialog box, you can actually specify a different type size for *each window* on your machine. You might want smaller type to fit more into a crammed-full icon view without scrolling, and larger type in less densely populated windows.

Note: Your choices range from 10 to 16 points, but, unfortunately, you can't choose a different font.

Windows XP–style Labeling

This feature lets you create, in effect, a *multiple-column* list view in a single window (see Figure 2-5).

Figure 2-5:
Thanks to the View Options palette (left), Mac OS X can now display icon names on the right, and even show a second line of file info, in any icon view. You now have all the draggable convenience of an icon view, along with the compact spacing of a list view. This is nothing new if you're used to Windows XP, where this attractive arrangement debuted.

"Show icon preview"

This option pertains primarily to graphics, which Mac OS X often displays only with a generic icon (stamped JPEG or TIFF or PDF). But if you turn on "Show icon preview," Mac OS X turns each icon into a miniature display of the image itself, as shown in Figure 2-5.

"Show item info"

While you've got the View Options dialog box open, try turning on "Show item info." Suddenly you get a new line of information about any disk or folder icon in the window, in tiny blue type. For example:

- **Folders.** The info line lets you know how many icons are inside each folder without having to open it up.

- **TIFF, JPEG, GIF, PDF files.** Certain graphics files may show a helpful info line, too—for example, graphics files display their dimensions, in pixels.

- **Sounds and QuickTime movies.** The light-blue bonus line tells you how long the sound or movie takes to play. For example, "02'49" means two minutes, 49 seconds.

You can see these effects illustrated in Figure 2-5.

Window Backgrounds

Here's another Mac OS X luxury: You can fill the background of any icon-view window on your Mac with a certain color—or even a photo.

Color-coordinating or "wallpapering" certain windows is more than just a cute gimmick; it can actually serve as a timesaving psychological cue. Once you've gotten used to the fact that your main Documents folder has a sky-blue background, you can pick it out like a sharpshooter from a screen filled with open windows. Color-coded Finder windows are also especially easy to distinguish at a glance when you've minimized them to the Dock.

Note: Background colors and pictures disappear in list or column view, and in windows that "belong" to Mac OS X itself, such as the hard drive window and the Users folder.

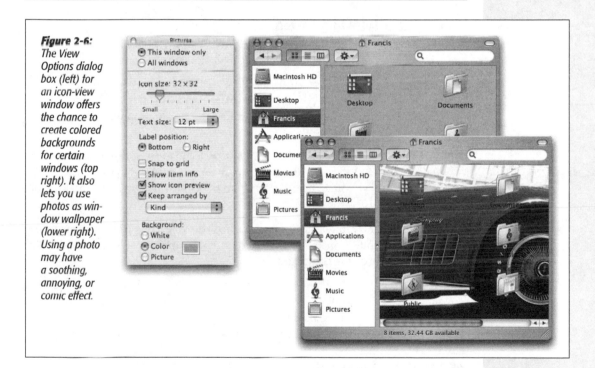

Figure 2-6:
The View Options dialog box (left) for an icon-view window offers the chance to create colored backgrounds for certain windows (top right). It also lets you use photos as window wallpaper (lower right). Using a photo may have a soothing, annoying, or comic effect.

The bottom of the View Options dialog box (Figure 2-6) offers three choices:

- **White.** This is the standard option.

- **Color.** When you click this button, you see a small rectangular button beside the word Color. Click it to open the Color Picker dialog box, which you can use to choose a new background color for the window. (Unless it's April Fool's day, pick a light color. If you choose a dark one—like black—you won't be able to make out the lettering of the icons' names.)

- **Picture.** If you choose this option, a Select button appears. Click it to open the Select a Picture dialog box, already open to your Library→Desktop Pictures folder. Choose a graphics file (one of Apple's—in the Desktop Pictures folder—or one of your own). When you click Select, you'll see that Mac OS X has superimposed the window's icons on the photo. As you can see in Figure 2-6, low-contrast or light-background photos work best for legibility.

Tip: The Mac has no idea what sizes and shapes your window may assume in its lifetime. Therefore, Mac OS X makes no attempt to scale down a selected photo to fit neatly into the window. If you have a high-res digital camera (a three- or four-megapixel model or higher), you may see only the upper-left corner of a photo as the window background. Use a graphics program like iPhoto (page 419) to scale the picture down to something smaller than your screen resolution for better results.

Keeping Icons Neat and Sorted

It's easy enough to request a visit from an electronic housekeeper who tidies up your icons, aligning them neatly to an invisible grid. For example:

- **Aligning individual icons to the grid.** Press the ⌘ key while dragging an icon or several highlighted icons. (Don't push down the key until after you begin to drag.) When you release the mouse, the icons you've moved all jump into neatly aligned positions.

- **Aligning all icons to the grid.** Choose View→Clean Up (if nothing is selected) or View→Clean Up Selection (if some icons are highlighted). Now *all* icons in the window (or those you've selected) jump to the closest positions on the invisible underlying grid.

  This is a temporary status, however. As soon as you drag icons around, or add more icons to the window, the newly moved icons wind up just as sloppily positioned as before you used the command.

  If you'd rather have icons snap to the nearest underlying grid positions *whenever* you move them, choose View→Show View Options. In the resulting dialog box, turn on "Snap to grid." Make sure the button you want is selected at the top of the window ("This window only" or "All windows"), and then close the window.

Note: You can override the grid setting by pressing the ⌘ key when you drag. In other words, when grid-snapping is turned *off,* ⌘ makes your icons snap into position; when grid-snapping is turned *on,* ⌘ lets you drag an icon freely.

Note, by the way, that neither of these grid-snapping commands—View→Clean Up and the "Snap to grid" option—moves icons into the most compact possible arrangement. If one or two icons have wandered off from the herd to a far corner of the window, they've merely been nudged to the grid points nearest their present locations. They aren't moved all the way back to the group of icons elsewhere in the window.

To make them jump back to the primary cluster, read on.

- **Sorting all icons for the moment.** If you choose View→Arrange By→Name, all icons in the window snap to the invisible grid *and* sort themselves alphabetically. Use this method to place the icons as close as possible to each other within the window, rounding up any strays. The other subcommands in the View→"Arrange By" menu, such as Size, Date Modified, and so on, work similarly, but sort the icons according to different criteria.

As with the Clean Up command, View→Arrange only reorganizes the icons in the window at this moment. Moving or adding icons in the window means you'll wind up with icons out of order. If you'd rather have all icons remain sorted *and* clustered, try this:

- **Sorting all icons permanently.** This arrangement is the ideal solution for neat freaks who can't stand seeing icons out of place. It maintains sorting and alignment of all icons in the window, present and future, so if you add more icons to the window, they jump into correct alphabetical position. If you remove icons, the remaining ones slide over to fill in the resulting gap.

To make it happen, choose View→Show View Options. In the resulting dialog box, turn on the "Keep arranged by" checkbox. From the pop-up menu, specify what order you want your icons to snap into. Close the window. As shown at right in Figure 2-7, your icons are now locked into sorted position, with no strays around the edges.

Figure 2-7:
Use the View Options dialog box (left) to turn on permanent-cleanliness mode (right). A tiny four-square icon (circled) appears in the Status bar. That symbol is supposed to remind you that you've turned on the Mac's spatial lockjaw feature, so that you don't get frustrated when you try to drag an icon into a new position and discover that it won't budge.

You can also apply any of the commands described in this section—Clean Up, Arrange, Keep Arranged, and so on—to icons lying loose on your *desktop*. Even though they don't seem to be in any window at all, you can specify small or large icons, automatic alphabetical arrangement, and so on. Just click the desktop before using the commands in the View menu.

List View

In windows that contain a lot of icons, the list view is a powerful weapon in the battle against chaos. It shows you a tidy table of your files' names, dates, sizes, and so on. Here's how to master these columns.

Sorting the List

As in Windows, the column headings in a list view aren't just signposts—they're buttons, too. Click Name for alphabetical order, Date Modified to view newest first, Size to put the largest files at the top, and so on.

It's especially important to note the tiny, dark gray triangle that appears in the column you've most recently clicked. It shows you which way the list is being sorted. For example, if the Size column is selected, an upward-pointing triangle means smallest things go first.

POWER USERS' CLINIC

Flippy Triangle Keystrokes

The keystrokes for opening and closing flippy triangles in a list view are worth committing to memory.

Pressing the Option key when you click a flippy triangle lets you view a folder's contents *and* the contents of any folders inside it. The result, in other words, is a longer list that may involve several levels of indentation.

If you prefer to use the keyboard, substitute the right-arrow key (to expand a selected folder's flippy triangle) or left-arrow key (to collapse the folder listing again). Here again, adding the Option key expands all levels of folders within the selected one.

Suppose, for example, that you want to find out how many files are in your Pictures folder. The trouble is, you have organized the graphics files within that folder in several category folders. And you realize that the "how many items" statistic in the status bar shows you how many icons are *visible* in the window. In other words, you won't know your

total photo count until you've *expanded* all the folders within the Pictures folder.

You could perform the entire routine from the keyboard like this: Get to your own Home folder by pressing Shift-⌘-H. Select the Pictures folder by typing the letter P. Open it by pressing ⌘-O (the shortcut for File→Open) or ⌘-down arrow. Highlight the entire contents by pressing ⌘-A (the shortcut for Edit→Select All).

Now that all folders are highlighted, press Option-right arrow. You may have to wait a moment for the Mac to open every subfolder of every subfolder. But eventually, the massive list appears, complete with many levels of indentation. At last, the "items" statistic in the status bar at the bottom of the window gives you a complete, updated tally of how many files are in all of those folders added together.

Finally, press Option-left arrow to close every flippy triangle in the Pictures folder.

Flippy Triangles

One of the Mac's most distinctive features is the tiny triangle that appears to the left of a folder's name in a list view. In its official documents, Apple calls these buttons *disclosure triangles;* internally, the programmers call them *flippy triangles.*

When you click one, you turn the list view into an outline, in which the contents of the folder are displayed in an indented list, as shown in Figure 2-8. Click the triangle again to collapse the folder listing. You're saved the trouble and clutter of having to open a window just to view the folder's contents.

By selectively clicking flippy triangles, you can, in effect, peer inside of two or more folders simultaneously, all within a single list view window. You can move files around by dragging them onto the tiny folder icons.

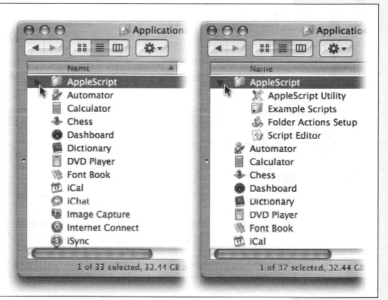

Figure 2-8:
Click a "flippy triangle" (left) to see the listing of the folders and files inside that folder (right). Or press the equivalent keystrokes: right arrow (to open) and left arrow (to close).

Which Columns Appear

Choose View→Show View Options. In the palette that appears, you're offered on/off checkboxes for the different columns of information that Mac OS X can display, as shown in Figure 2-9.

Other View Options

The View Options for a list view include several other useful settings (choose View→Show View Options, or press ⌘-J). As always, be sure to click either "All windows" or "This window only," so that your changes will have the scope of effect that you intended.

Column View

Icon view and list view should certainly be familiar from your old PC. But *column view* is probably something new—and welcome.

The goal is simple: Create a means of burrowing down through nested folders without leaving a trail of messy, overlapping windows in your wake.

The solution, a distant relative of the tree view known as Windows Explorer, is shown in Figure 2-10. It's a list view that's divided into several vertical panes. The first pane (not counting the Sidebar) shows the icons of all your disks, including your main hard drive.

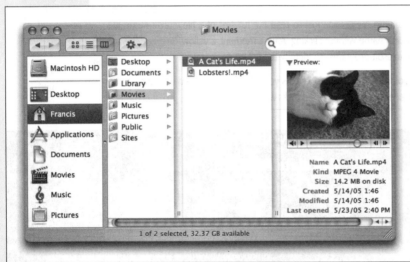

Figure 2-10:
If the rightmost folder contains pictures, sounds, or movies, Mac OS X even lets you look at them or play them, right there in the Finder. If it's a certain kind of text document (Apple-Works or PDF, for example), you actually see a tiny pre-view of the first page. If it's any other kind of document, you see a blowup of its icon and a few file statistics. You can drag this jumbo icon anywhere—into another folder, for example.

When you click a disk (once), the second pane shows a list of all the folders on it. Each time you click a folder in one pane, the pane to its right shows what's inside. The other panes slide to the left, sometimes out of view. (Use the horizontal scroll bar to bring them back.) You can keep clicking until you're looking at the file icons inside the most deeply nested folder.

If you discover that your hunt for a particular file has taken you down a blind alley, it's not a big deal to backtrack, since the trail of folders you've followed to get here is still sitting there before you on the screen. As soon as you click a different folder in one of the earlier panes, the panes to its right suddenly change, so that you can now burrow down a different rabbit hole.

Furthermore, the Sidebar (page 88) is always at the ready to help you jump to a new track; just click any disk or folder there to select a new first-column listing for column view.

The beauty of column view is, first of all, that it keeps your screen tidy. It effectively shows you several simultaneous folder levels, but contains them within a single window. With a quick ⌘-W, you can close the entire window, panes and all. Second, column view provides an excellent sense of where you are. Because your trail is visible at all times, it's much harder to get lost, wondering what folder you're in and how you got there, than in any other window view.

Note: Column view is always alphabetical. There's no way to sort the lists by date, for example, as you can in list view.

Column View by Keyboard

Efficiency fans can operate this entire process by keyboard alone. For example:

- You can jump from one pane to the next by pressing the right or left arrow keys. Each press highlights the first icon in the next or previous pane.

- You can use any of the commands in the Go menu, or their keyboard equivalents, or the icons in the Sidebar, to fill your columns with the contents of the corresponding folder—Home, Utilities, Applications, or whatever. (See page 26 for more on these important folders.)

- The Back command (clicking the Back button on the toolbar, pressing ⌘-[(left bracket) or choosing Go→Back) works just as it would in a Web browser, by letting you retrace your steps backward. You can use this command over and over again until you return to the column setup that appeared when you first switched to column view.

- Within a highlighted pane, press the up or down arrow keys to highlight successive icons in the list. Or type the first couple of letters of an icon's name to jump directly to it.

- When you finally highlight the icon you've been looking for, press ⌘-O or ⌘-down arrow to open it (or double-click it, of course). You can open any icon in any column, not just the one you've pinpointed in the rightmost column.

Manipulating the Columns

The number of columns you can see without scrolling depends on the width of the window. In no other view are the zoom button (page 30) and resize box (page 33) so important.

That's not to say, however, that you're limited to four columns (or whatever fits on your monitor). You can make the columns wider or narrower—either individually or all at once—to suit the situation, according to this scheme:

- To make a single column wider or narrower, drag its right-side handle (circled in Figure 2-11).

- To make *all* the columns wider or narrower simultaneously, hold down the Option key as you drag that right-side handle.

- Here's the tip of the week: *Double-click* one of the right-side handles to make the column precisely as wide as necessary to reveal all the names of its contents.

- And here's the tip of the month: Option-double-click any column's right-side handle to make *all* columns just as wide as necessary.

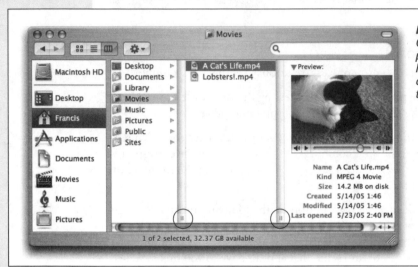

Figure 2-11:
Once again, the Option key proves its versatility. If you hold Option, you resize all columns at once, rather than one at a time.

View Options

Just as in icon and list view, you can choose View→Show View Options to open a dialog box—a Spartan one, in this case—offering a bit more control over your column views.

Note: Any changes you make here affect *all* column views; there's no "This window only" setting for column view.

- **Text size.** Choose your preferred size for icon labels in column views.

- **Show icons.** For maximum speed, turn off this option. Now you'll see only file names, not the tiny icons next to them, which can save your Mac a lot of work when you're loading a folder with hundreds or thousands of files.

- **Show preview column.** The far-right Preview column (Figure 2-11) can be handy when you're browsing graphics, sounds, or movie files. The rest of the time, it can get in the way, slowing down the works and pushing other, more useful columns off to the left side of the window. If you turn off this checkbox, the Preview column doesn't appear.

Tip: No matter what view you're in, remember this trick if you ever start dragging an icon and then change your mind: Press the Esc key while the mouse button is still down. The icon flies back to its precise starting place. (Too bad real life doesn't have a similar feature for returning a spilled glass of grape juice back to the tabletop.)

POWER USERS' CLINIC

The Go to Folder Command

Sometimes a Unix tentacle pokes through the user-friendly Aqua interface. Mac OS X has a number of places where you can use Unix shortcuts instead of the mouse.

One classic example is the Go→Go to Folder command (Shift-⌘-G). It brings up a box like the one shown here.

The purpose of this box is to let you jump to a certain folder on your Mac directly by typing its Unix *folder path.* Depending on your point of view, this special box is either a shortcut or a detour.

Go to Folder
Go to the folder:
/Users/Robin/
Cancel   Go

For example, if you want to see what's in the Documents folder of your Home folder, you could choose Go >Go to Folder, then type this:

/Users/mjones/Documents

Then click Go or press Return. (In this example, of course, *mjones* is your short account name.)

In other words, you're telling the Mac to open the Users folder in your main hard drive window, then your Home folder inside that, and then the Documents folder inside *that.* Each slash means, "and then open." (As in this example, you can leave off the name of your hard drive.) When you press Enter, the folder you specified pops open immediately.

Of course, if you really wanted to jump to your Documents folder, you'd be wasting your time by typing all that. Unix (and therefore Mac OS X) offers a handy shortcut that means, "home folder." It's the tilde character (~) at the upper-left corner of your keyboard.

To see what's in your Home folder, then, you could type just that ~ symbol into the "Go to" box and then press Return. Or you could add some slashes to it to specify a folder inside your Home folder, like this:

~/Documents

You can even jump to someone *else's* Home folder by typing a name after the ~ symbol, like this:

~chris

If you get into this sort of thing, here's another shortcut worth noting: If you type nothing but a slash (/) and then press Return, you jump immediately to the Computer window, which provides an overview of all your disks, plus a Network icon.

Note, too, that you don't have to type out the full path—only the part that drills down from the *window you're in.* If your Home folder window is already open, for example, you can open the Pictures folder just by typing *Pictures.*

But the Go to Folder trick *really* turns into a high-octane timesaver if you use *tab completion.* After each slash, you can type only enough letters of a folder's name to give Mac OS X the idea—*de* instead of *desktop,* for example—and then press the Tab key. Mac OS X instantly and automatically fills in the rest of the folder's name.

For example, instead of typing */Applications/Microsoft Office 2004/Clipart/Standard,* you could type nothing more than */ap/mi/cl/st,* remembering to press Tab after each pair of letters. Now *that's* how to feel like a Unix power-user.

What's in Your Home Folder

As noted in Chapter 1, your Home folder (choose Go→Home) will be your primary activity center on the Mac. It stores not only your documents, music files, photos, and so on, but also all of your preference settings for the programs you use. Because you'll be spending so much time here, it's worth learning about the folders that Apple puts inside here. As a convenience, Mac OS X creates the following folders:

- **Desktop folder.** When you drag an icon out of a window and onto your Mac OS X desktop, it may *appear* to show up on the desktop, but that's just an optical illusion. In truth, nothing in Mac OS X is ever *really* on the desktop. It's actually in this Desktop *folder,* and mirrored on the desktop area.

  You can entertain yourself for hours by proving this to yourself. If you drag something out of your Desktop folder, it also disappears from the actual desktop. And vice versa. (You're not allowed to delete or rename the Desktop folder.)

- **Documents.** Apple suggests that you keep your actual work files in this folder. Sure enough, whenever you save a new document (when you're working in AppleWorks or Word, for example), the Save As dialog box proposes storing the new file in this folder, as described in Chapter 4.

  Your programs may also create folders of their own here. For example, if Microsoft Entourage is your email program, you'll find a Microsoft User Data folder here (which contains your actual mail files). If you use a Palm organizer, you'll find a Palm folder here for your palmtop's calendar and phone book data. And so on.

- **Library.** The *main* Library folder (the one in your main hard drive window) contains folders for fonts, preferences, help files, and other files essential to the operation of Mac OS X.

  But you have your *own* Library folder, too, right there in your Home folder. It stores exactly the same kinds of things, but they're *your* fonts, *your* preferences, and so on.

  This setup may seem redundant if you're the only person who uses your Mac. But it makes perfect sense in the context of families, schools, or offices where numerous people share a single machine. Because you have your own Library folder, you can have a font collection, sounds, and other preference settings that are in effect only when *you're* using the Mac. (Because this folder is so important, you shouldn't move or rename it.)

- **Movies, Music, Pictures.** These folders, of course, are the precise equivalents of the Windows folders called My Movies, My Music, and My Pictures. The Mac OS X programs that deal with movies, music, and pictures will propose these specialized folders as storage locations. For example, when you plug a digital camera into a Mac OS X computer, the iPhoto program automatically begins to download the photos from it—and iPhoto stores them in the Pictures folder. Similarly, iMovie is programmed to look for the Movies folder when saving its files, and iTunes stores its MP3 files in the Music folder. (More on these programs in Chapter 14.)

- **Public.** If you're on a network, or if others use the same Mac when you're not around, this folder can be handy: It's the "Any of you guys can look at these files" folder. Other people on your network, as well as other people who sit down at your machine, are allowed to see whatever you've put in here, even if they don't have your password. (If your Mac isn't on an office network and isn't shared, you can safely throw away this folder.) Details on sharing the Mac are in Chapter 12, and those on networking are in Chapter 9.

- **Sites.** Mac OS X has a built-in *Web server*—software that turns your Mac into an Internet Web site that people all over the world can connect to. (This feature is practical only if your Mac has a full-time Internet connection.) This Mac OS X feature relies on a program called the Apache Web server, which is so highly regarded in the Unix community that programmers lower their voices when they mention it.

  This is the folder where you put the actual Web pages you want available to the Internet at large.

File and Folder Icons

Just as in Windows, every document, program, folder, and disk on your Mac is represented by an icon. In Mac OS X, icons look more like photos than cartoons, and you can scale them to just about any size (page 39). Otherwise, icons work just as they do in Windows. They're your ticket to moving, copying, and deleting your files and folders.

File Names

A Mac OS X icon's name can have up to 255 letters and spaces. Better yet, you're about to discover the first of many degrees of freedom that come with a move to the Mac: Punctuation is permitted. For the first time in your life, you can name a file, say, "Update 11/15/06," without getting yelled at by your operating system. In fact, you can use any symbol you want except for the colon (:), which the Mac uses behind the scenes for its own folder-hierarchy designation purposes.

To rename an icon, begin by highlighting it (with a single click, for example). Then do one of these two things:

- Click once on its name.

- Press Return or Enter.

Either way, a rectangle now appears around the name (see Figure 2-12). At this point, the existing name is highlighted; simply begin typing to replace it, as you do in Windows.

Tip: If you just want to add letters to the beginning or end of the file's existing name, press the left or right arrow key immediately after pressing Return or Enter. The insertion point jumps to the corresponding end of the file name.

A space is considered alphabetically *before* the letter A. To force a particular folder to appear at the top of a list view window, therefore, type a space before its name.

Selecting Icons

To highlight a single icon in preparation for printing, opening, duplicating, or deleting, click the icon once with the mouse. (In a list or column view, you can also click any visible piece of information about that file—its name, size, kind, date modified, and so on.) The icon darkens, and its name changes color.

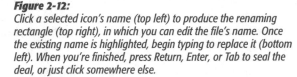

Figure 2-12:
Click a selected icon's name (top left) to produce the renaming rectangle (top right), in which you can edit the file's name. Once the existing name is highlighted, begin typing to replace it (bottom left). When you're finished, press Return, Enter, or Tab to seal the deal, or just click somewhere else.

You can highlight *multiple* files in preparation for moving or copying them en masse, using the same techniques you're used to in Windows. You can select all the ones in a window (press ⌘-A or choose Edit→Select All), drag diagonally to select a few (see Figure 2-13), or select individual icons by ⌘-clicking them one at a time. (If you include a particular icon by mistake, ⌘-click it to remove it from the selected cluster.)

The ⌘ key trick is especially handy if you want to select *almost* all the icons in a window. Press ⌘-A to select everything in the folder, then ⌘-click any unwanted icons to deselect them.

POWER USERS' CLINIC

Selecting Icons from the Keyboard

For the speed fanatic, using the mouse to click an icon is a hopeless waste of time. Fortunately, you can also select an icon by typing the first couple letters of its name.

When looking at your home window, for example, you can type *M* to highlight the Movies folder. If you actually intended to highlight the *Music* folder instead, press the Tab key to highlight the next icon in the window alphabetically. You

can use the arrow keys, too, to highlight a neighboring icon. (Pressing Tab has no effect in column view, however.)

After highlighting an icon in this way, you can manipulate it using the commands in the File menu or their keyboard equivalents: open (⌘-O), put in the Trash (⌘-Delete), Get Info (⌘-I), duplicate (⌘-D), or make an alias (⌘-L), as described later in this chapter.

Tip: In a list view, you can also select a group of consecutive files by clicking the first one you want, and then Shift-clicking the last file. All the files in between are automatically selected—along with the two icons you clicked.

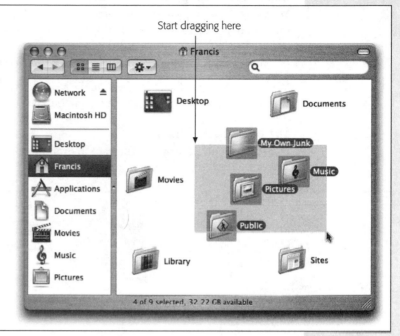

Figure 2-13:
You can highlight several icons simultaneously by dragging a box around them. To do so, drag diagonally across the targt icons, creating a transparent gray rectangle as you go. Any icons touched by this rectangle are selected when you release the mouse. If you press the Shift or ⌘ key as you do this, any previously highlighted icons remain selected.

Start dragging here

Moving and Copying Icons

In Mac OS X, there are two ways to move or copy icons from one place to another: by dragging them, or by using the Copy and Paste commands.

Copying by Dragging

You can drag icons from one folder to another, from one drive to another, from a drive to a folder on another drive, and so on. You can cancel the copying process by pressing either ⌘-period or the Esc key.

Understanding when the Mac copies a dragged icon and when it just *moves* the icon bewilders many a Windows refugee. However, the scheme is fairly simple:

- Dragging from one folder to another (on the same disk) *moves* the icon; dragging from one disk to another *copies* the folder or file. So far, this is the same as Windows.

- Option-dragging it (that is, pressing the Option key while dragging) *copies* the icon instead of moving it. Doing so within a single folder produces a duplicate of the file called "[Whatever its name was] copy."

• Dragging an icon from one disk to another while pressing ⌘ *moves* the file or folder, in the process deleting it from the original disk. (Press ⌘ just after you start to drag.)

Copying by Using Copy and Paste

You can use the Copy and Paste commands to get files from one window to another, too: Highlight the icon or icons you want to move, choose Edit→Copy, open the window where you want to put the icons, and then choose Edit→Paste. You get a second set of the copied icons, exactly as in Windows.

Well, almost exactly like Windows. On the Mac, you can't *cut* and paste icons to move them—you can only *copy* and paste them to make a copy of them.

Spring-Loaded Folders

Here's a common dilemma: you want to drag an icon not just into a folder, but into a folder nested *inside* that folder.

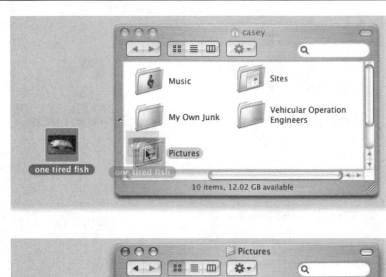

Figure 2-14:
Top: To make spring-loaded folders work, start by dragging an icon onto a folder or disk icon. Don't release the mouse button. Wait for the window to open automatically around your cursor. Bottom: Now you can either let go of the mouse button to release the file in its new window, or drag onto yet another, inner folder. It, too, will open. As long as you don't release the mouse button, you can continue until you've reached your folder-within-a-folder destination.

Instead of fiddling around, opening and closing one window after another, you can use the spring-loaded folders feature (see Figure 2-14), a Mac OS X delicacy with no Windows equivalent. It works like this: Drag the icon onto the first folder—but keep your mouse button pressed. After a few seconds, the folder window opens automatically, centered on your cursor. Still keeping the button down, drag onto the inner folder so that its window opens, too. Now drag onto the *inner* inner folder—and so on. (If the inner folder you intend to open isn't visible in the window, you can scroll by dragging your cursor close to any edge of the window.)

When you finally release the mouse, all the windows except the last one close automatically. You've neatly placed the icon into the core of the nested folders.

Aliases (Shortcuts)

Highlighting an icon and then choosing File→Make Alias (or pressing ⌘-L), generates an *alias,* a specially branded duplicate of the original icon (see Figure 2-15). It's the same idea as a file *shortcut* in Windows: When you double-click the alias, the original file opens. Since you can create as many aliases as you want of a single file, aliases let you, in effect, stash that file in many different folder locations simultaneously.

Tip: Another way to create an alias is by Control-clicking (or right-clicking) a normal icon and choosing Make Alias from the shortcut menu that appears. You can also create an alias by Option-⌘-dragging the icon out of its window.

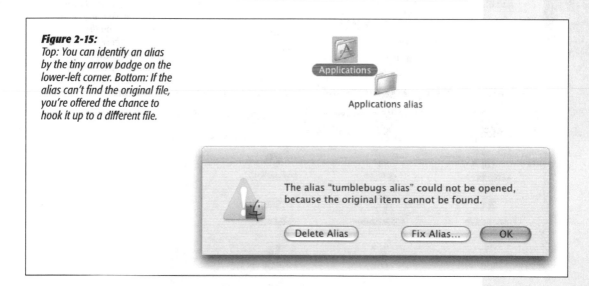

Figure 2-15:
Top: You can identify an alias by the tiny arrow badge on the lower-left corner. Bottom: If the alias can't find the original file, you're offered the chance to hook it up to a different file.

Applications

Applications alias

The alias "tumblebugs alias" could not be opened, because the original item cannot be found.

Delete Alias   Fix Alias...   OK

An alias takes up virtually no disk space—even if the original file is enormous—so you don't have to worry about filling up your hard drive. Aliases are smarter than Windows shortcuts, too: Even if you rename the alias, rename the original file, move the alias, and move the original, double-clicking the alias still opens the original icon.

That's just the beginning of alias intelligence. Suppose you make an alias of a file that's on a removable disk, such as an iPod. When you double-click the alias on your hard drive, the Mac requests that particular disk by name. And if you double-click the alias of a file that's stored on a different machine on your network, Mac OS X attempts to connect to the appropriate machine, prompting you for a password—even if the other machine is thousands of miles away and your Mac must dial the modem to connect.

Tip: Mac OS X makes it easy to find the file an alias "points" to without actually having to open it. Just highlight the alias and then choose File→Show Original (⌘-R). Mac OS X immediately displays the actual, original file, sitting patiently in its folder, wherever that may be.

And if for some reason your alias ever "breaks," you're offered the chance to connect it to a new file, as shown at the bottom of Figure 2-15.

Figure 2-16:
Top: Use the File menu or Action menu (the gear menu shown here) to apply a label to one icon—or even several at once.

Bottom: Instantly, the name takes on the selected shade. In a list or column view, the entire row takes on that shade, too, as shown in Figure 2-17. (If you choose the little X, you're removing any labels that you may have applied.)

Color Labels

Mac OS X includes a welcome feature that isn't available on Windows: icon labels. This feature lets you tag selected icons with one of seven different labels, each of which has both a text label and a color associated with it.

To do so, highlight the icons. Open the File menu (or the shortcut menu that appears when you Control-click the icons). There, under the heading Color Label, you'll see seven colored dots, which represent the seven different labels you can use. Figure 2-16 shows the routine.

What Labels are Good For

After you've applied labels to icons, you can perform some unique file-management tasks. For example:

- **Round up files with Spotlight.** Using the Spotlight file-finding command described later in this chapter, you can round up all icons with a particular label. Thereafter, moving these icons at once is a piece of cake: Choose Edit→Select All, and then drag any one of the highlighted icons out of the results window and into the target folder or disk.

- **Sort a list view by label.** No other Mac sorting method lets you create an arbitrary order for the icons in a window. When you sort by label, the Mac creates alphabetical clusters *within* each label grouping, as shown in Figure 2-17.

- **Track progress.** Use different color labels to track the status of files in a certain project. The first drafts have no labels at all. Once they've been edited and approved, make them blue. Once they've been sent to the home office, they turn purple.

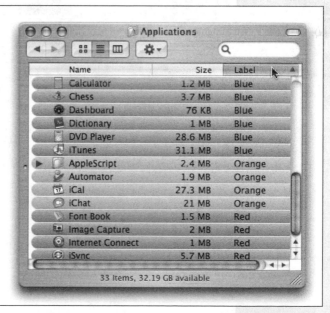

Figure 2-17:
Sorting by label lets you create several different alphabetical groups within a single list. (The ability to sort by label is available only if you first make the label column visible. Do so by choosing View→Show View Options and turning on the Label checkbox.)

Heck, you could have all kinds of fun with this: Money-losing projects get red tints; profitable ones get green; things that make you sad are blue.

Or maybe not.

Changing Labels

When you first install Mac OS X, the seven labels in the File menu are named for the colors they show: Red, Orange, Yellow, and so on. Clearly, the label feature would be much more useful if you could rewrite these labels, tailoring them to your purposes.

Doing so is easy. Choose Finder→Preferences. Click the Labels button. Now you see the dialog box shown in Figure 2-18, where you can edit the text of each label.

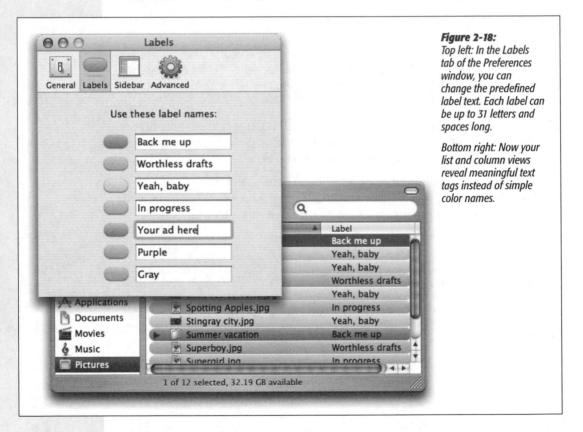

Figure 2-18:
Top left: In the Labels tab of the Preferences window, you can change the predefined label text. Each label can be up to 31 letters and spaces long.

Bottom right: Now your list and column views reveal meaningful text tags instead of simple color names.

The Trash

Few single elements of the Macintosh interface are as famous as the Trash, which now appears as a wire wastebasket at the end of the Dock. It's the same thing that Microsoft calls the Recycle Bin: a waiting room that holds files and folders you intend to delete.

You can either drag files or folders onto the Trash icon, or you can save a little effort by using the keyboard alternative: Highlight the icon and then press ⌘-Delete.

Rescuing Files and Folders from the Trash

File and folder icons sit in the Trash forever—or until you choose Finder→Empty Trash, whichever comes first. The Trash never reaches a fullness level where it empties automatically, as it does in Windows.

If you haven't yet emptied the Trash, you can open its window by clicking the wastebasket icon once. Now you can review its contents—namely, icons that you've placed on the waiting list for extinction. If you change your mind, you can rescue any of these items by dragging them out of the Trash window.

Tip: If dragging something to the Trash was the last thing you did, you can press ⌘-Z—the keyboard shortcut for the Edit→Undo command. This not only removes it from the Trash, but also returns it to the folder from whence it came. This trick works even if the Trash window isn't open.

Emptying the Trash

If you're confident that the items in the Trash window are worth deleting, use any of these three options:

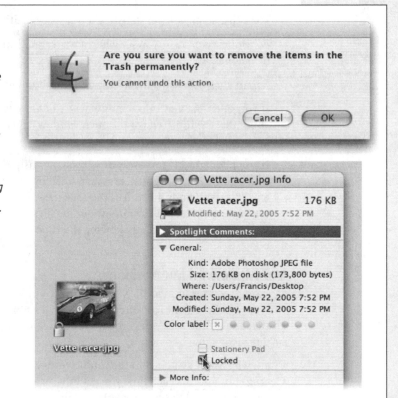

Figure 2-19:
Top: Your last warning. Unfortunately, Mac OS X doesn't tell you how many items are in the Trash or how much disk space they take up.

Bottom: The Get Info window for a locked file. Locking a file in this way isn't military-level security by any stretch—any passing evildoer can unlock the file the same way. But it does trigger a "You do not have sufficient privileges" warning when you try to put it into the Trash, providing at least one layer of protection against mistakes.

- Choose Finder→Empty Trash.

- Press Shift-⌘-Delete.

- Control-click (or right-click) the wastebasket icon, then choose Empty Trash from the shortcut menu. This method has two advantages. First, it doesn't bother asking "Are you sure?" (If you're clicking right on the Trash and choosing Empty Trash from the pop-up menu, it's pretty darned obvious you *are* sure.) Second, this method nukes any locked files (see the following Tip) without making you unlock them first.

If the Macintosh asks you to confirm your decision (see Figure 2-19), click OK.

Tip: By highlighting a file or folder, choosing File→Get Info, and turning on the Locked checkbox, you protect that file or folder from accidental deletion.

Get Info (Properties)

By clicking an icon and then choosing File→Get Info, you open an important window like the one shown in Figure 2-20. It's a collapsible, multi-pane palette that provides a wealth of information about a highlighted icon—the Mac version of icon properties. Click a triangle to expand a corresponding information panel. For example:

- For a disk icon, you get statistics about its capacity and how much of it is full.

- For a document icon, you see when it was created and modified, and what program it "belongs" to.

- For an alias, you learn the location of the actual icon it refers to.

- If you open the Get Info window when *nothing* is selected, you get information about the desktop itself (or the open window), including the amount of disk space consumed by everything sitting in or on it.

- If you highlight 11 icons or more simultaneously, the Get Info window shows you how many you highlighted, breaks it down by type ("23 documents, 3 folders," for example), and finds the sum of their file sizes. That's a great opportunity to change certain file characteristics on numerous files simultaneously, such as locking or unlocking them, hiding or showing their file name extensions (page 112), and so on.

Uni-window vs. Multi-window

In earlier versions of Mac OS X, a single Info window remained on the screen all the time as you clicked one icon after another. That single window was great for reducing clutter, but it didn't let you compare the statistics for the Get Info windows of two or three icons side by side.

That's why Apple switched to the multi-window approach for Get Info: Now, a new Get Info box appears each time you get info on an icon (unless you've highlighted 11 or more icons, as described above).

Still, the uni-window approach is available for those occasions when you don't need side-by-side Get Info windows—if you know the secret. Highlight the icon and then press Option-⌘-I (or choose File→Show Inspector). The new uni-window looks slightly different (the titlebar is thinner, for example) to provide a visual cue that it will change to reflect whatever icon you now click.

Figure 2-20:
Top: The Get Info window appears at first like this, with the information panes "collapsed."

Bottom: Click each flippy triangle to open its corresponding panel of information. The resulting dialog box can easily grow taller than your screen (shown here split in half because the book isn't tall enough). That's a good argument for either (a) closing the panels you don't need at any given moment or (b) running out to buy a really gigantic monitor.

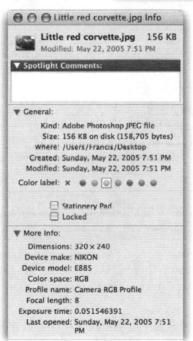

The Get Info Panels

Apple built the Get Info window out of a series of collapsed "flippy triangles," as shown in Figure 2-20. Click a triangle to reveal the information inside.

Depending on whether you selected a folder, file, picture, or whatever, these flippy-triangled panes may include the following:

- **Spotlight Comments.** Here you can type in random comments for your own reference. As described on page 46, you can then have these comments show up in list views, making it easy to pick out noteworthy files at a glance.

  Moreover, anything that you type in this field gets indexed by Spotlight, Mac OS X's super-useful searching tool. Then it's only a matter of hitting a quick keyboard shortcut to bring up a search box where you can locate files, folders, or the comments you just typed into the Spotlight Comments field.

- **General.** Here's where you can see the icon's size, creation date, most recent change date, locked status, and so on.

  If you click a disk, this info window shows you its capacity and how full it is. If you click the Trash, you see how much stuff is in it. If you click an alias, this panel shows you a Select New Original button and reveals where the original file is. The General pane always opens the first time you summon the Get Info window.

- **More Info.** Just as the name implies, here you'll find more information—most often the dimensions and color format of a graphics file and when the icon was last opened. These morsels, like the comments you can type in the uppermost pane, are easily Spotlight-searchable.

- **Name & Extension.** On this pane, you can read and edit the name of the icon in question. The "Hide extension" checkbox refers to the file name extension (*.doc* or *.txt,* for example).

  As described on page 110, many Mac OS X documents, behind the scenes, have file name extensions—but Mac OS X, like Windows XP, comes set to hide them. By turning off this checkbox, you can make the suffix reappear for an individual file. (You can also make file name extensions appear or disappear *globally,* as described on page 112.)

- **Open with.** This pane is available for documents only. Use it to specify which program will open when you double-click this document or all documents of this type. (Details on page 110.)

- **Preview.** On this pane, you see a large, handsome thumbnail image. In the case of spreadsheets, Microsoft Word files, HTML documents, and so on, this is nothing to write home about—you only see a magnified version of the generic document icon.

  But when you're examining pictures, text files, PDF files, sounds, clippings, and movies, this feature can be extremely useful. In those cases, you see a thumbnail version of what's actually *in* that document. A controller lets you play sounds and movies, where appropriate, for example.

- **Ownership & Permissions.** This is available for all kinds of icons. If other people have access to your Mac (either from across the network or when logging in in person), this panel lets you specify who is allowed to open or change this particular icon. Permissions is a hairy topic, or, if you're a system administrator, an exciting one.

Here and there, you may even see other panels in the Get Info window, especially when you get info on application icons. For example, iPhoto, iMovie, and iDVD each offer a Plugins panel that lets you manage add-on software modules.

Finding Files 1: Spotlight

Every computer offers a way to find files. Moreover, every computer offers a way to *open* files you've found. In Windows, the Search program achieves both tasks in a reasonably fast manner.

On Mac OS X, though, there's something even better. Spotlight, Apple's search technology, is designed to make searching so fast, efficient, and automatic that it reduces much of what you've read on the preceding pages to irrelevance.

That may sound like breathless hype, but wait until you try it.

The Spotlight Menu

See the little magnifying glass icon in your menu bar? That's the mouse-driven way to open the Spotlight search box.

The other way is to press ⌘-Space bar. If you can memorize only one keystroke on your Mac, that's the one to learn. It works at the desktop, but also when you're working in any other program.

In any case, the Spotlight text box appears just below your menu bar.

Begin typing to identify what you want to find and open. For example, if you're trying to find a file called *Pokémon Fantasy League.doc,* typing just *pok* or *leag* would probably suffice.

As you type, a menu immediately appears below the search box, listing everything Spotlight can find containing what you've typed so far. This is a live, interactive search; that is, Spotlight modifies the menu of search results *as you type.*

The menu lists every file, folder, program, email message, address book entry, calendar appointment, picture, movie, PDF document, music file, Web bookmark, Microsoft Office (Word, PowerPoint, Excel) document, System Preferences pane, and even font that contains what you typed, regardless of its name or folder location.

Note: Spotlight isn't just searching the *names* of your files and folders. It's actually searching their *contents*—the words inside your documents, for example. Technically speaking, Spotlight searches all your files' *metadata,* which is data about data: descriptive text information about what's in a file, like its height, width, size, creator, copyright holder, title, editor, created date, and last modification date. It also includes anything you've typed in the Spotlight Comments field of an icon's Get Info window.

If you see the icon you were hoping to dig up, click it to open it. Or use the arrow keys to "walk down" the menu, and then press Return or Enter to open the icon.

Tip: If you ⌘-click something in the results menu (or highlight something from the keyboard and then press ⌘-Enter), you *jump to* that item's icon, wherever it may be on your hard drive. That's a very handy trick when your purpose in finding something is, say, to trash it, copy it, label it, or back it up, rather than opening it.

If you open an application, well, that program pops onto the screen. If you open a System Preferences pane, System Preferences opens and presents that pane. If you choose an appointment, the iCal program opens, already set to the appropriate day and time. Selecting an email message opens that message in Mail. And so on.

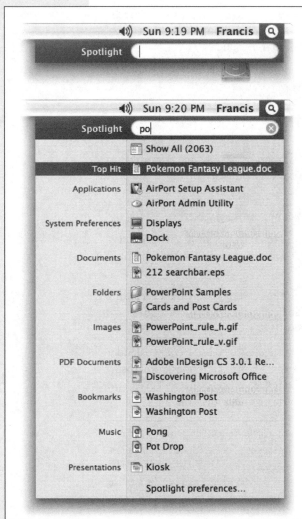

Figure 2-21:
Top: Press ⌘-Space, or click the magnifying glass icon, to make the search bar appear.

Bottom: As you type, Spotlight builds the list of every match it can find, neatly organized by type: programs, documents, folders, images, PDF documents, and so on. You can redefine the keystroke, which folders are "peeked into," and which categories appear here (and in which order) in System Preferences' Spotlight pane.

As you'll soon learn, Spotlight isn't just a fast Find command. It's an enhancement that's so deep, convenient and powerful, it threatens to make all that folders-in-folders business nearly pointless. Why burrow around in folders when you can open any file or program with a couple of keystrokes?

The Spotlight Window

As you may have noticed, the Spotlight menu doesn't list *every* match on your hard drive. Unless you own one of those extremely rare, 60-inch Apple Skyscraper Displays, there just isn't room.

Instead, Spotlight uses some fancy behind-the-scenes analysis to calculate and display the *20 most likely* matches for what you typed. But at the top of the menu, you usually see that there are many other possible matches; it says something like "Show All (423)," meaning that there are 423 other candidates.

Spotlight window from the Spotlight menu

If, indeed, the Spotlight menu—its Most Likely to Succeed list—doesn't include what you're looking for, click Show All (or just press Return or Enter). You've just opened the Spotlight *window,* shown in Figure 2-22.

Now you have access to the *complete* list of matches, neatly organized by category. (Even this view starts out showing only the top five matches in each category. If there's more to see, click the link that says "145 more…" beneath the list.)

Opening the Spotlight window directly

Choosing Show All from the Spotlight menu is one way to open the Spotlight window. But if you want to open the Spotlight window *directly,* using the Spotlight menu is a bit roundabout, since Mac OS X has to repeat your search all over again in the new window.

UP TO SPEED

Why Spotlight Isn't Windows Indexing Service

When certain crusty Windows fans hear about Spotlight, their first reaction runs along these lines: "We've had that in Windows for years," they say. "It's called Indexing Service."

But the truth is, Windows Indexing Service isn't even in the same league as Spotlight.

Indexing Service can indeed search *inside* the words of your documents, including Microsoft Office files and various kinds of text files.

But it's not integrated into the operating system, the way Spotlight is. For example, Indexing Service is harder to get to, even if you know how to turn it on; it isn't available from within any program, either. You can't open it with a keystroke. It doesn't search your address book, email, or

calendar. Above all, Indexing Service updates its internal database of what's on your hard drives at regular intervals, but it's not real-time. Spotlight, on the other hand, properly catalogs your system *every time* you create, save, move, copy, or delete a file. With Spotlight, search results reflect the up-to-the-second contents of your hard drive.

A much closer relative to Spotlight is Google Desktop Search, an add-on that creates a system-wide search box (and a keystroke that puts your cursor there), just like Spotlight. It doesn't search as many kinds of documents as Spotlight, and it's not as deeply integrated into the operating system (for example, it doesn't show up in the Open and Save boxes, as Spotlight does). But it's a very nice start.

Instead, press the *keystroke* for opening the Spotlight window. It's Option-⌘-Space bar, but you can change this keystroke to just about anything you like. (See page 72.)

When the Spotlight window opens, you can start typing whatever you're looking for into the Search box at the upper right.

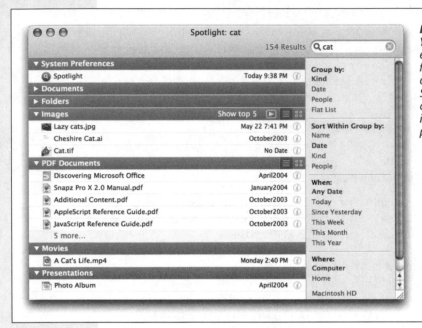

Figure 2-22:
You can open this window either by choosing Show All from the Spotlight menu, or by pressing Option-⌘-Space bar at any time. (You can change this keystroke, if you like, in the Spotlight pane of System Preferences.

As you type—or, more realistically, a second or two after you type each letter—the window changes to reveal, item by item, a list of the files and folders whose names contain what you typed.

Tip: If you're not sure about the spelling of the word you're typing, type as much as you know, and then hit Option-Escape. Mac OS X obligingly drops down its list of Every Word It Knows That Begins With Those Letters in a huge, scrolling menu!

If you've typed *decon,* for example, you'll see correctly spelled items for *decongest, decongestant,* and so on. You can click one to make it fill in the Search box.

While the searching is going on, a sprocket icon whirls away in the upper-left corner of the window. If a search is taking a long time, you're free to switch into another program while Spotlight keeps working in the background.

To cancel the search in progress, click the X button next to the phrase you typed (or press Escape). That button clears the box so you can type a different word or phrase.

Expand or collapse the list

Once you're looking at the search results, the Spotlight window may look clean and simple. But it's actually crawling with fun activities for the whole family.

For example, the flippy triangles next to each category (Documents, Images, and so on) are buttons. Clicking one hides or shows that category list. If you're looking for a photograph, you may as well collapse all the *other* headings to leave more room on your screen.

Tip: If you *Option*-click one of the flippy triangles, you collapse or expand *all* of the headings at once.

You can perform another sort of expansion, too: If you see "40 more…" at the bottom of a category list, click that phrase to expand the list so that you're seeing *all* matching items in that category. To return to the original, Top Five Only view, click the words "Show top 5" in the blue category-header bar.

At the right side of the Spotlight window, you'll find a skinny command panel with headings like "Group by," "Sort Within Group by," and so on. These are your tickets to

---

UP TO SPEED

What Spotlight Knows

The beauty of Spotlight is that it doesn't just find files whose *names* match what you've typed. That would be *so* 2004!

No, Spotlight actually looks *inside* the files. It can actually read and search the contents of text files, RTF and PDF documents, and documents from AppleWorks, Keynote, Pages, Photoshop, and Microsoft Office (Word, Excel, and PowerPoint).

As time goes on, software companies will develop bits of add-on software—plug-ins—that make their documents searchable by Spotlight, too. Check in periodically at, for example, *www.apple.com/downloads/macosx/spotlight*, to look for Spotlight plug-ins relevant to the kind of work you do. (Within a week of Tiger's release, for example, you could download free Spotlight plug-ins for OmniGraffle, OmniOutliner, TypeIt4Me, MacDraft, REALBasic, Painter, Wolfram Notebook, and others.)

But that's only the beginning. Spotlight searches not only the text you've typed, but also over 115 other bits of data—a staggering collection of information including the names of the layers in a Photoshop document, the tempo of an MP3

file, the shutter speed of a digital-camera photo, a movie's copyright holder, a document's page size, and on and on.

Technically, this sort of secondary information is called *meta-data*. It's usually invisible, although a lot of it shows up in the Get Info dialog box described earlier in this chapter.

You might think that typing something into the Spotlight bar triggers a search. But to be technically correct, Spotlight has *already done* its searching. In the first 15 to 30 minutes after you install Tiger—or in the minutes after you attach a new hard drive—Spotlight invisibly collected information about everything on your hard drive. Like a kid cramming for an exam, it read, took notes on, and memorized the contents of all your files. (During this time, the Spotlight icon in the menu bar pulses; if you click it, you'll be told that Spotlight is *indexing* the drives.) Once it has indexed your hard drive in this way, Spotlight can produce search results in seconds.

After that initial indexing process, Spotlight continues to monitor what's on your hard drive, indexing new and changed files in the background, in the microseconds between your keystrokes and clicks in other programs.

---

grouping and sorting the list of found stuff. (Figure 2-23 shows the difference between grouping and sorting.) Your options are Kind (folders, PDF, images, documents, and so on); Name (an alphabetical list); date (the *date you last opened it*, not the date you last made a change); People (authors of Microsoft Office documents, for example); and Flat List (no grouping at all.)

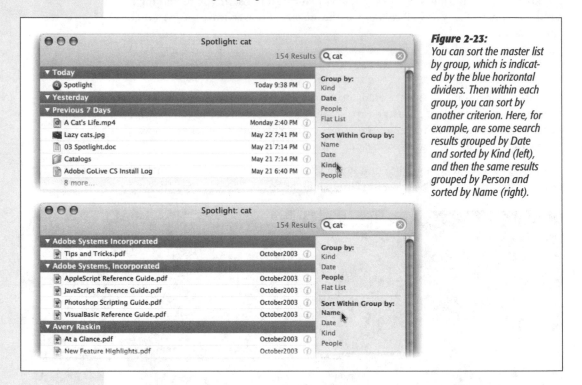

Figure 2-23:
You can sort the master list by group, which is indicated by the blue horizontal dividers. Then within each group, you can sort by another criterion. Here, for example, are some search results grouped by Date and sorted by Kind (left), and then the same results grouped by Person and sorted by Name (right).

See the pretty pictures

When you've grouped your results by Kind, the blue divider bars for Images and PDF Documents offer some useful little buttons at the right end. Figure 2-24 shows what they do.

Get more info

Click the ❶ button to the right of anything in the list to expand its listing. A sort of Get Info panel drops down, identifying where the item is on your hard drive and listing its authors, size, creation and modification dates, "last opened" date, dimensions (for graphics and PDF documents), duration (for music and movies), sender (for mail messages), date (for iCal appointments), and so on.

Filter the list

Filtering, in this case, means *winnowing down*—hiding some of the results so that you see only the good stuff. That's the purpose of the "When" and "Where" controls on the right side of the screen.

• **When.** If you click the Today link, for example, Spotlight cuts down the list so that you see only items you've opened today. Click This Week to see only items you've opened this week, and so on. (Click Any Date to restore the full list.)

Figure 2-24:
You can view groups of PDF documents either in a list, just like other documents, or as thumbnails, as shown here. Photos and other graphics files offer even more fun; you can view them as a list, as thumbnails, or as a full-screen slideshow.

• **Where.** These links let you restrict the listing to what's on your Home folder (click Home) or your main, internal hard drive (click Macintosh HD or whatever your drive is called). Click Computer to restore the full list of everything on all your drives.

Work with results

Most of the time, what people do with the results of a Spotlight search is *open them*. You find something, you open it.

But there are other things you can do with your search results. Try Control-clicking or right-clicking something in the list (or a highlighted group of somethings) to see a very useful little shortcut menu of options.

Tip: Everything in the Spotlight window is kind of like a regular Finder icon. You can work with anything as though you're looking at one big list view: Drag something to the Trash, drag something to the desktop (to move it there), drag something onto a Dock icon to open it with a certain program, Option-⌘-drag it to the desktop to create an alias, and so on.

Customizing Spotlight

You've just read about how Spotlight works fresh out of the box. But you can tailor its behavior, both for security reasons and to fit it to the kinds of work you do.

Here are three ways to open the Spotlight preferences center:

• Choose "Spotlight preferences" at the bottom of the Spotlight menu (that is, just after you've performed a search).

• Use Spotlight itself. Hit ⌘-Space, type *spotl,* press ⌘-Enter.

• Open System Preferences. Click Spotlight.

In any case, you wind up face-to-face with the dialog box shown in Figure 2-25.

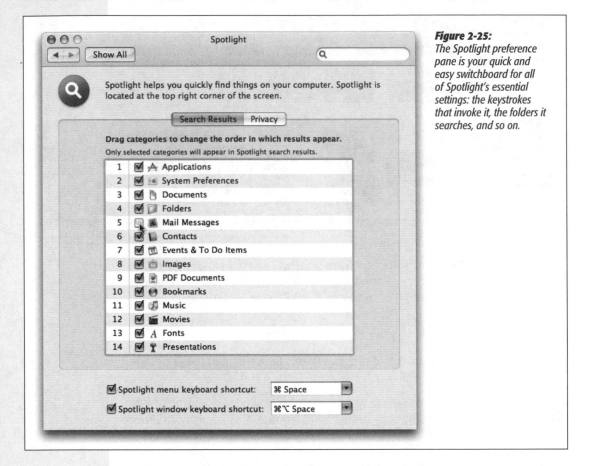

Figure 2-25:
The Spotlight preference pane is your quick and easy switchboard for all of Spotlight's essential settings: the keystrokes that invoke it, the folders it searches, and so on.

You can tweak Spotlight in three ways here, all very useful.

• **Turn off categories.** The list of checkboxes before you identifies all the kinds of things that Spotlight tracks. But if you find that Spotlight uses up precious menu space listing stuff you don't need to find very often—say, Web bookmarks or fonts—turn off their checkboxes. Now the Spotlight menu's precious 20 slots will be allotted to icon types you care more about.

• **Prioritize the categories.** This dialog box also lets you change the *order* of the category results: Just drag an individual list item up or down to change where it appears in the Spotlight menu.

• **Change the keystroke.** Ordinarily, pressing ⌘-Space highlights the Spotlight search box in your menu bar, and Option-⌘-Space opens the Spotlight window described above. If these keystrokes clash with some other key assignment in your software, though, you can reassign them to almost any other keystroke you like.

Most people notice only the pop-up menu that lets you select one of your F-keys (the function keys at the top of your keyboard). But you can also click inside the white box that lists the keystroke and then press *any* key combination—Control-S, for example—to choose something different. Whatever keystroke you choose *must* include at least one of the modifier keys—Option, Ctrl, or ⌘—or be an F-key.

Note: Don't use a keystroke that messes up some other function on your Mac. ⌘-S, for example, would *not* be a good choice.

Privacy settings

Ordinarily, Spotlight doesn't consider any corner of your hard drive off-limits. It looks for matches wherever it can (except in other people's Home folders, that is; you can't search through other people's stuff).

But even within your own Mac world, you can hide certain folders from Spotlight searches. Maybe you have privacy concerns—you don't want your spouse, for example, Spotlighting your stuff while you're away from your desk. Maybe you just want to

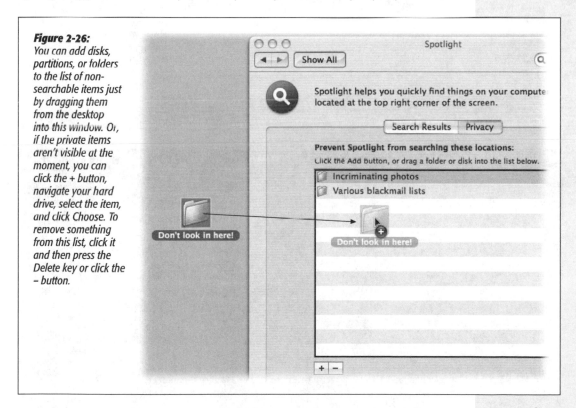

Figure 2-26:
You can add disks, partitions, or folders to the list of non-searchable items just by dragging them from the desktop into this window. Or, if the private items aren't visible at the moment, you can click the + button, navigate your hard drive, select the item, and click Choose. To remove something from this list, click it and then press the Delete key or click the – button.

create more focused Spotlight searches, removing a lot of old, extraneous junk from its database.

Either way, the steps are simple. Open the Spotlight panel of System Preferences, as described above. Click the Privacy tab. Figure 2-26 explains the remaining steps.

Once you've built up the list of private disks and folders, close System Preferences. Spotlight will pretend they don't even exist.

Finding Files 2: The Find Command

Mac OS X's File→Find command (⌘-F) opens the Search window shown in Figure 2-27. It's a lot more powerful (and complex) than the basic Spotlight menu, because it can hunt down icons using extremely specific criteria. If you spent enough time

Figure 2-27:
The first time you use it, the new Search dialog box opens up ready to search your entire hard drive (except other people's Home folders), regardless of file type. But don't settle—Spotlight has many more tricks up its software sleeve.

The Search Bar

See the ovalish text box at the top of every Finder window? This, too, is a piece of the Spotlight empire. The beauty of this bar, though, is that it can search *only the open window* (including any folders in it, and folders *within* folders, and so on).

To use it, just type a few letters of whatever you're looking for. The window instantly changes into the Search dialog box described on the previous pages, with one key difference: Among the search places listed along the top (Home, Computer, and so on), you'll see the name of the window you're searching. It will say, for example, "Folder 'Music.'"

What's so convenient about this feature is that you can narrow the scope of your search to just the current window by clicking that button. Spotlight doesn't even make you retype the search request.

Even better, once you've clicked the current-folder button in *one* Search window, Mac OS X will remember to narrow your results for each subsequent search you do. In other words, you've just told Mac OS X that you *always* want it to search only inside the current window—at least until you click a different button at the top of the window.

In any case, once you've rounded up a list of matches, you can work with them just as described on page 78.

setting up the search, you could use this feature to find a document whose name begins with the letters *Cro,* is over one megabyte in size, was created after August 24 but before the end of the year, was changed within the last week, has the file name suffix *.doc,* and contains the phrase "attitude adjustment." (Of course, if you knew *that* much about a file, you'd probably know where it is, too, without having to use the Search window. But you get the picture.)

Where to Look

The words at the top of the window—Servers, Computer, Home, and Others—are buttons. You click one to specify where you want Spotlight to do its searching. Here's what they mean:

- **Servers** refers to other computers on your network, assuming you've brought their icons to your screen as described on page 140.

- **Computer** means your entire hard drive, except what's in other people's Home folders.

- **Home** is your own Home folder (and not, say, the Applications folder, the Shared folder, or any other folders on your hard drive).

- **Others** lets you limit your search to certain disks or folders (see Figure 2-28). You could do that to make the search even faster, or just to avoid having to wade through a lot of irrelevant results.

Once you've added a new search location to the list, it sprouts its own button at the top of the window, so that it's available the next time you want to search. (If you dragged in a group of folders, the button says, for example, "3 folders.")

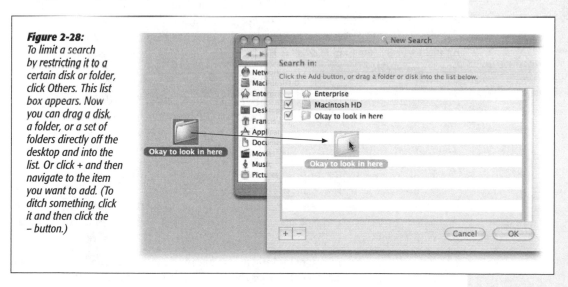

Figure 2-28:
To limit a search by restricting it to a certain disk or folder, click Others. This list box appears. Now you can drag a disk, a folder, or a set of folders directly off the desktop and into the list. Or click + and then navigate to the item you want to add. (To ditch something, click it and then click the – button.)

What to Look For

If all you want to do is search your entire computer for files containing certain text, you may as well use the Spotlight *menu* described at the beginning of this chapter.

The power of the Search *window,* though, is that it lets you design much more specific searches, using over 125 different search criteria: date modified, file size, the "last opened" date, color label, copyright holder's name, shutter speed (of a digital photo), tempo (of a music file), and so on. Figure 2-29 illustrates how detailed this kind of search can be.

Figure 2-29:
By repeatedly clicking the + button at the right end of the search-criteria rows, you can limit your search to files that were created before or after a certain date, that are larger or smaller than a certain size, and so forth.

To add a criterion to the list, click one of the + buttons at the right end of the dialog box. A new row appears in the window, whose pop-up menus you can use to specify *what* date, *what* file size, and so on. Figure 2-29 shows how you might build, for example, a search for all photo files that you've opened within the last week that contain a Photoshop layer named *Freckle Removal.*

To delete a row from the Find window, click the – button at its right end.

Here's a rundown of the ways you can restrict your search, according to the options you'll find in the first pop-up menu of a row. Note that after you choose from that first pop-up menu (Last Opened, for example), you're supposed to use the *second* pop-up menu to narrow the choice (Within the Last 2 weeks), as you'll read below.

- **Kind.** When the first pop-up menu says Kind, you can use the second pop-up menu to indicate *what* kind of file you're looking for: Images, Text files, PDF files, Movies, Music, Documents, Presentations, Folders, or Applications. For example, when you're trying to free up some space on your drive, you could round up all your gigantic movie files.

    And what if the item you're looking for isn't among the nine canned choices in the second pop-up menu? That's what the Others option is all about. It's the rabbit hole into a staggering array of hundreds of file types—ranging alphabetically from ".D document" to "ZIP archive"—that Spotlight knows about. To specify which of these oddball file types you want to round up, you can either choose from the Others pop-up menu shown in Figure 2-30, or you can type part of a file type's name into the text box; Mac OS X fills in the closest match automatically.

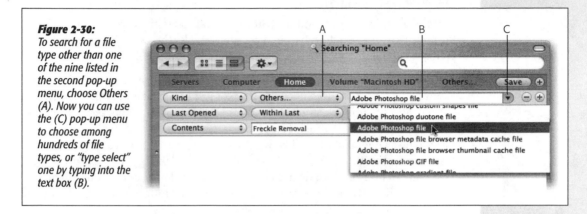

Figure 2-30:
To search for a file type other than one of the nine listed in the second pop-up menu, choose Others (A). Now you can use the (C) pop-up menu to choose among hundreds of file types, or "type select" one by typing into the text box (B).

- **Last Opened/Last Modified/Created.** When you choose one of these options from the first pop-up menu, the second pop-up menu lets you isolate files, programs, and folders according to the last time you opened them, the last time you changed them, or when they were created.

  The commands at the top of the pop-up menu (Today, Since Yesterday, This Month) offer canned time-limiting options. The commands at the bottom (Exactly, Before, After, Within Last) let you be more precise with your time-limiting.

  In any case, these are awesomely useful controls, because they let you specify a *chronological* window for whatever you're looking for. In fact, you're allowed to add *two* Date rows, which lets you round up files created before one date and after another.

- **Keywords.** You're most likely to encounter keywords in saved Web pages—they describe what the Web pages are *about,* rather than what specific words the pages contain.

- **Color Label.** Mac OS X lets you not only tag certain icons with color labels (page 59), but—perhaps even more importantly—lets you round them up later, for backing up, deleting, or burning to a CD en masse, for example. The criterion row sprouts seven colored dots—representing the seven available color labels—plus an X, which means "find all icons with no label applied."

- **Name.** The beauty of Spotlight is that it finds text *anywhere* in your files, no matter what their names are. That's why Apple demoted this option—the icon's name—to such a low position in the pop-up menu.

  Still, one nice thing about this criterion is that you can add it *more than once,* to create super-specific name searches. If you want to find file names that start with "Chewbacca" and also contain "nude," now you know how.

- **Contents.** You can think of this option as the opposite of Name. It finds *only* the text that's inside your files, and ignores their icon names. That's handy when you can't remember what you called a file, for example, or when a marauding toddler renames your doctoral thesis "xggrjpO#$5%////."

- **Size.** Using this control, and its "Greater than"/ "Less than" pop-up menu, you can restrict your search to files of a certain size. Use the second pop-up menu to choose KB (kilobytes), MB (megabytes), or GB (gigabytes).

- **Other.** Choosing Other from the first pop-up menu opens a special dialog box containing more than 100 *other* criteria. Not just the big kahunas like Name, Size, and Kind, but far more targeted (and obscure) criteria like "Bits per sample" (so you can round up MP3 music files of a certain quality), "Device make" (so you can round up all digital photos taken with, say, a Canon camera), "Key signature" (so you can find all the GarageBand songs you wrote in the key of F sharp), "Pages" (so you can find all Word documents that are really long), and so on. As you can see in Figure 2-31, each one comes with a short description.

You never know. Someday, you may remember *nothing* about a photo you're looking for except that you used the flash and an F-stop of 1.8.

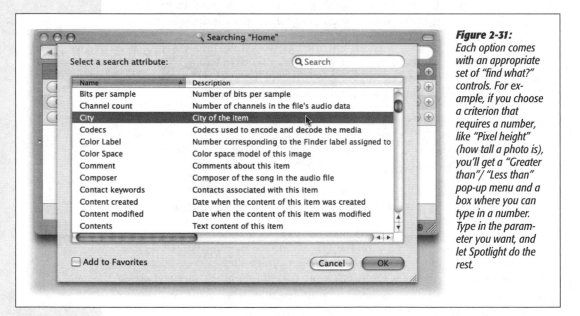

Figure 2-31:
Each option comes with an appropriate set of "find what?" controls. For example, if you choose a criterion that requires a number, like "Pixel height" (how tall a photo is), you'll get a "Greater than"/ "Less than" pop-up menu and a box where you can type in a number. Type in the parameter you want, and let Spotlight do the rest.

What to Do with Search Results

You can manipulate the list of search results much the way you'd approach a list of files in a standard Finder list view window. You can move up or down the list by pressing the arrow keys, scroll a "page" at a time with the Page Up and Page Down keys, and so on. You can also highlight multiple icons simultaneously, the same way you would in a Finder list view: Highlight all of them by choosing Edit→Select All, highlight individual items by ⌘-clicking them, drag diagonally to enclose a cluster of found items, and so on.

Or you can proceed in any one of these ways:

- **Find out where something is.** If you click *once* on any item in the results list, the bottom edge of the window becomes a folder map that shows you where that item is. To get your hands on the actual icon, just choose File→Open Enclosing Folder (⌘-R).

- **Open the file (or open one of the folders it's in).** If one of the found files is the one you were looking for, double-click it to open it (or highlight it and press either ⌘-O or ⌘-down arrow). In many cases, you'll never even know or care *where* the file was—you just want to get into it.

  You can also double-click to open any of the folders that appear in the folder map in the bottom half of the window.

- **Move or delete the file.** You can drag an item directly out of the found-files list and into a different folder, window, or disk—or straight to the Dock or Trash.

- **File-menu commands.** After highlighting an icon (or icons) in the list of found files, you can use the commands in the File menu, including Get Info, Add to Sidebar, and Move to Trash.

- **Collapse the list.** By clicking the flippy triangles, you can collapse or expand the category headings, just as in the regular Spotlight window. Once again, you can also Option-click a flippy triangle to expand or collapse *all* of them at once.

Note: This results window offers several other controls that should look familiar if you've experienced the thrill of the Spotlight window. For example, the blue heading for Images offers a slideshow button, a list-view button, and a thumbnails-view button. And every item offers an ❶ button at the far right of its row, for quick detailed information.

- **Copy a file.** To copy a file, Option-drag it out of the Search Results window and onto the desktop, into a different window, or onto a disk or folder icon. Alternatively, highlight the file and then choose Edit→Copy "Bunion Treatments.doc" (or whatever the file's name is). Then click inside a different folder window, or click a folder itself, before choosing Edit→Paste.

- **Make an alias.** You can make an alias for one of the found items exactly the way you would in a Finder window: Drag it out of the window while pressing ⌘-Option. The alias appears wherever you release the mouse (on the desktop, for example).

- **Start over.** If you'd like to repeat the search using a different search phrase, just edit the text in the Search bar (you can press Option-⌘-F to select the text). The results pane updates itself as you type.

- **Give up.** If none of these avenues suits your fancy, you can simply close the Search window as you would any other (⌘-W).

Smart Folders

Once you've grown comfortable with the layout of the Search dialog box, you may notice the little Save button in the upper-right corner. That button generates a *smart folder*—a self-updating folder that, in essence, performs a *continual, 24-hour search* for the criteria you specify. It's amazingly useful, and totally without precedent in the Windows world.

Here's the most common example. You choose File→Find. You set up the pop-up menus to say "Last Opened" and "This week." You click Save. You name the smart folder something like Current Crisis, and save it on your desktop (Figure 2-32).

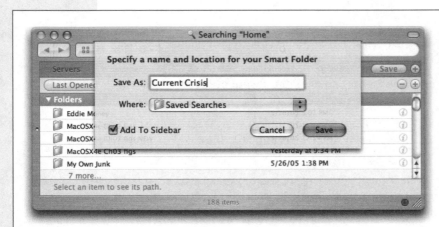

Figure 2-32:
When you click the Save button, Mac OS X offers to preserve your carefully structured search as a on the desktop. (If you turn on Add to Sidebar, you'll also make the smart folder available as a single-click icon in your Sidebar.)

From now on, whenever you double-click that smart folder, it opens to reveal all of the files you've worked on in the last week or so, neatly clustered into category groups the way Spotlight loves. The great part is that these items' *real* locations may be all over the map, scattered in folders all over your Mac and your network. But through the magic of the smart folder, they appear as though they're all in one neat folder.

Tip: If you decide your original search criteria need a little fine-tuning, open up the smart folder. At the upper-right corner of the window, click Edit. You're back on the original setting-up-the-search window. Use the pop-up menus and other controls to tweak your search setup, and then click the Save button once again.

The Dock, Desktop, Toolbar, and Sidebar

When you stop to think about it, the Mac OS X environment owes most of its different, photo-realistic looks to four key elements: the Dock at the bottom edge of the screen, the toolbar at the top of every Finder window, the Sidebar on the left side of every Finder window, and the shimmering, sometimes animated backdrop of the desktop itself. This chapter shows you how to use and control these most dramatic elements of Mac OS X.

The Dock

As noted briefly in Chapter 1, the Dock is a launcher (like the Windows Start menu) and a "what's open" listing (like the Windows taskbar) rolled into one. Only a tiny triangle beneath a program's icon tells you that it's open.

Apple starts the Dock off with a few icons it thinks you'll enjoy: QuickTime Player, iTunes, iChat, and so on. But using your Mac without putting your *own* favorite icons on the Dock is like buying an expensive suit and turning down the free alteration service. At the first opportunity, you should make the Dock your own.

The concept of the Dock is simple: Any icon you drag onto it (Figure 3-1) is installed there as a large button. A single click, not a double-click, opens the corresponding icon. In other words, the Dock is an ideal parking lot for the icons of disks, folders, documents, and programs you frequently use.

Tip: You can install batches of icons onto the Dock all at once—just drag them as a group.

Here are a few aspects of the Dock that may throw you at first:

- **It has two sides.** The fine dark line running down the middle of the Dock in Figure 3-1 is the divider. Everything on the left side is a program. Everything else goes on the right side: files, documents, folders, and disks.

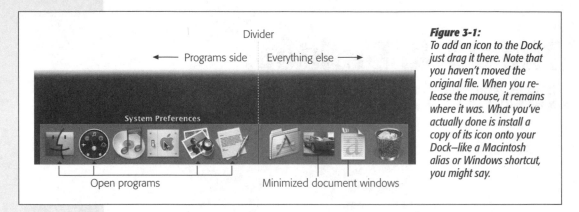

Divider

◄——— Programs side   Everything else ———►

System Preferences

Open programs   Minimized document windows

Figure 3-1:
To add an icon to the Dock, just drag it there. Note that you haven't moved the original file. When you release the mouse, it remains where it was. What you've actually done is install a copy of its icon onto your Dock—like a Macintosh alias or Windows shortcut, you might say.

- **Its icon names are hidden.** To see the name of a Dock icon, point to it without clicking. You'll see the name appear just above the icon.

- **Folders and disks are hierarchical.** If you retain nothing else in this chapter, remember this: If you *hold down* the mouse button on a folder or disk icon on the right side of the Dock, a list of its contents sprouts from the icon. It's a hierarchical list, meaning that you can burrow into folders within folders this way. See Figure 3-2 for an illustration.

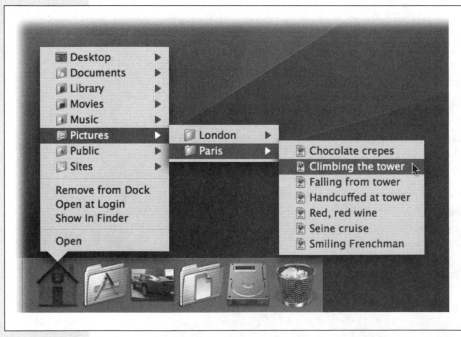

Figure 3-2:
As long as you keep the mouse button pressed, you can burrow into folders within folders—either with the intention of opening a file or folder (by releasing the mouse button as you point), or just to see what's inside.

Desktop ►
Documents ►
Library ►
Movies ►
Music ►
Pictures ►   London ►
Public ►   Paris ►   Chocolate crepes
Sites ►   Climbing the tower
                               Falling from tower
Remove from Dock   Handcuffed at tower
Open at Login   Red, red wine
Show In Finder   Seine cruise
                               Smiling Frenchman
Open

Tip: To make the pop-up menu appear instantly, just Control-click the Dock icon, or (if you have a two-button mouse) right-click it.

- **Programs appear there unsolicited.** Nobody but you can put icons on the *right* side of the Dock. But program icons appear on the left side of the Dock automatically whenever you open a program—even if it's one that you didn't put there. Its icon remains there for as long as the program is running.

Organizing and Removing Dock Icons

You can move the icons of the Dock around just by dragging them horizontally. As you drag, the other icons scoot aside to make room. When you're satisfied with its new position, drop the icon you've just dragged.

Tip: If you *don't* want the other icons to scoot away, then ⌘-drag it. In that case, the existing Dock icons freeze in place. This technique is absolutely essential when you're trying to drop a document into a *folder* on the Dock, rather than adding the document *to* the Dock. Without the ⌘ key, you wind up playing a frustrating game of chase-the-folder.

To remove a Dock icon, drag it away. Once your cursor has cleared the Dock, release the mouse button. The icon disappears, its passing marked by a charming little puff of animated cartoon smoke. (Mac OS X won't let you remove the Finder, the Trash, or the Dock icon of a program or document that's currently open, however.)

Weirdly enough, this technique (removing a Dock program's icon by dragging it away) works even while a program is still running. Granted, you won't see any change immediately, because the program is still open. But when you ultimately quit the program, you'll see that its previously installed icon is no longer on the Dock.

Three Ways to Get the Dock out of Your Hair

The bottom of the screen isn't necessarily the ideal location for the Dock. Because most screens are wider than they are tall, the Dock eats into your limited vertical screen space. Worse, a bottom-feeding Dock can actually overlap your document windows, interfering with your work.

In these situations, you have three ways out: Hide the Dock, shrink it, or rotate it 90 degrees.

Auto-hiding the Dock

To turn on the Dock's auto-hiding feature, choose →Dock→Turn Hiding On.

In other words, a hidden Dock works just like a hidden taskbar in Windows. When it's hidden, you can make it slide into view by moving the cursor to the Dock's edge of the screen. When you move the cursor back to the middle of the screen, the Dock slithers out of view once again. (Individual Dock icons may occasionally shoot upward into desktop territory when a program needs your attention—cute, very cute—but otherwise, the Dock lies low until you call for it.)

Tip: You may prefer to hide and show the Dock by pressing the hide/show keystroke, Option-⌘-D. The Dock pops on and off the screen without requiring you to move the cursor.

Shrinking and enlarging the Dock

Depending on your screen's size, you may prefer smaller or larger Dock buttons. The official way to resize them goes like this: Choose ⌘→Dock→Dock Preferences. In the resulting dialog box, drag the Dock Size slider, as shown in Figure 3-3.

There's a much faster way to resize the Dock, however: Just position your cursor directly on the Dock's divider line, so that it turns into a double-headed arrow (shown in Figure 3-3). Now drag up or down to shrink or enlarge the Dock.

Tip: If you press Option as you drag, the Dock snaps to certain canned icon sizes—those that the programmer actually drew.

Figure 3-3:
Look closely—you can see the secret cursor that resizes the Dock. If you don't see any change in the Dock size as you drag upward, you've reached the size limit: the Dock's edges are already approaching your screen sides.

As noted in Figure 3-3, you may not be able to *enlarge* the Dock, especially if it contains a lot of icons. But you can make it almost infinitely *smaller*. Which makes you wonder: How can you distinguish between icons if they're the size of molecules?

GEM IN THE ROUGH

Living Icons

Mac OS X brings to life a terrific idea, a new concept in mainstream operating systems: icons that *tell* you something. As shown here, for example, you can often tell documents apart just by looking at their icons.

Furthermore, some program icons actually change over time. The Mail icon (see Chapter 10) displays a live counter that indicates how many new email messages are waiting for you. (After all, why should you switch into the Mail program if you'll only be disappointed?) The iChat icon

sprouts an indicator to let you know that an instant message is waiting. And if you minimize a QuickTime movie while it's playing, it shrinks down and continues playing right there in the Dock.

Think of the possibilities. At this rate, one day the Safari icon could change to let us know when interesting new Web pages have appeared, the Quicken icon could display your current bank balance, and the Microsoft Word icon could change every time Microsoft posts a bug fix.

The answer lies in the →Dock→Turn Magnification On command. What you've just done is trigger the swelling effect shown in Figure 3-4. Now your Dock icons balloon to a much larger size as your cursor passes over them. It's a weird, rippling sort of animated effect that takes some getting used to. But it's yet another spectacular demonstration of the graphics technology in Mac OS X, and it can actually come in handy when you find your icons otherwise shrinking away to nothing.

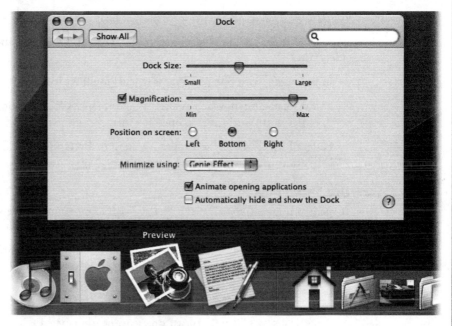

Figure 3-4:
To find a comfortable setting for the Magnification slider, choose →Dock→ Dock Preferences. Leave the Dock Preferences window open on the screen, as shown here. After each adjustment of the Dock Size slider, try out the Dock (which still works when the Dock Preferences window is open) to test your new settings.

Moving the Dock to the sides of the screen

Yet another approach to getting the Dock out of your way is to rotate it, so that it sits vertically against a side of your screen. You can rotate it in either of two ways:

- **The menu way.** From the →Dock submenu, choose "Position on Left," "Position on Right," or "Position on Bottom," as you see fit.

- **The mouse way.** While pressing Shift, drag the Dock's divider line, as though it's a handle, directly to either side of the screen.

You'll probably find that the right side of your screen works better than the left. (Most Mac OS X programs put their document windows against the left edge of the screen, where the Dock and its labels might get in the way.)

Note: When you position your Dock vertically, the "right" side of the horizontal Dock becomes the bottom of the vertical Dock. So if you use a vertical Dock, mentally substitute the phrase "bottom part of the Dock" when you read references to the "right side of the Dock."

Dock Features

Most of the time, you'll use the Dock as either a launcher (click an icon once to open the corresponding program, file, folder, or disk) or as a status indicator (the tiny black triangles, identified in Figure 3-1, indicate which programs are running).

But the Dock has more tricks than that up its sleeve. You can use it, for example, to pull off any of the following stunts.

Switch Applications

The Dock does much of what the Windows taskbar does—and more. For example, it lets you:

- Jump among your open programs by clicking their icons.

- ⌘-drag a document (such as a text file) onto a Dock application button (such as the Microsoft Word icon) to open the former with the latter.

- Hide all windows of the program you're in by Option-clicking another Dock icon.

Use Secret Menus

It turns out that if you Control-click a Dock icon—or, if you're in no hurry, hold down the mouse button on it—a hidden menu sprouts out (Figure 3-2).

If you've clicked a minimized window icon, this shortcut menu usually says only Open. But if you've clicked any other kind of icon, you get some very useful hidden commands. For example:

- **[Window names].** At the top of the shortcut menus of most running-application Dock icons, you'll find at least one tiny, neatly labeled window icon, as shown in Figure 3-5. This useful feature means that you can jump directly not just to a certain program, but to a certain *open window* in that program.

  For example, suppose you've been using Word to edit three different chapters. You can use Word's Dock icon as a Window menu to pull forward one particular chapter, or (if it's been minimized) to pull it up—even from within a different program.

Tip: The Finder tile that's always at the beginning of the Dock is, in effect, its own Window menu. By holding the mouse down on this icon for a moment, you produce a menu that lists all open desktop windows.

- **Keep In Dock/Remove from Dock.** Whenever you launch a program, Mac OS X puts its icon in the Dock—marked with a little black triangle—even if you don't normally keep the icon there. As soon as you quit the program, its icon disappears again from the Dock.

  If you understand that much, then the Keep In Dock command makes a lot of sense. It means, "Hello, I'm this program's icon. I know you don't normally keep me on your Dock, but I'd be happy to stay here even after you quit my program. Just say the word."

On the other hand, what if a program's icon is always on the Dock (even when it's not running) and you *don't* want it there? In that case, this command says Remove from Dock instead. It gets the program's icon off of the Dock, thereby returning the space it was using to other icons.

Use this last command on programs you rarely use. When you *do* want to run those programs, you can always use Spotlight to fire them up.

• **Open at Login.** This command lets you specify that you want this icon to open itself automatically each time you log in to the Mac. It's a great way to make sure that your email Inbox, your calendar, or the Microsoft Word thesis you've been working on is fired up and waiting, ready, on the screen when you sit down to work.

• **Show In Finder.** Choose this command to highlight the actual icon (in whatever folder window it happens to sit) of the application, alias, folder, or document you've clicked. You might want to do this when, for example, you're using a program that you can't quite figure out, and you want to jump to its desktop folder in hopes of finding a Read Me file there.

Tip: If you really want to reveal an icon in the Finder, there's a much faster way: ⌘-click its Dock icon. This takes you to the original instantly.

• **Hide/Show.** This operating system is crawling with ways to hide or reveal a selected batch of windows. Here's a case in point: You can hide all traces of the program you're using by choosing Hide from its Dock icon. (Page 100 lists several other methods, too.)

Figure 3-5:
Control-click a Dock icon, or click and hold on it, to open the secret menu. The names at the top of this shortcut menu are the names of the windows currently open in that program. The checkmark next to a window's name indicates that it's the frontmost window of that program (even if the program is in the background).

What's kind of cool here is that (a) you can even hide the Finder and all *its* windows, and (b) if you press Option, the command changes to say Hide Others. This, in its way, is a much more powerful command. It tells all of the programs you're *not* using—the ones in the background—to get out of your face. They hide themselves instantly.

Note: Once you've hidden a program's windows, this command changes to say Show, which is how you make them reappear.

- **Quit.** You can quit any program—besides the Finder and Dashboard—directly from its Dock shortcut menu. You don't have to switch into a program in order to access its Quit command. (Troubleshooting moment: If you get nothing but a beep when you use this Quit command, it's because you've hidden the windows of that program, and one of them has unsaved changes. Click the program's icon, save your document, and then try to quit again.)

Tip: If you hold down the Option key–even after you've opened the pop-up menu–the Quit command changes to say Force Quit. That's your emergency hatch for jettisoning a locked-up program.

Great Things to Put on Your Dock

Now that you know what the Dock's about, it's time to set up shop. Install the programs, folders, and disks you'll be using most often.

They can be whatever you want, of course, but don't miss these opportunities:

- **Your Home folder.** Many Mac fans immediately drag their hard drive icons onto the right side of the Dock—or, perhaps more practically, their Home folders (see page 26). Now they have quick access to every single file in every single folder they'll ever use.

- **The Applications folder.** Here's a no-brainer: Stash the Applications folder here, so you'll have quick pop-up menu access to any program on your machine.

- **The Documents folder.** The Documents folder in your Home folder is another primary center for your Mac activity. Stash it here for quick access.

- **The Shared folder.** If you're using the Mac's *accounts* feature (Chapter 12), this is your wormhole between all accounts—the one place you can put files where everybody can access them.

The Sidebar

As in Windows XP, the Sidebar is a pane at the left side of every navigation window. Unlike Windows, however, the Mac OS X Sidebar doesn't list operations you can perform on the current folder. (For that, you use the Finder's shortcut menu, which you summon by Control-clicking a folder.)

Instead, the Mac OS X Sidebar lists *places* where you might look for files and folders—that is, disks, folders, and network servers. Above the horizontal divider, you get the icons for your hard drives, iPods, flash drives, and other removable goodies.

Below the divider, you can stick the icons of anything else: files, programs, folders, or whatever.

Each icon is a shortcut. For example, click the Applications icon to view the contents of your Applications folder in the main part of the window (Figure 3-6). And if you click the icon of a file or program, it opens.

Figure 3-6:
The Sidebar makes navigation very quick, because you can jump back and forth between distant corners of your Mac with a single click.

In column view the Sidebar is especially handy, since it eliminates all of the columns to the left of the one you want, all the way back to your hard-drive level. You've just folded up your desktop!

Good things to put here: favorite programs, disks on the network to which you often connect, a document you're working on every day, and so on. Folder and disk icons here work just like the normal versions of those icons. You can drag a document onto a folder icon to file it there, drag a JPEG image file onto the Photoshop icon there, and so on.

In fact, the disks and folders here are spring-loaded (page 56).

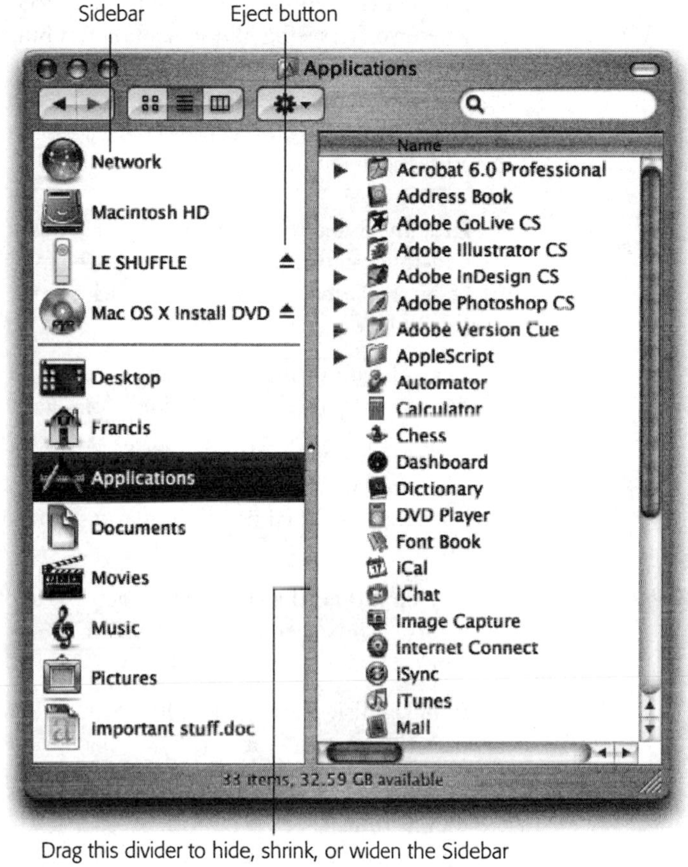

Sidebar   Eject button

Name
Network
Macintosh HD
LE SHUFFLE
Mac OS X Install DVD

Desktop
Francis
Applications
Documents
Movies
Music
Pictures
important stuff.doc

Acrobat 6.0 Professional
Address Book
Adobe GoLive CS
Adobe Illustrator CS
Adobe InDesign CS
Adobe Photoshop CS
Adobe Version Cue
AppleScript
Automator
Calculator
Chess
Dashboard
Dictionary
DVD Player
Font Book
iCal
iChat
Image Capture
Internet Connect
iSync
iTunes
Mail

33 items, 32.59 GB available

Drag this divider to hide, shrink, or widen the Sidebar

Fine-tuning the Sidebar

The beauty of this parking lot for containers is that it's so easy to set up with *your* favorite places. For example:

• **Remove** an icon by dragging it out of the Sidebar entirely. It vanishes with a puff of smoke (and even a little *whoof* sound effect). You haven't actually removed anything from your *Mac;* you've just unhitched its alias from the Sidebar.

• **Rearrange** the icons by dragging them up or down in the list.

- **Install a new icon** by dragging it off your desktop (or out of a window) into any spot in the appropriate half of the Sidebar: disks above the divider bar, everything else below.

  You can also highlight an icon wherever it happens to be and then choose File→Add to Sidebar (or just press ⌘-T).

- **Adjust the width** of the Sidebar by dragging the vertical divider bar (marked by the dot in its center) right or left. You'll "feel" a snap when the divider hits the spot where you're seeing all the icon names but not wasting any white space to their right.

Tip: If you drag carefully, you can position the divider bar just to the right of the disk and folder *icons*, thereby hiding their names.

- **Hide the Sidebar entirely** by double-clicking the vertical divider. The main file-and-folder-icons part of the window expands to exploit the freed-up space. (To bring the Sidebar back, double-click the left edge of the window; the telltale dot is still there to remind you.)

Then again, you probably wouldn't *want* to hide the Sidebar. It's one of the handiest navigation aids since the invention of the steering wheel. For example:

- **It takes a lot of pressure off the Dock.** Instead of filling up your Dock with folder icons (all of which look frustratingly alike), use the Sidebar to store them. You leave the Dock that much more room for programs and documents that you use often.

- **It's better than the Dock.** The Sidebar is a lot *like* the Dock, in that you can stash favorite icons there. But the Sidebar reveals the *names* of these icons, while the Dock doesn't.

- **It makes disk-ejecting easy.** Just click the ⏏ button next to any removable disk to make it pop out. (You can "eject" network disks the same way.)

- **It makes disc-burning easy.** When you've inserted a blank CD or DVD and loaded it up with stuff you want to copy, click the ☢ button next to its name. The Finder dutifully begins burning the disc.

- **You can drag onto its folders and disks.** You can use the Sidebar icons exactly as though they were the "real" disks, folders, and programs they represent.

- **It simplifies connecting to networked disks.** Park your other computers' hard drive icons here, as described in Chapter 5, and you shave several steps off the usual connecting-via-network ritual.

- **It lets you drag between distant folders.** See Figure 3-7 for details on this sneaky, yet highly efficient trick.

The Finger Toolbar

At the top of every Finder window is a small set of function icons, all in a brushed-aluminum row (Figure 3-8). The first time you run Mac OS X, you'll find only these icons on the toolbar:

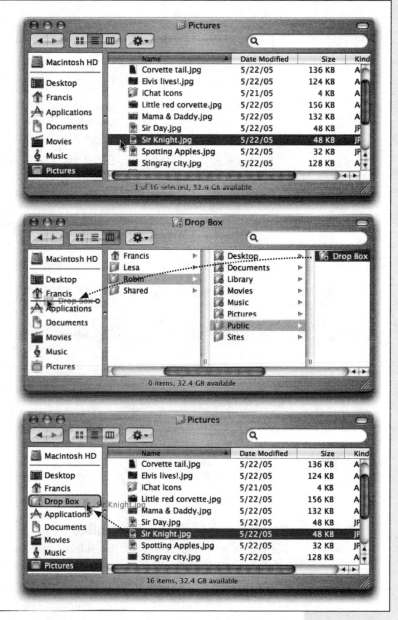

Figure 3-7:
Top: How are you supposed to drag the Sir Knight file (in your Home→Pictures folder) into a folder that's not visible at the moment—a folder that requires navigating down a totally different path? You could use spring-loaded folder-dragging (page 56), but if the two folders are distant, the following trick is faster. Middle: Start by dragging the destination folder into the Sidebar (in this case, the Public→Drop Box folder in Robin's Home folder.

Bottom: Drag the Sir Knight file onto the folder to complete the transition. Drag the Drop Box folder out of the Sidebar to get rid of it, if you wish.

• **Back, Forward.** As in Windows, the Mac OS X Finder works something like a Web browser. Only a single window remains open as you navigate the various folders on your hard drive.

The Back button returns you to whichever folder you were just looking at. (Instead of clicking Back, you can also press ⌘-[, or choose Go→Back—particularly handy if the toolbar is *hidden*.)

The Forward button springs to life only *after* you've used the Back button. Clicking it (or pressing ⌘-]) returns you to the window you just backed out of.

• **View controls.** The three tiny buttons next to the Forward button switch the current window into icon, list, or column view, respectively.

• **Action.** This pop-up menu shows the same commands as the Finder's shortcut menu, which you summon by Control-clicking inside a folder (or on the desktop).

• **Search bar.** This little round-ended text box is yet another entry point for the Spotlight feature described in Chapter 2. As you type into it, the window turns into a search-results window showing only matches within the *currently open window*. Once you've typed a couple of letters, you'll see the proof: The location bar (at the top of the window, where it says Servers, Computer, Home, and so on) identifies "Folder 'Pictures,'" or whatever the open window's name is.

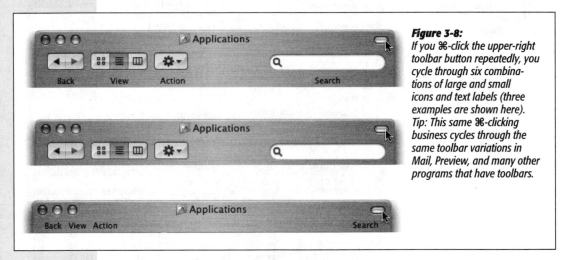

Figure 3-8:
If you ⌘-click the upper-right toolbar button repeatedly, you cycle through six combinations of large and small icons and text labels (three examples are shown here). Tip: This same ⌘-clicking business cycles through the same toolbar variations in Mail, Preview, and many other programs that have toolbars.

Removing or Shrinking the Toolbar

Between the toolbar, the Dock, the Sidebar, and the unusually large icons of Mac OS X, it almost seems like there's an Apple conspiracy to sell big screens.

Fortunately, the toolbar doesn't have to contribute to that impression. You can hide it with one click—on the white, oval "minimalist Finder window" button (Figure 3-8). You can also hide the toolbar by choosing View→Hide Toolbar or pressing Option-⌘-T. (The same keystroke, or choosing View→Show Toolbar, brings it back.)

But you don't have to do without the toolbar altogether. If its consumption of screen space is your main concern, you may prefer to simply collapse it—to delete the pictures but preserve the text buttons.

The trick is to ⌘-click the Old Finder Mode button. With each click, you make the toolbar take up less vertical space, cycling through six variations of shrinking icons, shrinking text labels, and finally labels without any icons at all (see Figure 3-8).

There's a long way to adjust the icon and label sizes, too: Choose View→Customize Toolbar (or Option-⌘ click the Old Finder Mode button). As shown in Figure 3-9, the dialog box that appears offers a Show pop-up menu at the bottom. It lets you choose picture-buttons with Icon Only, or, for the greatest space conservation, Text Only. You can see the results without even closing the dialog box. Click Done or press Enter to make your changes stick.

Note: In Text Only mode, the three View buttons become a little pop-up menu. Furthermore, the Search bar (page 74) turns into a one-word button called Search. Clicking it brings up the Finder-window version of the Spotlight dialog box (page 74).

Figure 3-9:
While this window is open, you can add additional icons to the toolbar by dragging them into place from the gallery before you. You can also remove icons from the toolbar by dragging them up or down off the toolbar, or rearrange them by dragging them horizontally.

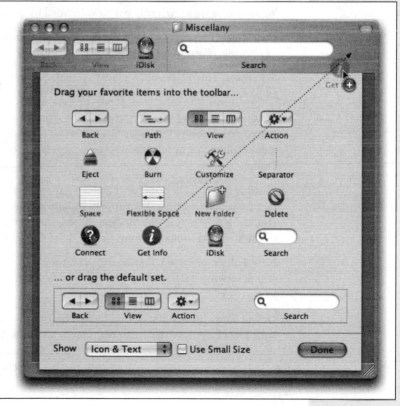

Adding New Icons to the Toolbar

Mac OS X not only offers a collection of beautifully designed icons for alternate (or additional) toolbar buttons, makes it easy for you to add *anything* to the toolbar, turning the toolbar into a supplementary Dock or Sidebar.

Apple's toolbar icon collection

To see the optional toolbar icons that Apple has prepared for you, choose View→ Customize Toolbar. The window shown in Figure 3-9 appears.

This is your chance to rearrange the existing toolbar icons or delete the ones you don't use. You can also add any of Apple's buttons to the toolbar simply by dragging them from the "gallery" upward onto the toolbar itself. The existing icons scoot out of your cursor's way, if necessary.

Most of the options listed in the gallery duplicate the functions of menu commands. Here are a few of the options that don't appear on the standard toolbar:

- **Path.** Most of the gallery elements are buttons, but this one creates a *pop-up menu* on the toolbar. When clicked, it reveals (and lets you navigate) the hierarchy—the *path*—of folders that you navigate to reach whichever window is open. (*Equivalent:* ⌘-clicking a window's title bar, as described on page 29.)

- **Customize.** This option opens the toolbar-customizing window that you're already examining. (*Equivalent:* The View→Customize Toolbar command.)

- **Separator.** This is the only gallery icon that doesn't actually do anything when clicked. It's designed to set apart groups of toolbar icons.

- **Space.** By dragging this mysterious-looking item into the toolbar, you add a gap between the icons to its sides. A space is about as wide as one icon. (The rectangular outline that appears when you drag it won't actually show up once you click Done.)

- **Flexible Space.** This icon, too, creates a gap between the toolbar buttons. The difference is that this time, the gap will expand as you make the window wider. Now you know how Apple got the Search box, for example, to appear off to the right of the standard toolbar, a long way from its clustered comrades to the left.

- **New Folder.** Clicking this button creates a new folder in whichever window you're viewing. (*Equivalent:* The File→New Folder command, or the Shift-⌘-N keystroke).

- **Delete.** This option puts the highlighted file or folder icons into the Trash. (*Equivalent:* The File→Move to Trash command, or the ⌘-Delete keystroke.)

Tip: The New Folder and Delete icons are among the most valuable ones to put on your toolbar. They represent functions you'll probably use often.

- **Connect.** If you're on an office network, opens the Connect to Server dialog box so that you can tap into another computer. (*Equivalent:* The Go→ Connect to Server command, or the ⌘-K keystroke.)

- **Default set.** If you've made a mess of your toolbar, you can reinstate its original, factory-installed arrangement just by dragging this rectangular strip directly upward onto your toolbar.

Note: If a window is too narrow to show all the icons on the toolbar, you will see, at the right end of the toolbar, a >> symbol. Click it for a pop-up menu that names whichever icons don't fit at the moment. (You'll find this toolbar behavior in many Mac OS X programs, not just the Finder: Preview, Mail, Activity Monitor, and so on.)

Adding your own stuff

You can drag *any icons at all* onto the toolbar—files, folders, disks, programs, or whatever—to turn them into one-click buttons. Figure 3-10 shows you how.

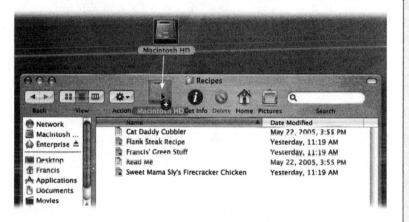

Figure 3-10:
You don't need to choose View →Customize Toolbar to add your own icons to the toolbar. Just drag them from the desktop or any folder window directly onto the toolbar, at any time. (Pause with your cursor on the toolbar for a moment before releasing the icon.)

Rearranging or Removing Toolbar Icons

You can drag toolbar icons around, rearranging them horizontally, by pressing ⌘ as you drag. Taking an icon off the toolbar is equally easy: While pressing the ⌘ key, just drag the icon clear away from the toolbar. It vanishes in a puff of cartoon smoke.

Designing Your Desktop

In some ways, just buying a Macintosh was a renegade act of self-expression. But that's only the beginning. Now it's time to fashion the computer screen itself according to your personal sense of design and fashion.

System Preferences

Cosmetically speaking, Mac OS X offers two dramatic full-screen features: desktop backgrounds and screen savers. (That's not counting the pictures and colors you can apply to individual folder windows, as described on page 42.)

The command center for both of these functions is the System Preferences program (the equivalent of the Windows Control Panel). Open it by clicking the System Preferences icon on the Dock, or by choosing its name from the menu.

When the System Preferences program opens, you can choose a desktop picture or screen saver by clicking the Desktop & Screen Saver button. For further details on these System Preferences settings, see page 359.

Desktop Sounds

Desktop *sounds* are the tiny sound effects that accompany certain mouse drags. And we're talking *tiny*—they're so subdued and sparse, you might not even have noticed them. For example, you hear a little *plink/crunch* when you drop an icon onto the Trash, a boingy *thud* when you drag something into a folder, a little *whoof!* when you drag something off the Dock and into oblivion, and so on. (The little thud that you hear at the end of a file-copying job is the only one that's actually useful, since it alerts you that the task is complete.)

If all that racket is keeping you awake, however, it's easy enough to get rid of it. Open System Preferences, click the Sound icon, and turn off "Play user interface sound effects."

And if you decide to leave them turned on, please—use discretion when working in a library, neurosurgical operating room, or church.

Menulets

Page 18 demystifies *menulets*, the Mac OS X replacement for icons in the Windows system tray.

Programs and Documents

T he beauty of life in the Era of Switchers is that most of the big-boy programs are available in nearly identical versions for both the Mac and Windows. Word, Excel, and PowerPoint; Photoshop, Illustrator, and InDesign; FileMaker Pro; Dreamweaver; and many other programs are available for both Mac and Windows. Sometimes you have to buy the Mac version separately; sometimes it's on the same CD.

The best part: The documents you create with the Mac versions are generally *identical in format* to the ones created in Windows. A Microsoft Word document, for example, requires no conversion when transferred from a Mac to a PC or vice-versa. It is what it is—a .doc file.

Same thing with Excel spreadsheets (.xls), PowerPoint slideshows (.ppt), Photoshop documents (.psd), and on and on. You may occasionally encounter a tiny formatting difference—a line thickness change, a movie file that requires a plug-in—but most documents open flawlessly when moved between Macs and PCs. (Chapter 7 offers more detail on finding Mac versions of your favorite PC programs.)

But even if switching to the Mac OS X versions of your programs is relatively easy, learning how Mac OS X programs *in general* operate may require some study. As this chapter makes clear, the relationship between programs and their documents differs in several substantial ways from the way things work in Windows.

Launching Mac OS X Programs

Many of the techniques for launching (opening) a program work just as they do in Windows. For example:

- Double-click an application's icon (in the Applications folder, for example).

- Click a program's icon on the Dock, Finder toolbar, or Sidebar (Chapter 3).

- If a program's icon is already highlighted, press ⌘-O (short for File→Open) or ⌘-down arrow.

- Use the ⌘ menu's Recent Items→Applications listing.

- Open a *document* icon in any of these ways, or drag a document onto the icon of a program that can open it (whether in the Dock, the Finder toolbar, or in a folder window).

As the program opens, its icon jumps up and down eagerly in your Dock (unless you've turned off the "Animate Opening Applications" checkbox in the System Preferences→Dock pane).

What happens next depends on the program you're using. Most present you with a new, blank, untitled document, just like most programs in Windows. Some, like iMovie and iDVD, automatically open the last file you worked on. And a few oddball programs don't open any window at all when first launched.

The Application Menu

Once a program is open, you'll notice a few changes to the menu bar at the top of the screen. The first menu appears with bold lettering and identifies the program you're using. It might say Safari, Word, or Mail, for example.

This Application menu (Figure 4-1) offers a number of commands pertaining to the entire program and its windows, including About, Quit, and Hide.

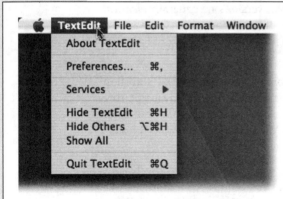

Figure 4-1:
The first menu in every program lets you know, at a glance, which program you're in.

Quitting Programs

In Macintosh lingo, you don't "exit" a program when you're finished with it, you "quit" it. And the command to do so isn't in the File menu—it's at the bottom of the Application menu.

But Mac OS X offers three much more fun ways to quit a program.

- Press ⌘-Q, which is the keyboard shortcut for the Quit command.

- Control-click a program's Dock icon and choose Quit from the pop-up menu.

- When you've pressed ⌘-Tab to summon Mac OS X's "heads-up display" of open programs (page 102), type the letter Q without releasing the ⌘ key. The highlighted program quits after a short pause.

Force Quitting Programs

Mac OS X is a rock-solid operating system, but that doesn't mean that *programs* never screw up. Individual programs are just as likely to freeze or lock up as they are in, say, Windows.

In such cases, you have no choice but to *force quit* the program—or, in Windows lingo, to terminate it or "end its task." Fortunately, doing so doesn't destabilize your Mac, meaning you don't have to restart it. In fact, you can almost always reopen the very same program and get on with your life.

You can force-quit a stuck program in any of several ways. First, you can Control-click its Dock icon (or just hold your mouse down on it). Once the pop up menu appears,

Figure 4-2:
Top: You can force quit a program from the Dock thanks to the Option key.

Bottom: When you press Option-⌘-Esc or choose Force Quit from the ⌘ menu, a tidy box listing all open programs appears. (This is the equivalent of the Windows Task Manager.) Just click the one you want to abort, click Force Quit, and click Force Quit again in the confirmation box.

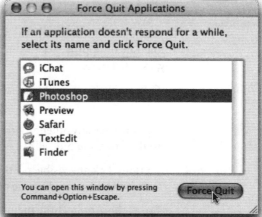

press Option so that the Quit command now says Force Quit (see Figure 4-2). Bingo: That program is outta here.

Second, you can press Option-⌘-Esc, the Mac's version of the Windows Control-Alt-Delete "three-fingered salute." Third, you can choose ⌘→Force Quit. Either way, proceed as shown in Figure 4-2.

Note: The only downside to force-quitting is that you lose any unsaved changes in the program you just killed.

Switching Programs

Mac OS X includes an elegant solution to tracking the programs you've opened: the Dock.

Chapter 3 describes the navigational features of this multipurpose icon row—but once you've actually opened a program or two, it takes on a whole new purpose in life.

Switching Programs

The primary purpose of the Dock is simple: to let you know which programs are running. Only one can be in front, or *active,* at a time.

One way to switch to a different program is to click its icon on the Dock. Doing so makes the program, along with any of its open windows and toolbars, pop to the front.

Hiding Programs

If the open programs on your Mac are like overlapping sheets of paper on a messy desk, then *hiding* a program makes that individual sheet transparent. When a program is hidden, all of its windows, palettes, and toolbars disappear. You can bring them back only by bringing the program to the front again (by clicking its Dock icon again, for example).

If your aim is to hide only the program you're *currently* using, Mac OS X offers a whole raft of approaches to the same problem. Many of them involve the Option key, as listed here:

- Option-click any visible portion of the desktop. The program you were in vanishes.

- Option-click any other program's icon on the Dock. You bring the clicked program to the front *and* hide all the windows of the program you were using.

- Option-click any visible portion of another program's windows. Once again, you switch programs, hiding the one you were using at first.

- From the Application menu—the boldfaced menu that bears the program's name—choose Hide [Program Name].

• Press ⌘-H. This may be the easiest and most useful trick of all (although it doesn't work in Photoshop and a few other oddball apps). Doing so hides the program you're in; you then "fall down" into the next running program.

To un-hide a program and its windows, click its Dock icon again, or choose the Show All command in the Application menu.

Hiding All Other Programs

Choosing Hide Others from your program's Application menu means, "hide the windows of every program but this one." It even hides your Finder (desktop) windows, although desktop *icons* remain visible. (In most programs, you're offered a keyboard shortcut for this command, too: Option-⌘-H.)

If this trick interests you, you might also enjoy its Mac OS X–only corollary, described next.

The Bring-Program-Forward, Hide-All-Others Trick

Here's a fantastic Mac OS X secret with no counterpart in Windows. It's a terrific technique that lets you bring one program to the front (along with all of its open windows), and hide all other windows of all *other* open programs—all with one click.

In any case, the trick is to Option-⌘-click the lucky program's icon on the Dock. As it jumps to the fore, all other windows on your Mac are instantly hidden. (You can bring them back, of course, by clicking the appropriate Dock icons, or by choosing Show All from the Application menu.)

Minimizing Individual Windows

In Mac OS X, you can hide or show individual windows, just as in Windows. In fact, Apple offers at least four ways to do so:

• Click the Minimize button on its title bar, as shown in Figure 4-3.

• Double-click the window's title bar.

• Choose Window→Minimize Window, if your program offers such a command.

• Press ⌘-M in almost any program.

In any case, the affected window shrinks down until it becomes a new icon on the right side of the Dock. Click that icon to bring the window back.

Tip: If you press the Option key as you perform any of these techniques, you minimize *all* of the program's open windows to the Dock. (If you had several document windows open, they turn into side-by-side document icons on the Dock.) This isn't the same thing as hiding the entire *program*, though; as described above, you remain in the same program, but now all of its windows are hidden.

Using the Dock for Drag-and-Drop

The Mac is smart about the relationship between documents and applications. If you double-click a Word document icon, for example, Microsoft Word opens automatically and shows you the document.

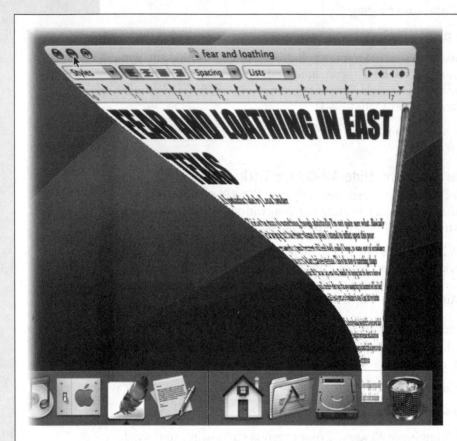

Figure 4-3:
When you click the center button on a window's title bar, you minimize that window, getting it out of your way and off your screen. It's now represented by an icon on your Dock, which you can click to reopen the window. You can change the animation that Mac OS X uses to minimize windows in the System Preferences→Dock pane.

But these days, it's occasionally useful to open a document using a program *other* than the one that created it. Perhaps, as is sometimes the case with downloaded Internet graphics, you don't *have* the program that created it, or you don't know which one was used.

In such cases, the Dock is handy: Just drag the mystery document onto one of the programs in the Dock, as shown in Figure 4-4. Doing so forces the program to open the document—if it can.

The New, Improved "Alt+Tab"

Exactly as in Windows, you can switch between programs with a keystroke—in Mac OS X, it's ⌘-Tab. And like Windows, if you hold *down* that keystroke, you can navigate through a "heads-up" display of all open programs using the Tab key. (To move backward through the open programs, press *Shift-⌘-Tab*.) Figure 4-5 shows the procedure.

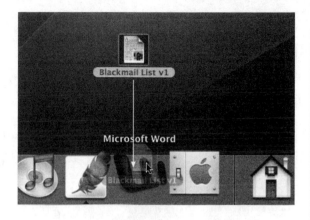

Figure 4-4:
To open a document using a program that didn't create it, drag the document icon onto the corresponding Dock icon. This technique is ideal for opening a downloaded graphics file into your favorite graphics program (such as Photoshop or iPhoto). It's also useful for opening a Read Me file into your word processor, such as Word, instead of the usual TextEdit program.

Figure 4-5:
The "heads-up" switcher lets you keep your eyes on your work, since the icons have translucent backgrounds. As you continue to hold down ⌘, you can click a program's icon to bring it forward; press H to hide a program; or press Q to quit one.

Better yet, a single press of ⌘-Tab takes you to the program you used *most recently*, and another press returns you to the program you started in. Imagine, for example, that you're doing a lot of switching between your Web browser and your email program. If you have five other programs open, you don't have to waste your time ⌘-Tabbing your way through *all* open programs just to get back to your Web browser.

Still, you can cycle through all open programs if you want to—the trick is to keep the ⌘ key pressed. Now, with each press of the Tab key, you highlight the Dock icon of another program, in left-to-right Dock order. Release both keys when you reach the one you want; Mac OS X brings the corresponding program to the front.

Exposé: The End of Window Clutter

Every operating system encounters the problem of overlapping windows—a problem that's a lot more common than it used to be, thanks to the proliferation of space-hog-

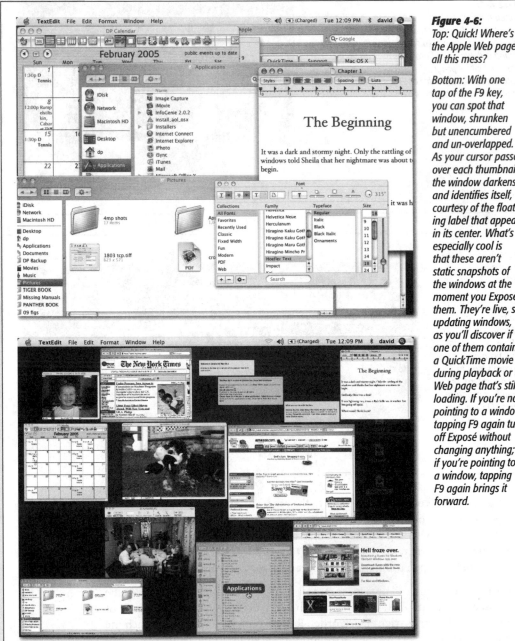

Figure 4-6:

Top: Quick! Where's the Apple Web page in all this mess?

Bottom: With one tap of the F9 key, you can spot that window, shrunken but unencumbered and un-overlapped. As your cursor passes over each thumbnail, the window darkens and identifies itself, courtesy of the floating label that appears in its center. What's especially cool is that these aren't static snapshots of the windows at the moment you Exposé'd them. They're live, still-updating windows, as you'll discover if one of them contains a QuickTime movie during playback or a Web page that's still loading. If you're not pointing to a window, tapping F9 again turns off Exposé without changing anything; if you're pointing to a window, tapping F9 again brings it forward.

ging palettes and panels in dozens of programs. Windows' attitude about this clutter can be summed up in three words: Deal with it.

Mac OS X, thankfully, is more proactive in eliminating window clutter. With a single press of the F9 key, Mac OS X shrinks *all windows in all programs* to a size that fits on the screen (Figure 4-6). You click the one you want, and you're there. It's called Exposé, and it's fast, efficient, animated, and a lot of fun.

Three Ways to Exposé

That business about finding a buried window on your screen is probably the way you'll use Exposé the most often. But it's actually only one of three Exposé functions. The other ways:

- **Find one window in the current program.** A second Exposé keystroke is designed to help you find a certain window only in the *program you're using*—a feature you'll probably find the most useful when you're Web browsing or word processing. When you tap F10 (the factory setting), all of the windows in the frontmost program spread out (and shrink, if necessary) so that you can see all of them simultaneously, in full—and so that you can click the one you want (see Figure 4-7, top).

  You can even mix this trick with the "heads-up" program switcher described earlier, using ⌘-Tab to switch to another program's windows.

- **Return to the desktop.** The third keystroke (F11 is the factory setting) may be the stealth breakthrough of Mac OS X. It sends *all* windows in *all* programs cowering to the edges of your screen, revealing the desktop beneath in all its uncluttered splendor (Figure 4-7, bottom). There the windows remain forever—or until you tap F11 again, click a visible window edge, click an icon, or take some other window-selection step.

  This feature is a *fantastic* timesaver. While you're writing an email message, for example, you can tap F11 to jump to the desktop and start dragging an attachment, then press F11 again to return to your message window and drop the file. Or, while you're on the Web, you can tap F11 to survey your desktop, to see if a file has finished downloading and decompressing itself. Finally, if you just get bored, you can just tap F11 to stare at your psychedelic desktop picture.

Tip: You can switch among the three Exposé modes (F9, F10, and F11) even after you've triggered one. For example, if you press F10 to shrink only *one* program's windows, you can then press F11 to see the desktop, and then press F9 to shrink *all* programs' windows.

Three Triggers for Exposé

Exposé is wonderful and all, but the standard keys for triggering its three functions—F9 to expose all windows, F10 for current-application windows, F11 for show-me-the-desktop—may leave something to be desired. For one thing, they may already be "taken" by other functions in your programs (like Microsoft Word) or even by your computer (like certain PowerBook G4 models, whose F9 and F10 keys adjust the keyboard illumination). For another thing, those keys are at the top of the keyboard where your typing fingers aren't used to going, and you may have to hunt to make sure you're pressing the right one.

Figure 4-7:
Top: When you press the F10 key, you get a clear shot at any window in the current program (Safari, in this example). In the meantime, the rest of your screen attractively dims, as though someone has just shined a floodlight onto the windows of the program in question. It's a stunning effect.

Bottom: Tap the F11 key when you need to duck back to the desktop for a quick administrative chore. Here's your chance to find a file, throw something away, eject a disc, or whatever, without having to disturb your application windows. In either case, tap the same function key again to turn off Exposé.

Fortunately, you can reassign the Exposé functions to a huge range of other keys, with or without modifier keys like Shift, Control, and Option. To view your options, choose ⌘→System Preferences and then click the Dashboard & Exposé icon (Figure 4-8).

Figure 4-8:
You can trigger Exposé in any of three ways: by twitching your cursor into a certain corner of the screen (top), pressing a key (middle), or clicking the extra buttons on a non-Apple mouse (bottom). Of course, there's nothing to stop you from setting up all three ways, so you can press in some situations and twitch or click in others.

Here, you'll discover that you can trigger Exposé's functions in any of three ways:

- **Screen Corners.** The four pop-up menus (Figure 4-8) represent the four corners of your screen. Using these menus, you can assign an Exposé trigger to each corner. If, for example you choose Desktop from the first pop-up menu, when your pointer hits the upper-left corner of the screen, you'll hide all windows and expose the desktop. (To make the windows come back, click any visible edge of a window, or twitch the cursor back into the same corner.) From that pop-up menu, you can pick other options, too, like turning on the screen saver or bringing forward Dashboard (page 108).

- **Keystrokes.** Also in the Exposé preferences, you'll find three pop-up menus—"All Windows," "Application Windows," and "Desktop"—that correspond to the three functions of Exposé as described above. You can't assign *any* old keystroke to Exposé, but you have far more options than the puny F9, F10, and F11 keys.

  Within each pop-up menu, for example, you'll discover that all of your F-keys are available as triggers: F1, F2, F3, and so on. If, while the pop-up menu is open, you press one or more of your modifier keys (Shift, Option, Control, or ⌘), all of these F-key choices *change* to reflect the key you're pressing; now the pop-up menu says

Shift-F1, Shift-F2, Shift-F3, and so on. That's how you can make *Shift*-F11 trigger the hide-all-windows function, for example.

- **Multiple-button mouse clicks.** If you've equipped your Mac with a replacement mouse—one with more than one button—you see a third pane in System Preferences, labeled Mouse. Use these pop-up menus to assign the three Exposé modes to the various clickers on your mouse: right-side click to hide all windows, left-side click to reveal the desktop, and so on.

Dashboard

The essence of using most operating systems is running *programs,* which often produce *documents.*

In Mac OS X, however, there's a third category: a set of weird, hybrid entities that Apple calls *widgets.* They appear, all at once, floating in front of your other windows, when your press the F12 key. Welcome to the Dashboard (Figure 4-9).

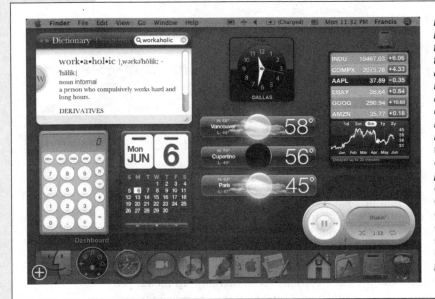

Figure 4-9:
Dashboard is a fleet of floating mini-programs that convey or convert all kinds of useful information. They appear and disappear all at once, on a tinted translucent sheet that floats in front of all your other windows. You get rid of Dashboard either by pressing the same key again (F12 or whatever) or by clicking anywhere on the screen except on a widget. (You can change this keystroke in the Dashboard & Exposé pane of System Preferences.)

What are widgets, anyway? They're not really programs, because they don't create documents or have Dock icons. They're certainly not documents, because you can't name or save them. What they *most* resemble, actually, is little Web pages. They're meant to display information, much of it from the Internet, and they're written using Web languages like HTML and JavaScript.

Mac OS X's starter widgets include a calculator, current weather reporter, stock ticker, clock, and so on. (You may have to wait a few seconds for them to "warm up," go online, and display any meaningful information.) The real beauty of the Dashboard, though, is that you can take your pick of over 1,000 additional, free widgets that bring you games, shopping, information, TV and movie schedules, sports, searching tools, and much more. (You'll find them at *www.apple.com/downloads/dashboard*.)

Mastering the basics of Dashboard won't take you long at all:

- **To move a widget,** drag it around the screen. (Click anywhere but on a button, menu, or text box.)

- **To close a widget,** press the Option key as you move the mouse across the widget's face. You'll see the circled X button appear at the widget's top left corner; click it.

- **To open a closed widget,** click the circled + button at the bottom of the screen, or just press ⌘-+. Now the entire screen image slides upward to make room for the *Widget Bar*: a "perforated metal" tray containing the full array of widgets, even the ones that aren't currently on the screen (Figure 4-10). Open one by clicking its icon, and enjoy the pond-rippling animation effect.

- **To rearrange your widgets** on the Widget Bar, open your hard drive→Library→ Widgets folder. Here you'll find the icons for your Dashboard widgets. Just rename them; they appear on the Widget Bar in alphabetical order.

Tip: The Dashboard icon also appears in your Dock, just in case you forget the F12 keystroke. Or, if you prefer the keystroke, you can drag the icon off your Dock to make room for more important stuff.

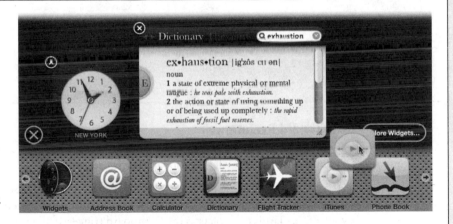

Figure 4-10:
You'll probably have to scroll the Widget Bar to see all the widgets, you can do this by clicking the arrows at either end. When you're finished opening new widgets, close the Widget Bar by clicking its circled X button at the left side of your screen.

Dashboard Tips

Dashboard is crawling with cool features. Here are a few of the biggies:

- If you just *click* an icon on the Widget Bar, the widget appears right in the middle of your screen. But if you *drag* the widget's icon off of the bar, you can deposit it anywhere you like on the screen.

- To refresh a certain widget—for example, to update its information from the Internet—click it and press ⌘-R. The widget instantly *twist-scrambles* itself into a sort of ice cream swirl (you've got to see it to believe it) and then untwists to reveal the new data.

- If you keep the Shift key pressed when you summon Dashboard, the widgets fly onto the screen in gorgeous, translucent, 3-D *slow motion*. Aren't you glad you're alive to see the day?

- Starting in Mac OS X 10.4.2, the Widget Bar includes a new widget just for managing *other* widgets. Figure 4-11 has the story.

Click to hide or show   Click to uninstall completely

Figure 4-11:
The Widget widget (whose icon appears at lower left in Figure 4-10) opens up this list of widgets. It lets you either hide or (if it's one you've downloaded yourself) completely uninstall any widget.

Dashboard Preferences

To change the Dashboard keystroke to something other than F12, choose ⌘→System Preferences, and then click Dashboard & Exposé.

Here, you'll discover that you can choose almost any other keyboard combination to summon and dismiss the Dashboard, or even choose a screen corner that, when your mouse lands there, acts as the Dashboard trigger. It all works just like setting up Exposé, as described earlier in this chapter.

How Documents Know Their Parents

Every operating system needs a mechanism to associate documents with the applications that created them. When you double-click a Microsoft Word document icon, for example, Mac OS X needs a way to know that you want Microsoft Word to launch and open the document.

In Windows, almost every document bears a three-letter file name suffix. If you double-click something called *memo.doc,* it opens in Microsoft Word. If you double-click *memo.wri,* it opens in Microsoft Write, and so on.

Mac OS 9 used a similar system, except that you never saw the identifying codes. Instead, it relied on invisible, four-letter *creator codes* and *type codes.* So why would you, a state-of-the-art Mac OS X maven, care what Mac OS 9 did? Because, as a Macintosh/Unix hybrid, Mac OS X uses both creator codes (like Mac OS 9) *and* file name suffixes (like Windows).

It's possible to live a long and happy life without knowing anything about these codes and suffixes. But if you're prepared for a little bit of technical bushwhacking, you may discover that understanding creator/type codes and file name suffixes can be useful in troubleshooting and customizing Mac OS X.

Type and Creator Codes

Many Macintosh documents come complete with invisible, behind-the-scenes, four-letter *type* and *creator* codes (see Figure 4-12).

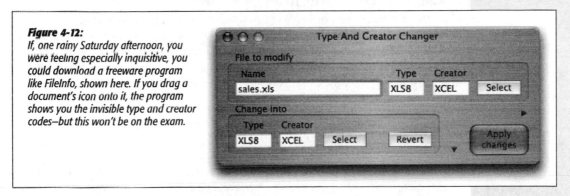

Figure 4-12:
If, one rainy Saturday afternoon, you were feeling especially inquisitive, you could download a freeware program like FileInfo, shown here. If you drag a document's icon onto it, the program shows you the invisible type and creator codes—but this won't be on the exam.

The *creator* code for a program and the documents it creates are identical—MSWD for Microsoft Word, 8BIM for Photoshop, and so on. That's the entire point: The creator code tells the Mac which program to open when you double-click a particular document.

The *type code,* on the other hand, specifies the document's file format. Photoshop, for example, can create graphics in a multitude of different formats: GIF, JPEG, TIFF, and so on. If you inspect your Photoshop documents, therefore, you'll discover that they all share the same creator code, but have a wide variety of type codes.

When you double-click a document, Mac OS X checks to see if it has a creator code. If so, it then consults an invisible database of icons and codes. This database is the master index that lists the correspondence between creator codes and the applications that generate them. Together, the type and creator codes also specify which *picture* appears on a particular icon.

If the desktop file discovers a match—if, say, you double-clicked a document with creator code BOBO, which corresponds to the AppleWorks entry in your desktop database—then the corresponding program opens the document, which now appears on your screen.

File Name Extensions

In Mac OS X, though, plenty of documents don't have type and creator codes. Documents created by *Cocoa* programs (page 120), for example, generally don't.

That's because Mac OS X is a Unix operating system. In Unix, type and creator codes are unheard of. Instead, what determines which program opens when you double-click a document is its *file name extension,* just as in Windows. A file name extension is identifiable by a suffix following a period in the file's name, as in *Letter to Mom.doc.*

The bottom line is that Mac OS X offers *two different* mechanisms that associate documents with the programs that created them. Mac OS X looks for type/creator codes first. Where they're absent, the file name suffixes kick in.

Hiding and Showing File Name Extensions

Exactly as in recent versions of Windows, Mac OS X comes set to *hide* most file name extensions, on the premise that they make the operating system look more technical and threatening. If you'd like to see them, however, choose Finder→Preferences→Advanced and turn on "Show all file extensions." Now examine a few of your documents; you'll see that their names display the previously hidden suffixes.

You can hide or show these suffixes on an icon-at-a-time basis, too (or a clump-at-a-time basis) using the Get Info window; see pages 63–64.

Reassigning Documents to Programs

Unfortunately, type and creator codes aren't of much use when you encounter a document created by a program you don't have. If your friend emails you a PowerPoint file, you won't be able to open it by double-clicking unless you have PowerPoint installed, too. Even if you have a different presentation program on your hard drive, just double-clicking the file won't always, by itself, open it.

The file name extension system, meanwhile, has problems of its own. File name extensions are even less likely to pinpoint which parent program should open a particular document. Suppose you've downloaded a graphic called Sunset.JPG. Well, almost any program these days can open a JPEG graphic—Word, Preview, Safari, and so on. How you tell Mac OS X which of these programs you want to open the file?

The solution is simple. You can *reassign* a document to a specific program (or all documents of its kind). Here's the rundown:

Reassigning a certain document—just once

Double-clicking a graphics file generally opens it in Preview, the graphics viewer included with Mac OS X (see page 427). Most of the time, that's a perfectly good arrangement. But Preview's photo-editing features don't hold a candle to a program like, say, iPhoto. If you wanted to edit such a file, you'd want it to open, just this once, into a different program—like iPhoto.

To do so, you must access the Open With command. You can find it in two places:

- Highlight the icon, and then choose File→Open With.

- Control-click the file's icon (or right-click it, if your mouse has two buttons). From the contextual menu, choose Open With.

In any case, study the submenu for a moment (Figure 4-13, top). The program whose name says "(default)" indicates which program *usually* opens this kind of document. From this pop-up menu, choose the name of the program you'd *rather* open this particular file, just this once.

Figure 4-13:
Top: The shortcut menu offers a list of programs capable of opening an icon. If you were to press the Option key right now, the words Open With would suddenly change to say Always Open With.

Bottom: If you choose Other, you'll be prompted to choose a different program. Turn on Always Open With if you always want this document to open in the new parent program. Otherwise, this is a one-time reassignment.

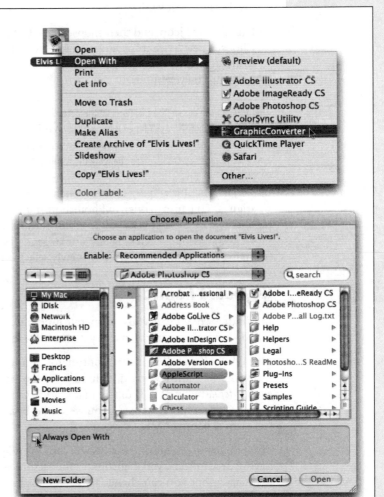

Reassigning a certain document—permanently

After opening a TIFF file in, say, Photoshop for editing, you haven't really made any changes in the fabric of your Mac universe. The next time you double-click that file, it will open once again in Preview.

If you wish this particular file would *always* open in Photoshop, the steps are slightly different. In fact, there are three different ways:

- In the Choose an Application dialog box, turn on "Always Open With" (shown at bottom in Figure 4-13).

- Start out with one of the techniques described above (File→Open With, or Control-click the file's icon and choose Open With)—but after you see the menu, press the Option key, too. Before your very eyes, the Open With command changes to say *Always* Open With.

- Highlight the icon, and then choose File→Get Info. Open the "Open with" panel. Choose a new "parent" program's name from the pop-up menu. You'll see that the word "(default)" changes position, now tacking itself onto the name of the new program you've chosen.

Tip: You can use this method to reassign the parenthood of a whole *flock* of selected icons at once. Once you've selected them, just hold the Option key, choose File→Show Inspector, open the "Open with" panel, and choose a new program from the pop-up menu. The message at the top of the window—"22 items," for example—reminds you that you're changing the whole batch at once.

In fact, if you follow up by clicking Change All beneath the pop-up menu, you can reassign *all* TIFF files to open in Photoshop, not just the specific one or batch that you highlighted. Mac OS X asks you to confirm by clicking Continue or pressing Enter. From now on, double-clicking any similar kind of document (one that has the same file name extension) opens it in the newly selected program.

Keyboard Control

In Windows, of course, you can operate every menu in every program from the keyboard—and every control in every dialog box—thanks to the power of the Alt key.

Mac OS X offers full keyboard control, too. You can operate every control in every dialog box from the keyboard, including pop-up menus and checkboxes. And you can even *redefine* many of the built-in Mac OS X keystrokes, like Shift-⌘-3 to capture the screen as a graphic. In short, if you were a keyboard power-user in Windows, you'll feel right at home in Mac OS X.

What follows are some of the ways you can control your Mac mouselessly. In the following descriptions, you'll encounter the factory settings for the keystrokes that do the magic—but you can change these combos to anything you want in the System Preferences→Keyboard & Mouse→Keyboard Shortcuts tab.

- **Control the menus.** When you press Control-F2, the ⌘ menu drops down. At this point, you can highlight individual commands on that menu by pressing the up or down arrow keys, or even typing the first couple letters. You move into a submenu by pressing the right or left arrow keys (or Tab). And you can "click" a menu command by pressing Enter, Return, or the Space bar. You can also close the menu without making a selection by pressing Escape or ⌘-period.

- **Control the Dock.** Once you've pressed Control-F3, you can move to highlight any icon on the Dock by pressing the appropriate arrow keys (or Tab and Shift-Tab). Then, once you've highlighted a Dock icon, you "click it" by pressing Enter or the Space bar. Again, if you change your mind, press Escape or ⌘-period.

Tip: Once you've highlighted a disk or folder icon, you can press the up or down arrow keys to make the list of its contents appear. (If you've positioned the Dock vertically, use the left or right arrow instead.)

- **Cycle through your windows.** Every time you press Control-F4, you bring the next window forward, eventually cycling through *every window in every open program*. Add the Shift key to cycle in the opposite order.

Note: This is different from the ⌘-` keystroke mentioned in Chapter 1, which just cycles through windows in the *current* program.

- **Control toolbars.** This one is on the unpredictable side, but it more or less works in most programs that display a Mac OS X–style toolbar: the Finder, Preview, Sherlock, the iPhoto editing window, and so on. When you press Control-F5, you highlight the first button on that toolbar. Move the "focus" by pressing the arrow keys or Tab and Shift-Tab. Then tap Enter or the Space bar to "click" the highlighted button.

- **Control tool palettes.** In a few programs that feature floating tool palettes, you can highlight the frontmost palette by pressing Control-F6. At this point, use the arrow keys to highlight the various buttons on the palette. You can see the effect when, for example you're editing text in TextEdit and you've also opened the Font palette. Pressing Control-F6 highlights the Font palette, taking the "focus" off your document.

- **Control dialog boxes.** Mac OS X also lets you navigate and manipulate any dialog box from the keyboard. When this feature is turned on, pressing the Tab key highlights the next control of any type, whatever it may be—radio button, pop-up menu, and so on. Press the Space bar to "click" a button or open a pop-up menu. Once a menu is open, use the arrow keys (or type letter keys) to highlight commands on it, and the Space bar to "click" your choice.

  At the bottom of the Keyboard & Mouse pane of System Preferences, there's a checkbox called "Turn on full keyboard access." When that checkbox is *off*, pressing the Tab key works only to move among text boxes in the dialog box. It skips over radio buttons, pop-up menus, and checkboxes.

The Save and Open Dialog Boxes

When you create a new document and then choose File→Save, you get Apple's version of the Save dialog box: the Save *sheet* (Figure 4-14).

Tip: In Mac OS X, a quick glance at the Close button in the upper-left corner of a document window tells you whether or not it's been saved (see Figure 4-14). When a small dot appears in the red button, it means you've made changes to the document that you haven't yet saved. Time to press ⌘-S! The dot disappears as soon as you save your work.

Figure 4-14:
Top: The Windows Save dialog box, an inevitable part of computing, displays a list of the folders on your hard drive. But how do you know where you are? What folder is this one inside of?

Bottom: In Mac OS X, you can see a familiar column display that matches the Finder, making it much easier to figure out what you're doing and how you got here.

In Windows, the Save dialog box appears dead center on the screen, where it commandeers your entire operation. You aren't allowed to do anything more in the current program until you click Save or Cancel to close the dialog box. Moreover, because it seems stuck to your *screen* rather than to a particular *document,* you can't clearly see which document you're saving—a real problem when you try to quit a program that has three unsaved documents open.

In most Mac OS X programs, a little Save dialog box called a *sheet* slides directly out of the document's title bar (see Figure 4-14). Now there's no mistaking which document you're saving.

Better still, you can think of this little Save box as a sticky note attached to the document. It will stay there, neatly attached and waiting, even if you switch to another program, another document within the same program, the desktop, or wherever. When you finally return to the document, the Save sheet will still be there, waiting for you to type a file name and save the document.

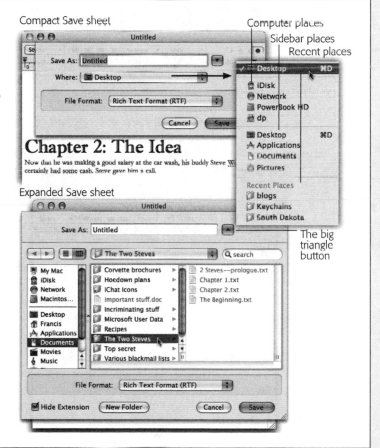

Figure 4-15:
Top: The Save dialog box, or sheet, initially appears in a compact view. Inset: To spare you from navigating your hard drive every time you save a file, your most recently accessed folders are listed in the Where pop-up menu.

Bottom: If you want to choose a different folder or create a new folder, click the Column-view triangle to open this Finder-like navigation view.

Compact Save sheet

Computer places
Sidebar places
Recent places

Expanded Save sheet

The big triangle button

Chapter 2: The Idea

Now that he was making a good salary at the car wash, his buddy Steve We certainly had some cash. Steve gave him a call.

Simplified Navigation

Of course, *you*, O savvy reader, have never saved a document into some deeply nested folder by accident, never to see it again. But millions of novices (and even a few experts) have fallen into this trap.

When the Save sheet appears, however, a pop-up menu shows you precisely where Mac OS X proposes putting your newly created document: in the Documents folder of your own Home folder—the Mac's version of the My Documents folder. For many people, this is an excellent suggestion. If you keep everything in your Documents folder, it will all be easy to find, and you'll be able to back up your work just by dragging a single folder (the Documents folder) to a backup disk.

But as described in Figure 4-15, the Where pop-up menu gives you direct access to some other places you might want to save a newly created file. (The keystrokes for the most important folders work here, too—Shift-⌘-H for your Home folder, for example.)

Tip: The Save box always displays whatever places you've put in your Sidebar. (In compact view, the Where pop-up menu lists them; in expanded view, you see the Sidebar itself.)

If you still can't find the folder you want, there's always the Search field in the upper-right corner of the dialog box—a direct descendant of the Spotlight box in the Finder. Just type a portion of the folder's name to display the matching result.

Column-View/List-View Navigation

When you save a file, the options in the Where pop-up menu have you covered 90 percent of the time. Most people work with a limited set of folders for active documents.

But when you want to save a new document into a *new* folder, or when you want to navigate to a folder that isn't listed in the Where pop-up menu, all is not lost. Click the large triangle identified in Figure 4-15.

After a moment, a familiar scene appears: a compact version of a Finder window. You should be on reassuring turf here: There's your Sidebar (page 88), there's your toggle switch between list and column views (although no icon view), there's the Back button, there's the Search bar, and so on. No other operating system on earth makes it so easy to navigate your folders from within the Save dialog box.

Highlight the name of the folder in which you want to save your newly created document. Alternatively, you can click the New Folder button to create a new folder *inside* whatever folder is highlighted in the column view. (The usual New Folder keystroke works here, too: Shift-⌘-N.) You'll be asked to type the new name for the folder. After you've done so, click Create (or press Enter). The new folder appears in the rightmost pane of the column view. You can now proceed with saving your new document into it, if you like.

The next time you save a new document, the Save sheet will reappear in whatever condition you left it. That is, if you used column view the last time, it will still be in column view. And at any time, you can collapse it into simplified view, shown at top in Figure 4-15, by again clicking the fat triangle to the right of the Where pop-up menu.

Tip: Whether you're using the mini-sheet or expanded view, you can always drag a folder directly from your *desktop* into the Save dialog box. Instantly, the dialog box changes to reflect the contents of that folder.

The Open File Dialog Box

The dialog box that appears when you choose File→Open is almost identical to the Save File sheet (see Figure 4-16). Because you encounter it only when you're opening an existing file, this dialog box lacks the New Folder button, Save button, file name field, and so on.

Most of the other Save File dialog box controls, however, are equally useful here. Once again, you can begin your navigation by seeing what's on the desktop (press ⌘-D) or in your Home folder (press Shift-⌘-H). Once again, you can find a folder or disk by beginning your quest with the Sidebar, and then navigate using either list or column view. And once again, you can drag a folder or disk off your desktop directly into the dialog box to specify where you want to look.

Figure 4-16:
Mac OS X's Open dialog box shows you only icons for disks, folders, and documents that you can actually open at this moment. For example, when using Preview as shown here, Word and TextEdit documents appear dimmed and unavailable, while picture files show up fine.

When you've finally located the file you want to open, do so by highlighting it (which you can do from the keyboard), and then pressing Return, Enter, or ⌘-O—or by just double-clicking it.

Three Kinds of Programs: Cocoa, Carbon, Classic

Mac OS X was supposed to make life simpler. It was supposed to eliminate the confusion and complexity that the old Mac OS had accumulated over the years—and replace it with a smooth, simple, solid system.

In a few years, that's exactly what Mac OS X will be. For the moment, however, you're stuck with running three different kinds of programs, each with different characteristics: *Cocoa, Carbon,* and *Classic.*

The explanation involves a little bit of history and a little bit of logic. To take full advantage of Mac OS X's considerable technical benefits, software companies must write new programs for it from scratch. So what should Apple do—send out an email to the authors of the 18,000 existing Mac programs, suggesting that they throw out their programs and rewrite them from the bottom up?

At big companies like Microsoft and Adobe, such a suggestion would wind up on the Joke of the Week bulletin board.

Instead, Apple gave software companies a break. It wrote Mac OS X to let programmers and software companies choose precisely how much work they wanted to put into compatibility with the new system. The various levels include:

- **Do nothing at all** (Classic). Let's face it: Software companies go out of business, unprofitable product lines are dropped, and shareware authors go off to law school. All of them leave behind orphaned programs that run only in the old Mac OS.

  Pre-Intel-chip Macs can still run this library of older software. When you try to open one of these older programs, Mac OS X launches a Mac OS 9 *simulator* called the Classic environment (page 123). Suddenly your screen is taken over by the ghost of Mac OS 9. Sure, you leave behind all the trappings (and benefits) of Mac OS X—its new look, most Exposé features, crash protection, and so on—but at least you're still running your favorite programs.

- **Update the existing programs** (Carbon). If software companies are willing to put *some* effort into getting with the Mac OS X program, they can simply adapt their existing software so that it works with Mac OS X. The resulting software looks and feels almost every bit like a true Mac OS X program—you get the crash protection, the good looks, the new Save dialog box, and so on—but behind the scenes, the bulk of the computer programming is the same as it was in Mac OS 9. These are what Apple calls *Carbonized* programs, named for the technology (Carbon) that permits them to run in Mac OS X.

  Carbonized programs include Microsoft Office, AppleWorks, iTunes, Photoshop, FileMaker, and, believe it or not, the Finder itself.

- **Write new programs from scratch (Cocoa).** As Mac OS X becomes a bigger and bigger hit, more and more programmers and software companies create new programs exclusively for it. The geeks call such programs *Cocoa* applications—and they're the best of all. Although they may look exactly like Carbonized programs, they feel a little bit more smooth and solid. More importantly, they offer a number of special features not offered by Carbonized programs.

  Many of the programs that come with Mac OS X are true Cocoa applications, including iChat, iCal, Safari, iPhoto, TextEdit, Stickies, Mail, Address Book, and so on. Any new programs Apple releases are also likely to be Cocoa applications.

Tip: Having trouble keeping the definitions of Carbon and Cocoa straight? You wouldn't be alone; it's like reading a novel where two characters' names start with the same letter. Here's one way to remember: *Carbon* programs are generally the *older* ones, those that might require Carbon-dating techniques to calculate their ages.

The Cocoa Difference

Here are some of the advantages offered by Cocoa programs. This section is worth reading—not to make you drool about a future when *all* Mac programs will fall into this category, but to help clear up any confusion you may have about why certain features seem to be only occasionally present.

Note: The occasional Carbon program may offer some of these features, too.

The Fonts Panel

Mac OS X comes with about 100 beautiful fonts that Apple licensed from commercial type companies—about $1,000 worth, according to Apple.

When you use a Carbon program, you usually access these fonts the same way as you do in Windows: using a Font menu. But when you use a Cocoa program, you get the Fonts panel, which makes it far easier to organize, search, and use your font collection (see Figure 4-17).

See how the Font panel is divided into columns, if the window is wide enough? The first column, Collections, contains the names of font-list subsets, such as Fun or Modern. This arrangement makes it easier to locate the kind of font you're looking for. You can make your own collections, too, by clicking the + button at the bottom of the panel.

The second column, Family, shows the names of the actual fonts in your system. The third, Typeface, shows the various style variations—Bold, Italic, Condensed, and so on—available in that type family. (Oblique and Italic are roughly the same thing; so are Bold and Black.)

The last column lists a sampling of point sizes. Of course, you can use any point size you want by typing any number into the box at the top of the Sizes list; the common sizes are just listed to save you a little typing.

Tip: You may have noticed that the Font panel doesn't actually *show* you the fonts you're working with—something of an oversight in a window designed to help you find your fonts. Never fear: The Show Preview command in the Action pop-up menu (the one that looks like a gear) adds a display section to the top of the Font panel, where you can see the font's name displayed in its *own* font.

Underline style | Strikethrough style | Text color | Background color | Shadow On/Off | Shadow darkness, blur, distance, angle

Action pop-up menu

Figure 4-17:
You'll find the Fonts panel only in Cocoa programs. As you adjust your font selections, you see the highlighted text in your program updated instantly. By clicking the name of a collection in the far left column, you can summon subsets of your fonts that make it much easier to home in on what you're looking for.

Services

Nestled in the Application menu of every Mac OS X program is a command called Services. These commands are dimmed when you use most *Carbonized* programs; they become available only when you use *Cocoa* programs.

Here's a sampling of the most useful commands in the Services menu.

Note: Not all of these Services work in all programs—even Cocoa programs. Implementing them is left partially to the discretion of the programmers.

Grab

Grab is a screen-capture program in your Applications→Utilities folder. You use it to turn what you see onscreen into graphics files. This is especially handy when writing computer books or training manuals.

Mail

This handy command springs to life only after you've highlighted some text in a Cocoa program—or a file in the Finder.

- **Send File.** This convenient option appears only if you've highlighted an icon in the Finder. In one swift step, this command opens the Mac OS X Mail program (Chapter 10), creates a new outgoing message, and attaches your highlighted file. All you have to do is address the message, click send, and exult in the tedium you've been spared.

- **Send Selection.** In one step, the Mail Text command launches Mail and pastes the highlighted text into the body of a new email message.

- **Send To.** This command is useful only if you've highlighted an email *address* in a text document. This command, too, switches to Mail and creates an outgoing message—but this time, Mac OS X pastes the text you've highlighted into the "To:" field.

Open URL

When you highlight a Web address in any program, choosing this command fires up your Web browser and takes you to the indicated page.

Speech

Mac OS X doesn't just display text onscreen—it can actually *read it* out loud.

- **Start Speaking Text.** Start by highlighting some text in a Cocoa program. Then choose this command, and presto: The Mac actually reads the text out loud, using the character voice you've chosen in System Preferences (page 349).

- **Stop Speaking.** This command makes the Mac shut up.

Summarize

Talk about intriguing: When you choose this command after highlighting some text, the Mac analyzes the sentences you've highlighted and, after a moment, launches Summary Service. This little program, which you probably never even knew you had, displays a greatly shortened version of the original text. Figure 4-18 offers details.

Tip: To save the summarized document as a TextEdit document, choose File→Save As.

How to Use Classic, If You Must

If only we could move into Mac OS X and live there! Unfortunately, *software* makes the world go 'round, and it could be a while before every program you'd ever want to use has been written or rewritten for Mac OS X.

That doesn't mean you can't use them at all, though. You can certainly run your old favorites within Mac OS X—by flipping back into Mac OS 9. (Note: The following pages apply to Macs *that do not contain an Intel chip*. Intel Macs can't run Classic.)

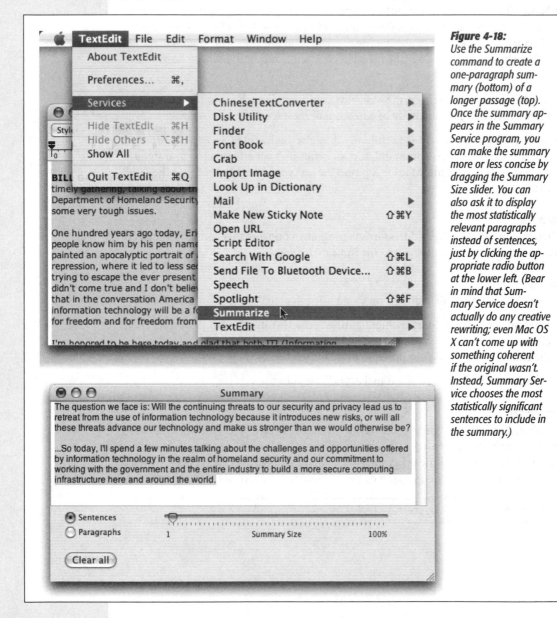

Figure 4-18:
Use the Summarize command to create a one-paragraph summary (bottom) of a longer passage (top). Once the summary appears in the Summary Service program, you can make the summary more or less concise by dragging the Summary Size slider. You can also ask it to display the most statistically relevant paragraphs instead of sentences, just by clicking the appropriate radio button at the lower left. (Bear in mind that Summary Service doesn't actually do any creative rewriting; even Mac OS X can't come up with something coherent if the original wasn't. Instead, Summary Service chooses the most statistically significant sentences to include in the summary.)

There are two ways to do that:

- **Run Classic.** You can think of the Classic program as a Mac OS 9 simulator or emulator. It runs automatically whenever you double-click the icon of a pre–Mac OS X program.

  At that point, the Classic (Mac OS 9) world takes over your screen, looking exactly like a 1999 Macintosh, complete with the old startup logo, old ⌘ menu, non-striped menu bar, and so on. Once it's running, you can launch most older Mac OS 9 programs without a hitch. Your Mac is running two operating systems at once, which requires quite a bit of memory.

  For most people, most of the time, Classic is the easiest, quickest, and most effective way to run really old Mac programs. (Except on Intel-based Macs, that is. Those computers can't run Classic programs at all.)

- **Restart the Mac in Mac OS 9.** Unfortunately, Classic is only a simulator. Because Mac OS X continues to run beneath it, it isn't actually *controlling* your Mac.

  Whenever a certain program "reaches for" a particular piece of circuitry on your Mac, such as the FireWire or USB jack, it may come up empty-handed. That's why many scanners, digitizing tablets, and even printers don't always work when you run programs in the Classic mode.

  In those situations, you might be able to use a second technique, although fewer and fewer people have this option with every passing month. If you bought a Mac model that was introduced before 2003, you can also restart your Mac in Mac OS 9, just as though you don't have Mac OS X installed at all. At this point, you've got just a Mac OS 9 machine, and all of that older gear works just as it always did. (Of course, you don't get any of the benefits of Mac OS X, such as its stability and multitasking prowess.)

  If you have the will and the Mac necessary to restart in Mac OS 9, open System Preferences→Startup Disk, click the Mac OS 9 System Folder you want to be in charge, and then click Restart. (To switch back to Mac OS X when you're done, choose ⌘→Control Panels→Startup Disk and click the specific Mac OS X System folder you want to be in charge. Then restart.)

Running Classic

If you've got a sufficiently old Mac, it's probably got Mac OS 9 installed already. In that case, when you double-click the icon of a pre–Mac OS X program, your Mac instantly concludes, "Well, this program won't run in Mac OS X, so I'll just go ahead and launch your Mac OS 9 simulator."

Otherwise, if you want to run a pre-Mac OS X program, you'll need to get and install a copy of Mac OS 9 yourself. (See *http://docs.info.apple.com/article.html?path=Mac/10.4/en/mh763.html* for assistance.) Once you've done that, you can double-click a Mac OS 9 program to get it going.

At this point, a progress bar appears in a floating window, as shown in Figure 4-20. During the startup process, you'll see a little Classic (numeral 9) icon in your Dock, just to help you understand what's going on.

Figure 4-19:
When you're running Mac OS X, the System Folder that contains Mac OS 9 is clearly marked by the golden 9. Only one System Folder per disk may bear this logo, which indicates that it's the only one officially recognized by the Mac. (As the programmers say, it's the "blessed" System Folder.)

When all the bouncing stops, you'll see a number of changes onscreen. Your Apple menu is now rainbow-striped, as it was in the days before Mac OS X. The menu bar is light gray, its fonts are smaller, and its menus and commands are different. In short, you've now gone back in time to Mac OS 9.

Note: As an entire operating system, Mac OS 9 could well be the subject of an entire book unto itself—like *Mac OS 9: The Missing Manual.*

Once Classic is running, you're free to use the Mac OS 9 program you originally double-clicked—or any other Mac OS 9 programs, for that matter.

Remember, though, that you're running two operating systems simultaneously. When you click a Mac OS X program's icon on the Dock, you bring forward both that program *and* Mac OS X itself. When you double-click a Mac OS 9's Dock icon (or click inside a Mac OS 9 program's window), you bring forward both that program *and* Mac OS 9. You can copy and paste information between the programs running in these two worlds—or even drag-and-drop highlighted material—but that's pretty much the extent of any cross-operating system communication.

Remember, though, that the old Mac OS is no more stable now than it ever was. One buggy program can still freeze or crash the entire Classic bubble. At that point, you may have to exit the Mac OS 9 portion of your machine, losing unsaved changes in *all* of your Mac OS 9 programs, just as though it were a Mac OS 9 machine that had locked up. (Mac OS X soldiers on, unaffected, and all your Mac OS X programs remain safe, open, and running.)

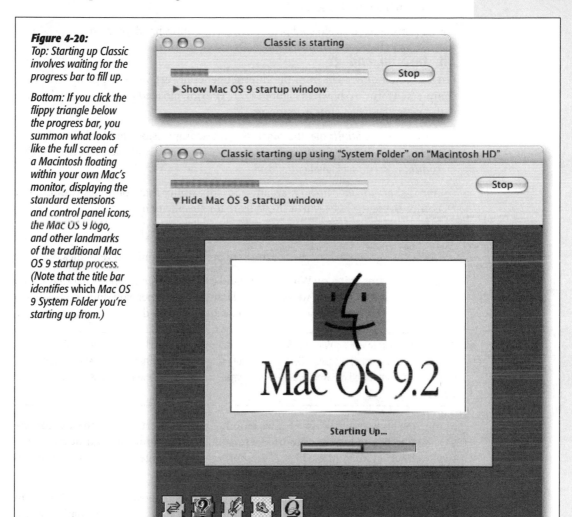

Figure 4-20:
Top: Starting up Classic involves waiting for the progress bar to fill up.

Bottom: If you click the flippy triangle below the progress bar, you summon what looks like the full screen of a Macintosh floating within your own Mac's monitor, displaying the standard extensions and control panel icons, the Mac OS 9 logo, and other landmarks of the traditional Mac OS 9 startup process. (Note that the title bar identifies which Mac OS 9 System Folder you're starting up from.)

There's really no good reason to quit the Classic simulator, ever. If you have a new Mac with plenty of memory, you may as well leave it open so that you won't have to wait for the startup process the next time you use a Mac OS 9 program.

Installing Mac OS X Programs

In general, new programs arrive on your Mac via one of two avenues: on a CD or via an Internet download. The CD method is slightly simpler; see "Performing the Installation" later in this section.

For help installing downloaded programs, on the other hand, read on.

.sit, .tar, .zip, and .gz

Programs you download from the Internet generally arrive in a specially encoded, compressed form, as shown in Figure 14-21. The downloaded file's name usually ends with one of these file name extensions:

- **.sit** indicates a *StuffIt* file, the Macintosh file-compression standard. You decompress such files with Stuffit Expander, a free program available from *www.stuffit.com/mac/expander/download3.html*.

- **.tar** is short for *tape archive,* an ancient Unix utility that combines (but doesn't compress) several files into a single icon, for simplicity in sending.

- **.gz** is short for *gzip,* a standard Unix compression format.

- **.tar.gz** or **.tgz** represents one compressed archive containing *several* files.

- **.zip** is the same as it is on Windows: a standard file-compression format that shows up in email attachments, web downloads, and so on. When you double-click a .zip file, Mac OS X launches a super-fast, background-only decompressing program.

Tip: Don't tell this to jealous Windows fans, but you can compress *any* file in the Finder by Control-clicking or right-clicking it and choosing "Create Archive of [whatever the file's name is]." After a few moments, you get a zip-compressed file, which you can then email to anyone in the world who uses either a Mac or a Windows PC.

Some Web browsers, including Safari, automatically convert some of these compression and archiving formats into usable form. Once you return to your desktop, you may well see *several* of these files, representing various stages of decompression and decoding (see Figure 4-21).

If not, just remember that StuffIt Expander, described above, can turn all of them back into usable form. If your browser didn't spur it into action automatically, just double-click your compressed file to get it back to the way it started.

Disk Images (.dmg files)

Once you've unstuffed (or untarred, or unzipped) a downloaded program, it often takes the form of a disk-image file, whose name ends with the letters *.dmg.* Disk images are extremely common in Mac OS X.

All you have to do is double-click the .dmg icon. After a moment, it magically turns into a disk icon on your desktop, which you can work with just as though it's a real disk (Figure 4-21). For example:

- Double-click it to open it. The software you downloaded is right inside.

- Remove it from your desktop by dragging it to the Trash (whose icon turns into a big silver Eject key as you drag), highlighting it and pressing ⌘-E (the shortcut for File→Eject), or Control-clicking it and choosing Eject from the shortcut menu. (You've still got the original .dmg *file* you downloaded, which you can use to resuscitate the disk image itself.)

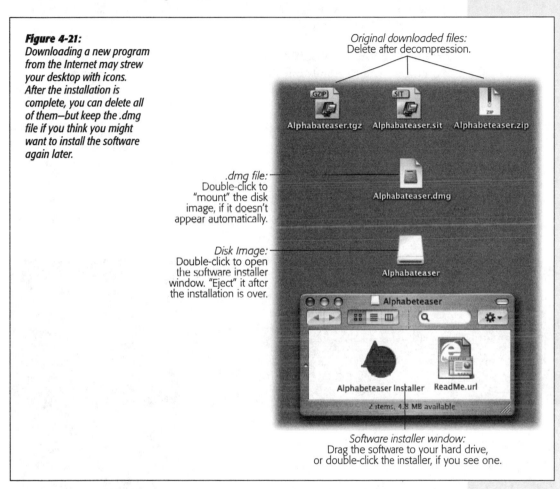

Figure 4-21:
Downloading a new program from the Internet may strew your desktop with icons. After the installation is complete, you can delete all of them—but keep the .dmg file if you think you might want to install the software again later.

Original downloaded files:
Delete after decompression.

Alphabateaser.tgz   Alphabateaser.sit   Alphabeteaser.zip

.dmg file:
Double-click to "mount" the disk image, if it doesn't appear automatically.

Alphabateaser.dmg

Disk Image:
Double-click to open the software installer window. "Eject" it after the installation is over.

Alphabateaser

Alphabeteaser

Alphabeteaser Installer   ReadMe.url

2 items, 4.8 MB available

Software installer window:
Drag the software to your hard drive, or double-click the installer, if you see one.

Cleaning Up After Decompression

When the StuffIt Expander progress-bar dialog box disappears, you may have several icons on your desktop. Some are useful, some you're free to trash.

- **The original compressed file.** As illustrated in Figure 4-21, it's safe to throw away the .sit, .tar, .gz, or .tgz file you originally downloaded (after it's decompressed, of course).

• **The .dmg file.** Once you've turned it into an actual disk-drive icon (Figure 4-21, bottom), installed the software from it, and ejected the disk-drive icon, you can delete the .dmg file. Keep it only if you think you might need to reinstall the software someday.

• **The disk image itself.** This final icon, the one that contains the actual software or its installer, doesn't exist as a file on your hard drive. It's a phantom drive, held in memory, that will go away by itself when you log out. So after installing its software, feel free to drag it to the Trash.

Performing the Installation

Working with .tar, .gz, and .dmg files are all skills unique to downloading Mac OS X programs from the Internet. Installing software from a CD is much more straightforward.

In either case, once you've got a disk icon on your desktop (either a pseudo-disk from a disk image or a real CD you've inserted), you're ready to install the software. You can install many Mac OS X programs just by dragging their icons or folders to your hard drive. Others offer a traditional installer program that requires you to double-click, read and accept a license agreement, and so on.

In both cases, *where* you decide to install the new program is suddenly a big issue. You have the following choices:

POWER USERS' CLINIC

When Programs Are Actually Folders

You may have noticed that OS X programs don't seem to have 50,000 support files strewn across your hard drive. To open Safari, you don't first open a Safari *folder;* you can just double-click the Safari icon itself. That's a much better arrangement than in Mac OS 9 or Windows, where many programs must remain in special folders, surrounded by libraries, dictionaries, foreign language components, and other support files and folders.

The question is: Where did all those support files go?

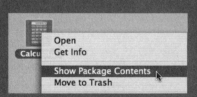

Mac OS X features so-called *packages* or *bundles,* which are folders that behave like single files. Every properly written Mac OS X program looks like a single, double-clickable application icon. Yet to the Mac, it's actually a folder that contains both the actual application icon *and* all of its support files, which are hidden for your convenience.

If you'd like to prove this to yourself, try this. Choose Go→Applications. See the Calculator program in the list? Control-click it. From the contextual menu, choose Show Package Contents. You're asking Mac OS X to show you what's inside the Calculator "application icon" folder.

The Calculator package window opens, revealing a Contents folder full of strange-looking, Unixy folders and files that, behind the scenes, are pieces of the Calculator program itself.

The application-as-folder trick is convenient, because it means that you can uninstall the program by dragging this single icon to the Trash without worrying that you're leaving behind its entourage of support files. (That is, unless you use Microsoft Office, which still keeps a separate stash of support files just like it does in Windows.)

- **In the Applications folder.** Most programs sit in your Applications folder. Almost always, this is where you'll want to install new programs. Putting them in the Applications folder makes it available to anyone who uses the Mac.

Note: You can't put anything in your Applications folder unless you have an *administrator account,* as described on page 323.

- **In your Home folder.** This option is valuable only if you share your Mac with other people, as described in Chapter 12. If that's your situation, you may occasionally want to install a program privately, reserving it for your own use only. In that case, just install or drag it into your Home folder (see page 26). When other people log onto the machine, they won't even know that you've installed that new program.

Note: If you don't have an administrator account, this is your *only* option.

Removing Mac OS X Programs

There's no Add/Remove Programs tool on the Macintosh, and there never was one. To uninstall a program, you just drag it (or its folder) to the Trash.

In general, this simple act removes all traces of a program (except perhaps its preference file, which may remain in your Home→Preferences folder). The Macintosh doesn't have a Registry, and most pieces of an application are actually hidden inside its icon (see the box on the facing page). What that means for most people is a *lot* fewer headaches.

Part Two:
Making the Move

2

Five Ways to Transfer Your Files

A huge percentage of "switchers" do not, in fact, *switch*. Often, they just *add*. They may get a Macintosh (and get *into* the Macintosh), but they keep the old Windows PC around, at least for a while. If you're in that category, get psyched. It turns out that communicating with a Windows PC is one of the Mac's most polished talents.

That's especially good news in the early days of your Mac experience. You probably have a good deal of stuff on the Windows machine that you'd like to bring over to the Mac. Somewhere along the line, somebody probably told you how easy this is to do. In fact, the Mac's reputation for simplicity may even have played a part in your decision to switch.

In any case, this chapter describes the process of building a bridge from the PC to the Mac, so that you can bring all your files and settings into their new home. It also tells you where to *put* all of them. (The next chapter is dedicated to the slightly hairier process of getting your email and addresses copied over.)

As it turns out, files can take one of several roads from your old PC to your new Mac. For example, you can transfer them on a disk (such as a CD or iPod), by a network, or as an attachment to an email message.

Transfers by Disk

One way to transfer Windows files to the Mac is to put them onto a disk that you then pop into the Mac. (Although Windows can't read all Mac disks without special software, the Mac can read Windows disks.)

This disk can take any of these forms:

- **A floppy disk.** Apple eliminated built-in floppy drives from its computers in 1997, but any Mac can be equipped with an external, add-on floppy drive for about $50. Of course, if all of your old Windows files fit on a floppy disk, you must be a casual PC user indeed!

- **An external hard drive or iPod.** If you have an external USB or IEEE 1394 (what Apple calls *FireWire*) hard drive, you're in great shape. While it's connected to the PC, drag files and folders onto it. Then unhook the drive from the PC, attach it to the Mac, and marvel as its icon pops up on your desktop, its contents ready for dragging to your Mac's built-in hard drive. (An iPod music player works great for this process, too, because it *is* an external hard drive.)

WORKAROUND WORKSHOP

How to Save Some Effort—for $50

This chapter is all about (a) hooking up your PC to your Mac so that you can transport your files across the great divide, and (b) figuring out where to *put* the files that you bring over.

If you're willing to spend a little money, however, it's possible to automate some of this process. The ticket is a software-and-cable kit called Move2Mac (from a company called Detto, which you can visit at *www.detto.com/ move2mac/*).

You install the software on both your PC and your Mac, and then you connect the two with the included, specialized USB cable (or parallel-to-USB cable, if your PC is too old for USB).

At this point, a wizard guides you through the process of choosing which PC files you want brought over to the Mac—and the list of options is enormous. You can tell the program to bring over your documents, pictures, music, video

files, desktop wallpaper, sounds, Internet Explorer favorites, Internet connection settings, Outlook Express address book, AIM screen names, and many other kinds of files.

(Notably absent from the list: email messages. Move2Mac can bring over your email *settings,* but it can't bring over the messages from any Windows email program, and it can't bring over the address book from any program except Outlook Express. For details on making these sorts of transfers, see Chapter 6.)

As part of the process, Move2Mac does everything it can to put the moved files and folders into the right places on the Mac. For example, the PC's My Documents folder arrives in your Home→Documents folder, with most of its folders-within-folders structure intact.

Move2Mac requires Windows 98 or later on the PC (a Windows 95 version is available separately with a parallel-to-USB cable) and costs about $50.

The only downsides here are that USB hard drives are pretty slow (except for the newer, USB 2.0 versions, which require newer computers), and not very many PCs have FireWire connectors.

- **A USB flash drive.** These small keychainy sticks, once popular only among hard-core geeks, have become so cheap and capacious that even Apple makes them—in the form of the $99 iPod Shuffle. Like a mini-external hard drive, a flash drive plugs directly into your USB port, at which point it shows up on your desktop just like a normal disk. You copy files to it from your PC, plug it into your Mac, and copy the files off, just like you would for any other disk. And, like an external hard drive, you're left with a backup copy of the data on the drive itself.

- **A Zip, Jaz, or Peerless drive.** One great thing about these various old backup drives from Iomega is that they're cross-platform. Copy stuff onto a disk while the drive is connected to the PC. Then, if the drive has a USB or FireWire connector, simply move the whole drive over to the Mac. (For best results, install Iomega's Macintosh driver software beforehand.)

Unfortunately, if your drive connects to the PC using a *parallel* connector, scratch this idea off the list; the Mac has no parallel port. (You could, in theory, get an adapter, but it's not worth the trouble or the cost when you can buy an entire external hard drive for about $100.)

Figure 5-1:
Burned CDs generally show up with equal aplomb on both Mac and Windows, regardless of which machine you used to burn it. Here's a CD burned on a Windows XP Pro machine (bottom), and what it looks like on the Mac (top)—same stuff, just a different look and different sorting order. Double-click this disk icon to open its window and then drag files to and from it, rename files, delete files, and so on.

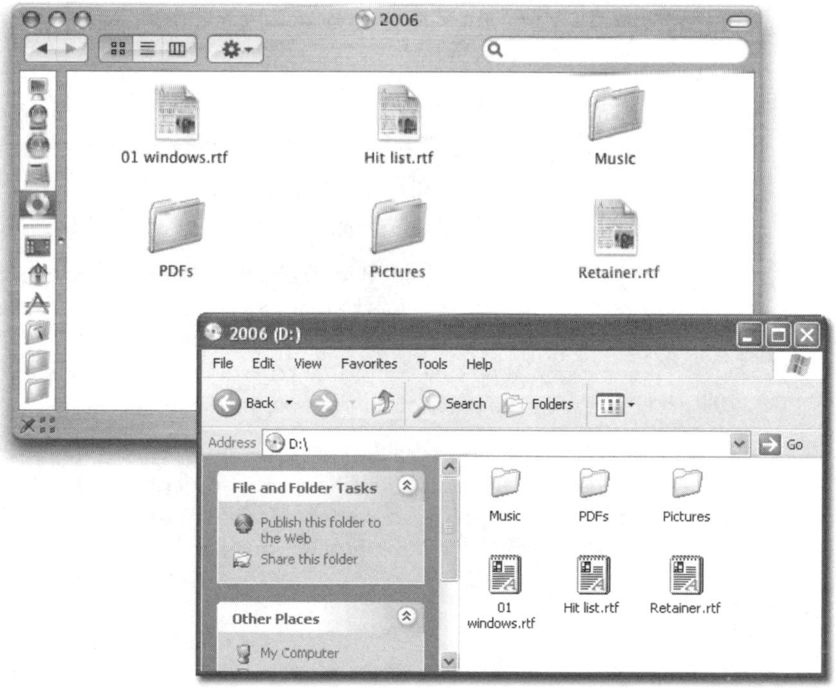

• **A CD or DVD.** If your Windows PC has a CD or DVD burner, here's another convenient method. Burn a disc in Windows, eject it, and then pop it into the Mac (see Figure 5-1). As a bonus, you wind up with a backup of your data on the disc itself.

Note: If you're given a choice of file format when you burn the disc in Windows, choose ISO9660. That's the standard format that the Macintosh can read.

• **Move the hard drive itself.** This is a grisly, very technical maneuver best undertaken by serious wireheads—but it can work. You can install your PC's hard drive directly into a Power Mac, as long as it was prepared using the older FAT or FAT32 formatting scheme. (The Mac can handle FAT hard drives just fine, but chokes with NTFS hard drives.)

When you insert a Windows-formatted disk, whatever the type, its icon appears at the upper-right corner of your desktop, where Mac disks like to hang out. (If it doesn't appear, you or someone you love has probably fiddled with the "Show these items on the Desktop" settings in the Finder→Preferences→General tab.)

Transfers by Network

Here's one of the best features of Mac OS X: It can "see" shared disks and folders on Windows PCs that are on the same network. Seated at the Mac, you can open or copy files from a PC. In fact, you can go in the other direction, too: Your old PC can see shared folders on your Mac.

This isn't a networking book, but there's enough room here for a crash course.

Ethernet Networks

Most people connect their personal computers using either of two connection systems: Ethernet or Wi-Fi (that is, 802.11 networking or, in Apple's terminology, AirPort).

If you connect all of the Macs, PCs, and Ethernet printers in your small office to a central *Ethernet hub*—a compact $25 box with jacks for five, ten, or even more computers and printers—you've got yourself a very fast, very reliable network. Most people wind up trying to hide the Ethernet hub in the closet, and running the wiring either along the edges of the room or inside the walls.

You can buy Ethernet cables, plus the Ethernet hub, in any computer store or, less expensively, from an Internet-based mail-order house. Hubs aren't platform-specific. (And a word of advice: All recent Macs offer built-in *100BaseT* and some offer *Gigabit Ethernet* cards, so don't hobble your network speed by buying a slower, *10baseT* hub.)

Tip: If you want to connect only two machines—your PC and your Mac, for example—you don't need an Ethernet hub at all. Instead, you can connect a standard Ethernet cable directly from your Mac to your PC's Ethernet adapter. This is a sensational system that places no limits on the amount of data that you can transfer—and it's *fast.*

That's if your Mac was made in 2002 or later. If you have an older model (Power Mac or PowerBook G3, colored iMac or iBook, 15-inch flat-panel iMac, and so on), you have to use an Ethernet *crossover cable* rather than a regular Ethernet cable—about $8 from a computer store or online mail-order supplier. Run it directly between the Ethernet jacks of the two computers.

Figure 5-2:
*If your PC has an Ethernet jack
(left), you're in for some easy
networking. It looks like an
overweight telephone jack, and
every Mac OS X–compatible
Macintosh has one. It connects
to an Ethernet hub (right) via
Ethernet cable (also known
as RJ-45), which looks like a
pudgy telephone wire.*

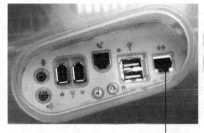 

Ethernet jack   Ethernet hub

Ethernet is the best networking system for many offices. It's fast, easy, and cheap.

Wireless Networks

By buying a $70 Wi-Fi (802.11) base station for your office, you catapult yourself into the most modern home-networking arrangement: *wireless* networking. Once you've installed a corresponding wireless card into both the Mac and the PC, they can then communicate without a cable in sight, as long as the machines are within 150 feet (as the termite burrows) from the base station. This system is a lot like a cordless phone; the computers are the "handsets."

Apple, having recognized that both "Wi-Fi" and "802.11" are extremely geeky names, made up its own term for this kind of networking: AirPort. For example, the card that you buy for your Mac is called an AirPort card, and Apple's version of the base station is called an AirPort base station. (Macs almost always require Apple's wireless cards, but they can connect to *any* brand of base station.)

Note: Technically, there are two Mac-compatible wireless standards: 802.11*b* ("AirPort") and 802.11*g* ("AirPort Extreme"). The AirPort Extreme standard is about five times faster than regular AirPort (54 MB/second versus 11 MB/second), but in order to take advantage of the increased speed, both of the computers *and* the base station have to offer it. If any of the three components operates at the slower AirPort speed, all three will revert to the slower mode—the case, for example, when you're using a Mac released before 2003.

After wiring your network (or unwiring it, as the case may be), your network is ready. Your Mac should "see" any Ethernet or shared USB printers, in readiness to print. You can now play network games or use a network calendar. And you can now turn on *file sharing,* one of the most useful and sophisticated features of the Mac OS.

Seated at the Mac: Seeing the PC

Suppose you have a Windows machine on the network. Thanks to Mac OS X's networking smarts, you can bring selected folder icons from the PC onto your Mac's screen, and manipulate their contents just as though they were sitting on your Mac's own hard drive.

Before the Mac and PC can begin chatting, though, Windows must be made ready to share its folders—and that entails installing a special software blob called File and Printer Sharing for Microsoft Networks. Do you have it? Here's how to tell:

- **Windows XP, Windows Me, Windows 2000.** You have this software already. Skip ahead to step 1.

- **Windows 95, 98, or NT.** If your PC has never been part of an office network, then it probably *doesn't* have the necessary software installed.

    To install it, choose Start→Control Panel; in the Control Panel window, open Network. If you don't see "File and printer sharing for Microsoft Networks," click the Add button, double-click Service, select "File and printer sharing for Microsoft Networks," click OK, and insert the Windows installation CD when you're asked for it. See Windows Help for details.

In any case, you should now be ready to commence the cross-platform network hookup, like this:

1. **On your Windows PC, share a folder.**

    You have to specify which folders you want to make available on the network. In Windows XP, for example, you right-click a folder, choose Properties from the shortcut menu, click the Sharing tab, and turn on "Share this folder on the network" (Figure 5-3, top). In the "Share name" box, type a name for the folder as it will appear on the network (no spaces are allowed).

Note: If you've never shared a folder on this PC before, you may not see the "Share this folder" option. In its place, you'll see a link that runs the Network Setup Wizard. Go ahead and run that, supplying a computer and workgroup name when prompted, and then restart the PC to turn on sharing. Then start over with step 1.

    Repeat for any other folders you want to make available to your Mac.

2. **On the Mac, in any desktop window's Sidebar, click the Network icon.**

    Any PCs on your network should show up automatically in the list at right (Figure 5-3, bottom), although it may take a minute or so for your Mac to "notice" your PCs.

They may appear as individual computer names, or—if you've used Microsoft's Network Setup Assistant—you may see only the icon of their *workgroup* (network cluster). Unless you (or a network administrator) changed it, the workgroup name is probably MSHOME or WORKGROUP.

Tip: If you don't see any sign of your PCs, read the troubleshooting box on page 143.

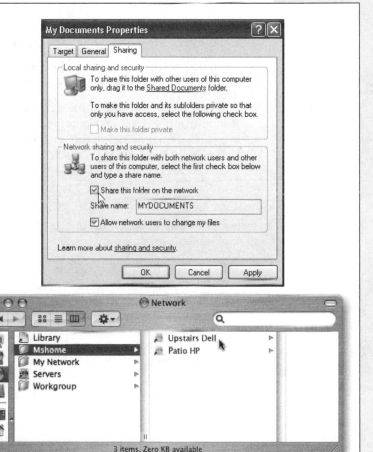

Figure 5-3:
Top: To share a folder in Windows, right-click it, choose Properties, and turn on "Share this folder on the network."

Bottom: Back in the safety of Mac OS X, open the Network window. What you see here depends on the complexity and structure of your network. You may see individual computers listed, network "clusters" as shown here, or a mix of the two.

Tip: While you're learning how to share files on the network, you might as well take note of the My Network icon shown here. That's how you connect to other Macs on your network. They'll all appear in this "folder," provided you've turned on the Personal File Sharing checkbox for each one. (You'll find this box on the Sharing panel of System Preferences.)

3. **Click the Windows workgroup name, if necessary.**

   Now the names of the individual PCs on the network appear on the right side of the window (Figure 5-3, bottom).

4. **Double-click the name of the computer you want.**

   The Authentication dialog box appears, as shown at top in Figure 5-4.

5. **Type your name and password, if necessary, and then click OK.**

If you have an account on the Windows PC, great—use that name and password. If the PC isn't in a corporation where somebody administers access to each machine, though, you may be able to leave the password blank.

Tip: If you do have to enter a password, consider turning on "Remember password in keychain." That way, you won't need to type the password again.

The SMB Mount dialog box now appears (Figure 5-4, lower left). Its pop-up menu lists the *shares* (that is, shared folders and disks) on the selected PC.

6. **From the pop-up menu, choose the name of the shared folder that you want to bring to your Mac desktop (Figure 5-4, bottom left). Click OK.**

At long last, the shared folder on the Windows machine appears on your desktop with a network-drive icon (Figure 5-4, lower right). From here, it's a simple matter to drag files from one machine's icon to another, to open Word documents that live on the PC using Word for the Mac, and so on.

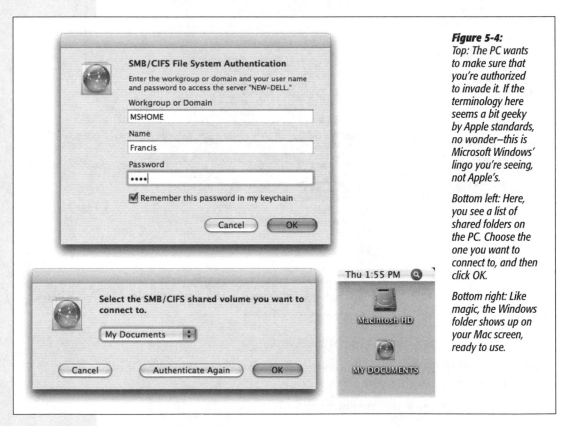

Figure 5-4:
Top: The PC wants to make sure that you're authorized to invade it. If the terminology here seems a bit geeky by Apple standards, no wonder—this is Microsoft Windows' lingo you're seeing, not Apple's.

Bottom left: Here, you see a list of shared folders on the PC. Choose the one you want to connect to, and then click OK.

Bottom right: Like magic, the Windows folder shows up on your Mac screen, ready to use.

Seated at the PC: Seeing the Mac

Not only can your Mac see other PCs on the network, but they can see the Mac, too. Here's how you prepare the Mac for visitation from a PC, if that idea appeals to you.

1. **On the Mac, open System Preferences. Click the Sharing icon, and then click the Services tab.**

   Now you see a list of the different ways your Mac can share its goodies with the outside world via network.

2. **Turn on Windows Sharing (Figure 5-5, top).**

   If there are other *Macs* on the network, you may want to turn on Personal File Sharing, too. Now your Mac will be available for visitation by all kinds of computers.

3. **Click Enable Accounts.**

   The small box shown in the middle of Figure 5-5 appears, listing all of the *accounts* (Chapter 12) on your Mac.

TROUBLESHOOTING MOMENT

When Your Mac Can't See the PC

For most people, the magic of Mac OS X's "Macs and PCs can see each other on the network" feature works automatically, the first time, every time.

But if Network window doesn't show the PCs on the network, it may be that you need to introduce your Mac to the Windows workgroup.

Open the Directory Access program in your Applications→Utilities folder. Click the padlock, sign in as an administrator, and then double-click the SMB/CIFS item in the list.

When you get the dialog box shown here, type (or choose) the precise name of the Windows workgroup you'd like your Mac to "belong" to, and then click OK. Quit

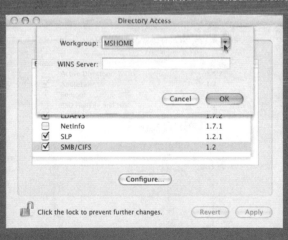

Directory Access and choose Go→Network once again. This time, your Mac should see the PCs.

Finally, note that the PC won't show up in the Network window if it's not on the same network segment as your Mac—a possibility if you work in a big corporation. In that case, ask your network administrator what the PC's *IP address* is (its numerical network address).

Once you know that key piece of information, you can bring that PC to your Mac desktop by choosing Go→Connect to Server, typing *smb://111.222.33.4444* into the text box at the top of the dialog box (substitute the real IP address, of course), and clicking Connect.

4. **Turn on the "On" checkbox for the accounts that you want to show up on the screen of your Windows PC. Click Done.**

You return to the Sharing dialog box.

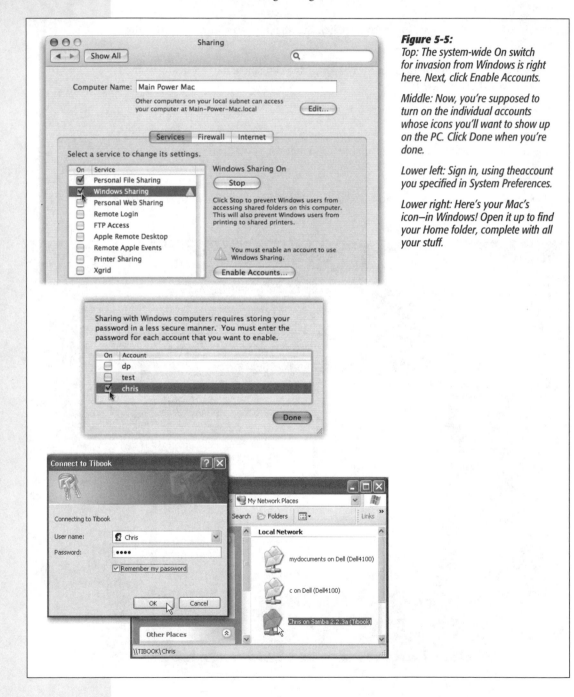

Figure 5-5:
Top: The system-wide On switch for invasion from Windows is right here. Next, click Enable Accounts.

Middle: Now, you're supposed to turn on the individual accounts whose icons you'll want to show up on the PC. Click Done when you're done.

Lower left: Sign in, using the account you specified in System Preferences.

Lower right: Here's your Mac's icon—in Windows! Open it up to find your Home folder, complete with all your stuff.

5. **On the Windows machine, open the My Network Places or Network Neighborhood icon.**

   Your Mac's icon should appear here, bearing a name like "Samba 2.2.3a (Robinscomputer)." No, Microsoft isn't trying to give you dance lessons. Samba is the Mac's version of the SMB file-sharing protocol that Windows uses.

6. **Double-click the icon's name, sign in (Figure 5-5, bottom), and then go to town.**

   In the final window, you see your Mac's actual Home folder—on a Windows PC. You're ready to open its files, copy them back and forth, or whatever.

Transfers by File-Sending Web Site

There's a new breed of file-shuttling Web site prowling the Net—and a new option for transferring large amounts of data between machines.

They're free Web sites, like *yousendit.com* and *sendthisfile.com,* that are specifically designed for sending huge files from one computer to another, without worrying about email file attachments or size limits.

On the Windows PC, zip up your files into a great big .zip file. Upload it to one of these free sites, and provide your Mac's email address.

On the Mac, click the link that arrives by email—and presto, that huge zip file gets downloaded onto your Mac. It's free, there's no file-size limit, and you can download the big file(s) within three days of sending them. The only price you pay is a little bit of waiting while the stuff gets uploaded and then downloaded.

TROUBLESHOOTING MOMENT

When Your PC Can't See the Mac

If your Mac doesn't show up in the My Network Places (or Network Neighborhood) window of the PC, you may have to knock it into submission.

If this is your first attempt at Mac–PC communication, try restarting the PC. The My Network Places window updates itself only once per session.

If that doesn't work, on the PC, click the "View workgroup computers" link in the left-side task pane. In the next window, click the "Microsoft Windows Network" link.

Finally, you arrive at the Microsoft Windows Network window, which contains icons for the various workgroups on the network. Double-click the icons until you find your Mac. Log in as described in Figure 5-5. Thereafter, your

Home folder will show up like any other folder in the My Network Places window, saving you the trouble of going through all this again.

If your PC sees the Mac but doesn't let you sign in, on the other hand, the troubleshooting tactic is slightly different. Go to the Mac and open System Preferences. Open the Accounts pane, click Change Password, and change your password to something else. Click Change Password—and then change the password *back again,* if you like. The point here is that changing your password (even if you change it right back) usually shocks both the Mac and PC into re-memorizing it.

Now when you sign in from the PC, the Mac should recognize you—and let you in.

Tip: If you have your own Web site—a *.com* of your own, for example, or a free site through a university—you can also use *that* Web space as a transfer tool. Follow the uploading instructions that you were given when you signed up for the space. (Hint: It usually involves a so-called *FTP* program.) Then, once all your files are on the site, download them onto your Mac.

Transfers by Email

Although sending files as email attachments might seem to be a logical plan, it's very slow. Furthermore, remember that most email providers limit your attachment size to 5 or 10 megabytes. Trying to send more than that at once will clog your system. If you've got a lot of stuff to bring over from your PC, use one of the disk- or network-based transfer systems described earlier in this chapter.

But for smaller transfer jobs or individual files, sending files as plain old email attachments works just fine.

If you have trouble, or if you can't open the attachments at the other end, consider the following potential snags.

File Compression and Encoding

The technology behind email attachments is somewhat technical, but it's extremely useful in understanding why some attachments don't make it through the Internet alive.

When you send an email attachment, your email program does two things. First, surprising as it may seem, the Internet cannot technically transmit *files*—only pure text. Your email program, therefore, takes a moment to *encode* your file attachment, converting it into a stream of text code to be reconstructed by your recipient's email program.

This encoding business is a problem chiefly when sending files *from* a Mac *to* a Windows machine—and only rarely a problem, at that. The Mac can understand almost any encoding format—MIME, Base64, AppleDouble, whatever—but Windows machines don't understand something called BinHex. If your Mac-to-Windows attachments aren't coming through alive, make sure your Mac email program isn't using the BinHex scheme for attachments. (Fortunately, no popular Mac email program uses BinHex unless you explicitly tell it to.)

But there's a second, more common problem: Your email program may also *compress* the attached file so that it takes less time to send and receive. Many Mac email programs compress outgoing files using the StuffIt method—but few Windows recipients can open StuffIt files.

When sending files from the Mac to Windows, therefore, you should turn off the StuffIt compression option in your email program. (Alternatively, you can download StuffIt Expander for Windows, available at no charge from *www.stuffit.com,* which can open StuffIt attachments.)

Note: America Online is a particular problem. When you attach multiple files to a single email message, AOL uses StuffIt compression automatically. When sending files to Windows from AOL, therefore, attach only a single file per email message.

Or, use the workaround: Select all the files you want to attach in the Finder. Control-click (or right-click) one of them and choose "Create Archive of [however many] items." After a short delay, your Mac spits out a single .zip file—the Windows file-compression standard—which you can then attach to your message. Problem solved.

Problems Receiving Windows Files

When your Mac receives Windows files by email, the problems aren't so severe. Most email programs, including Mail and Entourage, decompress and decode most file attachments automatically. When they don't, you can drag the downloaded files onto the icon of the free utility program StuffIt Expander, as described on page 128. StuffIt Expander can convert most Internet files back into human form.

It's worth noting again, however, that not every Windows file *can* be opened on a Macintosh, and vice versa. A file whose name ends in *.exe,* for example, is almost always a double-clickable Windows application that doesn't run on the Mac (at least, not unless you've gone to the expense and trouble of installing a Windows emulator program like Virtual PC). See the table on page 156 for some examples of files that transfer well from Windows to Mac and don't need conversion or adapters of any kind.

Transfers by iDisk

If your Windows PC isn't in the same building as the Mac, connecting the two using an Ethernet or a wireless network may not be a practical proposition. But even if you can't connect them into *a* network, you can still connect them via *the* network: the Internet.

It turns out that, for $100 per year, Apple will be happy to admit you to a club it calls *.Mac* ("dot-mac"). It offers a number of handy Internet features that tie in nicely to Mac OS X (Figure 5-6). For example, you can turn a group of your digital pictures in Apple's free iPhoto program into a full-blown Web page, posted online for all the world to see, with only two mouse clicks. You also get an email account *(yourname@mac. com)* that you can access either from the .Mac Web site anywhere in the world, or using a standard email program. And you get a backup program that automatically backs up designated files and folders onto a safe, Internet-based hard drive that will still be there even if your office goes up in flames.

For many people, though, the crown jewel of the .Mac services is the iDisk, which appears on your desktop as though it's a 250 MB hard drive. Anything you drag into the folders inside this "drive" gets copied to Apple's secure servers on the Internet. (If that's not enough space for you, Apple will rent you a larger allotment in exchange for more money.)

Because you can pull the iDisk onto *any* computer's screen—Mac or Windows—anywhere in the world, it makes a handy universal transfer disk.

The iDisk from Windows

You can bring your iDisk onto the screen of any computer, even a Windows PC. That's what makes it such a handy file-transfer vehicle when you're making the big move to Mac: You can bring the iDisk icon to your PC's screen, fill it up with files, and then retrieve those files on the Mac when you get back home.

The procedure varies by Windows version, like this:

Links to primary .Mac features

Figure 5-6:
The .Mac Web site features special links across the side. For example, the iCards feature lets you send attractively designed electronic greeting cards by email to anyone on the Internet. The Backup feature works in conjunction with a basic backup program that you can download from this site. Bookmarks and HomePage are other second-tier features. The most useful feature for transferring files, however, is iDisk.

Signing Up for .Mac

To sign up for a .Mac account, open System Preferences. When you click Internet, the .Mac tab is staring you in the face. Click Learn More.

You now go online, where your Web browser has opened up to the .Mac sign-up screen. Fill in your name and address,

make up an account name and password, and so on.

When you return to System Preferences, you'll see that your account name and password are all filled in. You're now ready to use .Mac.

- **Windows XP:** Download iDisk Utility for Windows from *www.mac.com/1/iDiskUtility_WindowsXP.zip*. Open it, provide your account name and password, and then see Figure 5-7.

- **Windows 2000:** In any folder window, choose Tools→Map Network Drive. Click "Web folder or FTP site," and type *http://idisk.mac.com/yourname/*, where *yourname* is your .Mac account name.

- **Windows 98:** Open My Computer. Double-click the Web Folders icon, double-click Add Web Folder, and type the same URL as for Windows 2000.

At this point, click Browse, OK, or whatever button looks promising. Figure 5-7 shows the idea.

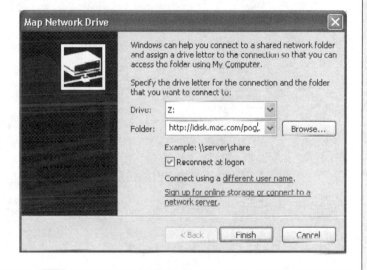

Figure 5-7:
You can think of the iDisk as an Internet-based data bucket that lets you slosh files back and forth between distant computers, such as a Mac and a PC.

If you're asked for a name and password, type in your usual .Mac name and password.

After a minute or two, you'll find the icon for your iDisk in the My Computer window, sitting there as though it's a very slow hard drive attached to the PC. (In Windows XP, for example, it's in the Network Drives category, called something like "Frank23 on 'idisk.mac.com.'")

Tip: From now on, you'll be able to summon your iDisk by double-clicking its icon in the Network Places folder.

When you're ready to copy your files onto the iDisk, there's only one rule: You can't create your own folders on the iDisk. You must put your files and folders into one of the folders *already on the iDisk,* such as Documents or Pictures. If you try to drag an icon directly into the iDisk window, or onto the iDisk icon, for example, you'll get an error message.

Otherwise, only the iDisk's 250-megabyte ceiling can stand in your way. (And even then, Apple is happy to expand your storage space—for a fee.)

The iDisk on the Mac

Apple must really love the iDisk concept, because it has devised about 300 different ways to pull the iDisk icon onto your Mac's screen:

- Choose Go→iDisk→My iDisk (or press Shift-⌘-I), as shown in Figure 5-8.

- Click the iDisk icon in the Sidebar of any Finder window. (If you don't see it there, turn on the iDisk checkbox in Finder→Preferences→Sidebar.)

- From within any program, choose File→Save As or File→Open. In the Save or Open dialog box, choose iDisk from the Sidebar (in full-size mode), or from the pop-up menu (in shortened mode; see Figure 5-8).

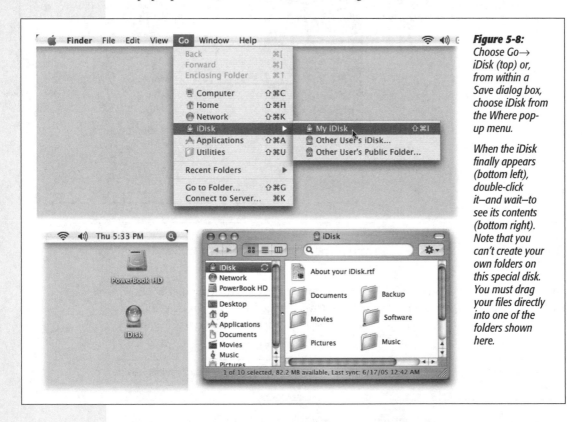

Figure 5-8:
Choose Go→ iDisk (top) or, from within a Save dialog box, choose iDisk from the Where pop-up menu.

When the iDisk finally appears (bottom left), double-click it—and wait—to see its contents (bottom right). Note that you can't create your own folders on this special disk. You must drag your files directly into one of the folders shown here.

- Choose Go→Connect to Server (⌘-K). At the bottom of the resulting dialog box, type *http://idisk.mac.com/yourname* (substitute your actual account name for *your-name*). Press Enter. In the next dialog box, type your .Mac name and password, and then click Connect.

- Choose Go→iDisk→Other User's iDisk. Type your name and password, and click Connect. (This is the quickest approach if you're using somebody else's Mac OS X machine, or if you haven't set up your information in System Preferences→Internet.)

- Visit *www.mac.com* and click the iDisk icon. Type in your name and password, and then click Enter. Finally, click Open Your iDisk. (Clearly, this is a lot more work than the one-click methods described above. Use this technique when you're using a Mac OS 9 machine away from home, for example.)

At this point, using iDisk is exactly like using a very slow—but very safe—hard drive. You can drag files or folders from your hard drive into one of the folders that appears on the iDisk, or, more to the point, copy your old Windows files *from* the iDisk to your *Mac's* hard drive (into your Home folder, for example).

Tip: Inside the Software folder on your iDisk is an entire software collection you didn't even know you had. Inside are various folders containing both Apple software updates and the most popular Mac OS X shareware and freeware programs. After reviewing these programs, drag the software you want to your hard drive or your desktop. You can open or install it from there. (Fortunately, none of this software eats into your 250 MB limit, since it's actually stored on Apple's software servers, not your iDisk itself.)

You can leave the iDisk's icon onscreen for as long as you like. If you have a full-time Internet connection, great: You can consider the iDisk a permanent fixture of your Macintosh. But even if you have a dial-up Internet account, you can leave the iDisk on your screen. Whenever you double-click it or save something onto it, your modem automatically dials the Internet and opens the pipes you need to feed your iDisk.

Transfers by Bluetooth

Bluetooth isn't really designed to be a networking technology; it's designed to eliminate cables between various gadgets. But if your Mac and a PC each have Bluetooth adapters, you can share files between them as though there's no language barrier at all. (Apple sells a Bluetooth adapter for any USB Mac for $50, and builds it directly into certain models, like new PowerBook models.)

The Mac's Bluetooth adapter comes with a nondenominational file-exchange program called Bluetooth File Exchange; not all Windows Bluetooth adapters come with such a program. But if yours does (3Com's adapters do, for example), you should be able to shoot files between the machines with the greatest of ease, if not the greatest of speed.

Where to Put Your Copied Files

Where to put your copied files? Easy one: in your Home folder.

Actually, it's a good idea to keep just about *everything* in your Mac's Home folder. That way, it's protected from inspection by other people who use the computer, it's easy to find, and it's easy to back up.

Some of the more specific "where to put it" answers are pretty obvious:

- **My Documents.** Put the files and folders from the PC's My Documents folder into your Home→Documents folder. Here's where you should keep all your Microsoft Office files, PDF files, and other day-to-day masterpieces, for example.

- **My Music.** In recent versions of Windows, a My Music folder is designed to hold all of your MP3 files, AIFF files, WAV files, and other music. As you could probably guess, you should copy these files into your Home→Music folder.

  After that, you can import the music directly into iTunes. If you used iTunes on your old PC, for example, just open iTunes on your Mac and choose iTunes→Preferences→Advanced. Then click Change, and navigate to the place where you moved your old iTunes library.

  If you used some *other* music program on your PC (like Windows Media Player or MusicMatch), things are a little different. On your Mac, choose iTunes→Import, and navigate to the folder that contains all your music. (In either case, click Choose in the resulting dialog box.)

- **My Pictures.** The latest Windows versions also offer a My Pictures folder, which is where your digital camera photos probably wound up. Mac OS X has a similar folder: the Home→Pictures folder.

  Here again, after copying your photos and other graphics faves over to the Mac, you're only halfway home. If you fire up iPhoto (in your Applications folder), choose File→Import, and choose the Pictures folder, you'll *then* be able to find, organize, and present your photos in spectacular ways.

- **My Videos.** The My Videos folder of Windows XP contains the video clips you've downloaded from your camcorder (presumably so that you can edit them with, for example, Microsoft's Movie Maker software). Once you've moved them to your Home→Movies folder, though, you're in for a real treat: You can now edit your footage (if it's *digital* footage) with iMovie, which, to put it kindly, runs rings around Movie Maker.

Other elements of your Windows world, though, are trickier to bring over. For example:

Desktop Pictures (Wallpaper)

You can say whatever you like about Microsoft's sense of design (and devoted Macintosh fans have plenty to say on this topic). But especially in recent versions of Windows, the desktop pictures, better known in the Windows world as wallpaper, are pretty cool. Fortunately, you're welcome to bring them over to your Mac and use them on your own desktop.

To find the graphics files that make up the wallpaper choices in Windows XP and Windows Me, for example, proceed like this:

1. **Open My Computer, double-click your hard drive's icon, and open the WINDOWS or WINNT folder.**

If you see a huge "These files are hidden" message at this point, or if the window appears empty, click "Show the contents of this folder" or "View the entire contents of this folder" at the left side of the window.

2. **In the Windows or WINNT window, open the Web folder.**

You're looking for a folder inside it called Wallpaper.

3. **Open the Wallpaper folder.**

It's filled with .bmp or .jpg files ready for you to rescue and use on the Mac. See page 359 for instructions on choosing wallpaper for your Mac.

Note: In Windows 95 or 98, the wallpaper files are in your Program Files→Plus!→Themes folder instead.

Sound Effects

The Mac doesn't let you associate your own sound effects to individual system events, as Windows does (Low Battery Alarm, Maximize, Minimize, and so on). It lets you choose *one* sound effect for all of its attention-getting purposes, using the Sound pane of System Preferences (page 377).

Still, there's nothing to stop you from harvesting all of the fun little sounds from your Windows machine for use as the Mac's error beep.

To find them on the PC, repeat step 1 of the preceding instructions. But in the WINDOWS or WINNT folder, open the Media folder to find the .wav files (standard Windows sound files).

Once you've copied them to your Mac, you can double-click one to listen to it. (It opens up in something called QuickTime Player, which is the rough equivalent of Windows Media Player. Press the Space bar to listen to the sound.)

To use these sounds as error beeps, follow these two steps:

1. **Open your hard drive icon. Open the Library folder. Choose File→New Folder, and create a folder named Sounds (if there isn't one already).**

This process assumes that you have an *administrator account* (page 323).

2. **Drag the .wav files into the Sounds folder.**

Now open System Preferences (by choosing its name from the menu, for example). Click the Sound icon, and then scroll down. There are your new error beeps, reporting for duty. You don't even have to convert them to a different music format!

Web Browser Favorites

There's no automatic way way to transfer your PC's bookmarks (favorites) list to your Mac's Web browser. There is, however, a way to make sure that, at the very least, you don't lose them.

As it turns out, each Web site you've bookmarked in Internet Explorer becomes a special icon, an Internet shortcut, on your PC. To find your stash of them, proceed like this:

- **Windows 2000, XP.** On the PC, open your My Computer icon; double-click your main hard drive icon; open the Documents and Settings folder. Inside, you'll see one folder for each person who has an account on your PC. Open yours, then open the Favorites folder within.

- **Windows 95, 98, Me.** Open My Computer; double-click your main hard drive icon; open the WINDOWS folder. Open the Favorites folder within. (In Windows Me, you may have to click the "View the entire contents of this folder" at the left side of the window to make the WINDOWS folder's contents appear.)

Once you've copied these shortcuts to your Mac, you can double-click to open any of them in Safari, Apple's Web browser. To permanently add these favorites (or "bookmarks") to Safari, however, proceed like this:

1. **Open Applications→Safari. Choose Bookmarks→Show All Bookmarks (Option-⌘-B).**

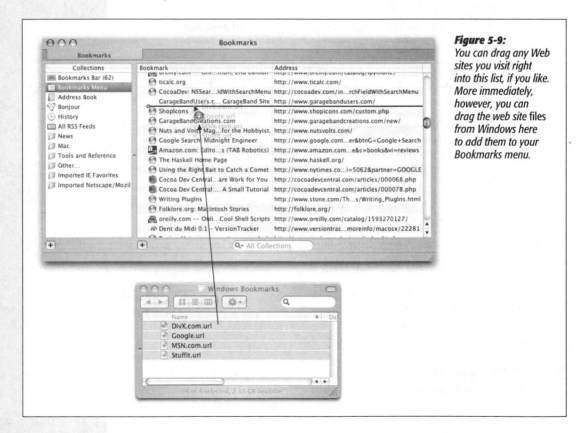

Figure 5-9:
You can drag any Web sites you visit right into this list, if you like. More immediately, however, you can drag the web site files from Windows here to add them to your Bookmarks menu.

You now see the Bookmarks pane, where you can edit your collection of favorite Web sites.

2. **In the Collections column, click Bookmarks Menu.**

You now see a list of the Web sites that appear in the Bookmarks menu at the top of the screen. By adding your Windows bookmarks into this list, *they* will appear in the Bookmarks menu, too.

Tip: If you only have a small collection of favorites, click Bookmarks Bar instead. Adding favorites to the Bookmarks bar makes them appear right underneath the Address box, where you can access them with a single click.

---

3. **Select all the shortcuts in the Finder and drag them into the Safari window (Figure 5-9).**

Once you've completed that, you can delete the shortcuts from the Finder and close the current Safari window. Now, whenever you want to open one of your favorites from Windows, just open the Bookmarks menu.

FREQUENTLY ASKED QUESTION

Importing Bookmarks from Firefox

On my PC, I use Firefox instead of Internet Explorer. How can I get those bookmarks into Mac OS X?

Firefox is a truly great Web browser, renowned for its speed and reliability. It's cross-platform, too—there's a Mac OS X version that's just as free and fast as the Windows version. Or, if you like, you can switch to Safari.

In any case, the first step in transferring your bookmarks is opening it on your PC. Choose Bookmarks→Manage Bookmarks, and then File→Export. Choose a place to save your bookmarks file, and then copy the file to your Mac as described earlier in this chapter.

At this point, you have a decision:

Keep using Firefox. Since Firefox is available for both Windows and Mac OS X, you don't have to switch to a new Web browser at all. Just download the Mac version from *www.getfirefox.com.*

Now open Firefox (on your Mac) and choose Bookmarks→ Manage Bookmarks. Choose File→Import, and click From

File. Finally, select the file you exported from Windows and click Choose.

Once Firefox finishes importing the bookmarks, you're all set; continue browsing as you always have, with your bookmarks right where you expect them.

Switch to Safari. If you're up for something new, Safari offers a few more features than Firefox. You get a regular Mac toolbar, the ability to share bookmarks over a network, and a great RSS-reading feature (page 300), for example.

If you're willing to make the leap, just open Safari and choose File→Import Bookmarks. Select the file you exported from Firefox, and click Import. All your old bookmarks now get stored in Safari's Bookmarks menu. (See page 293 for the lowdown on using this feature and the rest of Safari.)

If you ever want to switch *back* to Firefox, on the other hand, you can use Safari's File→Export Bookmarks command to save a bookmarks file, and then import the file into Firefox as described above.

Everything Else

See Chapter 6 for details on copying your email, address book, and Outlook calendar information to the Mac.

Document-Conversion Issues

As described in Chapter 4, most big-name programs are sold in both Mac and Windows flavors, and the documents they create are freely interchangeable.

Files in program-agnostic, standard exchange formats don't need conversion either. These formats include JPEG (the photo format used on Web pages), GIF (the cartoon/logo format used on Web pages), PNG (a newer image format used on Web pages), HTML (raw Web-page documents), Rich Text Format (a word-processor exchange format that maintains bold, italic, and other formatting), plain text (no formatting at all), QIF (Quicken Interchange Format), MIDI files (for music), and so on.

UP TO SPEED

Moving Data Within the Mac

Most of this chapter concerns the act of moving files between *machines.* Once you've settled in on the Mac, though, you'll frequently want to move data between *documents.*

Fortunately, the Cut, Copy, and Paste commands work almost exactly as they do in Windows. You still can't paste a Web page into your image editor, and you can't paste MIDI music information into your word processor. But you *can* put graphics into your word processor, paste movies into your database, insert text into Photoshop Elements, and combine a surprising variety of seemingly dissimilar kinds of data. All you have to do is get used to the Macintosh keyboard shortcuts, which use the ⌘ key instead of the Ctrl key: ⌘-X for Cut, ⌘-C for Copy, and ⌘-V for paste.

You can also drag highlighted text or graphics to another place in the document, into a different window, or into a dif-

ferent application, as shown here—a satisfyingly direct feature that works in even more Macintosh programs than Windows programs. Just note that in some Mac OS X programs (*Cocoa* programs; see page 120), you must press the mouse button for half a second before beginning to drag.

You can also drag text, graphics, sounds, and even movie clips out of your document windows and directly onto the *desktop.* Once there, your dragged material generally becomes an icon called a *clipping file.* (In Windows, it's called a Scrap file.)

Later, when you drag a clipping from your desktop *back* into an application window, the material in that clipping reappears. Drag-and-drop, in other words, lets you treat your desktop itself as a giant, computer-wide pasteboard—an area where you can temporarily stash pieces of text or graphics as you work.

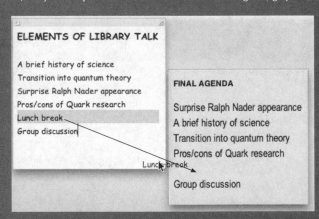

Part of this blessing stems from the fact that both Windows and Mac OS X use file name extensions to identify documents. ("Letter to the Editor.doc", for example, is a Microsoft Word document on *either* operating system.) Common suffixes include:

Kind of document	Suffix	Example
Microsoft Word	.doc	Letter to Mom.doc
text	.txt	Database Export.txt
Rich Text Format	.rtf	Senior Thesis.rtf
Excel	.xls	Profit Projection.xls
PowerPoint	.ppt	Slide Show.ppt
FileMaker Pro	.fp5, fp6, fp7 . . .	Recipe file.fp7
JPEG photo	.jpg	Baby Portrait.jpg
GIF graphic	.gif	Logo.gif
PNG graphic	.png	Dried fish.png
Web page	.htm	Index.htm

The beauty of Mac OS X is that most Mac programs add these file name suffixes automatically and invisibly—and recognize such suffixes from Windows with equal ease. You and your Windows comrades can freely exchange documents without ever worrying about this former snag in the Macintosh/Windows relationship.

You may, however, encounter snags in the form of documents made by Windows programs that don't exist on the Mac, such as Microsoft Access. Chapter 7 tackles these special cases one by one.

FireWire Disk Mode (Target Disk Mode)

FireWire Disk Mode is by far the fastest method yet for transferring a lot of data—even faster than copying files over a network—but it works only between two Macs, which is why it occupies this lonely spot at the end of this chapter. FireWire Disk Mode is extremely useful in any of these situations:

- **You're traveling with a laptop.** You want to copy your life onto it from your main Mac, including your entire 2 GB email folder and project files, before taking it on a trip, and then unload it when you return.

- **You have a new Mac.** You want to copy everything off the old one, without having to wait all night.

- **One Mac won't start up.** You want to repair it, using another Mac as a "front end."

In the following steps, suppose your main Mac is an iMac, and you want to use a PowerBook as an external hard drive for it.

1. **Using a FireWire cable, connect the FireWire jacks of both computers.**

   For this trick, you need a *6-pin* FireWire cable—*not* the one that connects a camcorder to a Mac. The one you need has the same, large connector on both ends.

Note: If both Macs have Apple's new FireWire 800 jacks, use a 9-pin FireWire cable instead for much greater speed. If only one Mac has a FireWire 800 jack, use that computer's traditional FireWire 400 connector instead. Otherwise, you need either a special FireWire 800–to–FireWire 400 cable, or the 400-to-800 adapter that came with your Mac.

2. **On the PowerBook, choose →System Preferences. Click Startup Disk.**

   The bottom of this screen is all new in Tiger, including the button you're about to click.

3. **Click Target Disk Mode. In the confirmation box, click Restart.**

   The PowerBook turns off, then on again. A giant, yellow, Y-shaped FireWire icon bounces around the laptop screen.

   Now take a look at the iMac's screen: Sure enough, there's the PowerBook's hard drive icon on the desktop. You're ready to copy files onto or off of it, at extremely high speeds, and go on with your life.

4. **When you're finished working with the PowerBook, eject it from the iMac's screen as you would any disk. Then turn off the laptop by pressing the power button.**

   The next time you turn on the PowerBook, it will start up from its own copy of Mac OS X, even if the FireWire cable is still attached. (You can disconnect the cable whenever.)

Transferring Email and Contacts

If you use your PC for email, good news: Switching to a Mac doesn't mean you have to reconfigure your email accounts from scratch or manually retype the hundreds of names and addresses tucked away in Microsoft Outlook, Outlook Express, Eudora, or another email program. This chapter covers the secrets of moving your entire email life over to the Mac—messages, addresses, settings, everything—with as little hassle as possible.

As you read this chapter, it's important to keep straight the two leading Windows email programs, which many people don't realize are actually two entirely different beasts:

- **Microsoft Outlook.** This program is part of Microsoft Office for Windows. It's a sprawling, network-based email, contact, and calendar program that's ubiquitous in corporate offices and many schools. You, or somebody who employs you, paid good money for this software.

- **Outlook Express.** This Windows program is a free, scaled-down version of Outlook. It comes with Microsoft Windows, and is therefore sitting on practically every PC sold. It doesn't have a calendar, a To Do list, or other bells and whistles of Outlook—but it's free.

(From a security standpoint, both of these programs are at the bottom of the list.)

Unfortunately, each Windows email program requires a different method of exporting its email and addresses. Each Macintosh email program requires a different piece of go-between Windows software to ease the transition, too.

There are so many permutations of the "to/from" issue, in fact, that you'd practically need a table or two to keep them straight. They might look something like this:

Ways to Move Your Email

	From Outlook	From Outlook Express	From Eudora
To Apple Mail	Outlook2Mac or Netscape 7	Netscape 7	Netscape 7
To Entourage	Outlook2Mac or Netscape 7	Netscape 7	Netscape 7
To Eudora for Mac	Outlook2Mac or Eudora for Windows	Netscape 7 or Eudora for Windows	Copy files

Ways to Move Your Address Book

	From Outlook	From Outlook Express	From Eudora
To Mac OS X Address Book	Outlook2Mac or Netscape 7	Move2Mac or Netscape 7	Netscape 7
To Entourage	Outlook2Mac or CSV Method or	CSV Method	CSV Method
To Eudora for Mac	Outlook2Mac or Eudora for Windows	Eudora for Windows	Copy files

It's a complex matrix. But if you know what program you've been using on the PC, and which one you want to use on the Mac, you'll find the steps you need later in this chapter.

Transferring Your Outlook Mail

If Microsoft Outlook has been your Windows address book/email program, you're in luck: You have two options for importing your stuff.

Both of these methods bring over your entire backlog of existing email—the contents of your Inbox, Sent items, archived mail and, perhaps, even deleted items that are still in your email program's Trash.

Outlook2Mac Method (Quick, Simple, $10)

If you value your time, buy Outlook2Mac—a $10 utility that streamlines the process of bringing Outlook data to your Mac. (You can download it right now from *www. littlemachines.com.*)

With Outlook2Mac, you're spared the lengthy, sometimes tricky steps required by the free conversion methods described in the following pages. The program takes a wizard-like approach to transferring your Outlook data, gently stepping you through the whole process, as shown in Figure 6-1. It saves all the exported data into one folder (called My_Outlook_Files), making it simple to grab the files you need and move them to your Mac.

Outlook2Mac also provides far more options than you get using other methods. For example, it lets you choose messages from only a specific date range—all your 2004 and 2005 email, for example, but nothing older. It lets you choose whether or not you want to include attachments with the transferred messages. It can even filter out certain attachments based on type (so that you can filter out, for example, .exe files, which can't run on the Mac OS).

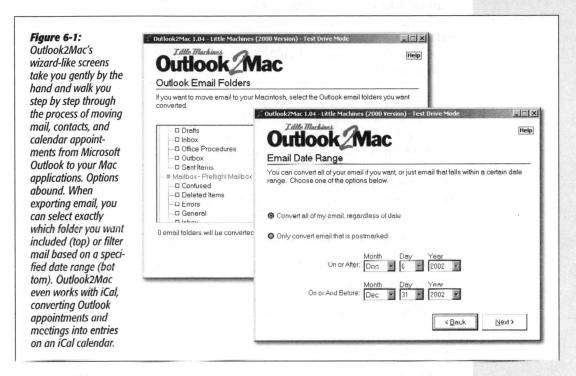

Figure 6-1:
Outlook2Mac's wizard-like screens take you gently by the hand and walk you step by step through the process of moving mail, contacts, and calendar appointments from Microsoft Outlook to your Mac applications. Options abound. When exporting email, you can select exactly which folder you want included (top) or filter mail based on a specified date range (bottom). Outlook2Mac even works with iCal, converting Outlook appointments and meetings into entries on an iCal calendar.

Outlook2Mac's other selling point is that it can handle more than just your email messages. It can also convert calendar entries and your address book, which can be imported directly into iCal, Entourage, or the Mac's Address Book.

As a final perk, the program moves email to and from just about any programs: *from* Outlook 97, 98, 2000, 2002, or 2003 *to* Apple Mail, Entourage, MailSmith, PowerMail, or iCal.

Netscape Method (Time-Consuming, Free)

If you're on a *very* tight budget, too tight for a $10 piece of shareware, you can also transfer your email to the Mac for free. The trick is to import it first into—don't laugh—Netscape 7 for Windows.

But wait, you're thinking, isn't Netscape a *Web browser*? In its newest version, yes. But as it turns out, previous versions of Netscape (version 7 and earlier) double as contacts-and-email importers. Netscape 7 even preserves any hierarchical folders you may have set up in programs like Outlook (or Outlook Express) to sort and organize your messages. In other words, your email arrives on your Mac just as well organized as it was when it left your Windows machine.

If you don't have some version of Netscape 7 (preferably 7.2) on your Windows machine, download a free copy from *http://browser.netscape.com/ns8/download/archive. jsp*. It works with Windows 98 or later. (If your machine has Windows 95, opt for the Outlook2Mac method described earlier.)

Note: You don't need Netscape on the *Mac* for this process. Furthermore, when installing Netscape on Windows, you don't have to opt for any of the Custom install options—the default installation will give you everything you need.

When you've got Netscape 7 installed on the PC, you're ready to follow the three big steps: First, you import your email into Netscape. Next, you copy the Netscape email to your Mac. You import the mail into Apple's Mail program—and then, optionally, Microsoft Entourage. Take a deep breath, and read on.

Phase 1: Import to Netscape

Your first job is to bring your existing Outlook mail into Netscape 7. (This method also works for transferring Outlook Express or Eudora mail.) Here's how you do it:

1. **Open Netscape. Choose Window→Mail & Newsgroups.**

   As you'd expect, the Mail & Newsgroups window appears.

2. **Choose Tools→Import.**

   A dialog box opens, allowing you to select the type of information you want to import.

3. **Choose Mail. Click Next.**

   Don't worry about the Address Books or Settings options at this point. You can move those items over separately.

4. **Select the program from which you want to import messages.**

   Netscape can handle email from Outlook, Outlook Express, Eudora, and easier versions of Netscape Communicator. Pick the appropriate program from among the ones listed.

5. **Click Next to start the import process—and be patient.**

   Netscape now starts doing its thing, obediently sucking every last email message into its own email folder. If you've got a hefty stash of email—thousands of messages organized in lots of nested folders—this will take a while. It may even look as if Netscape has stalled, but it hasn't. Wait patiently as the progress bar creeps forward.

   When the process is finally over, Netscape displays a dialog box listing all the different mailboxes, folders, and subfolders that it has successfully ingested, as shown in Figure 6-2. Click Finish to wrap things up.

When you return to Netscape's Mail & Newsgroups window, you'll see your imported mailboxes listed in the pane on the left (you might have to expand the Local Folders flippy triangle first). Clicking a mailbox icon displays the corresponding messages in the main window.

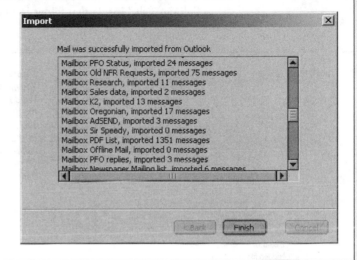

Figure 6-2:
This is Netscape's way of telling you that everything went OK when it imported all your mailboxes and messages. Review this list before forging ahead with your Mac migration to make sure Netscape grabbed all the mail you want brought over to your Mac.

Phase 2: Copy to the Mac

Your next task is to transfer Netscape's copy of your mail to your Mac.

1. **Open your Application Data folder.**

   The steps depend on your version of Windows. For example:

   Windows 98 or 98SE: Open the My Computer→your hard drive icon→Win98 →Application Data folder.

   Windows Me: Open the My Computer→your hard drive icon→WINDOWS→ Application Data folder.

   Windows 2000: Open the My Computer→your hard drive icon→Documents and Settings→*your name*→Application Data folder, where *your name* is your Windows user account name (the name you use to log into Windows at startup).

   Windows XP: Microsoft's assumption is that you, the lowly, technically ignorant PC user, have no businesses mucking around in the important operating-system folders— so Windows hides them from you. To expose the hidden files, follow the steps shown in Figure 6-3.

   Once that's done, open the My Computer→your hard drive icon→Documents and Settings→*your name*→Application Data, where *your name* is your Windows user account name.

2. **Once you've opened the Application Data folder, open your Mozilla→Profiles folder. Finally, open the folder that corresponds with the profile name you chose when you started running Netscape. (If you didn't bother to set up a profile, it's just called "default".)**

Inside that folder, you'll find a jumble-named subfolder, something like "h4m2ny3s. slt" or "6lihjgy3.slt." Inside *that* folder is a folder called Mail. That's the one you want.

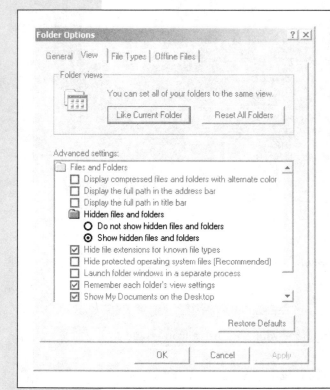

Figure 6-3:
You must uncloak the hidden folders lurking in Windows in order to copy your email files. Here's the trick: In any open folder window, choose Tools→Folder Options. Switch to the View tab, as shown here. In the Advanced settings, turn on "Show hidden files and folders," and then click OK. Now you can see all the previously hidden folders—including the Netscape ones.

3. **Copy the Mail folder to your Mac.**

Once again, Chapter 5 describes various ways to go about it.

Once the mail files are on your Mac, you're ready to bring them into the program of your choice. Exactly how you do this depends on the email program you're using; read on.

Phase 3: Import into Apple Mail

Mail, the email program that comes free with Mac OS X, does an elegant job of importing the files generated by Netscape 7. (If you plan to use Microsoft Entourage, you have to start with this step, too; that is, you must first bring the mail into Mail.)

Here are the steps for feeding the mail from your PC to the Mail program:

1. **Open Mail.**

   It's in the Applications folder, and its icon is probably on the Dock.

2. **In Mail, choose File→Import Mailboxes.**

   The Import Mailboxes dialog box appears.

3. **Click the Netscape/Mozilla radio button.**

   You can also import mail from a variety of *Mac* email programs, including Entourage, Outlook Express, and Eudora.

4. **Click the Continue button.**

   You're presented with a standard Open dialog box.

5. **Locate and select the folder named Local Folders inside the Mail folder you brought over from your PC. Click the Choose button.**

   Mail finds all the Netscape mailboxes it finds within the folder you chose and displays a list of them, as shown in Figure 6-4.

6. **Turn on the checkboxes of the email folders you want to bring into the Mail program.**

   All the checkboxes start out turned on, meaning that Mail will grab everything you brought over from Netscape. But if you decide at this point that you don't want to include, say, the messages that were in the Trash folder, you can filter them out by turning off the appropriate checkboxes.

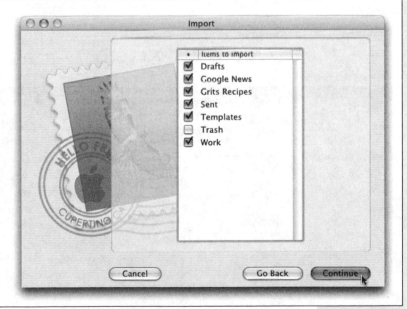

Figure 6-4:
When importing mail messages from Netscape 7, Mail first shows you all the mailboxes it found, ready for import. Turn off the checkboxes next to any folders that you don't want included during the import process.

Tip: You can use the up and down arrow keys to navigate through a long list of mailboxes and folders in the Import Mailboxes window.

7. **Click the Continue button to start importing.**

   The import process now begins. Mail shows you the subject line of each message it brings in.

When the process is complete, your imported mailboxes appear in the Mailboxes column on the left side of the window. (See Chapter 10 for more on the Mail program.) By selecting an imported mailbox, you can refile its contents into other mailbox folders, if you like.

Phase 4: Import into Entourage (optional)

If you have Microsoft Office for Macintosh, you may prefer its more powerful Entourage email program. No problem: You can bring the Netscape files that you brought over from your PC—and then imported into Mail—into Microsoft Entourage.

1. **In Entourage, choose File→Import.**

   The Begin Import dialog box appears. Click the right arrow.

2. **Choose "Import information from a program."**

   Since your messages are already stored in Mail—with all the folders and subfolders intact—you can have Entourage go from there. Click the right arrow.

3. **Choose "Apple Mail."**

   Make sure Messages and Accounts are turned on. (The other two checkboxes are only useful if you've started customizing Mail as described in Chapter 10.) Click the right arrow again.

4. **Wait until the import is finished, and then click OK.**

FREQUENTLY ASKED QUESTION

From the Outlook Archives

I've got about five years' worth of old Outlook email archived on my hard drive. Is there any way to get the contents of these archives into my Mac's email program?

Absolutely.

When you're in Outlook (on your Windows PC), choose File→Open→Personal Folders File to open any of the Outlook-generated archive files that you want to bring over to your Mac. (Outlook archives have *.pst* file name extensions.) Once you open an archive file, a "mailbox"

icon called Archive Folders appears in Outlook's Folder List, allowing you to access any of the individual messages within the archive.

Simply import your Outlook mail into Netscape, as explained earlier in this chapter, *after* opening the archive files. Their contents will be included when you bring the mail into Netscape and when you later transfer your mail folders to your Mac.

If everything went according to plan, your messages now show up in the main pane of Entourage's window.

Alternative Method (Free, to Eudora Only)

At this writing, Outlook2Mac—the delightful $10 utility described earlier in this chapter—doesn't yet talk to Eudora for Mac. (Check out *www.littlemachines.com* for current status.)

Here's the convoluted workaround: Start by importing your Outlook (or Outlook Express) email and addresses into Eudora for *Windows*. (To import from Outlook Express, choose File→Import; to import from Outlook, choose File→Import and then click Advanced.) Use the most recent Eudora version, if possible.

Now that your mail and contacts are in Eudora for Windows, see page 174 for instructions on getting it all into Eudora for Mac OS X.

Outlook and Exchange

If you run Microsoft Outlook on your office PC, you may be able to transfer the contents of your entire mailbox to your Mac *without* going through any of the import-export pyrotechnics described in this chapter.

On most office networks, Outlook accesses mail through a *Microsoft Exchange Server*—a central computer that stores all the email moving through the network. When you use Outlook in conjunction with Exchange, your mail, appointments, and contacts actually reside on the Exchange server itself—not on your PC's hard drive.

The same thing's possible in Entourage. To set up your Mac so that it checks your Exchange email, proceed like this:

1. **Open Entourage and choose Tools→Accounts.**

   This is the setup window for all your email accounts.

2. **Click the arrow next to New and choose Mail from the pop-up menu.**

   That's how you tell Entourage, "I want to input the settings for an email account."

3. **Turn on the "My account is on an Exchange server" checkbox.**

   If you had wanted to set up any other kind of email account—like one given by your Internet Service Provider—you'd leave the checkbox off.

4. **Call your network administrator over and ask her to give you information for all the required fields.**

   When you're done inputting everything and Entourage is satisfied, you should see a list of all your network-based email—the same messages you saw in Outlook.

Tip: If Entourage isn't your thing, you can tap into your network's Exchange Server with Mac OS X's built-in Mail program. In Mail, just choose File→Add Account, pick Exchange for the Account Type, and proceed with step 4 above.

Now you can download the contents of your Outlook folders directly to your Mac without having to manually copy them from machine to machine. You won't be able to see the Exchange Server's calendar or address book this way, but at least you'll get the messages.

Transferring Your Outlook Address Book

The contents of your Contacts list may represent years of typing and compiling. The last thing you want to do is leave that valuable info behind or—heaven forbid—manually retype each entry as you set up your Mac email program.

Here are the steps for bringing all those names, phone numbers, email addresses, notes, and other details from Outlook into your favorite Mac contact manager.

Outlook2Mac Method (Easy, $10)

If you took the advice on page 160 and bought the Outlook2Mac program, you're already done; this ingenious utility brings over both your email *and* your Outlook addresses to your choice of Mac programs.

Netscape 7 Method (Lengthy, Free)

Once again, Netscape 7 for Windows comes to the rescue. Its address book module can extract contact info directly from the most popular PC email programs—not just Outlook, but also Outlook Express and Eudora. Better yet, it converts that data into a format that Apple's Address Book understands perfectly (Figure 6-5).

Figure 6-5:
Mac OS X comes with a free Address Book program, ready and waiting to receive the contacts you export from Windows programs like Outlook, Outlook Express, or Eudora.

Note: These steps guide your little-black-book data into Mac OS X's built-in Address Book program. If your aim is to transfer it into Entourage on the Mac instead, see page 171.

When you've got Netscape 7 installed, you're ready to transfer your contacts, like this:

1. **On your PC, open Netscape 7's Address Book.**

   To get Netscape's Address Book running, choose Start→All Programs→Netscape 7.0 (or 7.2)→Address Book. Or, if you've already got Netscape running, choose Window→Address Book.

2. **Choose Tools→Import.**

   The Netscape Import dialog box appears, introducing a wizard-like series of screens to guide you through the quick import process.

Note: If you don't see an Import command in the Tools menu, make sure you're in Netscape's Address Book window and not the main Navigator window.

3. **Click the Address Books radio button, and then click Next.**

   Now Netscape wants to know the name of the email program whose addresses you want to snag.

4. **Choose the program from which you want to import addresses (Figure 6-6).**

   You can choose Outlook, Outlook Express, Eudora, or Communicator (an earlier version of the Netscape software).

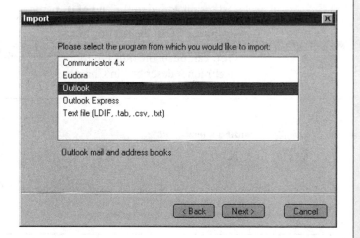

Figure 6-6:
Netscape, the Swiss Army software, is happy to open the address book of almost any email program, or even a text file containing addresses (such as tab- or comma-delimited text).

5. **Click Next.**

   Netscape now sniffs out your contacts and pulls all the information into its own Address Book. If all goes well, the Import dialog box displays a message indicating that your contacts were successfully imported.

6. **Click the Finish button to close the dialog box.**

   You return to the Address Book window.

Tip: You can confirm that you've successfully imported all your contacts into Netscape by clicking the icon in the Address Books pane of the Netscape window that matches your imported batch of contacts. The name of the icon depends on the program from which you imported the contacts; it may be something like "Contacts" (if from Outlook), "Eudora Nicknames," or "Outlook Express Address Book."

   With your contacts safely stored in Netscape, you're halfway home. Next, you need to get these contacts out of Netscape and onto your Mac. To do this, you must save them into an *LDIF* file. LDIF stands for Lightweight Directory Interchange Format—a text format mostly used by network administrators to synchronize directory information across large networks. It's also a format that Apple's Address Book recognizes.

7. **With your imported contacts displayed in the Netscape Address book, choose Tools→Export.**

   The Export dialog box appears.

8. **From the "Save as type" drop-down menu, choose LDIF. Type a name for the file, select a destination, and click Save.**

   Netscape writes all your contact data into a single self-contained file with an *.ldif* extension added to the end of its name.

9. **Copy the LDIF file to your Mac.**

   You can burn the *.ldif* file to a CD, transfer it via a network, or use any of the techniques described in Chapter 5.

Figure 6-7:
Apple's Address Book program can slurp up your Windows contacts in one gulp by importing an LDIF file, which you can easily generate using Netscape 7 on Windows.

10. On the Mac, open Address Book (it's in the Applications folder, and its icon is probably on the Dock). Choose File→Import→LDIF.

The Open dialog box appears.

11. Locate and open the .ldif file you brought over from Windows.

Moments later, all the contacts you brought over from your Windows machine are converted into Address Book entries (see Figure 6-8).

CSV Method (Free, to Entourage Only)

If your email program of choice on the Mac is Microsoft Entourage, and you can't find the $10 you need to buy Outlook2Mac (page 160), the Netscape 7 method described above isn't enough. Entourage *can't* import LDIF files.

The best way to transfer contacts into Entourage, then, is to import them in *CSV* format. CSV is short for Comma-Separated Values, and it's a format that many contact programs can import and export these days. (In fact, *Address Book* can attempt to import CSV files, but it's picky about formatting to a fault—which is why the Netscape method described above is a lot more reliable if you use Address Book.)

Here's the procedure:

1. On your PC, export your contacts in CSV format.

If you use Outlook Express, for example, choose File→Export Address Book and then select "Text File (Comma Separated Values)." Save the file. (Same goes if you use Outlook.)

If you use Eudora on Windows, you're in for a bit more fun. Since Eudora can't directly export CSV files, you have to move your contacts into Netscape 7 *first*, as described above. When you get to step 8 above, however, choose "Comma Separated" for the type of file you'd like to export, rather than LDIF. You now have a CSV file on your PC with your contacts inside, so read on.

2. Move the CSV file to your Mac.

The file should end in .csv if you did everything right.

3. Open Entourage and choose File→Import. Click "Import information from a text file."

Click the right arrow.

4. Make sure "Import contacts from a tab- or comma-delimited text file" is selected.

Again, click the right arrow.

5. Select the CSV file you copied to your Mac in step 2.

Press Return to dismiss the dialog box.

6. **"Map" any information that's confusing Entourage (Figure 6-8).**

Even though Entourage and Outlook are both made by Microsoft, there's still room for Entourage to get confused by your contacts—and mapping is how you fix it.

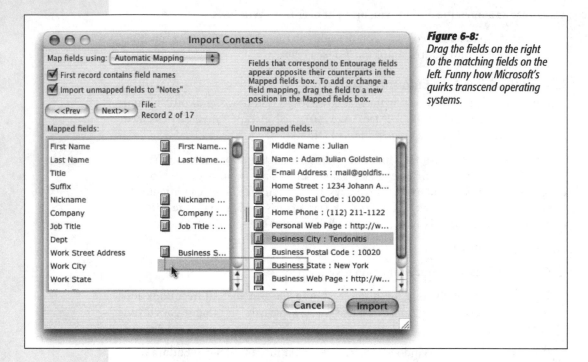

Figure 6-8:
Drag the fields on the right to the matching fields on the left. Funny how Microsoft's quirks transcend operating systems.

For instance, if you exported your contacts from Outlook Express, one field on the right might be called "E-mail Address" which confuses Entourage because it's not called "Email Address 1." To eliminate the confusion, drag the gray handle from the E-mail Address line on the right so it's next to the Email Address 1 line on the left. You've just told Entourage, in essence, "'E-mail' and 'Email' are the same thing, so let me get on with my life."

7. **Click Import.**

Dismiss the dialog box that appears by clicking Don't Save.

8. **Click Finish.**

Your contacts are now ready and waiting in Entourage.

Eudora Method (Free)

If your aim is to get your contacts into Eudora for Macintosh, see "Alternative Method (Free, to Eudora Only)" on page 167. The instructions transfer your address book exactly the same way they transfer your messages.

Transferring from Outlook Express

If you've been using Outlook Express (Microsoft's free email program) on the Windows PC, you'll have very little trouble moving into any of the Mac's email programs.

Moving Your Address Book

You have two alternatives at your disposal:

- **The free method.** You can use free Windows software as a go-between—but which Mac address book you've adopted will determine which program to use.

  To import your Outlook Express addresses into Apple's *Address Book,* follow the instructions in "Netscape 7 Method (Lengthy, Free)" on page 168.

  To import them into *Microsoft Entourage* instead, see "CSV Method (Free, to Entourage Only)" on page 170.

- **The Move2Mac method.** The Move2Mac kit is described on page 136 (and discounted at the back of this book). It does an elegant job of transferring contacts from Outlook Express on your PC to the Mac's Address Book program.

  Those are, however, the only email programs it handles. Move2Mac won't import the addresses into Entourage instead of Address Book.

Moving Your Mail

Outlook Express is also a pleasant partner when it comes to moving the messages themselves over to the Mac. Here again, you use Netscape 7 as a sort of translator. Follow the steps listed under "Netscape Method (Time-Consuming, Free)," beginning on page 161.

To Eudora for Mac

Getting your mail and addresses from Outlook Express (Windows) into Eudora (Macintosh) involves moving it first into Eudora for Windows, and then into Eudora for Macintosh. See "Alternative Method (Free, to Eudora Only)" on page 167 for instructions; they cover moving both your messages and addresses out of Outlook Express.

Transferring Your Eudora Mail

Eudora, an email program written at the University of Illinois in the eighties, used to be wildly popular because it was free and full-featured. Today, this venerable email client, now sold by Qualcomm, is available for both Windows and Mac OS X.

Moving Email into Entourage or Mac OS X Mail

If you'd like your mail to wind up in a Mac email program like Entourage or Mail, it's good old Netscape 7 to the rescue. Follow the steps in "Netscape Method (Time-Consuming, Free)," beginning on page 161.

Moving Email to Eudora for the Mac

If you use Eudora on Windows and want to move your existing messages into the Mac version of Eudora, you can copy them straight over to your Mac. All you need to know is where to find the necessary files and how to set them up on your Mac.

Here's the most direct path for converting your Eudora mailboxes from Windows to Mac:

1. **Find the Eudora .MBX files on your PC.**

   The folder names depend on your version of Windows, but here's the gist:

   Windows 98 or 98SE: Open the My Computer→your hard drive icon→Win98 →Application Data→Qualcomm→Eudora folder.

   Windows Me: Open the My Computer→your hard drive icon→WINDOWS→ Application Data→Qualcomm→Eudora folder.

   Windows 2000, Windows XP: Turn on the hidden files, as shown in Figure 6-3. Then open the My Computer→your hard drive icon→Documents and Settings→*your name*→Application Data→Qualcomm→Eudora.

   All versions: In the Eudora folder, you'll find several mailbox files that—depending on your version of Eudora—may end with the filename extension .mbx: In, Out, and Trash, as shown in Figure 6-9. These are the files you want, whether they end in .mbx or not.

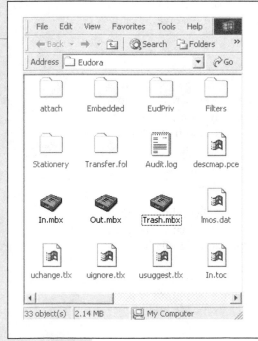

Figure 6-9:
Drill down into the your PC's Applications Data folder to find the Eudora folder, where your Eudora mailbox files live. The Trash file contains messages you've already thrown into Eudora's trash can. There's no need to copy that file over to your Mac unless you want to preserve those trashed messages.

Note: Can't find an Application Data folder inside your user folder? That's because Application Data is a hidden folder and you have the "Do not show hidden files and folders" option turned on in Windows. See the instructions for copying Netscape 7 files on page 164 to learn how to change this setting.

1. **Copy the files to your Mac.**

   Don't worry about all the other stuff in the Eudora folder. The mailbox files contain all your messages, so they're the only ones you need to convert.

2. **Fix the carriage returns in the .mbx files.**

   Here's where things get a little bit ugly. While these mailbox files are really just text files containing your email messages, Windows handles *line breaks*—the invisible "this is the end of a line!" symbol—differently than the Mac. In order for the Mac version of Eudora to read the files correctly, you have to convert the *hard returns* in the text files into *line breaks*. You can accomplish this by doing a simple find-and-replace in a program like Microsoft Word, as shown in Figure 6-10.

Tip: If you don't have Microsoft Word, you can also run the mailbox files through a shareware conversion program like BBEdit, which is available on the "Missing CD" page at *www.missingmanuals.com,* among other places.

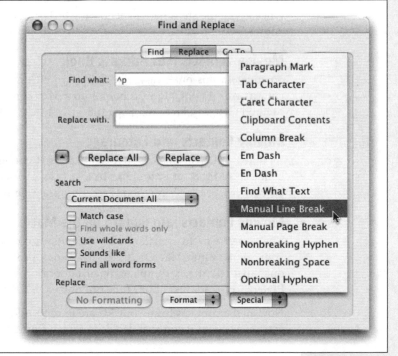

Figure 6-10:
Here's how you'd use Word to convert Eudora mailbox (.mbx) files from Windows to Mac format. Open a mailbox file and choose Edit→Replace. Search for all paragraph marks and replace them all with manual line breaks—or, to be precise, search for ^p and replace with ^l. (You can also choose these symbols by name from the Special menu, as shown here.) Click Replace All to run the conversion, which may take some time; then save the modified text file.

3. **Remove the .mbx extension from the file names.**

   On the Mac side, Eudora expects the file to be called In, not In.mbx. Remove the extension, if it exists, from each of the mailbox files you've brought over.

4. **Drop the converted mailbox files into Eudora's Mail Folder folder on your Mac.**

   Starting from your Home folder, go to Documents→Eudora Folder→Mail Folder, and replace the existing mailbox files with the ones you copied and converted from your PC.

Note: If you don't see a folder called "Mail Folder" inside the Eudora folder, it's probably because you're looking in the Eudora application folder (in the *Applications* folder) instead of the Eudora folder inside your *Documents* folder.

---

5. **Launch Eudora and read your mail.**

   When you launch Eudora, your converted mail should now be accessible. Unfortunately, the status of each message (read, unread, forwarded, and so on) is not preserved, nor are any labels you may have applied to organize the messages within Eudora. Oh well.

Transferring Your Eudora Address Book

Once again, the steps here depend on which program you'll be using as your Mac address book.

Moving Contacts into Address Book

Fortunately, this one's easy. The Swiss Army Converter known as Netscape 7 can convert your Eudora address book into a Mac-compatible format; see "Netscape 7 Method (Lengthy, Free)" on page 168.

Moving Contacts into Entourage

As noted earlier in this chapter, Netscape isn't enough if the landing site for your contacts is Microsoft Entourage. In that case, you should use the CSV format as a go-between. See "CSV Method (Free, Entourage Only)" on page 171.

Moving Contacts into Eudora on the Mac

The easiest way to transfer your old Eudora contacts to the Mac is to *first* get your contacts into Mac OS X's Address Book program, as described above. Then, once that transfer is complete, open Eudora on your Mac and choose Eudora→Preferences→Address Book. Turn on "Show OS X AddressBook."

Now all the contacts from your PC are in both Address Book *and* Eudora, which is extra convenient if you ever decide to switch from Eudora to Mail.

Email Settings

Chapter 9 guides you through the painless process of plugging your Internet settings—whether by dial-up connection, cable modem, DSL, or network connection—from the PC to your Mac.

But even after you've done that, you can't start sending and receiving email on your Mac until you've transferred some vital email account *settings* from your PC.

Fortunately, there's only a handful of settings you need to grab—and hunting these down and moving them to your Mac is pretty quick work. Here's all the information you need to gather in order to get yourself set up:

- **Account name (or user name).** This is the name you use when you log into your email account, such as *Joe63* or *kjackson*.

- **Password.** This is the password that you have to enter along with your account name to get into your email account. Passwords can't be copied and pasted or directly exported, so you'll need to remember this password and type it in when configuring your Mac email software.

- **Account type.** There are two main kinds of email server protocols—*POP* (which stands for post-office protocol—by far most common) and IMAP (Internet Message Access Protocol). You'll need to know which type you've been using on your PC, so that you can set up accounts on your Mac the same way.

WORKAROUND WORKSHOP

Netscape to Netscape

The email programs for Mac OS X are so clean, effortless, and powerful, it's hard to imagine that you might want to commit your email life to Netscape for Mac OS X.

But if you're a dyed-in-the-wool Netscape fiend from way back, it turns out that bringing your addresses over from the Windows version to the Mac version is easy. Both Mac and Windows versions read LDIF files (page 170), so you can use the Window→Address Book and then Tools→Import command in Netscape to open and import the LDIF file you exported from the Windows version of Netscape.

Transferring mail, however, is more complicated. The Mac version of Netscape imports messages only from Eudora or earlier Mac versions of Netscape Communicator.

So the best route for bringing in your mail is, believe it or not, this:

1. In Windows, import your Netscape Mail from Netscape into *Eudora*. (Download it, if you have to; it's free from *www.eudora.com*.) In Eudora for Windows, choose File→Import, and then click Advanced, to bring in your Netscape messages.

2. Transfer your mail into Eudora for Macintosh, following the instructions on page 174. (Again, you can download a free copy of Eudora for Macintosh for this purpose, if necessary.)

3. Open Netscape 7 on your Mac. Use the Tools→ Import command to import the mail from the Mac version of Eudora.

It's ridiculously convoluted, but it usually works.

Note: Exchange servers are another choice popular in big organizations. If your email is stored on an Exchange server, see page 167.

- **Incoming and outgoing mail servers** are the names of the computers that route email to and from you, such as *mail.earthlink.net* or *mailserve.photorabbit.com*. (The incoming and outgoing servers sometimes have the same address, but they *can* be two different servers with different names.)

Finding the Settings on Windows

Each of the popular Windows email programs stores these nuggets of email account info differently. Here's how to find the items you need:

Outlook Express

Choose Tools→Accounts→Mail to open the dialog box containing the list of your current email accounts. Select the name of the account you want, then click the Properties button. In the Properties dialog box, click the Servers tab to reveal the Server Information pane, where you'll find all the info you need, as shown in Figure 6-11.

Tip: If you're using Move2Mac (see the box on page 136), you can transfer Outlook Express's email settings directly from your PC to Apple's Mail program on your Mac. Move2Mac saves you the trouble of having to retype these settings.

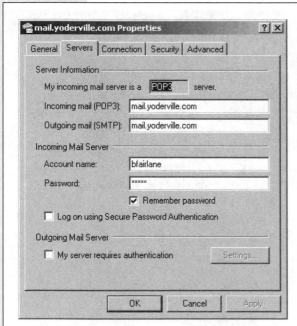

Figure 6-11:
Here's where Outlook Express for Windows keeps all the settings you need to harvest in order to configure your Mac email. Note that you can't copy the contents of the password field—that's prohibited for security reasons. You'll have to type your password in again when moving to your new machines.

Outlook

If you're connected to a Microsoft Exchange Server computer—and you probably are if you're running Outlook in a corporate workplace—your user name and password are exactly the same as the ones you use to log into the network when you start up your computer. You'll have to check with your network administrator to get the name of the mail servers being used on the network.

If you're running Outlook in any other situation—at home, for example—choose Tools→E-mail Accounts. Click "View or change existing e-mail accounts," click Next, click your account's name on the E-mail Accounts page, and then click Change. You'll find your name, email address, incoming and outgoing servers, and other key settings staring you in the face. (Click Cancel after you've finished copying it down.)

Eudora

Choose Tools→Options. Click the Getting Started icon, if it's not already selected, to find your incoming and outgoing mail server names. Then click the Incoming Mail icon to display the Server configuration setting—either POP or IMAP—at the top of the window.

Figure 6-12:
Once you've stepped through the five screens of the Entourage Account Setup Wizard, you end up here, with your account settings all in place and ready to connect up.

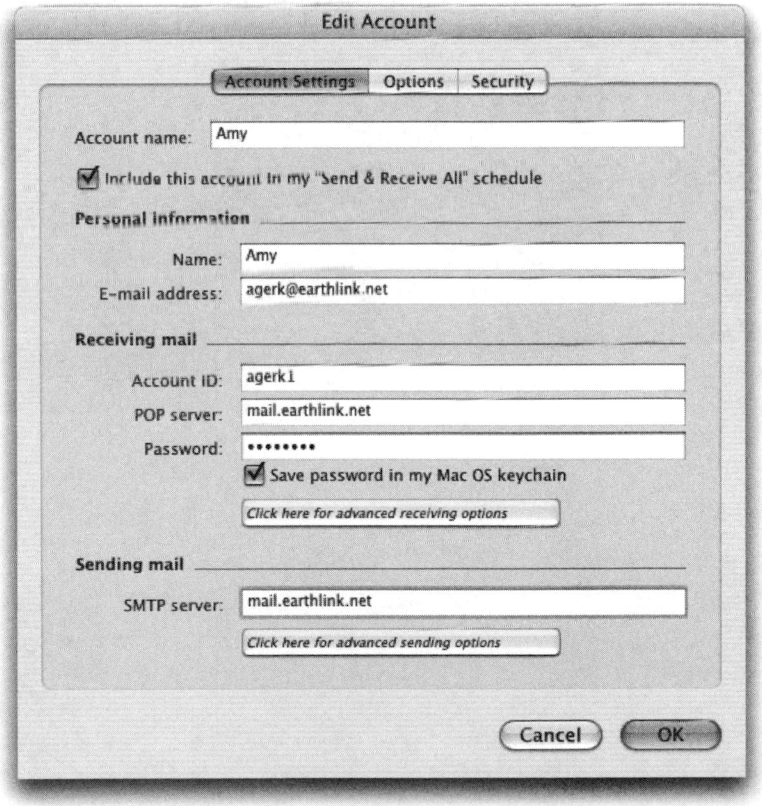

Netscape 7

Choose Window→Mail & Newsgroups, and then choose Edit→Mail and Newsgroups Account Settings. Each email account you use is listed in the field on the left side of the window. Click one to display its information on the right.

Configuring the Settings on Your Mac

Once you've found and copied the email settings on your PC, you can plug them into the appropriate places in your Mac email programs:

Apple Mail

Once you've opened Mail (in the Applications folder), choose File→Add Account. Proceed through the various screens, inputting the information from your old PC.

Microsoft Entourage

Choose Tools→Accounts. Click the New button in the Accounts window to start the Account Setup Assistant. Follow the screen-by-screen directions to fill in the user name, password, and server information, as shown in Figure 6-12.

Eudora for Macintosh

Choose Eudora→Preferences and click the Checking Mail icon. Fill in the necessary details here, and then click Sending Mail to fill in the rest.

Special Software, Special Problems

Be glad you waited so long to switch to the Mac. By now, all the big-name programs look and work almost exactly the same on the Mac as they do on the PC. Once you've mastered the basic differences between the Mac and Windows (keyboard shortcuts, the menu bar, and so on), you'll find that programs from Microsoft, Adobe, and other major software companies feel distinctly familiar in their Mac incarnations. In fact, the documents that they create are in the same format and generally need no conversion.

But one fact is unassailable: There are more software programs available for Windows than for the Mac. Sooner or later, you'll probably run into a familiar Windows program for which there's no equivalent on the Mac.

The purpose of this chapter is to make that discovery less painful: to identify the Mac equivalents of the most popular Windows programs, and to guide you in bringing over your settings from Windows to the Mac whenever possible.

Note: On the other hand, remember that you *can* still run your old-favorite Windows programs—if you have a 2006-or-later Mac. See Appendix B.

ACDSee

As digital photography becomes more popular, so do programs like ACDSee, a popular Windows program that serves as a digital shoebox and basic retouching program for digital photos. Your Mac, of course, stands ready to run a far more elegant equivalent: iPhoto, described on page 419. It's one of the world's most pleasant photo-organizing programs—and it's free.

In its most recent incarnation, iPhoto has a pretty complete set of image-retouching features. Still, if you need more editing power, consider Photoshop Elements, a program that's available for both Mac and Windows and has won rave reviews on both platforms.

In any case, ACDSee doesn't have any documents of its own—it does all its work on your existing digital photos, wherever you keep them on your hard drive. All you have to do, then, is move the photos themselves to the Mac, using any of the techniques described in Chapter 5. From there, drag them into the iPhoto Window to import them.

Acrobat Reader

Acrobat Reader, which lets you read Acrobat (PDF) files, works precisely the same on the Mac as it does in Windows (except that it looks a little nicer on the Mac). If you'd like, you can download Acrobat Reader from *www.adobe.com/products/acrobat/readstep2.html.*

There are fewer and fewer reasons to use Acrobat Reader, though; you have a much nicer PDF-reading program right there in your Applications folder, called Preview.

Preview can read PDFs like the best of them—but it's also got Acrobat Reader covered on several other counts. Preview can annotate PDFs with virtual yellow sticky-notes—a great tool for marking up book layouts before they go to press, for example. Also, Preview's search feature is so fast and convenient, it blows Acrobat Reader out of the water. And finally, Preview opens in a matter of seconds, while Acrobat Reader can take over a minute to launch. (For more on Preview, see page 427.)

ACT

No Mac version of this address book/calendar program is available, but don't let that stop you. Export and Import commands are the bread and butter of address and calendar programs. Your ACT life can find a happy home in any of several Mac address books:

- Mac OS X's free, built-in Address Book.

- Palm Desktop for Mac OS X (a free address book/calendar/to-do program from *www.palm.com,* which works with—but doesn't require—an actual Palm organizer).

- Microsoft Entourage (part of Microsoft Office for Mac).

- Now Contact *(www.nowsoftware.com)*, which is networkable. That is, if you have more than one computer in the house, you can check your Rolodex from any machine on the network (Mac or Windows).

In any case, here are the instructions for transferring your addresses from ACT (version 5 or later) to the Mac:

1. **In ACT for Windows, start by choosing File→Data Exchange→Export.**

   The Export Wizard dialog box appears.

2. **From the "File type" drop-down list, choose Text-Delimited. Specify a folder location and name for your exported file (call it Exported Contacts, for example). Click Next, and click Next on the next screen, too.**

   Now you're asked "Which contact or group records do you want to export?"

3. **Click "All records," and then click Next.**

   Now you see a list of the *fields* (information tidbits like City, State, and Zip) that ACT is prepared to export. You can save yourself time later if you take a moment now to remove the ones you don't need (click its name and then click Remove Field).

4. **Click Finish.**

   If you plan to import your addresses into a commercial program like Now Contact, transfer the Exported Contacts file to the Mac (see Chapter 5), and then import them into Now Contact. The tricky part is making sure that the order of the fields appears in the order Now Contact expects, which may entail some trial, error, and returning to the ACT Export Wizard screen described in step 3 (where you can rearrange the field order).

   If your aim is to import the addresses into Microsoft Entourage on the Mac, or Mac OS X's own Address Book program, though, read on.

5. **Open Outlook Express.**

   Yes, Outlook Express for Windows, the free program that comes on every PC. (It's also a free download from Microsoft's Web site.) You'll use it as a glorified converter program.

6. **Follow the instructions on page 173 for exporting the contacts into a format suitable for your Mac.**

   That page outlines two ways (one free, one fast) to get your contacts from Outlook Express into Mac OS X's Address Book—your ACT info's final resting place.

Ad Subtract (Pop-up Stopper)

Nothing quite spoils the fun of the Web like pop-ups—those annoying miniature advertising windows that sprout in front of the Web page you're trying to read.

Safari, Mac OS X's Web browser, has a simple menu command for blocking pop-ups: Safari→Block Pop-Up Windows. Nowadays, so does just about every other Web browser made for the Mac—Firefox, Netscape, Camino, and so on. In other words, you don't even *need* Ad Subtract.

The one exception, though, is Internet Explorer for Mac (a program that is no longer supported by Microsoft). If you can't bear to stop using Internet Explorer, use a shareware program like Pop-up Zapper (which you can download from the "Missing CD" page of *www.missingmanuals.com*) to kill off pop-ups.

Adobe [your favorite program here]

If anyone has jumped onto the Mac OS X bandwagon, it's Adobe, which reflects the massive size of its customers in the graphic arts business. Most of its bestsellers are available in Mac OS X versions, including Photoshop, Photoshop Elements, After Effects, Illustrator, InDesign, GoLive, Acrobat, Acrobat Reader, and so on.

Note: One notable exception is Premier, an Adobe video-editing program that's only available for Windows. The closest Mac equivalent is Final Cut Pro, a $1,000 program made by Apple. (If you're coming from Premier *Elements,* the closest equivalent is Final Cut *Express*, which is only $300.) Or you may find that the newly beefed-up iMovie HD program (free on all Macs; see page 409) handles all the video editing you need.

Regardless, you almost never have to do any document conversion. A Windows Photoshop document is exactly the same thing as a Macintosh Photoshop document, for example.

America Online

America Online is available for both Windows and Mac OS X. In fact, the Mac OS X version may have come preinstalled on your Mac (look in the Applications folder). If not, you can download it from *http://downloads.channel.aol.com/macproducts*, or pick up a free AOL starter CD at your local Circuit City.

When you use the Macintosh version of the software for the first time, just plug in your existing screen name and password.

The beauty of AOL is that it stores your mail, address book, buddy list, and favorites *online.* You can check your email one day at the office on a PC and the following night at home on the Mac, and you'll always see the same messages there. It makes no difference if you connect to the service using a Windows PC, a Macintosh, or a kerosene-powered abacus.

Tip: Your Favorites (bookmarks) are stored online only if you use AOL for Windows version 8 and later. If you've been using an earlier version on your PC, your Favorites won't be waiting for you when you switch the Mac.

If your PC meets the system requirements, you'd be wise to upgrade its copy of America Online to version 8 or later before switching to the Macintosh. (This is a free upgrade; you can download the software at *www.aol.com/downloads*.) If you do so, you'll find the Favorites waiting for you in AOL for Mac OS X.

This is all really good news, of course, but you may have one headache in performing the switch: your Personal Filing Cabinet. If you've been saving email messages into this virtual filing drawer, the news isn't quite as good: these messages are saved on the PC, not online. So when you switch to the Macintosh, your Personal Filing Cabinet will be empty.

Here are your options at this point:

- Be content with only the last 30 days' worth of old mail, and the last week's worth of new mail. This is what lives on the America Online computers, no matter what computer you use to access it. When you move to the Mac, that much email will immediately appear the first time you use AOL.

- Fire up your old PC and open each message in your Personal Filing Cabinet. Click the Forward button, and type in your own AOL address. You're basically emailing each message to yourself.

  Once the messages have arrived on the Mac, you can save them into *its* Personal Filing Cabinet. Of course, you were the sender, so you can no longer click Reply to send a response to whoever originally wrote you. (If that's ever necessary, you can always copy and paste the sender's address into your reply.)

Once all your information is in AOL for Mac OS X, you can, if you want, move the information into Apple's *own* Internet programs: iChat, Address Book, Mail, and Safari. Just download AOL Service Assistant from *http://downloads.channel.aol.com/ macproducts,* and click through the various steps.

By the final screen, all your bookmarks, contacts, screen names, and email settings will be waiting for you in Apple's programs, which are a lot more powerful (not to mention attractive) than the AOL software itself.

AIM (AOL Instant Messenger)

If you're an online chat junkie, switching to the Mac involves very little disruption to your routine. AIM is available for the Mac, too, and it awaits your download at *www.aim.com.* Better yet, the minute you fire it up, you'll discover that your entire Windows-version buddy list is intact and ready to use. (That's because it actually lives on the America Online network, not on your Windows PC.)

Tip: Before you sink fully into the Mac version of AIM, give iChat a try, too. It's a free Mac OS X chat program that's compatible with the whole AIM network, as described on page 304.

Children's Software

Thanks to the vast number of Macs in schools, a huge percentage of educational software programs are available in both Mac and Windows versions—often on the same CD. That includes most programs from The Learning Company (including the Arthur, Carmen Sandiego, Little Bear, and Reader Rabbit series), Broderbund (Kid Pix, Mavis Beacon, Print Shop, and so on), Humongous Entertainment (series like Blue's Clues, Dora the Explorer, Putt-Putt, Backyard Sports), and other major educational publishers.

Note: Some of these programs aren't actually Mac OS X programs. They generally run just fine on current Macs, but they do so in the Classic mode described on page 123. (They reflect the operating-system situation in the world of education, which is to say, usually a couple of versions out of date.)

Earthlink Total Access

If Earthlink is your Internet service provider, and you're a fan of its Total Access software (which provides access to email, blocks pop-up ads, lets you switch to other family members' accounts, and so on), you're in luck. Hie thee to *www.earthlink. net/home/software/mac* to download the Macintosh version. (And then see Chapter 9 for details on transferring your Windows account settings to the Mac.)

Easy CD Creator

You don't actually need any add-on software at all to burn CDs in Mac OS X. You can just drag files and folders onto the icon of a blank CD, as described on page 223.

If you want fancier features—recording less common disc formats, for example—what you need is Toast for the Macintosh. It comes from the same company that makes Easy CD Creator.

Its main rival is DiScribe *(www.charismac.com)*. Both programs can create audio CDs, video CDs, data DVDs, and so on. Both come with a program that helps you turn old vinyl records and tapes into digital CDs, too.

The only disappointment: Neither program can treat a CD as a glorified floppy disk, as Easy CD Creator for Windows can, so that you can add and delete files freely (rather than burning the CD all at once).

There's a workaround, though: Copy the contents of a rewriteable CD (a CD-RW disc) to a folder on your desktop; make whatever changes you like to the contents of this folder; and then burn the CD-RW again. (Use the Disk Utility program in your Applications→Utilities folder to erase the disc first.)

Tip: Ordinarily, the CD-burning feature of Mac OS X burns the entire CD each time, even if you've only filled a small portion of it. But if you download the handy $17 shareware program called CD Session Burner, you can perform additional "mini-burns" of new data to the CD until all the space is used up. Each such *session* shows up on your desktop with its own icon, as though it's a separate disc. You can download this program from *www.sentman.com/burner/*.

Encarta

Microsoft's best-selling encyclopedia program isn't available for the Macintosh. The World Book Encyclopedia is, however. (Details at *www2.worldbook.com.*)

Of course, you can also use the Web-based versions of either encyclopedia, which are Mac OS X–compatible.

Eudora

You want Eudora? You got Eudora! It's available on the Mac, as it is in Windows. Chapter 6 even tells you how to move your mail and address book over to the Mac version.

Excel

See "Microsoft Office" in this chapter.

Firefox

On Windows, Firefox is a faster, more secure, better-featured Web-browsing alternative to Internet Explorer. If you'd like, you can download the Mac version from *www. getfirefox.com,* and then follow the instructions on page 153 for transferring your bookmarks.

Alternatively, you can switch to Mac OS X's built-in, super-fast Safari browser, which offers a more Mac-like browsing experience. Page 289 begins the coverage of the Safari adventure.

Games

Nobody switches to the Mac to play games; of the top 250 computer games for Windows, only about 150 are available for the Macintosh.

Still, that number includes the majority of the big-name titles and series, including Civilization, Quake, Harry Potter, Spider-Man, Tomb Raider, The Sims, WarCraft, Jedi Knight, Soldier of Fortune, Max Payne, Links Championship Edition, Age of Empires, Medal of Honor, Return to Castle Wolfenstein, and dozens of others.

And once you do get these programs going on the Mac, you're likely to be impressed. Recent Macs generally come equipped with pleasantly high-horsepower graphics cards—the kind that serious computer games crave.

If you're a game nut, you can stay in touch with what's new and upcoming by reading the articles (and watching the game "trailers") at *www.apple.com/games,* not to mention *www.insidemacgames.com, macgamer.com,* and *macgamefiles.com.*

Google Desktop Search

Mac OS X's Spotlight feature does everything that Google Desktop does—searching inside files, finding favorite Web sites, and so on. Spotlight just does it better.

See page 67 for an explanation of the differences between these two tools.

ICQ

If you're a fan of this Internet-wide chat program, look no further than ICQ for Mac or one of its many shareware rivals. To grab them, visit *www.versiontracker.com* and perform a search, on the Mac OS X tab, for *ICQ*.

Internet Explorer

Internet Explorer is available for the Mac, but you'd be silly to use it. Safari (Apple's built-in Web browser) blocks pop-up windows, loads pages more quickly, and doubles as an RSS reader for news sites. Coverage starts on page 289.

If some Web site (like a banking site) accommodates only Internet Explorer for Mac, however, you can download it from *www.microsoft.com/mac*.

iTunes

If you grew used to iTunes on Windows, you'll be glad to know that the Mac version is already sitting in your Applications folder. It works absolutely identically to the PC version.

Kazaa

Kazaa, of course, is the "new Napster." People use it to swap music and video files online, hard drive to hard drive—illegally, in many cases. You know who you are.

If you visit *www.kazaa.com*, you won't find a Macintosh version of the Kazaa program that you need to do file swapping. There are such programs, however, including a program called Poisoned, which you can download (at this writing, anyway) from *www.gottsilla.net*. Or try Limewire, described next.

Limewire

Limewire is the same idea as Kazaa (see above), but it runs on something called the Gnutella network—and there's a nice Mac version of the downloading program. You can get it at *www.limewire.com*.

Macromedia [your favorite program here]

Here's another company that knows who its customers are, and therefore has created Mac OS X versions of its best-known programs: Dreamweaver, Director, Flash, Fireworks, FreeHand, and so on. The documents are freely interchangeable between the Mac and Windows—no conversion is necessary.

Note: Macromedia's programs will soon become part of the Adobe family, but you can still expect Mac versions of Adobe Dreamweaver, Adobe Flash, and so on.

MacAfee VirusScan

The Mac version is called MacAfee Virex—but read the box on the next page first to see whether or not you even need a virus program for Mac OS X.

Microsoft Access

Microsoft has never been much interested in creating a Macintosh equivalent of its flag-ship database program (which it includes with the higher-priced versions of Microsoft Office for Windows). FileMaker, a much easier-to-use database program, towers over the Macintosh database market like the Jolly Green Giant (and has a decent following on the Windows side, too). Resistance, Microsoft apparently assumes, is futile.

It's easy enough to get your data out of Microsoft Access; just choose File→Export. In the resulting dialog box, you can choose from a number of common export formats that can serve as intermediaries between the Windows and Mac worlds (see Figure 7-1).

Figure 7-1:
When you export your data from Access, you can choose from any of several formats. The idea is that you'll transfer the resulting exported file onto your Mac, and then import it into a proper database program there.

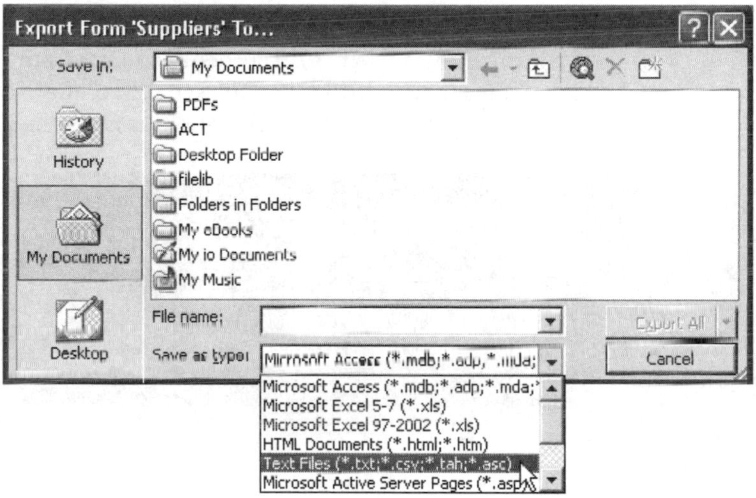

Among them is Microsoft Excel—that is, you can turn your database into a spreadsheet. The beauty here is that FileMaker on the Macintosh can turn Excel documents into FileMaker databases without even batting an eye. You just drag the exported Excel document onto the FileMaker icon, and FileMaker does the rest.

Tip: If you don't need such a full-fledged database program on the Mac—for example, if you're just managing a mailing list you've exported from Access—you might be perfectly happy with AppleWorks, a Swiss Army knife program with a word processor, graphics, and database all built-in. AppleWorks comes with every iMac and iBook computer, and you can equip other Mac models with it for about $80. In this case, you'll want to export your data from Access as a tab-delimited text file, as shown in Figure 7-1.

Unfortunately, there's more to an Access database than just its data. Your database may well have fancy forms (layouts), complete with letterhead and other graphic elements, not to mention relational links between database files. In these situations, the situation isn't quite so hopeful—there's no way to export layouts and relational links to the Macintosh.

In this situation, your best bet might be to run Microsoft Access itself on the Macintosh using VirtualPC, which is described on page 202.

Microsoft Money

Microsoft doesn't make Money for the Macintosh (although it certainly makes money *from* the Macintosh). If you're looking for a home-finances program for Mac OS X, though, look no further than Quicken *(www.intuit.com)*.

You can even export your Money data into Quicken, although not every scrap of information comes through alive. You'll lose your Money abbreviations, comments, and Lifetime Planner information. Fortunately, the important stuff—your accounts and the transactions in them, including categories, classes, and stocks that you've set up—come through in one piece.

Unfortunately, you have to export one account at a time. Furthermore, you'll be creating something called a QIF (Quicken Interchange Format) file as an intermediary between Windows and the Mac—and this file format can't handle category names

---

UP TO SPEED

Viruses in Mac OS X (Not!)

One of the greatest perks of moving to Macintosh is that viruses are practically nonexistent. There have been a handful over the last 15 years—but only for Mac OS 9, and generally of the "I'll display a funny message on December 13th" variety, rather than the "I'll eat all your files and make you wish you were never born" type.

At this writing, in fact, not a *single virus* for Mac OS X has been reported.

The one kind of virus that manages to sneak into Mac OS X are Microsoft Word macro viruses that hide in ordinary Word files sent to you by your Windows friends.

Fortunately, on the Mac version of Word, most of these either don't run at all or don't run the way they were intended. Second, whenever you try to open a document that contains macros that you didn't create yourself, you see the error message shown here. All you have to do is click Disable Macros. The file opens normally, 100 percent virus free.

If you have Apple's .Mac service (described on page 147), you have free access to McAfee's antivirus software—just in case. Otherwise, it usually doesn't make financial sense to buy an antivirus program at all.

> **Warning**
>
> The document you are opening contains macros or customizations. Some macros may contain viruses that could harm your computer.
>
> If you are sure this document is from a trusted source, click Enable Macros. If you are not sure and want to prevent any macros from running, click Disable Macros.
>
> [Enable Macros] [Do Not Open] [Disable Macros] [Tell Me More]

---

longer than 15 characters. Before you begin, then, you might want to take a moment either to shorten them or to make a note of which ones might get truncated in the transfer.

Ready? Fire up Money on your Windows PC and then proceed like this:

1. **Choose File→Export.**

   The Export dialog box appears. It wants to know if you are exporting your information to another version of Money ("Loose QIF") or to some other, rival financial program that shall, as far as Microsoft is concerned, remain nameless.

2. **In the resulting dialog box (Figure 7-2), choose Strict QIF, and then click OK.**

   In the resulting dialog box, you're supposed to name and save the exported file. Make sure you give each account a descriptive name (like Citibank Savings).

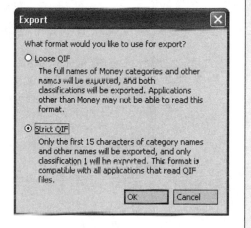

Figure 7-2:
Use the Strict QIF option. It lops off category names longer than 15 characters.

3. **Specify a name and folder on your PC for the exported file, and then click OK.**

   Repeat these three steps for each of your Money accounts.

4. **Transfer the exported files to the Mac.**

   You can do it via network, burned CD, or any of the other techniques described in Chapter 5. Then move to the Macintosh, open Quicken 2003 or later, and create a new file (see the Quicken instructions). Then, once you've got an empty "check register" before you, continue like this:

5. **Choose File→Import QIF. In the "Select a QIF file" dialog box, navigate to, and open, the first exported account file.**

   If all goes well, you should see a progress bar appear and then disappear. When the dust settles, you'll see your Money transactions safely ensconced in Quicken.

(If you see a message that some transactions couldn't be completed, don't worry; it's usually just telling you that some of your category names were longer than 15 characters. and have been marked with asterisks to make them easier for you to find and correct.)

If you have more than one account, choose File→New Account to set it up, and then repeat step 5 to bring in your other Money accounts.

Microsoft Office

Microsoft Office is available for the Mac in what some critics have declared to be a more attractive, less frustrating version than the Windows incarnation. At this writing, the current version is called Office 2004 for Macintosh.

As noted elsewhere in this book, the beauty of Microsoft Word, Excel, and PowerPoint documents is that their format is the same on Mac and Windows. You can freely exchange files without having to go through any kind of conversion. (The big exception, as noted earlier, is Access; Microsoft doesn't make a database program for the Mac.)

In heavily formatted documents, you may occasionally see some strange differences: Documents containing many numbered paragraphs sometimes become confused when switched across the platform divide, for example. And if the Mac and the originating PC don't have the fonts installed, you'll see different fonts, too. Otherwise, documents look identical despite having been shuttled through the ether to a different kind of computer.

Microsoft Publisher

Microsoft Publisher is a comprehensive page-layout program, complete with canned designs, clip art, and so on.

There's no Mac version of it, but you can perform most of the same tasks using Pages. (Pages is part of Apple's $100 iWork software suite, and it comes preinstalled on new iBook, eMac, and iMac models.) The older AppleWorks 6 is a good choice, too; it comes preinstalled on those same Macs, and costs $80 otherwise.

When it comes to page layout, AppleWorks isn't as comprehensive as Microsoft Publisher. It doesn't offer nearly as many templates, wizards, layouts, and clip-art pieces. It does, however, offer several dozen ready-to-go designs and thousands of pieces of art—not to mention a full-fledged database, spreadsheet, word processor, and slideshow program.

Pages offers a lot more templates—and a lot more good-looking ones at that—but the 2005 version doesn't have a spreadsheet. Also, you have to use Keynote (a separate program included with iWork) to create presentations.

There are also plenty of standalone page-design programs—this is the Mac, after all—from Ready, Set, Go! (*www.diwan.com*) to professional powerhouses like Adobe InDesign and QuarkXPress.

Microsoft Visio

If flowcharts, org charts, network diagrams, family trees, project processes, office layouts and similar diagrams are part of your own personal workflow, you're in luck—at least some luck. Microsoft Visio isn't available in a Macintosh version, but you'll probably find that OmniGraffle for Mac OS X is a satisfactory, even delightful, replacement (see Figure 7-3). The Pro version even lets you import and export Visio documents.

Figure 7-3: OmniGraffle comes preinstalled in the Applications folders of many new Mac models, or you can download the latest version from www.omnigroup.com.

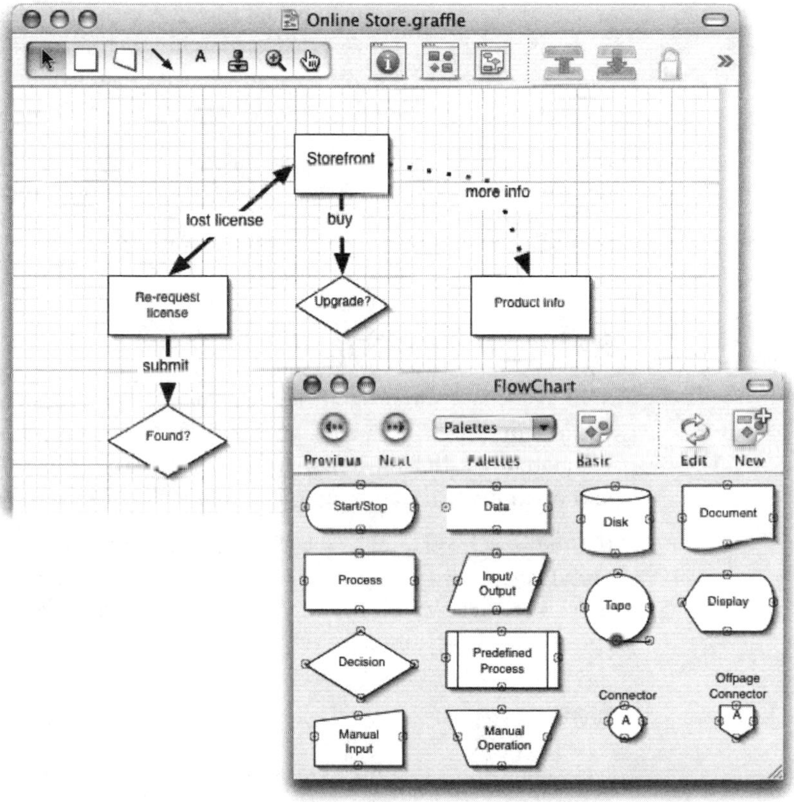

Minesweeper

Time wasters, rejoice! There are a number of free Minesweeper programs for Mac OS X, including CocoaMines and Aqua Mines. You can download them from a site like *www.versiontracker.com* (search for *minesweeper*).

MSN Messenger

Online chat-aholics have nothing to worry about on the Mac. MSN Messenger, the instant-messaging program, is alive and well in a Mac OS X version that you can download from *www.microsoft.com/mac*. Like AOL Instant Messenger described earlier in this chapter, you don't even have to worry about your carefully assembled buddy list. From the instant you start up MSN Messenger for Mac OS X, you'll see your Buddy list in place (because the list is actually stored on the Internet, not on your computer).

MSN (Service)

Microsoft is dead serious about challenging America Online for dominance in the easy-to-use online service market. MSN 8 is proving a hit with Windows users: in one single, attractive program, it brings together Web browsing, email (junk mail filters) and multimedia features, plus links to useful Web sites. A key feature for families: The software can email parents a list of what Web sites their kids have visited, and how much time they've spent in chat rooms.

MSN for Mac OS X is no longer a self-standing program; instead, you're supposed to use *www.msn.com* to access your news, sports information, and so on.

Mac OS X's parental-control features, meanwhile, work regardless of whether you're using MSN or not. You can find them in System Preferences→Accounts.

NaturallySpeaking

Speech-recognition programs are far more advanced on Windows than they are on the Macintosh. Windows programs like Dragon NaturallySpeaking transcribe your dictated text with almost Star Trek–like accuracy, and even let you make corrections and manipulate the computer itself using all voice commands.

On the Mac, your choices are IBM ViaVoice (*www-3.ibm.com/software/speech/mac*) and iListen (*www.macspeech.com*). If you just can't use the keyboard, or don't want to, you can get by with either program. But neither, alas, offers anything close to the speed or accuracy of their Windows rivals.

Netscape

Netscape comes in a Mac OS X version—free, of course, from *www.netscape.com*. (Mozilla, which is like a Netscape cousin without all the AOL promotional material, is also available for the Mac, too, from *www.mozilla.org*. So is the Firefox Web browser, described earlier in this chapter.)

Newsgroup Readers

If you're a fan of the online bulletin boards known as *newsgroups,* you've come to the right place. The Mac is crawling with newsgroup-reading programs. Microsoft Entourage, for instance, has one built in. In the shareware world (search *www.versiontracker.com),* you can take your pick of MT-NewsWatcher X, NewsHunter, and Halime, to name a few.

Norton AntiVirus

You can buy Norton Antivirus for the Macintosh, no problem (*www.symantec.com*). The question is, why? See the box on page 190.

Norton Utilities

This program, too, is available in a Mac OS X version. It does the same kinds of things it does in Windows: defragments your hard drive, helps recover files in case of disaster, and repairs disk problems.

In times of trouble, though, you may prefer Disk Warrior, a similar (and, many experts feel, superior) program that you can buy from *www.alsoft.com.*

Notepad

If you're an aficionado of this beloved note-taking tool in the standard Windows Start menu, you're in luck. Mac OS X's Stickies program is even more powerful, because it offers formatting and even graphics. Or, for more of a word processor effect, check out TextEdit.

Outlook/Outlook Express

Mac OS X's built-in Mail program is similar to Outlook Express for Windows, just more powerful and a lot better-looking. Chapter 6 describes the process of switching, and Chapter 10 covers the rest of the Mail experience.

If you want all the features from *Outlook,* though, you'd probably be better off using Microsoft Entourage, which is available as part of Microsoft Office for Mac.

Paint Shop Pro

If your goal is to retouch and edit digital photos, the closest you can come to Paint Shop on the Mac is probably Photoshop Elements, a sensational Mac OS X program (about $100) that belongs on the hard drive of any serious digital camera owner. (Any digital camera owner who doesn't also own the full-blown Photoshop program, that is.)

If your goal is to organize and *use* your photos, rather than paint on them, remember that the newest version of iPhoto is either already on your hard drive or available as part of Apple's iLife suite ($80).

Finally, if opening and converting graphics to other formats is your main concern, try Preview (page 289), whose exporting feature is surprisingly powerful. You may also want to investigate the beloved shareware program GraphicConverter (find and download it at *www.versiontracker.com*), which may be the last graphics editing/converting program you'll ever need.

Palm Desktop

The CD that came with your Palm organizer included both Mac and Windows versions of this calendar/address book/to-do list/notepad program. Put another way, if you have a Palm, you probably already have Palm Desktop for Mac OS X.

But you don't have to buy a Palm to enjoy Palm Desktop's power, good looks, and amazing variety of printing options. You're welcome to use it as a standalone information manager. (It's a free download from *www.palm.com/support/Macintosh.*)

Picasa

Picasa, one of several Windows photo-organizers, isn't available for the Mac, but don't worry. On Mac OS X, you can edit, organize, and order prints of your images with iPhoto (page 419).

Pocket PC

The world of palmtop computers falls into two broad camps: Palm compatibles (from Palm, Sony, Kyocera, and others) and Pocket PC (from Dell, HP, ViewSonic, and others). Pocket PC machines are loaded with useful features. Unfortunately, they also run a tiny (but still confusing) version of Windows—and they can't exchange information with a Macintosh.

Or at least they can't right out of the box. Once you've added the program called PocketMac *(www.pocketmac.net),* though, you can synchronize your Pocket PC with the appointments, calendar, and to do list from any of the popular Mac OS X programs that handle this kind of information: Microsoft Entourage, Address Book, and iCal. You can even load up the pocket PC with files from Word and Excel for viewing and editing on the road, and MP3 files for music listening in transit. (Depending on the features you want, you'll pay anywhere from $15 to $42.)

PowerPoint

See "Microsoft Office" in this chapter. Remember, too, that Apple's own Keynote presentation program (available as part of iWork for $100) is the same idea as PowerPoint, but with much more spectacular graphic effects.

QuickBooks

If you've been happily using QuickBooks for Windows to manage your small business—to prepare estimates and invoices, track bills, maintain lists of inventory and customers, and so on—there's good news and bad news. The good news is that QuickBooks is available on the Mac, and, at least at this writing, comes free with many high-end Mac models.

The bad news is that the software, by itself, doesn't let you transfer your old QuickBooks data to the Mac version. You have several choices:

- Visit an Apple retailer and pay the guys at the Genius bar to perform the conversion for you ($75).

- Pay Intuit to do the conversion for you ($99 if you can wait 10 days, $250 if you can only wait three days). See *www.quickbooks.com/support/index/win2mac/* for details.

- Follow the rather involved do-it-yourself procedure at *www.quickbooks.com/support/index/win2mac/*.

Quicken

If you've been keeping track of your personal finances in Quicken on your PC, you'll feel right at home when you move to the Mac. Quicken 2003 and later versions are available for Mac OS X.

In general, switching over is quick and painless. You can import into the Mac version of Quicken all of the actual transaction information, including accounts, the categories and classes you've used to group them, and stock holdings. Certain kinds of Windows Quicken information—like schedule transactions, QuickFill transactions, online account information, stock histories, and loan information—don't make it, however.

Here's how to transfer your financial life to the Mac:

1. **Open up your Quicken file on the PC and choose List→Account List. Click Options, and then turn on the View Hidden Accounts checkbox. Edit your account names, if necessary, so that none is longer than 15 letters and spaces long.**

   That's a limit imposed by the Quicken Interchange Format, which you're going to use to transfer the data.

2. **Choose List→Security. Make sure that your stock symbols appear in ALL CAPITAL letters.**

   If you've been using Quicken to track your investments, Intuit advises that you take a few minutes to edit those transactions in some fairly technical and tweaky ways. Full instructions appear (at least at this writing) on the Quicken help Web site: *www.intuit.com/support/quicken/2003/mac/2159.html*.

3. **Clean up your file before exporting.**

"Clean up" means accepting all online transactions into the register, clearing up any outstanding transactions in the Online Center and Compare to Register windows, and deleting any pending payments.

4. **Export your data to a QIF file.**

To do so, choose File→Export. Choose QIF File as the format. You'll be asked what range of dates you want to include, which accounts, and which lists (categories, accounts, securities, and so on). Choose a location and name for the file you're about to export (such as *Quicken Windows Export*), and then click OK.

5. **Transfer your Quicken Windows Export file to the Mac.**

Chapter 5 describes a number of ways you can go about it.

6. **On the Macintosh, fire up Quicken. Choose File→New. Create and save a new document.**

When the Accounts window appears, click Cancel.

7. **Choose File→Import QIF. Find and double-click your Quicken Windows Export document.**

If the technology gods are smiling, the Mac version of Quicken should take a moment to import all of your Windows data, which now appears neatly in your Register windows, ready to use. Make sure the final balances match the final balances in Quicken for Windows. (If they don't, scan your Mac registers for duplicate or missing transactions.)

RealPlayer

Want to listen to Internet music and watch Internet video in Real format, just as you did on your PC? No sweat. Visit *www.real.com* and download RealPlayer for Mac OS X, either in the free basic edition or the fancy paid version.

If you just want to listen to music on your *hard drive,* though, you'd be better off using iTunes (page 227).

RssReader

RSS is a technology for reading quick Web site summaries, and it's taking the Net by storm. RSS returns the Internet to real utility, free from pop-up ads and the other annoyances of Web life.

To take advantage of RSS, however, you need a program to *subscribe* to Web sites that support RSS—and then to display the resulting summaries. On Windows, you might use a program like RssReader, or a Web site like *www.pluck.com.*

On Mac OS X, however, Apple's way ahead of you. Safari, described in detail in Chapter 11, provides a fantastic built-in RSS reader, and can subscribe to RSS sites with ease.

Skype

For making Internet-based phone calls, it's hard to beat Skype. If you call from one computer to another, you pay absolutely nothing—no matter how far away your recipient is.

Luckily, you can download a Mac version from *www.skype.com*. From there, you can audio-chat with all your Mac- and PC-using Skype buddies until you lose your voice.

Tip: iChat, Apple's own instant-messaging program, also offers free audio chats. If you and your buddy both have Web cams or videocameras, in fact, you can make free, Internet *video* calls. See page 313 for the details.

SnagIt

If you prepare instructions for using any kind of computer or software—computer books, magazine articles, or how-to materials of any kind—you may already be familiar with this amazing screen-capture program. It captures any window, menu, or area of the Windows screen and saves it as a graphics file that you can print or pop into a layout program.

In Mac OS X, this feature is built right in. Here's how to capture:

- **The whole screen.** Press Shift-⌘-3 to create a picture file on your desktop, in PNG format, that depicts the entire screen image. A satisfying camera-shutter sound tells you that you were successful.

  The file is called *Picture 1*. Each time you press Shift-⌘-3, you get another file, called Picture 2, Picture 3, and so on. You can open these files in Preview, Photoshop, or another graphics program, in readiness for editing or printing.

- **One section of the screen.** You can capture only a rectangular *region* of the screen by pressing Shift-⌘-4. When you drag and release the mouse, you hear the camera-click sound, and the Picture file appears on your desktop as usual.

- **One menu, window, icon (with its name), or dialog box.** Once you've got your menu or window open onscreen, or the icon visible (even if it's on the Dock), press Shift-⌘-4. But instead of dragging diagonally, press the Space bar.

  Now your cursor turns into a tiny camera. Move it so that the misty highlighting fills the window or menu you want to capture—and then click. The resulting Picture file snips the window or menu neatly from its background. (Press the Space bar a second time to exit "snip one screen element" mode and return to "drag across an area" mode.)

Tip: If you hold down the Control key as you click or drag (using any of the techniques described above), you copy the screenshot to your *clipboard,* ready for pasting, rather than saving it as a new graphics file on your desktop.

Mac OS X also offers another way to create screenshots: a program called Grab, which offers a timer option that lets you set up the screen before it takes the shot. It's in your Applications→Utilities folder.

But if you're really serious about capturing screenshots, you should opt instead for Snapz Pro X (*www.ambrosiasw.com*), which can capture virtually anything on the screen—even movies of onscreen procedures, along with your narration—and save it your choice of format.

Solitaire

Ah yes, Solitaire: possibly the most overused Windows software in the world.

The Mac doesn't come with a preinstalled copy of Solitaire, but the Web is crawling with free and shareware solitaire games for the Mac. Luckily, there's a quick way to unearth the most popular 20 or so. On the Web, visit *www.versiontracker.com* (one of most popular sources for freeware and shareware Mac programs). Click the Mac OS X tab if it's not already selected, and then, in the Search box, type *solitaire.*

When you click Go or press Enter, you'll see a substantial list of solitaire games, ready to download: FreeCell, MacSolitaire, Klondike, and so on.

Street Atlas USA

This popular mapping and routing software is also available for the Macintosh, although its features aren't quite as complete as they are in the Windows version.

And if it's Europe you want, it's Route 66 you need (*http://rs108.66.com/route66.*)

Tip: If you're looking for driving directions and maps, don't forget about *www.mapquest.com.* It's fast, it's convenient, it works the same on both Mac and Windows, and it's free. You can say the same for Google Maps (*http://maps.google.com*).

Also, don't forget about the Yellow Pages feature of the Dashboard (page 108). It's ready to print directions and draw maps.

TaxCut, TurboTax

Both of these popular tax programs are available for the Mac. You can even buy state versions for the many states that require income tax returns. You can buy them wherever fine Mac programs are sold: *www.macmall.com, www.macwarehouse.com, www.macconnection.com,* and so on.

WinAmp, MusicMatch

When it comes to playing MP3 files, creating MP3 files, burning music CDs, and otherwise organizing your music library, you'd be hard-pressed to beat iTunes, the free Mac OS X program that's already on your Mac (and a free download from *www. apple.com/itunes*).

Windows Media Player

The Macintosh equivalent for Windows Media Player is, of course, QuickTime Player. It handily plays and shows almost any kind of movie, picture, or sound (although you'll want to use iTunes for most music playback).

There are a few entertainment sources that work only with Windows Media Player, though—certain Internet radio stations, for example. Fortunately, Microsoft has gone to the trouble of creating a Macintosh version of Windows Media Player (never mind the irony of its name). You can download it from *www.microsoft.com/mac*.

WinZip

In Mac OS X, you create a .zip file by Control-clicking or right-clicking any Finder icon and choosing "Make Archive of [the icon's name]" from the shortcut menu. You decompress a .zip file by simply double-clicking its icon in the Finder.

Sometimes, however, you'll encounter compressed files on the Mac that end in *.sit*. You decompress such files with StuffIt Expander, a free download from *www.stuffit.com*.

Word

See "Microsoft Office" in this chapter.

WordPerfect

Unfortunately, WordPerfect lost the battle with Microsoft Word on the Mac side pretty much the same way it did on the Windows side. In the end, before discontinuing WordPerfect for the Mac completely, Corel made it a free download—in something called WordPerfect 3.5e, which you can still find floating around the Web if you look hard enough.

Even that version, however, is not a true Mac OS X program, and instead runs in Classic mode (page 123). If you're a die-hard WordPerfect fan, your best bet might be to invest in Microsoft Word and capitalize on its keystroke-customizing features to turn it into a living simulation of WordPerfect.

Or, if you'd rather not spend a significant portion of your life's savings on a word processor, use the free Word-importing and exporting features of TextEdit (page 435).

Yahoo Messenger

The equivalent chat program on the Mac is, of course, Yahoo Messenger for Mac OS X. It's a free download from *http://messenger.yahoo.com.*

VirtualPC: The Program of Last Resort

If you absolutely can't find a replacement for your favorite Windows programs, and you don't have an Intel Mac that can run Windows programs at full speed (Appendix A), you have one last choice: an emulation program that runs a simulated PC inside your Mac. Such programs hog memory and hard drive space, and are slow as a sedated sloth, but sometimes nothing else will do.

Virtual PC, a program made by Microsoft, is the most popular choice for emulating a PC. Depending on the version of Windows you buy with it, though, you could end up paying over $200—a point at which, honestly, you might be better off buying a year-old PC on eBay.

Still, if you decide to install Virtual PC, you can run almost any proprietary Windows software you had on your old PC on the same machine that you're running great Mac-only software like iMovie and iPhoto.

In other words, it's the best of both worlds, but only barely.

Hardware on the Mac

Most of the discussion in this book so far has covered *software*—not only the Mac OS X operating system that may be new to you, but also the programs and documents you'll be using on it. But there's more to life with a computer than software. This chapter covers the finer points of using Macintosh-compatible printers, cameras, disks, monitors, and keyboards.

Printers and Printing

Today's Mac OS X comes preinstalled with hundreds of printer drivers, including those for all current printer models from Epson, HP, Canon, and Lexmark. All you have to do is connect your printer and start printing, without installing a single piece of printer software. Now *that's* plug and play.

The situation is trickier if you have an older printer—the one you've been using with Windows, for example—that you'd like to make work with your new Mac. If it connects via a cable that the Mac recognizes (USB, for example, or Ethernet if it's an office laser printer), you can probably find Mac OS X–compatible driver software for it in one of these locations:

- *http://gimp-print.sourceforge.net.* That's the Web site for Gimp-Print. It may have an unappetizing name but it is, in fact, a collection of Mac OS X printer drivers for hundreds of Mac and Windows printers.

- The printer company's Web site.

Introducing the Printer

When you're ready to hook up your printer, follow this guide:

1. **Connect the printer to the Mac, and then turn the printer on.**

   Inkjet printers usually connect to your USB jack. Laser printers generally hook up to your Ethernet connector. (If you're on an office network, the laser printer may already be connected somewhere else on the network, saving you this step. If you're hooking the printer straight into your Mac's Ethernet jack, you may need an Ethernet *crossover cable* to connect it, rather than a standard Ethernet cable.)

Note: Some Ethernet- or network-connected laser printers communicate with your Mac using a language called AppleTalk. If you have such a printer, here is step 1.5: Open the Network pane of System Preferences. Double-click your current connection (like Built-in Ethernet or AirPort), and click the AppleTalk tab. Turn on Make AppleTalk Active, and then click Apply Now. (If you omit this step, Print Center will nag you about it later.)

---

2. **Open the document you want to print. Choose File→Print. In the Print dialog box, choose your printer's name from the Printer pop-up menu (or one of its submenus, if any).**

   Cool! Wasn't that easy? Very nice how the Mac auto-discovers, auto-configures, and auto-lists almost any USB, FireWire, Bluetooth, or Bonjour printer.

   Have a nice afternoon. The End.

   Oh—unless your printer *isn't* listed in the Printer pop-up menu. (Hey, it can happen.)

3. **From the Printer pop-up menu, choose Add Printer (Figure 8-1, top).**

   A program called Printer Setup Utility opens automatically. (You could also have opened it manually from your Applications→Utilities folder, or by opening the Print & Fax pane of System Preferences and clicking Printer Setup.)

WORKAROUND WORKSHOP

Parallel-Printer Hell

If you have a parallel printer, you might assume that you're out of luck; the Mac has no parallel port.

The technically oriented make old parallel printers work by buying a $150 component called a *network print server;* plugging it into the Ethernet network; and using CUPS and Gimp-Print to print to that printer. (See the tip on page 210 for more on CUPS.)

The non-technical and stingy, however, do just fine with a parallel-to-USB adapter, which plugs into your printer's parallel port and your Mac's USB port. You can get one for under $30, and if your printer is made by a name-brand manufacturer, your Mac will usually work with it as easily as it would with a regular USB printer.

All this effort may not be worth the trouble, though, if the old printer is an inkjet printer. New inkjets are so cheap these days, they practically fall out of specially marked boxes of Frosted Mini-Wheats.

But if it's a parallel printer that you have a special admiration for, or some specialty printer that's supposedly Mac-incompatible (like a dot-matrix printer that you *need* for printing carbon-paper forms), you'll be happy to have these two options.

It's even better at auto-detecting printers available to your Mac. If you see the printer's name now, in the Printer Browser window, click it and then click Add (Figure 8-1, middle). You've just designated that printer as the *default* printer—the one that you'll print on most of the time.

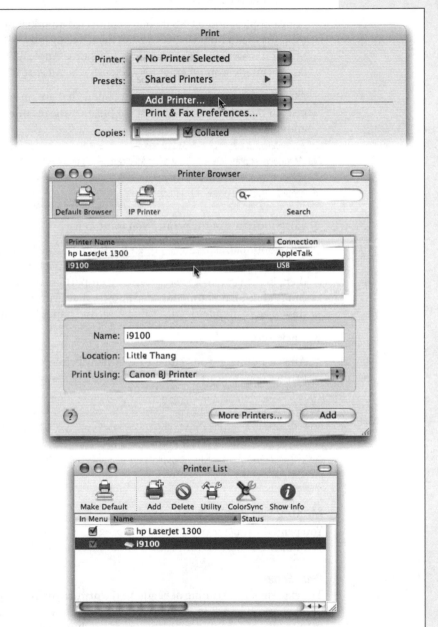

Figure 8-1:
Top: To introduce your Mac to a new printer, try to print some-thing–and then choose Add Printer from this pop-up menu.

Middle: Your Mac should automatically "see" any printers that are hooked up and turned on. Click the one you want, and then click Add. (If you have some oddball printer whose driver doesn't come built into Mac OS X, a "Driver not installed" message ap-pears. Find the driver, if it exists, on the printer's Web site.)

Bottom: If you've set up more than one printer in this way, you'll see all of them listed in the Printer List. (To get there from the Printer Browser shown above, choose View→Printer List.) The one whose name appears in bold is the default printer–the one destined to produce your next printout unless you choose a different one from the Print pop-up menu.

You're all set. Have a good time.

Unless your printer *still* isn't showing up. In that case, proceed to step 4.

4. **Click More Printers. In the next dialog box, use the pop-up menu to specify how the printer is connected to your Mac.**

   For example, choose USB if you've connected an inkjet printer to your USB port. (You may see a brand-name version here, like Epson USB or Canon USB; choose that, if it matches your printer brand.) Choose AppleTalk if you're connected to a laser printer via an Ethernet network cable or AirPort wireless network.

   After a moment, the names of any printers that are turned on and connected appear in the printer list. For most people, that means only one printer—but one's enough.

   Tip: Windows Printing means, "Hey, your Mac can send printouts to a Windows-only printer out there on your office network!" Just choose this option, click the name of the network group you're in, and then type an account name and password, if necessary.

   ---

5. **Click the name of the printer you want to use.**

   As an optional step, you can open the Printer Model pop-up menu at the bottom of the dialog box. Choose your printer's manufacturer (like HP or Canon), and then, in the list that appears, choose your particular printer's model name, if you can find it. That's how your Mac knows what printing features to offer when the time comes: double-sided, legal size, second paper tray, and so on.

6. **Click Add.**

   After a moment, you return to the main Printer Browser window, where your printer now appears (Figure 8-1, top). You're ready to print.

   Note: If you *still* don't see your printer's name, ask yourself: Is my Mac on a corporate network? Does the network have an LPR (Line Printer) printer? If you and your company's network nerd determine that the printer you want to use is, in fact, an LPR printer, click IP Printing at the top of the Printer Browser dialog box (Figure 8-1, middle). Fill in the appropriate IP address and other settings, as directed by your cheerful network administrator.

Making the Printout

You print documents from within the programs you use to create them, exactly as in Windows. The options for printing should feel distinctly familiar.

Page Setup

The experience of printing depends on the printer you're using—laser printer, inkjet, or whatever. In every case, however, all the printing options hide behind two commands: File→Page Setup, which you need to adjust only occasionally, and File→Print, which you generally use every time you print.

The Page Setup dialog box lets you specify some key characteristics about the document you're going to print: orientation, paper dimensions, and so on (see Figure 8-2).

The options here vary by program and printer. The Page Setup options for an Epson inkjet, for example, differ dramatically from those for a laser printer. Only your printer's user manual can tell you exactly what these choices do.

Note: Unless you're happy with Apple's defaults, you must set the Page Setup options differently for *each* program you use.

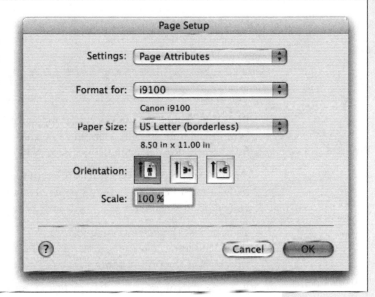

Figure 8-2:
Here in Page Setup are the controls you need to print a document rotated sideways on the page, so that it prints "the long way." The Scale control, which lets you reduce or enlarge your document, can be handy if the program you're using doesn't offer such a control. And the Paper Size pop-up menu, of course, specifies the size of the paper you're printing on—US Letter, US Legal, envelopes, or one of the standard European or Japanese paper sizes.

The Print command

Although you can grow to a ripe old age without ever seeing the Page Setup dialog box, you can't avoid the Print dialog box. It appears, like it or not, whenever you choose File→Print in one of your programs.

Once again, the options you encounter depend on the printer you're using. But here's what you may find on the box's main screen (the screen you see when the pop-up menu reads Copies & Pages):

- **Printer.** If you have more than one printer connected to your Mac, you can indicate which you want to use for a particular printout by choosing its name from this pop-up menu.

- **Presets.** Here's a way to preserve your favorite print settings. Once you've proceeded through this dialog box—specifying the number of copies, which printer trays you want the paper taken from, and so on—you can choose Save As from the pop-up menu shown in Figure 8-3, and then assign your settings a name (like "Borderless,

2 copies"). Thereafter, you'll be able to re-create that elaborate suite of settings just by choosing its name from this pop-up menu.

- **Copies.** Type the number of copies you want printed. The Collated checkbox controls the printing order for the various pages. For example, if you print two copies of a three-page document, the Mac will generally print the pages in this order: 1, 2, 3, 1, 2, 3. If you turn on Collated, on the other hand, it'll print in this order: 1, 1, 2, 2, 3, 3.

- **Pages.** You don't have to print an entire document—you can print, say, only pages 2 through 15.

Tip: You don't have to type numbers into both the From and To boxes. If you leave the first box blank, the Mac assumes that you mean "from page 1." If you leave the second box blank, the Mac understands you mean "to the end." To print only the first three pages, in other words, leave the first box blank, and type 3 into the second box. (These page numbers refer to the physical pages you're printing, not to any fancy numbering you've set up in your word processor.)

- **PDF.** A *PDF* file, of course, is an Adobe Acrobat document—a file that any Mac, Windows, Linux, or Unix user can view, read, and print using either Preview or the free Acrobat Reader (included with every PC and earlier Mac operating system).

  One of Mac OS X's most useful features, though, is its ability to *create* PDF files—a truly beautiful feature that saves paper, ink, and time. The document remains on your hard drive, and the text inside is even searchable using Spotlight.

  To access all the PDF-creating features for a document, click the pop-up *button* shown in Figure 8-3. The command you'll use most often is probably Save as PDF, which turns the printout into a PDF file instead of sending it to the printer.

- **Preview.** This button provides a print-preview function to almost every Mac OS X program on earth, which, in the course of your life, could save huge swaths of the Brazilian rainforest and a swimming pool's worth of ink in wasted printouts.

  Technically, the Preview button sends your printout to the Preview *program*. Preview, an expert graphics viewer, lets you zoom in or zoom out, rotate, or otherwise process your preview. When you're satisfied with how it looks, you can print it (File→Print), cancel it (File→Close), or turn it into a PDF (File→Save as, Format: PDF).

- **Supplies.** This new Tiger feature will strike you either as blissfully convenient or disgustingly mercenary. It's a button that takes you directly to a Web page where you can buy new cartridges for your specific printer model.

If you examine the unnamed pop-up menu just below the Presets pop-up menu, you find dozens of additional options. They depend on your printer model and the program you're using at the moment, but here are some typical choices:

- **Layout.** As described in Figure 8-3, you can save paper and ink or toner cartridges by printing several miniature pages on a single sheet of paper.

- **Scheduler.** This option lets you specify *when* you want your document to print. If you're a freelancer, sitting at home with an inkjet on your desk, you might not immediately grasp why anyone wouldn't want the printouts *right now.* But try to print a 400-page catalog in a big office where other people on the network might resent you for tying up the laser printer all afternoon, and you'll get the idea.

- **Paper Handling.** You can opt to print out your pages in reverse order so that they stack correctly, or you can print just odd or even pages so that you can run them through again for double-sided printing.

- **ColorSync.** Most color printers offer this pane, where you can adjust the color settings—a little more red, perhaps. This is also where you indicate whose *color-matching system* you want to use: Apple's ColorSync, your printer manufacturer's, or none at all.

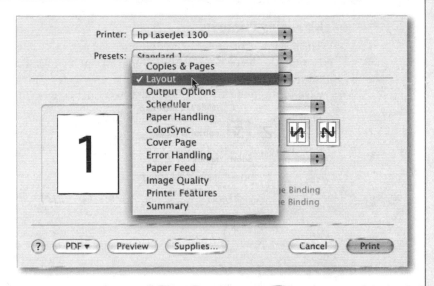

Figure 8-3:
The options included in this dialog box depend on the printer model you're using. On the Layout pane, you can choose from the Pages per Sheet pop-up menu to indicate how many miniature virtual pages you want printed on each sheet, to save paper and ink.

- **Quality & Media** (inkjet printers only). Here's where you specify the print quality you want, the kind of paper you're printing on, and so on. (The name of this pane varies by manufacturer.)

- **Error Handling.** Using these controls, you can specify that you want a technical message to print out when the laser printer reports a PostScript error (when your document is too complex for the printer's memory, for example). Depending on your printer, you may also be able to specify what kind of notification you want to receive if your specified paper tray runs out of paper.

- **Paper Feed.** If you chose the correct printer model when setting up your printer, then this screen already "knows about" your printer's various paper trays. Here's where you specify which pages you want to come from which paper tray. (By far the most popular use for this feature is printing the first page of a letter on company letterhead, and the following pages on blank paper from a second tray.)

- **[Program Name].** Whichever program you're using—Mail, Word, AppleWorks, or anything else—may offer its own special printing options on this screen. Some HP printers, for example, offer Cover Page, Finishing, and other choices.

- **Summary.** This command summons a text summary of all your settings so far.

Tip: Here's one for the technically inclined. Open your Web browser (Safari, for example) and enter this address: *http://127.0.0.1:631.* You find yourself at a secret "front end" for CUPS (Common Unix Printing System), the underlying printing technology for Mac OS X—and the one that lets your Mac communicate with a huge array of older printers that don't yet have Mac OS X drivers. Using this administration screen, you can print a test page, stop your printer in its tracks, manage your networked printers and print jobs, and more. Very slick.

Managing Printouts

The real fun of printing begins only after you've used the Print command (and clicked Print in the dialog box). At this point, you can manage the printouts-in-waiting in a number of ways—ways that are useful primarily for people who do a lot of printing, have connections to a lot of printers, or share printers with many other people.

Start by opening Printer Setup Utility. In the list of printers, the Status column shows you which printers are busy. Double-click a printer's name to see something like Figure 8-4; the printouts that will soon be sliding out of your printer appear in a tidy list.

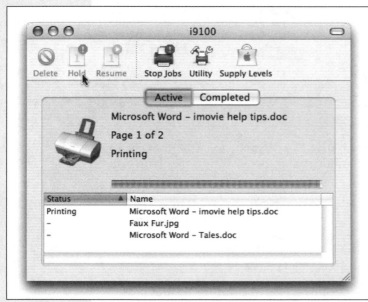

Figure 8-4:
Waiting printouts appear in this Printer Setup Utility window. You can sort the list by clicking the column headings Name or Status; make the columns wider or narrower by dragging the column-heading dividers horizontally; or reverse the sorting order by clicking the column name a second time. The Supply Level button shows you how much ink each cartridge has remaining (certain printer models only).

Here are some of the ways in which you can control these waiting printouts, which Apple affectionately calls the *print queue:*

- **Delete them.** By clicking an icon (or ⌘-clicking several) and then clicking the Delete toolbar button, you remove items from the list of waiting printouts. Now they don't print.

- **Pause them.** By highlighting a printout and then clicking the Hold button, you pause the printout. It doesn't print out until you highlight it again and click the Resume button. This pausing business could be useful when, for example, you need time to check or refill the printer, or when you're about to print your resignation as your boss drops by to offer you a promotion.

Tip: If you pause one printout, the others lined up behind it continue to print.

- **Halt them all.** You can stop all printouts from a printer by clicking Stop Jobs. (They resume when you click the button again, which now says Start Jobs.)

Faxing

Mac OS X's built-in faxing feature saves you the price of a *real* fax machine, plus all the paper and cartridges that go with it. Faxing from the Mac also eliminates the silly ritual of printing something out just so that you can feed it into a fax machine. And because your fax originates directly from the heart of Mac OS X instead of some crummy 200-dpi fax-machine scanner, it blesses your recipient with a good-looking document.

Here's the basic idea: When faxes come in, you can read them on the screen, opt to have them printed automatically, or even have them emailed to you so that you can get them wherever you are in the world. (Try *that* with a regular fax machine.) And sending a fax is even easier on a Mac than it is on a regular fax machine. You just use the File→Print command, exactly like you're making a printout of the onscreen document.

There are two downsides to using a Mac as a fax machine, though:

- **The Mac needs its own phone line.** Otherwise, when your Mac answers each incoming call, your friends and relatives will get a screeching earful as they try to call to express their love.

Tip: You can avoid this prerequisite if you use your Mac exclusively for *sending* faxes, since it won't pick up the phone when people call.

- **You can't fax from a book or magazine.** The one big limitation of computer-based faxing is that you can only transmit documents that are, in fact, *on the computer.* That pretty much rules out faxing notes scribbled on a legal pad, clippings from *People* magazine, and so on (unless you scan them in first).

Setting Up Faxing

Open System Preferences. Click Print & Fax. Click the Faxing tab.

If you intend to *send* faxes from the Mac, type in your return fax number. If you intend to *receive* faxes, turn on "Receive faxes on this computer." Then specify how you want to handle incoming faxes, as described in Figure 8-5.

Tip: If you're smart, you'll also turn on "Show fax status in menu bar." It installs a fax menulet that lets you monitor and control your faxing.

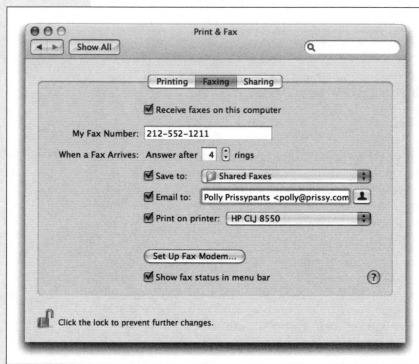

Figure 8-5:
When your Mac answers the fax line, there are three things it can do with the incoming fax. Option 1: Save it as a PDF file that you can open with Preview. (The Mac proposes saving these files into the Users→Shared→Shared Faxes folder, but you can set up a more convenient folder.) Option 2: Email it to you, so that you can get your faxes even when you're not home (and so you can forward them easily). Option 3: Print it out automatically, just like a real fax machine.

Sending a Fax

When you're ready to send a fax, type up the document you want to send. Choose File→Print. In the Print dialog box (Figure 8-3), open the PDF pop-up button and choose Fax PDF.

The dialog box shown at bottom in Figure 8-6 appears. Here are the boxes you can fill in:

- **To.** If you like, you can simply type the fax number into the To box, exactly the way it should be dialed: *1-212-553-2999,* for example. Or you can send a single fax to more than one number by separating each with a comma and a space.

- **Presets, Settings.** Most of the time, fiddling with the lower pop-up menu, let alone saving your settings as a Preset, isn't relevant to sending a fax. (ColorSync? On a black-and-white fax? Get real!) But the standard printing controls are here for your convenience. You can use the Scheduler pane to specify a time for your outgoing fax, the Layout pane to print more than one "page" per sheet, and so on.

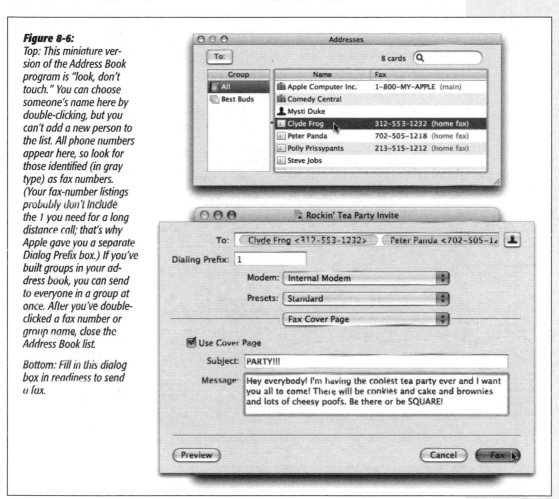

Figure 8-6:
Top: This miniature version of the Address Book program is "look, don't touch." You can choose someone's name here by double-clicking, but you can't add a new person to the list. All phone numbers appear here, so look for those identified (in gray type) as fax numbers. (Your fax-number listings probably don't include the 1 you need for a long distance call; that's why Apple gave you a separate Dialog Prefix box.) If you've built groups in your address book, you can send to everyone in a group at once. After you've double-clicked a fax number or group name, close the Address Book list.

Bottom: Fill in this dialog box in readiness to send a fax.

- **Use Cover Page, Subject, Message.** If you turn on this checkbox, you're allowed to type a little message into the Subject and Message boxes.

- **Preview.** This button opens your outgoing fax in Preview (page 427), so you can see exactly what it will look like. Choose File→Save As at this point to keep a copy of the fax you're sending.

Sending

When everything looks good, hit the Fax button. Although it may look like nothing is happening, check your Dock, where the icon of a secret program called Internal Modem has appeared. If you click it, you'll see a clone of the dialog box shown in Figure 8-7, indicating the progress of your fax. Here you can pause the faxing, delete it, or hold it exactly as you would a printout. (Your Fax menulet, if you've installed it, also keeps you apprised of the fax's progress; see the tip on page 212.)

Otherwise, you don't get much feedback on the faxing process. Once the connection sounds are complete, you don't hear anything, see anything, or receive any notice that the fax was successful.

(If your fax was *not* successful, the Internal Modem window automatically reschedules the fax to go out in five minutes.)

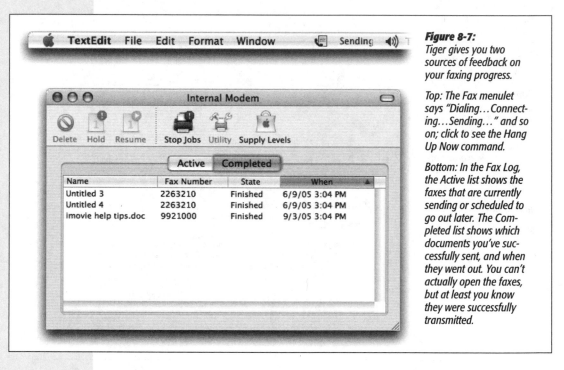

Figure 8-7:
Tiger gives you two sources of feedback on your faxing progress.

Top: The Fax menulet says "Dialing...Connecting...Sending..." and so on; click to see the Hang Up Now command.

Bottom: In the Fax Log, the Active list shows the faxes that are currently sending or scheduled to go out later. The Completed list shows which documents you've successfully sent, and when they went out. You can't actually open the faxes, but at least you know they were successfully transmitted.

Checking the log, checking the queue

To see Mac OS X's record of sent and received faxes, you have to open the Fax List. Here are two ways to get there:

- Open the Print & Fax pane of System Preferences. Click Faxing. Click Set Up Fax Modem. In the Fax List window, double-click Internal Modem.

- In your Applications→Utilities folder, open Printer Setup Utility. Choose View→Show Fax List. Double-click Internal Modem.

Either way, you now get a status window that looks a lot like the one for a regular printer (Figure 8-4).

Receiving a Fax

A Mac that's been set up to answer calls does a very good impersonation of a fax machine. You don't even have to be logged in to get faxes, although the Mac does have to be turned on. In System Preferences→Energy Saver, turn on "Wake when modem detects a ring" to prevent your Mac from being asleep at the big moment.

When a fax comes in, the Mac answers it after the number of rings you've specified. Then it treats the incoming fax image in the way you've specified in System Preferences—by sending it to your email program, printing it automatically, or just saving it as a PDF file in a folder that you've specified.

Scanning

In theory, you should be able to use your old Windows scanner with your new Mac—if it connects with USB, FireWire (IEEE 1394), or some other connection that physically fits into the Mac.

But in practice, scanning is often a sore spot for Mac OS X fans. Most *current* scanner models (Epson, Canon, Agfa, Nikon, Microtek, Umax) work with Mac OS X, but hundreds of older ones still don't have Mac OS X drivers.

If your scanner model isn't one of the lucky ones, pay a visit to *www.hamrick.com* to download VueScan. It's a $40 shareware program that makes dozens of scanners work with Mac OS X, including:

- **SCSI models** including SCSI scanners from Apple, Epson, Canon, HP, Microtek, UMAX, LinoType-Hell, Acer, and AGFA.

- **USB models** including scanners from Epson and many from Canon, HP, Microtek, Umax, and others.

- **FireWire models** including scanners from Epson, Microtek, UMAX, and LinoType-Hell.

If your scanner model isn't on the VueScan list, it may be on the list of SilverFast (*www.silverfast.com*), which restores to life 150 older SCSI and USB scanners from Acer, AGFA, EPSON, Linotype, Microtek, PFU, Polaroid, Quato, and UMAX.

PDF Files

Even before your switch from Windows, you probably ran into PDF (portable document format) files at some point. Many a software manual, Read Me file, and downloadable "white paper" comes in this format. And no wonder: When you distribute PDF files to other people, they see precisely the same fonts, colors, page design, and other elements that you did in your original document—even if they don't own the programs used to create the PDF file. Better yet, the same PDF file opens identically on the Mac, in Windows, and even on Unix/Linux machines.

In Windows, you need the free program called Acrobat Reader if you hoped to open or print these files. But PDF files are one of Mac OS X's common forms of currency. The Mac's built-in PDF reader, called Preview, is a joy to use. Better yet, you can turn *any document,* in any program with a Print command, *into* a PDF file—a trick that once required the $250 program called Adobe Acrobat Distiller.

Opening PDF files

There's nothing to opening up a PDF file on the Mac: Just double-click it. Preview takes over from there, and opens the PDF file on your screen.

Creating PDF files

Opening, schmopening—what's really exciting in Mac OS X is the ability to create your *own* PDF files. The easiest way is to click the PDF pop-up button in the standard Print dialog box (Figure 8-8). When you click it, you're offered a world of interesting PDF-creation possibilities:

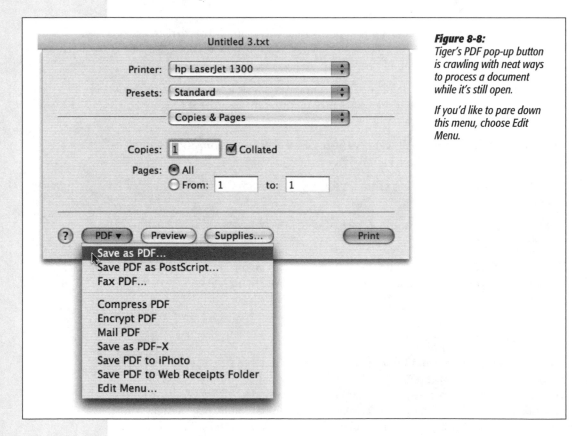

Figure 8-8:
Tiger's PDF pop-up button is crawling with neat ways to process a document while it's still open.

If you'd like to pare down this menu, choose Edit Menu.

- **Save as PDF.** Mac OS X saves your printout-to-be to the disk as a PDF document instead of printing it.

- **Save PDF as PostScript.** PostScript is a format preferred by some designers and print shops. It consists of highly precise "what to draw" instructions for PostScript laser printers.

- **Fax PDF** *faxes* a document instead of printing it, as described on the preceding pages.

- **Compress PDF** creates a PDF that takes up less disk space—at some expense of resolution (visual quality), especially in the graphics department. Ideal for emailing, not so hot for printing.

- **Encrypt PDF** lets you password-protect the resulting PDF document for added security. (Just don't forget the password; there's no back door.)

- **Mail PDF** generates a PDF and then attaches it to an outgoing message in Mail.

- **Save as PDF-X** creates a specialized PDF format, popular in the printing industry, that's extra compact because it contains the minimum data needed to print the document.

- **Save PDF to iPhoto** creates a PDF version of the document and then exports it to iPhoto. That's not such a bad idea; iPhoto is great at managing and finding any kind of graphics documents, including PDFs.

- **Save PDF to Web Receipts Folder** is a great option when you've just bought something on a Web site and the "Print this Receipt" screen is staring you in the face, but you don't really feel like wasting paper and ink on it. With this command, you get a perfectly usable PDF version, stored in your Home→Documents→Web Receipts folder, where you can consult or print it later if your gray-market goods never arrive.

- **Edit Menu** lets you prune this very list to remove the options you never use.

Fonts—and Font Book

Mac OS X type always looks smooth onscreen, no matter what the point size, and always looks smooth in printouts, no matter what kind of printer you use. (That's because Mac OS X accepts only always-smooth type formats like TrueType, PostScript Type 1, and OpenType.)

To help you keep its fonts organized, Mac OS X comes with a program that's just for installing, removing, inspecting, and organizing fonts. It's called Font Book (Figure 8-9), and it's waiting in your Applications folder.

Where Fonts Live

If you're used to Windows, one of the most confusing changes is that there is no longer one single Fonts folder for your computer. There are now *five* Fonts folders.

The fonts you actually see listed in the Font menus and panels of your programs are combinations of these Fonts folders' contents. They include:

- **Your private fonts (your Home folder→Library→Fonts).** You're free to add your own custom fonts to this folder. Go wild—it's your font collection and yours alone. Nobody else who uses the Mac will be able to use these fonts, and nobody will even know that you have them.

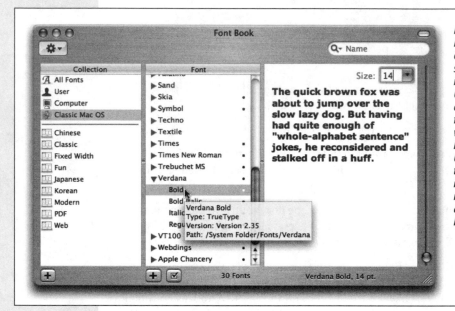

Figure 8-9:
Each account holder can have a separate set of fonts; your set is represented by the User icon. You can drag fonts and font families between the various Fonts folders here—from your User account folder to the Computer icon, for example—to make them available to all account holders.

- **Main font collection (Library→Fonts).** This, for all intents and purposes, is the equivalent of the traditional Fonts folder. Any fonts in this folder are available to everyone to use in every program. (As with most features that affect everybody who shares your Macintosh, however, only people with Administrator accounts are allowed to change the contents of this folder.)

- **Network fonts (Network→Library→Fonts).** In certain corporations, a network administrator may have set up a central font collection on another computer on the network, to which your Mac and others can "subscribe." The beauty of this system, of course, is that everybody on the network will be able to rely on a consistent set of fonts.

- **Essential system fonts (System→Library→Fonts).** This folder contains the fonts that the Mac itself needs: the typefaces you see in your menus, dialog boxes, icons, and so on. You can open this folder to *see* these font suitcases, but you can't do anything with them, such as opening, moving, or adding to them.

- **Classic fonts (Mac OS 9 System Folder→Fonts).** Mac OS X automatically notices and incorporates any fonts in the System Folder that you've designated for use by the Classic environment (page 123). This folder is also, of course, the source of fonts that appear in the Font menus of your Classic programs (page 120).

With the exception of essential system fonts, you'll find an icon representing each of these locations in your Font Book program, described next.

Font Book: Installing and Managing Fonts

One of the biggest perks of Mac OS X is its preinstalled collection of great-looking fonts—"over $1,000 worth," according to Apple, which licensed them from type companies. Font Book is your ticket to making the most of them.

Looking over your fonts

Right off the bat, Font Book is great for one enjoyable pursuit: looking at samples of each typeface. Click Computer, for example; click the first font name, and then press the down-arrow key. As you walk down the list, the rightmost pane shows you a sample of each font (Figure 8-9).

You can also open any font family's flippy triangle (or highlight its name and then press the right arrow) to see the font *variations* it includes: Italic, Bold, and so on.

Tip: Don't miss the Preview menu, which lets you substitute a full display of every character in the rightmost pane (choose Repertoire)—or, if you choose Custom, substitute your own text.

Eliminating duplicates

Since your Mac accesses up to five folders containing fonts, you might wonder what happens in the case of *conflicts*. For example, suppose you have two slightly different fonts, both called Optima, which came from different type companies, and are housed in different Fonts folders on your system. Which font do you actually get when you use it in your documents?

The scheme is actually fairly simple: Mac OS X proceeds down the list of Fonts folders in the order described on the facing page, beginning with your own home Fonts folder. It only acknowledges the existence of the *first* instance of the font it finds.

Tip: If you'd rather have more control, open Font Book. A bullet (•) next to a font's name is Font Book's charming way of telling you that you've got copies of the same font in more than one place. Click the one that you want to *keep* and then choose Edit→Resolve Duplicates.

Adding fonts

You can use most of your old Windows fonts on the Mac, too, since most of them use the same file format. (The Mac accepts the TrueType and OpenType fonts from your PC, but not Windows PostScript Type 1. You can find out a font's type by right-clicking its icon in the Windows Fonts folder and choosing Properties from the shortcut menu.)

To find your PC's fonts, proceed like this:

- **Windows XP, Windows Me, Windows 2000.** Open My Computer→[your hard drive]→Windows (or WINNT)→Fonts folder.

- **Windows 95, 98.** Choose Start→Settings→Control Panel→Fonts.

Copy the font files, using any of the techniques described in Chapter 5, onto your Mac. Then, when you double-click a font's file in the Finder, Font Book opens and presents the typeface for your inspecting pleasure. If you like it, click Install font.

You've just installed it into *your account's* Fonts folder, so that it appears in the Font menus and panels of all *your* programs.

Removing and hiding fonts

Removing a font from your machine is easy: Highlight it in Font Book and then press the Delete key. (You're asked to confirm the decision.)

Before taking such a drastic step, however, consider this: When you *disable* a font, you simply hide it from your programs. You might want to disable a font so that you can use a different version of it (a copy from a different company, for example), or to make your Font menus shorter, or to make a program like Microsoft Word start up faster.

To disable a font, just click it and then click the checkbox button beneath the list (or press Shift-⌘-D). Confirm your decision by clicking Disable in the confirmation box.

The font's name now appears gray, and the word Off appears next to it, making it absolutely clear what you've just done. (To turn the font on again, highlight its name and then click the now-empty checkbox button, or press Shift-⌘-D again.)

Note: When you install, remove, disable, or enable a font using Font Book, you see the changes in the Font panels of your *Cocoa* programs (page 120) immediately. You won't see the changes in open Carbon programs, however, until you quit and reopen them.

Digital Cameras

Just like Windows XP, Mac OS X is extremely camera-friendly. The simple act of connecting a digital camera to its USB cable stirs Mac OS X into action—namely, it opens iPhoto, Apple's digital-photo shoebox program. See page 419 for a crash course.

If it's a digital *video* camera you plugged in, Mac OS X opens iMovie instead. Page 409 has an overview of this useful video editor.

Disks

Floppy drives disappeared from Macs beginning in 1997—and these days, they're disappearing from Windows PCs, too.

If you miss having a floppy drive, you can always buy a USB-based one for your Mac. In the meantime, there are all kinds of other disks you can connect to a Mac these days: FireWire (IEEE 1394) external hard drives, iPods, USB flash drives, and so on.

When you insert any kind of disk, its icon shows up on the right side of the screen; there's no My Computer icon to open when you want to find the inserted disk's icon. Similarly, *no icon* for a drive appears if there's no disc in it. If you've used only Windows, this behavior may throw you at first.

Note: You *can* use Mac OS X like Windows if you choose. To open a single window containing icons of all currently inserted disks, choose Go→Computer. To complete the illusion that you're running Windows, you can even tell Mac OS X not to put disk icons on the desktop at all. Just choose Finder→Preferences→General and turn off the three top checkboxes—"Hard disks," "CDs, DVDs, and iPods" and "Connected servers." They'll no longer appear on the desktop—only in your Computer window.

To remove a disk from your Mac, use one of these methods:

- **Drag its icon onto the Trash icon.** For years, this technique has confused and frightened first-time Mac users. Their typical reaction: "Doesn't the *Trash* mean *delete?*" Yes, but only when you drag document or folder icons there—not disk icons. Dragging disk icons onto the Trash (at the right end of the Dock) makes the Mac spit them out.

  Actually, all you can really do is *intend* to drag it onto the Trash can. The instant you begin dragging a disk icon, the Trash icon on the Dock changes form, as though

---

FREQUENTLY ASKED QUESTION

The Eject Button That Doesn't

When I push the Eject button on my keyboard (or on my CD-ROM drawer), how come the CD doesn't come out?

There might be two things going on. First of all, to prevent accidental pushings, the ⏏ key on the modern Mac keyboard is designed to work only when you hold it down steadily for a second or two. Just tapping it doesn't work.

Second, remember that once you've inserted a CD, DVD, or Zip disk, the Mac won't let go unless you eject it in one of the official ways. On Mac models with a CD tray, pushing the button on the CD-ROM *door* opens the drawer only when it's *empty*. If there's a disc in it, you can push that button till doomsday, but the Mac will simply ignore you.

That behavior especially confuses people who are used to working with Windows. (On a Windows PC, pushing the CD button does indeed eject the disc.) On the Mac, push-

ing the CD door button ejects an inserted disc only when the disc wasn't seated properly (or when the disk drive's driver software isn't installed), and the disc's icon never did appear onscreen.

The ⏏ key on the modern Mac keyboard, however, isn't so fussy. It pops out whatever CD or DVD is in the drive.

Finally, if a CD or DVD won't come out at all (and its icon doesn't show up on the desktop), restart the Mac. When the computer is finished loading, it will either recognize the disc or generate an error message containing an Eject button. (Most drives also feature a tiny pinhole in or around the slot. Inserting a straightened paper clip, slowly and firmly, will also make the disc pop out.) Keeping the mouse button pressed as the Mac restarts also does the trick, as well.

---

to reassure the novice that it will merely eject a disk icon, not erase it. As you drag, the wastebasket icon turns into a giant-sized ⏏ logo (which matches the symbol on the upper-rightmost key of current Mac keyboards).

- **Press the ⏏/F12 key on your keyboard.** Recent Mac keyboards, both on laptops and desktops, have a special Eject key (⏏) in the upper-right corner; on older Macs, you use the F12 key instead (if this conflicts with your Dashboard keystroke, see page 107). Either way, hold it down for a moment to make a CD or DVD pop out.

- **Highlight the disk icon, and then choose File→"Eject [the disk's name]," or press ⌘-E.** The disk now pops out.

- **Control-click or right-click the disk icon.** Choose "Eject [the disk's name]" from the contextual menu.

Startup Disks

When you turn the Mac on, it hunts for a *startup disk*—that is, a disk containing a copy of Mac OS X. And, as you know, a computer without an operating system is like a machine that's had a lobotomy.

Selecting a startup disk

It's perfectly possible to have more than one startup disk simultaneously attached to your Mac. Some veteran Mac fans deliberately create other startup disks—on burnable DVDs, for example—so that they can easily start the Mac up from a backup startup disk, or a different version of the OS.

Figure 8-10:
In the Startup Disk pane of System Preferences, the currently selected disk—the one that will be "in force" the next time the machine starts up—is always highlighted. You see the Mac OS X version number and the name of the drive it's on, but not its actual name—until you point to an icon without clicking.

Only one System folder can be operational at a time, though. So how does the Mac know which to use as its startup disk? You make your selection in the Startup Disk pane of System Preferences (Figure 8-10). Use it to specify which disk you want the Mac to start up from the next time you turn it on.

Erasing, Formatting, and Initializing

When you want to erase a disk (such as a CD-RW disc) in Mac OS X, use Disk Utility, which is located in your Applications→Utilities folder.

You can use this program to erase, repair, or subdivide (*partition*) a hard drive, or any other kind of disk.

To erase a CD-RW or DVD-RW disc, open Disk Utility, click the Erase tab, click the name of the CD (in the left-side list), and click the Erase button.

Burning CDs and DVDs

If your Mac contains a CD-RW drive or an Apple SuperDrive (a drive that plays and burns CDs *and* DVDs), you've got yourself the world's most convenient and elegant backup system. It's like having a floppy disk drive, except that a blank CD holds at least 450 times as many files—and a blank DVD about 3,250 times as many files—as a floppy disk.

You can buy blank CDs very inexpensively in bulk via the Web—$20 for 100 discs, for example. (To find the best prices, visit *www.shopper.com* or *www.buy.com* and search for *blank CD-R.*) Blank DVDs are more expensive—about $25 for 50 (at *www.cdrdvdrmedia.com,* for example)—but that's not ridiculous, considering their capacity.

Burning a CD or DVD is great for backing stuff up, transferring stuff to another computer, mailing to somebody, or offloading (archiving) older files to free up hard

---

UP TO SPEED

Mac OS Extended Formatting

Whenever you use Disk Utility to erase a disk (or when you first install Mac OS X and elect to erase the hard drive in the process), you'll be confronted with a choice between formatting options called Mac OS Extended and UNIX File System (UFS). (Depending on the kind of disk, you may also get an option to create a DOS-formatted disk for use in Windows machines.)

Mac OS Extended or Mac OS Extended (Journaled) refers to the HFS Plus filing system, a disk format that's been proudly maximizing disk space for Mac fans since Mac OS

8.1. ("Journaled" just means that the disk pays even closer attention to reading and writing files, so that it can repair the disk better in the event of a crash.)

Mac OS X still accepts disks that were prepared using the older, Mac OS Standard formatting—the ancient HFS (hierarchical filing system) format—but such disks are considered collector's items nowadays.

As for the UNIX File System option, it's exclusively for use on computers that run Unix (the pure variety, not the dressed-up version that is Mac OS X).

---

drive space. (If you've used Easy CD Creator to burn discs on Windows, you should be on home turf here.)

To make things as convenient as possible, Mac OS X actually provides two *different* ways to burn a disc: with the disc inserted or without. Read on.

Burn Folders: Without the Disc

Burn folders are a Mac OS X concept that's foreign to most Windows refugees. It's a special folder that you fill up by dragging file and folder icons to it. Then, when you're ready to burn, you just insert the blank disc and go.

This burn-folder system has a number of benefits:

- **No wasted hard drive space.** A burn disc simply contains *aliases* of the files you intend to burn—and aliases, as you know, take up almost no space. When you finally burn the disc, the Mac copies the *original* files to the CD or DVD, creating a true backup of your files.

- **Easy re-use.** You can keep a burn folder on your desktop, prestocked with the files and folders you like to back up. Each time you burn a disc, you get the latest version of those files' contents, without having to gather them each time.

- **Prepare ahead of time.** You can get a CD or DVD ready to burn without having a blank disc readily available.

Here's how you use burn folders:

1. **Create a burn folder.**

   To make a burn folder appear on your desktop, choose File→New Burn Folder. To create one in any other window, Control-click (or right-click) a blank spot inside the window and, from the shortcut menu, choose New Burn Folder.

   Either way, a new folder icon appears, bearing the universal Mac radioactive "burn" symbol (Figure 8-11, top).

2. **Rename it.**

   Its name is automatically highlighted, so you can just start typing to rename it. Press Return when you're finished.

3. **Load up the folder by dragging files and folders onto it.**

   If you double-click the burn folder to open its window, you'll notice that you're not actually copying the huge files. You're simply making a list of aliases (page 57).

Tip: To check how many megabytes' worth of stuff you've added so far—so you don't overflow your CD or DVD—click the Burn button in the upper-right corner of the burn folder's window *before* inserting a disc. The resulting message, shown at bottom in Figure 8-11, tells you the current total. (Hit the Enter key, or click Cancel, to close the dialog box.)

---

4. **Decorate the window, if you like.**

   You can choose list view or icon view; you can drag the icons into an arrangement that you like; you can change the background color of the window; and so on. One welcome feature of Mac OS X: the look of a window is preserved when you burn it to a disc.

5. **Click the Burn button in the upper-right corner of the window, or choose File→ Burn Disc.**

   The message shown at bottom in Figure 8-11 appears.

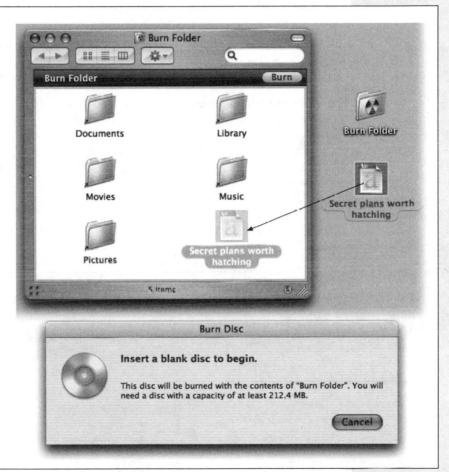

Figure 8-11:
Top: A burn folder looks like any ordinary folder, except that it has that radioactive logo on it. You can drag files and folders right into its window; Tiger displays only aliases for now, but when you burn the disc, the actual files and folders will be there.

Bottom: If you open the burn folder, you find an unusual strip across the top which, when you click the Burn button, results in this dialog box.

6. **Insert a blank disc.**

   If you have a slot-loading Mac, slip the disc into the slot. If your Mac has a sliding disc tray instead, open it first by pressing the button on the tray, or by pressing your ⏏ key for about one second. (Once you've inserted a disc into the tray, you can close it either by pushing gently on the tray or pressing the ⏏ key again.)

7. **Click Burn (or press Enter).**

The Mac proceeds to record the CD or DVD, which can take some time. Feel free to switch into another program and continue using your Mac. When it's all over, you have a freshly minted CD or DVD, whose files and folders you can open on any Mac or Windows PC.

Burn Folders: With a Blank Disc on Hand

If you have a blank disc ready to go, burn folders are even simpler to use. In fact, you may not even be aware that you're using them.

Start by inserting the disc. After a moment, the Mac displays a dialog box asking, in effect, what you want to do with this blank disc. See Figure 8-12 for instructions.

If you choose Open Finder, you'll see the disc's icon appear on the desktop after a moment; its icon also appears in the Sidebar, complete with a round Burn symbol that looks like a radioactivity logo.

At this point, you can begin dragging files and folders onto the disc's icon, or (if you double-click the icon) into its window. You can add, remove, reorganize, and rename the files on it just as you would any standard Finder window. You can also rename the CD or DVD itself just as you would rename any other icon (page 53).

Tip: The status bar at the bottom of the window gives you a running tally of the disk space you've filled up so far. At last, you have an effortless way to exploit the blank disc's capacity with precision.

When the disk contains the files and folders you want to immortalize, do one of these things:

Figure 8-12:
Top left: Choose Open Finder *if you plan to copy regular Mac files onto the CD, or* Open iTunes *if you plan to burn a music CD. Click OK.*

Right: Drag the disc onto the Burn icon in the Dock, or Control-click it and choose Burn Disc.

Lower left: Confirm your choice in this box.

- Choose File→Burn Disc.

- Click the Burn button next to the disc's name in the Sidebar.

- Drag the disc's icon toward the Trash icon in the Dock. As soon as you begin to drag, the Trash icon turns into that yellow fallout-shelter logo. Drop the disc's icon onto it.

- Control-click (right-click) the disc's icon and choose Burn Disc from the shortcut menu (shown in Figure 8-12).

In any case, the dialog box shown at bottom left in Figure 8-12 now appears. Click Burn. When the recording process is over, you'll have yourself a DVD or CD that works in any Mac or PC.

Tip: Not sure what kinds of discs your Mac can burn? Open System Profiler (in your Applications→Utilities folder) and expand the Hardware triangle. The Disc Burning category lists every format your machine can read and write (that is, read and burn).

---

iTunes: The Digital Jukebox

iTunes, in your Applications folder, is the ultimate software jukebox (Figure 8-13). It can play music CDs, tune in to Internet radio stations, load up your iPod music player, and play back digital sound files (including the Internet's favorite format, MP3).

It can also turn selected tracks from your music CDs *into* MP3 files, so that you can store favorite songs on your hard drive to play back anytime—without having to dig up the original CDs. If your Mac can burn CDs, iTunes lets you record your own custom audio CD mixes that contain only the good songs. Finally, of course, iTunes is the shop window for Apple's popular iTunes Music Store ($1 a song).

iTunes can also burn *MP3 CDs:* music CDs that fit much more than the usual 74 or 80 minutes of music onto a disc, since they store songs as MP3 files. (Not all CD players can play MP3 discs, however, and the sound quality is somewhat lower than standard CDs.)

The first time you run iTunes you're asked (a) whether you want iTunes to be the program your Mac uses for playing music files from the Internet, (b) whether you want it to ask your permission every time it wants to connect to the Internet, and (c) whether you want the program to scan your Home folder for all music files already in it (the files you've brought over from Windows, for example).

Tip: If you used iTunes on Windows, good news: The Mac version is nearly a pixel-for-pixel duplicate of the PC version. You can safely skip this section if you already know how to use iTunes for Windows.

MP3 Files and Company

The iTunes screen itself is set up to be a list—a database—of every song you've got in formats like MP3, AIFF, WAV, AC3, AAC, and Apple Lossless. iTunes automatically finds, recognizes, and lists all such files in your Home folder→Documents→iTunes Music folder.

> **Tip:** You can instruct iTunes to display the contents of other folders, too, by choosing File→Add to Library. It promptly copies any sound files from the folder you "show" it into your Home folder→Music→iTunes folder.

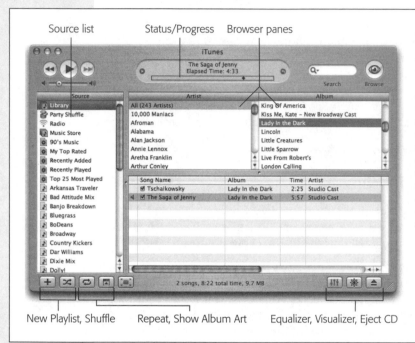

Source list   Status/Progress   Browser panes

New Playlist, Shuffle   Repeat, Show Album Art   Equalizer, Visualizer, Eject CD

Figure 8-13:
When the Library icon is selected in the Source list, you can click the Browse button (upper-right) to produce a handy, supplementary view of your music database, organized like a Finder column view. It lets you drill down from a performer's name (left column) to an album by that artist (right column) to the individual songs on that album (bottom half, beneath the browser panes).

Audio CDs

If you're not into collecting MP3 files, you can also populate the main list here simply by inserting a music CD. The songs on it immediately show up in the list.

FREQUENTLY ASKED QUESTION

Auto-Playing Music CDs

How do I make my Mac play music CDs automatically when they're inserted?

First, make sure iTunes is slated to open automatically when you insert a music CD. You do that on the CDs & DVDs panel of System Preferences (use the "When you insert a music CD" pop-up menu).

Then all you have to do is make sure iTunes knows to begin playing automatically once it launches. Choose iTunes→Preferences, click the General icon, and from the On CD Insert pop-up menu, choose Begin Playing. Click OK.

From now on, whenever you insert a music CD, iTunes will launch automatically and begin playing.

At first, they may appear with the exciting names "Track 01," "Track 02," and so on. But after a moment, iTunes connects to the Internet and compares your CD with the listings at *www.cddb.com,* a global database of music CDs and their contents. If it finds a match among the thousands of CDs there, it copies the album and song names into iTunes, where they reappear every time you use this particular CD.

Tip: If you connect an iTunes-compatible portable MP3 player or cell phone to your Mac, its name, too, shows up in the left-side Source list. You can add songs to your player (by dragging them onto its icon), rename or reorder them, and so on.

The iPod

Unless you're just off the shuttle from Alpha Centauri, you probably already know that the iPod is Apple's beautiful, tiny, elegant music player, whose built-in hard drive can hold thousands of songs. (The iPod *Shuffle* doesn't have an actual hard drive—and, as a result, it stores only a couple hundred songs—but it's a lot smaller.) iPods are designed to integrate seamlessly with iTunes.

All you have to do is connect the iPod to the Mac via its FireWire or USB port. You'll see the iPod's icon show up on your desktop as though it's a hard drive. You'll also see an iPod icon show up in the iTunes Source list. Click its icon to view its contents.

The iTunes Music Store

The iTunes Music Store is incredibly easy to figure out. Right from within iTunes, you can search for or browse over 1.5 million pop songs, classical pieces, and even comedy excerpts—and then buy them for $1 apiece. There are no monthly fees, and your downloads don't go *poof!* into the ether if you decide to stop using the store, as they do with some rival services.

Start by clicking the Music Store icon in the iTunes Source list. You go online and land on the home page, which looks and works like a Web page. Use the Search Music Store box (top right corner) to find the songs or performers you're interested in. Double-click a song to hear a 30-second sample (for audio books, you get a 90-second excerpt).

Buying music

If you decide to buy a song, you need an Apple account. Click the Account: Sign In button on the right side of the iTunes window to get started. (If you've ever bought or registered an Apple product on the company's Web site, signed up for AppleCare, ordered an iPhoto book, or had a .Mac membership, you probably have an Apple Account already. All you have to do is remember your username—usually your email address—and password.)

When you click the Buy button next to a song's name, iTunes downloads it into your Home→Music→iTunes Music folder. It also shows up in the Purchased Music "playlist" in the Source list for convenient access.

Restrictions

In an attempt to keep downloaded songs from being shared willy-nilly, Apple copy-protects them—but gently. You can only listen to iTunes-bought songs on up to five computers, for example. (You have to *authorize* those machines by typing your Apple account name and password on them.) Also, if a playlist has purchased songs in it, you can't burn more than ten copies of that playlist onto blank CDs. (Big deal!)

Podcasts

Podcasts are little self-contained radio shows put together by all sorts of people—from professional radio personalities down to little kids—that you can listen to on your Mac or iPod. (The name "podcasts" is a bit of a misnomer; you don't actually need an iPod to listen to them.)

Besides the fact that you can't "lose a signal" with a podcast like you can with a radio station, three things make podcasts different (and better) than normal radio shows:

- You can listen to podcasts *whenever you want.* They're just MP3 or AAC audio files on your hard drive.

- There's a podcast for just about every taste you could imagine: politics, cooking, investing, and even some topics too risqué for the public airwaves.

- Podcasts almost never have ads.

To get in on the podcasting action, just click Podcasts in the iTunes Music Store's main page. Browse around the different categories. Once you find a podcast you like, click Subscribe. Repeat the process until you're satisfied with your batch of podcasts.

Now click Podcasts in iTunes' left-hand Source pane. All your podcasts are listed here; a blue dot next to a podcast's name means "this podcast has a new installment that you haven't listened to." To go ahead and start listening, just double-click the podcast's row.

Tip: To list old installments, click the flippy triangle next to a podcast's name. (You can customize how long iTunes holds onto old shows—and how often it checks for new ones–in iTunes→Preferences→Podcasts.)

You can use podcasts just like normal audio tracks, too: add them to playlists, burn them onto CDs, and take them along on your commute with a portable MP3 player.

Playing Music

To turn your Mac into a music player, click iTunes's Play button (▶) or press the Space bar. The Mac immediately begins to play the songs whose names have checkmarks in the main list (Figure 8-13), or the CD that's currently in your Mac.

Tip: The central display at the top of the window shows not only the name of the song and album, but also where you are in the song, as represented by the diamond in the horizontal strip. Drag this diamond, or click elsewhere in the strip, to jump around in the song.

Visuals

As music plays, you can control and manipulate the music and the visuals of your Mac in all kinds of interesting ways. Some people don't move from their Macs for months at a time.

Visuals, for example, are onscreen light shows that pulse, beat, and dance in sync to the music. The effect is hypnotic and wild. (For real party fun, invite some people who grew up in the sixties to your house to watch.)

To summon this psychedelic display, click the flower-power icon in the lower-right corner of the window (see Figure 8-13). The show begins immediately—although it's much more fun if you choose Visuals→Full Screen so that the movie takes over your whole monitor. True, you won't get a lot of work done, but when it comes to stress relief, visuals are a lot cheaper than a hot tub.

Copying (Ripping) CD Songs to Your Hard Drive

iTunes lets you convert your favorite songs from audio CDs into files on your hard drive. Once they've been transferred to your Mac, you can play them whenever you like, without inserting the original CD.

To *rip* a CD (as aficionados would say) to your hard drive, make sure that only the songs you want to capture have checkmarks in the main list. Choose a format for the files you're about to create using the pop-up menu on the iTunes→ Preferences→Importing tab. Then click the Import button at the upper-right corner of the window (see Figure 8-14).

Figure 8-14:
Watch the display at the top of the window to see how long the conversion is going to take and which song iTunes is working on. As iTunes finishes processing each song, you see a small, circled checkmark next to its name in the main list to remind you that you've got it on board and no longer need its CD in your machine.

Done   Stop ripping

In progress

When it's all over, you'll find the imported songs listed in your Library (click the Library icon in the left-side Source list). From there, you can drag them into any other "folder" (playlist), as described next.

Playlists—and Smart Playlists

When you click the Library icon in the left-side Source list, the main part of the screen displays every music file iTunes knows about. It's organized much like a Finder window, with columns indicating the song length, singer or band, album, and so on. As always, you can rearrange these columns by dragging their headings, sort your list by one of these criteria by clicking its heading, reverse the sorting order by clicking the heading a second time, and so on. To find a particular song, just type a few letters into the Search blank above the list. iTunes hides all but the ones that match.

Apple recognizes that you may not want to listen to *all* your songs every time you need some tunes. That's why iTunes lets you create *playlists*—folders in the Source list that contain only certain songs. You might create one called Party Tunes, another called Blind Date Music, and so on.

Creating playlists

To create a new playlist, click the New Playlist button in the lower-left corner of the window, or choose File→New Playlist (⌘-N). A new playlist appears as an icon in the list at the left side of the screen. You can rename one by clicking, and add songs to one by dragging them out of the main list.

Playing with criteria

Smart Playlists constantly rebuild themselves according to criteria you specify. You might tell one Smart Playlist to assemble 45 minutes' worth of songs that you've rated higher than four stars but rarely listen to, and another to play your most oft-played songs from the eighties.

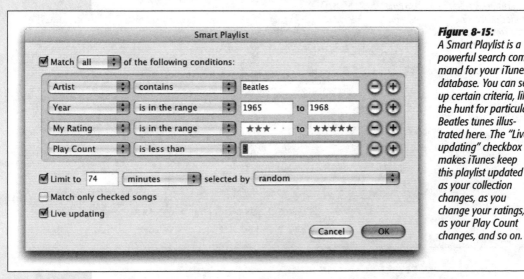

Figure 8-15:
A Smart Playlist is a powerful search command for your iTunes database. You can set up certain criteria, like the hunt for particular Beatles tunes illustrated here. The "Live updating" checkbox makes iTunes keep this playlist updated as your collection changes, as you change your ratings, as your Play Count changes, and so on.

Tip: To *rate* a song, make the window wide enough that you can see the My Rating column. Then just click the My Rating column for a selected song. The appropriate number of stars appears (one, two, three, four, or five) depending on the position of your click. You can change a song's rating as many times as you like—a good thing, considering the short shelf life of many a pop hit these days.

To make a smart playlist, choose File→New Smart Playlist (Option-⌘-N). The dialog box shown in Figure 8-15 appears. The controls here are designed to set up a search of your music database. Figure 8-15, for example, illustrates how you'd find up to 74 Beatles tunes, released between 1965 and 1968, that you've rated three starts or higher and that you've listened to exactly twice.

When you click OK, your Smart Playlist is ready to show off. When you click its name in the Source list, the main song list updates itself according to your criteria and any changes in your music collection. (Smart Playlists get transferred to your iPod, but don't continue to update themselves there.)

iTunes: Burning Music CDs

iTunes can record selected sets of songs, no matter what the original source, onto a blank CD. When it's all over, you can play the burned CD on any standard CD player just as you would a CD from Tower Records—but this time, you hear only the songs you like, in the order you like, with all the annoying ones eliminated.

Tip: Use CD-R discs. CD-RW discs are not only more expensive, but may not work in standard CD players. (Not all players recognize CD-R discs either, but the odds are better.)

Start by creating a playlist for the CD you're about to make. Drag the songs you want onto its "folder icon" (out of your Library list, for example). Click its icon in the left-side Source list to see the list you've built. Take a moment to drag them up or down in the list to reflect their playback order. Keep an eye on the readout at the bottom of the list, which tells you how much time the songs will take. (About 74 minutes of AIFF audio files fit on one CD. But if you make an MP3 CD instead, as described in the following tip, you can hold ten times as much, or more.)

Tip: You can control how many seconds of silence iTunes leaves between tracks on your custom CD. Choose iTunes→Preferences, click the Burning icon, and make a selection from the Gap Between Tracks pop-up menu. This is also where you specify whether you want to make a standard audio CD or a CD in the newer, less compatible MP3 CD format (which holds much more music per disc).

When everything is set up, click the Burn CD button in the playlist window. Insert a blank CD into the Mac and then click Burn CD again.

The burning process takes some time. Feel free to work in other programs while iTunes chugs away.

DVD Movies

If your Mac has a DVD drive (a combo drive or SuperDrive), you're in for a treat. Your Mac can play rented or purchased movies on DVD as though it were born to do so.

Watching movies on your Mac screen couldn't be simpler: Just insert the DVD. The Mac detects that it's a video DVD (as opposed to, say, a music DVD) and, unless you've fiddled with your preference settings, opens the DVD Player program (Figure 8-16).

Figure 8-16:
Top: A DVD on your screen! Use your mouse to click the buttons, if you like; that's a lot more direct than having to use the arrow keys on a remote control.

Bottom: You can orient this controller either horizontally or vertically on your screen by choosing Controls→Use Vertical Controller.

Slo-mo   Subtitles
Frame Advance   Language
Return to Movie   Angle

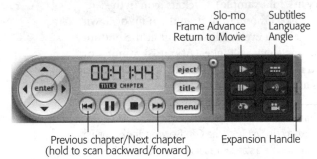

Previous chapter/Next chapter   Expansion Handle
(hold to scan backward/forward)

If DVD Player starts out playing your movie in a window, your first act should be to choose Video→Enter Full Screen (⌘-0). At this point, the movie screen fills your entire monitor—even the menu bar disappears. (To make it reappear, just move your cursor near the top of the screen.)

At this point, you're ready to play the movie. By far the easiest way is to just press the Space bar—once to start, again to pause, again to start again. You can also use the onscreen remote control. (Use the commands in the Controls menu to choose a vertical or horizontal orientation for the remote.)

Tip: Watching a movie while sitting in front of your iMac or Power Mac is not exactly the great American movie-watching dream. But remember that you can connect the video-output jacks of your Mac (most models) to your TV for a much more comfortable movie-watching experience.

Just be sure to connect the cables from the Mac's video-output jacks *directly* to the TV. If you connect them to your VCR instead, you may get a horrible, murky, color-shifting picture—the result of the built-in copy-protection circuitry on your VCR.

Keyboard

As you know by now, switching to the Mac entails switching your brain, especially when it comes to the old keyboard shortcuts. All of those Ctrl-key sequences become, on the Mac, ⌘-key sequences. (Check your Macintosh keyboard: The ⌘ key is right next to the Space bar, usually on both sides.)

But plenty of other Mac keys may seem unfamiliar. For your reassurance pleasure, here's a rundown of what they do:

- **F1, F2, F3…** These function keys do pretty much the same thing they do in most Windows programs: Nothing.

  There are exceptions, though. F9, F10, and F11, for example, invoke the Exposé window-hiding mode (page 104), and F12 brings up the Dashboard (page 108).

  You can also buy programs like QuicKeys X or iKey that let you attach these keys to your favorite programs, so that pressing F5 opens up Word, F6 launches your Web browser, and so on.

  On many Macs, designated function keys also correspond to the Dimmer/Brighter controls for your screen, and the Mute, Softer, and Louder commands for your built-in speaker. (You'll know if your keyboard offers these functions by the presence of little ☼ and ☀ icons for brightness, ◀) and ◀)) icons for sound, and—on some new PowerBooks—little glowing bar icons for *keyboard* brightness.)

- **⏏.** This is the Eject key; it spits out whatever disc is in your drive. (If *nothing* is in your drive, it doesn't do anything—unless you have a tray-loading Mac, in which case holding it down for about a second makes the CD/DVD tray slide open.) When there *is* a disc in there, press the key once to make the computer spit it out—unless the disc is currently in use.

- **Home, End.** In a desktop (Finder) window, Home and End are ways of saying "jump to the top or bottom of the window." If you're word processing, the Home and End keys are supposed to jump to the first or last word of the file, although some programs require you to press Ctrl or ⌘ too, as described in a moment.

- **Pg Up, Pg Down:** These keys scroll the current window up or down by one screenful, just as on Windows. Once again, the idea is to let you scroll through word-processing documents, Web pages, and lists without having to use the mouse.

- **NumLock, Clear:** Clear means "get rid of this text I've highlighted, but don't put a copy on the invisible Clipboard, as the Cut command would do."

  The Num Lock key is just as much of an oddball on the Mac as it is on the PC. In certain versions of Microsoft Word, the NumLock key works like a Forward Delete key, erasing the next character *after* the insertion point. In Microsoft Excel, the NumLock key actually does something unique, but you're free to nuzzle up to the online help for the details.

- **Esc:** *Esc* stands for *Escape*, and means "Click the Cancel button," such as the one found in most dialog boxes. In other words: same as in Windows.

- **Delete:** This is the Mac's name for the Backspace key.

- **Del:** This is your Forward Delete key; it erases whatever letter is just *after* the insertion point in text. (If your keyboard lacks a Del key—for example, if you have a laptop—then you produce the Forward Delete function by pressing the *regular* Delete key along with the Fn key in the lower-left corner of the keyboard.)

- **Return and Enter:** In general, these keys do the same thing: wrap your typing to the next line. Be careful, though: Some programs distinguish between the two. In AppleWorks, for example, Return begins a new paragraph, but Enter makes a *page break*, forcing the next typing to begin on a fresh page.

- **Command (⌘):** This key triggers keyboard shortcuts for menu items, as described in Chapter 1.

- **Control, Option:** The Control key triggers contextual menus (like shortcut menus), as described in Chapter 1; the Option key lets you type special symbols and access secret features.

- **Help:** This key opens the online help screens (at least in certain programs).

Text-Navigation Keystrokes

In Windows, you may have grown accustomed to certain common keystrokes for navigating text—key combinations that make the insertion point jump to the beginning or end of a word, line, or document, for example.

Mac OS X programs offer similar navigation keystrokes, as you can see here:

Function	Windows keys	Mac keys
Move to previous/next word	Ctrl+arrow keys	Option-arrow keys
Move to beginning/end of line	Home/End	Home/End*
Move to previous/next paragraph	Ctrl+up/down arrows*	Option-up/down arrows*
Move to top/bottom of window	Home/End	Home/End (but see below)
Select all text	Ctrl+A	⌘-A

Select text, one letter at a time	Shift+arrow keys	Shift-arrow keys
Select text, one word at a time	Ctrl+Shift+arrow keys	Option-Shift-arrow keys
Undo	Ctrl+Z	⌘-Z
Cut, Copy, Paste	Ctrl+X, C, P	⌘-X, C, P
Close window	Alt+F4	⌘-W
Switch open programs	Alt+Tab	⌘-Tab
Hide all windows	⊞+D	F11

* in some programs

Incidentally, the keystroke for jumping to the *top or bottom* of a window varies widely on the program. You need ⌘-Home/End in Microsoft Word, ⌘-up/down arrow in TextEdit and Stickies, and Home/End in iPhoto and Finder list windows.

As a consolation prize, though, here's a bit of good news: All *Cocoa* programs (page 120)—TextEdit, Stickies, iPhoto, iDVD, Safari, Keynote, iChat, iCal, Mail, Address Book, and so on—offer an amazing quantity of consistent, Unix-based navigation keystrokes that should last you the rest of your life. Here they are:

- **Control-A.** Moves your insertion point to the beginning of the paragraph. (*Mnemonic:* A = beginning of the alphabet.)

- **Control-E.** Deposits your insertion point at the end of the paragraph. (*Mnemonic:* E = End.)

- **Control-D.** Forward delete. Deletes the letter to the *right* of the insertion point.

- **Control-K.** Instantly deletes all text from the insertion point to the right end of the line. (*Mnemonic:* K = Kills the rest of the line.)

- **Control-O.** Inserts a paragraph break, much like Return, but leaves the insertion point where it was, above the break. This is the ideal trick for breaking a paragraph in half when you've just thought of a better ending for the first part.

- **Control-T.** Moves the insertion point one letter to the right—and along with it, drags whichever letter was to its left. (*Mnemonic:* T = Transpose letters.)

- **Option-Delete.** Deletes the entire word to the left of the insertion point. When you're typing along in a hurry, and you discover that you've just made a typo, this is the keystroke you want. It's much faster to nuke the previous word and retype it than to fiddle around with the mouse and the insertion point just to fix one letter.

Four additional keystrokes duplicate the functions of the arrow keys. Still, as long as you've got your pinky on that Control key…

- **Control-B, Control-F.** Moves the insertion point one character to the left or right, just like the left and right arrow keys. (*Mnemonic:* Back, Forward).

• **Control-N, Control-P.** Moves the insertion point one row down or up, like the down and up arrow keys. (*Mnemonic:* Next, Previous).

Mouse

Most USB mice work as soon as you plug them into your Mac—even two-button, scroll-wheel mice. Using System Preferences, you can even program your spare mouse buttons to invoke cool features like Exposé and the Dashboard.

That's not to say, however, that you shouldn't install your mouse's driver software. If your mouse *came* with such software (or if you find it on the manufacturer's Web site), you may well find that your mouse learns a few new tricks—making its "back" and "forward" buttons work properly in Safari, for example. Otherwise, a shareware program like USB Overdrive ($20, from *www.usboverdrive.com*) can unlock those features.

Monitors

Your Mac can use standard monitors of the type found in the Windows world. Every Macintosh can drive *multiple* screens at the same time, too, meaning that you can use your old PC screen either as your Mac's main monitor (if it's a Power Mac, Mini, or Cube) or as a second, external screen (if it's a laptop or any other model).

If one of those arrangements appeals to you, the only complication might be the connector. Most PC screens, of course, have a standard VGA connector (or a more modern DVI connector) at the tip of their tails. Your Mac may or may not have a place to plug in that VGA or DVI cable:

• Flat-panel iMacs, recent Mac laptops, and the Mac Mini come with a short adapter cable. One end clicks into the Mac; the other end mates with your monitor's VGA cable.

• If you have a Power Mac, you may have both a proprietary Apple monitor connector *and* a VGA connector, or you may have at least one DVI connector. (If not, you can always buy a second graphics card.)

• Some older Mac models come with an ADC connector (a proprietary Apple monitor connector), but you can buy an ADC-to-DVI converter for use with any DVI-connected monitor. (For example, you can buy the $35 DVI Extractor adapter from *www.drbott.com*.)

Tip: It's even possible to connect *both* your Mac and your PC to the *same* monitor, and switch from one to the other at will. If this arrangement appeals to you, you'll need a so-called KVM switch (which also lets you switch your keyboard and mouse between your two computers). You can find KVM switches for sale at electronics stores, and online from manufacturers like Belkin (*www.belkin.com*).

In any case, most recent Mac models (except for iBooks, eMacs, and some iMacs) let you choose either *mirror mode* (where both screens show the same thing—a handy setup in classroom situations) or *desktop extension mode* (where one screen acts as additional real estate, an annex to the first). You specify which mode you want using the Displays pane of System Preferences, or using the Displays menu-bar icon. (See page 364 for some caveats of this multi-monitor arrangement.)

Part Three:
Making Connections

3

Getting Online

Millions of people still connect to the Internet using a modem that dials out over ordinary phone lines. But the balance is rapidly tipping in favor of people connecting over higher-speed wires, using so-called *broadband* connections that are always on: cable modems, DSL, or corporate networks. This chapter explains how to set up each one (and how to use each with a wireless AirPort system).

Connecting by Dial-up Modem

If you're used to connecting to the Internet via ordinary phone lines, courtesy of your PC's modem and an Internet service provider (ISP) like Earthlink or Verizon, you'll have to transfer your PC's connection settings to the Mac. Set aside—oh, a good six minutes for this task.

Note: You don't have to fool with any settings at all if you use America Online. When you first run AOL for Mac OS X, it guides you through the setup process automatically.

If MSN is your provider, on the other hand, you're in unsupported territory. There's no Mac OS X version of the MSN software, so you're best off switching to a new provider. Still, if you copy the connection settings from your PC as described on the following pages, you *may* be able to get your MSN connection to work—albeit without any of MSN's bells and whistles.

Phase 1: The TCP/IP Tab

Start by choosing →System Preferences and clicking the Network icon. From the Show pop-up menu, choose Internal Modem, and then click the TCP/IP tab. Unless your ISP has told you otherwise, keep "Using PPP" selected in the Configure IPv4 pop-up menu.

Your main mission here is to fill in the DNS numbers provided by your Internet service provider (ISP). You can get these numbers either from your ISP or by consulting your old PC, assuming it's still set up to go online:

- **Windows XP.** Choose Start→Control Panel, then open Network Connections. Right-click the icon for your dial-up connection and, from the shortcut menu, choose Properties. Double-click the row that says "Internet Protocol (TCP/IP)." The numbers you want appear in the "Use the following DNS server addresses." (If "Obtain DNS server address automatically" is selected instead, then you don't have to put *anything* into the Domain Name Server boxes on the Mac.)

- **Windows 2000.** Choose Start→Settings→Network and Dial-up Connections. Right-click the icon for your Internet connection; from the shortcut menu, choose Properties. Click the Networking tab. Double-click the row that says "Internet Protocol (TCP/IP)." Once again, copy the numbers that show up in the "Use the following DNS server addresses." (Once again, don't put anything into the Domain Name Server boxes on the Mac if "Obtain DNS server address automatically" is selected.)

- **Windows 98, Windows Me.** Choose Start→Settings→Control Panel. In the Control Panel window, double-click Network. Double-click the "TCP/IP→Dial-Up Adapter" row. You'll see your DNS numbers on the DNS Configuration tab.

Phase 2: The PPP Tab

Now click the PPP tab (Figure 9-1). Your job here is to fill in the blanks—but how are you supposed to know what to fill?

Here's a listing of the blanks you find here, and where, on your old Windows machine, to find the necessary information (assuming you were able to get online with that machine).

Service Provider

This is the name of your ISP, and it doesn't have to be exact (*EarthLink*, for example).

Account Name, Password, Telephone Number

These are the three key pieces of account information that your Mac needs to dial up. They're easy enough to find in Windows:

- **Windows XP.** Choose Start→Control Panel. Open Network Connections. Double-click the icon for your dial-up connection.

- **Windows 2000.** Choose Start→Settings→Network and Dial-up Connections. Double-click the icon for your Internet connection.

- **Windows Me.** Choose Start→Settings→Dial-Up Networking. In the Control Panel, double-click the icon for your dial-up connection.

- **Windows 98.** Open My Computer→Dial-Up Networking. Double-click the icon for your Internet connection.

In each case, the Connect dialog box appears, with connection information staring you in the face. Copy this information into the corresponding boxes on the PPP tab on the Mac, as shown in Figure 9-1. When you're finished making your settings, click Apply Now.

Note: Only an administrator can make changes to the Internet dial-up settings. To make a change, therefore, you may have to click the little padlock in the lower-left corner of the dialog box to input an administrator's name and password.

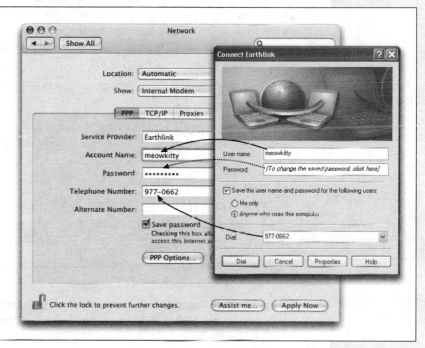

Figure 9-1:
As you copy your ISP details from Windows (XP, shown at right) to the Mac (left), note that your password is blanked out to prevent evildoers from copying it. You'll have to either remember it or submit yourself to your ISP's mercy, because there's no way to copy it directly out of Windows.

Incidentally, if you click the PPP Options button, you bring up a special Options box, filled with checkboxes that control your online sessions. Here, for example, you can specify how long the Mac waits before hanging up the phone line after your last online activity, and how many times the Mac should dial if the ISP phone number is busy.

One checkbox here that you'll almost certainly want to turn on is "Connect automatically when needed." It makes your Mac dial the Internet automatically whenever you check your email or open your Web browser. (Otherwise, you'd have to establish the Internet call manually, using the Internet Connect program described on page 418. Only then could you check your email or use your Web browser.)

Alternate Number

If your ISP gave you a backup phone number when you signed up for service, enter it here. If your Mac can't connect using your ISP's main number, it'll try your alternate number before giving up completely.

Phase 3: The Modem Tab

This is where you specify the kind of modem you have. Every Mac OS X–compatible Mac has a built-in Apple modems, which is why the pop-up menu already says "Apple Internal 56K Modem (v.90)" or "Apple Internal 56K Modem (v.92)."

Some of the other settings that can be handy include:

- **Wait for dial tone before dialing.** This one's for you, North American laptop owners. Because the dial tones in certain foreign countries sound weird to the Mac, it won't dial because it's still listening for that good old North American dial tone. In that case, turning off this checkbox makes the Mac dial bravely even though it hasn't heard the sound it's listening for.

- **Dialing.** Specify what kind of phone service you have—Tone or, in a few rural locations, Pulse.

- **Sound.** By clicking Off, you make your Mac dial the Internet silently, sparing sleeping family members or dorm roommates from having to listen to your modem shriek as it connects.

Going Online

That's all there is to it. If you turned on "Connect automatically when needed," your Mac dials and connects to the Internet automatically whenever an Internet-related program tries to connect (a Web browser or email program, for example).

If you didn't turn on that option, then you can make your Mac dial the Internet in one of these ways:

- **Using Internet Connect.** This little program is in your Applications folder. The main item of interest here is the Connect button (on the Internal Modem pane), which makes the Mac dial.

    If you're smart, however, you'll turn on the "Show modem status on menu bar" checkbox found here. It adds a tiny telephone icon—the Modem Status menulet—to the upper-right corner of your screen, which lets you completely bypass Internet Connect the next time you want to go online or disconnect (Figure 9-2).

- **Use the menu-bar icon.** Just click the Modem Status menulet and choose Connect from the pop-up menu. Your Mac dials without even blocking your desktop picture with a dialog box.

Disconnecting

The Mac automatically drops the phone line 10 minutes after your last activity online (or whatever interval you specified in the PPP Options dialog box). If other people have accounts on your Mac, the Mac doesn't even hang up when you log out. It maintains the connection so that the next person can Net-surf without redialing.

Of course, if other people in your household are screaming for you to get off the line so that they can make a call, you can also disconnect manually. Either choose Disconnect from the Modem Status menulet or click Disconnect in the Internet Connect window (both shown in Figure 9-2).

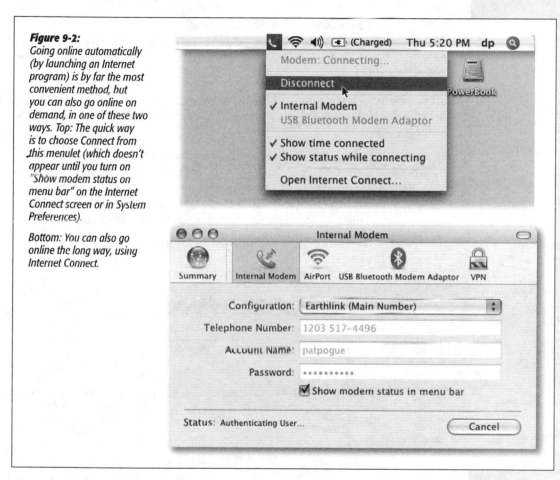

Figure 9-2:
Going online automatically (by launching an Internet program) is by far the most convenient method, but you can also go online on demand, in one of these two ways. Top: The quick way is to choose Connect from this menulet (which doesn't appear until you turn on "Show modem status on menu bar" on the Internet Connect screen or in System Preferences).

Bottom: You can also go online the long way, using Internet Connect.

Broadband Connections

If you get online via cable modem, DSL, or office network, you're one of the lucky ones. You have a high-speed connection to the Internet that's always available. You never have to wait to dial, to disconnect, or to download—everything happens on demand.

You set up your account on the Mac like this: Open System Preferences; click the Network icon; from the Show pop-up menu, choose either AirPort or Built-in Ethernet, depending on how your Mac is connected to the broadband modem. Click the TCP/IP tab.

Then make a selection from the Configure IPv4 pop-up menu—and fill in the boxes. You can find out how to set this up either from your service provider (cable TV company or phone company, for example) or by checking your Windows configuration like this:

Settings from Windows XP, Windows 2000

If you have Windows XP, choose Start→Control Panel. Open Network Connections. If you have Windows 2000, choose Start→Settings→Network and Dial-up Connections.

Either way, continue by right-clicking the icon for your broadband connection and, from the shortcut menu, choose Properties. Double-click the row that says "Internet Protocol (TCP/IP)."

If the resulting screen says "Obtain an IP address automatically" (see Figure 9-3), then you should choose Using DHCP from the Mac's Configure IPv4 pop-up menu. (DHCP stands for *dynamic host configuration protocol*, with the operative word being *dynamic*. Your modem or router, behind the scenes, assigns your Mac a different IP address [that is, Internet address] every time you turn on the machine.)

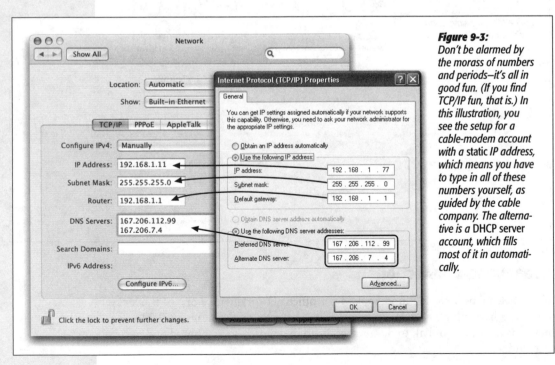

Figure 9-3:
Don't be alarmed by the morass of numbers and periods–it's all in good fun. (If you find TCP/IP fun, that is.) In this illustration, you see the setup for a cable-modem account with a static IP address, which means you have to type in all of these numbers yourself, as guided by the cable company. The alternative is a DHCP server account, which fills most of it in automatically.

The good news is that this option saves you from having to fill in any of the other boxes in this control panel. Instead, all the settings will come to you magically over the Internet. (One occasional exception: the DNS Servers box.)

If the Windows screen says, "Use the following IP address" instead, select Manually from the Mac's IPv4 pop-up menu, and copy the following numbers into the Mac's Network panel like this (see Figure 9-3):

Copy this Windows setting:	**Into this Mac text box:**
IP address	IP Address
Subnet mask	Subnet Mask
Default gateway	Router

Similarly, if the Internet Protocol (TCP/IP Properties) dialog box says, "Use the following DNS server addresses," type the numbers from the "Preferred DNS server" and "Alternate DNS server" boxes into the Mac's DNS Servers text box. (Press Return to make a new line for the second number.)

Note: If your Mac plugs directly into the cable modem (that is, you don't use a router), you'll have to turn the cable modem or DSL box off and then on again when you've switched from the PC to the Mac.

Settings from Windows 98, Windows Me

Choose Start→Settings→Control Panel. In the Control Panel window, double-click Network. Double-click the TCP/IP row that identifies how your PC is connected to the broadband modem. (It may say "TCP/IP→3Com Ethernet Adapter," for example.)

Click the IP Address tab. If "Obtain an IP address automatically" is selected, then you should choose Using DHCP from the Mac's Configure IPv4 pop-up menu.

If it says "Specify an IP address" instead, copy the IP Address and Subnet Mask numbers into the same ones on the Mac's Network panel. Then click the Gateway tab, and copy the "Installed gateway" number into the Mac's Router box.

Finally, click the DNS Configuration tab. Copy the strings of numbers you see here into the Mac's DNS Servers text box. (Press Return to make a new line for the second number, if necessary.)

POWER USERS' CLINIC

PPPoE and DSL

If you have DSL service, you may be directed to click the PPPoE tab (located in the Network pane of System Preferences). It stands for *PPP over Ethernet,* meaning that although your DSL modem is connected to your Ethernet port, you still have to make and break your Internet connections manually, as though you had a dial-up modem. In other words, you're not online full-time.

Fill in the PPPoE tab as directed by your ISP (usually just click "Connect using PPPoE" and fill in your account name and password). From here on in, you start and end your Internet connections exactly as though you had a dial-up modem, as described on page 246 (except that the menu-bar pop-up menu that you want is the PPPoE Status menulet, not the Modem Status menulet).

Applying the Settings

That's all the setup—click Apply Now. If your settings are correct, you're online, now and forever. You never have to worry about connecting or disconnecting.

If you have a wireless laptop, you'll really love life. Any time you're in a wireless "hot spot" (in a hotel lobby or airport, say), your AirPort menu-bar icon (🛜) will light up as a signal-strength indicator, and a message will invite you to join the wireless network you've just found. Sometimes you have to open your Web browser and supply a credit-card number; sometimes you need a name and password. But sometimes, you get lucky and find a wide-open, free patch of high-speed wireless Internet goodness.

The Firewall

If you have a broadband, always-on connection, you're connected to the Internet 24 hours a day. It's theoretically possible—although very unlikely—for some cretin to use automated hacking software to take control of your machine.

If your Mac is connected to a router as described on page 138, its *firewall* circuitry is probably protecting you. If not, Mac OS X's firewall *software* can put up a simpler, but effective, barrier.

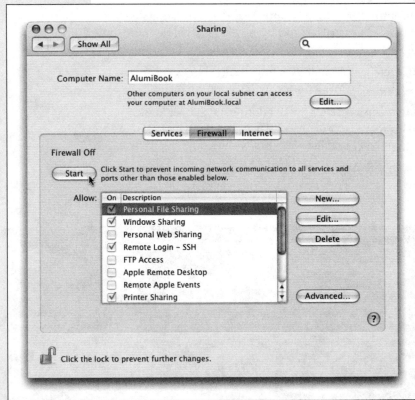

Figure 9-4:
Like Windows XP, Mac OS X comes with a built-in firewall, sparing you the trouble of installing a shareware one like Firewalk or BrickHouse. Click Start to turn it on.

If you click Advanced, you get even more ways to make your Mac invisible to Internet evildoers. Stealth Mode, for example, makes your Mac not respond to ping. (Pings are "are you there?" signals sent by spammers who are looking for unsuspecting, always-on PCs that they can make part of their junk-mailing network.)

To turn it on, open the Sharing pane of System Preferences. Click the Firewall tab (Figure 9-4), and then click Start. That's all there is to it: You're protected.

Note: If you're using Mac OS X's Internet connection-sharing feature, turn on the firewall only for the *first* Mac—the one that's the gateway to the Internet. Leave the firewall turned off on all the Macs "downstream" from it.

And if you have some program that's raising trouble because it can't get through your firewall (an online game, for example), head back to the Sharing pane and click Add. In the dialog box that appears, choose Other from the Port Name menu and fill in the lower fields as instructed in the program's help files. You've now allowed that program's traffic to pass unimpeded through your Mac's firewall.

Switching Locations

If you travel with a laptop, you may wind up connecting to the Internet differently in each location: Ethernet at the office, dial-up in the hotel room. Or maybe you

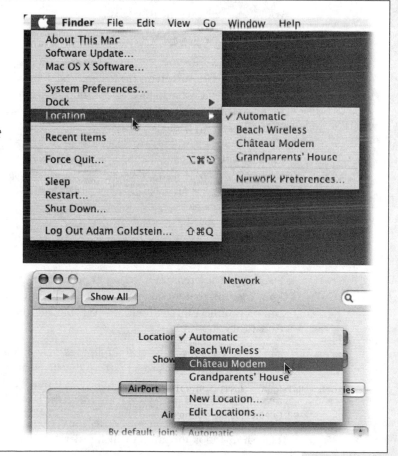

Figure 9-5:
The Location feature lets you switch from one "location" to another just by choosing its name—either from the menu (top) or from this pop-up menu in System Preferences (bottom). The Automatic location just means "the standard, default one you originally set up." (Don't be fooled: Despite its name, Automatic isn't the only location that offers multihoming, which is described later in this chapter.)

simply visit the branch office from time to time, and you're getting tired of having to change the local access number for your ISP each time you leave home (and return home again).

The simple solution is the →Location submenu. As Figure 9-5 illustrates, all you have to do is tell it where you are. Mac OS X handles the details of switching to the correct Internet connection and phone number.

Creating a New Location

To create a *Location*, which is nothing more than a set of memorized settings, open System Preferences, click Network, and choose New Location from the Location pop-up menu. You'll be asked to provide a name for your new location, such as *Chicago Office* or *Dining Room Floor*.

When you click OK, you return to the Network pane, which is now blank. Take this opportunity to set up the kind of Internet connection you use at the corresponding location, just as described on the first pages of this chapter. If you travel frequently, in fact, you can use Location Manager to build a long list of city locations, each of which "knows" the local phone number for your Internet access company (because you've entered it on the PPP tab).

Making the Switch

Once you've set up your various locations, you can switch among them using either the Location pop-up menu (in System Preferences→Network) or the →Location submenu, as shown in Figure 9-5. As soon as you do so, your Mac is automatically set to connect using the new phone number or whatever method you specified.

Tip: If you have a laptop, create a connection called Offline. From the Show pop-up menu, choose Network Port Configurations and turn off *all* the connection methods you see in the list. When you're finished, you've got yourself a laptop that will *never* attempt to go online. This setup will save you the occasional interruption of a program that tries to dial but takes three minutes to discover you're on Flight 751 to Miami and have no phone line available.

Multihoming

Speaking of different ways to get online, Mac OS X offers one of the coolest features known to Internet-loving mankind: *multihoming*. That's the ability to detect which Internet connection methods are available and then switch to the fastest one—automatically.

This feature is especially ideal for laptops. When you open your Web browser, your laptop might first check to see if it's at the office, plugged into a cable modem via the Ethernet—the fastest possible connection. If not, it automatically looks for an AirPort network. Finally, if it draws a blank there, the laptop dials the modem.

In short, for each location you create, you can specify which network connections the Mac should look for, and in which order. You can even turn off some connections entirely. For example, if you have a desktop Mac that's always connected to a cable modem, you may never want your Mac to dial using its built-in modem. In that case, you could turn off the modem entirely.

Here's how to go about using this multihoming feature:

1. **Open System Preferences. Click the Network icon.**

   Make sure the appropriate location is selected in the Location pop-up menu.

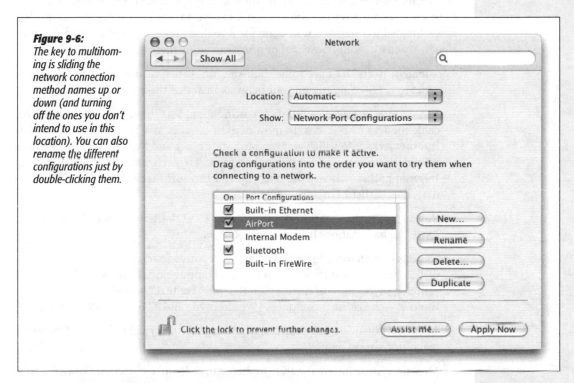

Figure 9-6:
The key to multihoming is sliding the network connection method names up or down (and turning off the ones you don't intend to use in this location). You can also rename the different configurations just by double-clicking them.

2. **From the Show pop-up menu, choose Network Port Configurations.**

   Now you see the display shown in Figure 9-6. It lists all the different ways your Mac knows how to get online, or onto an office network.

3. **Drag the items up and down in the list into priority order.**

   If you have a cable modem, DSL, or office network connection, for example, you might want to drag Built-in Ethernet to the top of the list, since that's almost always the fastest way to get online.

   At this point, you can also *turn off* any connections you don't want your Mac to use when it's in this location—the internal modem, for example.

4. **Click Apply Now.**

That's all there is to it. Your Mac will now switch connections—not just each time you go online, but even during a single Internet session, if a faster connection becomes available.

Internet Sharing

If you have cable modem or DSL service, you're a very lucky individual. Not only do you benefit from spectacular speed when surfing the Web or processing email, but your connection is on full-time. You never have to wait for some modem to dial, screeching all the way, and wait again for it to disconnect. It's just too bad that only one computer in your household or office can enjoy these luxuries.

Fortunately, it doesn't have to be that way. You can spread the joy of high-speed Internet to every computer on your network in any of these ways:

- **Buy a router.** A *router* is a little box, costing about $40, that connects directly to the cable modem or DSL box. In most cases, it doubles as a hub, providing multiple Internet jacks into which you can plug your Macs and PCs. As a bonus, a router provides excellent security, serving as a firewall to keep out unsolicited visits from Internet hackers. (If you use one, you can turn off Mac OS X's *own* firewall, as described earlier in this chapter.)

- **Buy an AirPort base station.** Apple's wireless 802.11b (AirPort) or 802.11g (AirPort Extreme) base stations have a router built in.

- **Use Internet Sharing.** Internet Sharing is the software version of a router, in that it distributes a single Internet signal to every computer on the network. But unlike a router, it's free. You just fire it up on the one Mac that's connected directly to the Internet—the *gateway* computer. (Windows Me and XP offer a similar feature.)

  There is a downside, however: If the gateway Mac is turned off, none of the other machines can get online.

  Most people use Internet Sharing to share a broadband connection like a cable modem or DSL. But in fact, Internet Sharing works even if the gateway Mac connects to the Internet via dial-up modem or Bluetooth cell phone. The only requirement is that the gateway Mac *also* has a network connection (Ethernet or AirPort, for example) to the Macs that will share the connection.

Turning on Internet Sharing

To turn on Internet Sharing on the gateway Mac, open the Sharing pane of System Preferences. Click the Internet tab.

Now select the appropriate settings from the "Share your connection from" pop-up menu (how your Mac connects to the Internet) and the checkboxes beneath (how other computers will connect to yours), as shown in Figure 9-7. Two possibilities:

- **Share your Internet connection with AirPort-equipped computers.** Choose Built-in Ethernet from the pop-up menu and turn on the AirPort checkbox. This is the software base-station effect described in the next section.

• **Share the connection with other computers on Built-in Ethernet.** Select Built-in Ethernet from the pop-up menu, and then turn on the Built-in Ethernet checkbox. This option is for *wired* networks. In other words, it gives Internet access to other Macs or PCs on the same Ethernet network as the gateway Mac. (That could mean a group of them all connected to the same Ethernet *hub*, or a single other Mac connected to the gateway machine with an Ethernet *crossover cable*.)

Figure 9-7:
Top: Ka-ching! Mac OS X's new Internet Sharing button just saved you the cost of a hardware router.

Bottom: All of the missing information here will be supplied by the gateway Mac—the one Mac that's directly connected to the broadband modem.

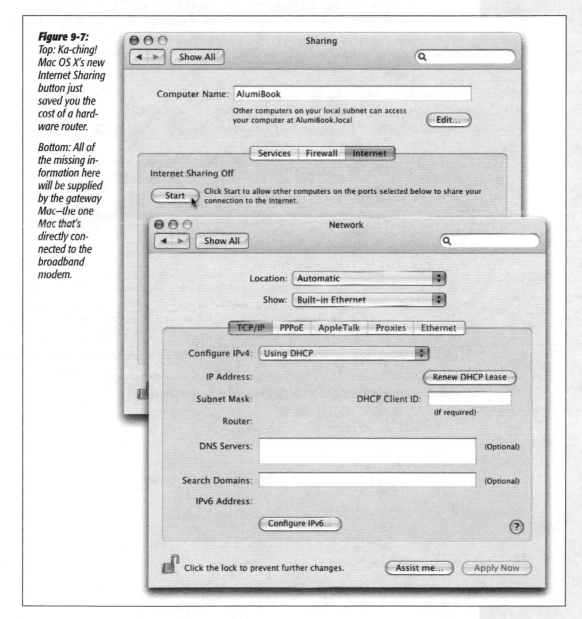

Note: Which checkboxes appear here depends on which kinds of Internet connections are turned on in the Network pane of System Preferences. For example, if the gateway Mac doesn't have an AirPort card installed or if AirPort is turned off in the current configuration, the AirPort option doesn't appear.

To begin the sharing, click Start.

Now visit each of the other Macs on the same network. Open the Network pane of System Preferences. Using the Show pop-up menu, choose AirPort or Built-in Ethernet—whichever reflects how each Mac is connected to your network. Then, from the Configure pop-up menu, choose Using DHCP. Leave everything else blank, as shown in Figure 9-7. Finally, click Apply Now.

As long as the gateway Mac remains turned on, you should find that both it and your other Macs can get onto the Internet simultaneously, all at high speed. (Even Windows PCs on the same network can get online, as long as you set them up to use DHCP just as you did on your "downstream" Macs.)

Note: You may wonder how you can plug in both the cable modem and the local network, if your gateway Mac only has one Ethernet port.

One approach is to install a second Ethernet card. The more economical approach: Connect the cable modem to the *Uplink* or *WAN* jack on your Ethernet hub. Your gateway Mac plugs into the hub as usual.

The Software Base Station Effect

If the gateway Mac has an AirPort card, turning on Internet Sharing (and selecting Built-in Ethernet from the pop-up menu and AirPort below) has another profound effect: It creates a *software* base station. The Mac itself is now the transmitter for Internet signals to and from any other wirelessly equipped Macs or PCs within range. You just saved yourself the $200 cost of a physical, flying saucer Apple base station!

As long as the gateway Mac remains turned on, you should find that both it and your PCs or other Macs can get onto the Internet simultaneously, all at high speed.

Mail and Address Book

You know how every copy of Windows comes with Outlook Express, a basic, free email program? Well, every copy of Mac OS X comes with Mail, a slightly fancier email program that's also free. Mail is a surprisingly complete, refreshingly attractive program, filled with shortcuts and surprises. Together with the high-octane Address Book program included with Mac OS X 10.4, you may never pine for your Windows setup again.

Note: This chapter assumes that you've already transferred your email, addresses, and email account settings to Mail and the Address Book, as described in Chapter 6.

Checking Your Mail

You can get new mail and send mail you've already written in any of several ways:

- Click Get Mail on the toolbar.
- Choose Mailbox→Get All New Mail (or press Shift-⌘-N).

Note: If you have multiple email accounts, you can also use the Mailbox→Get New Mail submenu to pick just *one* account to check for new mail.

- Control-click (or right-click) Mail's Dock icon, and choose Get New Mail from the shortcut menu. (You can use this method from any program, as long as Mail is already open.)

- Wait. Mail comes set to check your email automatically every few minutes. To adjust its timing or turn it off completely, choose Mail→Preferences, click General, and choose a time interval from the "Check for new mail" pop-up menu.

At this point, Mail contacts the mail servers listed in the Accounts pane of Mail's Preferences window, retrieving new messages and downloading any files attached to those messages. It also *sends* any outgoing messages that couldn't be sent when you wrote them.

Tip: If you'd like to keep tabs on Mail's doings, choose Window→Activity Viewer (⌘-0). You get a Stop button, progress bar, and other useful information for each task that Mail is working on.

Also, if you're having trouble connecting to some (or all) of your email accounts, choose Window→Connection Doctor. Mail does its best to explain the problem.

The Mighty Morphing Interface

You don't have to be content with the factory-installed design of the Mail screen. You can control almost every aspect of its look and layout.

For example, you can control the main window's information columns exactly as you would in a Finder list view window—make a column narrower or wider by dragging the right edge of its column heading, rearrange the columns by dragging their titles, and so on. You can also control which columns appear using the commands in the View→Columns menu. Similarly, you can *sort* your email by clicking these column headings, exactly as in the Finder. (Click a second time to reverse the sorting order.)

The various panes of the main window are also under your control. For example, you can drag the divider bar between the Messages list and the Preview pane up or down to adjust the relative proportions, as shown here. In fact, you can get rid of the Preview pane altogether by double-clicking the divider line, double-clicking just above the vertical scroll bar, or dragging the divider line's handle all the way to the bottom of the screen. Bring it back by dragging the divider line up from the bottom.

You can also control the Mailboxes column. Drag its thin vertical line (or the fatter ribbed handle at the bottom) inward or outward to make the column wider or narrower, for example; you can even drag it so tightly that you see only the mailboxes' icons. Make the column disappear or reappear by choosing View→Hide Mailboxes (or →Show Mailboxes), or by pressing Shift-⌘-M. And if you're super-tight on screen space, you can make your mailbox icons a quarter of their normal size by choosing View→Use Small Mailbox Icons.

Finally, you have full control over the toolbar, which works much like the Finder toolbar. You can rearrange or remove buttons (by ⌘-dragging them); add interesting new buttons to the toolbar (by choosing View→Customize Toolbar); change its display to show *just* text labels or *just* icons—either large or small (by repeatedly ⌘-clicking the white, oval, upper-right toolbar button); or hide the toolbar entirely (by clicking that white button or using the View→Hide Toolbar command).

And if Mail's all-gray toolbar buttons make you pine for the more colorful toolbar of Outlook Express, download Mail Stamps from *www.andrewescobar.com/mailstamps/* to restore Mail to its older, multicolored toolbar.

The Mailboxes Column

Mail, like Outlook Express, lists your various email folders in a column on the left-hand side of the window. In this Mailboxes column, you'll find the usual suspects, sometimes hidden by flippy triangles: Inbox, Outbox, Sent, Drafts, and so on. Only a few of these mailboxes may be new to you:

- **Junk** appears automatically when you use Mail's spam filter, as described later in this chapter.

- **Trash** works a lot like the Trash on your desktop, in that messages you put there don't actually disappear. They remain in the Trash folder until you permanently delete them or move them somewhere else—or until Mail's automatic trash-cleaning service deletes them for you (page 274).

- **Anything else** is usually a folder that's stored on your Mac for mail-filing convenience. You can set these folders up yourself, as explained on page 270.

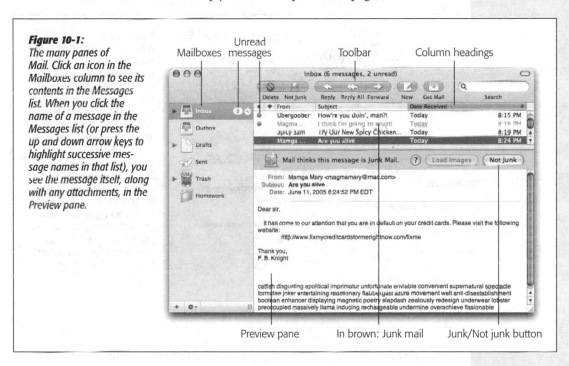

Figure 10-1:
The many panes of Mail. Click an icon in the Mailboxes column to see its contents in the Messages list. When you click the name of a message in the Messages list (or press the up and down arrow keys to highlight successive message names in that list), you see the message itself, along with any attachments, in the Preview pane.

To see what's in one of these folders, click it once. The list of its messages appears in the top half of the main window. When you click a message name, the message itself appears in the top half of the right side of the window (this is the Messages list). When you click a message name, the message *itself* appears in the bottom half of the main window (the Preview pane). Figure 10-1 shows the idea.

Writing Messages

To send email to a recipient, click the New icon on the toolbar. The New Message form, shown in Figure 10-2, opens. If you've ever sent email from a Windows PC, this should all feel familiar. Here are a few notes:

- To send this message to more than one person, separate their addresses in the "To:" box with commas: *bob@earthlink.net, billg@microsoft.com, steve@apple.com.*

- Mail offers Auto-complete. If somebody is in your Address Book (page 279), just type the first couple letters of his name or email address; Mail automatically completes the address. (If the first guess is wrong, type another letter or two until Mail revises its proposal.)

- As in most dialog boxes, you can jump from blank to blank (from the "To:" field to the "Cc:" field, for example) by pressing the Tab key.

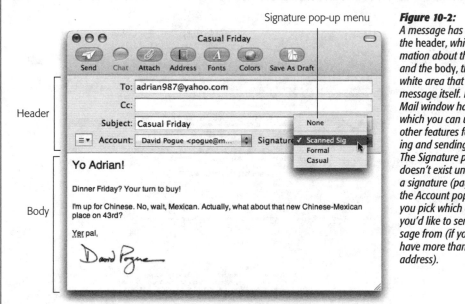

Figure 10-2:
A message has two sections: the header, which holds information about the message; and the body, the big empty white area that contains the message itself. In addition, the Mail window has a toolbar, which you can use to access other features for composing and sending messages. The Signature pop-up menu doesn't exist until you create a signature (page 263), and the Account pop-up menu lets you pick which email address you'd like to send the message from (if you do, in fact, have more than one email address).

- A *blind carbon copy* ("Bcc") lets you send a message to someone on the sly (none of the "To" and "Cc" recipients will know that you sent the message to the "Bcc" recipients). If you're sending a message from a different email address than usual, "Reply-to" lets you specify an email address that your recipient should, well, reply to. And a message's Priority lets you tell your recipients how urgent the message is.

If you would find these fields helpful while composing a message, click the three-lined pop-up menu on the left side of the New Message window. Click Customize.

Now just turn on the checkboxes next to whichever fields you want visible, and click OK.

- There are two main kinds of email: *plain text* and *formatted* (what Apple calls Rich Text). Plain text messages are faster to send and open, universally compatible with the world's email programs, and greatly preferred by many veteran computer fans. And even though the message is plain, you can still attach pictures and other files.

By contrast, formatted messages (see Figure 10-3) sometimes open slowly, and in some email programs the formatting doesn't come through at all.

To control which kind of mail you send on a message-by-message basis, choose, from the Format menu, either Make Plain Text or Make Rich Text. To change the factory setting for new outgoing messages, choose Mail→Preferences, click the Composing icon, and choose from the Message Format pop-up menu.

Figure 10-3:
If you really want to use formatting, click the Fonts icon on the toolbar to open the Font panel described on page 121, or the Colors icon to open the Color Picker dialog box. The Format menu (in the menu bar) contains even more controls—paragraph alignment (left, right, or justify), and even Copy and Paste Style commands that let you transfer formatting from one block of text to another.

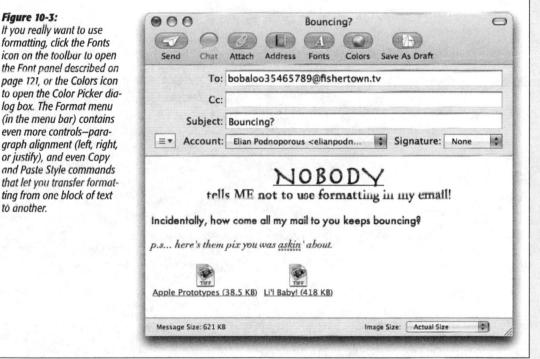

- As you type your message, Mail checks your spelling, using a dotted red underline to mark questionable words (also shown in Figure 10-3). To check for alternative spellings for a suspect word, Control-click or right-click it. From the list of suggestions in the shortcut menu, click the word you really intended, or choose Learn Spelling to add the word to the Mac OS X dictionary shared by all Cocoa programs (page 120).

Tip: To turn off automatic spell check, choose Edit→Spelling→Check Spelling→Never. Or, if you'd rather Mail wait until you're *done* composing your messages before spell checking, choose Edit→Spelling→Check Spelling→When You Click Send.

- When you click Send (or press Shift-⌘-D), your Mac connects to the Internet and sends the message.

  If you'd rather have Mail place each message you write in the Outbox folder, quietly collecting them instead of connecting to the Net the moment you click Send, choose Mailbox→Go Offline. While you're offline, Mail will refrain from trying to connect, which is a great feature when you're working on a laptop at 39,000 feet. (Choose Mailbox→Go Online to reverse the procedure.)

Sending File Attachments

Sending little text messages is fine, but it's not much help when you want to send somebody a photograph, a sound, or a Word document. To attach a file to a message you've written, use one of these methods:

- Drag the icons you want to attach directly off the desktop (or out of a folder window) into the New Message window. There your attachments appear with their

---

Attachment Tricks

Nowadays, what's attached to a message is often more important than the message itself. That's why it's such a pain when email attachments don't go through properly—or when they're too big to send at all. Luckily, Mac OS X provides three tools for making attachments smaller and more compatible for your Windows-using friends.

If you're sending images along with your message, you can shrink them down right in Mail. Use the Image Size pop-up menu in the lower-right corner of the window to pick a smaller size for the images (like Medium or Small). Keep tabs on the total size of your attachments in the lower-left corner of the window; ideally, you should keep the total under 2 MB, so dial-up users don't get annoyed—and so your message doesn't get rejected by your recipient's ISP for being too big.

Use the Finder to compress big files before you send them. You can Control-click or right-click a file, group of highlighted files, or a folder right in the Finder—and, from the shortcut menu, choose Create Archive. The Finder creates Windows-compatible .zip files, which generally take up much less space than the originals.

You can pick from two different formats for your attachments: normal or Windows-friendly. Normal attachments open correctly on both Macs and Windows PCs. Trouble is, a normal attachment may show up on a PC accompanied by a useless, second attachment whose name starts with "._". (Your recipients should just ignore it.)

Windows-friendly attachments, on the other hand, always work correctly on PCs—but may not open at all on Macs. Unless you work in an all-Windows company, then, stick with the normal setting.

To use the Windows-friendly setting for an open message, choose Edit→Attachments→Send Windows Friendly Attachments. (If no message is open, the command says "*Always* Send Windows Friendly Attachments" instead.) You can also adjust the setting on a per-email basis using the Send Windows Friendly Attachments checkbox at the bottom of the attachment dialog box.

---

own hyperlinked icons (Figure 10-3), meaning that your recipient can simply click to open them.

Tip: Exposé (page 104) was *born* for this moment. Hit the F11 key to make all open windows flee to the edges of the screen, revealing the desktop. Root around until you find the file you want to send. Begin dragging it; without releasing the mouse, press F11 again to bring your message window back into view. Complete your drag into the message window.

Mail makes it look as though you can park the attached file's icon (or the full image of a graphics file) *inside* the text of the message, mingled with your typing. Don't be fooled, however; on the receiving end, all of the attachments will probably be clumped together at the end of the message (unless your recipient also uses Mail).

- Drag the icons you want to attach from the desktop onto Mail's Dock icon. Mail dutifully creates a new, outgoing message, with the files already attached.

- Click the Attach icon on the New Message toolbar, choose File→Attach File, or press Shift-⌘-A. The standard Open sheet now appears, so that you can navigate to and select the files you want to include. (You can choose multiple files simultaneously in this dialog box. Just ⌘-click or Shift-click the individual files you want as though you were selecting them in a Finder window.)

Once you've selected the files, click Choose File (or press Enter). You return to the New Message window, where the attachments' icons appear, ready to ride along when you send the message.

To remove an attachment, drag across its icon to highlight it, and then press the Delete key. (You can also drag an attachment icon clear out of the window onto your Dock's Trash, or choose Message→Remove Attachments.)

Signatures

Signatures are bits of text that get stamped at the bottom of your outgoing email messages. A signature may contain your name, contact information, a pithy quote, or some combination of the three.

You can customize your signatures by choosing Mail→Preferences, and then clicking the Signatures icon. Here's what you should know:

- **To build up a library of signatures that you can use in any of your accounts:** Select All Signatures in the leftmost pane, and then click the + button to add each new signature (Figure 10-4, top). Give each new signature a name in the middle pane, and then customize the signatures' text in the rightmost pane (Figure 10-4, bottom).

- **To make a signature available in one of your email accounts:** Drag the signature's name from the middle pane onto the name of the account in the leftmost pane. In other words, you can make certain signatures available to only your personal account, so you never accidentally end up appending your secret FBI contact signature to the bottom of a birthday invitation you send out.

- **To mark a particular signature as the default for one account:** In the left pane, click the account; then select from the Choose Signature pop-up menu. Each time you compose a message from that account, Mail will insert the signature you selected.

Tip: *To make things more interesting for your recipients, pick At Random; now Mail will select a different signature each time you send a message. Or, if you're not that much of a risk-taker, choose In Sequential Order; Mail will pick subsequent signatures for each new message you write.*

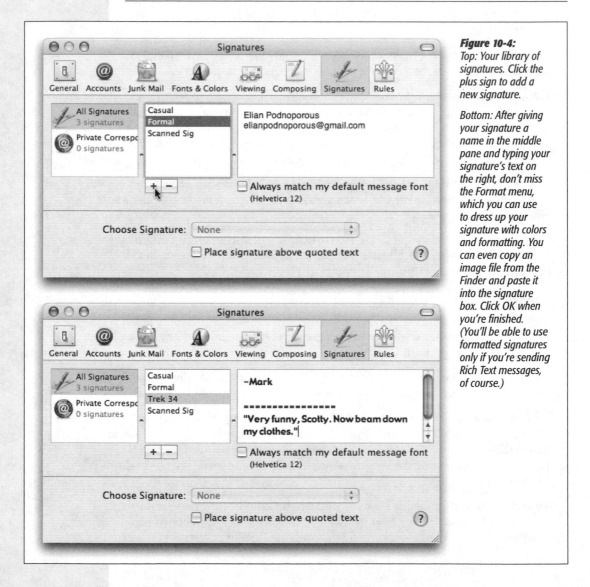

Figure 10-4:
Top: Your library of signatures. Click the plus sign to add a new signature.

Bottom: After giving your signature a name in the middle pane and typing your signature's text on the right, don't miss the Format menu, which you can use to dress up your signature with colors and formatting. You can even copy an image file from the Finder and paste it into the signature box. Click OK when you're finished. (You'll be able to use formatted signatures only if you're sending Rich Text messages, of course.)

- **To use the signature feature as a prefix in replies:** Turn on "Place signature above quoted text." If you turn on this setting, your signature will get inserted *above* any of the text that you're replying to, rather than below. You'd use this setting if your signature said something like, "Hi there! You wrote this to me—".

Reading Email

Mail puts all the email you get into your Inbox. The statistic after the word *Inbox* lets you know how many of its messages you haven't yet read. These new messages are also marked with light blue dots in the main list.

Tip: The Mail icon in the Dock also shows you how many new messages you have waiting—it's the number in the red circle.

Click the Inbox folder to see a list of received messages. If it's a long list, press Control-Page Up and Control-Page Down to scroll. Click the name of a message once to read it in the Preview pane, or double-click a message to open it into a separate window. (If a message is already selected, pressing Return or Enter also opens it in a separate window.)

Tip: Instead of reading your mail, you might prefer to have Mac OS X read it *to* you, as you sit back in your chair and sip your strawberry daiquiri. Highlight the text you want to hear (or choose Edit→Select All), and then choose Edit→Speech→Start Speaking. You'll hear the message read aloud, in the voice you've selected in the Speech pane of System Preferences (Chapter 13).

To stop the insanity, choose Stop Speaking from the same menu.

GEM IN THE ROUGH

All the Little Symbols

The first column of the main email list shows little symbols that let you know at a glance how you've processed certain messages. The most common one is, of course, the light blue dot (●), which means "new message." (After reading a message, you can mark it once again as an *unread* message by choosing Message→Mark As Unread—or Control-clicking the message's name and choosing Mark→As Unread from the shortcut menu.)

You might also see these symbols, which represent messages that you've replied to (↰), forwarded (→), redirected (↱), or flagged (⚑).

A well-guarded secret, however, is that the "replied to" and "forwarded" symbols aren't just indictors—they're *buttons*.

When you see one of these symbols next to your original message, click it to jump straight to your reply (or forwarded message). You're spared the trouble of having to search through all your mailboxes.

Incidentally, you may have noticed that Mail marks a message as having been read the moment you click it. You can change it back to unread by using its shortcut menu—but there's also a more permanent workaround.

If you hide the Preview pane by double-clicking the divider bar just above it, Mail no longer marks messages "read" just because you clicked them in the list. (You can bring back the Preview pane by double-clicking just above the vertical scroll bar, or by dragging the divider bar back up from the bottom.)

Once you've viewed a message, you can respond to it, delete it, print it, file it, and so on. The following pages should get you started.

Threading

Depending on what email program you used in Windows, you may already be familiar with *threading*—one of the most useful mail-sorting methods to come along in a long time. When threading is turned on, Mail groups emails with the same subject (like "Raccoons" and "Re: Raccoons") as a *single item* in the main message list.

To turn on threading, choose View→Organize by Thread. If several messages have the same subject, they all turn light blue to indicate their membership in a thread (see Figure 10-5).

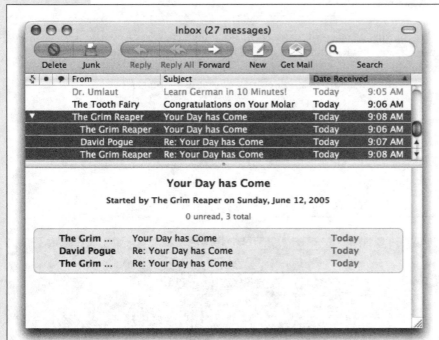

Figure 10-5:
Threads have two parts: a heading (the subject of the thread, listed in dark blue when not selected) and members (the individual messages in the thread, listed in light blue and indented). Often, the main list shows only a thread's heading; click the flippy triangle to reveal its members.

Here are some powerful ways to use threading:

- **View a list of all the messages in a thread** by clicking its heading. In the Preview pane, you'll see a comprehensive inventory of the thread (Figure 10-5). You can click a message's name in this list to jump right to it.

- **Move all the members of a thread to a new mailbox** by moving just its heading. You might find this useful, for example, when you've just finished a project and want to file away all the email related to it quickly. (A circled number tells you how many messages you're moving as you drag the heading.) You can even delete all the messages in a thread at once by deleting its heading.

- **Examine thread members from multiple mailboxes.** Normally, threads only display messages held in the *same* mailbox, but that's not especially convenient when you want to see both messages (from your Inbox) and your replies (in your Sent box).

  To work around that problem, click Inbox and then ⌘-click the Sent mailbox (or any other mailboxes you want to include). Your threads will seamlessly combine related messages from all of the selected mailboxes.

- **Quickly collapse all threads** by choosing View→Collapse All Threads. If your main list gets cluttered with too many expanded threads, this is a quick way to force it into order.

- **Send someone all the messages in a thread** by selecting the thread's heading and clicking Forward. Mail automatically copies all the messages of the thread into a new message, putting the oldest at the top. You might find this useful when you want to send your boss all the correspondence you've had with a coworker about a certain project.

Adding the Sender to Your Address Book

When you choose the Message→Add Sender To Address Book command, Mail memorizes the email address of the person whose message is on the screen. In fact, you can highlight a huge number of messages and add *all* the senders simultaneously using this technique.

Thereafter, you'll be able to write new messages to somebody just by typing the first couple letters of the name.

Opening Attachments

Just as you can attach files to an outgoing message, so people can send file attachments to you. Sometimes they don't even bother to type a message; you wind up receiving an empty email message with a file attached. Only the presence of the file's icon in the message body tells you that there's something attached.

Tip: Mail doesn't ordinarily indicate the presence of attachments in the main mail list. It can if you want it to, however. Just choose View→Columns→Attachments. A new column appears in the email list—at the far right—where you'll see a paper clip icon and the number of file attachments listed for each message.

Like Outlook Express for Windows, Mail doesn't store downloaded files as normal file icons on your hard drive. They're actually encoded right into the *.mbox* mailbox databases described on page 275. To extract an attached file from this mass of software, you must proceed in one of these ways:

- Control-click (right-click) the attachment's icon, and choose Save Attachment from the shortcut menu. You'll be asked to specify where to put it.

- Drag the attachment icon out of the message window and onto any visible portion of your desktop (or any visible folder).

- Click the Save button at the top of the email, or choose File→Save Attachments. (If the message has more than one attachment, this maneuver will save all of them.)

Tip: The Save button at the top of the Preview pane doubles as a pop-up menu. If you hold down the mouse over it, you can select from several other options for saving the attachments—like importing them into iPhoto or downloading only one of them.

- Double-click the attachment's icon, or single click the blue link underneath the icon. If you were sent a document (such as a photo, Word file, or Excel file), it now opens in the corresponding program (Preview, Word, Excel, or whatever).

Warning: After the attachment is open, use the *File→Save As* command to save the file into a folder of your choice. Otherwise, any changes you make won't be visible in the file except when you open it from within Mail.

- Control-click (right-click) the attachment's icon. From the shortcut menu, you can specify which programs you want to use for opening it, using the Open With submenu.

Tip: If the attachments you want to open are just pictures, you don't have to open them in a separate program at all. Tiger's Slideshow button can play a full-screen slideshow of every attached image.

If you jiggle the mouse a little during the slideshow, you get a useful row of buttons along the bottom of the screen, too. Fit to Screen, for example, makes small images bigger, and Index Sheet gives you an Exposé-like view of all the attached images at once.

And if you want to show off to your PC-using friends, click Add to iPhoto. The current image slickly slides to the bottom of the screen—and gets copied to iPhoto in the background, without even disrupting the progress of your slideshow.

When attachments don't open

If you're having trouble opening a file attachment, you may be dealing with a Windows file that requires some effort to open. For example:

- **.exe** files are Windows programs. Without an emulator like Virtual PC (page 202), your Mac can't run Windows programs, just as Windows computers can't run Macintosh programs.

- **.html.** A file whose name ends in .html or .htm is a Web page. In the beginning, Web pages hung out only on the Internet. These days, however, you're increasingly likely to find that you've downloaded one to your Mac's hard drive (it may be a software manual for some shareware, for example). You can open it just by double-clicking; Mac OS X comes set to open all .htm and .html files in Safari.

- **.vcf.** A "business-card" file; see page 282.

If you were sent a file with a three-letter code not listed here, you may well have a file that can be opened only by a Windows program. You might consider asking your correspondent to resend it in one of the more universal formats, such as the graphics formats JPEG and TIFF, or the text formats RTF and TXT. (Mac OS X opens all of these formats easily.) In addition, just about *any* layout, graphics, or text file can be turned into a PDF. If you're still having trouble opening the attachment, ask your correspondent to send the attachment in that format instead.

Replying to a Message

To answer a message, click the Reply button on the message toolbar (or choose Message→Reply, or just press ⌘-R). If the message was originally addressed to multiple recipients, you can address your reply to everyone simultaneously by clicking the Reply to All button instead.

A new message window opens, already addressed. As a courtesy to your correspondent, Mail places the original message at the bottom of the window, denoted by a vertical bar, as shown in Figure 10-6.

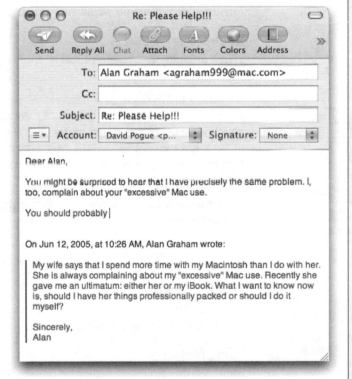

Figure 10-6:
In Rich Text–formatted Mail messages (not to be confused with RTF [Rich Text Format] word processing format, which is different), a reply includes the original message, marked in a special color (which you can change in Mail→Preferences) and with a vertical bar to differentiate it from the text of your reply. (In plain-text messages, each line of the reply is >denoted >with >brackets, although only your recipient will see them.)

The original sender's name is automatically placed in the "To:" field. The subject is the same as the original subject with the addition of "Re:" (shorthand for Regarding). You're ready to type your response.

Tip: If you highlight some text before clicking Reply, Mail pastes only that portion of the original message into your reply. That's a great convenience to your correspondent, who now knows exactly which part of the message you're responding to.

At this point, you can add or delete recipients, edit the Subject line or the original message, attach a file, and so on.

When you're finished, click Send. (If you click Reply to All in the message window's toolbar, your message goes to everyone who received the original note, *even* if you began the reply process by clicking Reply. Mac OS X, in other words, gives you a second chance to address your reply to everyone.)

Forwarding Messages

To pass the note on to a third person, click the Forward toolbar button (or choose Message→Forward, or press Shift-⌘-F). A new message opens, looking a lot like the one that appears when you reply. You may wish to precede the original message with a comment of your own, along the lines of, "Frank: I thought you'd be interested in this joke about Congress."

Finally, address it as you would any outgoing piece of mail.

Redirecting Messages

Here's a handy feature you probably never encountered in Windows: *redirecting* a message.

It's similar to forwarding a message, with one extremely useful difference. When you *forward* a message, your recipient sees that it came from you. When you *redirect* it, your recipient sees the original writer's name as the sender. The message bears no trace of your involvement (unless the recipient thinks to choose View→Message→Long Headers). In other words, a redirected message uses you as a low-profile relay station between two other people.

Treasure this feature. You can use it to transfer messages from one of your own accounts to another, or to pass along a message that came to you by mistake.

To redirect a message, choose Message→Redirect, or press Shift-⌘-E. You get an outgoing copy of the message—this time without any quoting marks.

Printing Messages

Sometimes there's no substitute for a printout. Choose File→Print, or press ⌘-P, to summon the Print dialog box (page 207).

Filing Messages

Mail lets you create new mailboxes in the Mailboxes column. You might create one for important messages, another for order confirmations from Web shopping, still another for friends and family, and so on. Mail also lets you create mailboxes *inside* these mailboxes, a feature beloved by the hopelessly organized.

Mail even offers *smart mailboxes*—self-updating folders that show you all your mail from your boss, for example, or every message with "mortgage" in its subject. It's the same idea as smart folders in the Finder (page 80) or smart playlists in iTunes (page 232): folders whose contents are based on criteria that you specify (see Figure 10-7).

Figure 10-7:
Just like iTunes, iPhoto, and the Finder, Mail lets you create self-populating folders. In this example, the "New Mail from Steve" smart mailbox will automatically display all messages from Steve Jobs at Apple that you've received in the past week.

Smart Mailbox Name: New Mail from Steve

Contains messages which match [all ▲▼] of the following conditions:

[From ▲▼] [Contains ▲▼] steve@apple.com ⊖ ⊕
[Date Received ▲▼] [is this week ▲▼] ⊖ ⊕

☐ Include messages from Trash
☐ Include messages from Sent [Cancel] (OK)

The commands you need are all in the Mailboxes menu. For example, to create a new mailbox folder, choose Mailbox→New Mailbox, or click the + button at the bottom of the drawer. To create a smart mailbox, choose Mailbox→New Smart Mailbox.

Mail asks you to name the new mailbox. If you have more than one email account, you can specify which one will contain the new folder. (Smart mailboxes, however, always sit outside your other mailboxes.)

Tip: If you want to create a folder-inside-a-folder, use slashes in the name of your new mailbox. (If you use the name *Cephalopods/Squid*, for example, Mail will create a folder called Cephalopods, with a subfolder called Squid.) You can also drag the mailbox icons up and down in the drawer to place one inside another.

None of these tricks works for smart mailboxes, however. The only way to organize smart mailboxes is to put them inside a smart mailbox *folder*, which you create using Mailbox→New Smart Mailbox Folder. You might do that if you have several smart mailboxes for mail from your co-workers ("From Jim," "From Anne," and so on) and want to put them together in one collapsible group to save space.

When you click OK, a new icon appears in the Mailboxes column, ready for use.

You can move a message (or a group of messages) into a mailbox folder by dragging it (or them) out of the main list or by using the Message→Move To submenu, which lists all your mailboxes.

The only way to change the contents of a *smart* mailbox is to change the criteria that it uses to populate itself. To do so, double-click the smart mailbox icon and use the dialog box that appears.

Flagging Messages

Sometimes you'll receive email that prompts you to some sort of action, but you may not have the time (or the fortitude) to face the task at the moment. ("Hi there…it's me, your accountant. Would you mind rounding up your expenses for 1995 through 2005 and sending me a list by email?")

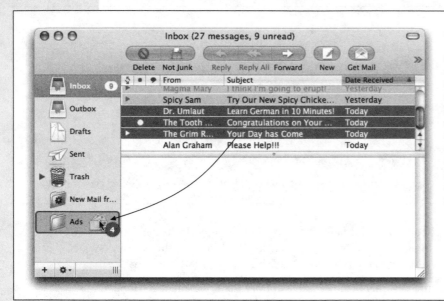

Figure 10-8:
You can use any part of a message's "row" as a handle; the envelope tells you that Mail knows what's happening. You can also drag messages en masse onto a folder. If you Option-drag a message into a folder, you make a copy, leaving the original message where it is.

That's why Mail lets you *flag* a message, summoning a little flag icon in a new column next to a message's name. These indicators can mean anything you like—they simply call attention to certain messages. You can sort your mail list so that all your flagged messages are listed first; click the flag at the top of the column heading.

To flag a message in this way, select the message (or several messages) and choose Message→Mark→As Flagged, or press Option-⌘-L, or Control-click the message's name in the list and choose Mark→As Flagged from the shortcut menu. (To clear the flags, repeat the procedure, but use the Mark→As Unflagged command instead.)

Finding Messages

As noted earlier in this chapter, you can sort the columns in your main email list just by clicking the headings (From, Subject, Date & Time, and so on). The smart mailbox feature described on page 270 is another useful way of sorting your messages, provided you know that you're going to be looking for the same kind of messages over and over again.

But when dealing with masses of email, you may find it easier to process your messages using Mail's *dedicated* searching tools. They're fast and convenient, and when you're done with them, you can go right back to browsing your Message list as it was.

Finding messages within a mailbox

See the little text box in the upper-right corner of your main mail window? You can use it to hide all but certain messages, as shown in Figure 10-9.

Tip: You can also set up Mail to show you only certain messages that you've *manually* selected, hiding all the others in the list. To do so, highlight the messages you want (Shift-click the first and last message of a block to make contiguous cselections, or ⌘-click to make noncontiguous selections.) Then choose View→Display Selected Messages Only. (To see all of them again, choose View→Display All Messages.)

Figure 10-9:
You can jump to the search box by pressing Option-⌘-F. As you type, Mail shrinks the list to include only the matches. You can fine tune your results using the buttons just above the list. To return to the full message list, click the tiny X at the right side of search box.

This search box has a number of useful features:

- When you're searching, a thin row of buttons appears underneath the toolbar. You can use these buttons to narrow down your results to only messages with your search term in their *subject*, for example, or to only those messages in the currently selected mailbox.

- When you select a message in the search view, the Preview pane pops up from the bottom of the window. If you click Show in Mailbox, on the other hand, you exit the search view and jump straight to the message in whatever mailbox it came from. That's perfect if the message is part of a thread, since jumping to the message will also display all the other messages from its thread.

- If you think you'll want to perform the current search again sometime, click Save in the upper-right corner of the window. Mail displays a dialog box with your search term and criteria filled in; all you have to do is give it a name and click OK to transform your search into a smart mailbox that you can open anytime.

Finding text within an open message

You can also search for certain text within a single message. Choose Edit→Find→Find (or press ⌘-F) to bring up the Find dialog box (Figure 10-10).

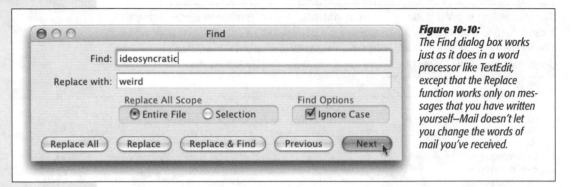

Figure 10-10:
The Find dialog box works just as it does in a word processor like TextEdit, except that the Replace function works only on messages that you have written yourself—Mail doesn't let you change the words of mail you've received.

Deleting Messages

It's a snap to delete a selected message, several selected messages, or a message that's currently before you on the screen. You can press the Delete key (with or without the ⌘ key), click the Delete button on the toolbar, choose Edit→Delete, or drag messages out of the list window and into your Trash mailbox—or even onto the Dock's Trash icon.

Tip: If you delete a message by accident, the Undo command (Edit→Undo or ⌘-Z) restores it.

All of these commands move the message to the Trash folder. If you like, you can then click its icon to view a list of the messages you've deleted. You can even rescue messages by dragging them back into another mailbox (back to the Inbox, for example).

Method 1: Emptying the Trash folder

Mail doesn't vaporize messages in the Trash folder until you "empty the trash," just like in the Finder. You can empty it in any of several ways:

- Click a message (or several), within the Trash folder list and then click the Delete icon on the toolbar (or press the Delete key). Now those messages are *really* gone.

- Choose Mailbox→Erase Deleted Message (⌘-K). Or, if you have multiple accounts, choose Erase Deleted Messages→In All Accounts.

- Control-click (right-click) the Trash mailbox icon and choose Erase Deleted Messages from the shortcut menu. (Mail sports an Action pop-up button at the bottom, too, just like the Finder toolbar. You can also choose Erase Deleted Messages from there.)

- Wait. Mail will permanently delete these messages automatically after a week.

If a week is too long (or not long enough), you can change this interval. Choose Mail→Preferences, click Accounts, and select the account name from the list at left. Then click Mailbox Behaviors, and change the "Erase deleted messages when" pop-up menu. If you choose Quitting Mail from the pop-up menu, Mail will take out the trash every time you quit the program.

Method 2: Deleted mail turns invisible

Mail offers a second—and very unusual—method of deleting messages that doesn't involve the Trash folder at all. Using this method, pressing the Delete key (or clicking the Delete toolbar button) simply hides the selected message in the list. Hidden messages remain hidden, but don't go away for good until you use the Rebuild Mailbox command described in the box on page 279.

If this arrangement sounds useful, choose Mail→Preferences and click Accounts. Now select the account from the list on the left, click Mailbox Behaviors, and turn off the checkbox called "Move deleted messages to a separate folder" or "Move deleted messages to the Trash mailbox." (The checkbox's wording depends on what kind of account you have.) From now on, messages you delete vanish from the list.

Figure 10-11:
To resurrect a deleted message (indicated in light gray type), Control-click it and choose Undelete from the shortcut menu.

TROUBLESHOOTING MOMENT

Secrets of the Mbox Files

Mail keeps your messages in a series of mailbox database files in your Home→Library→Mail→Mailboxes folder, inside folders named for your accounts (Outbox, Sent, and so on).

Knowing this permits you to perform a number of interesting tricks. First of all, now you know what files to back up for safekeeping.

Second, you now have yourself a beautiful monthly archiving system. Each month, create a new mailbox folder in Mail, named for a certain month ("June2005.mbox," for example).

Drag into it all the mail you want to archive, and then back up just that mailbox file from your hard drive—instant archiving system! (If you ever want to work with these messages again, just drag that .mbox file back into your Home→Library→ Mail folder before opening Mail.)

Third, now you know which files to copy to your laptop to maintain email continuity when you travel.

And finally, if you have messages on an old Mac that you want to copy to a new one, you now know where they're stored.

They're not really gone, however. You can bring them back, at least in ghostly form, by choosing View→Show Deleted Messages (or pressing ⌘-L). Figure 10-11 shows the idea.

Using this system, in other words, you never truly delete messages; you just hide them

The advantage of this arrangement is that, at some point, almost everyone wishes they could resurrect a deleted message—maybe months later, maybe years later. Using the hide-deleted-message system, your old messages are always around for reference. (The downside to this system, of course, is that SEC investigators can use it to find incriminating evidence that you thought you'd deleted.)

When you do want to purge these messages for good, you can always return to the Special Mailboxes pane and turn the "Move deleted mail to a separate folder" checkbox back on.

Using Message Rules

Like most Windows email programs, Mail lets you create *message rules* (filters) that file, answer, or delete incoming messages automatically based on their contents (such as their subject, address, and/or size). Message rules require you to think like the distant relative of a programmer, but the mental effort can reward you many times over. Message rules turn Mail into a surprisingly smart and efficient secretary.

Setting up message rules

Here's how to set up a message rule:

1. **Choose Mail→Preferences, and then click the Rules icon.**

   The Rules pane appears, as shown at top in Figure 10-12.

2. **Click Add Rule.**

   Now the dialog box shown at bottom in Figure 10-12 appears.

3. **Use the criteria options (the ones at the top) to specify how Mail should select messages to process.**

   For example, if you'd like the program to watch out for messages from a particular person, you would set up the first two pop-up menus to say "From" and "Contains," respectively.

   To flag messages containing *loan, $$$$, XXX, !!!!,* and so on, set the pop-up menus to say "Subject" and "Contains."

   You can set up *multiple* criteria here, so you flag messages whose subjects contain any one of those command spam triggers. (If you change the "any" pop-up menu to say "all," then *all* of the criteria must be true for the rule to kick in.)

4. **Specify *which* words or people you want the message rule to watch for.**

In the text box to the right of the two pop-up menus, type the word, address, name, or phrase you want Mail to watch for—a person's name, or *$$$$*, in the previous examples.

5. **In the lower half of the box, specify what you want to happen to messages that match the criteria.**

   If, in steps 1 and 2, you've instructed your rule to watch for junk mail containing *$$$$* in the Subject line, here's where you can tell Mail to delete it or move it into, say, the Junk folder.

   With a little imagination, you'll see how the options in this pop-up menu can do absolutely amazing things with your incoming email. Mail can colorize, delete,

Figure 10-12:
Top: Mail rules can screen out junk mail, serve as an email answering machine, or call important messages to your attention. All mail message rules you've created appear in this list. (The color shading for each rule is a reflection of the colorizing options you set up, if any.)

Bottom: Double-click a rule to open the Edit Rule dialog box, where you can specify what should set off the rule and what it should do in response.

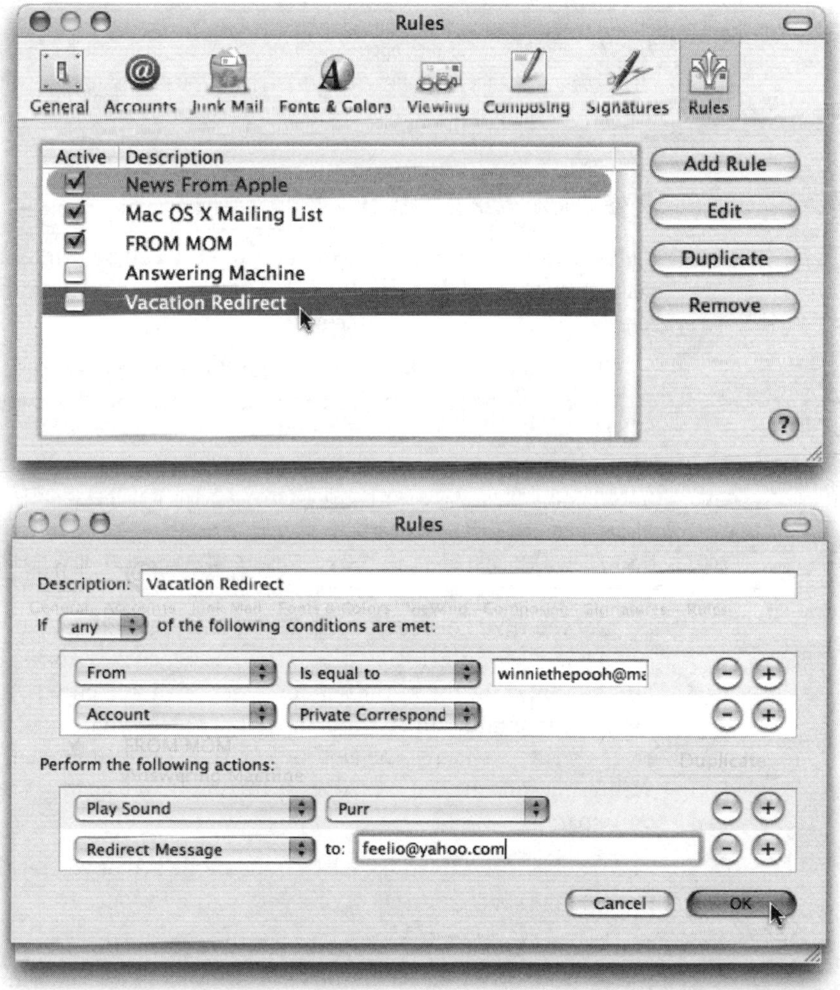

move, redirect, or forward messages—or even play a sound when you get a certain message.

Consider, for example, what happens when you go on a trip. By setting up the controls as shown in Figure 10-12, you'll have specified that messages your boss (identified as Winnie the Pooh in the illustration), sends to your .Mac account are to be redirected to your vacation email address, *feelio@yahoo.com*. (The rest of the mail will just have to wait until you're home again.)

6. **In the very top box, name your mail rule. Click OK.**

Now you're back to the Rules pane (Figure 10-12, top). Here you can choose a sequence for the rules you've created by dragging them up and down. Here, too, you can turn off the ones you won't be needing at the moment, but may use again one day.

Tip: Mail applies rules as they appear, from top to bottom, in the list. If a rule doesn't seem to be working properly, it may be that an earlier rule is intercepting and processing some message before the "broken" rule even sees it. To fix this, try dragging the bad rule up or down in the list.

The Junk Mail Filter

Spam is the junk that now makes up more than 80 percent of all email, and it's only getting worse. Luckily, you, along with Mail's advanced spam filters, can make it better—at least for *your* email accounts.

You'll see the effects of Mail's spam filter the first time you check your mail: A certain swath of message titles appear in color. These are the messages that Mail considers junk.

Note: Out of the box, Mail doesn't apply its spam-targeting features to people whose addresses are in your address book, to people you've emailed recently, or to messages sent to you by *name* rather than just by email address. You can adjust these settings in Mail→Preferences→Junk Mail tab.

During your first couple of weeks with Mail, your job is to supervise Mail's coloring job. That is, if you get spam that Mail misses, click the message and then click the Junk button at the top of the window (identified in Figure 10-1), or the Junk icon on the toolbar. On the other hand, if Mail flags legitimate mail as spam, slap it gently on the wrist by clicking the Not Junk button. Over time, Mail gets better and better at filtering your mail; it even does surprisingly well against the new breed of image-only spam.

The trouble with this so-called Training mode is that you're still left with the task of trashing the spam yourself, saving you no time whatsoever.

Once Mail has perfected its filtering skills to your satisfaction, therefore, open Mail's preferences, click Junk Mail, and click "Move it to the Junk mailbox." From now on,

Mail automatically files what it deems junk into a Junk mailbox, where it's much easier to scan and delete the messages en masse.

Tip: Don't miss the "Trust Junk Mail headers sent by your Internet Service Provider" option in the Junk Mail pane of the preference window. If you turn on that checkbox, Mail will take your ISP's word that certain messages are spam, giving you a *double* layer of protection.

Address Book

Address Book is Mac OS X's little-black-book program—an electronic Rolodex where you can conveniently stash the names, job titles, addresses, phone numbers, email addresses, and Internet chat screen names of all the people in your life (Figure 10-13). Of course, Address Book can hold other related information too, such as birthdays and anniversaries, as well as any other tidbits of personal data you'd like to keep at your fingertips.

Once you make Address Book the central repository of all your personal contact information, you can call up this information in a number of convenient ways:

- You can open Address Book and search for any contact by typing just a few letters in the Search box.

- Regardless of what program you're in, you can use a single keystroke (F12 by default) to summon the Address Book Dashboard widget (page 108). There, you can search for any contact you want, and hide the widget with the same quick keystroke when you're done.

- When you're composing messages in Mac OS X's Mail program, Address Book automatically fills in email addresses for you when you type the first few letters.

TROUBLESHOOTING MOMENT

Rebuilding Your Mail Databases

As noted earlier in this chapter, Mail keeps your messages in a series of mailbox database files in your Home→Library→Mail→Mailboxes folder.

Over time, as you add and delete hundreds of messages from these database files, some digital sawdust gets left behind, resulting in peculiarities when addressing messages or general Mail sluggishness. You also wind up with *massive* message files hidden on your hard drive, which can consume hundreds of megabytes of disk space. That's a particular bummer if you like to copy your message database to your laptop when you go on a trip.

Fortunately, it's easy enough to *rebuild the message databases.* Doing so cleanses, repairs, and purges your message files. As a result, you wind up with a much more compact and healthy database.

To rebuild a mailbox, highlight it in the Mailboxes column. (Highlight several by ⌘-clicking, if you like.) Then choose Mailbox→Rebuild. Mac OS X takes several minutes (or hours, depending on the size of your mailboxes) to repair and compact your database—but if you're experiencing Mail weirdness or slowness, it's well worth the sacrifice.

Tip: If you choose Window→Address Panel (Option-⌘-A) from within Mail, you can browse all of your addresses without even launching the Address Book program. Once you've selected the people you want to contact, just click the "To:" button to address an email to them—or, if you already have a new email message open, to add them to the recipients.

- If you have a subscription to the .Mac service (page 147), you can synchronize your contacts to the Web, so you can see them while you're away from your Mac.

- Address Book can send its information to an iPod, giving you a little white "little black book" that fits in your shirt pocket, can be operated one-handed, and comes with built-in musical accompaniment. (To set this up, open iTunes while your iPod is connected. Choose iTunes→Preferences, click iPod, click the Contacts tab, and turn on "Synchronize Address Book Contacts.")

- If you have a Bluetooth cellphone, Address Book can exchange information with your phone and even dial it for you. Incoming calls to your phone wirelessly trigger Address Book to display the number or name of the caller. Using the same wireless connection, you can also exchange contact information between Address Book and Palm-compatible handhelds.

You can find Address Book in your Applications folder or (in a fresh installation of Mac OS X) in the Dock.

Tip: See Chapter 6 for details on importing addresses from other programs into Address Book.

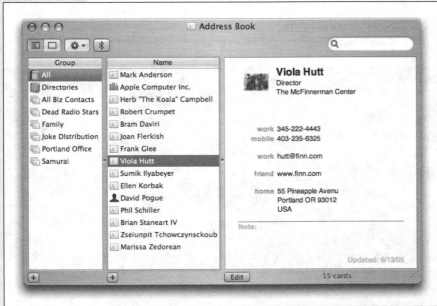

Figure 10-13:
The big question: Why isn't this program named iContact? With its three-paned view, soft rounded buttons and brushed-aluminum style windows, it certainly looks like a close cousin of iPhoto and iTunes.

Creating Address Cards

Each entry in Address Book is called a *card*—an electronic version of a paper Rolodex card, with predefined spaces to hold all the standard contact information.

To add a new person to your collection, choose File→New Card (or press ⌘-N, or click the + button beneath the Name column). Then type in the contact information, pressing the Tab key to move from field to field, as shown in Figure 10-14.

Tip: If you find yourself constantly adding the same fields to new cards, check out the Template pane of Address Book→Preferences. There, you can customize exactly which fields appear for new cards.

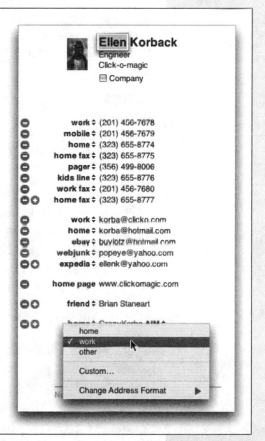

Figure 10-14:
If one of your contacts happens to have three office phone extensions, a pager number, two home phone lines, a cellphone and a couple of fax machines, no problem—you can add as many fields as you need. Click the little green + buttons when editing a card to add more phone, email, chat name, and address fields. (The buttons appear only when existing fields are filled.) Click a field's name to change its label; you can select one of the standard labels from the pop-up menu (Home, Work, and so on) or make up your own labels by choosing Custom, as seen in the lower portion of this figure.

Each card also contains a free-form Notes field at the bottom, where you can type any other random crumbs of information you'd like to store about the person (spouse's name, embarrassing nicknames, favorite Chinese restaurant, and so on).

Editing an address

When you create a new address card, you're automatically in Edit mode, which means you can add and remove fields and change the information on the card. To switch into Browse Mode (where you can view and copy contact information but not change it), click the Edit button or choose Edit→Edit Card (⌘-L). You can also switch *out* of Browse Mode in the same ways.

Tip: Regardless of which mode you're in—Edit or Browse—you can *always* type, drag, or paste text into the Notes field.

Adding addresses from Mail

As mentioned earlier in this chapter, you can also make new contacts in Address Book directly from the Mail program, saving you the trouble of having to type names and email addresses manually. Select an email address in Mail, then choose Message→Add Sender to Address Book (or press ⌘-Y). Presto, Mac OS X automatically adds a new card to Address Book, with the name and email address fields already filled in. Later, you can edit the card in Address Book to add phone numbers, street addresses, and so on.

Groups

A *group* is a collection of related address cards, saved under a single descriptive name. Organizing your contact entries into groups can make them much easier to find and use—especially when your database of addresses climbs into the hundreds. For example, if you regularly send out a family newsletter to 35 relatives, you might gather the address cards of all your assorted siblings, cousins, nieces, nephews, uncles, and aunts into a single group called Family. When addressing an outgoing message using Mail, you can type this group name to reach all of your kin at once. As a bonus, a person can be a member of as many different groups as you want.

To create a group, click the + button at the bottom of the Group column in the Address Book window, or choose File→New Group (Shift-⌘-N). Type a name for the newly spawned group icon in the Group column, and then populate it with address cards by dragging entries from the Name list into the group. If you're familiar with iTunes, you'll feel right at home doing this; it's just like adding songs to a playlist.

UP TO SPEED

About vCards

Address Book exchanges contact information with other programs primarily through *vCards*. (vCard is short for *virtual business card*.) More and more email programs send and receive these electronic business cards, which you can easily spot by the .vcf extension on their names.

If you ever receive an email to which a vCard file is attached, drag the .vcf file into your Address Book window to create an instant entry with a complete set of information.

You can create vCards of your own, too. Just drag a name out of Address Book and onto the desktop (or into a piece of outgoing mail). You can even select *several* entries and drag them, en masse, to the desktop, where they appear as a single vCard. (Keep that trick in mind if you ever want to copy all your contacts to a new Mac.)

Clicking on a group automatically locates and displays (in the Name column) all the names that are a part of that group—and hides any that aren't.

Tip: To turn a set of address cards into a group very quickly, select multiple entries from the Name column—by either Shift-clicking the names (to make contiguous selections) or ⌘-clicking (for noncontiguous selections)—then choose File→New Group From Selection. You end up with a new group containing all the selected names.

You can even create *smart groups,* which automatically populate themselves with items that match criteria you specify. For example, you might create a smart group called Apple Employees that lists all your contacts with "apple.com" in their email addresses.

To create a smart group, choose File→New Smart Group (Option-⌘-N). Then use the resulting dialog box (which looks a lot like Mail's smart mailbox dialog box) to specify how you'd like the group to fill itself.

Removing someone from a group

To take someone out of a group, first click the group name, and then click the person's name in the Name column and press the Delete key. If you want to remove the person from Address Book *itself,* click Delete in the resulting dialog box. Otherwise, just click "Remove from Group" or press Return. Address Book will keep the card, but remove it from the currently selected group.

Note: If you selected All in the Group column, rather than a specific group, Mac OS X doesn't give you a "Remove from Group" option. Instead, it just lets you confirm whether you do, in fact, want to permanently remove the card.

Pictures

You can dress up each Address Book entry not only with textual information, but also with a photo. Whenever you're editing somebody's address-book card, just drag a digital photo—preferably 64 pixels square, or a multiple of it—onto the current address card; the image will show up in the picture well to the left of the person's name, as shown in Figure 10-14. Or you can double-click the picture well and browse to a picture yourself by clicking Choose.

Tip: You can also drag a snapshot directly from iPhoto into the picture frame.

You don't necessarily have to use a photo, of course. You could add any graphic that you want to represent someone, even if it's a Bart Simpson face or a skull and crossbones. You can use any standard image file in an address card—a JPEG, GIF, TIFF, or even a PDF.

From now on, if you receive an email from that person, the photo shows up right in the email message.

Finding an Address

You can search for an Address Book entry inside the currently selected group by typing a few letters of the name (or address, or any other snippet of contact information) in the capsule-shaped Search box (see Figure 10-15). To search *all* your contacts instead of just the current group, click All in the Group list.

Tip: For time-saving convenience, press ⌘-F to jump to the Search field.

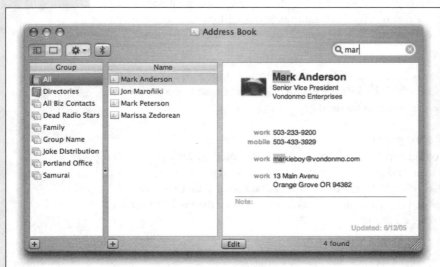

Figure 10-15:
With each letter you type, Address Book filters your social circle and displays the number of matches at the bottom. The matching records themselves appear in the Name column, the first of the matching card entries appears in the far-right pane, and the matching text itself appears highlighted in the matching card.

If Address Book finds more than one matching card, use the up and down arrow keys (or the Return and Shift-Return keystrokes) to navigate through them.

Once you've found the card you're looking for, Address Book lets you perform some interesting stunts. If you click the label of a phone number ("home" or "office," for example), you see the Large Type option: Address Book displays the phone number in an absurdly gigantic font that fills the entire width of your screen, making it all but impossible to misread the number as you dial the phone from across the room. You can also click the label of an email address to create a preaddressed email message, or click a home-page label to launch your Web browser and go to a contact's site. Clicking an address label even gives you the option of getting a map of the address via your Web browser (Figure 10-16).

You can also just copy and paste address card info, or drag it into another program.

Changing the Address Book Display

You can't do much to customize Address Book's appearance, but the Preferences window (Address Book→Preferences) gives you at least a couple of options in the General pane that are worth checking out:

- **Display Order.** Choose to have names displayed with the first name followed by the last, or vice versa.

- **Sort By.** Sort the entries in Address Book by either first or last name.

- **Font Size.** Choose from Regular, Large, or Extra Large. (Unfortunately, you can't change anything else about the font used in Address Book; the color, face, and style are all locked down.)

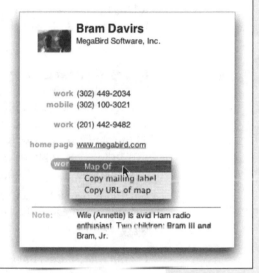

Figure 10-16:
The options that become available when you click the field labels on an address card vary according to field type. Pop-up menus let you send email, open Web pages, or view a map, depending on the particular field you've clicked.

Printing Options

When you choose File→Print, you can use the Styles pop-up menu to select from four different printing approaches: mailing labels, envelopes, no-nonsense printed lists, and pocket address books. If, when using this last feature, you choose Indexed from the Flip Style pop-up menu, each page's edge will even list the first letters of the last names listed on the page, making it a cinch to find the page with the address you want.

No matter which mode you choose, the only cards that will be printed are the ones that were selected when you chose File→Print. If you want to print *all* your cards, therefore, make sure to select "All" in the Group column before you print.

Address Book Backups

When you think about it, the contents of your Address Book may represent *years* of typing and compiling on several computers. Losing all that information to a corrupted database or a hard drive crash could be devastating. Here, then, are two ways to protect your Address Book data:

- **Use the Backup command.** Periodically choose File→Back up Address Book. If something goes wrong—say, a batch of important contacts gets inadvertently deleted—you can go back to a previously saved version to rescue the data by choosing File→Revert to Address Book Backup.

- **Make a backup copy of your entire Address Book database.** Open your Home→Library→Application Support folder. Copy the entire AddressBook folder to another disk—burn it to a CD, download it to your iPod, or upload it to a file server, for example. Now your contact data is safe even in the event of a hard drive failure.

Address Book and Bluetooth

Address Book can do far more than just store, retrieve, and display phone numbers. It can actually *dial* them using your cellphone, thanks to Bluetooth wireless technology.

Getting Bluetooth-enabled

To make Address Book talk to the outside world in this way, you have to *pair* it with a Bluetooth-enabled cellphone. (And your Mac, of course, must have a Bluetooth adapter, like the one that comes preinstalled on new laptops.) Once you've turned on all the hardware, your cellphone and Mac have to "find" each other on the wireless network—a task managed by the Bluetooth pane of System Preferences.

Once your computer and phone have mated for life, open Address Book. You see a Bluetooth logo in the Address Book window, letting you know that your phone and computer "see" each other and that you can now make calls and send cellphone messages from your computer.

Dialing with Address Book

To make a phone call, click any phone number field label on an address card and choose Dial from the pop-up menu. Then pick up your cellphone and wait for the person you're calling to answer.

Texting from Address Book

You can also use Address Book to send SMS text messages directly to other cellphones. (SMS stands for "short message service," and as anyone under 20 can tell you, refers to the feature of cellphones that lets you send and receive short text messages.) To send an SMS message, click a phone number field on an address card and choose SMS menu from the pop-up menu. Type your message and send it off.

Receiving calls

Once your cellphone and Mac have met, Address Book can notify you of *incoming* calls, too. It's Caller ID on the Mac!

When a call comes in, a window opens (assuming Address Book is open), showing the caller's number in jumbo type. If it's somebody in your Address Book, you even see the caller's name.

Click Answer and then pick up your cellphone to begin your conversation. If you click Send to Voicemail instead, your phone stops ringing and you dump the caller into your cell service's answering machine, just as though you'd pressed the voicemail button on the phone.

Sometimes, you may prefer to send the caller to voicemail *and* create a new SMS message to reply. In that case, click Send SMS Reply. This way, you shut up the ringing phone while your family is sleeping, but still manage to type out a reply (like "It's 3:35 AM, for God's sake! What are you doing?!").

SWITCHING TO THE MAC: THE MISSING MANUAL

Safari, iChat, and Sherlock

Apple is obviously intrigued by the possibilities of the Internet. With each new release of Mac OS X, more clever tendrils reach out from the Mac to the world's biggest network. You don't have to look any further than the Dashboard (page 108) to see how much Apple loves integrating the Internet into every nook and cranny of Mac OS X.

Still, some of the Mac's most powerful Internet tools are full-fledged *programs,* not widgets. In addition to Mail (Chapter 10), Mac OS X includes the Safari Web browser; iChat for instant messaging, voice chatting, and videoconferencing; and the aging, somewhat superfluous Sherlock program for targeted Web searches.

This chapter tackles the latter three members of this motley crew one by one.

Safari

If you want something done right, you have to do it yourself.

That must be what Apple was thinking when it wrote its own Web browser, which so annoyed Microsoft that it promptly ceased all further work on its own Mac version of Internet Explorer.

Safari is beautiful, very fast, and filled with delicious features. Unless you visit the handful of sites that still require Internet Explorer (like some banking sites), you'll be *glad* not to use the poky Internet Explorer for Mac.

To move your Web bookmarks over from Windows to the Mac, see page 153. Then, when you're ready to get going, read on.

Tip: If you'd like to use a different Web browser on the Mac—Firefox, for example—open Safari, and then choose Safari→Preferences→General. Pick your favorite Web browser from the Default Web Browser pop-up menu. Now, any time you click a link in an email message (or anywhere else), *your* favorite browser will open up instead of Safari.

Browsing Basics

Navigating the Web requires little more than clicking buttons and/or hyperlinks, as shown in Figure 11-1. Most Web pages, in fact, look almost identical in Safari and Internet Explorer, so buttons and hyperlinks should be right where you expect them.

Tip: If you're not sure whether something on a page is a hyperlink, just move your cursor over it. If the arrow turns into a pointing finger, you've found yourself a link.

Bookmarks bar Address bar RSS button Google search

Graphic link Text link Form

Figure 11-1:
The Safari window offers tools and features that let you navigate the Web almost effortlessly. These various toolbars and buttons are described in this chapter. One difference that may throw you if you're used to Internet Explorer: When you're loading a Web page, the progress bar appears as a colored stripe that gradually darkens the Address bar itself, rather than as a strip at the bottom of the window.

Saving graphics

If you ever find a graphic that you want to save to your hard drive, just Control-click (or right-click) it, and then choose Save Image to the Desktop from the shortcut menu. (You can tell Safari where to save all such files in the Safari→Preferences→General tab.)

Even better: If you know exactly *where* you want a graphic stored, just drag the image straight off the Web page and into the desired folder in the Finder.

Scrolling

Scrolling a Web page in Safari is virtually identical to scrolling in Internet Explorer. You can use the scroll bar on the right—by clicking the arrow buttons, dragging the little slider, or clicking inside the scroll bar itself—or use the arrow keys on your keyboard. You can even use the Page Up and Page Down keys to scroll in full-screen increments—a stunt that also works if you press Space and Shift-Space

Finally, if you have a mouse with a scroll wheel, that'll work in Safari, too. You can even scroll *horizontally* by holding Shift as you scroll.

Safari Toolbars

Many of Safari's most useful controls come parked on toolbars and buttons that you summon or hide by choosing their names from the View menu. Here's what they do:

Address bar

When you type a new Web page address (URL) into this strip and press Enter, the corresponding Web site appears.

Because typing out Internet addresses is so central to the Internet experience and such a typo-prone hassle, the Address bar is rich with features that minimize keystrokes. For example:

- You don't have to click the Address bar before typing; just press ⌘-L.

- You can highlight the entire address (so it's ready to be typed over with a new one) by clicking the very upper or lower edge of the Address bar text box. Alternatively, you can click the small icon just to the left of the current address, or triple-click the Address bar.

- You don't have to type out the whole Internet address. You can omit the *http://*, *www*, and *.com* portions; Safari fills in those standard address bits for you. To visit NYTimes.com, for example, a speed freak might press ⌘-L to highlight the Address bar, type *nytimes*, and then press Enter.

- When you begin to type into the Address bar, the AutoComplete feature compares what you're typing against a list of Web sites you've recently visited or that you've saved as bookmarks. Safari displays a drop-down list of Web addresses that seem to match what you're typing. To spare yourself the tedium of typing out the whole thing, click the correct complete address with your mouse, or use the down arrow key to reach the desired listing and then press Enter. The complete address you select then pops into the Address bar.

You can summon or dismiss a number of individual buttons on the Address bar, in effect customizing it (Figure 11-2):

- **Back/Forward.** As usual, click the Back button to revisit the page you were just on. *Keyboard shortcut:* Delete, or ⌘-left arrow, or ⌘-left bracket.

Once you've clicked Back, you can then click the Forward button (or press ⌘-right arrow, or ⌘-right bracket) to return to the page you were on before you clicked the Back button. Click (and hold on) the Back button for a drop-down list of the Web pages you've visited during this online session. (Hold Option as you hold down the mouse to see the actual *addresses*—as opposed to the names—of the Web pages you've visited.)

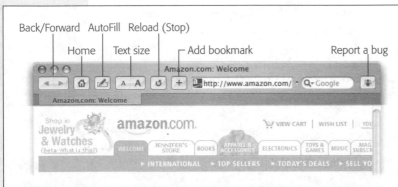

Back/Forward AutoFill Reload (Stop)

Home Text size Add bookmark Report a bug

Amazon.com: Welcome

http://www.amazon.com/ Google

Amazon.com: Welcome

Figure 11-2:
You summon or hide these buttons by choosing View→ Customize Address Bar and dragging buttons onto or off of the Address bar. Some of them lack text labels, but all offer tooltip labels that you can read by pointing to the button without clicking.

GEM IN THE ROUGH

Let AutoFill Do the Typing

Safari can remember user names, passwords, and other information you type into the text boxes you encounter in your Web travels.

To turn on this awesome feature, visit the Safari→Preferences→AutoFill tab. If you turn on "Using info from my Address Book card," whenever you're supposed to fill in your shipping address on a Web form, you can click the AutoFill button in the Address bar to have Safari fill in the blanks for you automatically. (If you don't see the AutoFill button—as shown in Figure 11-2—add it using View→Customize Address Bar, or use Edit→AutoFill Form to do the deed instead.)

Alternatively, just click a text box—"Name," for example—and start typing. As soon as Safari recognizes a familiar scrap of your contact information, it fills out the rest of the word automatically. (If it guessed wrong, just keep typing.)

If, in Preferences, you turn on "User names and passwords," then each time you type a password into a Web page, Safari offers to memorize it for you. It's a great time and brain saver, even though it doesn't work on all Web sites. (Of course, use it with caution if you share an account on your Mac with other people.)

When you want Safari to "forget" your passwords—for security reasons, for example—revisit that Safari→Preferences→AutoFill tab. Click one of the Edit buttons, and then delete the Web site names for which your information has been stored.

Turn on Other Forms if you'd like Safari to remember the terms you've typed into search engines, shopping sites, online gaming sites, and so on.

- **Home.** Click to bring up the Web page you've designated as your home page (in Safari→Preferences→General tab).

- **AutoFill.** Click this button to make Safari fill in Web order forms with your name, address, and other information. See the box on the facing page.

- **Text Size.** You can adjust the point size of a Web page's text using these buttons. When you visit a Web site designed for Windows computers—whose text often looks too small on Mac screens—you can use these buttons to bump up the size. *Keyboard shortcut: ⌘-R.*

- **Add Bookmark.** When you find a Web page you might like to visit again, click this button. You can also press ⌘-D, or choose Bookmarks→Add Bookmark, or drag the tiny icon from the Address bar directly onto your Bookmarks bar.

  As shown in Figure 11-3, Safari offers to add this Web page's name (or a shorter name that you specify for it) either to the Bookmarks menu or to the Bookmarks *bar* described below. The next time you want to visit that page, just select its name in whichever location you chose.

Tip: Press Shift-⌘-D to add the bookmark to the menu instantly—no questions asked, no dialog box presented.

  You can rearrange the names in your Bookmarks menu easily: Just choose Bookmarks→Show All Bookmarks (Option-⌘-B), or click the tiny book icon shown in Figure 11-3. In the resulting organization window, drag the bookmarks up and down.

  For more dramatic management tasks—to edit, rename, or delete your bookmarks, for example—also see Figure 11-3.

- **Google Search.** Here's one of Safari's most useful features—a Search box that automatically sends your search request to Google.com, the world's most popular Web search page. It's kind of like the MSN Search Toolbar for Internet Explorer, just more compact and more convenient.

  In any case, press Option-⌘-F to deposit your insertion point inside this rounded text box, type something you're looking for, and then press Enter. Safari takes you straight to the Google results page.

Tip: Click the tiny triangle at the left end of the Google bar to produce a pop-up menu of your most recent searches.

Bonus Tip: If you Control-click (right-click) a highlighted word or phrase on a Web page, you can choose Google Search from the shortcut menu to search for that text. And, even cooler, this trick works in *all* Cocoa programs—not just in Safari.

- **Bug.** Ladies and gentleman, Apple at its most humble. This insect-shaped button opens a tiny "Dear Apple" box, where you can tell Apple about a Safari feature or

Web page that doesn't work. If you click Options, you can even send Apple a screen illustration of, for example, a screwy Web-page layout that Safari delivered.

Bookmarks bar

The Bookmarks menu is one way to maintaining a list of Web sites you visit frequently. But opening a Web page from that menu requires *two mouse clicks*—an exorbitant expenditure of energy. The Bookmarks bar (View→Bookmarks Bar), on the other hand, lets you summon a few *very* favorite Web pages with only one click.

Figure 11-3 illustrates how to add buttons to, and remove them from, this toolbar.

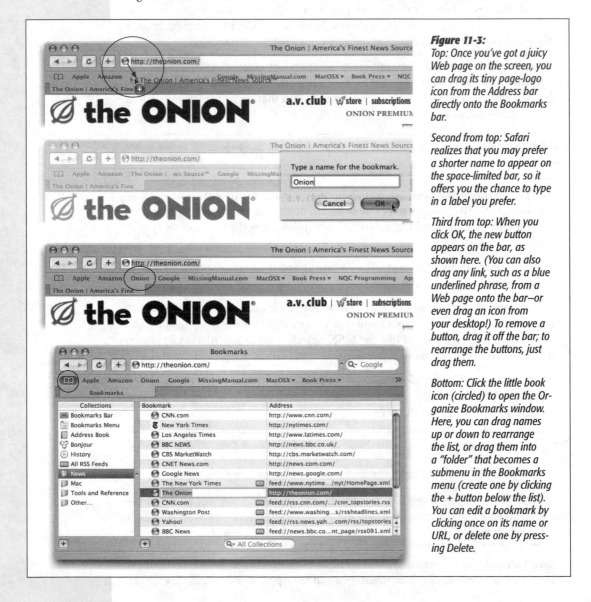

Figure 11-3:

Top: Once you've got a juicy Web page on the screen, you can drag its tiny page-logo icon from the Address bar directly onto the Bookmarks bar.

Second from top: Safari realizes that you may prefer a shorter name to appear on the space-limited bar, so it offers you the chance to type in a label you prefer.

Third from top: When you click OK, the new button appears on the bar, as shown here. (You can also drag any link, such as a blue underlined phrase, from a Web page onto the bar—or even drag an icon from your desktop!) To remove a button, drag it off the bar; to rearrange the buttons, just drag them.

Bottom: Click the little book icon (circled) to open the Organize Bookmarks window. Here, you can drag names up or down to rearrange the list, or drag them into a "folder" that becomes a submenu in the Bookmarks menu (create one by clicking the + button below the list). You can edit a bookmark by clicking once on its name or URL, or delete one by pressing Delete.

Status Bar

The Status bar at the bottom of the window tells you what Safari is doing (such as "Opening page…" or "Done"). When you point to a link without clicking, the Status bar also tells you which URL will open when you click it. For those two reasons, it's a very useful strip, but it doesn't appear when you first run Safari. You have to summon it by choosing View→Show Status Bar.

Tips for Better Surfing

Safari is filled with shortcuts and tricks for better speed and more pleasant surfing. For example:

SnapBack

The little orange SnapBack button ( ), at the right end of the Address bar or Google search bar, takes you instantly back to the Web page whose address you last typed (or whose bookmark you last clicked), or to your first Google results page. The point here is that, after burrowing from one link to another in pursuit of some Google result or Amazon listing, you can return to your starting point without having to mash the Back button over and over again. (The SnapBack button doesn't appear until you've actually clicked away from the first page you visited.)

Tip: At any time, you can designate your current page as the new SnapBack page. To do so, choose History→Mark Page for SnapBack (Option-⌘-K)

Stifle pop-ups and pop-unders

The world's smarmiest advertisers have begun inundating us with *pop-up* and *pop-under* ads—nasty little windows that appear in front of the browser window, or, worse, behind it, waiting to jump out the moment you close your current window. They're often deceptive, masquerading as error messages or dialog boxes, and they'll do absolutely anything to get you to click inside them.

If this kind of thing drives you crazy, choose Safari→Block Pop-Up Windows, so that a checkmark appears next to the command. It's a war out there—but at least you now have some ammunition.

Note: Unbidden pop-up windows are sometimes legitimate (and not ads)—notices of new banking features, warnings that the instructions to a site have changed, and so on. Safari can't tell these from ads and stifles them too. So if a site you trust says "Please turn off pop-up blockers and reload this page," you know you're probably missing out on a *useful* pop-up message.

Also, while Safari's pop-up blocker is better than Internet Explorer's on Windows, it's not perfect. You may, from time to time, encounter a pop-up that manages to sneak by.

Impersonating Internet Explorer

Sooner or later, you'll run into a Web site that doesn't work in Safari. Why? When you arrive at a Web site, your browser identifies itself. That's because many commercial

Web sites display a different version of the page depending on which browser your using, thanks to differences in the way various browsers interpret Web layouts.

But because you're still using the relatively unknown Safari browser, your otherwise beloved Web site tells you, "Sorry, browser not supported."

In such times of trouble, you can make Safari *impersonate* any other browser, which is usually good enough to fool the picky Web site into letting you in.

The key to this trick is Safari's Debug menu, which is generally hidden. You can make it appear using TinkerTool, a free program available on this book's "Missing CD" page at *www.missingmanuals.com*. TinkerTool offers a simple checkbox that turns on the Debug menu.

When you next open Safari, the new Debug menu appears right next to Help. Most of its commands are designed to appeal to programmers, but the submenu you want—User Agent—is useful to everyone. It lets Safari masquerade as a different browser. Choose User Agent→Mac MSIE 5.22, for example, to assume the identity of Internet Explorer for Macintosh.

Note: Unfortunately, there's a dark side to using this User Agent trick. If enough people pretend that they're using Internet Explorer, whoever created the Web site will never know how many people are actually using Safari–and will never get around to fixing the Web site.

Whenever you encounter a Web site that gives Safari trouble, therefore, you should also (a) take a moment to notify Apple of the problem and (b) notify the Webmaster of the site you're trying to visit that you want Safari compatibility.

Where am I?

As you dig your way down into a Web site, you may wish you could have left a trail of bread crumbs to mark your path. Ah, but Safari has already thought of that. See Figure 11-4.

Figure 11-4:
If you ⌘-click the title bar (centered just above the Address bar), Safari displays the "ladder" of pages you descended to arrive at the current one.

Faster browsing without graphics

Graphics are part of what makes the Web so compelling. But they're also responsible for making Web pages take so long to arrive on the screen. Without them, Web pages appear almost instantly—and you still get fully laid-out Web pages with all their text and headlines.

To turn off graphics, choose Safari→Preferences and click the Appearance tab. Turn off "Display images when the page opens," and close the Preferences window. Now try visiting a few Web pages and enjoy the substantial speed boost. (And if you wind up on a Web page that's nothing without its pictures, return to Safari→Preferences, turn the same checkbox on, and reload the page.)

Viewing Web pages offline

You don't have to be connected to the Net to read a favorite Web page. You can save a certain Web page on your hard drive so that you can peruse it later—on your laptop during your commute, for example—just by choosing File→Save As.

If you want to save the *entire* page, along with all its images, movies, and so on, be sure to choose Web Archive from the Format pop-up menu. If you're tight on hard drive space, though, choose Page Source instead; you'll still get all the text of the page, but without the fatty multimedia.

Tip: Whenever you buy something online, don't waste paper by printing out the final "This is your receipt" page. Instead, choose File→Print and, from the PDF pop-up menu, choose Save PDF to Web Receipts folder. Safari saves it as a PDF file into a tidy folder (in your Home→Documents folder) called Web Receipts.

Sending a page to a friend

Safari provides two different ways of telling a friend about the page you're looking at. You might find that feature useful when you come across a particularly interesting news story, op-ed piece, or burrito recipe.

- **The send-the-whole-page method.** While looking at a page, choose File→Mail Contents of This Page (⌘-I) to open a new Mail message with a copy of the *actual* Web page in the body. Address the message and click Send.

  Bear in mind that your recipient might not be so thrilled about this method. HTML messages (like the ones you send with this technique) are bandwidth-clogging monstrosities, so the message can take a while to download on the other end—especially over a dial-up connection. And even once it's downloaded, there's no guarantee your recipient will even be able to see the message, since some email programs can't display HTML messages at all.

- **The send-a-link method.** To send just a *link* to the page you're looking at, choose File→Mail Link to This Page (Shift-⌘-I). Then proceed as usual, addressing the message and clicking Send.

Links take only a split second for your recipient to download, and they're guaranteed to display properly in all email programs. All your recipients have to do is click the link to open it in their Web browsers.

Designate your home page

The first Web site you encounter when Safari connects to the Internet is an Apple Web site. This site is your *home page.* You'll probably find Web browsing more fun, though, if you specify your favorite Web page as your home page.

To do that, navigate your way to the page you prefer. Google, or its news page *http:// news.google.com,* is a good starting place. So is your favorite newspaper home page, or *www.macsurfer.com,* a summary of the day's Mac news coverage from around the world, or maybe *www.dilbert.com,* for today's Dilbert cartoon.

Then choose Safari→Preferences, click the General tab, and click Set to Current Page (or type the address into the box).

FREQUENTLY ASKED QUESTION

Erasing Your Tracks—And Private Browsing

So about this History menu: I'd just as soon my wife/husband/boss/parent/kid not know what Web sites I've been visiting. Must that History menu display my movements quite so proudly?

Some people find it creepy that Safari maintains a complete list of every Web site they've seen recently, right there in plain view of any family member or co-worker who wanders by.

To delete just one particularly incriminating History listing, click the book icon at the left end of the Bookmarks bar; in the resulting Bookmarks organizer window, click History. Expand the relevant date triangle, highlight the offending address, and then press the Delete key. Click the book icon again to return to normal browsing. You've just rewritten History!

Or, to erase the *entire* History menu, choose History→Clear History.

Of course, the History menu isn't the only place where you've left footprints. If you choose Safari→Reset Safari instead, you also erase all *other* shreds of your activities: any *cookies* (Web-page preference files) you've accumulated, your list of past downloads, the *cache* files (tiny Web graphics files on your hard drive that the browser stores to save time when you return to the page they came from), and so on. This is

good information to know; after all, you might be nominated to the Supreme Court some day.

That's a lot of work just to cover my tracks; it also erases a lot of valuable cookies, passwords, and History things I'd like to keep. Is all of that really necessary just so I can duck in for an occasional look at the Hot Bods of the Midwestern Tax Preparer's Association home page?

No, it's not. A new Tiger feature called *private browsing* lets you surf without adding any pages to your History list, any searches to your Google search box, any passwords to Safari's saved password list, or any cookies to your virtual cookie jar. (Apple says that this feature is intended for use at public Macs, where you don't want to reveal anything personal to subsequent visitors. Likely story.)

The trick is to choose Safari→Private Browsing *before* you start browsing. Once you OK the explanation box, Safari records nothing while you surf.

When you're ready to browse "publicly" again, choose Safari→Private Browsing so the checkmark goes away. Safari once again begins taking note of the pages you visit—but it never remembers the earlier ones. In other words, what happens in Private Browsing stays in Private Browsing.

If you can't decide on a home page, or your mood changes from day to day, use the "New window open with" pop-up menu to choose Empty Page. Some people prefer this setup, which makes Safari load very quickly when you first open it. Once the empty window opens, *then* you can tell the browser where you want to go today.

Tip: In the Safari→Preferences→General tab, you can also choose Bookmarks. Then, whenever you open a new window or launch Safari, you can choose exactly which page you want to open by choosing from a list of your bookmarks.

Return to the past

The History menu lists the Web sites you've visited in the last week or so, neatly organized into subfolders like "Earlier Today" and "Yesterday." (A similar menu appears when you click and *hold* on the Back or Forward button.) These are great features if you can't recall the URL for a Web site that you remember having visited recently.

Tabbed Browsing

Beloved by hard-core surfers the world over (and famously lacking in Internet Explorer) is *tabbed browsing*, a way to keep a bunch of Web pages open simultaneously in a single, neat window. Figure 11-5 illustrates the concept.

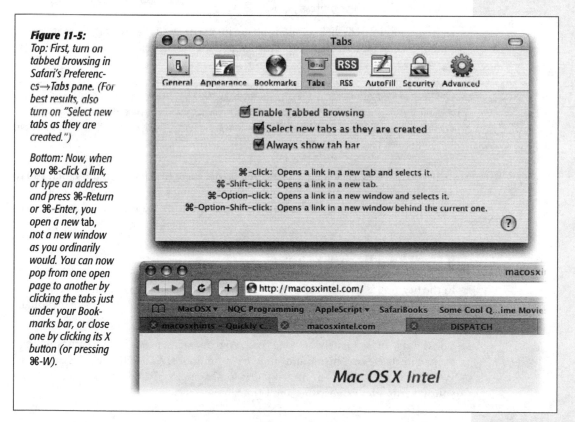

Figure 11-5:
Top: First, turn on tabbed browsing in Safari's Preferences→Tabs pane. (For best results, also turn on "Select new tabs as they are created.")

Bottom: Now, when you ⌘-click a link, or type an address and press ⌘-Return or ⌘-Enter, you open a new tab, not a new window as you ordinarily would. You can now pop from one open page to another by clicking the tabs just under your Bookmarks bar, or close one by clicking its X button (or pressing ⌘-W).

Turning on tabbed browsing unlocks a whole raft of Safari shortcuts and tricks, which are just the sort of thing power surfers gulp down like Gatorade:

- If there's a certain set of Web sites you like to visit daily, put the bookmarks into one folder, using the Bookmarks organizer window (Figure 11-5). You can then load all of them at once into a single tabbed window, simply by selecting the resulting "folder" in the Bookmarks menu—or the Bookmarks bar—and choosing Open in Tabs from the submenu.

  The beauty of this arrangement is that you can start reading the first Web page while all of the others load into their own tabs in the background.

Tip: Click the book icon at the left end of the Bookmarks bar. In the Bookmarks organizer, click the Bookmarks Bar icon in the left-side list. Now you can see an Auto-Click checkbox for each listed folder.

If you turn on this checkmark, you can then open all the bookmarks in that folder into tabs, all at once, merely by clicking the folder's name in the Bookmarks bar. (If you want to summon the *normal* menu from the folder, just hold the mouse button down.)

- If you Option-click a tab's X (close) button, you close all tabs *except* the one you clicked. The same thing happens if you hold down Option and choose File→Close Other Tabs, or if you press Option-⌘-W.

- If you Option-⌘-click a link, it opens in a separate window, rather than a new tab. (When tabbed browsing is turned *off*, you just ⌘-click a link to open a new window.)

Tip: Deep in the guts of Safari is a neatly formatted page that lists nearly every keyboard shortcut in the program. If you've installed the Debug menu as described on page 296, just choose Debug→Keyboard and Mouse shortcuts. Otherwise, Control-click the Safari icon in the Finder, choose Show Package Contents from the shortcut menu, and open Contents→Resources→Shortcuts.html.

- If you Shift-⌘-click a link, Safari opens that page in a tab *behind* the one you're reading. That's a fantastic trick when you're reading a Web page and see a reference you want to set aside for reading next, but you don't want to interrupt whatever you're reading.

RSS: The Missing Manual

In the beginning, the Internet was an informational Garden of Eden. There were no banner ads, pop-ups, flashy animations, or spam messages. Back then, people thought the Internet was the greatest idea ever.

Those days, unfortunately, are long gone. Web browsing now entails a constant battle against intrusive advertising and annoying animations. And with the proliferation of Web sites of every kind—from news sites to personal Web logs (*blogs*)—just reading your favorite sites can become a full-time job.

Enter RSS, a technology that lets you subscribe to *feeds*—summary blurbs provided by thousands of sources around the world, from Reuters to Apple to your nerdy next-door neighbor. You use a program like Safari to "subscribe" to updates from such feeds, and then read any new articles or postings at your leisure.

The result: You spare yourself the tedium of checking for updates manually, plus you get to read short summaries of new articles without ads and blinking animations. And if you want to read a full article, you can click its link in the RSS feed to jump straight to the main Web site.

> **Note:** RSS either stands for Rich Site Summary or Really Simple Syndication. Each abbreviation explains one aspect of RSS—either its summarizing talent or its simplicity.

Viewing an RSS Feed

So how do you sign up for these free, automatic RSS "broadcasts?" Watch your Address bar as you're surfing the Web. When you see a blue RSS button appear (identified in Figure 11-6), Safari is telling you, "This site has an RSS feed available."

To see what all the fuss is about, click that button. Safari switches into RSS-viewing mode, as shown in Figure 11-6.

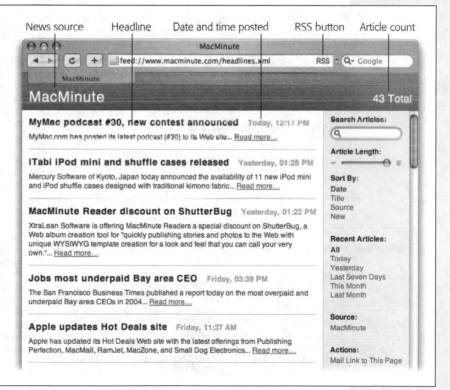

Figure 11-6:
The Length slider controls how much text appears for each RSS blurb, if you drag it all the way to the left, you're left with nothing but the headlines. To change the number and order of the articles being displayed, use the search options on the right. And if you feel a sudden desire to tell your friends about an amazing RSS feed you've just discovered, use the "Mail Link to This Page" link in the lower-right section of the window.

At this point, you have two choices:

- **Add the RSS feed as a bookmark.** Use the Bookmarks→Add Bookmark command, and add the feed to your Bookmarks menu or Bookmarks bar as you would any Web page. From now on, you'll be able to see whether the RSS feed has had any new articles posted—without actually having to visit the site. Figure 11-6 has the details.

- **Close the RSS feed altogether.** To do so, just click the RSS button again. You're back where you started, at whatever Web page you were visiting.

RSS Tricks

RSS is a tremendously flexible and powerful technology, especially in Safari's able hands. The fun never ends, as these tricks illustrate.

Creating RSS summaries

If you create a new bookmark folder and fill it with RSS feeds, you can see the total number of new articles right next to the folder's name (Figure 11-7, bottom). You

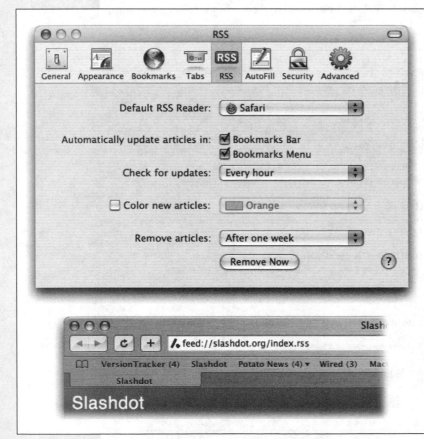

Figure 11-7:
Top: Want to specify when Safari should check for updates to your RSS bookmarks? In Safari→ Preferences, click RSS. Turn on Bookmarks Bar and Bookmarks Menu. (If you're an especially impatient person, select "Every 30 minutes" from the "Check for updates" pop-up menu.)

Bottom: Next to your RSS feeds' names (in this screenshot, VersionTracker and Wired), a number tells you how many new articles are waiting for you. If you have a bookmark folder containing several RSS feeds in it (here, Potato News), the number reflects the total number of new articles in that folder's feeds. Never again will you have to check a Web site for updates the old-fashioned way.

might create a folder of Mac news feeds, for instance, so you know whenever there's an important event in the Mac world.

From then on, by clicking the folder's name (and opening its pop-up menus), you can see which feeds have new articles; they're the ones with numbers next to their names. If you ⌘-click a bookmark folder's name—in either the Bookmarks bar or the Bookmarks menu—Safari shows you *all* of the feeds, neatly collated into one big, easily digestible list for your perusing pleasure. (If you're billing by the hour, you can also choose View All RSS Articles from the folder's pop-up menu to achieve the same effect.)

Tip: To make the merged list more useful, click New under the "Sort By" heading. Now Safari displays any new articles at the top of the list, regardless of what site they came from, so you don't have to hunt through the list for new articles yourself.

The personal clipping service

The search box at the right of any RSS-viewing window works pretty much as you'd expect: It narrows down the list of articles to only those that contain your search terms.

But that's barely scratching the surface of the search field's power. If you've adopted the feed-merging trick described above, the Search box can search *several* feeds at once—perfect, for example, if you want to see all the news from Mac sites that has to do with iTunes.

But get this—you can then save the search *itself* as a bookmark. Use the Bookmark This Search link at the lower-right corner of the window. Give the bookmark a name, choose where it should appear in Safari, and click Add.

You've just turned Safari into a high-tech personal clipping service. With one click on your new bookmark, you can search all of your favorite news sources simultaneously—the feeds you've just selected—for the terms you want. You've just saved yourself *hours* of daily searching—not to mention the expense of a real clipping service.

The RSS screen saver

In System Preferences→Desktop & Screen Saver, you'll find the RSS Visualizer screen saver, one of the most impressive displays of Mac OS X technology you'll ever see. When you click Options and select an RSS feed (and enable screen savers, as described on page 361), you set up Mac OS X to get news from that feed whenever you're away from your Mac. When the screen saver comes on, you're treated to a three-dimensional animation of the news from that site—along with astonished gazes from your co-workers.

If the news story grabs your interest, press the number key mentioned at the bottom of the screen. The screen saver fades out, and Safari comes forward to display the associated article.

Tip: If the feed you want isn't part of System Preferences' repertoire, just add the feed to your *Safari* bookmarks and relaunch System Preferences.

Make feeds open automatically

As described on page 298, you can easily set up any favorite Web site as your home page, the page that opens automatically whenever you start Safari or create a new window.

It turns out, though, that you can also make an RSS feed—or a list of feeds—your home page. Open the feeds you want, choose Safari→Preferences, click General, and click Set to Current Page.

If you started by opening a list of local, national, international, business, and sports news feeds, you've just made yourself a great imitation of a newspaper, but tailored to *your* interests. Plus, articles in this Safari-newspaper arrangement are timelier than anything you could read in print—and they're completely free.

Tip: To find more RSS feeds, visit a site like *www.feedster.com,* or just watch for the appearance of the blue RSS button in the Address bar.

By the way, Safari isn't the only RSS reader for Mac OS X. If you catch the RSS bug, you might want to try a program like NetNewsWire (*http://ranchero.com/netnewswire/*), which offers a more advanced layout and many more options.

iChat

If you're an instant-messaging junkie, good news: All three of the biggies, AIM (America Online Instant Messenger), MSN Messenger, and Yahoo Messenger are available for Mac OS X—and you use them exactly as you did in Windows. (Download them from *www.aim.com, www.microsoft.com/mac,* and *http://messenger.yahoo.com,* respectively.) Once you start using the Mac versions of these programs, you'll find that your old buddy lists are intact and ready to use—no importing necessary.

AIM, Yahoo, and MSN Messenger are not, however, the only chat games in town. Apple has created its own take on instant messaging—something called iChat.

Of course, Apple would be nuts to create a fourth, mutually incompatible network standard. Fortunately, it wasn't quite that crazy: iChat is AIM-compatible, so you can type back and forth with any of AIM's millions of members. But iChat's visual design is pure Apple, complete with comic strip–style word balloons and a candy-coated interface.

You'll find, too, that iChat supports three *different* types of communication:

- **Instant messaging.** This is what you've come to expect from chat programs on Windows: it's like live email.

- **Free long distance.** If your Mac has a microphone—and so does your buddy—the two of you can also chat *out loud,* using the Internet as a free long-distance telephone. (Thanks to Mac OS X's beefed-up audio conferencing features, you can have up to *ten* participants, provided you have a recent Mac model.)

- **Free videoconferencing.** If you and your buddies each have broadband Internet connections and a FireWire camera—like Apple's own iSight camera, or (if you have a recent Mac model) even a digital camcorder—up to four participants can join in *video* chats, all on screen at once, no matter where they happen to be in the world. This arrangement is a jaw-dropping visual stunt that can bring distant collaborators face-to-face without plane tickets.

Three Chat Networks

iChat lets you reach out to chat partners on three different networks:

- **The AIM network.** If you've signed up for a .Mac address (the free kind or the paid kind) or a free AOL Instant Messenger account, you can chat with anyone in the huge AOL Instant Messenger network.

- **The Jabber network.** Jabber is another chat network, whose key virtue is its *open source* origins. In other words, it wasn't masterminded by some corporate media behemoth; it's an all-volunteer effort, joined by thousands of programmers around the world. There's no one Jabber chat program (like AOL Instant Messenger). There are dozens, available for Mac OS X, Windows, Linux, Unix, Palm and PocketPC organizers, and so on. All of them can chat with each other across the Internet in one glorious frenzy of typing. Now iChat joins the crowd.

- **Your own local network.** Thanks to the Bonjour network-recognition technology, you can communicate with other Macs on your own office network without signing up for anything at all—and without being online. This is a terrific feature when you're sitting around a conference table, using your wireless laptop to idly chat with colleagues (and the boss thinks you're taking notes).

These three kinds of chats operate in parallel. Each network (AIM, Jabber, and Bonjour) has its own separate Buddy List window and its own chat window. You log into each network separately.

Otherwise, however, chatting works identically on all three networks. Keep that in mind as you read the following pages.

Signing Up

When you open iChat for the first time, you see the "Welcome To iChat" window (Figure 11-8). This is the first of several screens in the iChat setup sequence, during which you're supposed to enter which kinds of chat accounts you have, and set up a camera (if you have one).

An *account* is a name and password. Fortunately, chatting accounts are free, and there are several ways to acquire one.

Tip: The easiest procedure is to get an account *before* you open iChat for the first time, because then you can just plug in your names and passwords in the setup screens.

You *can* input your account information later, though. Choose iChat→Preferences, click the Accounts button, click the + button, and choose the right account type (Jabber, .Mac, or AIM) from the Account Type pop-up menu.

How to get a free .Mac account

If you're already a member of Apple's .Mac service (page 147), iChat fills in your Mac.com user name and password automatically.

If not, you can get an iChat-only .Mac account for free. To get started, do one of these two things:

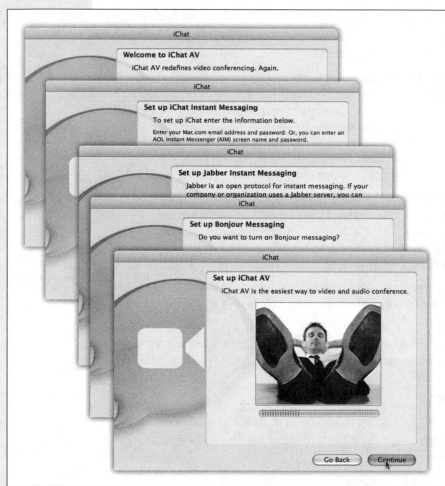

Figure 11-8:
The iChat setup assistant gives you the chance to input your account names and passwords—if you already have them. Only one of these screens ("Set up iChat instant messaging") offers you the chance to create a chat account—in this case, a free .Mac account. Otherwise, you're expected to have a name and password (for AIM or Jabber, for example) already. Finally, if you have an iSight camera or camcorder attached, you get the chance to test it out. The volume meter at the bottom bounces in response to your Mac's or camcorder's microphone.

- Click the "Get an iChat Account" button that appears on the second Setup Assistant screen.

- Choose iChat→Preferences, click the Accounts button, click the + button, and click Create New .Mac Account.

Either way, you go to an Apple Web page where you can sign up for a free iChat account name. You'll also get 60 days of the more complete .Mac treatment (usually $100 a year). When your trial period ends, you'll lose all of the other stuff that .Mac provides, but you'll get to keep your iChat name.

Note: If your .Mac name is *missingmanualguy,* you'll actually appear to everyone else as *missingmanualguy@mac.com.* The software tacks on the "@mac.com" automatically.

How to get a free Jabber account

You can't create a Jabber account using iChat. Apple expects that, if you're that interested in Jabber, you already have an account that's been set up by the company you work for (Jabber is popular in corporations) or by you, using one of the free Jabber programs.

For example, at *www.adiumx.com*, you can download a great chat program for Mac OS X that presents you, the first time you open it, with a Preferences:Accounts screen. Click the + button, choose Jabber, type in any screen name and password you like—and when you're told that your account doesn't exist, mutter "I know, I know," and click Register. Your account is now created (your account name is *Francis@jabber.com,* for example), and you can plug that screen name and password into iChat.

How to get a free AIM account

You can't create an AIM account in iChat either. If you're an America Online member, your existing screen name and password work fine; if you've used AIM before, you can use your existing name and password from there.

If you've never had an AIM account, you can sign up at *my.screenname.aol.com.* Click "Create one FREE now" to make up an AIM screen name.

The Buddy List

Once you've entered your account information, you're technically ready to start chatting. All you need now is a chatting companion, or what's called a *buddy* in instant-messaging circles. iChat comes complete with a Buddy List window in which you can house the chat addresses for all your friends, relatives, and colleagues out there on the Internet.

Actually, to be precise, iChat comes with *three* buddy lists (Figure 11-9):

- **Buddy List.** This window lists all of your chat pals who have either .Mac or AIM accounts; they all share the same buddy list. You see the same list whether you log into your .Mac or your AIM account. (You can't log into both simultaneously.)

- **Jabber List.** Same idea, except that all of your contacts in this window must have Jabber accounts.

- **Bonjour.** This list is limited to your local network buddies—most likely the ones in the same building, and on the same network. You can't add names to your Bonjour list; anyone who's on the network and running iChat appears automatically in the Bonjour list.

Making a list

When you start iChat, your buddy lists automatically appear (Figure 11-9). If you don't see them, choose the list you want from the Window menu: Buddy List, Bonjour, or Jabber. (Or press their keyboard shortcuts: ⌘-1, ⌘-2, or ⌘-3.)

Adding a buddy to this list entails knowing that person's account name, and whether it's on AIM, Mac.com, or Jabber. Once you know that, you can either choose Buddies→Add a Buddy (Shift-⌘-A) or click the + button at the bottom-left corner of the window.

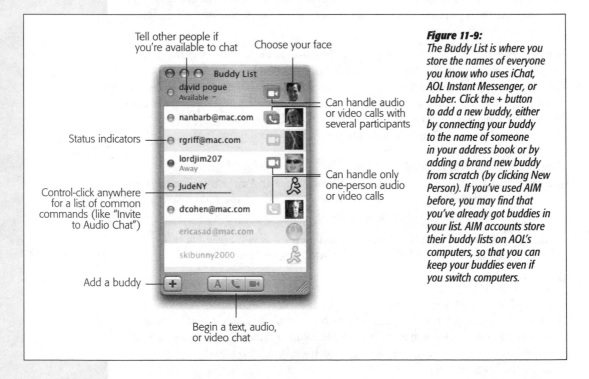

Tell other people if you're available to chat

Choose your face

Status indicators

Control-click anywhere for a list of common commands (like "Invite to Audio Chat")

Add a buddy

Can handle audio or video calls with several participants

Can handle only one-person audio or video calls

Begin a text, audio, or video chat

Figure 11-9:
The Buddy List is where you store the names of everyone you know who uses iChat, AOL Instant Messenger, or Jabber. Click the + button to add a new buddy, either by connecting your buddy to the name of someone in your address book or by adding a brand new buddy from scratch (by clicking New Person). If you've used AIM before, you may find that you've already got buddies in your list. AIM accounts store their buddy lists on AOL's computers, so that you can keep your buddies even if you switch computers.

Out slides a sheet attached to the Buddy List window, offering a window into the Mac OS X Address Book program (Chapter 10).

If your chat companion is already in Address Book, scroll through the list until you find the name you want (or enter the first few letters into the Search box), click the name, and then click Select Buddy.

If not, click New Person and enter the buddy's AIM address, .Mac address, or (if you're in the Jabber list) Jabber address. You're adding this person to both your Buddy List and Address Book.

Tip: Using the pop-up menu just below your name, you can broadcast your status to *other* people's buddy lists. You can announce that you're Available, Away, or (by choosing Custom or Edit Status Menu) Drunk.

Cooler still, if you have music playing in iTunes, you can tell the world what you're listening to at the moment by choosing Current Track. (Your buddy can even click that song's name to open its screen on the iTunes Music Store.)

Let the Chat Begin

As with any conversation, somebody has to talk first. In chat circles, that's called *inviting* someone to a chat.

They invite you

To "turn on your pager" so that you'll be notified when someone wants to chat with you, run iChat. Hide its windows, if you like, by pressing ⌘-H.

When someone tries to "page" you for a chat, iChat comes forward automatically and shows you an invitation message like the one in Figure 11-10. If the person initiating a chat isn't already in your Buddy List, you'll simply see a note that says "Message from *[name of the person]*."

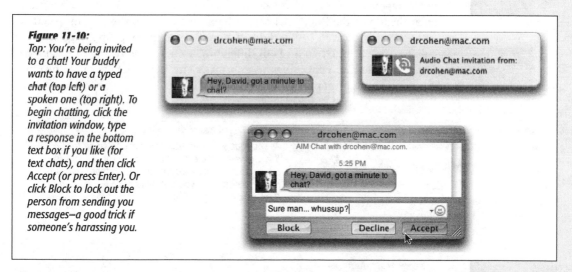

Figure 11-10:
Top: You're being invited to a chat! Your buddy wants to have a typed chat (top left) or a spoken one (top right). To begin chatting, click the invitation window, type a response in the bottom text box if you like (for text chats), and then click Accept (or press Enter). Or click Block to lock out the person from sending you messages—a good trick if someone's harassing you.

You invite them

To invite somebody in your Buddy List to a chat:

- For a text chat, double-click the person's *name,* type a quick invite ("You there?"), and press Enter.

Tip: You can invite more than one person to the chat. Each time you click the + button at the bottom of the Participants list, you can choose another person to invite. (Or ⌘-click each name in the buddy list to select several people at once and then click the A button at the bottom of the list to start the text chat.)

Everyone sees all the messages everyone sends.

- To start an audio or video chat, click the microphone or movie-camera icon in your Buddy List (shown in Figure 11-9).

To initiate a chat with someone who *isn't* in the Buddy List, choose File→New Chat With Person. Type the account name of the person and click OK to send the invitation.

Either way, you can have more than one chat going at once. Real iChat nerds wind up with screens overflowing with individual chat windows. Juggling them all, and keeping them all current, is just part of the fun.

Text Chatting

A typed chat works like this: Each time you or your chat partner types something and then presses Enter, the text appears on both your screens (Figure 11-11). iChat displays each typed comment next to an icon. The icon may be one your chat partner added, a picture *you* added (in Address Book, for example), or a generic icon if neither of you has put any effort into it.

To use a graphic as your *own* icon, click the square picture to the right of your own name at the top of the Buddy, Jabber, or Bonjour list. From the pop-up palette of recently selected pictures, choose Edit Picture to open the pop-up image selection palette. Feel free to build an array of different graphics to represent yourself—and to change them in mid-chat using this pop-up palette, to the delight or confusion of your conversation partner.

Figure 11-11:
As you chat, your comments always appear on the right. If you haven't yet created a custom icon, you'll look like a blue globe or an androgynous AOL cartoon. You can choose a picture for yourself either in your own Address Book card or right in iChat.

Tip: When you minimize the iChat message window, its Dock icon displays the icon of the person you're chatting with—a handy reminder of who it actually is.

In-chat fun

Typing back and forth isn't the only thing you can do during a chat. You can also perform any of these stunts:

- **Open the drawer.** Choose View→Show Chat Participants to hide or show the "drawer" that lists every person in your current chat. To invite somebody new to the chat, click the + button at the bottom of the drawer, or drag the person's icon out of the Buddy List window and into this drawer.

- **Format your text.** You can press ⌘-B or ⌘- to make your next typed utterance bold or italic. Or change your color or font by choosing Format→Show Colors or Format→Show Fonts, which summons the standard Mac OS X color or font palettes. (If you use some weird font that your chat partners don't have installed, they won't see the same typeface.)

- **Insert a smiley.** When you choose a face (like Undecided, Angry, or Frown) from this quick-access menu of smiley options (at the right end of the text-reply box), iChat inserts it as a graphic into your response.

  On the other hand, if you know the correct symbols to produce smileys—where :) means a smiling face, for example—you can save time by typing them instead of using the pop-up menu. iChat converts them into smiley icons on the fly, as soon as you send your reply.

- **Send a File.** Choosing Buddies→Send File lets you send a file to *all* the participants of your chat. Better yet, just drag the file's icon from the Finder into the box where you normally type, or, onto the buddy's name in the Buddy list. (This trick works well with pictures, because they appear right in your pal's iChat window.)

Tip: This is a fantastic way to transfer a file that would be too big to send by email. A chat window never gets "full," and no attachment is too large to send. This method halves the time of transfer, too, since your recipients get the file *as* you upload it.

Note, though, that this feature doesn't always work if your recipient is using an old version of the AOL Instant Messenger program.

- **Get Info on someone.** If you click the name of someone in your Buddy list and then choose Buddies → Get Info, you get a little Info window about your buddy, where you can edit her name, address, and picture.

  If you choose Actions from the Show pop-up menu, at this point, you can make iChat react when this particular buddy logs in, logs out, or changes status—for example, by playing a sound or saying, "She's here! She's here!"

- **Send an Instant Message.** Not everything in a chat session has to be "heard" by all participants. If you choose Buddies → Send an Instant Message, you'll get a *private* chat window, where you can "whisper" something directly to a special someone behind the other chatters' backs.

- **Send Direct Message.** A Direct Message (Buddies→Send Direct Message) is exactly like an Instant Message, except that it sends a message *Mac to Mac*, rather than via AOL's central server (which is what happens during an Instant Message session).

- **Send Email.** If someone messages you, "Hey, will you email me directions?" you can do so on the spot by choosing Buddies→Send Email. Your email program opens up automatically so you can send the note along; if your buddy's email address is part of his Address Book card, the message is preaddressed.

- **Send an SMS message to a cellphone.** If you're using an AIM screen name, and you know somebody whose cell phone can get SMS (Short Message Service) notes, try this wacky variation: Choose File→New Chat with Person. In the address box that pops up, type +1 and then the full cell phone number. For (212) 555-1212, you'd type this: *+12125551212*.

Press Enter to return to the chat window. Type a very short message (a couple of sentences, tops) and then press Enter.

Popping the balloons

The words you might have for iChat's word-balloon design might be "cute" and "distinctive." But it's equally likely that your choice of words includes "juvenile" and "annoying."

Fortunately, behind iChat's candy coating are enough options that you'll certainly find one that works for you (Figure 11-12).

You can even change iChat's white background to any image using View→Set Chat Background. Better yet, find a picture you like and drag it into your chat window; iChat immediately makes it the background of your chat. To get rid of the background and revert to soothing white, choose View→Clear Chat Background.

Audio Chats

iChat becomes much more exciting when you exploit the audiovisual features. Even over a dial-up modem connection, you can conduct audio chats, where you speak into your microphone and listen to the responses from your speaker.

If you have a broadband connection, though, you get a much more satisfying experience—and, if you have a pretty recent Mac, up to 10 of you can join in one massive, free conference call from across the Internet.

A telephone icon next to a name in your Buddy List tells you that the buddy has a microphone, and is ready for a free Internet "phone call." If you see what appear to be stacked phone icons, then your pal's Mac has enough horsepower to handle a *multiple-person* conference call. (You can see these icons back in Figure 11-9).

To begin an audio chat, click the telephone icon next to the buddy's name, or highlight someone in the Buddy List and then click the telephone icon at the bottom of the list, or (if you're already in a text chat) choose Buddies→Invite to Audio Chat.

Once your invitation is accepted, you can begin speaking to each other. The bars of the sound-level meter let you know that the microphone—which you've specified in the iChat→Preferences→Video tab—is working.

Note: Although the audio is *full-duplex* (you can hear and speak simultaneously, like a phone but unlike a walkie-talkie), there may be a delay, like you're calling overseas on a bad connection.

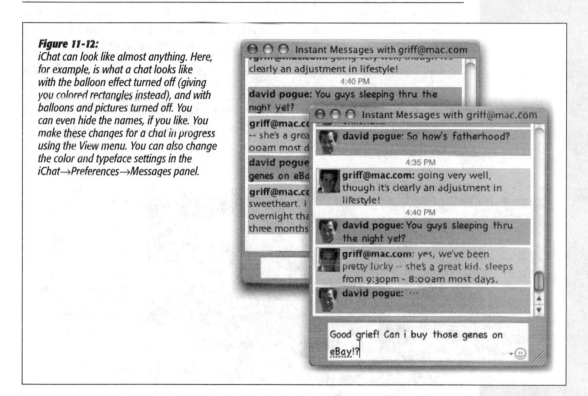

Figure 11-12:
iChat can look like almost anything. Here, for example, is what a chat looks like with the balloon effect turned off (giving you colored rectangles instead), and with balloons and pictures turned off. You can even hide the names, if you like. You make these changes for a chat in progress using the View menu. You can also change the color and typeface settings in the iChat→Preferences→Messages panel.

Video Chats

If you and your partner both have broadband Internet connections, even more impressive feats await. You can conduct a free video chat with up to four people, who show up on three vertical panes, gorgeously reflected on a shiny black table surface. This isn't the jerky, out-of-audio-sync, Triscuit-sized video of Windows videoconferencing. If you've got the Mac muscle and bandwidth, your partners are as crisp, clear, bright, and smooth as television—and as big as your screen, if you like.

People can come and go; as they enter and leave the "videosphere," iChat slides their glistening screens aside, enlarging or shrinking them as necessary to fit on your screen.

Apple offers this luxurious experience, however, only if you have both a video camera with a FireWire connector and Mac with a 600-megahertz G3 processor (for one-on-one video chats) or a G4- or G5-based Mac made in the past few years (for multi-person video chats).

Tip: You don't both need the same gear. If only you have a camera, for example, you can choose Buddies→Invite to One-Way Video Chat (or Audio Chat). Your less-equipped buddy can see (or hear) you, but has to speak or type in response.

If you see a camcorder icon next to a buddy's name, you can have a full-screen, high-quality video chat with that person, because he, like you, has a camcorder or FireWire camera and a high-speed Internet connection. If you see a *stacked* camera icon, then that person has a fast enough Mac to join a four-way video chat.

To begin a video chat, click the camera icon next to a buddy's name. Or, if you're already in a text chat, choose Buddies→Invite to Video Chat.

A window opens, showing *you.* This preview mode is intended to show you what your buddy will see. (You'll probably discover that you need some kind of light in front of you to avoid being too shadowy.)

Figure 11-13:
That's you in the smaller window. To move your own mini-window, click a different corner, or drag yourself to a different corner. If you need to blow your nose or do something unseemly, Option-click the microphone button to freeze the video and mute the audio. Click again to resume.

And now, some video-chat notes:

- If your conversation partners seem unwilling to make eye contact, it's not because they're lying. They're just looking at *you,* on the screen, rather than at the camera—and chances are that you aren't looking into your camera, either.
- Don't miss the Video→Full Screen command! Wild.

- You can have video chats with Windows computers, too, as long as they're using a recent version of AOL Instant Messenger. Be prepared for disappointment, though; the video is generally jerky, small, and slightly out of sync.

- If you use iChat with a camcorder, you can set the camera to VTR (playback) mode and play a tape right over the Internet to whoever's on the other end. (The video appears flipped horizontally on your screen, but looks right to the other person.)

- You can't record audio or video—at least not without a screen-recording shareware program like Snapz Pro X (*www.ambrosiasw.com*). But you can capture a still "photo" of a video chat by ⌘-dragging the image to your desktop, or by choosing Video→Take Snapshot (Option-⌘-S).

- If you're having network trouble (or getting poor-fidelity chats), the Video→ Connection Doctor may be able to help. Otherwise, check iChat's help files for connection tips.

iChat Tweaks

If you've done nothing but chat in iChat, you haven't even scratched the surface. The iChat→Preferences window gives you plenty of additional control. For example:

- **General pane.** If you turn on **Show status in menu bar,** you bring the iChat *menulet* to your menu bar. It lets you change your iChat status (Available, Away, and so on), whether you're in iChat or not.

- **Accounts pane.** If you have more than one AIM, Jabber, or .Mac account, you can switch among them here. Your passwords are conveniently saved in your Mac OS X Keychain.

- **Messages pane.** The Messages pane lets you design your chat windows—the background color, word balloon color, and typeface and size of text you type.

- **Alerts pane.** Here, you can choose how iChat responds to various events. For example, it can play a sound, bounce its Dock icon, or say something out loud whenever you log in, log out, receive new messages, or whatever.

- **Video pane.** This is where you get a preview of your own camera's output, limit the amount of bandwidth (signal-hogging data) the camera uses (a troubleshooting step), and specify that you want iChat to fire up automatically whenever you switch on the camera.

Sherlock

Sherlock is like a Web browser that's specifically fine-tuned to bring you the most popular kinds of Web info, without the waiting, without the navigation hassle, and without the ads. With Dashboard (page 108), however, you have most of the same features at your fingertips in *any* program, with a single keystroke. Sherlock, therefore, is quickly losing any edge it ever had in the information-access department.

Among the channels that can safely be ignored are Stocks, Phone Book, Flights, Dictionary, Translation (all of which are now in Dashboard), and Internet (a basic Web search, supplanted by Safari's Google toolbar). Even Sherlock's eBay tracker is a lame duck, since Dashboard has several terrific widgets that do the same thing. (Check *www.apple.com/downloads/dashboard.*)

But three remaining Sherlock modules are still useful, in some cases because they're not yet available as Dashboard modules. Here's a rundown.

Pictures

Need a photo of something? Type in whatever you're looking for into this channel's "Picture Topic or Description" box—*Santa Claus, October squash, Keanu Reeves*—and then press Enter. In a flash, you see thumbnails of photographs from commercial stock-photo Web pages all over the Internet that match your search (see Figure 11-14). Double-click one to view its Web page in your browser, so that you can download it—and pay for it.

Tip: For noncommercial use, the Image Search tab of Google.com is far more powerful. It finds far more pictures on the topic you're seeking, because it grabs them from thousands of everyday Web pages, rather than limiting its search to stock-photo companies. (Yes, you should ask permission from one of the Web sites whose pictures appear before you use it for some other purpose.)

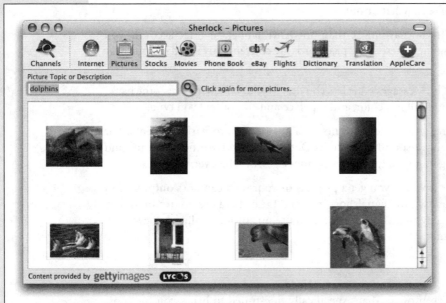

Figure 11-14:
If you're a busy graphic designer with the money to pay for professionally captured, professional-resolution digital images, this channel can be very useful. It's like having the searchable catalogs of several stock-art companies at your fingertips.

Movies

This channel makes finding a movie or theater in your neighborhood so easy and efficient that Moviefone.com looks positively antique by comparison. As you can see in Figure 11-15, it's an instantly updated database of movies and show times for your neighborhood.

True enough, you can download Dashboard widgets that show local movie times. But Sherlock also shows movie descriptions, ratings, cast lists, and even QuickTime video previews, which is nothing to sneeze at.

The only thing stopping this module from becoming an international smash hit is that...well, it doesn't work internationally. It knows only about movie theaters in the United States.

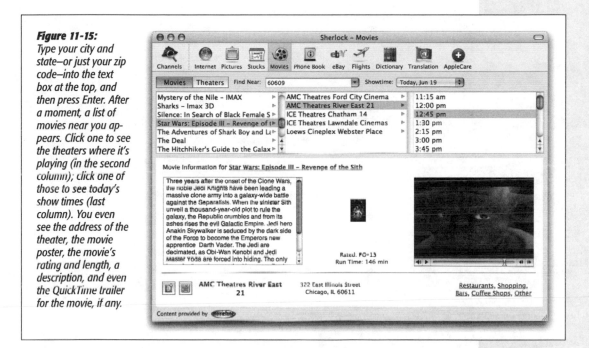

Figure 11-15:
Type your city and state–or just your zip code–into the text box at the top, and then press Enter. After a moment, a list of movies near you appears. Click one to see the theaters where it's playing (in the second column); click one of those to see today's show times (last column). You even see the address of the theater, the movie poster, the movie's rating and length, a description, and even the QuickTime trailer for the movie, if any.

AppleCare

This module gives you a direct line to Apple's Knowledge Base, a huge collection of answers, troubleshooting tips, and feature explanations for every Mac model ever made. It's based on the same technical library consulted by Apple's tech-support representatives, so you may as well check it before you call the Apple help line.

The trick is to use just a few words in the Topic or Description box—you might type *Simple Finder*, for example, or *Windows networking*. When you press Enter, you see a list of the articles from the library. Click one to read the article in the bottom half of the window.

SWITCHING TO THE MAC: THE MISSING MANUAL

Part Four:
Putting Down Roots

4

Accounts and Security

In an era where *security* is a high-tech buzzword, Apple was smart to make security a focal point for Mac OS X. The built-in security features in Mac OS X can protect you from hacker attacks; erase your hard drive so no one can ever recover your private information; and clean up the digital tracks you leave as you browse the Web. You'll be grateful for Mac OS X's protection when you hear horror stories about security breaches from your Windows-using friends—or on the evening news.

Another important component of Mac OS X's security scheme involves *accounts,* which let each person who uses your Mac keep his information private. In combination, therefore, Mac OS X's protections keep your data safe from nosy co-workers *and* from malevolent hackers.

This chapter covers Mac OS X's security features in all their various incarnations.

Introducing Accounts

Like the Unix under its skin (and also like Windows XP and Windows 2000), Mac OS X is designed from the ground up to be a multiple-user operating system. A Mac OS X machine can be configured so that everyone must *log in*—click or type her name and type in a password—when the computer turns on. And you're doing so, you discover the Macintosh universe just as you left it, which includes these elements:

- Your documents, files, and folders

- Your preference settings in every program you use; Web browser bookmarks; desktop picture; screen saver; language choice; icons on the desktop and in the Dock; and so on

• Email accounts, including personal information and mailboxes.

• Your personally installed programs and fonts.

• Your choice of programs that launch automatically at startup.

If you're the only person who uses your Mac, you can safely skip this chapter. The Mac will never ask you for the name and password you made up when you installed Mac OS X, because Apple's installer automatically turns on something called *automatic login* (page 334). You *will* be using one of these accounts, though, whether you realize it or not.

Furthermore, when you're stuck in line at the Department of Motor Vehicles, you may find the concepts presented here worth skimming, as certain elements of this multiple-user operating system may intrude upon your solo activities—and the discussions in this book—from time to time.

Tip: Even if you don't share your Mac with anyone and don't create any other accounts, you might still be tempted to learn about this feature because of its ability to password-protect the entire computer. All you have to do is to turn *off* the automatic login feature described on page 334. Thereafter, your Mac is protected from unauthorized fiddling when you're away from your desk or when your laptop is stolen.

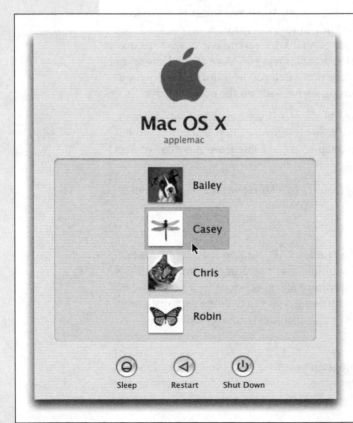

Figure 12-1:
When you set up several accounts, you don't turn on the Mac so much as sign into *it. A command in the* *menu called Log Out summons this sign-in screen. Click your own name and then type your password to get past this box and into your own stuff.*

The First Account

The first time you turn on a Mac OS X Mac (or install Mac OS X), the screen asks you for a name and password. You may not have realized it at the time, but you were creating the first *user account* on your Macintosh. Since that fateful day, you may have made a number of changes to your Mac's appearance—adjusted the Dock settings, set up your folders and desktop the way you like them, added some favorites to your Web browser, and so on—without realizing that you were actually making these changes only to *your account.*

You've probably been saving your documents into your own Home folder, which is the cornerstone of your account. This folder, generally named after you and stashed in the Users folder on your hard drive, stores not only your work, but also your preference settings for all the programs you use, special fonts that you've installed, your own email collection, and so on.

Now then: Suppose you create an account for a second person. When she turns on the computer and signs in, she'll find the desktop exactly the way it was factory-installed by Apple—blue swirling desktop picture, Dock along the bottom, the default Web browser home page, and so on. She can make the same kinds of changes to the Mac that you've made, but nothing she does will affect *your* environment the next time you log in.

In other words, the multiple-accounts feature has two components: first, a convenience element that hides everyone else's junk; and second, a security element that protects both the Mac's system software and everybody's work.

All of this works much the same way it does in Windows 2000 and Windows XP. There are just a few differences, as explained on the following pages.

Administrator vs. Standard Accounts

If you like the idea of this multiple-accounts business, begin by opening System Preferences (Chapter 13). In the System Preferences window, click Accounts.

The screen shown in Figure 12-2 appears, displaying the list of everyone who has an account. If you're new at this, there's probably just one account listed here: yours. This is the account that Mac OS X created when you first installed it.

Administrator Accounts

It's important to understand the phrase you see in the Kind column. On your own personal Mac, it probably says *Admin* next to your name. This, as you could probably guess, stands for Administrator.

Because you're the person who installed Mac OS X to begin with, the Mac assumes that you are its administrator—the technical wizard who's in charge of it. Only an administrator is allowed to:

• Install new programs into the Applications folder.

• Add fonts that everybody can use.

- Make changes to certain System Preferences panes (including Network, Date & Time, Energy Saver, Login, and Startup Disk).

- Create new folders outside of your Home folder.

- Decide who gets to have accounts on the Mac.

- Open, change, or delete anyone else's files (page 472).

The notion of administrators is an important one. For one thing, you'll find certain settings all over Mac OS X that you can change *only* if you're an administrator—including many in the Accounts panel itself (see Figure 12-2). For another thing, administrator status plays an enormous role when you want to network your Mac to other kinds of computers.

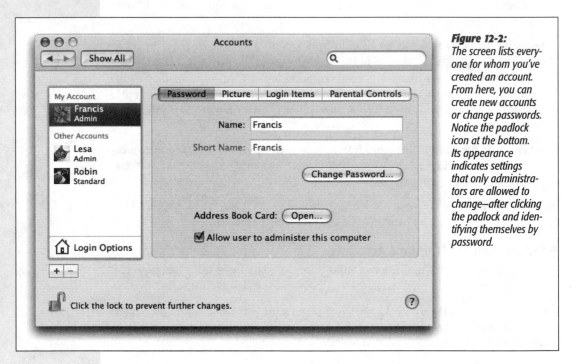

Figure 12-2:
The screen lists everyone for whom you've created an account. From here, you can create new accounts or change passwords. Notice the padlock icon at the bottom. Its appearance indicates settings that only administrators are allowed to change—after clicking the padlock and identifying themselves by password.

As you create accounts for other people who'll use this Mac, you'll be offered the opportunity to make each one an administrator just like you. Needless to say, use discretion. Bestow these powers only upon people as responsible and technically masterful as you.

Standard Accounts

Anyone who isn't an administrator is probably an ordinary *Standard* account holder (Figure 12-2). These people have everyday access to their own Home folders and to some of System Preferences, but most other areas of the Mac are off-limits. Mac OS X won't even let them create new folders on the main hard drive, except inside their own Home folders (or in the Shared folder described later).

A few of the System Preferences panes contain a padlock icon like the one in Figure 12-2. If you're a Standard account holder, you can't make changes to these settings without the assistance of an administrator. Fortunately, you aren't required to log out so that an administrator can log in and make changes. You can just call the administrator over, click the padlock icon, and let him type in his name and password—if, indeed, he feels comfortable with you making the changes you're about to make.

Creating an Account

To create a new account, start by unlocking the Accounts panel. That is, click the little padlock at the lower-left, and fill in your own account name and password.

Now you can click the + button beneath the list of accounts. The little panel shown in Figure 12-3 appears.

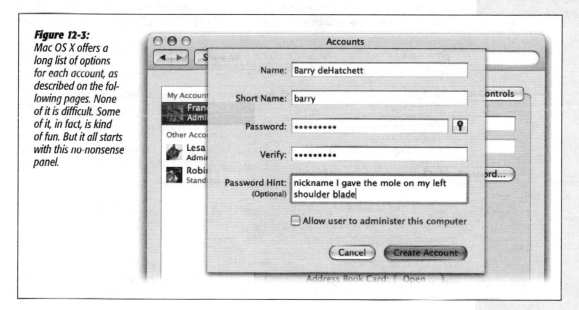

Figure 12-3:
Mac OS X offers a long list of options for each account, as described on the following pages. None of it is difficult. Some of it, in fact, is kind of fun. But it all starts with this no-nonsense panel.

Phase 1: Name, password, and status

In this starter sheet, you'll fill in the most critical information about the new account holder.

- **Name.** If it's just the family, this could be Chris or Robin. If it's a corporation or school, you'll probably want to use both first and last names.

- **Short Name.** You'll quickly discover the value of having a short name—an abbreviation of your actual name—particularly if your name is, say, Alexandra Stephonopolous. When you sign into your Mac in person, you can use either your long or short name. When you access this Mac by dialing into it or connecting from across the network (as described in the next chapter), the short variation is all you need.

As soon as you tab into this field, the Mac proposes a short name for you. You can replace the suggestion with whatever you like, as long as it doesn't have punctuation marks.

- **Password, Verify.** Here's where you type this new account holder's password (Figure 12-3). In fact, you're supposed to type it twice, to make sure you didn't introduce a typo the first time. (The Mac displays only dots as you type, to guard against the possibility that somebody is watching over your shoulder.)

  The usual computer book takes this opportunity to stress the importance of a long, complex password—a phrase that isn't in the dictionary, something made up of mixed letters and numbers. This is excellent advice if you create sensitive documents and work in a big corporation.

  But if you share the Mac only with a spouse or a few trusted colleagues in a small office, you may have nothing to hide. You may see the multiple-users feature more as a convenience (keeping your settings and files separate) than a protector of secrecy and security. In these situations, there's no particular urgency to the mission of thwarting the world's hackers with a convoluted password.

  In that case, you may want to consider setting up *no* password—leaving both password blanks empty. Later, whenever you're asked for your password, just leave the Password box blank. You'll be able to log in that much faster each day.

- **Password Hint.** If you gave yourself a password, you can leave yourself a hint in this box. Later, if you ever forget your password, the Mac will show you this cue to jog your memory (if this option is turned on, as described on page 335).

- **Allow user to administer this computer.** This checkbox is the most important item here. It's the master switch that turns this ordinary, unsuspecting computer user into an administrator, as described above.

When you finish setting up these essential items, click Create Account. (If you left the password boxes empty, the Mac asks for reassurance that you know what you're doing; click OK.)

You now return to the Accounts pane, where you see the new account name in the list at the left side.

Phase 2: Choose a picture

The usual Mac OS X sign-in screen (Figure 12-1) displays each account holder's name, accompanied by a little picture.

On the Picture tab, you can choose a little graphic for yourself. It becomes not only your icon on the sign-in screen, but also your "card" photo in Mac OS X's Address Book program, and your icon in iChat.

If you like the selections that Apple has provided at the right side of the window (drag the scroll bar to see them all), just click one to select it. If you'd rather supply your own graphics file—a digital photo of your own head, for example—follow one of these paths:

- Drag the graphics file directly into the "picture well" (Figure 12-4). Use the resulting Images window to frame your picture.

- Click the Edit button. In the Images dialog box that appears, click Choose. You're shown a list of what's on your hard drive so you can select an image file.

- If you have an iSight camera (or a digital camcorder) hooked up to your FireWire jack, click Edit. Use the resulting Images window to frame yourself, and then click the Take Video Snapshot button.

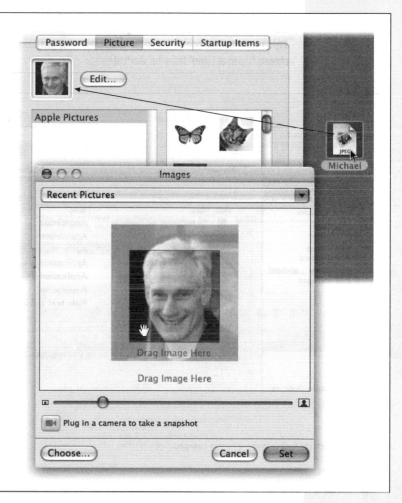

Figure 12-4:
Once you've selected a photo to represent yourself (left), you can adjust its position relative to the square "frame" (right), or adjust its size by dragging the slider. Finally, when the picture looks correctly framed, click Set. (The next time you return to the Images dialog box, you can recall the new image using the Recent Pictures pop-up menu.)

Phase 3: Login Items

There's one additional System Preferences setting that your account holders can set up for themselves: which programs or documents open automatically upon login. (This is one decision an administrator *can't* make for other people. It's available only to whoever is logged in at the moment.)

Now turn on "Send permission emails to." With this setting enabled, anytime your youngster uses Apple's Mail program to send a message to someone who's *not* on the approved list, he gets the message shown at top in Figure 12-6. If he clicks Ask Permission, then *your* copy of Mail receives a permissions-request message (Figure 12-6, middle). If you add that person's address to the list of approved correspondents, then your young apprentice can click the message in his Drafts folder and send it on its merry way (Figure 12-6, bottom).

- **Finder & System.** When you turn on this checkbox, you see the options shown in Figure 12-7. Use these options to limit what your Standard-account flock is allowed to do. You can limit them to using certain programs, for example, or prevent them from burning DVDs, changing settings, or fiddling with your printer setups.

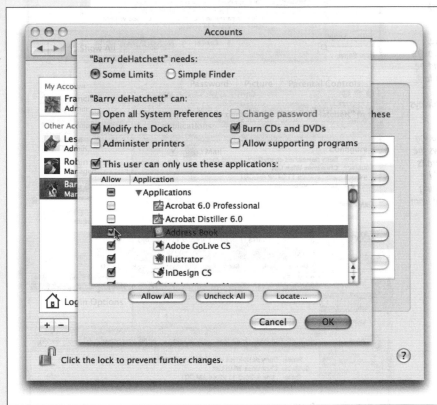

Figure 12-7:
From the Limitations window, you can control the capabilities of any user of your system. In the lower half of the Finder & System window, you can choose applications by turning on the boxes next to their names. (Expand the flippy triangles as necessary.) Those are the only programs these account holders will be allowed to use.

In fact, if you're *really* concerned about someone's ability to survive the Mac—or the Mac's ability to survive them—click the Simple Finder button (shown at top in Figure 12-7); then turn on the checkboxes of the programs that person is allowed to use. Now your victim sees the bare-bones Finder shown in Figure 12-8, which is so simple that even a literate 5-year-old could probably figure it out.

- **iChat.** When you turn on the iChat checkbox, an empty list appears, which you can fill with the buddy-list names of everyone it's OK for your kid to chat with.

This time, though, Mac OS X makes things easy: When you click the + button, your own Address Book list pops open. You can add a name to the list by clicking it and then clicking Select Buddy (assuming the person has an AIM-compatible address, of course).

Now, when your underling fires up iChat, she discovers that her Buddy List is empty except for the people you've identified. If she tries to click the + button to add a buddy, she gets only an error message.

- **Safari.** This feature is designed to limit which Web sites your kid is allowed to visit. But you don't have to build the list of approved Web sites right into the dialog box. Instead, you're supposed to set up your kid's copy of Safari (after logging in with his account). Turn off parental controls for the moment by choosing Safari→Preferences, clicking Security, and turning off "Enable parental controls." Enter your administrator's name and password.

Now set up his copy of Safari so that all of the approved sites appear on the *Bookmarks bar* (page 294 has instructions). Everything else will be off-limits. When you're finished building the Bookmarks bar, return to System Preferences and turn Safari's parental control back on.

Now, if your child tries to visit a page on a site you haven't permitted, he'll see a message that invites him to *add* the desired Web site to the Bookmarks bar, thereby making it an approved site—but he can only do it with an Administrator's name and password. Put simply, your kid needs to call you over to do the job.

Figure 12-8:
The Simple Finder doesn't feel like home—unless you've got one of those Spartan, space-age, Dr. Evil-type pads. But it can be just the ticket for less-skilled Mac users, with few options, a basic interface, and no access to powerful (and potentially confusing) features like Spotlight. Every program in the My Applications folder is actually an alias to the real program, which is safely ensconced in the off-limits Applications folder.

- **Dictionary.** As you know from Chapter 14, Mac OS X comes with a complete electronic copy of the *New Oxford American Dictionary.* And "complete," in this case, means "it even has swear words."

  Turning on this checkbox is like having an Insta-Censor™. It hides most of the naughty words from the dictionary whenever your young account holder is logged in (Figure 12-9).

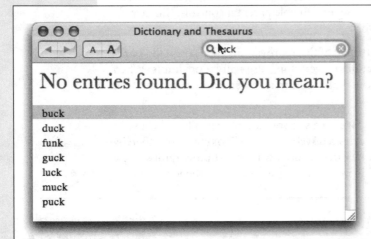

Figure 12-9:
Something's oddly missing from the Dictionary when parental controls are turned on: dirty words.

Editing Accounts

Administrators have all the fun. Although Standard account holders are permitted to change their startup pictures and passwords, *administrators* can change virtually anything about any account—its long name, its Simple Finder settings, its password, and so on (not, however, its short name).

If you're a Standard account holder and you want to make changes, you'll have to ask an administrator to log in, make the changes to your account, and then turn the computer back over to you.

Deleting User Accounts

When that time comes, click the account name in the Accounts list and then click the minus-sign button beneath the list. Tiger asks what to do with all of the dearly departed's files and settings (Figure 12-10):

- **Delete Immediately.** This button offers the "Hasta la vista, baby" approach. The account and all of its files and settings are vaporized forever, on the spot.

- **OK.** This button presents the "I'll be back" approach. Mac OS X preserves the user's folders on the Mac, in a tidy digital envelope that won't clutter your hard drive, and that can be reopened in case of emergency.

The file resides in the Users→Deleted Users folder, and it's a disk image file (.dmg) like the ones described on page 128. If fate ever brings that person back into your life, you can use this disk image to reinstate the deleted person's account.

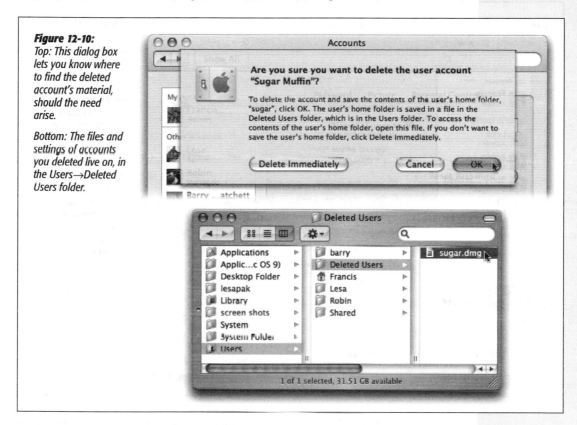

Figure 12-10:
Top: This dialog box lets you know where to find the deleted account's material, should the need arise.

Bottom: The files and settings of accounts you deleted live on, in the Users→Deleted Users folder.

Setting Up the Login Process

Once you've set up more than one account, the dialog box shown in Figure 12-1 appears whenever you turn on the Mac, whenever you choose →Log Out, or whenever the Mac logs you out automatically (page 344). But a few extra controls let you, an administrator, set up either more or less security at the login screen—or, put another way, build in less or more convenience.

Open System Preferences, click Accounts, and then click the Login Options button (Figure 12-11). Here are some of the ways you can shape the login experience for greater security (or greater convenience):

Once you're in, the world of the Mac looks just the way you left it (or the way an administrator set it for you). Everything in your Home folder, all your email and bookmarks, your desktop picture and Dock settings—all of it is unique to you. Your Home folder even contains its own Library folder, which maintains a separate (additional) set of fonts and preference settings just for you. Your Applications folder may even have programs that other account holders don't see.

Unless you're an administrator, you're not allowed to install any new programs into the Applications folder. That folder, after all, is a central software repository for *everybody* who uses your Mac, and the Mac forbids everyday account holders from moving or changing all such universally shared folders.

The Shared Folder

Every Mac OS X machine has a Users folder in the main hard drive window. It contains the individual Home folders of every account on the Mac.

If you try to open anybody else's Home folder, you'll see a tiny red "no go here" icon superimposed on almost every folder inside, telling you: "Look, but don't touch."

There are exceptions, though. As shown in Figure 12-12, two folders are designed to be distribution points for files your co-workers want you to see: Public and Sites.

You, too, have Public and Sites folders in your own Home folder. Here again, anything you put into these folders is available for inspection—although not for changing—by anyone else who uses this Mac.

DON'T PANIC

The Case of the Forgotten Password

Help—I forgot my password! And I never told it to anybody, so even the administrator can't help me!

No problem. Your administrator can simply open up System Preferences, click Accounts, click the name of the person who forgot the password, and then click Reset Password to re-establish the password.

But you don't understand. I am the administrator! And I'm the only account!

Aha—that's a different story. All right, no big deal. At the login screen, type a gibberish password three times. On the last attempt, the Mac will offer you the chance to reset the password. All you have to do is type in your master password (page 336) to prove your credentials.

Um—I never set up a master password.

All right then. That's actually good news, because it means you didn't turn on FileVault. (If you had, and you'd also forgotten the master password, your account would now be locked away forever.)

Insert the Mac OS X DVD. Restart the Mac while pressing down the letter C key, which starts the Mac up from the DVD and launches the Mac OS X installer.

On the first installer screen, choose Installer→Reset Password. When the Reset Password screen appears, click the hard drive that contains Mac OS X. From the first pop-up menu, choose the name of your account. Now make up a new password and type it into both boxes. Click Save, close the window, click the installer, and restart.

And next time, be more careful! Write down your password on a Post-it note and affix it to your monitor. (Joke—that's a joke!)

Sitting in the Users folder is one folder that doesn't correspond to any particular person: Shared. This is the one and only folder that everybody can access, freely inserting and extracting files. It's the common ground among all the account holders. It's Central Park, the farmer's market, and the grocery store bulletin board.

Tip: If several people on your machine want to share the same iTunes music, move the library from your Home→Music folder into the Users→Shared folder. Now open iTunes→Preferences→Advanced, click Change, and direct iTunes to the new location of your music folder.

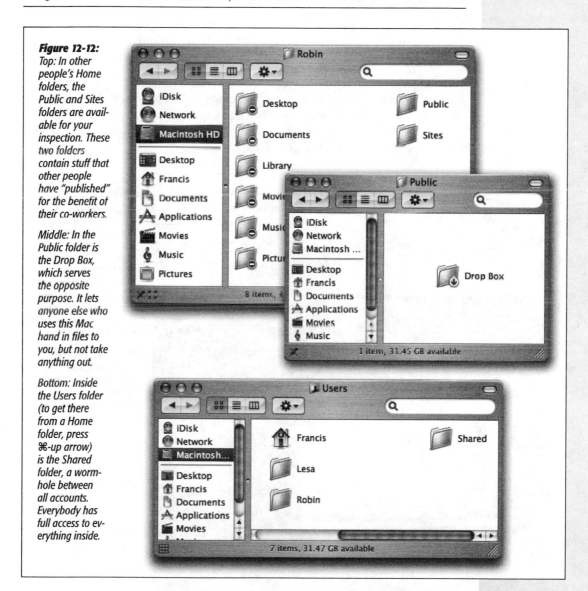

Figure 12-12:
Top: In other people's Home folders, the Public and Sites folders are available for your inspection. These two folders contain stuff that other people have "published" for the benefit of their co-workers.

Middle: In the Public folder is the Drop Box, which serves the opposite purpose. It lets anyone else who uses this Mac hand in files to you, but not take anything out.

Bottom: Inside the Users folder (to get there from a Home folder, press ⌘-up arrow) is the Shared folder, a wormhole between all accounts. Everybody has full access to everything inside.

Logging Out

When you're finished using the Mac, choose →Log Out (or press Shift-⌘-Q). A confirmation message appears; if you click Cancel or press Esc, you return to whatever you were doing. If you click Log Out, or press Return, you return to the screen shown in Figure 12-1, and the entire sign-in cycle begins anew.

Fast User Switching

The account system described so far in this chapter has its charms. It keeps everyone's stuff separate, it keeps your files safe, and, most importantly, it lets you have the desktop picture of your choice.

Unfortunately, it can go from handy to hassle in one split second. That's when you're logged in, and someone else wants to duck in for just a second—to check email or a calendar, for example. What are you supposed to do—log out completely, closing all of your documents and quitting all of your programs, just so the interloper can look something up? Even *Windows* doesn't make you do that.

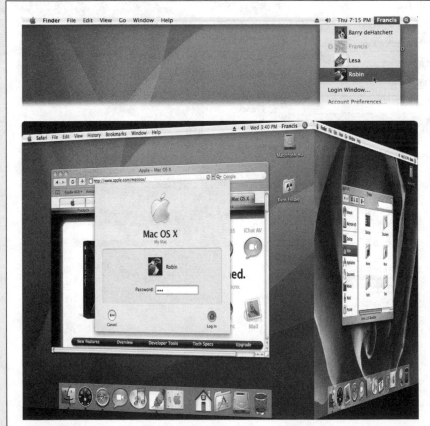

Figure 12-13:
Top: The existence of the Accounts menulet lets you know that Fast User Switching is turned on. The circled checkmark indicates a person who has already logged in. The dimmed account name shows who's logged in right now.

Bottom: Fast User Switching lets one account holder "cut in" without requiring someone else to log out first. When the screen changes from your account to someone else's, your entire world slides visibly offscreen although it's mounted on the side of a rotating cube—a spectacular feature made available by the Quartz Extreme graphics software available on new Macs.

Luckily, Apple took a cue from Microsoft and added Fast User Switching to Mac OS X. Now Person B can log in and use the Mac for a little while, while all of *your* stuff, Person A, simply slides into the background (Figure 12-13).

When Person B is finished working, you can bring your whole work environment back to the screen without having to reopen anything. All your windows and programs are still open, just as you left them.

To turn on this feature, open the Accounts panel of System Preferences (and click the padlock, if necessary, to unlock the pane). Click Login Options, and turn on "Enable fast user switching."

The only change you notice immediately is the appearance of your own account name in the upper-right corner of the screen (Figure 12-13, top). (You can change what this menu looks like by using the "View as" pop-up menu, also shown in Figure 12-13.)

That's all there is to it. Next time you need a fellow account holder to relinquish control so that you can duck in for a little work, just choose your name from the Accounts menu. Type your password, if one is required, and feel guiltless about the interruption.

The Root Account

An administrator's account isn't exactly a skeleton key that gives unfettered access to every corner of the Mac. Even an administrator isn't allowed to remove files from the System folder, or other files whose removal could hobble the machine.

It turns out that Normal and Administrator aren't the only kinds of accounts. There's one account that wields ultimate power, one person who can do anything to any file anywhere. This person is called the *superuser*.

Unix fans speak of the superuser account—also called the *root* account—in hushed tones, because it offers absolutely unrestricted power. The root account holder can move, delete, rename, or otherwise mangle any file on the machine, no matter what folder it's in. One wrong move—or one Internet hacker who manages to seize the root account—and you've got yourself a $2,500 doorstop. That's why Mac OS X's root account is completely hidden and, in fact, deactivated from the start.

Still, if you know what you're doing, and you see no alternative, you might be glad the root account is available.

You turn on the root account like this:

1. **In your Applications →Utilities folder, open the NetInfo Manager program. Click the tiny padlock in the lower-left corner of its screen.**

   A dialog box asks you for an administrator's name and password. After all, you wouldn't want ordinary underlings fooling around with the superuser account.

2. **Type your name and password, and then click OK. Choose Security→Enable Root User.**

If this is the first time you've performed this particular surgery, you'll be told, "The root password is currently blank." You're asked to make up a "non-trivial" (meaning virtually impossible for anyone to guess) password for the newly created root account.

3. **Click OK and then type the password in both of the bottom Password boxes. Click OK two more times.**

   The second dialog box simply tells you that if you intend to make any *more* changes in NetInfo Manager, you'll have to sign in as an administrator *again*. But your work here is done.

4. **Quit NetInfo Manager.**

   You've just brought the dormant root account to life.

5. **Log out. Log back in again as root.**

   That is, when the login screen appears, click Other User (a choice that magically appears once you've turned on the root account). In the first text box, type *root*. In the second, type the password you made up in step 4. Click Log In.

That's it—you arrive at the desktop, where no matter what you do, no error messages regarding access privileges or ownership will interrupt the proceedings. In the words of every movie hero's sidekick: Be careful out there.

When you're finished going about your business as a root user, immediately log out again. It's important to rule out the possibility that some clueless or malicious person might wander up to the Mac while you're still logged in as the superuser.

In fact, if you don't anticipate needing your superuser powers again soon, consider turning off the root account altogether. (Just repeat steps 1 and 2 on the preceding page. But in step 2, choose Security→Disable Root User.)

Six Mac OS X Security Shields

Mac OS X has always had a spectacular reputation for stability and security. Not a single Mac OS X virus had emerged as of 2005—a spectacular feature that is, in itself, a compelling reason to switch from Windows. (The Mac doesn't have any Windows-esque plague of spyware, either.)

The usual rap is, "Well, that's because Windows is a much bigger target. What virus writer is going to waste his time on a computer with five percent market share?"

That may be part of the reason. But Mac OS X has always been built more intelligently from the ground up. Thoughtful features abound, like the Finder's File→Secure Empty Trash command, which erase deleted files so thoroughly from your hard drive that they're irrecoverable.

But that's just one example. Here are the big-ticket defenses.

The Firewall

If you have a broadband, always-on connection (cable modem or DSL, for example), you're connected to the Internet 24 hours a day. It's theoretically possible for some cretin to use automated hacking software to flood you with files or take control of your machine. Fortunately, Mac OS X's *firewall* feature puts up a barrier to such mischief. It's described on page 250.

Tip: For extra protection, click the Advanced button and enable Stealth Mode. That shuts your Mac's backdoor to the Internet, so that hackers who check to see if your Mac exists get no response at all.

FileVault

The Security pane of System Preferences is one of Tiger's most powerful security features. Understanding what it does, however, may take a little slogging.

As you know, the Mac OS X accounts system is designed to keep people out of each other's files. Ordinarily, for example, Chris isn't allowed to go rooting through Robin's stuff.

Until FileVault came along, though, there were all kinds of ways to circumvent this protection system. For one thing, someone could just remove the hard drive from your Mac and attach it to a Mac OS 9–based computer, where all the advanced user settings would be moot. For people with sensitive or private files, the result was a security hole bigger than Steve Jobs' bank account.

FileVault is an extra line of defense. When you turn it on, your Mac automatically *encrypts* (scrambles) everything in your Home folder, using something called AES-128 encryption. (How secure is that? It would take a password-guessing computer *149 trillion years* before hitting paydirt.)

This means that unless someone knows your password, FileVault renders your files unreadable for anyone but you and your computer's administrator—no matter what sneaky tricks they try to pull.

You won't notice much difference when FileVault is turned on. You log in as usual, clicking your name and typing your password. Only a slight pause indicates that Mac OS X is decoding your entire Home folder.

Here are some things you should know about FileVault's protection:

- **It's useful only if you've logged out.** Once you've logged in, your files are *not* encrypted. If you want the protection, log out before you wander away from your Mac.

- **It covers only your Home folder.** Anything in your Applications, System, or Library folders is exempt from protection.

- **An administrator can access your files, too.** According to Mac OS X's caste system, anyone with an Administrator account can have virtually unhindered access to his peasants' files—even with FileVault on—because the administrator has the master password described below.

- **It doesn't let you access your files from anything other than Mac OS X.** In exchange for protection against evildoers, Mac OS X doesn't let you get to the stuff in your Home folder when the Mac starts up in Mac OS 9, or when you access it via FireWire disk mode (page 157). (That, after all, is the whole point.)

- **It keeps other people from opening your files, not from deleting them.** It's still possible for someone to trash all your files, without ever seeing what they are. There's not much you can do about this with FileVault on *or* off.

- **Any shared folders in your Home folder will no longer be available on the network.** That is, any folders you've shared won't be available to your co-workers except when you're at your Mac and logged in.

- **Backup programs may throw a tizzy.** FileVault's job is to "stuff" and "unstuff" your Home folder as you log in and out. Backup programs that work by backing up files and folders that have changed may therefore get very confused.

- **If you forget your password *and* your administrator forgets the master password, you're toast.** If this happens, your data is *permanently lost.* You'll have no choice but to erase your hard drive and start from scratch.

To turn FileVault on, proceed like this:

1. **In System Preferences, click Security. Click Set Master Password.**

   If you're the first person to try to turn on FileVault, you need to create a *master* password first. The master password is an override password that gives an ad-

---

UP TO SPEED

Password Hell

With the introduction of the master password, you now have quite a few different passwords to keep straight. Each one, however, has a specific purpose:

Account password. You type this password in at the normal login screen. You can't get into anyone else's account with it—only yours. Entering this password unlocks FileVault, too.

Administrator password. You're asked to enter this password whenever you try to install new software or modify certain system settings. If you're the only one who uses your computer (or you're the one who controls it), your administrator password is your account password. Other-

wise, you're supposed to go find an administrator, and ask him to type in his name and password once he's assessed what you're trying to do.

Master password. Think of this password as a master key. If anyone with FileVault forgets her account password, the administrator who knows the master password can unlock the account. The master password also lets an administrator change an account's password right at the sign-in screen, whether FileVault is turned on or not.

Root password. This password is rarely necessary for anything other than programmery system modifying, and you turn it on as described earlier in this chapter.

---

ministrator full power to access any account, even without knowing the account holder's password, or to turn off FileVault for any account.

When you click Set Master Password, the dialog box shown at top in Figure 12-14 appears.

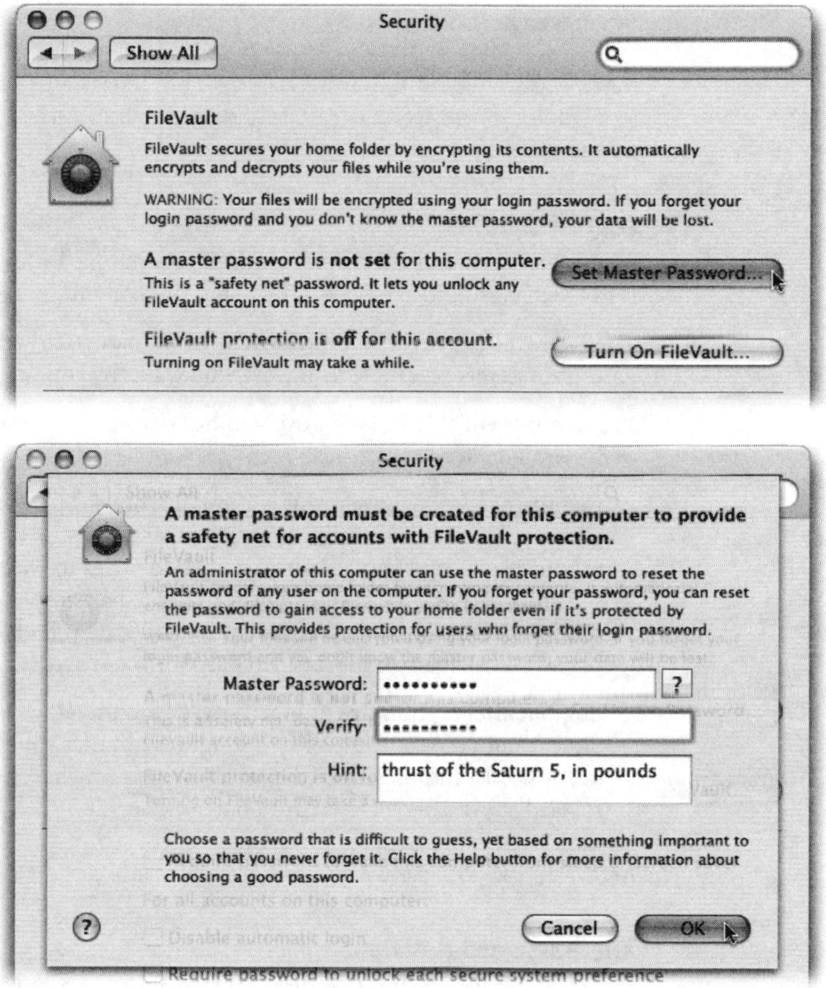

Figure 12-14:
Top: The Security pane is the gateway to Mac OS X's beefed-up security features.

Bottom: Type in your master password twice, and give yourself a hint. (In the event of an emergency, the hint appears with the third unsuccessful attempt to type in the master password.) When you click OK, you see that the Security pane now says, "A master password is set for the computer."

Security

Show All

FileVault

FileVault secures your home folder by encrypting its contents. It automatically encrypts and decrypts your files while you're using them.

WARNING: Your files will be encrypted using your login password. If you forget your login password and you don't know the master password, your data will be lost.

A master password is **not set** for this computer.
This is a "safety net" password. It lets you unlock any FileVault account on this computer.

Set Master Password...

FileVault protection is **off** for this account.
Turning on FileVault may take a while.

Turn On FileVault...

Security

A master password must be created for this computer to provide a safety net for accounts with FileVault protection.

An administrator of this computer can use the master password to reset the password of any user on the computer. If you forget your password, you can reset the password to gain access to your home folder even if it's protected by FileVault. This provides protection for users who forget their login password.

Master Password: •••••••••• **?**

Verify: ••••••••••

Hint: thrust of the Saturn 5, in pounds

Choose a password that is difficult to guess, yet based on something important to you so that you never forget it. Click the Help button for more information about choosing a good password.

Cancel **OK**

2. **Click Turn On FileVault.**

   Some time passes as Mac OS X tries to figure out whether or not you have enough free disk space to encrypt your Home folder. If you *do* have enough space, an explanatory dialog box appears.

3. **Click Turn on FileVault in the dialog box.**

Now Mac OS X logs you out of your own account. (It can't encrypt a folder that's in use.) Some time will pass while it converts your Home folder into a protected state, during which you can't do anything but wait.

After a few minutes, you arrive at the standard login window, where you can see that your account picture is now adorned by the FileVault logo. Sign in as usual, confident that your stuff is securely locked away from anyone who tries to get at it when you're not logged in.

Note: To turn off FileVault, open System Preferences, click Security, and click Turn Off FileVault. Enter your password and click OK. (The master password sticks around, though, in case you ever want to turn FileVault on again.)

Logout Options

As you read earlier in this chapter, the usual procedure for finishing up a work session is for each person to choose →Log Out. But sometimes people forget.

The next thing you know, you've left your Mac unattended but logged in, with all your life's secrets accessible to anyone who walks by your desk.

You can prevent this situation using either of two checkboxes in the Security pane of System Preferences:

- **Require password to wake this computer from sleep or screen saver.** This option gives you a password-protected screen saver that locks your Mac after a few minutes of inactivity. Now, whenever somebody tries to wake up your Mac after the screen saver has appeared (or when the Mac has simply gone to sleep according to your settings in the Energy Saver pane of System Preferences), the "Enter your password" dialog box appears. No password? No access.

- **Log out after __ minutes of inactivity.** If you prefer, you can make the Mac sign out of your account completely if it figures out that you've wandered off (and it's been, say, 15 minutes since the last time you touched the mouse or keyboard). Instead, it presents the standard Login screen.

Note: If there are open, unsaved documents at the moment of truth, the Mac won't auto-log out.

The Password Assistant

Plenty of software features require you to make up a password: Web sites, accounts, networked disks, and so on. No wonder most people wind up trying to use the same password in as many situations as possible. Worse, they use something easily guessable, like their kids' names. Even regular English words aren't very secure, because hackers routinely use *dictionary attacks*—software that tries to guess your password by running through every word in the dictionary—to break in.

To prevent evildoers from guessing your passwords, Mac OS X comes with a good-password suggestion feature called the Password Assistant. It cheerfully generates one suggestion after another for impossible-to-guess passwords. ("*recharges8@exch angeability*," anyone?)

Fortunately, you won't have to remember most of them, thanks to the Keychain password-memorizing feature described at the end of this chapter. (The only password you have to memorize is your account password.)

See Figure 12-15 for details on the Password Assistant.

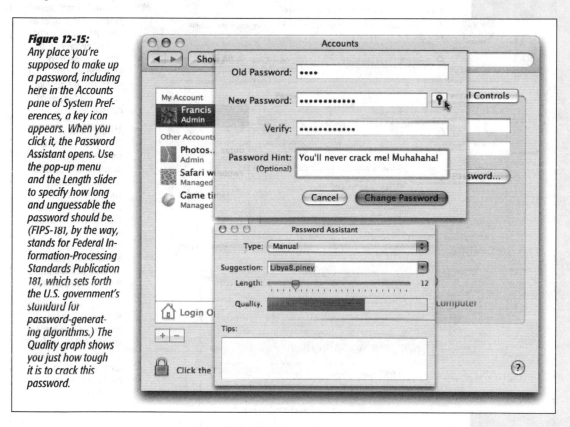

Figure 12-15:
Any place you're supposed to make up a password, including here in the Accounts pane of System Preferences, a key icon appears. When you click it, the Password Assistant opens. Use the pop-up menu and the Length slider to specify how long and unguessable the password should be. (FIPS-181, by the way, stands for Federal Information-Processing Standards Publication 181, which sets forth the U.S. government's standard for password-generating algorithms.) The Quality graph shows you just how tough it is to crack this password.

The Keychain

The information explosion of the computer age has one colossal annoyance: the proliferation of *passwords* we have to memorize. Shared folders on the network, Web sites, your iDisk, FTP sites—each requires another password.

Apple has done the world a mighty favor with its *Keychain* feature. The concept is brilliant: Whenever you log into Mac OS X and type in your password, you've typed the master code that tells the computer, "It's really me. I'm at my computer now." From that moment on, the Mac *automatically* fills in every password blank you encounter, whether it's a Web site in Safari, a shared disk on your network, a wireless network, an encrypted disk image, or an FTP program like Fetch. With only a few exceptions, you can safely forget all of your passwords except your login password.

These days, all kinds of programs and services know about the Keychain and offer to store your passwords there. Figure 12-16 shows two prime examples.

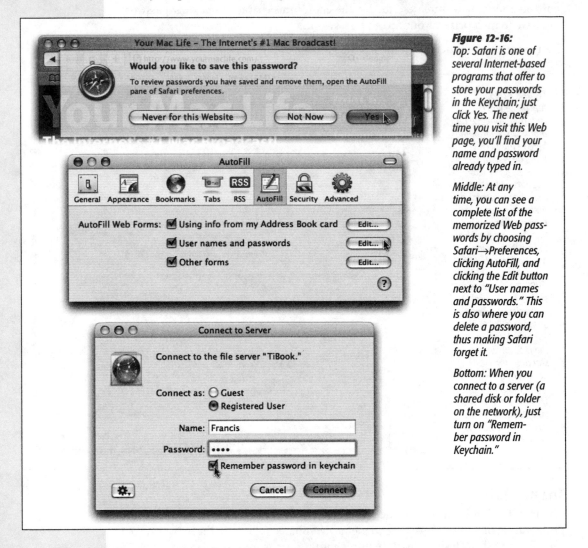

Figure 12-16:
Top: Safari is one of several Internet-based programs that offer to store your passwords in the Keychain; just click Yes. The next time you visit this Web page, you'll find your name and password already typed in.

Middle: At any time, you can see a complete list of the memorized Web passwords by choosing Safari→Preferences, clicking AutoFill, and clicking the Edit button next to "User names and passwords." This is also where you can delete a password, thus making Safari forget it.

Bottom: When you connect to a server (a shared disk or folder on the network), just turn on "Remember password in Keychain."

Locking and unlocking the Keychain

If you work alone, the Keychain is automatic, invisible, and generally wonderful. Logging in is the only time you have to type a password. After that, the Mac figures: "Hey, I know it's you; you proved it by entering your account password. That ID is good enough for me. I'll fill in all your other passwords automatically." In Apple parlance, you've *unlocked* your keychain just by logging in.

If you want to *lock* the keychain, so that passwords aren't autofilled anymore, open Applications→Utilities→Keychain Access. Choose Keychain Access→Preferences→ General. Now choose File→Lock Keychain.

Tip: You can make the Keychain lock *itself* (after a period of inactivity) by choosing Edit→Change Settings for Keychain [your name].

Managing Keychains

To take a look at your Keychain, open the Keychain Access program. By clicking one of the password rows, you get to see its attributes—name, kind, account, and so on.

While you're here, you might as well record any *other* private information (ATM numbers, credit card numbers, and so on). No, the Mac won't automatically fill them in for you, but it will maintain them in one central, password-protected location.

Secure Virtual Memory

Here's another security feature in Tiger: *secure virtual memory.*

Virtual memory is a trick that computers use to keep open a lot of programs at once—more, in fact, than they technically have enough memory (RAM) for. To compensate, they set some memory down on the hard drive.

Sophisticated snoopers could, in theory, sneak up to the Mac while you're logged in but away from your desk. Using a built-in Unix command, the intruder could actually *read* what's stored in that virtual memory "swap file"—in particular, your passwords.

But the "Use secure virtual memory" checkbox (on the Security pane of System Preferences) takes away all their fun; it encrypts your virtual memory like FileVault does for your personal files. (You may find that it slows down your Mac, though, especially when you switch from one program to another.)

System Preferences

R emember the Control Panel on the PC? On the Mac, it's called System Preferences, but it's still the same thing: a collection of little icons that open various
preference panes. Some are extremely important, because their settings determine whether or not you can connect to a network or go online to exchange email.
Others handle the more cosmetic aspects of customizing Mac OS X. This chapter
guides you through the entire System Preferences program, panel by panel.

Tip: Only someone with an Administrator account (page 323) can change settings that affect everyone who
shares a certain machine: its Internet settings, Energy Saver settings, and so on. If you see a bunch of controls
that are dimmed and unavailable, now you know why.

A tiny padlock in the lower-left corner of a pane is the other telltale sign. If you, a nonadministrator, would
like to edit some settings, call an administrator over to your Mac and ask him to click the lock, input his
password, and supervise your tweaks.

The System Preferences Window

You can open System Preferences by choosing its name from the menu, clicking its
"light-switch" icon in the Dock, or double-clicking its icon in the Applications folder.
At first, the rows of icons are grouped according to function: Personal, Hardware,
and so on.

But you can also view them in tidy alphabetical order, as shown at bottom in Figure
13-2. That can spare you the ritual of hunting through various rows just to find a
certain panel icon whose name you already know. (This alphabetical arrangement
matches the way the various panels are organized in this chapter, too.)

Either way, when you click one of the icons, the corresponding controls appear in the main System Preferences window. To access a different preference pane, you have a number of options:

- *Fast:* When System Preferences first opens, the insertion point is blinking in the System Preferences search box. Type a few letters of *volume, resolution, wallpaper, wireless,* or whatever feature you want to adjust. In a literal illustration of Spotlight's power, the System Preferences window darkens except for the icons where you'll find relevant controls (see Figure 13-1). Click the name or icon of the one that looks most promising.

Note: If the insertion point is *not* blinking in the Spotlight box, press ⌘-F.

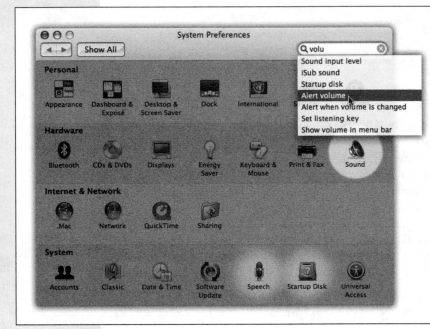

Figure 13-1:
Even if you don't know which System Preferences pane contains the settings you want to change, Spotlight can help. Type into the box at the top, and watch as the "spotlight" shines on the relevant icons. At that point, you can either click an icon, click a name in the pop-up menu, or arrow down the menu and press Enter to choose the pane you want.

- *Equally fast:* Click the Show All icon in the upper-left corner of the window (or press ⌘-L, a shortcut worth learning). Then click the icon of the new pane you want.

Tip: Shift-click any System Preferences icon to make its pane appear in luxurious slow motion.

- *Faster:* Choose any pane's name from the View menu—or, if System Preferences is already open, from the menu that sprouts from the System Preferences *Dock icon.*

- *Fastest:* Highlight the first System Preferences icon by pressing Tab. (The highlighting is very faint, but it's there.) Then type the first couple of letters of the icon you want to highlight—*p* for Print & Fax, *di* for Displays, or whatever—and then press the Space bar to open that pane.

Note: This trick works only if you've turned on "Full keyboard access" in the Keyboard & Mouse pane of System Preferences.

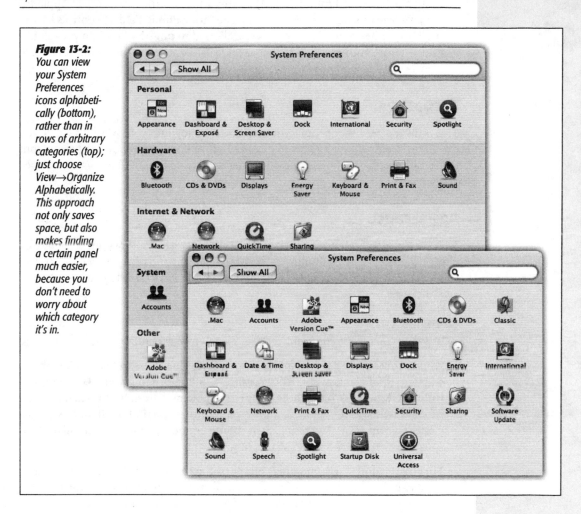

Figure 13-2:
You can view your System Preferences icons alphabetically (bottom), rather than in rows of arbitrary categories (top); just choose View→Organize Alphabetically. This approach not only saves space, but also makes finding a certain panel much easier, because you don't need to worry about which category it's in.

.Mac

This pane is of no value unless you've signed up for a .Mac account (page 147). This pane offers four tabs:

- **Account.** This is where you fill in your member name and password for your .Mac account, if you've subscribed. If you're not yet a member, you can click the Learn More button to get started.

- **Sync, Advanced.** Here's where you tell Tiger which elements of your digital world (calendar, address book, email, and so on) you want synchronized—via the .Mac service—with a cellphone, iPod, Palm organizer, or another Mac.

- **iDisk.** The Disk Space graph indicates how full your electronic iDisk is. (And if it approaches your limit of 250 MB, a Buy More button lets you pay Apple for the privilege of gaining more storage.) The "Your Public Folder" controls let you specify whether or not other people are allowed to put new files into your Public folder (a sort of Internet-wide Shared folder), and whether or not outsiders need a password to see what's in your Public folder.

Accounts

This is the master list of people who are allowed to log into your Mac. It's where you can adjust their passwords, startup pictures, self-opening startup items, permissions to use various features of the Mac, and other security features. All of this is described in Chapter 12.

Appearance

This pane is mostly about how things look on the screen: windows, menus, buttons, scroll bars, and fonts. Nothing you find here lets you perform any *radical* surgery on the overall Mac OS X look—but you can tweak certain settings to match your personal style.

Changing Colors

Two pop-up menus let you crank up or tone down Mac OS X's overall colorfulness:

- **Appearance.** Choose between Blue or Graphite. Blue refers to Mac OS X's factory setting—bright, candy-colored scroll-bar handles, progress bars, 🍎 menu, and pulsing OK buttons—and those shiny red, yellow, and green buttons in the corner of every window. If you, like some graphics professionals, find all of this circus-poster coloring a bit distracting, then choose Graphite, which renders all of those interface elements in various shades of gray.

- **Highlight color.** When you drag your cursor across text, its background changes color to indicate that you've selected it. Exactly what color the background becomes is up to you—just choose the shade you want using this pop-up menu.

Tweaking the Scroll Bars

These radio buttons control the scroll-bar arrow buttons of all your windows. You can keep these arrows together at one end of the scroll bar, or you can split them up so that the "up" arrow sits at the top of the scroll bar, and the "down" arrow is at the bottom—a much more Windows-like arrangement. (Horizontal scroll bars are similarly affected.)

Tip: For details on the "Jump to the next page" and "Scroll to here" options, see page 33.

You can also turn on one or both of the following checkboxes:

- **Use smooth scrolling.** This option makes pages lurch with slight accelerations when you click in the scroll bar, rather than with jerky scrolling motions.

- **Minimize when double clicking a window title bar.** This option provides an extra way to minimize a window. In addition to the tiny yellow Minimize button at the upper-left corner of the window, you now have a much bigger target—the entire title bar.

Number of Recent Items

Just how many of your recently opened documents and applications do you want the Mac to show using the Recent Items command in the menu? Pick a number from the pop-up menus. (You'll probably find that 5 is too few; 30 is more practical.)

Font Smoothing Style

The Mac's built-in text-smoothing (*antialiasing*) feature is supposed to produce smoother, more commercial-looking text anywhere it appears on your Mac: in word processing documents, email messages, Web pages, and so on. Yet one of the most common complaints about Mac OS X is that it actually makes text look *blurry* to people who aren't used to the effect.

Figure 13-3:
Top: The same 12-point type with text smoothing turned on (top) and off, shown magnified for your inspection pleasure.

Smoothing off   **Krakatoa:** A New Musical

Smoothing on   **Krakatoa:** A New Musical

Bottom: Here's the widest difference in text-smoothing styles: Light smoothing vs. Strong. Standard and Medium, of course, are in between.

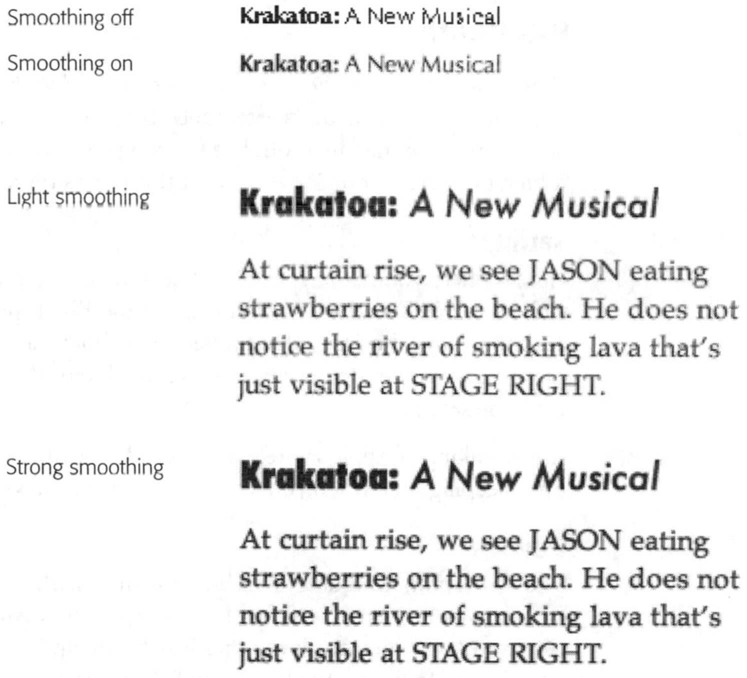

Light smoothing

Krakatoa: A New Musical

At curtain rise, we see JASON eating strawberries on the beach. He does not notice the river of smoking lava that's just visible at STAGE RIGHT.

Strong smoothing

Krakatoa: A New Musical

At curtain rise, we see JASON eating strawberries on the beach. He does not notice the river of smoking lava that's just visible at STAGE RIGHT.

Fortunately, you can control the degree to which text gets smoothed. Use the pop-up menu to choose a setting that suits your eyes—and your monitor. For example, Apple offers Standard for CRT screens (cathode-ray tube—that is, traditional, bulky, television-style screens), and Medium for flat-panel screens like laptops and almost all current desktop Macs. Or just leave the setting at Automatic, to have Mac OS X use its best choice.

Either way, the differences are fairly subtle (see Figure 13-3). Furthermore, unlike most System Preferences, this one has no effect until the next time you open the program in question. In the Finder, for example, you won't notice the difference until you log out and log back in again.

Turning Off Smoothing on Tiny Fonts

At smaller type sizes (10-point and smaller), you might find that text is *less* readable with font smoothing turned on. It all depends upon the font, the size, and your taste. For that reason, this pop-up menu lets you choose a cutoff point for font smoothing. If you choose 12 here, for example, then 12-point (and smaller) type still appears crisp and sharp; only larger type, such as headlines, displays the graceful edge smoothing. You can choose a size cutoff as low as 4 points.

Note: None of these settings affects your printouts, only the onscreen display.

Bluetooth

This pane shows up only if your Mac is equipped with a Bluetooth transmitter, either built-in or in the form of an external USB gadget. The thrill of using Bluetooth to send files stems from the Bluetooth File Exchange program in your Applications→Utilties folder, but here's a quick overview of this pane's three tabs:

Settings

Here's where you make your Mac *discoverable* (that is, "visible" to other Bluetooth gadgets). Here's also where you can tell the Bluetooth Setup Assistant to open up automatically when the Mac thinks no keyboard and mouse are attached. (In that case, it assumes that you have a wireless Bluetooth keyboard and mouse that have yet to be set up.)

And speaking of Apple's wireless keyboard: The third checkbox here allows it to wake up a sleeping Mac when you press a key, just like a wired keyboard does.

Devices

The whole point of Bluetooth is hooking up—with phones, other Macs, wireless keyboards, wireless phone headsets, Bluetooth printers, palmtops, and so on. On this pane (Figure 13-4), you introduce other Bluetooth equipment to your Mac. Click "Set up new device" to fire up the Bluetooth Setup Assistant, which scouts the local airwaves for Bluetooth gear in your vicinity and lets you add them to your Mac's list.

In any case, once you've introduced the Mac to a Bluetooth companion, you'll see the new device listed on this pane—and the buttons on the right let you delete it, disconnect from it, change its settings, and so on.

Figure 13-4:
Top: This panel reveals a list of every Bluetooth gadget your Mac knows about. Click a name to see, in the lower box, what sort of device it is (phone, palmtop, etc.), and whether it's turned on and available. The heart symbols denote Favorites—the ones that you've paired so that you don't have to re-enter a password every time you need the connection.

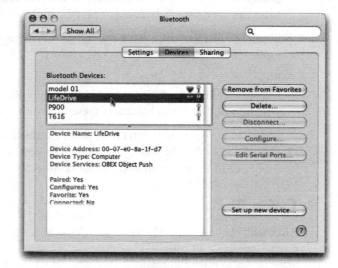

Middle: The Setup Assistant scans for other Bluetooth gadgets, and, after a moment, lists them. Click one and then continue.

Bottom: Where security is an issue—like when you plan to use your cellphone as an Internet antenna for your PowerBook, and you don't want other people nearby surfing the Web via your cellphone—the Assistant offers you the chance to pair your Bluetooth device with the Mac. You're asked to make up a one-time password, which you have 60 seconds to type into both the Mac and the phone. Thereafter, no more muss, fuss, or passwords.

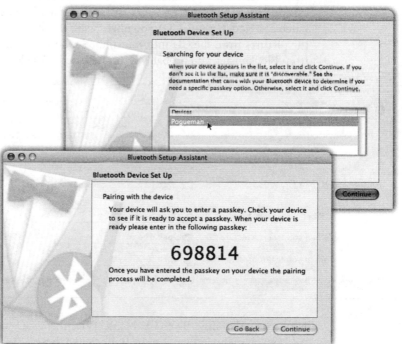

Sharing

This pane lists all the ways you can use Bluetooth to exchange files wirelessly, and lets you fiddle with how they work. These methods include:

- **Bluetooth File Transfer.** When this option is turned on, other people with Bluetooth Macs can see a list of what's in your Public folder, and help themselves.

- **Bluetooth File Exchange.** This option lets other people send files to you by Bluetooth.

- **Bluetooth-PDA-Sync.** PDA stands for personal digital assistant, but in this dialog box, it actually means "Palm organizer." Many Palms offer Bluetooth wireless syncing with Bluetooth Macs, and these controls make it possible.

  For most purposes, you don't have to do anything but make sure this feature is turned on (so that the top-right button says Stop Serial Port). The Mac creates a simulated modem (serial) port that can connect to the Palm wirelessly.

CDs & DVDs

This handy pane (Figure 13-5) lets you tell the Mac what it should do when it detects you've inserted a CD or DVD. For example, when you insert a music CD, you might want iTunes to open automatically so that you can listen to the CD or convert its musical contents to MP3 files on your hard drive. Similarly, when you insert a picture CD (such as a Kodak Photo CD), you might want iPhoto to open in readiness to import the pictures from the CD into your photo collection. And when you insert a DVD from Blockbuster, you probably want the Mac's DVD Player program to open.

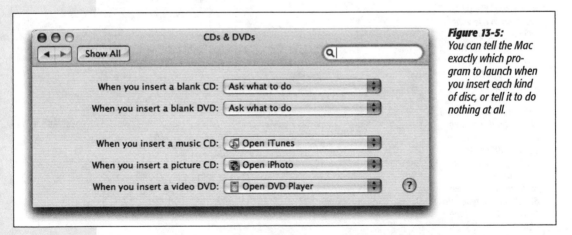

Figure 13-5:
You can tell the Mac exactly which program to launch when you insert each kind of disc, or tell it to do nothing at all.

For each kind of disk (blank CD, blank DVD, music CD, picture CD, or video DVD), the pop-up menu lets you choose options like these:

- **Ask what to do.** A dialog box will appear that asks what you want to do with the newly inserted disc.

- **Open (iDVD, iTunes, iPhoto, DVD Player...).** The Mac can open a certain program automatically when you insert the disc. When the day comes that somebody writes a better music player than iTunes, or a better digital shoebox than iPhoto, you can use the "Open other application" option.

- **Run script.** If you become handy writing AppleScripts (little automated software robots, described on page 388), you can schedule one of your own scripts to take over when you insert a disc. For example, you can set things up so that inserting a blank CD automatically copies your Home folder onto it for backup purposes.

- **Ignore.** The Mac won't do anything when you insert a disc except to display its icon on the desktop.

Classic

Pre–Mac OS X programs can still run under Mac OS X, thanks to a feature called Classic (page 123). This pane lets you start, stop, and restart Classic. And, in the unlikely event that you have more than one Mac OS 9 System Folder installed, it lets you choose which one you want to fire up whenever you open a pre–Mac OS X program.

Dashboard & Exposé

Here's where you specify how you want to trigger Dashboard (page 108) and Exposé (page 104): by pressing certain keys, or by shoving your cursor into a corner of the screen. Full details on changing these keystrokes or corners appear on page 110.

Date & Time

Your Mac's conception of what time it is can be very important. Every file you create or save is stamped with this time, and every email you send or receive is marked with this time. As you might expect, setting your Mac's clock is what the Date & Time panel is all about.

Date & Time tab

Click the Date & Time tab. If your Mac is online, turn on "Set Date & Time automatically," and be done with it. Your Mac sets its own clock by consulting a highly accurate scientific clock on the Internet. (No need to worry about Daylight Saving Time, either, as your Mac takes that into account.)

You can also set the date and time manually. To change the month, day, or year, you can click the digit that needs changing and then either (a) type a new number or (b) click the little arrow buttons. Press the Tab key to highlight the next number. (You can also specify the day of the month by clicking a date on the minicalendar.)

To set the time of day, use the same technique—or, for more geeky fun, try dragging the hour, minute, or second hands on the analog clock. Finally, click Save. (Click the Revert button to restore the panel settings.)

Tip: If you're frustrated that the Mac is showing you the 24-hour "military time" on your menu bar (that is, *17:30* instead of *5:30 p.m.*)—or it *isn't* showing military time when you'd like it to—click the Clock tab button and turn "Use a 24-hour clock" on or off.

Time Zone tab

If you don't set up this tab, the email and documents you send out—and the Mac's conception of what documents are older and newer—could be hopelessly skewed. Teach your Mac where it lives using the Time Zone map, as shown in Figure 13-6.

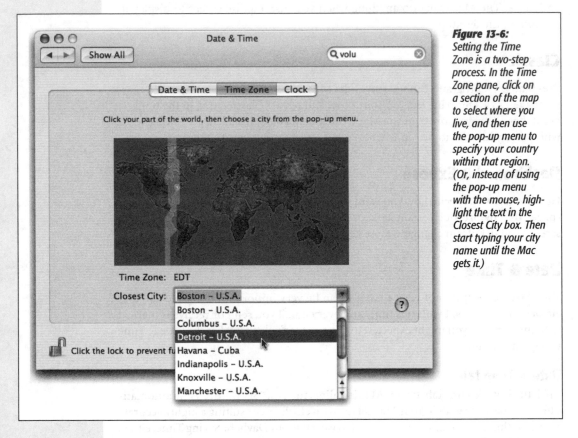

Figure 13-6:
Setting the Time Zone is a two-step process. In the Time Zone pane, click on a section of the map to select where you live, and then use the pop-up menu to specify your country within that region. (Or, instead of using the pop-up menu with the mouse, highlight the text in the Closest City box. Then start typing your city name until the Mac gets it.)

Clock tab

In the Clock pane, you can specify whether or not you want the current time to appear, at all times, at the right end of your menu bar or in a small floating window, whose transparency you can control with the slider here. You can choose between two different clock styles: digital (3:53 p.m.) or analog (a round clock face).

Tip: At the bottom of the dialog box, you'll find a feature called "Announce the time." At the intervals you specify, the Mac will speak, out loud, the current time: "It's ten o'clock." If you tend to get so immersed in "working" that you lose track of time, Mac OS X just removed your last excuse.

And by the way, your menu-bar clock always shows the current *time*. When you need to know today's *date*, just click the clock. A menu drops down revealing the complete date.

Desktop & Screen Saver

This pane offers two ways to show off Mac OS X's glamorous graphics features: *desktop pictures* and *screen savers*.

Desktop

Mac OS X comes with several ready-to-use collections of desktop pictures, ranging from National Geographic–style nature photos to plain solid colors. To install a new background picture, first choose one of the image categories in the list at the left side of the window, as shown in Figure 13-7.

Note: Several of Apple's ready-to-use desktop pictures come in two sizes. The elongated versions (with the flatter, squashed-down thumbnails) are designed to perfectly fill the extra-wide screens on 15- and 17-inch PowerBooks, Apple Cinema Displays, and other unusually wide screens.

Figure 13-7:
Using the list of picture sources at left, you can preview an entire folder of your own images before installing one specific image as your new desktop picture. Use the Choose Folder option to select a folder of assorted graphics—or, if you're an iPhoto veteran, click an iPhoto album name, as shown here. Clicking one of the thumbnails installs the corresponding picture on the desktop.

Using your own pictures

Of course, you may feel that decorating your Mac desktop is much more fun if you use one of your *own* pictures. You can use any digital photo, scanned image, or graphic you want in almost any graphics format (JPEG, PICT, GIF, TIFF, Photoshop, and even PDF).

That's why your own Pictures folder is also listed here. (If you use iPhoto to manage your digital camera shots, you'll welcome the appearance of the Library, Last Import, and iPhoto album icons here, too.)

In any case, when you click one of these icons, you see thumbnail versions of its contents in the main screen to its right. Just click the thumbnail of any picture to apply it immediately to the desktop. (There's no need to remove the previously installed picture first.)

Tip: If there's one certain picture you like, but it's not in any of the listed sources, you can drag its image file onto the *well* (the mini-desktop displayed in the Desktop panel). A thumbnail of your picture instantly appears in the well and, a moment later, the picture is plastered across your monitor.

Making the picture fit

No matter which source you use to choose a photo of your own, you have one more issue to deal with. Unless you've gone to the trouble of editing your chosen photo so that it matches the precise dimensions of your screen (1280 x 854 pixels, for example), it probably isn't exactly the same size as your screen.

Tip: The top 23 pixels of your graphic are hidden by the menu bar—something to keep in mind when you prepare the graphic.

Fortunately, Mac OS X offers a number of solutions to this problem. Using the pop-up menu just to the right of the desktop preview well, you can choose Fill Screen, Stretch, Center, or Tile, each of which enlarges the picture (relative to your screen) in a different way.

Auto-picture changing

The novelty of any desktop picture, no matter how interesting, is likely to fade after several months of all-day viewing. That's why the randomizing function is so delightful.

Turn on "Change picture" at the bottom of the dialog box. From the pop-up menu, specify when you want your background picture to change: "every day," "every 15 minutes," or, if you're *really* having trouble staying awake at your Mac, "every 5 seconds." (The option called "when waking from sleep" refers to the *Mac* waking from sleep, not its owner.)

Finally, turn on "Random order," if you like. If you leave it off, your desktop pictures will change in alphabetical order by file name.

That's all there is to it. Now, at the intervals you specified, your desktop picture will change automatically, smoothly cross-fading between the pictures in your chosen source folder like a slideshow. You may never want to open another window again, because you'll hate to block your view of the show.

Screen Saver

On the Screen Saver pane, you can create your own screen-saver slideshows—an absolute must if you have an Apple Cinema Display and a cool Manhattan loft apartment.

Tip: A screen saver doesn't really save your screen. LCD flat-panel screens—practically the only kind Apple sells—are incapable of "burning in" a stationary image of the sort that originally inspired the creation of screen savers years ago. (And even on CRT screens, you'd have to leave the same picture up for two solid years before the image would begin to burn in.)

No, these screen savers offer two unrelated functions. First, they mask what's on your screen from passersby whenever you leave your desk. Second, they're a blast.

Apple provides a few displays to get you started. Some of the most interesting:

- **Flurry.** You get flaming, colorful, undulating arms of fire, which resemble a cross between an octopus and somebody arc welding in the dark.

- **Abstract, Beach, Cosmos, Forest, Nature Patterns, Paper Shadow.** These are photographic screen savers, featuring gorgeous pictures that slowly zoom and softly cross-fade into each other.

- **iTunes Artwork.** Now you can fill your screen with a grid of CD album covers culled from your iTunes music collection, if you have one. They periodically flip around, just to keep the image changing.

- **RSS Visualizer.** This amazing screen saver, for seeing quick summaries of Web sites, is described on page 303.

- **.Mac.** One of the perks for paying $100 per year for a .Mac membership is the ability to create slideshows online, which can play back either on your own Mac or (if you opted to make it public) on anybody else's. Yes, that's right: You can now enjoy a screen saver composed of photos taken by *somebody else on the Internet.* ("Oh, look, honey, here's some shots of Uncle Jed's crops this summer!")

- **Pictures Folder, Choose Folder, iPhoto Selection.** This is one of the coolest modules. It lets you transform your *own* collection of pictures—whatever you've got in your Home→Pictures folder—into a self-playing slideshow, complete with spectacular zooming and dissolving effects. If you've created a slideshow *in* iPhoto, it also appears here.

- **Library, Last Import, album list.** If you're using iPhoto to organize your digital photos, you'll see its familiar album list here, making it a snap to choose any of your own photo collections for use as a screen saver.

When you click a module's name in the Screen Savers list, you see a mini-version of it playing back in the Preview screen. Click Test to give the module a dry run on your full monitor screen.

Tip: To customize a screen saver, click Options.

When you've had enough of the preview, just jiggle the mouse or press any key. You return to the Screen Saver panel.

Activating the screen saver

You can control when your screen saver takes over your monitor in a couple of ways:

- **After a period of inactivity.** Using the "Start screen saver" slider, you can set the amount of time that has to pass without keyboard or mouse activity before the screen saver starts. You can drag the slider to Never to prevent the screen saver from ever turning on by itself.

- **When you park your cursor in the corner of the screen.** If you click the Hot Corners button, you'll see that you can turn each corner of your monitor into a hot corner (see Figure 13-8).

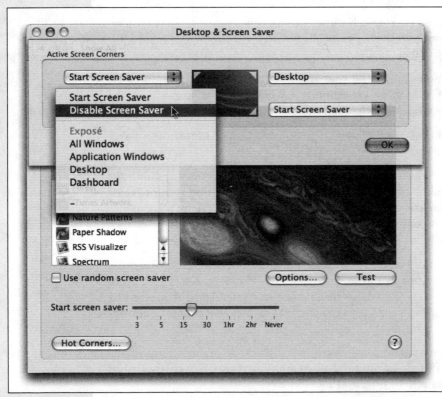

Figure 13-8:
Click the Hot Corners button to open this sheet, which lets you designate certain corners of your screen as instant-activation spots, or never-come-on spots. Sliding the mouse to the Start Screen Saver corner, for example, turns on your screen saver right away. (You can use the remaining corners to control Exposé, as described on page 104.)

Tip: You can find dozens more screen saver modules at *www.epicware.com/macosxsavers.html.*

Displays

Displays is the center of operations for all your monitor settings. Here, you set your monitor's *resolution*, determine how many colors are displayed onscreen, and calibrate color balance and brightness.

Tip: On a laptop, you can open up this panel with a quick keystroke from anywhere on the Mac. Just press Option as you tap one of the screen-brightness keys (F1 or F2) on the top row of your keyboard.

The specific controls you'll see here depend on the kind of monitor you're using, but here are the ones you'll most likely see.

Display Tab

This tab is the main headquarters for your screen controls. It governs these settings:

- **Resolutions.** All Mac screens can make the screen picture larger or smaller, thus accommodating different kinds of work. You perform this magnification or reduction by switching among different *resolutions* (measurements of the number of dots that compose the screen). The Resolutions list displays the various resolution settings your monitor can accommodate: 800 x 600, 1024 x 768, and so on (Figure 13-9).

Figure 13-9:
In the early days of computing, higher color settings entailed a speed hit, since it took time to compute the color for thousands of individual pixels. Today, there's little downside to leaving your screen at its maximum depth setting ("Millions" of colors). Photos, especially, look best at higher depth settings. (The Detect Displays button appears primarily on laptops; it means, "Check to see if I've attached an external monitor or projector.")

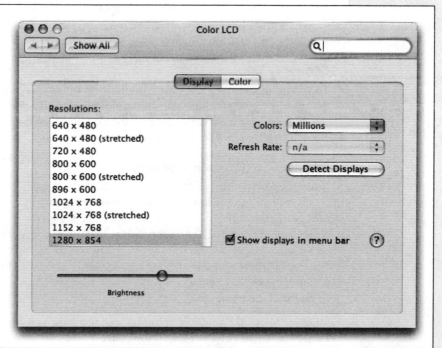

When you use a low-resolution setting, such as 800 x 600, the dots of your screen image get larger, thus enlarging (zooming in on) the picture—but showing a smaller slice of the page.

- **Colors.** Today's Mac monitors offer different *color depth* settings, each of which permits the screen to display a different number of colors simultaneously. The Colors pop-up menu generally offers three choices: 256 Colors, Thousands, and Millions.

- **Refresh Rate.** This pop-up menu (available for CRT screens only—that is, not flat panels) lets you adjust how many times per second your screen image is repainted by your monitor's electron gun. Choose a setting that minimizes flicker.

- **Brightness, Contrast.** Use these sliders to make the screen look good in the prevailing lighting conditions. The Contrast control appears only on CRT monitors, and you'll usually want it all the way up. The Brightness slider is usually best near the middle.

Of course, most Apple keyboards have brightness-adjustment *keys,* so these software controls are included just for the sake of completeness.

Tip: You can adjust the color depth and resolution of your monitor without having to open System Preferences. Just turn on "Show displays in menu bar," which adds a Monitors pop-up menu (a *menulet* [page 18]) to the right end of your menu bar for quick adjustments.

- **Automatically adjust brightness as ambient light changes.** This option appears only if you have a PowerBook with a light-up keyboard. In that case, your laptop's light sensor also dims the screen automatically in dark rooms—*if* this checkbox is turned on.

Geometry Tab

This pane appears only on Macs with built-in, non-flat screens—for the most part, that means eMacs and the older, fruit-colored iMacs. It lets you adjust the position, size, and angle of the screen image on the glass itself—controls that can be useful in counteracting distortion in aging monitors.

Arrange Tab (Multiple Monitors)

From the dawn of the color-monitor era, Macs have had a terrific feature: the ability to exploit multiple monitors all plugged into the computer at the same time. All Macs can project the same thing on both screens (*mirror mode*), which is useful in presentations when the "external monitor" is a projector. A few lucky models permit one monitor to act as an extension of the next. For example, you might have your Photoshop image window on your big monitor, but keep all the Photoshop controls and tool palettes on a smaller screen. Your cursor passes from one screen to another as it crosses the boundary.

To bring about the multiple-monitor arrangement, you need a Mac with a video output jack. (All current Mac laptops have one, as do iMacs and eMacs. And with the installation of additional video cards, a desktop Mac can have three or even more monitors all going at once.) You don't have to shut down the Mac to hook up another monitor—just put it to sleep. Or just hook up the monitor or projector and then choose Detect Displays from the Displays menulet.

When you open System Preferences, you see a different Displays window on each screen, so that you can change the color and resolution settings independently for each. Your Displays menulet shows two sets of resolutions, too, one for each screen.

If your Mac can show different images on each screen, your Displays panel offers an Arrange tab, showing a miniature version of each monitor. By dragging these icons around relative to each other, you can specify how you want the second monitor's image "attached" to the first. Most people position the second monitor's image to the right of the first, but you're also free to position it on the left, above, below, or even directly on top of the first monitor's icon (the last of which produces a video-mirroring setup).

For committed multiple-monitor fanatics, the fun doesn't stop there. See the microscopic menu bar on the first-monitor icon? You can drag that tiny strip onto a different monitor icon, if you like, to tell Displays where you'd like your menu bar to appear.

Color Tab

The Color pane lets you choose an accurate ColorSync profile for your screen (page 444), and calibrate it for correct color display.

Dock

See Chapter 3 for details on the Dock and its System Preferences pane.

Energy Saver

The Energy Saver program helps you and your Mac in a number of ways. By blacking out the screen after a period of inactivity, it prolongs the life of your monitor. By putting the Mac to sleep half an hour after you've stopped using it, Energy Saver cuts down on electricity costs and pollution. On a laptop, Energy Saver extends the length of the battery charge by controlling the activity of the hard drive and screen. You even have the option to have your computer turn off each night automatically, and turn on again at a specified time in anticipation of your arrival at the desk.

Sleep Tab

The Energy Saver controls are very different on a laptop Mac and a desktop. On a desktop Mac, you see a pair of sliders; on a laptop, you have to click Show Details to see them (Figure 13-10).

In any case, the top slider controls when the Mac will automatically go to sleep—anywhere from one minute after your last activity to Never. (Activity can be mouse movement, keyboard action, or Internet data transfer; Energy Saver won't put your Mac to sleep in the middle of a download.)

At that time, the screen goes dark, the hard drive stops spinning, and your processor chip slows to a crawl. Your Mac is now in sleep mode (page 15), using only a fraction of its usual electricity consumption. To wake it up when you return to your desk, press any key. Everything you were working on, including open programs and documents, is still onscreen, exactly as it was. (To turn off this automatic sleep feature entirely, drag the slider to Never.)

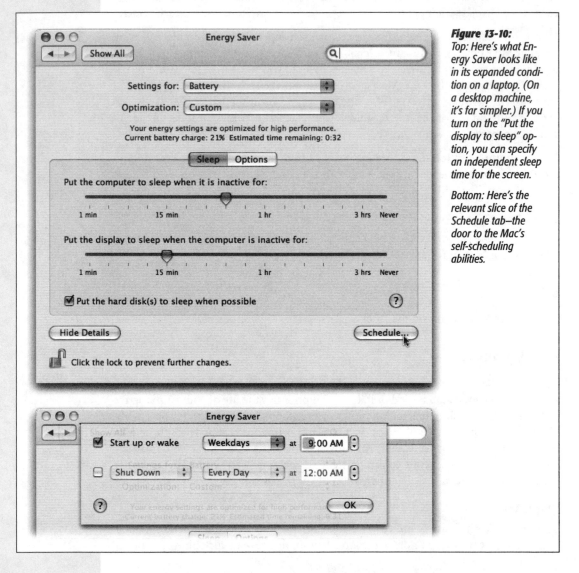

Figure 13-10:
Top: Here's what Energy Saver looks like in its expanded condition on a laptop. (On a desktop machine, it's far simpler.) If you turn on the "Put the display to sleep" option, you can specify an independent sleep time for the screen.

Bottom: Here's the relevant slice of the Schedule tab—the door to the Mac's self-scheduling abilities.

Finally, "Put the hard disk(s) to sleep when possible" saves even more juice—and noise—by stopping your drives from spinning when not in use. The downside is a longer pause when you return to work and wake the thing up, because it takes a few seconds for your hard drive to "spin up" again.

Laptop Options

As noted above, Energy Saver on a laptop offers quite a few additional controls (see Figure 13-10). That's because power management is ten times more important on a laptop, where every drop of battery power counts.

The pop-up menus at the top of the dialog box, for example, let you create different settings for the two states of life for a laptop: when it's plugged in (Power Adapter) and when it's running on battery power (Battery).

Once you've indicated which setting you want to adjust, you can then use the Optimization pop-up menu to choose a canned Energy Saver setting, depending on where you want to fall on the speed-vs.-battery-life spectrum. For example, when you're adjusting the settings for battery-only operation, you can choose Better Battery Life (screen and laptop go to sleep relatively quickly, your processor chip slows down, and the screen brightness dims) or Better Performance (screen sleeps after 10 minutes, laptop after 15, processor runs at normal speed).

The Custom option just means "none of the above." Whenever you adjust one of the sliders or checkboxes, Energy Saver automatically changes the pop-up menu to say Custom. (Mac OS X remembers your settings here, too. If you choose one of the presets and then choose Custom again, your hand-adjusted settings remain in place.)

Scheduled Startup and Shutdown

By clicking the Schedule tab button, you can set up the Mac to shut itself down and turn itself back on automatically (Figure 13-10, bottom).

If you work 9 to 5, for example, set the Mac to turn itself on at 8:45 a.m., and shut itself down at 5:15 p.m.—an arrangement that conserves electricity, saves money, and reduces pollution, but doesn't inconvenience you in the least. In fact, you may come to forget that you've set up the Mac this way, since you'll never actually see it turned off.

Note: The Mac doesn't shut down automatically if you've left unsaved documents open onscreen. It *will* go to sleep, though.

Waking and Other Options

Click the Options tab button to summon a few more controls, including "Wake when the modem detects a ring" (handy if you use your Mac as a fax machine), "Restart automatically after a power failure," and "Processor Performance." This last item is the quick fix for the thigh-scalding heat of a PowerBook's metal case: Choose Reduced from this pop-up menu. Your chip doesn't run nearly as fast now, but it's still plenty fast for email, word processing, and so on—and it runs at about half the temperature. (You'll gain some battery life, too.)

International

The International pane lets you set up your Mac to work in other languages. If you bought your Mac with a *localized* operating system—a version that already runs in your own language—and you're already using the only language, number format, and keyboard layout you'll ever need, then you can ignore most of this pane.

But at the very least, check it out. When it comes to showing off Mac OS X to your friends and loved ones, the "wow" factor on the Mac's polyglot features is huge.

Another Language—Instantly

The Mac has always been able to run software in multiple languages—if you installed the correct fonts, keyboard layouts, and localized software (a French copy of the Mac OS, a French version of Entourage, and so on). But in Mac OS X, you can shift from language to language in certain programs on the fly, without reinstalling the operating system or even restarting the computer.

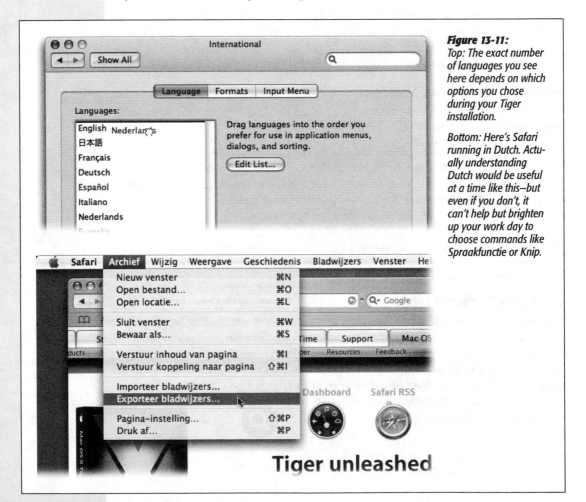

Figure 13-11:
Top: The exact number of languages you see here depends on which options you chose during your Tiger installation.

Bottom: Here's Safari running in Dutch. Actually understanding Dutch would be useful at a time like this—but even if you don't, it can't help but brighten up your work day to choose commands like Spraakfunctie or Knip.

Open the International pane. On the Language tab, you see a listing of the different languages the Mac can switch into—French, German, Spanish, and so on. Just drag one of the languages to the top of the list to select it as the target language, as shown in Figure 13-11.

Now open Safari, TextEdit, or Stickies. Every menu, button, and dialog box is now in the new language you selected! If you log out and back in (or restart) at this point, the entire Finder will be in the new language, too.

Note: Not all programs are language-switching aware. Also note that, while you can add other languages to the Language list using the Edit button, they don't actually work unless you install additional language kit software using the Mac OS X Install disc.

Input Menu Tab

While the Mac can display many different languages at the same time, *typing* in those languages is another matter. The symbols you use when you're typing Swedish aren't the same as when you're typing English. Apple solved this problem by creating different *keyboard layouts*, one for each language. Each rearranges the letters that appear when you press the keys. For example, when you use the Swedish layout and press the semicolon key, you don't get a semicolon (;)—you get an ö.

Apple even includes a Dvorak layout—a scientific rearrangement of the standard English layout that puts the most common letters directly under your fingertips on the home row. Fans of the Dvorak layout claim greater accuracy, better speed, and less fatigue.

Use the list in the Input Menu pane to indicate which keyboard layout you want. If you check off more than one keyboard layout, a tiny flag icon appears in your menu bar—a keyboard *menulet* that lets you switch from one layout to another just by choosing its name.

Tip: Instead of using the keyboard menu, you can switch back and forth between the most recently selected pair of keyboard layouts by pressing ⌘-Space bar. Alternatively, you can "walk down" the list of layouts by pressing Option-⌘-Space.

Of course, these keystrokes are exactly the same as Tiger's preassigned keystrokes for the Spotlight menu and Spotlight window (Chapter 2). There's not much you can do about it, other than changing the Spotlight key assignments as described on page 71.

Keyboard Viewer

Keyboard Viewer consists of a single window containing a tiny onscreen keyboard (Figure 13-12). When you hold down any of the modifier keys on your keyboard (like ⌘, Option, Shift, or Control), you can see exactly which keys produce which characters. The point, of course, is to help you learn which keys to press when you need special symbols or non-English characters, such as © or ¢, in each font.

Note: Keyboard Viewer shows only the symbols you can produce by typing *keystrokes*. A font may contain thousands of other characters that can't actually be typed; the Character Palette (page 369) is the only way to access these other symbols.

It's a great tool—if you can find it.

To do so, open the International pane of System Preferences, click Input Menu, and turn on the Keyboard Viewer checkbox. The window shown at top in Figure 13-12 appears. (Thereafter, you'll be able to choose its name from the flag menulet at the top of the screen, also shown at top in Figure 13-12.)

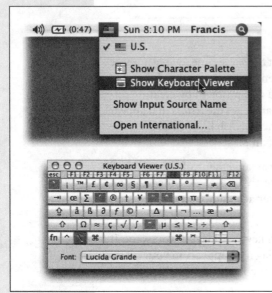

Figure 13-12:
How do you make a π symbol?

Top: Open Keyboard Viewer by choosing its name from the International (flag) menulet.

Bottom: Keyboard Viewer reveals the answer. When you press the Option key, the Keyboard Viewer keyboard shows that the pi character (π) is mapped to the P key.

To see the effect of typing while pressing the modifier keys, either click the onscreen keys or type on your actual keyboard. The corresponding keys on the onscreen keyboard light up as they're pressed.

Change the Keyboard Viewer font

Different fonts contain different hidden characters. For example, Palatino contains an character (pressing Shift-Option-K), yet Adobe Garamond does not.

Fortunately, Keyboard Viewer lets you see the characters lurking within *almost* any installed font; just choose a font's name from the Font pop-up menu to see all of its modifier-key characters. Alas, this feature doesn't work in a few of the fonts where it would be the most useful—certain symbol fonts like Symbol and Zapf Dingbats.

Tip: You're not stuck viewing all characters in 12-point size—a good thing, because some of them are hard to read when displayed that small. Just "zoom" the Key Caps window by clicking its Zoom button. You magnify the Key Caps window and its font.

Keyboard & Mouse

This pane lets you do some fine-tuning of your mouse, keyboard, and (for laptops) trackpad. It also unlocks Mac OS X's strange and remarkable Full Keyboard Access feature, which lets you control your Mac's menus, windows, dialog boxes, buttons, the Dock, and the toolbar, all from the keyboard. Here's a tour of the Keyboard & Mouse panel's various tab buttons.

Keyboard Tab

The changes you make are teeny tiny, but can have a cumulatively big impact on your daily typing routine.

GEM IN THE ROUGH

The Character Palette

There you are, two-thirds of the way through your local chess-club newsletter, when it hits you: You need an arrow symbol. Right now.

You know there's one in one of your symbol fonts, but you're not about to take two weeks off from work just to hunt through your fonts, typing every single combination of keys until you produce the arrow symbol. You can't help wishing there was an easier way to find those special symbols that hide among your fonts—fancy brackets, math symbols, special stars and asterisks, heart shapes, and so on.

The Keyboard Viewer display described on the facing page is one solution. But there's a better one: the Character Palette.

To make it appear, open System Preferences, click the International icon, click the Input Menu tab, and turn on the Character Palette and "Show input menu in menu bar" checkboxes. Now inspect your menu bar. You've just added the keyboard menu.

Next time you're word processing or doing page layout, choose Show Character Palette from this menu. (In most programs, you can choose Edit→Special Characters to summon the palette, too.)

The resulting window rounds up all symbols from all your fonts at once. To find a particular symbol, click the "by Category" tab, choose Roman from the View pop-up menu, and then click the various category headings: Arrows, Stars/Asterisks, Math, and so on. (You can preview various styles of the same symbol by opening the Font Variations triangle.) You can also use the Spotlight-ish Search box at the bottom of the window to find a symbol by name: "heart" or "yen" or "asterisk," for example. When you find the symbol you want, double-click it.

If you're using a Cocoa program, the correct symbol pops into your document. (If not, you may get only the correct character, but not in the correct font. In that case, you'll have to change the font of the inserted character manually. To find out what font it came from, click the Font Variation flippy triangle.)

CHAPTER 13: SYSTEM PREFERENCES

- **Key Repeat Rate, Delay Until Repeat.** Hold down any key long enough, and it starts spitting out repetitions, making it easy to type, for example, "No WAAAAAAAY!" or "You go, girrrrrrrrl!" These two sliders govern this behavior. On the right: a slider that determines how long you must hold down the key before it starts repeating (to prevent triggering repetitions accidentally, in other words). On the left: a slider that governs how fast each key spits out letters once the spitting has begun.

- **Use the F1-F12 keys to control software features.** On Mac laptops, many of the F-keys on the top row perform laptop-related functions. For example, the F1 and F2 keys adjust the screen brightness; F3, F4, and F5 control the speaker volume; and so on.

  So what if you want to use those keys for other functions? For example, the F1 key is the Help key in many programs. In those situations, you're supposed to add the Fn key in the lower-right corner of your keyboard. On a desktop Mac, F1 opens Help; on a laptop, Fn-F1 does the job.

  If you find yourself using the software features (like Help) more often than the hardware features (like brightness), you can reverse this logic. Turning on "Use the F1-F12 keys to control software features" (an option that appears *only* on laptops) lets the F-keys be F-keys, so that they behave exactly as they do on a desktop Mac. Now F1 by itself opens Help—but now you need to add the Fn key for the *hardware* functions like brightness and volume.

- **Illuminate keyboard in low light conditions.** This setting appears only if your Mac's keyboard does, in fact, light up when you're working in the dark—a showy feature of, for instance, some 15- and 17-inch PowerBook models. You can specify that you want the internal lighting to shut off after a period of activity (to save power when you've wandered away, for example), or you can turn the lighting off altogether.

Tip: The Modifier Keys button lets you change the behavior of special keys—Control and Caps Lock, for example—to something that performs a more useful operation.

Mouse Tab

It may surprise you that the cursor on the screen doesn't move five inches when you move the mouse five inches on the desk. Instead, the cursor moves farther when you move the mouse faster.

How *much* farther depends on how you set the first slider here. The Fast setting is nice if you have an enormous monitor, since you don't need an equally large mouse pad to get from one corner to another. The Slow setting, on the other hand, forces you to pick up and put down the mouse frequently as you scoot across the screen. It offers almost no acceleration at all, but it can be great for highly detailed work like pixel-by-pixel editing in Photoshop.

The Double-Click Speed setting specifies how much time you have to complete a double-click. If you click too slowly—beyond the time you've allotted yourself with this slider—the Mac "hears" two *single* clicks instead.

Note: If you've bought a Mighty Mouse (Apple's two-button mouse) and installed its software, this pane looks quite a bit different. Now it lets you assign different functions to the mouse's four programmable buttons.

Trackpad Tab

This pane shows up only if you have a laptop. At the top, you find duplicates of the same Tracking Speed and Double-Click Speed sliders described above—but these let you establish independent tracking and clicking speeds for the *trackpad*.

Trackpad gestures

Under normal circumstances, you touch your laptop's trackpad exclusively to move the cursor. For clicking and dragging, you're supposed to use the clicking button *beneath* the trackpad.

Many people find, however, that it's more direct to tap and drag directly on the trackpad, using the same finger that's been moving the cursor. That's the purpose of these three checkboxes:

- **Clicking.** When this box is turned on, you can tap the trackpad surface to register a mouse click at the location of the cursor. Double-tap to double-click.

- **Dragging.** Turn on this option if you want to move icons, highlight text, or pull down menus—in other words, to drag, not just click—using the trackpad. Start by tapping twice on the trackpad, then *immediately* after the second tap, begin dragging your finger. (If you don't start moving promptly, the laptop assumes that you were double-clicking, which could wind up opening an icon you didn't intend to open.) You can stroke the trackpad repeatedly to continue your movement, as long as your finger never leaves the trackpad surface for more than about one second. When you finally stop touching the pad, you "let go," and the drag is considered complete. (All of this is much easier to do than to describe.)

- **Drag lock.** If the dragging maneuver described above makes you nervous that you're going to "drop" what you're dragging if you stop moving your finger for a fraction of a second, turn on this option instead. Once again, begin your drag by double-clicking, then move your finger immediately after the second click.

  When this option is on, however, you can take your sweet time in continuing the movement. In between strokes of the trackpad, you can take your finger off the laptop for as long as you like. You can take a phone call, a shower, or a vacation; the Mac still thinks that you're in the middle of a drag. Only when you tap *again* does the laptop consider the drag a done deal.

- **Use two fingers to scroll.** Starting on the mid-2005 PowerBook models, the trackpad harbors a little secret: You can scroll any window that has scroll bars by moving two adjoining fingers on the trackpad (vertically or horizontally, depending on the settings you make here).

Trackpad options

- **Ignore accidental trackpad input.** This option addresses a chronic syndrome of laptop owners who turn on the Clicking option. When you type along and a finger accidentally brushes the trackpad, it sends the insertion point onto a different line of text. Before you even notice, you've typed over, or typed into, some random part of your document.

  This ingenious option locks out the click-and-drag trackpad functions when you're actually typing on the keyboard—an elegantly simple solution.

- **Ignore trackpad when mouse is present.** Here's another ingenious advance in laptop technology: When you hook up a mouse, trackball, or tablet to your laptop, the trackpad is deactivated. If you're using a mouse, then you probably won't want to use the trackpad—and by turning on this checkbox, you're no longer susceptible to accidentally brushing it.

Tip: If you're lucky enough to have one of the newer PowerBooks that supports two-finger scrolling, you can customize it here, too.

Bluetooth Tab

People have named their Macs for years (Voyager, Li'l Abner, PowerThang G5). Now they can name their keyboards and mice—and, indeed, must—thanks to Apple's introduction of its cordless Bluetooth keyboard and mouse. Here's where you type in their names (so that Mac knows which wireless keyboard and mouse it's "listening" to in a room full of them) and monitor their battery levels.

Keyboard Shortcuts

Mac OS X comes loaded with keyboard shortcuts for common tasks—and now you can reassign them to shortcuts you prefer. For a full discussion of the options on this pane, see page 114.

Network

The Network panel is the brain of your Mac's Internet and local networking connections. See Chapter 9 for the settings you need to plug in.

Print & Fax

Chapter 8 describes printing and faxing in detail. This panel's purpose in life is to offer a few miscellaneous printing options, such as which printer and paper size you use most of the time, which printers you want to share on the network, and faxing settings like your fax number and whether you want received faxes to print out automatically.

QuickTime

The settings in the QuickTime panel affect the way movies are played back on your Mac, including movies that stream to you from a Web page and movies that you watch using QuickTime Player (page 431). Very few of these settings are worth tweaking.

Security

Mac OS X turns out to be one of the most secure operating systems on earth—and this panel helps to explain why. See Chapter 12 for details on locking up your Mac.

Sharing

Mac OS X is an upstanding network citizen, flexible enough to share its contents with other Macs, Windows PCs, people dialing in from the road, people dialing in from the Internet, and so on. The various checkboxes you'll encounter are:

- **Personal File Sharing.** Turning on this checkbox makes your Mac accessible to *other* Macs. Someone using another Mac on your network can simply choose Go→Network to browse the list of accessible networked computers, double-click your Mac's name, and enter his username and password to get access to his files on your Mac.

Tip: You can even connect to your home Mac from over the *Internet*, provided you have the home Mac's I.P. address (It's the four numbers separated by periods at the bottom of your Sharing window). On the Internet-connected Mac, choose Go→Connect to Server (⌘-K), type *afp://111.121.131.141/* (substituting the correct I.P. address), click Connect, and enter your username and password.

A hard drive icon representing your home Mac now appears on your screen, which you use just like any connected disk—copying files to and from it, for example, and dragging it to the Trash when you're done.

- **Windows Sharing.** Page 140 explains this magic technology, which allows any networked Windows PC to get to the files on your Mac.

- **Personal Web Sharing.** This single checkbox turns your Mac into a full-fledged Web server—a computer that provides Web pages to any visitors on the Internet.

  Place the actual Web pages (in HTML format) into your Home→Sites folder. Then give out the URL at the bottom of the Sharing pane to any prospective visitors: family members, neighbors, and so on.

Note: Unless you have an Internet connection that's on all the time (like a DSL or cable connection), your visitors will only be able to access the Web site when you are *also* online.

- **Remote Login.** Warning: This checkbox is for Unix nerds only. When turned on, it enables you to tap into your Mac's Unix underbelly from anywhere in the world, using a cryptic command called *ssh*. If you have no aspirations of ever becoming a command-line user, you can safely ignore this checkbox.

• **FTP Access:** This checkbox transforms your Mac into an *FTP server*—a specialized computer for transferring files (not Web pages) over the Internet. Any visitors must know the URL provided at the bottom of your System Preferences window, but once they've entered it into their Web browser or FTP program—and typed in an administrator's username and password—they can download files from your Mac at very high speed.

• **Apple Remote Desktop:** This geeky feature allows network administrators to manage groups of Macs remotely. Ignore it.

• **Remote Apple Events:** When this checkbox is turned on, other Macs can send *Apple Events*—quick activity requests—to your Mac. If you have any reason to turn this on, your network administrator will let you know.

• **Printer Sharing:** You can learn more about this useful feature (for transforming a USB printer into a networked printer) on page 489.

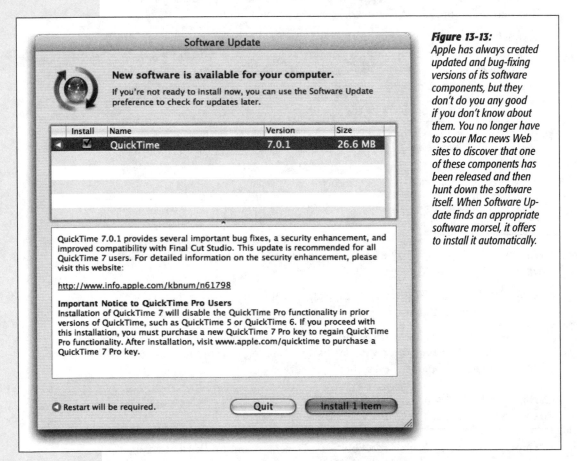

Figure 13-13:
Apple has always created updated and bug-fixing versions of its software components, but they don't do you any good if you don't know about them. You no longer have to scour Mac news Web sites to discover that one of these components has been released and then hunt down the software itself. When Software Update finds an appropriate software morsel, it offers to install it automatically.

- **Xgrid:** This feature is another one that should be labeled "nerds only." Avoid it unless you have software especially designed for large-scale network processing tasks.

The Firewall tab is described starting on page 250, and the Internet tab is explained on page 254.

Software Update

In any project as complex as an operating system, there are always bugs to be fixed, features to be sped up, and enhancements to add. That's why Windows has Automatic Updates—and why Apple has Software Update.

Whenever Apple comes up with a new software fix, this program can notify you, download the update, and install it into your System automatically.

Software Update doesn't automatically download the new software unless you turn on the "Download important updates in the background" checkbox. No matter what, though, Software Update always asks you before *installing* an update, as shown in Figure 13-13.

For maximum effortlessness, turn on the "Check for updates" checkbox and then select a frequency from the pop-up menu—daily, weekly, or monthly

---

Note: Software Update also keeps a meticulous log of everything it drops into your system. On the Install Updates tab, you see them listed, just in case some tech-support person ever asks.

Sound

Using the tabs of the Sound pane, you can configure the sound system of your Mac in the following ways.

Sound Effects

"Sound effects" means *error beeps*—the sound you hear when the Mac wants your attention, or when you click someplace you shouldn't. Just click the sound of your choice to make it your standard system beep. Most are funny and clever, yet subdued enough to be of practical value as alert sounds.

As for the other controls on the Sound Effects panel, they include:

- **Alert Volume slider.** The *main* volume slider for your Mac is at the bottom of the Sound panel, called "Output volume." The slider on the Sound Effects pane is *just* for error beeps.

- **Play user interface sound effects.** This option produces a few subtle sound effects when you perform certain Finder operations: dragging something off of the Dock, for example, or dropping something into the Trash.

• **Play feedback when volume keys are pressed.** Most Mac keyboards have little speaker icons that, when pressed, adjust the overall volume louder or softer. Each time you press one of these keys, the Mac beeps to help you gauge the current speaker level.

That's all fine when you're working at home. But more than one person has been humiliated in an important meeting when the Mac made a sudden, inappropriately loud sonic outburst—only to amplify that embarrassment by furiously and repeatedly pressing the volume-down key, beeping all the way.

If you turn off this checkbox, the Mac won't make any sound at all as you adjust its volume. Instead, you'll see only a visual representation of the steadily decreasing (or increasing) volume level.

Tip: This System Preferences pane is another one that offers a "Show in menu bar" option at the bottom. It installs a volume control right in your menu bar, making the volume control instantly accessible from any program.

Output Tab

"Output" means speakers or headphones. For 99 percent of the Mac-using community, this pane offers nothing useful except the Balance slider, with which you can set the balance between your Mac's left and right stereo speakers.

Input Tab

This panel lets you specify which microphone you want the Mac to "listen to," if, indeed, you have more than one connected. It also lets you adjust the sensitivity of that microphone—its "input volume"—by dragging the slider and watching the real-time Input Level meter above it change as you speak.

Speech

The Mac's speech features—both listening and talking back—are far more extensive than what you're probably used to from Windows. Depending on the kind of work you do, these features might give you both a productivity boost and a good giggle along the way.

Speech Recognition

The Apple marketing machine may have been working too hard when it called this feature "speech recognition." The Mac OS feature called PlainTalk doesn't take dictation, typing out what you say. Instead, PlainTalk is what's known as a *command-and-control* feature. It lets you open programs, choose menu commands, trigger keystrokes, and click dialog box buttons and tabs—just by speaking their names.

Truth is, very few people use PlainTalk speech recognition. But if your Mac has a microphone, PlainTalk is worth at least a 15-minute test drive. It may become a part of your work routine forever.

The on/off switch for speech recognition in Mac OS X is the Speech pane of System Preferences. Where you see "Speakable Items," click On. (The first time you do this, a small instructions sheet appears. Read it if you like, and then click Continue. If you ever want to see these tips again, click the Helpful Tips button on this pane.)

The Feedback window

Check out the right side of your screen: A small, microphone-ish window now appears (Figure 13-14). The word *Esc* in its center indicates the "listen" key—the key you're supposed to hold down when you want the Mac to respond to your voice. (You wouldn't want the Mac listening all the time—even when you said, for example, "Hey, it's cold in here. *Close the window.*" Therefore, the Mac comes ready to listen only when you're pressing that key.)

You can specify a different key, if you wish, or eliminate the requirement to press a key altogether, as described in the next section.

When you start talking, you'll also see the Mac's interpretation of what you said written out in a yellow balloon just over the Feedback window.

Tip: The Feedback window lacks the standard Close and Minimize buttons. If it's in your way, just double-click it (or say "minimize speech window") to shrink it onto your Dock.

The Speakable Commands window

The only commands the Mac understands are those listed in the Speakable Commands window, which generally appears automatically when you turn on speech recognition. Keeping your eye on the Speakable Commands window is absolutely essential, because it offers a complete list of everything your Mac understands. As you can see, some of them represent shortcuts that would take several steps if you had to perform them manually.

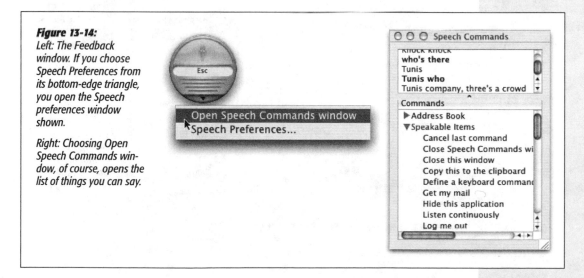

Figure 13-14:
Left: The Feedback window. If you choose Speech Preferences from its bottom-edge triangle, you open the Speech preferences window shown.

Right: Choosing Open Speech Commands window, of course, opens the list of things you can say.

To open this list if it's not open, click the tiny arrow at the bottom of the Feedback window and choose "Open Speech Commands window" from the pop-up menu. The entries you find here correspond to the various commands you can speak in the current program—and the sets of commands you've enabled in the System Preferences→Speech→Speech Recognition tab→Commands tab.

Speaking to the Mac

When you're ready to talk to your computer, position the microphone between one and three feet from your mouth. If it's a headset, make sure it's plugged in. (If it's built-in, speech recognition may not be as accurate.)

In any case, finish up by opening the Speech pane of System Preferences. Click the Speech Recognition tab, click the Settings tab, and use the Microphone pop-up menu to specify which microphone you'll be using (if you have a choice).

Now you're ready to begin. While pressing the Esc key (if that's still the one identified in the Feedback window), begin speaking. Speak normally; don't exaggerate or shout. Try one of the commands in the Speakable Commands list—perhaps "What time is it?" If the Feedback window doesn't display animated sound waves, indicating that the Mac is hearing you, something's wrong with your microphone setup. Open the Speech pane again, and confirm that the correct microphone is selected.

Improving the PlainTalk vocabulary

By putting an alias of the favorite document, folder, disk, or program into the Home→Library→Speakable Items folder, you can teach PlainTalk to recognize its name and open it for you on command. You can name these icons anything you want.

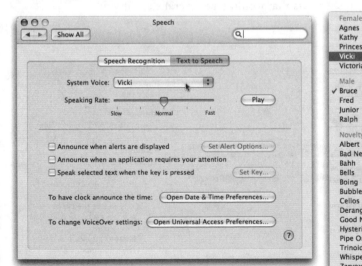

Figure 13-15:
For 15 minutes of hilarious fun, try clicking the Mac's voices in turn (or press the up and down arrow keys) to hear a sample sentence spoken in that voice. Drag the slider to affect how fast he or she speaks. (Clearly, Apple's programmers had some fun with this assignment.)

You can also rename the starter set that Apple provides. You'll have the best luck with polysyllabic names—"Microsoft Word," not just "Word."

The Mac Talks Back

The conversation doesn't have to be one-way, though; it's even easier to make the *Mac* talk.

The Mac can read almost anything you like: text that you pass your cursor over, alert messages, menus, and *any text document in any program*. It can speak in your choice of 23 synthesizer voices, ages 8 to 50. The Mac's voice comes out of its speakers, reading with a twangy, charmingly Norwegian accent.

To set this up, click the Text to Speech tab (Figure 13-15), Here, you can control which voice your Mac uses, as well as how fast it should speak. Click "Speak selected text when the key is pressed"; you'll be asked to press the keys you want to use as a trigger (like Option-S). From now on, the Mac will read aloud any highlighted text, in any program, when you press Option-S!

Spotlight

Here's how you tell the Mac (a) which categories of files and information you want the Spotlight search feature to search, (b) which folders you *don't* want searched, for privacy or speed reasons, and (c) which key combination you want to use for summoning the Spotlight menu or dialog box. Details appear on page 73.

Startup Disk

Use this panel to pick the System Folder your Mac will use the next time you start your Mac, swapping between Mac OS X and Mac OS 9.2, for example. Check out the details on page 222.

Universal Access

The Universal Access pane is designed for people who type with one hand, find it difficult to use a mouse, or have trouble seeing or hearing. (These features can also be handy when the mouse is broken or missing.)

Seeing Tab (Magnifying the Screen)

If you have trouble seeing the screen, then boy, does the Mac have features for you.

VoiceOver

The Mac has always been able to read stuff on the screen out loud. But in Tiger, Apple took this feature light-years farther, turning it into a full-blown *screen reader* for the benefit of people who can't see. VoiceOver doesn't just read every scrap of text it finds on the screen, it also lets you control everything on the screen (menus, buttons, and so on) without ever needing the mouse.

As you can guess, learning VoiceOver means learning a *lot* of new keyboard shortcuts. (Most of them involve the same two modifier keys pressed together: Control-Option.) Click "Open VoiceOver Utility" to configure this feature's settings (you may want someone to set this up for you, if you have trouble seeing the screen). You'll want to spend a good deal of time with the online help screens reading about how VoiceOver works (choose Help→Mac Help, and search for *voiceover*).

Magnify the screen

Another quick solution is to reduce your monitor's *resolution*—thus magnifying the image—using the Displays panel described earlier in this chapter. If you have a 17-inch or larger monitor set to, say, 640 x 480, the result is a greatly magnified picture.

That method doesn't give you much flexibility, however, and it's something of a hassle to adjust. For a better solution, try the Zoom feature that appears here; it lets you enlarge the area surrounding your cursor in any increment.

To make it work, press Option-⌘-8 as you're working. Or, if the Seeing panel is open, click the On button under the word "Zoom." That's the master switch.

No zooming actually takes place, however, until you press Option-⌘-plus sign (to zoom in) or Option-⌘-minus sign (to zoom out). With each press, the entire screen image gets larger or smaller, creating a virtual monitor that follows your cursor around the screen.

If you click Options, you'll find miles and miles of choices that control when the enlarged screen image pans (all the time, or only when the pointer hits a screen edge), the maximum or minimum degree of enlargement, and so on.

Inverted colors

While you're at it, pressing Control-Option-⌘-* (asterisk), or clicking the "Switch to Black on White" button, inverts the colors of the screen, so that text appears white on black—an effect that some people find easier to read. (This option also freaks out many Mac fans who turn it on by mistake, somehow pressing Control-Option-⌘-* by accident during everyday work. They think that the Mac's expensive monitor has just gone loco. Now you know better.)

Tip: There's also a button called Use Grayscale, which banishes all color from your screen. This is another feature designed to improve text clarity, but it's also a dandy way to see how a color document will look when printed on a monochrome laser printer.

No matter which color mode you choose, the "Enhance contrast" slider is another option that can help. It makes blacks blacker and whites whiter, further eliminating in-between shades and thereby making the screen easier to see. (If the Universal Access pane doesn't happen to be open, you can always use the keystrokes Ctrl-Option-⌘-< and > to decrease or increase contrast.)

Hearing Tab (Flashing the Screen)

If you have trouble hearing the Mac's sounds, the obvious solution is to increase the volume, which is why this panel offers a direct link to the Sound preferences pane. (If your Mac doesn't have external speakers, consider getting some.)

Fortunately, hearing your computer usually isn't critical (except when working in music and audio, of course). The only time audio is especially important is when the Mac tries to get your attention by beeping. For those situations, turn on "Flash the screen when an alert sound occurs" (an effect you can try out by clicking Flash Screen). Now you'll see a white flash across the entire monitor whenever the Mac would otherwise beep—not a bad idea on laptops, actually, so that you don't miss beeps when you've got the speakers muted.

Keyboard Tab (Typing Assistance)

This panel offers two clever features designed to help people who have trouble using the keyboard.

- *Sticky Keys* lets you press multiple-key shortcuts (involving keys like Shift, Option, Control, and ⌘) one at a time instead of all together.

  To make Sticky Keys work, first turn on the master switch at the top of the window. Then go to work on the Mac, triggering keyboard commands as shown in Figure 13-16.

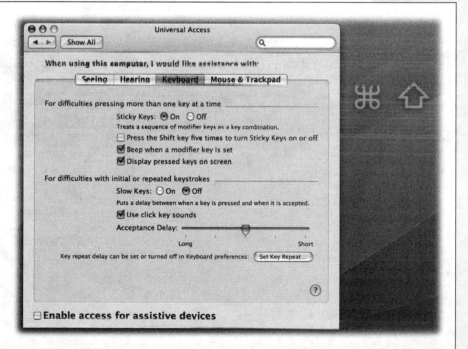

Figure 13-16:
Whenever you want to press a multiple-key keystroke like Shift-Option-⌘-D, press them one at a time. You'll see ghost images of these keys superimposed on your screen, to show you which keystrokes you've added to your temporary collection. To "un-press" a key you've already pressed, press it again twice.

If you press a modifier key *twice*, meanwhile, you lock it down. (Its onscreen symbol gets brighter to let you know.) When a key is locked, you can use it for several commands in a row. For example, if a folder icon is highlighted, you could double-press ⌘ to lock it down—and then type O (to open the folder), look around, and then press W (to close the window). Press the ⌘ key a third time to "un-press" it.

Tip: The checkbox called "Press the Shift key five times to turn Sticky Keys on or off" gives you the flexibility of turning Sticky Keys on and off at will, without even taking a trip to System Preferences. Whenever you want to turn on Sticky Keys, press the Shift key five times in succession. You'll hear a special clacking sound effect alerting you that you just turned on Sticky Keys. (Repeat the five presses to turn Sticky Keys off again.)

- *Slow Keys,* on the other hand, doesn't register a key press at all until you've held down the key for more than a second or so—a feature designed to screen out accidental key presses.

If "Use click key sounds" is turned on, you'll hear a little typing sound each time you press a key—but none of these key presses registers unless you hold the key down for a moment. (Use the Acceptance Delay slider to govern this threshold.) You hear a different sound when the Mac actually accepts the key press—and, of course, you'll see the letter you typed appear onscreen.

Mouse & Trackpad Tab (Cursor Control from the Keyboard)

Mouse Keys is designed to help people who can't use the mouse—or who want more precision when working in graphics programs. It lets you click, drag, and otherwise manipulate the cursor by pressing the keys on your numeric keypad.

POWER USERS' CLINIC

Direct System Preferences Access from the Dock

Pining for the days of Windows, when all control panels were only a click away (in the menu or Start→Control Panel menu)? Pine no more. Within one minute, you can have yourself a tidy pop-up menu of System Preferences panes right there in your Dock.

Make a new folder (in your Home folder, for example). Name it whatever you want the Dock icon to say—Control Panel, for example.

Now open your System→Library→PreferencePanes folder, which contains the icons for the various System Preferences panes. Select all of them—or only the ones you actually use.

Drag them into your Control Panel folder, taking care to hold Option-⌘ before you release the mouse. (Option-⌘-dragging makes aliases of them.) If the .prefPane suffix on the aliases bugs you, select all of the aliases, press ⌘-I, open the Name & Extension panel in the Get Info window, and turn on "Hide extension."

Finally, drag the Control Panel folder onto the right side of your Dock. Now, whenever you want to open a particular pane, just Control-click (or hold the mouse button down on) this Dock icon. You get a handy pop-up list, as shown here.

When Mouse Keys is turned on, the 5 key acts as the clicker—hold it down for a moment to "click the mouse," do that twice to double-click, and so on. Hold down the 0 key to lock down the mouse button, and the period key to unlock it. (The amount of time you have to hold them down depends on how you've set the Initial Display slider.)

Move the cursor around the screen by pressing the eight keys that surround the 5 key. (For example, hold down the 9 key to move the cursor diagonally up and to the right.) If you hold one of these keys down continuously, the cursor, after a pause, begins to move smoothly in that direction—according to the way you have adjusted the sliders called Initial Delay and Maximum Speed.

Tip: The checkbox called "Press the Option key five times to turn Mouse Keys on or off" saves you the trouble of opening System Preferences.

The Freebie Programs

R ight out of the box, Mac OS X comes with a healthy assortment of nearly 50 freebies: programs for sending email, writing documents, doing math, even playing games. Some are dressed-up versions of Mac programs that have been around for years. Others, though, are new programs that not only show off some of Mac OS X's most dramatic new technologies, but also let you get real work done without having to invest in additional software.

These programs reside in two important folders on your hard drive: Applications (in the main hard drive window) and Utilities (within the Applications folder). The Applications folder houses the productivity programs; Utilities holds a couple of dozen maintenance programs for setting up printers and network connections, fixing problems on your hard disk, and so on.

Tip: You can jump straight to the Applications folder in the Finder by pressing Shift-⌘-A, or by clicking the Applications button in the Finder Sidebar (it's the icon that looks like an *A*). Similarly, Shift-⌘-U takes you to the Utilities folder.

You might consider adding the Application and Utilities folders' icons to the right side of your Dock, too, so that you can access them no matter what program you're in.

This chapter guides you through every item in your new software library, one program at a time. (Depending on your Mac model, you may find other programs in your Applications folder; Apple occasionally licenses software from other companies to spice up the collection for, say, iMacs or Power Macs.)

Address Book

The Address Book is a database that stores names, addresses, email addresses, phone numbers, and other contact information. Chapter 6 covers the process of importing your Windows contacts into Address Book, and Chapter 10 can help you use them once they're there.

AppleScript

AppleScript may be hard for a Windows switcher to grasp right away, because there's simply nothing like it in Windows. It's a programming language that's both very simple and very powerful, because it lets Mac programs send instructions or data to *each other*. A simple AppleScript program might perform some simple daily task for you: backing up your Documents folder, for example. A more complex script can be pages long. In professional printing and publishing, where AppleScript enjoys its greatest popularity, a script might connect to a photographer's hard drive elsewhere on the Internet, download a photo from a predetermined folder, color-correct it in Photoshop, import it into a specified page-layout document, print a proof copy, and send a notification email to the editor—automatically.

Ready-made AppleScripts

Mac OS X comes with several dozen prewritten scripts that are genuinely useful—and all you have to do is choose their names from a menu. "Playing back" an AppleScript in this way requires about as much technical skill as pressing an elevator button.

To sample some of these cool starter scripts, you must first bring the Script menu to your menu bar. To do so, open your Applications→AppleScript folder. Inside, double-click the icon called AppleScript Utility. Turn on "Show Script Menu in menu bar."

Now open the newly installed Script menu, whose icon looks like a scroll, to see the list of prewritten scripts (Figure 14-1).

Some of the scripts in this menu operate on familiar components of the Mac OS, like the Finder; others show off applications or features that are new in Mac OS X. Here are a few of the best:

- **Basics→Open Script Editor** launches Script Editor, a program that you can use to edit and write your own AppleScript programs.

- **Finder Scripts→Add to File Names, Finder→Add to Folder Names.** These scripts tack on a prefix or suffix to the name of every file or folder in the frontmost Finder window (or, if no windows are open, on the desktop). Now you're starting to see the power of AppleScript: You could use this script to add the word *draft* or *final* or *old* to all of the files in a certain folder.

- **Finder Scripts→Replace Text in Item Names** lets you do a search-and-replace of text bits inside file names, folder names, or both. When one publisher rejects your 45-chapter book proposal, you can use this script to change all 45 chapter files from, for example, "A History of Mouse Pads—A Proposal for Random House, Chapter 1" to "A History of Mouse Pads—A Proposal for Simon & Schuster, Chapter 1."

- **Info Scripts→Font Sampler** is designed to show you what all your fonts look like (see Figure 14-2).

Figure 14-1:
Mac OS X comes with an assortment of useful scripts to try. The Script menu (which you install from your Applications→AppleScript folder) lets you launch AppleScripts, just by choosing their names, from within any application.

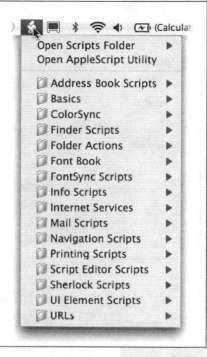

Figure 14-2:
The Font Sampler script launches TextEdit, opens a new document, and fills it with dozens of copies of the classic "What does this font look like?" test sentence: The quick brown fox jumped over the lazy dog. Then, as you watch, it formats each line with a different font—a good page to print out and keep as a reference.

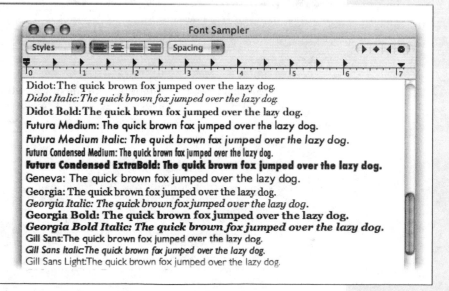

- **Mail Scripts→Crazy Message Text** is Apple at its wackiest. When you run it, a dialog box asks you what message you want to send ("Happy Birthday," for example). Mail then creates a colorful, zany, outgoing formatted message in which each letter has a random typeface, style, color, and size. It's ideal for making people think you spent a long time with your Format menu for their entertainment.

- **URLs→CNN** and the other commands in the URLs submenu simply open your browser, connect to the Internet if necessary, and then open the specified Web page.

  Another script here, Download Weather Map, is much cooler. In a flash, it downloads the current U.S. weather-map image and then opens the file in the Preview program for viewing.

Writing Your Own AppleScripts

As programming languages go, AppleScript is easy to understand. It takes only a few weeks, not years, to become comfortable with AppleScript. And the power AppleScript places in your hands is well worth the effort you'll expend learning it.

For example, here's a fragment of actual AppleScript code:

```
open folder "AppleScript" of folder "Applications" of startup
disk
```

You probably don't need a manual to tell you what this line from an AppleScript program does. It opens the Applications→AppleScript folder on your hard drive. (That's the folder that contains Script Editor, the Mac OS X program that lets you write your own AppleScripts.)

Tip: AppleScript is too big of a topic to cover in just a few pages. If you're serious about learning to script on the Mac—to control Photoshop, Word, and iChat automatically, for example—a book like *AppleScript: The Missing Manual* is a near-necessity.

Calculator

The Mac OS X Calculator is useful for performing quick arithmetic without having to open a spreadsheet, but it can also act as a scientific calculator for students and scientists, a conversion calculator for metric and U.S. measures, even a currency calculator for world travelers.

Here's everything you need to know for basic math:

- The calculator has three modes: Basic, Advanced (Figure 14-3), and Programmer. Switch among them by choosing the appropriate commands from the View menu (or, more conveniently, using the keyboard shortcuts ⌘-1, ⌘-2, and ⌘-3).

- You can operate the Calculator by clicking the onscreen buttons, but it's much easier to press the corresponding number and symbol keys on your keyboard.

Tip: If you have a Mac laptop, don't miss the embedded numeric keypad, superimposed on the right side of the keyboard and labeled on the keys in a different color ink. When you press the Fn key in the lower-left corner of the keyboard, typing these keys produces the numbers instead of the letters.

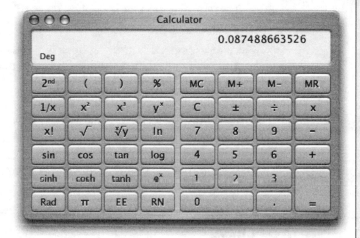

Figure 14-3:
The Calculator program offers a four-function Basic mode, a full-blown scientific calculator mode (shown here), and a programmer's hex calculator. Each one offers a "paper tape" feature (View→Show Paper Tape) that lets you correct errors made way back in a calculation. To edit one of these numbers, drag through it, retype, and then click Recalculate Totals.

- As you go, you can make your calculator speak each key you press. This is a sensational feature; the Mac's voice ensures that you don't mistype as you keep your eyes on the receipts in front of you, typing by touch.

  Just choose Speech→Speak Button Pressed to turn this feature on or off. (You can choose the voice in the Speech pane of System Preferences.)

- Once you've calculated a result, you can copy it (using File→Copy, or ⌘-C) and paste your answer directly into another program.

- If you don't need anything more than a basic calculator, just use the calculator Dashboard widget instead (page 108). You can access it from any program by pressing F12 (and, if the calculator isn't already on the screen, dragging it there from the bar that appears when you click the + button).

Conversions

Calculator is more than a calculator; it's also a conversion program. No matter what units you're trying to convert—meters, grams, inches, miles per hour—the Calculator is ready. Proceed like this:

1. **Clear the calculator. Type in the starting measurement.**

   To convert 48 degrees Celsius to Fahrenheit, for example, type *48.*

2. **From the Convert menu, choose the kind of conversion you want.**

   In this case, choose Temperature. A little dialog box appears.

3. **Use the pop-up menus to specify which units you want to convert to and from.**

To convert Celsius to Fahrenheit, for example, choose Celsius from the first pop-up menu, and Fahrenheit from the second.

4. **Click OK.**

That's it. The calculator displays the result—in degrees Fahrenheit, in this example.

Calculator is especially amazing when it comes to *currency* conversions—from pesos to American dollars, for example—because it actually does its homework. It goes online to download up-to-the-minute currency rates to ensure that the conversion is accurate.

All you have to do is choose Convert→Update Currency Exchange Rates. Then, when you use the Convert→Currency command, your numbers will be the very latest.

Tip: Again, the Dashboard offers a unit-converter widget that's more useful, because you can access it from any program with a single keystroke (F12).

Chess

Mac OS X comes with only one game, but it's a beauty (Figure 14-4). Chess is a traditional chess game played on a gorgeously rendered board with a set of realistic 3-D pieces. The program is actually a 15-year-old Unix-based chess program, GNU Chess, that Apple packaged up in a new wrapper.

GEM IN THE ROUGH

Talking to Chess

If your friends and co-workers are, for some reason, still unimpressed by Mac OS X and your mastery of it, invite them over to watch you play a game of chess with your Mac—by *talking* to it.

Open the Chess program. Unless you've turned it off (in Chess→Preferences), the game's speech-recognition feature is already turned on. When it's on, the round Feedback window should be visible onscreen.

To learn how to speak commands in a way that Chess will understand, click the small gray triangle at the bottom of the Speech Feedback panel to open the Speech Commands window. As usual, it lists all the commands that Chess can

comprehend.

You specify the location of pieces using the grid of numbers and letters that appears along the edges of the chessboard. The White King, for example, starts on square e1 because he's in the first row (1) and the fifth column (e). To move the King forward by one square, you'd say: "King e1 to e2."

As the Speech Commands window should make clear, a few other commands are at your disposal. "Take back move" is one of the most useful. When you're ready to close in for the kill, the syntax is, "Pawn e5 takes f6."

And smile when you say that.

When you launch Chess, you're presented with a fresh, new game that's set up in Human vs. Computer mode—meaning that you (the Human, with the white pieces) get to play against the Computer (your Mac, on the black side). Drag the chess piece of your choice into position on the board, and the game is afoot.

Tip: Choose Chess→Preferences to change the difficulty level, and to customize the appearance of the board and pieces (fur pawns, anyone?).

Figure 14-4:
Chess isn't just another computerized chess game; it's also one of the more visually striking programs you get with Mac OS X. You don't have to be terribly exact about grabbing the chess pieces when it's time to make your move. Just click anywhere within a piece's current square to drag it into a new position on the board.

Francis – Computer (White to Move)

Dictionary

For word nerds everywhere, the Dictionary (and Thesaurus) is one of Mac OS X's most welcome features. You can look up word definitions, pronunciations, and synonyms—all through an electronic version of the entire New Oxford American Dictionary and Oxford American Writers Thesaurus.

Mac OS X also comes with about a million ways to look up a word:

- **Double-click the Dictionary icon.** The Dictionary's no-nonsense lookup window appears. As you type into the Spotlight-y search box, you home in on matching words; double-click a word, or select it and press Enter, to view a complete, typographically elegant definition, complete with sample sentence and pronunciation guide.

Tip: If you don't recognize a word in the definition, double-click *that* to look up *its* definition. You can then double-click again in *that* definition—and on, and on, and on.

(You can then use the History menu, the ⌘-[and ⌘-] keystrokes, or the Back and forward buttons on the toolbar, to go back and forward in your chain of lookups.)

It's worth exploring the Dictionary→Preferences dialog box, by the way. There, you can choose U.S. or British pronunciations, adjust the font size, and indicate whether you prefer synonyms or definitions.

- **Press F12.** That's right: The Dictionary is one of the widgets in Dashboard (page 108).

- **Control-click a highlighted word in a Cocoa program.** From the shortcut menu, choose Look Up in Dictionary. The Dictionary program opens to that word. (And if hauling open the entire Dictionary application seems a bit overkill, visit its Preferences dialog box and choose "Open Dictionary panel." Now you'll get a compact, handy panel that pops right out of the highlighted word instead.)

- **Point to a word in any Cocoa program and press Ctrl-⌘-D.** That keystroke makes the definition panel sprout right out of the word you were pointing to. (The advantage of this technique, of course, is that you don't have to highlight the word first.)

DVD Player

DVD Player, your Mac's built-in movie projector, is described on page 234.

Font Book

This delightful program lets you install or uninstall fonts, or sets of fonts, as the whim suits you. It's also great for examining your fonts to see what they look like. Details on page 219.

iCal

In many ways, iCal, Mac OS X's calendar program, is not so different from those "Hunks of the Midwest Police Stations" paper calendars we leave hanging on our walls for months past their natural life span. But iCal offers several advantages over paper calendars. For example:

- It can automate the process of entering repeating events, such as weekly staff meetings or gym workout dates.

- iCal can give you a gentle nudge (with a sound, a dialog box, or even an email) when an important appointment is approaching.

- iCal can share information with your Address Book program, with Mail, with your iPod, with other Macs, with "published" calendars on the Internet, or with a Palm organizer. Some of these features require one of those .Mac accounts described on page 147, and some require iSync (described later in this chapter). But iCal also works just fine on a single Mac, even without an Internet connection.

When you open iCal, you see something like Figure 14-5. By clicking one of the View buttons on the bottom edge of the calendar, you can switch among any of the standard calendar-software views: Day, Week, or Month.

Tip: iCal provides a quick way to get to the current day's date: Choose Calendar→Go to Today, or press ⌘-T.

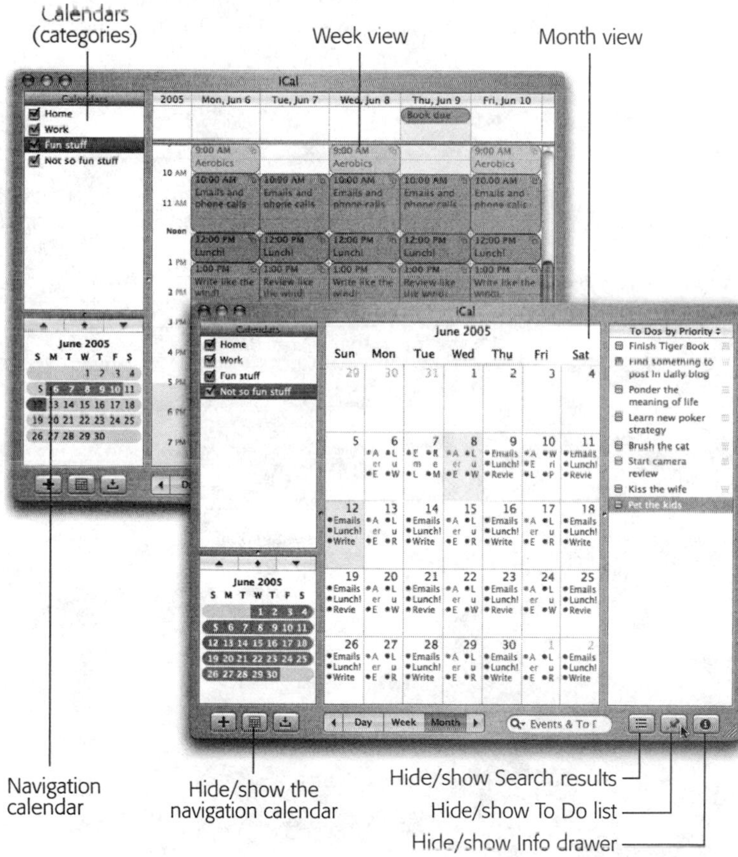

Figure 14-5.
Left: Week view. The miniature navigation calendar provides an overview of adjacent months. You can jump to a different week or day by clicking the triangle buttons, and then clicking within the numbers. If the event is recurring, its upper "grip strip" shows two stacked squares.

Right: Month view. You can hide the To Do list either using the Window→Hide To Dos command, or just by clicking the thumbtack button identified here.

Labels: Calendars (categories); Week view; Month view; Navigation calendar; Hide/show the navigation calendar; Hide/show Search results; Hide/show To Do list; Hide/show Info drawer

Making an Appointment

You can quickly record an appointment using any of several techniques, listed here in order of decreasing efficiency:

- Double-click the appointed time on the calendar, in any view. A colored box appears, where you type the name for your new appointment.

- When viewing a day or week view, drag vertically through the time slots that represent the appointment's duration, and then type inside the newly created colored box.

- Using the month view, double-click the appropriate date, and then type in the newly created colored bar.

- Choose File→New (or press ⌘-N). A new appointment appears on the currently selected day, regardless of the current view.

Unless you use the drag-over-hours method, a new event believes itself to be one hour long, but you can adjust its duration by dragging the bottom edge vertically. Drag the dark top bar up or down to adjust the start time.

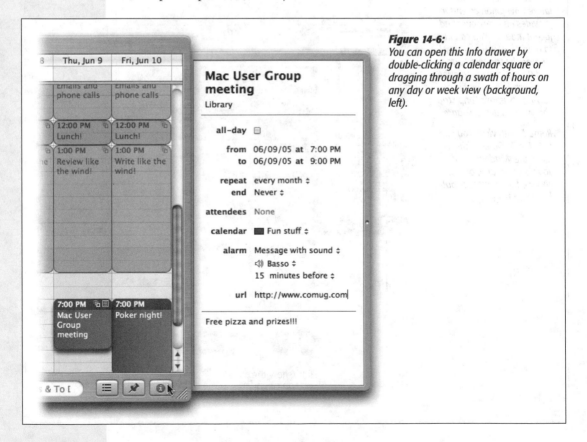

Figure 14-6:
You can open this Info drawer by double-clicking a calendar square or dragging through a swath of hours on any day or week view (background, left).

In many cases, that's all there is to it. You have just specified the day, time, and title of the appointment.

But if you double-click an appointment's title bar, or if you double-click a Month-view square, you bring up the Event Info pane shown in Figure 14-6. Using it, you can create far more specific appointments, decked out with far more bells and whistles. For example:

- **Subject.** That's the large, bold type at the top—the name of your appointment. For example, you might type *Fly to Phoenix.*

- **location.** This field makes a lot of sense; if you think about it, almost everyone needs to record *where* a meeting is to take place whenever such an appointment comes up. You might type a reminder for yourself like *My place,* a specific address like *212 East 23,* or some other helpful information like a contact phone number or flight number.

- **all day.** An "all-day" event, of course, refers to something that has no specific time of day associated with it: a holiday, a birthday, or a book deadline.

Tip: *If you turn on "All-day event," the lower Date box becomes un-dimmed so that you can specify a different ending date. This way, you can create* banners *like the one shown in Figure 14-5.*

- **from, to.** You can adjust the times shown here by typing, clicking buttons, or both. (Press Tab to jump from one setting to another, and from there to the hours and minutes of the starting time.)

- **repeat.** The pop-up menu here (which starts out saying None) contains common options for recurring events: every day, every week, and so on.

  Once you've made a selection, you get an **end** pop-up menu that lets you specify when this event should *stop* repeating. If you choose "Never," you'll be stuck seeing this event repeating on your calendar until the end of time (a good choice for recording, say, your anniversary, especially if your spouse might be consulting the same calendar). You can also turn on "after" (a certain number of times), which is a useful option for car and mortgage payments. And if you choose "on date," you can specify the date that the repetitions come to an end; use this option to indicate the last day of school, for example.

- **attendees.** If the appointment is a meeting or some other gathering, you can type the participants' names here. If a name is already in your Address Book program, iCal proposes auto-completing the name for you; if you type in fresh names and separate them by commas, iCal automatically turns each into a shaded oval pop-up button. You can click it for a pop-up menu of commands like Remove Attendee and Send Email. (That last option appears only if the person in your Address Book has an email address, or if you typed a name *with* an email address in brackets, like this: *Chris Smith <chris@yahoo.com>.*)

Tip: *You can also drag people out of your Address Book list directly into this Attendees area.*

- **calendar.** A *calendar*, in iCal's confusing terminology, is a subset—a category—into which you can place various appointments. You can create one for yourself, another for family-only events, another for book-club appointments, and so on. Later, you'll be able to hide and show these categories at will, adding or removing them from the calendar with a single click.

Tip: Use this same pop-up menu to *change* an appointment's category. If you filed something in Company Memos that should have been in Sweet Nothings for Honey-Poo, open the appointment's information drawer and reassign it.

- **alarm.** This pop-up menu tells iCal how to notify you when a certain appointment is about to begin. iCal can send four kinds of flags to get your attention: It can display a message on the screen (with a sound, if you like); send you an email; open a file on your hard drive (to remind you of work you have to do, for example); or run an AppleScript (page 388).

  Once you've specified an alarm mechanism, a new pop-up menu appears to let you specify how much advance notice you want for this particular appointment.

- **url.** What Apple really means here, of course, is *URL*—a Uniform Resource Locator, better known as a Web address like *www.apple.com*. If there's a URL relevant to this appointment, by all means type it here. Type more than one, if it will help you (separate each with a comma).

- **notes.** Here's your chance to customize your calendar event. You can type, paste, or drag any text that you like in the notes area—driving directions, contact phone numbers, a call history, or whatever.

Your newly scheduled event now shows up on the calendar, complete with the color coding that corresponds to the calendar category you've assigned.

What to Do with an Appointment

Once you've entrusted your agenda to iCal, you can start putting it to work. iCal is only too pleased to remind you of your events, reschedule them, print them out, and so on. Here are a few of the possibilities.

- **Editing events.** To edit a calendar event's name, just double-click it. To edit any of the appointment's other characteristics, you have to open its Event Info pane. To do that in day or week view, double-click the event's top bar (where its time appears); in month view, double-click the dot before the name (in either view, you can also select the event and choose View→Show Info). The calendar event pops up in the Info pane, where you can alter any of its settings as you see fit.

Tip: If you simply want to change an appointment's "calendar" category, you can bypass the event dialog box. Instead, just Control-click the appointment's name (or anywhere on its block), and choose the category you want from the resulting contextual menu.

- **Rescheduling.** If an event in your life gets rescheduled, you can drag an appointment vertically in its column to make it later or earlier the same day, or horizontally to another date, using its "time bar" as a handle in day or week view. If something is postponed for, say, a month or two, you can cut it from its original date (Edit→Cut) and paste it in the new date (Edit→Paste).

- **Lengthening or shortening events.** If a scheduled meeting becomes shorter or your lunch hour becomes a lunch hour-and-a-half (in your dreams), changing the length of the representative calendar event is as easy as dragging the top or bottom border of its block in any column view.

- **Printing events.** To commit your calendar to paper, choose File→Print, or press ⌘-P.

- **Deleting events.** To delete an appointment, just select it and then press the Delete key. If a confirmation dialog box appears, click Delete (or press Enter).

- **Searching for events.** You should recognize the oval text box at the bottom of the iCal screen immediately: it's almost identical to the Spotlight box. This search box is designed to let you hide all appointments except those matching what you type into it. Figure 14-7 has the details.

Figure 14-7:
As you type into the search box, iCal filters your calendar until only events with matching text are visible. It screens out both the text list and the colored boxes on the calendar itself, so that you can produce, in seconds, a calendar that shows only events pertaining to a particular client or project. (You can also open up this list view by clicking the button identified here at right.)

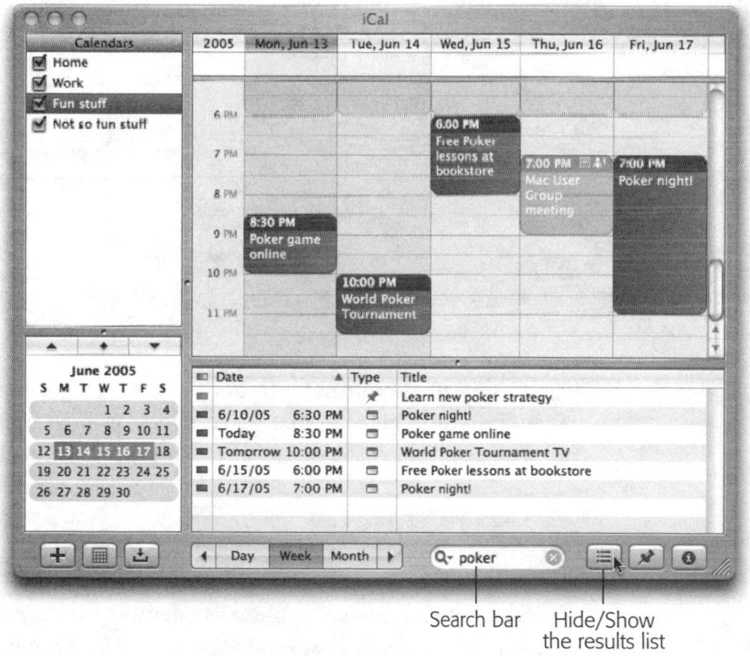

Search bar   Hide/Show the results list

The "Calendar" Calendar Concept

Just as iTunes has *playlists* that let you organize songs into subsets, and iPhoto has *albums* that let you organize photos into subsets, iCal has something called *calendars* that let you organize appointments into subsets. One person might have calendars called Home, Work, and TV Reminders. Another might have Me, Spouse 'n' Me, and Whole Family. A small business could have categories called Deductible Travel, R&D, and R&R. They can be anything you like.

To create a calendar, double-click any white space in the Calendar list (below the others), or click the + button at the lower-left corner of the iCal window. Type a name that defines the category in your mind (see Figure 14-8).

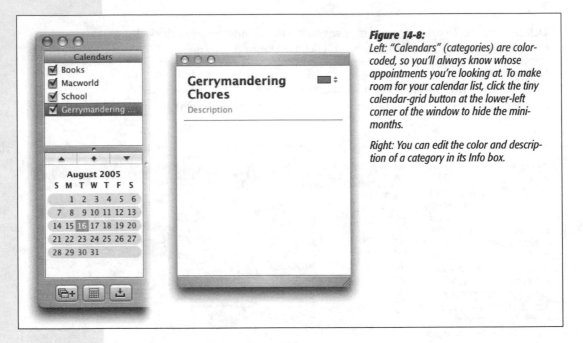

Figure 14-8:
Left: "Calendars" (categories) are color-coded, so you'll always know whose appointments you're looking at. To make room for your calendar list, click the tiny calendar-grid button at the lower-left corner of the window to hide the mini-months.

Right: You can edit the color and description of a category in its Info box.

You assign an appointment to one of these categories using the pop-up menu on its Event Info window. After that, you can hide or show an entire category of appointments at once just by turning on or off the appropriate checkbox in the Calendars list.

Tip: Click a calendar name *before* you create an appointment. That way, the appointment will already belong to the correct calendar.

You can even have what Apple calls calendar *groups:* calendar containers that contain the appointments from several *other* calendars, to make it easier to manage many appointments. To create a calendar group, just choose File→New Calendar Group and give it a name in the Calendar list. Drag other calendar names into it to include them, and use the flippy triangle to hide or show the component calendars.

"Publishing" Calendars to the Web

One of iCal's best features is its ability to post your calendar on the Web, so that other people—or you, using a different computer—can subscribe to it, which adds *your* appointments to *their* calendars. If you have a .Mac account, then anyone with a Web browser can also *view* your calendar, right online.

For example, you might use this feature to post the meeting schedule for a group or club that you manage, or to make clear the agenda for a series of financial meetings coming up that all of your co-workers will need to consult.

Publishing

Begin by clicking the calendar category you want in the left-side list. (To publish more than one calendar, create a calendar group.)

Then choose Calendar→Publish; the dialog box shown in Figure 14-9 appears. Here you customize how your saved calendar is going to look and work. You can even turn on "Publish changes automatically," so that whenever you edit the calendar, iCal connects to the Internet and updates the calendar.

Tip: CalSync ($5, *www.itoast.de/eng/calSync*) lets you publish your calendars to any FTP server and have them updated automatically, in full subscribable form. If you have Web space from anyone *besides* Apple, that's your ticket to sharing your calendars.

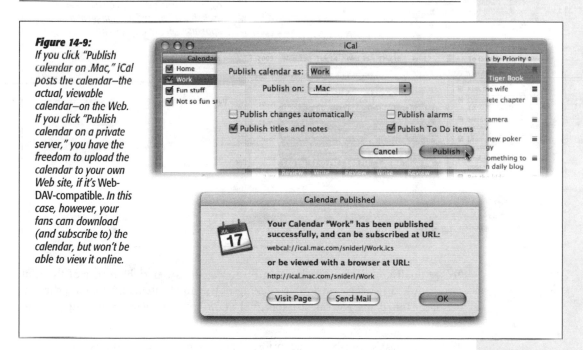

Figure 14-9:
If you click "Publish calendar on .Mac," iCal posts the calendar–the actual, viewable calendar–on the Web. If you click "Publish calendar on a private server," you have the freedom to upload the calendar to your own Web site, if it's Web-DAV-compatible. In this case, however, your fans can download (and subscribe to) the calendar, but won't be able to view it online.

Subscribing

If somebody else has published a calendar, you subscribe to it by choosing Calendar→Subscribe. In the Subscribe to Calendar dialog box, type in the Internet address you received from the person who published the calendar. Alternatively, click the Subscribe button in any iCal Web page.

When it's all over, you see a new "calendar" category in your left-side list, representing the appointments from the published calendar.

Tip: This feature of iCal is a brilliant solution to the old, "My spouse and I each have a Palm, but we can't see each other's calendars" problem. In conjunction with iSync (described later in this chapter), each person can now summon the other's calendar to the screen on demand.

To-Do Lists

iCal's Tasks feature lets you make a to-do list and then shepherds you along by giving you gentle reminders, if you so desire (Figure 14-10).

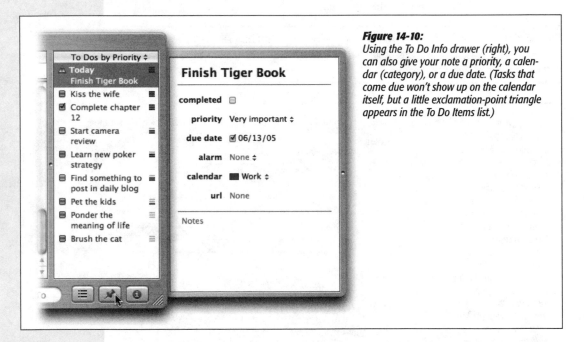

Figure 14-10:
Using the To Do Info drawer (right), you can also give your note a priority, a calendar (category), or a due date. (Tasks that come due won't show up on the calendar itself, but a little exclamation-point triangle appears in the To Do Items list.)

To see the list, click the little pushpin button at the lower-right corner of the iCal screen. Add a new task by double-clicking in the To Do Items list that appears. In this same Info panel, you can also specify the task's priority, alarm, repeating pattern, and so on.

To change a task's priority, use the "priority" pop-up menu. To sort the list (by priority, for example), use the pop-up menu at the top of the to-do list. To delete a task, click it and then press the Delete key.

iChat

This instant-messaging program is described starting on page 304.

iDVD

You have iDVD only if you bought a new Mac containing a SuperDrive DVD burner, or you bought Apple's iLife software suite. In any case, iDVD is designed to let you turn your digital photos or camcorder movies into DVDs that work on almost any DVD player, complete with menus, slideshow controls, and other navigation features. iDVD handles the technology; you control the style.

Sure, you can export your finished iMovie project back to an old VHS cassette. But preserving your work on a DVD gives you a boatload of benefits, including better durability, dramatically better quality, no need for rewinding, duplication without quality loss, and cheaper shipping. (And besides, you can fit a lot more DVDs on a shelf than VHS tapes.)

Note: DVD players sold since 2002 are generally a safe bet for playing back homemade DVDs, but check the master player compatibility list at *www.dvdrhelp.com* if you're ever in doubt. Some players are fussy about which DVD-R brand discs they play, too.

Here's the basic routine for converting an iMovie movie into a Blockbuster-style DVD.

Phase 1: Insert Chapter Markers

DVD *chapters* let viewers skip to predefined starting points within a movie, either using a Scene menu or pressing the Next Chapter or Previous Chapter buttons on the remote control. Thanks to the partnership of iMovie and iDVD, you can add chapter markers to your own movies markers, perfectly replicating this feature.

1. **In iMovie, click the iDVD button to open the iDVD palette.**

    You'll find it among the other palette buttons, just to the right of the Effects button, as shown in Figure 14-11.

2. **Drag the playhead to the position for your new chapter. Click Add Chapter. Type a chapter title into the Chapter Title box.**

    Whatever you type here will wind up as the chapter name in the finished DVD menu.

3. **Repeat step 2 until you've created all the chapters for your movie. Save your project.**

    If you've added a chapter in error, click it and then click Remove Chapter.

Phase 2: Hand Off to iDVD

Now you're ready to hand off the movie to iDVD, where you do your menu design and DVD burning.

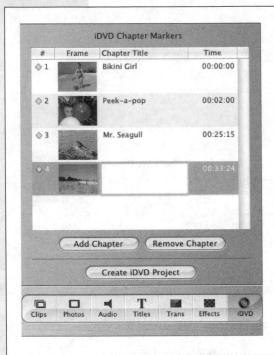

Figure 14-11:
The iDVD palette lets you add, remove, and name chapters—and then publish your iMovies to iDVD. New iMovie chapters are numbered sequentially, as they appear in your movie from left to right. Chapter references appear in your timeline as small yellow diamonds, just above the video track. iMovie can add up to 99 chapters per movie with the iDVD palette.

Save your project, and then click Create iDVD Project at the bottom of the chapter list. Your hard drive whirs, thunder rolls somewhere, and after a few minutes, you wind up in iDVD itself. You'll know when you get there: Empty postcards scroll slowly from right to left, confirming your arrival in iDVD land. (This is the Travel 1 *theme*, described in a moment.)

Tip: To turn off the Apple logo that appears in the lower-right corner of every iDVD Project, choose iDVD→Preferences and turn off "Show Apple logo watermark."

Phase 3: Design the Menu Screen

The moving postcards, the music that's playing, and the font for your buttons are all part of a *theme:* a unified design scheme that governs how the menus look and behave.

A wide range of canned themes awaits your inspection. To see them, click Customize to open the Customize drawer, if it isn't already open (Figure 14-12). Then, from the pop-up menu at the top of the Themes part of the drawer, choose All.

Scroll through the list of themes, clicking each one to see what it looks like in the main work area, or just rely on the little thumbnail icons to get a sense of the theme's overall flavor.

Figure 14-12:
The Customize button reveals iDVD's Customize drawer. When you click one of the buttons at the top, the pane changes to show its contents. For example, Themes lets you choose a design scheme. The Settings pane lets you choose motion menu duration, background video and audio, title fonts, and the look and placement of buttons. The Media pane links directly to iTunes and iPhoto.

Select a theme by clicking its thumbnail. The main menu screen takes on your chosen theme instantly. If your DVD menu system has other screens—a scene-selection screen that lists your chapter markers, for example—choose Advanced→Apply Theme to Project, so that every screen looks alike.

Phase 4: Edit Titles and Buttons

On the main menu screen now before you, you'll find two buttons:

- **Play.** On the finished DVD, this button will mean, "Play the movie from the beginning."

- **Scene Selection.** On the finished DVD, this button will take your audience to a second screen, which is filled with individual buttons for the chapters you created. (In fact, this second screen may well have arrows that lead to third and fourth screens, because iDVD can fit only six buttons per screen.)

You can edit these text buttons just as you would Finder icon names: Click inside the text to open up an editing box, type your changes, and then press Enter or Return.

Editing button names works almost the same way, except that you single-click the button first, and then click the text itself to open the editing box.

Button images and button videos

Almost every button displays an icon, picture, or tiny movie clip to give viewers a hint as to what lies in store if they click it. To specify what that image is, see Figure 14-13.

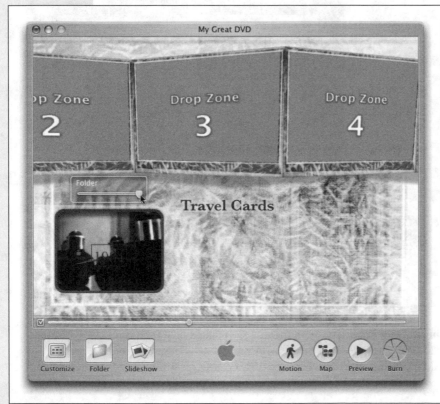

Figure 14-13:
iDVD can display up to 30 seconds of a movie right there on the button. Turn on Movie, and then use the slider to specify where you want the tiny button movie to begin looping. To make your button's face a still image instead, turn off the Movie checkbox, and then drag any graphics file right onto the button; you'll see the image change instantly.

Phase 5: Burning Your DVD

Once your menu screens are looking pretty good, you're almost ready to burn the DVD. Before you go using up a blank disc, however, you should test your creation to make sure that it works on the virtual DVD player known as the Macintosh.

- **Preview the DVD.** iDVD's Preview button lets you test your menu system to avoid unpleasant surprises. When you click it, iDVD enters Preview mode, which simulates how your DVD works on a standalone set-top DVD player. You even get a simulated remote control to help you navigate. Click Stop (the filled square) or reclick Preview to return to iDVD's Edit mode.

- **Check the length.** iDVD prefers to burn 60-minute DVDs, because they have the best quality. The instant you try to add the sixty-first minute of footage to your project, though, iDVD invites you to switch to 90-minute mode—at lower quality—or to delete some video from the project to make it fit within 60 minutes again.

When you've finished editing your disc and testing it thoroughly, it's time to proceed with your burn.

1. **Check your Motion setting.**

   The Motion button at the bottom of the window determines whether or not your finished DVD will have animated menus, buttons, and backgrounds, and whether or not music will play. If the Motion button is green, you'll get all of the above. If you click to turn the Motion button off (gray), then motion and audio features won't appear on the final disc.

2. **Choose File→Save. Click the Burn button twice.**

   The first click on the gray, closed Burn button "opens" it, revealing a throbbing yellow-and-black button. The second click begins the burning process.

3. **Insert a blank DVD-R disc when the Mac asks for it.**

   Be sure you're using the correct kind of blank DVD for the speed of your DVD burner. For example, don't attempt to burn 1x or 2x blanks at 4x speed.

Tip: Depending on your Mac model, you may be able to use *either* blank DVD-R discs *or* blank DVD+R discs. (Yes, these are really two different kinds—note the punctuation. They're essentially identical after burning—but some Macs can't burn DVD+R.)

To find out which kinds of discs your Mac can burn, open Applications→Utilities→System Profiler, click Disc Burning, and look at the formats listed next to "DVD-Write."

After a while, or a bit more than a while, a freshly burned DVD automatically ejects from your SuperDrive.

Image Capture

This unsung little program is something of an orphan. It was designed to download pictures from a USB digital camera and then process them automatically (turning them into a Web page, scaling them to emailable size, and so on). Of course, since Image Capture's birth, iPhoto came along, generally blowing its predecessor out of the water. Even so, Apple still includes Image Capture with Mac OS X for these reasons:

- Image Capture makes it easy to download only *some* pictures from your camera. iPhoto, by contrast, always downloads the *entire* contents of your camera's memory card. (Figure 14-14 shows how to choose individual pictures.)

- Image Capture can grab images from Mac OS X–compatible scanners, too, not just digital cameras.

- Image Capture can turn a compatible digital camera into a Webcam, broadcasting whatever it "sees" to anyone on your office network—or the whole Internet. Similarly, it can share a scanner with all the networked Macs in your office.

Once Image Capture is open, it looks like Figure 14-14.

Figure 14-14:
Top: You can set up Image Capture to open automatically when you attach a USB camera to your Mac. One click (on Download All) transfers its pictures to your hard drive.

Bottom: If you click Download Some, you get this "slide-sorter" window, where you can choose the individual pictures you want to download, use the buttons at the top to rotate selected shots, or delete shots from the camera. In slide-sorter view, Shift-click or ⌘-click the thumbnails of the pictures you want. In list view, Shift-click or ⌘-click as though they're Finder list-view files.

Here, you can use the pop-up menus to specify a destination folder for downloaded pictures and specify what happens automatically after they arrive ("Build slide show" or "Build Web page," for example).

iMovie HD

If you have a digital camcorder (MiniDV, Digital8, or high-definition format) and a few hours of free time—all right, a few weekends of it—iMovie helps you make astonishingly high-quality, fully edited movies. Digital video is great; you can transfer the footage back and forth between the Mac and the camcorder a hundred times, but you'll never see any deterioration in quality.

Phase 1: Set Up iMovie

The first time you run iMovie, it asks you whether you want to open an existing iMovie file (called a *project*) or start a new one. After that, each time you launch iMovie, it automatically opens up the movie you most recently worked on.

If you click Create Project, you're asked to select a name and location for the movie you're about to make. (You can ignore the "Video format" pop-up menu; iMovie autodetects what kind of camcorder you have once you begin importing footage.)

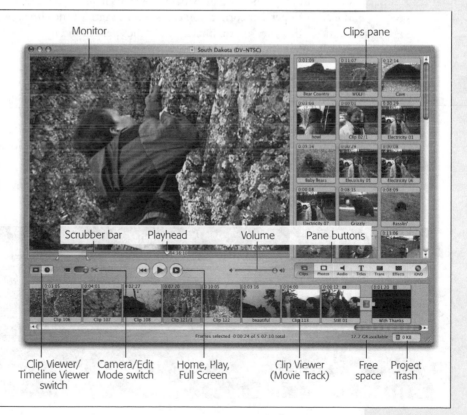

Figure 14-15:
Here's iMovie in a nutshell. Save your project onto the drive that has the most space (if, indeed, you have more than one), because digital video files are enormous. They require 3.6 MB of hard drive space per second or 13 gigabytes per one-hour tape. Choose a monitor resolution that's 1024 x 768 or larger (using, for example, the Displays panel of System Preferences). Poor iMovie can't even run at any lower setting.

Monitor   Clips pane

Scrubber bar   Playhead   Volume   Pane buttons

Clip Viewer/   Camera/Edit   Home, Play,   Clip Viewer   Free   Project
Timeline Viewer   Mode switch   Full Screen   (Movie Track)   space   Trash
switch

Once you've saved your project, you finally arrive at the main iMovie window (Figure 14-15).

Phase 2: Import Camcorder Footage

After you've shot some footage, connect the camcorder to the Mac using a FireWire cable. If you have the proper cable, one end (the six-pin connector) fits your Mac, and the much smaller end (the four-pin connector) goes into the FireWire connector on your camcorder, which, depending on the brand, may be labeled FireWire, i.Link, DV In/Out, or IEEE 1394.

Put the camcorder into VTR mode (also known as VCR or Playback mode). If necessary, click iMovie's Camera button, identified in Figure 14-15.

The Monitor window says, "Camera Connected." Now you can click the Play, Rewind, Fast Forward, and other buttons on the screen to control the camcorder. Scan your tape to find the sections that you'll want to include in your edited movie.

Every time you click the Import button—or tap the Space bar—iMovie imports the footage you're watching, saving it as a series of digital-video movie files on the Mac's hard drive. For each scene, iMovie creates what looks like a slide in the Clips pane, as shown in Figure 14-15. That's a *clip*—a single piece of footage that makes up one of the building blocks of an iMovie movie. Its icon is a picture of the first frame. On the clip's upper-left corner, you can see the length of the clip expressed as "seconds: frames" (there are approximately 30 frames per second in North American video or HDTV; 25 in the European format).

Phase 3: Arrange the Clips

As you're building your movie, you can store your clips in either of two places: the Clips pane or the storyboard strip—the *Movie Track,* for want of an official name—at the bottom of the window (Figure 14-15). You put clips on the Clips pane before deciding what to do with them, and drag them down to the Movie Track area once you've decided where they fit into your movie.

The Movie Track can appear in either of two ways, depending on which tab you click (the film strip or the clock, respectively):

GEM IN THE ROUGH

Automatic Scene Detection

If you let the tape continue to roll, you'll notice that each time a new scene begins, a new clip icon appears in the Clips pane.

iMovie is studying the *date and time stamp* that DV camcorders record into every frame. When iMovie detects a break in time, it assumes that you stopped recording, if only for a moment—and therefore that the next piece of footage should be considered a new shot. It turns each new shot into a new clip.

If you'd prefer manual control over when each clip begins and ends, choose iMovie→Preferences, click Import, and turn off "Start a new clip at each scene break."

- **Clip Viewer.** In this view, each clip appears as an icon, like a slide on a slide viewer. Each is sized identically, regardless of length.

- **Timeline Viewer.** Here, each clip is represented by a horizontal bar that's as wide as the clip is long. Parallel bars below the clips indicate the soundtracks playing simultaneously.

You can do several things to a clip, whether it's in the Clips pane or the Movie Track. For example:

- **Select a clip.** Click a clip's icon to view its first frame and, down below the Movie Track, some statistics (for example, when the scene was filmed).

  To highlight several consecutive clips in the Movie Track, click one clip, and then Shift-click the last one. You can also drag diagonally across a batch of them.

- **Play a clip.** To play a highlighted clip, press the Space bar. You can also drag the *playhead* (see Figure 14-15) to view earlier or later parts of the clip. By pressing the right and left arrow keys when playback is stopped, you can view your clip one frame at a time, as though you're watching the world's least interesting slideshow.

Tip: Adding the Shift key to your arrow-key presses is often more useful—it lets you jump *ten* frames at a time.

- **Reorganize the clips.** You can drag clips from cubbyhole to cubbyhole on the Clips pane. In fact, you can even drag a clip (or even a mass of highlighted clips) onto

---

FREQUENTLY ASKED QUESTION

Why Emptying the Trash Doesn't Restore Disk Space

When I emptied the trash, the little "free disk space remaining" counter didn't change at all! I had 532 megs available before I emptied the Trash, and the same amount after!

In iMovie HD, you can use the Revert Clip to Original command any time, even after emptying the Trash, even months or years later. You can also add back a missing chunk from the middle of a clip that you'd previously lobotomized—again, even after emptying the Trash. You can chop, truncate, split, and shorten clips to your heart's content, and at any time, restore what you'd eliminated. (In previous iMovie versions, emptying the Trash meant that portions you cut from clips were gone forever.)

These features work because iMovie quietly preserves the *entire copy* of every clip you import. If you split a clip in half, drag the second part to the Trash, and then empty the Trash,

you don't get back one single byte of disk space. iMovie is hanging onto the entire original clip, just in case you change your mind someday.

The *only* time emptying the Trash actually frees up disk space, in fact, is if you've put an entire clip into it. (Even then, you may have to empty the *Finder* Trash to complete the transaction.) If even one frame of it appears in the Timeline, iMovie still preserves the entire original clip on your hard drive.

So what if you've imported a 40-minute tape all in one clip and you intend to work with only the first five minutes' worth? Will that iMovie project occupy 40 minutes' worth of space on your hard drive forever?

Yes, unless you export the entire movie project as a full-quality DV clip and then reimport it.

---

an *occupied* cubbyhole. iMovie automatically creates enough new cubbyholes to hold them all, and shuffles existing clips out of the way if necessary.

- **Trash a clip.** You can get rid of a clip either by selecting it and then pressing the Delete key or by dragging it directly onto the project Trash icon (once again, shown in Figure 14-15).

  The iMovie Trash has a lot in common with the iPhoto Trash, the Finder's Trash, or the Windows Recycle Bin: it's a safety net. It's a holding tank for clips, photos, and sounds that you intend to throw out. They're not really gone, though, until you use the File→Empty Trash command.

  To open the Trash window *before* you empty it, click the Trash icon or choose File→Show Trash.

Warning: Emptying the Trash saves your project—and whenever you save your file, *you lose the ability to Undo your previous steps.* In fact, emptying the Trash also disables the Revert to Saved command and vaporizes whatever's on your Clipboard. (You can still use the Revert Clip to Original command, however.)

- **Trim a clip (Clips pane, Clips viewer).** Unless you have some godlike ability to control precisely *when* the subjects of your life—your pets, your children, your geysers—are at their most video-worthy, you probably don't need to preserve every frame of your captured footage for future generations.

  To target some footage for deletion, click a clip, position your cursor within the Scrubber bar, and drag horizontally until the triangle handles surround the footage you want to keep (Figure 14-15). If you choose Cut or Clear from the Edit menu, iMovie promptly trims away whatever was highlighted between the triangles. (If you choose Edit→Crop instead, iMovie deletes whatever was *outside* the highlighted portion.)

- **Trim a clip (Timeline viewer).** Drag the edges of a clip's colored bar inward to shorten it from either end. (Drag outward again if you change your mind.)

Phase 4: Assemble the Movie

Drag the edited clips out of the Clips pane and into the correct order on the Movie Track, exactly as though you're building a storyboard or timeline. (To magnify the Timeline Viewer for a better look, drag the slider at the lower-left corner of the window. It adjusts the relative sizes of the bars that represent your clips.)

As you work, you'll want to play back your movie to check its flow. You may discover that, in the context of the whole movie, some clips are too long, too short, in the wrong order, and so on. To play back your entire Movie Track, press the Home key, which means Rewind. When you tap the Space bar, iMovie plays your movie from the beginning, one clip after another, seamlessly.

Or just click the Play Full Screen button (the darkened triangle to the right of the round Play button). It makes the playback—even if it's already underway—fill the entire computer screen. To interrupt the movie showing, press Escape.

Phase 5: Transitions, Effects, Titles, Audio, and Photos

Professional film and video editors have at their disposal a wide range of *transitions*—special effects that smooth the juncture between one clip and the next. For example, apart from a simple *cut*, the world's most popular transition is the *crossfade* or *dissolve*, in which the end of one clip gradually fades away as the next one fades in.

iMovie offers a long list of transitions, of which crossfades are only the beginning. To see them, click the Trans button (Figure 14-16).

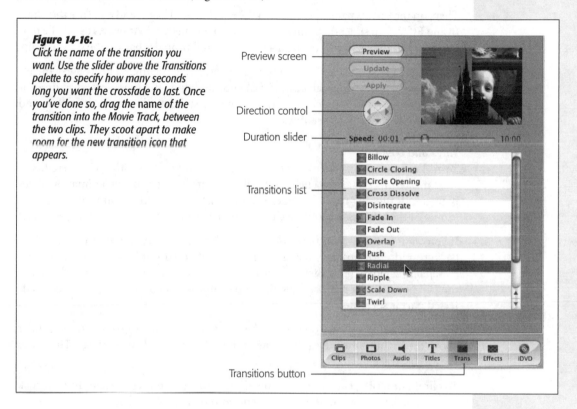

Figure 14-16:
Click the name of the transition you want. Use the slider above the Transitions palette to specify how many seconds long you want the crossfade to last. Once you've done so, drag the name of the transition into the Movie Track, between the two clips. They scoot apart to make room for the new transition icon that appears.

Preview screen

Direction control

Duration slider

Transitions list

Transitions button

When you drag a transition into your Movie Track, the Mac now creates the crossfade—*renders* it—by superimposing the end of one clip with the beginning of the next. When the red progress bar is finished, click in your timeline just before the transition, press the Space bar to play, and marvel in your new ability to make home movies look pro.

Tip: You can continue working on other parts of your movie, or even switch into another Mac OS X program, while the rendering is going on.

To delete a transition, click its icon in the timeline and then press Delete. To edit it (by changing its length, for example), click its icon, return to the Transitions palette, make the adjustment, and then click Update.

Effects

The Effects button summons a pane full of additional visual effects. Most are designed to create actual special effects that simulate fog, rain, earthquakes, lightning, flashbulbs, and bad LSD. (Most are weird and distracting. Use sparingly.)

To apply an effect, first specify which lucky region of footage you want to be affected. (iMovie can apply effects only to *entire* clips, so it may have to split your clip at the endpoints of the selection, and then apply the effect to the central clip.)

Then, on the Effects pane, specify when the effect should begin and end (use the Effect In and Effect Out sliders), its intensity, and so on. Finally, click Apply. As usual, the rendering telegraphs its progress with a miniature red progress bar on the selected clip.

If you click a clip and then press the Delete key, you're saying: "Throw away the effect. Bring back my original, unmodified clip." To adjust the start time, stop time, or other parameters of a special effect, you must first delete the effect altogether, and then reapply it using new settings.

Titles and credits

To add rolling credits, opening titles, subtitles, or MTV-style music video credits to your masterpiece, start by clicking the Titles button. A list of title animation styles pops up. In the tiny text box underneath the list, type the text you want to appear. (Some of the effects, like Rolling Credits, offer *pairs* of text blobs; see Figure 14-17.)

If you want to insert this title *at the end of* a clip, so that the text appears on a black background, turn on the Over Black checkbox. If you'd rather have the text appear *on top of* the video, leave that box unchecked. (Superimposing a title usually breaks the clip in half—the part with the title superimposed is now one clip, and the unaffected part is separate.)

Click the Preview button to see what the title will look like. Adjust the timing slider above the list, and then drag the *name* of the title type (such as Centered Title) into the Movie Track.

To eliminate a title, click its icon in the timeline and then press Delete. To edit, click its icon, make changes in the Titles palette, and then click Update.

Audio

The top horizontal band of the Timeline Viewer displays the *video* component of your movie. For the most part, you won't do much with this strip when you're editing audio; its primary purpose is to show where you are in the movie.

The two skinnier horizontal strips underneath it are your playground for audio clips (Figure 14-18). Both audio tracks play in tandem. Each can hold sound from any of these sources:

- **iTunes tracks.** When you click the Audio button, iMovie shows you your complete iTunes music collection, including playlists, making it easy for you to choose background music for your flick. Double-click a song to listen to it; drag its name onto one of the audio tracks to use it in your movie.

- **Narration.** This can be anything that you've recorded with your microphone. Drag the Playhead to a spot just before you want the narration to begin, click the round Record Voice button on the Audio pane, and begin to speak. You can watch the video play as you narrate. (If the level meter isn't dancing as you speak, check the selected sound source in the Sound panel of System Preferences.)

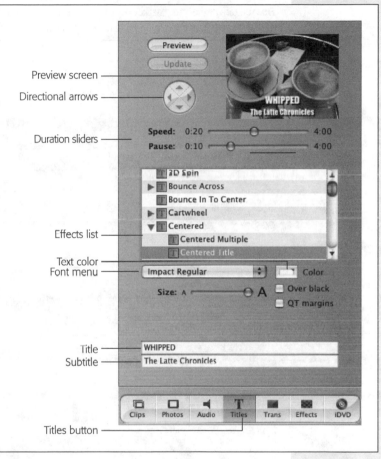

Figure 14-17:
After you've typed in a couple of pairs, click the + button to tack on yet another pair to your credits. The program automatically adds the dots and lines up the names (just like real credits!), or places the subtitle beneath the main title, as shown here.

Preview screen

Directional arrows

Duration sliders

Effects list

Text color
Font menu

Title
Subtitle

Titles button

- **Sound effects.** From the pop-up menu at the top of the iMovie Audio pane, choose iMovie Sound Effects. Now you can add any of iMovie's sound effects (laughing, crickets, and so on) to your movie just by dragging them into an audio track.

- **MP3, WAV, AAC, and AIFF audio files.** Import these popular music formats using the File→Import command.

- **Music from a CD.** You can insert a standard audio CD and transfer a song into iMovie to serve as the music for a scene. (Its contents appear in the Audio palette, and iTunes usually opens automatically to help you catalog the CD.) As usual, drag the name of a song to an audio track to install it there.

- **Your camcorder audio.** You can turn the ordinarily invisible audio portion of a video clip into an independent sound clip, which you can manipulate just like any other kind of sound clip (great for creating voice-overs, echoes, audio flashbacks, and so on). To do that, highlight the audio clip and then choose Advanced→Extract Audio.

Tip: You can use the three checkboxes at the right end of these tracks to control which ones play back. When you want to watch or listen to only one track, turn off the other two checkboxes.

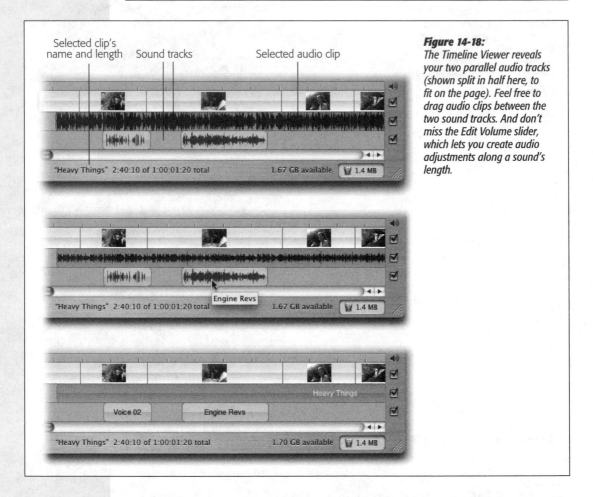

Selected clip's name and length   Sound tracks   Selected audio clip

Figure 14-18:
The Timeline Viewer reveals your two parallel audio tracks (shown split in half here, to fit on the page). Feel free to drag audio clips between the two sound tracks. And don't miss the Edit Volume slider, which lets you create audio adjustments along a sound's length.

Fortunately, you can do more with your audio clips than just insert them into the Timeline Viewer:

- **Whole-clip volume adjustments.** To make a selected clip louder or quieter, use the Clip Volume pop-up menu at the bottom of the screen. You can make it so quiet that it's absolutely silent, or you can boost it up to 50 percent louder than the original.

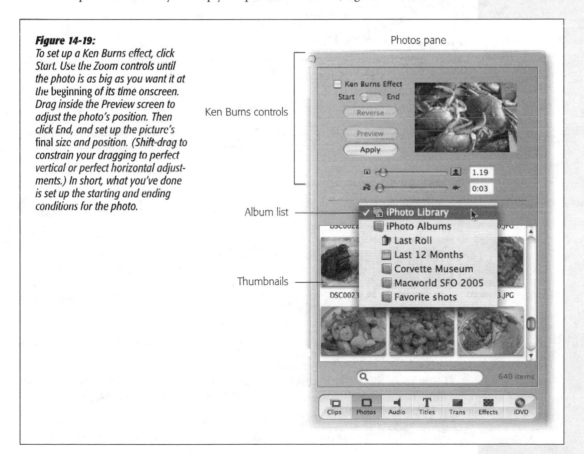
・ **Volume adjustments within a clip.** You can also make the volume of a clip rise and fall along its length. For example, you can "pull back" the music when somebody is speaking, and then bring it back to full volume in between speeches.

When you choose View→Show Clip Volume Levels (Shift-⌘-L), a horizontal line appears on every audio clip, stretching from edge to edge (and your video clips, too). This line is a graph of the clip's volume.

Click directly on the line and drag upward or downward to produce a temporary volume fluctuation.

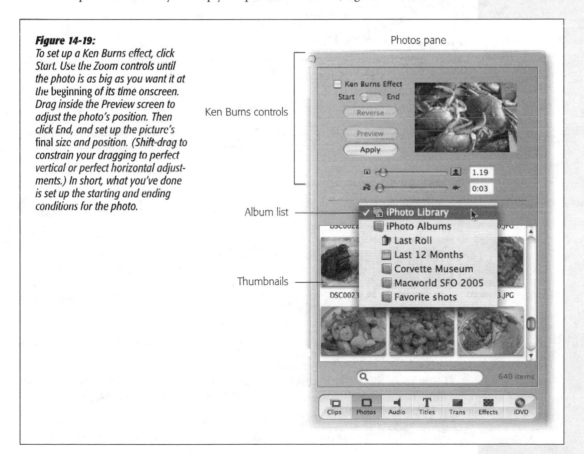

iMovie HD

Note: When Show Clip Volume Levels is turned on, you can't drag clips' edges to shorten or lengthen them in the Timeline Viewer.

Photos

You might want to import a graphics file into iMovie for any number of reasons—to use as a less distracting still image behind your titles and credits, for example, or to create a video photo album. If you keep your pictures in iPhoto, a great feature awaits.

Figure 14-19:
To set up a Ken Burns effect, click Start. Use the Zoom controls until the photo is as big as you want it at the beginning of its time onscreen. Drag inside the Preview screen to adjust the photo's position. Then click End, and set up the picture's final size and position. (Shift-drag to constrain your dragging to perfect vertical or perfect horizontal adjustments.) In short, what you've done is set up the starting and ending conditions for the photo.

When you click the Photos button (Figure 14-19), you're shown the contents of your entire iPhoto Library. Using the pop-up menu, you can even limit your view to the contents of one iPhoto *album* or another.

Once you've pinpointed the picture you want, use the controls at the top of the Photos palette to specify the amount of time the photo will remain on the screen, and whether or not you want the *Ken Burns effect,* where the "movie camera" pans and zooms smoothly across photos, in essence animating them and directing the viewer's attention. (Ken Burns is the creator of PBS documentaries like *The Civil War* and *Baseball,* which use this effect in abundance.)

Finally, drag the photo out of the thumbnail palette and into the Movie Track. The other clips scoot out of the way to make room, and the photo becomes, in effect, a new silent video clip with the duration you specified. (If you turned on the Ken Burns effect, iMovie takes a few moments to render the animation. The familiar red progress bar inches across the face of the clip.)

Note: If you don't routinely keep your photos in iPhoto, you can also import a graphics file, or even a QuickTime movie, right from your hard drive by choosing File→Import.

Phase 6: Meet Your Public

When the movie's looking good on your Mac screen, you're ready to distribute it to the adoring masses. Choose File→Share, pick how you'd like to export the movie (back to your video camera, say, or as a QuickTime movie that you can send by email or play off your hard drive), set any options, and click Share.

Then wait while iMovie does its business. It could take hours, depending on the length of your movie and the export format you chose.

Internet Connect

If you have a full-time, wired Internet connection (cable modem, DSL, or corporate network, for example), skip this section.

If, on the other hand, you have a dial-up modem or connect via AirPort, read on. Internet Connect shows your current status and settings (as configured in the Network pane of your System Preferences), and provides a Connect/Disconnect button for opening or closing a connection. Here's what you can accomplish with Internet Connect:

- Choose Internal Modem and then click Connect to dial out using your current modem settings.

- Once you're hooked up, check the status display to confirm whether or not your modem successfully connected to your ISP—or if you've been disconnected.

- You can also see your connection *speed,* to find out if you really connected up at 56 K (ha!), or if your modem was only able to negotiate a 28 K connection.

- Internet Connect keeps a neat log of your connection activity (choose Window→ Connection Log). Reading this log is about as exciting as reading random entries from the White Pages. Nonetheless, if you're having serious connection problems, it can be a useful troubleshooting tool.

- The "Show modem status in menu bar" checkbox lets you use a menu-bar icon to dial and observe your connections—without using Internet Connect at all.

- Internet Connect is your gateway to Virtual Private Networking, a feature that lets you tunnel into corporate networks from the road. Ask your network administrator for the settings you need.

- Click the AirPort tab to see your wireless network's strength, pick a new network, or turn off AirPort altogether to save power.

Of course, even in these cases, you don't really need Internet Connect to get online. If your Internet settings are configured correctly (see page 246), your Mac will automatically connect whenever you launch a program that needs to get online (such as Safari).

iPhoto

iPhoto is a rich, flexible, "digital shoebox" for your digital photos. It's a glorious program that could easily be the topic of its own book. In fact, it is a book—*iPhoto 5* (or whatever the current version number is): *The Missing Manual*.

Figure 14-20:
Here's what iPhoto looks like when you first open it. The large photo-viewing area is where thumbnails of your imported photos will appear. The icons at the bottom of the window represent all the stuff you can do with your photos.

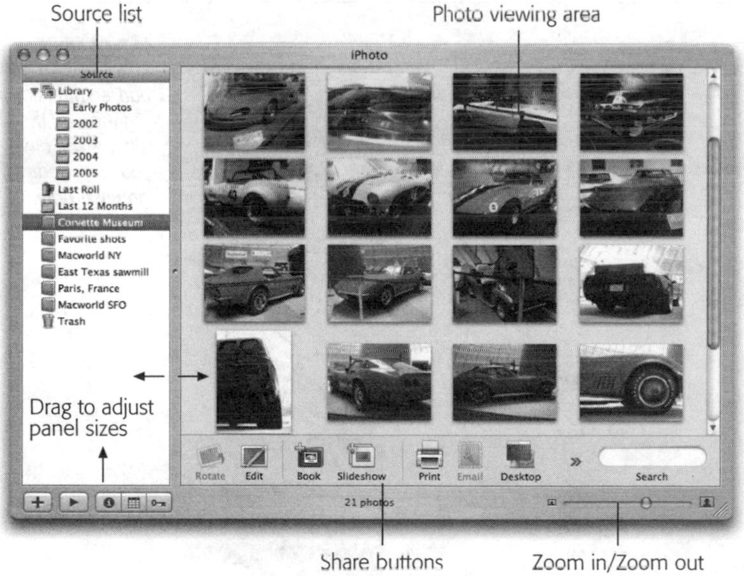

But the basics are easy enough. When you connect a recent-model USB camera and click Import (Figure 14-20), this program automatically sucks the pictures into your Mac. (Using the appropriate checkbox, you can also opt to have them erased from the camera after being transferred.)

Organizing Photos

You now see a neatly arranged grid of thumbnails (Figure 14-21). You're looking at what iPhoto refers to as your *Photo Library*—your entire photo collection, including every last picture you've ever imported. Use the Size slider at lower right to adjust the thumbnail size.

Tip: To see the pictures you just imported, click Last Import. To return to the full list, click Library.

Albums

An *album* is a subset of pictures from your Photo Library, grouped together for easy access and viewing. It's represented by a little album-book icon in the album list. (If you've used playlists in iTunes, or mailboxes in Mail, you'll recognize the concept.) Albums make finding photos much faster. Furthermore, only in an album can you drag your photos into a different *order*.

To create an iPhoto album, choose File→New Album (⌘-N), or click the + button in the iPhoto window, below the album list. Type a descriptive name (*Yellowstone 2005, Edna in Paris,* or whatever), click OK, and watch as a new album icon appears in the Album pane. (See Figure 14-21.)

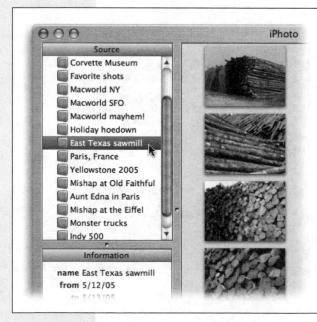

Figure 14-21:
There's no limit to the number of albums you can add, so make as many as you need to logically organize all the photos in your Photo Library. New albums are always added to the end of the list, but you can change the order in which they appear by simply dragging them up or down.

To rename an album, double-click its name or icon. A renaming rectangle appears, with text highlighted and ready to be edited.

To add photos to an album, drag them onto its icon. (Putting photos in an album doesn't *move or copy* them. You're just creating *references* to, or aliases of, the photos in your master Photo Library. In other words, each photo can appear in as many different albums as you want.)

Tip: To delete a photo or album, just click it and press Delete. Note, however, that deleting a photo from one album doesn't delete it from your entire *Library*.

Editing Photos

Once they're in iPhoto, there's no end to the fun you can have with your pictures.

- **Enhance.** With one click, this tool endeavors to make photos look more vibrant by tweaking the brightness and contrast settings and adjusting the saturation to compensate for washed-out or oversaturated colors.

- **Cropping.** The cropping tool lets you cut away the outer portions of a photo to improve its composition or to make it the right size for a printout or Web page. (Choose a fixed proportion from the Constrain menu, if you like, then drag across the photo to indicate how you want it cropped. Finally, click Crop.)

- **Retouch.** This little brush lets you paint out minor imperfections like blemishes, freckles, and scratches.

- **Red-Eye.** This little filter gets rid of a very common photo glitch—those shining red dots that sometimes appear in a person's eyes as the result of flash photography. Who wants to look like a werewolf?

- **B & W.** Turns your color photos into moody black-and-white art shots.

- **Sepia.** Makes new photos look faded and brownish, for that old-time photography look.

- **Adjust.** Opens the new Adjust panel, whose sliders offer ridiculous amounts of control over color balance, exposure, and other parameters.

Tip: By pressing and releasing the Control key, you can toggle between the "before" and "after" versions of the photo in order to assess the results of the enhancement. Remember, too, that no matter what changes you make to a photo, you can always restore it to its original camera condition—even years later—by clicking it and then choosing Photos→Revert to Original. That's *quite* a nice safety net.

Presenting Your Photos

iPhoto provides a number of different features for bringing your photos to a wider audience. Most are available in both the Share menu and the "toolbar" at the bottom of the window.

- **Print.** iPhoto offers more print options than just about any other program. For example, you can cluster several photos on the same piece of paper, to save ink.

- **Slideshow.** You can create three different kinds of slideshows in iPhoto: *instant* (no options, just pictures), *quick* (some options in a dialog box), and *saved* (tons of control in a full-window editor).

  To make an instant show, just Option-click the Play button in the lower-left corner of the window. When you've had enough, click the mouse.

  For more control, click the Play button *without* pressing Option. You get to fine-tune the slideshow, from the soundtrack to the transition.

  Finally, if you'd like to organize the specific images that appear in your slideshow—and save them for display later—click the Slideshow icon at the bottom of the window. It tosses you into the Slideshow editing mode, which has some features of Edit mode and some of regular old thumbnail-organizing mode.

- **Email.** Start by selecting one picture, or a few. Then click the Email button. (Its icon reflects your choice of email program, as you've specified in the iPhoto→Preferences command.)

  iPhoto asks you what size you want the photo to be—an extremely friendly gesture, because sending a *full-size* digital camera picture is grossly overblown for viewing onscreen, and will probably choke your recipient's email account. That's why iPhoto offers to scale the picture down to reasonable size, such as 640 by 480 dots.

  Click Compose. After a moment, an empty piece of email appears, with the file already attached, ready for you to type in the address and any comments you want to include.

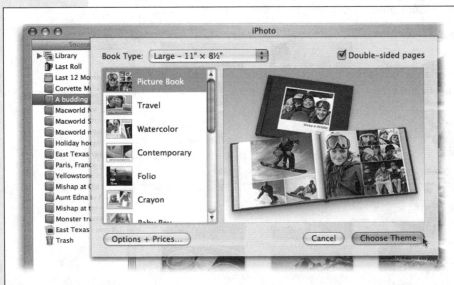

Figure 14-22:
You can change these settings later, even after you've started laying out your book pages. But if you have the confidence to make these decisions now, you'll save time, effort, and (if you want captions for your photos) possibly a lot of typing.

- **Order prints.** This option uploads your selected photos and—for a fee—converts them into handsome Kodak prints that get mailed back to you.

- **Book.** iPhoto's Book feature lets you design and order (via the Internet) a gorgeous, linen-covered, 8½-by-11–inch book, printed at a real bindery and shipped back to you in a slipcover. Your photos are printed on the glossy, acid-free pages, complete with captions, if you like.

  Book prices start at $10—not counting mini-books, which start at $4 in bulk. That's about the least you could hope to pay for a handsome, emotionally powerful gift *guaranteed* never to wind up in an attic, garage sale, or eBay.

  Once you've selected an album or a batch of photos, click the Book button below the main picture area, or choose File→New Book. Now you see something like Figure 14-22: a dialog box in which you can specify what you want your book to look like. You can choose hardcover or softcover, single- or double-sided pages, and which design scheme you want.

  When you click Choose Theme, a message appears to let you know you have two choices for placing photos onto the book-page layouts: either click the Autoflow button (to make the Mac do the job for you), or drag photos individually into the placeholders. Click OK.

  Now a new icon appears in the Source list (at the left side of the window) to represent your book. You also see something like Figure 14-23, where the page you're working on appears at full size, for your editing pleasure

  At this point, you can choose a page type (from the Page Type pop-up menu), pick a variation for the current layout (from the Page Design pop-up menu), and, most importantly, drag images from the list at the top of the window into the picture spaces on each of your pages.

Tip: You can also move pictures around within the book by dragging their thumbnails horizontally in the list at top. Similarly, you can remove a page by clicking its *icon* in the list at top and pressing Delete, or insert a new page by clicking the Add Page button at the bottom of the window.

  When you think your book is ready for birth, click Buy Book—and wait several minutes as iPhoto converts your design into an Internet-transmittable file.

- **HomePage.** If you have a .Mac account (page 147), you can turn an album or a selection of photos into an instant Web-page gallery, complete with fast-downloading thumbnail images that your visitors can click to magnify. All you have to do is send your fans the Web address provided by the .Mac account.

Tip: If you already have a Web site (not a .Mac account), you can create the same attractive online gallery by choosing Share→Export and clicking the HTML tab. iPhoto will save, to your hard drive, a complete set of HTML documents and linked, nested folders (containing both thumbnails and full-size images), ready to upload to your site.

• **.Mac slides.** When you send your photos out into the world as .Mac slides, other Mac OS X users can *subscribe* to your show, displaying *your* pictures as *their* screen saver. (Of course, you must have a .Mac account, as described on page 147, for this to work.)

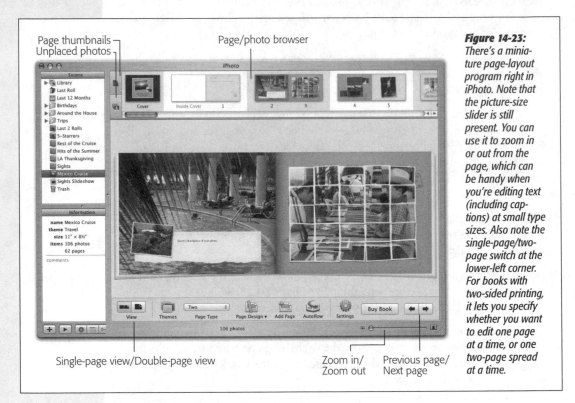

Page thumbnails
Unplaced photos

Page/photo browser

Single-page view/Double-page view

Zoom in/
Zoom out

Previous page/
Next page

Figure 14-23:
There's a minia-ture page-layout program right in iPhoto. Note that the picture-size slider is still present. You can use it to zoom in or out from the page, which can be handy when you're editing text (including cap-tions) at small type sizes. Also note the single-page/two-page switch at the lower-left corner. For books with two-sided printing, it lets you specify whether you want to edit one page at a time, or one two-page spread at a time.

To create a .Mac slideshow, select the album or photos you want to share, and then click this button (or, if you don't see it, choose Share→.Mac Slides). Click Publish to begin uploading your photos. When the process is complete, click Announce Slideshow to email your friends to let them know about your slides.

• **Desktop.** Click one photo and then click this button. iPhoto instantly fills your desktop background with that photo.

If you click one *album* and then click this button, you turn that album's contents into a spectacular screen saver feature that fills your screen with animated, gently flowing photographs when your iMac isn't in use.

• **Burn Disc.** *iPhoto CDs* are discs (either CDs or DVDs) that you can create directly from within iPhoto to archive your entire Photo Library—or any selected portion of it—with just a few mouse clicks. This is a great way to back up your photos; transfer them to another Mac without losing all your keywords, descriptions, and titles; share discs with other iPhoto fans; offload photos to CD or DVD as your photo collection grows; or merge separate Photo Libraries (such as the one on your iBook and the one on your iMac) into a single master library.

These discs *do not play* in Windows or Mac OS 9. They're *exclusively* for iPhoto's use.

Note: The Burn Disc button doesn't start out installed at the bottom of the iPhoto screen. Use the Share→Show in Toolbar submenu to specify which icons appear there.

Select the albums or photos that you want to include on the disc, and then click the Burn icon. Pop in a blank CD or DVD.

Now take a look at the Info panel just below the Albums list (you might have to click the ❶ button to summon the panel). If the set of photos you want to burn is larger than 650 or 700 megabytes (for a CD) or about 4.3 gigabytes (for a DVD), it's not going to fit. You'll have to split your backup operation across multiple discs. Select whatever number of photo albums or individual pictures you can that *will* fit on a single disc, then, after burning the first disc, select the next set of photos, and then burn another CD or DVD.

Finally, click the Burn icon again. When the process is done, your Mac spits out the finished CD (named "iPhoto Disc"), ready to use. Later, if you want to view the contents of your finished CD in iPhoto, pop the disc back into the drive.

iSync

If Apple ever had evidence to back up its "digital hub" hype, iSync is it.

This attractive, simple program is designed to keep the calendars and phone lists on your various computers, Palm organizer, and cellphone in perfect synchronization, sparing you the biggest headache of the modern age: inputting the same information over and over again. (See Figure 14-24.) Here's what it can keep synched:

- **A Bluetooth phone.** Of course, this also requires a Bluetooth adapter for your Mac (some models have it built in, or you can buy an Apple USB Bluetooth module for $50). And it requires a certain amount of technical setup (creating a phone profile, pairing the phone with your Mac, opening iSync and choosing Device→Add Device, and selecting the phone). You'll find detailed instructions on the iSync Help screens.

- **Other Macs.** This part requires a .Mac account, but it can be fantastically useful. It means that you and a colleague (or you and a spouse, or you and yourself at the office) can keep your calendars in sync, using the Internet as an intermediary.

  To set this up, just open iSync and click the .Mac icon. Click Register, type a name for your Mac, and then click Continue.

Tip: In order to use this feature, you need one of those $100-a-year .Mac accounts.

- **A Palm organizer.** iSync can also keep iCal and Address Book synched with a Palm-compatible organizer. It doesn't do the work itself; it relies, behind the scenes, on Palm's own HotSync software, which must be installed and properly configured beforehand. (You must also install the separate iSync_Palm.pkg software after installing iSync and Palm Desktop.)

Once that's done, open HotSync Manager in your Palm folder. Choose Hotsync→Conduit Settings. See where it says Address Book, Date Book, and To Do List? Double-click each one, select Do Nothing, and click Make Default.

Then double-click iSync Conduit; turn on Synchronize Contacts and Synchronize Calendars; click OK; and quit HotSync Manager. You've just told Palm's own syncing software to butt out. From now on, iSync will handle these data types (Address Book, Date Book, and To Do List).

Finally, in iSync, use the Devices→Add Device command to make iSync "see" your Palm, which you've put into its cradle, attached to its cable, or (if it's a Bluetooth

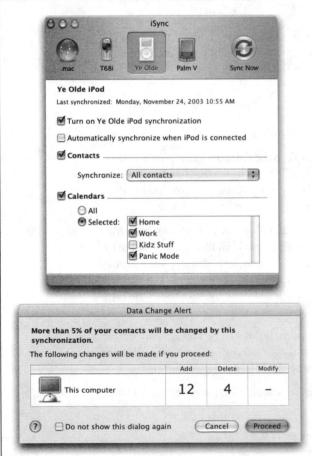

Figure 14-24:
Top: For each gadget, you can specify which iCal calendar categories you want synched, which contacts, and (for a .Mac account) whether or not you want the synching to be automatic.

Bottom: This safeguard window warns you about exactly how many changes you're about to make. (You can turn off this confirmation box in the iSync→Preferences window.)

Palm) made discoverable. To start the synchronization, press the physical HotSync button on the palmtop's cradle, cable, or HotSync screen.

Note: All of this leaves your Palm memos unsynched, because neither Address Book nor iCal has a place for memos. The workaround: Use Palm Desktop to view and edit them.

- **An iPod.** iTunes 4.8 and later versions handle the task of keeping your iPod updated with your iCal and Address Book info directly. (To get started, connect the iPod to the Mac and then choose iTunes→Preferences and click the iPod button.) In other words, this iSync feature is an orphan, exclusively for people who don't, for some reason, have iTunes 4.8 or later.

When you open iSync, its toolbar shows the icons of any synchable devices connected to your Mac at the moment. Click the appropriate gadget on the toolbar—your iPod, for example—to see the synching options available. Turn on the checkboxes you want, and then click the Sync Devices button. iSync does the deed.

iSync is plenty smart when it comes to resolving conflicts among your gadgets. For example, if you edit somebody's home phone number on your Palm, and your spouse simultaneously edits the same person's office number on the Mac, iSync will smoothly incorporate both changes into all copies of your address book. Unless you and your spouse *both* change the home number in different ways; then iSync will present a Resolve Conflicts button. Click it, and choose which info you believe should prevail.

iTunes

iTunes is Apple's beloved digital music-library program. Page 227 tells all

Mail

Mail, the Mac OS X email program, is described in detail in Chapter 10.

Preview

Preview began life as Mac OS X's built-in graphics viewer—but now, it's much more than that. It's the program you use to view incoming faxes as well as a nearly full-blown clone of Acrobat Reader (the free Adobe program that you used to read PDF files with).

In fact, because Preview now includes searching PDF documents, copying text out of them, adding comments, filling in forms, and clicking live hyperlinks—features that used to be available only in Acrobat Reader—you'd be silly to use Acrobat Reader at *all*.

Preview as Graphics Viewer

Preview's hallmark is its surprising versatility. It can display and manipulate pictures saved in a wide variety of formats, including common painting formats like JPEG,

TIFF, PICT, and GIF (or even animated ones, since you can add a Play button to the toolbar, as described below); less commonly used formats like BMP, PNG, SGI, TGA, and MacPaint; and even Photoshop, EPS, and PDF graphics.

Cropping graphics

To crop graphics in Preview, chopping out unwanted sections, drag across the part of the graphic that you want to keep, and then choose Tools→Crop (⌘-K).

If you don't think you'll ever need the original again, save the document. Otherwise, choose File→Save As to spin the cropped image out as a separate file, preserving the original in the process.

Tip: You can also rotate an image—even a PDF document—in 90-degree increments and then flip it vertically or horizontally, using the commands in the Tools menu.

Converting file formats

Preview doesn't just open all these file formats—it can also convert between most of them. You can pop open some old Windows BMP files and turn them into JPEGs for use on your Web site, and so on.

Tip: What's even cooler, you can open raw PostScript files right into Preview, which converts them into PDF files on the spot. You no longer need a PostScript laser printer to print out high-end diagrams and page layouts that come to you as PostScript files. Thanks to Preview, even an inkjet printer can handle them.

All you have to do is open the file you want to convert and choose File→Save As. In the dialog box that appears, choose the new format for the image using the Format pop-up menu. Finally, click Save to export the file.

The Thumbnails drawer

The Thumbnails drawer slides out from the side of the main Preview window whenever (a) you open a multipage PDF or TIFF file, or (b) you highlight a bunch of graphics files in the Finder and open them all at once. (If your PDF file has been prepared with a table of contents, the drawer shows that.)

The idea is that these thumbnails (miniatures) let you navigate pages or graphics without having to open a rat's nest of individual windows. Figure 14-25 expands on the idea.

Preview as PDF Reader

Preview is a nearly full-blown equivalent of Acrobat Reader, the free program used by millions to read PDF documents. Here are the basics:

- Zoom in and out using ⌘-plus and ⌘-minus.

- Use the View→PDF Display submenu to control how the PDF document appears: as two-page spreads, single scrolling sheets of paper towel, with borders that indicate ends of pages, and so on.

- Use ⌘-up arrow and ⌘-down arrow to page through a document. (Page Up and Page Down aren't quite the same thing; they shift to the previous or next part of the *same* page, if it wasn't already visible.) You can use the up arrow and down arrow keys alone to walk through the miniature images in the Thumbnails drawer, or to scroll within the same page.

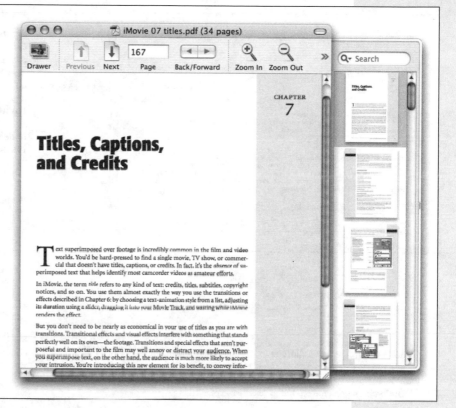

Figure 14-25:
To open or close the new Thumbnails drawer (right), click the Thumbnails icon at the left end of the toolbar. Incidentally, you can change the size of these miniatures by choosing Preview→Preferences and adjusting the slider.

- Bookmark your place by choosing Bookmarks→Add Bookmark (⌘-D); now type a clever name. Thereafter, you'll be able to return to that spot by choosing its name from the Bookmarks menu.

- Type in little notes as shown in Figure 14-26.

Note: Once you save the document, you can't move or change the notes or ovals you've added. If being able to restore the original document is important to you, use the File→Save As to spin out a copy of it before you annotate.

- Turn antialiasing (font smoothing) on or off to improve readability; to find the on/off switch, choose Preview→Preferences and click the PDF tab. (Though antialiased text generally looks great, it's sometimes easier to read very small type with antialiasing turned off. It's a little jaggy, but clearer nonetheless.)

- Turn on View→PDF Display→Continuous to scroll through multipage PDF documents in one continuous stream, instead of jumping from page to page when you use the scroll bars.

- To find a word or phrase somewhere in a PDF document, press ⌘-F (or choose Edit→Find→Find) to open the Find drawer. Proceed as shown in Figure 14-27.

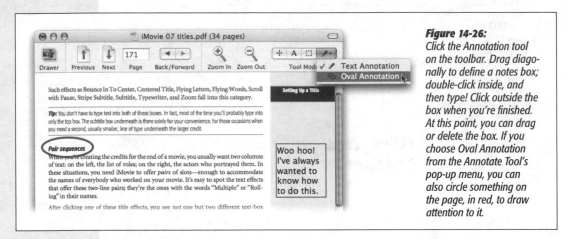

Figure 14-26:
Click the Annotation tool on the toolbar. Drag diagonally to define a notes box; double-click inside, and then type! Click outside the box when you're finished. At this point, you can drag or delete the box. If you choose Oval Annotation from the Annotate Tool's pop-up menu, you can also circle something on the page, in red, to draw attention to it.

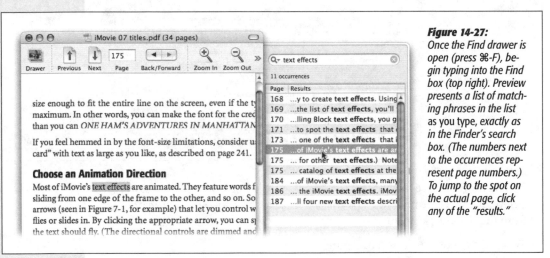

Figure 14-27:
Once the Find drawer is open (press ⌘-F), begin typing into the Find box (top right). Preview presents a list of matching phrases in the list as you type, exactly as in the Finder's search box. (The numbers next to the occurrences represent page numbers.) To jump to the spot on the actual page, click any of the "results."

- If you want to copy some text out of a PDF document—for pasting into a word processor, for example, where you can edit it—click the Text tool (the letter A on the toolbar) or choose Tools→Text Tool. Now you can drag through some text and then choose Edit→Copy, just as though the PDF document is a Web page. (You can even drag across page boundaries.)

- Preview is now a mini-iPhoto, complete with color-correction tools. With a photo on the screen, choose Tools→Image Correction. A passel of sliders appears (Saturation, Contrast, Exposure, and so on), for your image-tweaking pleasure.

- You can export a single page from a PDF as a TIFF file, so that you can use it in other graphics, word processing, or page layout programs—some of which might not directly support PDF.

  To extract a page, use the usual File→Save As command, making sure to choose the new file format from the pop-up menu. (If you choose a format like Photoshop or JPEG, Preview only converts the current page. That's because there's no such thing as a multipage Photoshop or JPEG graphic. But you already knew that.)

The toolbar

You can have hours of fun with Preview's toolbar. Exactly as with the Finder toolbar, you can customize it (by choosing View→Customize Toolbar—or by Option-⌘-clicking the upper-right toolbar button), rearrange its icons (by ⌘-dragging them sideways), and remove icons (by ⌘-dragging them downward).

Tip: Unhappy about the full inch of screen space consumed by the toolbar? No problem. Just ⌘-click the toolbar button (the white capsule in the upper-right corner). With each click, you cycle to the next toolbar style: large icons, small icons, no text labels, only text labels, and so on.

QuickTime Player

Dozens of Mac OS X programs can open QuickTime movies, play them back, and sometimes even incorporate them into documents: Word, FileMaker, AppleWorks, PowerPoint, Safari, America Online, and so on.

But the cornerstone of Mac OS X's movie-, sound-, and photo-playback software is QuickTime Player, which sits in your Applications→QuickTime folder (and comes factory-installed on the Dock). It does exactly what you'd expect: show pictures, play movies, and play sounds. You might think of it as Apple's take on Windows Media Player.

Playing Movies

You can open a movie file by double-clicking it, dragging it onto the QuickTime Player icon, or by launching QuickTime Player and then choosing File→Open File (⌘-O). The most important controls (Figure 14-28) are:

- **Scroll bar.** Drag the playhead to jump to a different spot in the movie.

- **Play/Stop button.** Click once to start, and again to stop. You can also press the Space bar, Return key, or ⌘-right arrow for this purpose. (Or avoid the buttons altogether and double-click the movie itself to start or stop playback.)

Tip: You can make any movie automatically play when opened, so that you avoid clicking the Play button. To do so, choose QuickTime Player→Preferences→Player Preferences, and turn on "Automatically play movies when opened."

Figure 14-28:
Some of the controls you see here are available only in the Pro version of QuickTime Player. They appear as soon as you type in your registration code (which you get when you pay $30).

- **Selection handles.** These tiny black triangles appear only in the $30 Pro version. You use them to highlight stretches of footage.

- **Volume.** If you like, you can make the soundtrack louder or softer by dragging this slider with your mouse or clicking in its "track." You may find it easier, however, to press the up or down arrow keys.

Tip: Try minimizing a QuickTime Player window while a movie is playing. It shrinks to the Dock—and *keeps on playing.* Do this enough times, and you'll know what it's like to be Steve Jobs on stage.

QuickTime Pro

If you've spent the $30 to upgrade your free copy of QuickTime Player to the Pro version—and to shut up the "Upgrade Now!" advertisement that appears the first time you open QuickTime Player each day—you've unlocked a number of useful features. For example:

- Your Movie menu contains additional playback options, including full-screen playback.

- When you find a QuickTime movie on a Web page, you can usually save it to your hard drive. (Click on the movie; hold down the mouse button until a pop-up menu appears; choose Save Movie to Disk, or the equivalent in your browser.)

- Using the commands in the Edit menu, you can view, turn on and off, add, or delete the individual *tracks* in a particular movie. (Most movies have nothing but a video track and a soundtrack. But a few specialized movies may also contain a text track, an animation track, alternate soundtracks, and so on.)

By far the most powerful feature you gain in the Pro version, however, is its ability to *edit* QuickTime movies. You can rearrange scenes, eliminate others, and save the result as a new movie with its own name. (Even QuickTime Player Pro doesn't let you *create* live-action QuickTime movies with your camcorder. For that, you need iMovie or a more complex editing program like Final Cut Express. QuickTime Player Pro simply lets you edit *existing* movies.)

Sherlock

Sherlock is one of Mac OS X's Web-information mini-browsers, as described in Chapter 11.

Stickies

Stickies lets you create virtual Post-it notes that you can stick anywhere on your screen—a triumphant software answer to the thousands of people who stick notes on the edges of their *actual* monitors. If you're a fan of the Windows Notepad, you might find yourself getting heavily into Stickies instead.

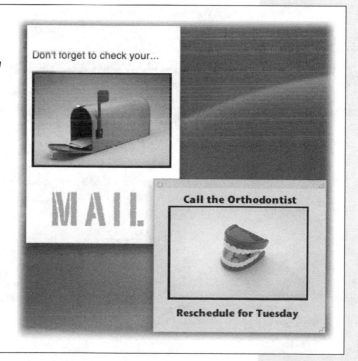

Figure 14-29:
Thanks to full-text formatting features and support for graphics and multimedia, even the humble to-do item can display a certain graphic sophistication in Mac OS X. You've come a long way from Notepad, baby.

You can use Stickies to type quick notes and to-do items, paste in Web addresses or phone numbers you need to remember, or store any other little scraps and snippets of text you come across. Your electronic Post-its show up whenever the Stickies program is running.

You can use a mix of fonts, text colors, and styles within each note. You can even copy and paste (or drag) *pictures, movies, and sounds* into your notes, producing the world's most elaborate reminders and to-do lists. You can even spell check your notes and search-and-replace text.

Creating Sticky Notes

The first time you launch Stickies, a few sample notes appear automatically, describing some of the program's features. You can quickly dispose of each sample by clicking the close button in the upper-left corner of each note or by choosing File→Close (⌘-W). Each time you close a note, a dialog box asks if you want to save the note. If you click Don't Save, the note disappears permanently.

Note: The Stickies module that's part of Dashboard (page 108) is extremely similar, and it's arguably quicker to open (just press F12). But it's also far more limited.

To create a new note, choose File→New Note (⌘-N) and start typing, pasting, or dragging text (or graphics, movies, or sounds) in from other programs.

Organizing Stickies

Once you start plastering your Mac with notes, it doesn't take long to find yourself plagued with desktop clutter. Fortunately, Stickies includes a few built-in tricks for managing a deskful of notes:

- There's a small resize handle on the lower-right corner of each note. Drag it to make notes larger or smaller onscreen.

- Use the small triangle in the upper-right corner of each note to zoom and shrink note windows with a single click. The first click collapses a note down to a more compact size. Another click pops the note back open to normal size.

- The best option: Double-click anywhere along the dark strip at the top of each note to miniaturize it into a compact one-line mini-note, as shown in Figure 14-30. You also can miniaturize a selected note by choosing Window→Miniaturize Window (⌘-M).

Figure 14-30:
If the first line of text gets truncated, as in the third note shown here, you can tug the right corner of the note and drag it wider without de-miniaturizing it.

- If your notes are scattered randomly across the desktop, you can bring them all forward with the Window→Bring All to Front command.

Tip: The most efficient way to use Stickies is to keep the notes in their miniaturized state, as shown in Figure 14-30. When a note is miniaturized, the first line of text shows up in tiny type right in the collapsed title bar of the note, so you don't have to expand the note to remember what's in it. And since many—if not most—of your notes can probably be summed up in a couple of words ("pick up dry cleaning," "call mom"), it's perfectly possible to keep your sticky notes in their miniaturized state permanently.

Formatting Notes

Stickies has several word processor–like commands for creating designer sticky notes, with any combination of fonts, colors, and styles. (You can also choose from six different background colors from the Color menu.) For the full scoop on Mac OS X's Font panel, see page 121.

Saving Sticky Notes

The notes you create in Stickies last only as long as you keep them open. If you close a note to get it out of the way, it vanishes permanently.

If you want to preserve the information you've stuffed into your notes in a more permanent form, use File→Export Text to save each note as a standalone text document. When you use the Export Text command, you can save the file as a plain text file, RTF (a special format recognized by most word processors), and RTFD (a strange and powerful variant of RTF that can contain *attachments*—graphics, files, and even programs you've dragged into the note).

System Preferences

This program opens the door to the very nerve center of Mac OS X's various user preferences, settings, and options. Chapter 13 covers every option in detail.

TextEdit

TextEdit is a word processor—a pretty darn powerful one, at that, considering you didn't have to pay a cent extra for it. You can create real documents with real formatting, using style sheets, colors, automatic numbering and bullets, tables, and customized line spacing, and—get this—even save the result as a Microsoft Word document. If you need to use Word files, but you can't stand bloated Microsoft interfaces, welcome.

Tip: Not only can TextEdit open and save Microsoft Word documents, but it even recognizes some of the very same keyboard shortcuts. For example, you can advance through documents one word at a time by pressing Option-left arrow or Option-right arrow. Adding the Shift key to those key combinations lets you *select* one whole word at a time. You can also use the ⌘ key in conjunction with the right and left arrow keys to jump to the beginning or end of a line.

TextEdit's Two Personalities

The one confusing aspect of TextEdit is that it's both a *plain-text editor* (no formatting; globally compatible) and a true *word processor* (fonts, sizes, styles; compatible with other word processors). You need to keep your wits about you as you edit, because the minute you add formatting to your document, TextEdit no longer lets you save it as a plain text file.

Here's the scheme:

- You can change a plain-text document to a formatted one by choosing Format→Make Rich Text. The ruler appears automatically to remind you that a new world of formatting has just become available.

- Conversely, you can change a formatted document (a Word file you've opened, for example) to a plain-text document by choosing Format→Make Plain Text. An alert message appears to point out that you're about to lose all formatting.

- If you know what kind of document you *always* want to open, go to the TextEdit→ Preferences dialog box and select "Rich text" or "Plain text" from the New Document pane. That's what kind of document you'll get every time you choose File→New.

Working in TextEdit

As you begin typing, all the usual word processing rules apply, with a few twists:

- Choose Bold, Italic, and font sizes using the Format→Font submenu, or choose Format→Font→Show Fonts (⌘-T) to open up the standard Mac OS X Font panel

---

UP TO SPEED

The Deal with Microsoft Word

Yes, you read that correctly: Humble TextEdit can *open and create* Microsoft Word documents! Your savings: the $400 price of Microsoft Office!

Well, sort of.

When you open a Microsoft Word document, most of the formatting comes through alive: bold, italic, font choices, colors, line spacing, alignment, and so on. Even very basic tables make it into TextEdit, although with different column widths.

A lot of Word-specific formatting does not survive crossing the chasm, however: borders, style sheets, footnotes, and the like. Bullets and numbered lists don't make it, either, even though TextEdit can create its own version of these.

Saving a TextEdit document as a Word document (File→Save As) is a better bet, because Word understands *all* of the kinds of formatting that TextEdit can produce—including bullets, numbering, and tables. The one disappointment is that Word doesn't recognize any style sheets you've set up in TextEdit. The formatting *applied* by those style names survives—just not the style names themselves.

Even so, a built-in Word-document editor is a huge, huge step for the Mac OS. It means that for the most part, you can be a first-class citizen on the great playing field of American business. Nobody ever needs to know that you're (a) using a Mac, and (b) *not* using the real Microsoft Word.

(page 121). You can even use subscript or superscript formatting, change the color of the text (Format→Font→Show Colors), and so on.

- Common paragraph-alignment options—Align Left, Align Right, Center, Justify—are all available as ruler buttons (and also in the Format→Text submenu). Adjust the line spacing (single, double, or any fraction or multiple) using the Spacing pop-up menu in the ruler.

- The ruler offers automatic bulleting and numbering of highlighted (or about-to-be-typed) paragraphs. Just choose the numbering style you prefer from the Lists pop-up menu.

- You can select several bits of text *simultaneously*. To pull this off, highlight your first piece of text by dragging, and then press ⌘ as you use the mouse to select more text. Bingo: You've highlighted two separate chunks of text.

When you're done selecting bits of text here and there, you can operate on them en masse. For example, you can make them all bold or italic with one fell swoop. You can use the Cut, Copy, and Paste commands, as described in the next section. When you cut or copy, the command acts upon all your multi-selections at once.

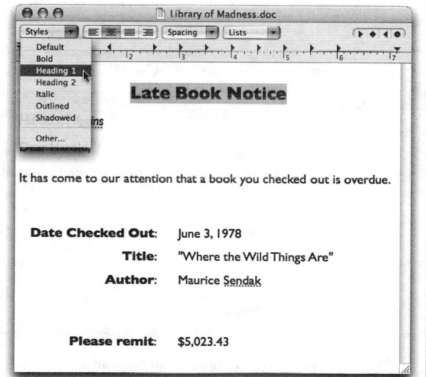

Figure 14-31:
The text ruler gives you control over tab stops, line spacing, paragraph justification, and so on. Pressing ⌘-R makes it appear and disappear. The Style pop-up menu lists canned sets of character and paragraph formatting, so that you can apply them consistently throughout a document.

You can also drag any *one* of the highlighted portions to a new area, confident that the other chunks will come along for the ride. All of the selected areas will wind up consolidated in their new location.

Tip: If you *Option*-drag one of the highlighted bits, you *copy* them, leaving the originals in place.

- Similarly, you can use the Find command to highlight a certain term everywhere it appears in a document. To do that, choose Edit→Find→Find (or just press ⌘-F). Fill in the "Find" and "Replace with" boxes—and then press the Control key. The Replace All button changes to say Select All.

Style Sheets

A *style* is a prepackaged collection of formatting attributes that you can apply and reapply with a click of the mouse: bold, 24-point Optima, double-spaced, centered (for example). You can create as many styles as you need: chapter headings, sidebar styles, and so on. You end up with a collection of custom-tailored styles for each of the repeating elements of your document.

Once you've created your styles, you can apply them as you need them, safe in the knowledge that they'll be consistent throughout the document. During the editing process, if you notice you accidentally styled, say, a *headline* using the *Subhead* style, you can fix the problem by simply reapplying the correct style.

Note: Unlike a "real" word processor, TextEdit doesn't let you *change* a style's formatting and thereby update every occurrence of it. You can't search and replace by style, either.

- **Creating a named style.** To create a style, start by formatting some text so that it looks the way you like it, complete with font, color, line spacing, tab settings, and so on.

  Then, from the Styles pop-up menu in the ruler, choose Other. Click Add to Favorites, type a name for the style, turn on both checkboxes (Figure 14-32), and click Add.

- **Applying a style.** Later, when you want to reuse the formatting you set up, just highlight some text and then choose the appropriate name from the Styles pop-up menu. TextEdit applies the formatting immediately.

Tip: If you simply click *inside a paragraph,* applying a style affects only *paragraph* attributes like line spacing, tab stops, and alignment. If you *highlight text* instead, applying a style affects only *character* attributes like the font and type size.

If you highlight an *entire* paragraph, however, both text and paragraph formatting appears.

- **Deleting a style.** To delete superfluous styles, choose Other from the Styles pop-up menu on the ruler. Click the Favorite Styles button, choose the unwanted style's name from the pop-up menu, and click Remove From Favorites. (Deleting a style doesn't affect any formatting that's already in your document; it just removes the name from the Styles menu.)

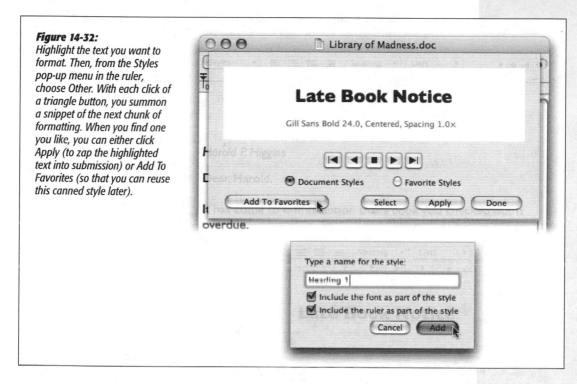

Figure 14-32:
Highlight the text you want to format. Then, from the Styles pop-up menu in the ruler, choose Other. With each click of a triangle button, you summon a snippet of the next chunk of formatting. When you find one you like, you can either click Apply (to zap the highlighted text into submission) or Add To Favorites (so that you can reuse this canned style later).

Tables

As shown in Figure 14-33, *tables* can make life a heck of a lot easier when you want to create a résumé, agenda, program booklet, list, multiple-choice test, Web page, or other document where numbers, words, and phrases must be aligned across the page. In the bad old days, people did it by pressing the Tab key to line up columns—a technique that turned into a nightmare as soon as you tried to add or delete text. But using a word processor's *table* feature is light-years easier and more flexible, because each row of a table expands infinitely to contain whatever you put into it. Everything else on its row remains aligned.

Tip: Tables are also critical for designing Web pages, as any Web designer can tell you. Even though you can't see the table outlines, many a Web page is filled with columns of text that are aligned, invisibly, by tables. And since TextEdit can save your work as an HTML document (File→Save As, File Format: HTML), it's a viable candidate for designing basic Web pages.

TextEdit's table feature, new in Tiger, is not what you'd call polished and sophisticated, but it works well enough:

- **Create a table** by choosing Format→Text→Table. The little floating Table palette appears (Figure 14-33). Use it to specify how many rows and columns you want; the placeholder table in your document adjusts itself in real time.

- **Format the table** using the other controls in the Table palette. The Alignment controls let you specify how the text in one of the table cells hugs its border; Cell Border controls the thickness of the line around the selected cells' borders (or, if you enter 0, to make the table walls invisible); the color swatch next to Cell Border specifies the color of the solid lines; and the Cell Background controls let you color in the table cells with colors of your choice. (Choose Color Fill from the pop-up menu, and then click the color swatch.)

- **Adjust the rows and columns** by dragging the cell borders.

- **Merge two selected cells** by clicking Merge Cells in the Table palette. To undo a merge, click Split Cell.

- **Nest one table inside a cell of another** by clicking in the cell and then clicking Nest Table. Change the numbers in the Rows and Columns boxes to set up its dimensions.

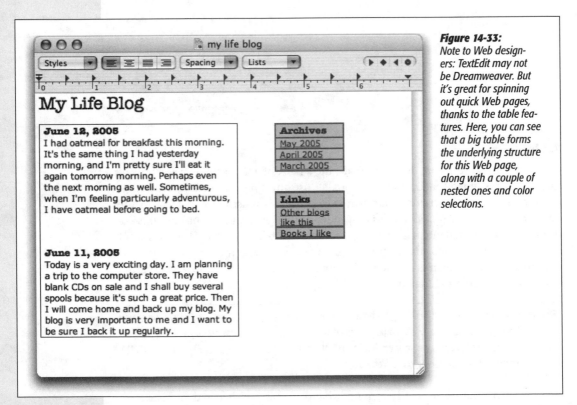

Figure 14-33:
Note to Web designers: TextEdit may not be Dreamweaver. But it's great for spinning out quick Web pages, thanks to the table features. Here, you can see that a big table forms the underlying structure for this Web page, along with a couple of nested ones and color selections.

Spell Checking

If the Edit→Spelling→Check Spelling As You Type command is turned on, you get interactive spell-checking, just as in Microsoft Word and other word processors. That is, misspelled words get flagged with a dashed red line the moment you type them.

To open the full Spelling panel at any time, choose Edit→Spelling→Spelling (or press Shift-⌘-;). Using the panel, you can correct errors (choosing from the suggestions generated by Apple's built-in spelling dictionary) or tell TextEdit to learn or ignore other suspected misspellings.

However, the quickest way to handle spelling corrections is shown in Figure 14-34.

Tip: This feature isn't really a TextEdit function—it's a system-wide spelling checker that you'll also find in Stickies, Mail, iCal, iPhoto, and other programs. You learn it once, you've learned it forever.

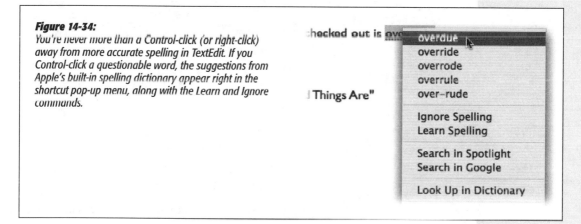

Figure 14-34:
You're never more than a Control-click (or right-click) away from more accurate spelling in TextEdit. If you Control-click a questionable word, the suggestions from Apple's built-in spelling dictionary appear right in the shortcut pop-up menu, along with the Learn and Ignore commands.

AutoComplete

This feature is great for anyone who's in a hurry, who's unsure of a spelling, or who's trying to solve a crossword puzzle. See Figure 14-35 for details, and note that Auto-Complete is actually available in almost every Cocoa program.

Utilities: Your Mac OS X Toolbox

The Utilities folder (inside your Applications folder) is home to another batch of freebies: another couple dozen tools for monitoring, tuning, tweaking, and trouble-shooting your Mac.

The truth is, though, that you're likely to use only about six of these utilities. The rest are very specialized gizmos primarily of interest only to network administrators or Unix geeks who are obsessed with knowing what kind of computer-code gibberish is going on behind the scenes.

Activity Monitor

Activity Monitor is designed to let the technologically savvy Mac fan see how much of the Mac's available power is being tapped at any given moment.

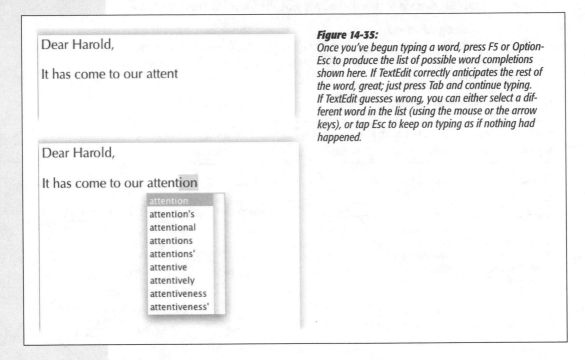

Dear Harold,

It has come to our attent

Dear Harold,

It has come to our attention

attention
attention's
attentional
attentions
attentions'
attentive
attentively
attentiveness
attentiveness'

Figure 14-35:
Once you've begun typing a word, press F5 or Option-Esc to produce the list of possible word completions shown here. If TextEdit correctly anticipates the rest of the word, great; just press Tab and continue typing. If TextEdit guesses wrong, you can either select a different word in the list (using the mouse or the arrow keys), or tap Esc to keep on typing as if nothing had happened.

The Processes table

Even when you're only running a program or two on your Mac, dozens of computational tasks (*processes*) are going on in the background. The top half of the dialog box, which looks like a table, shows you all the different processes—visible and invisible—that your Mac is handling at the moment. For each item, you can see the percentage of CPU being used, who's using it (either your account name, someone else's, or *root*, meaning the Mac itself), and the quantity of memory it's using.

The System monitor tabs

At the bottom of Activity Monitor, you're offered five tabs that reveal intimate details about your Mac and its behind-the-scenes efforts: CPU (how much work your processor is doing), System Memory (the state of your Mac's RAM at the moment), Disk Activity (meaning your hard drive), Disk Usage (how full your hard drive is), and Network.

AirPort Admin Utility

Don't even think about this program unless you've equipped your Mac with (or your Mac came with) the hardware necessary for Apple's wireless AirPort networking technology—namely, an AirPort wireless card.

Even then, you don't use the AirPort Admin Utility to set up AirPort connections for the first time. For that task, use the AirPort Setup Assistant described on the next page.

After you're set up, you can use AirPort Admin Utility to monitor the connections in an existing AirPort network. (You can also use this utility to set up new connections manually, rather than using the step-by-step approach offered by the Assistant.)

Figure 14-36:
The many faces of Activity Monitor. Top: It can be a graph of your processor (CPU) activity, your RAM usage at the moment, your disk capacity, and so on.

Bottom: If you double-click a process's name, you're treated to a three-tab dialog box that offers stunningly complete reams of data, mostly of interest only to programmers, about what that program is up to. (The Open Files and Ports tab, for example, shows you how many files that program has opened, often invisibly.) The most handy feature of this dialog box is the Quit button. It's a handy way to jettison a locked-up program when all else fails.

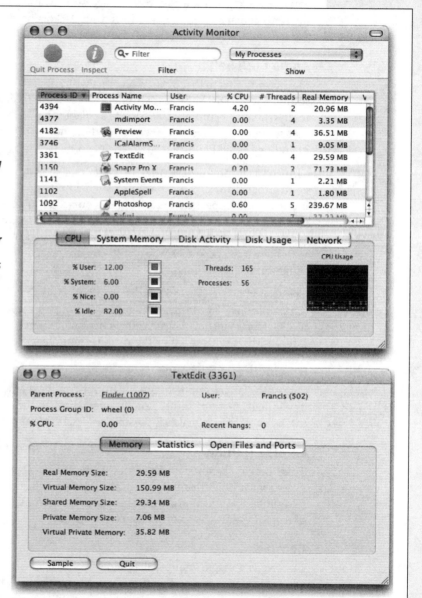

AirPort Setup Assistant

An assistant, in Apple-ese, is what you'd call a wizard in Windows. It presents a series of screens, posing one question at a time.

The AirPort Setup Assistant is the screen-by-screen guide that walks you through the steps needed to set up and use AirPort wireless networking. You'll be asked to name your network, provide a password for accessing it, and so on. When you've followed the steps and answered the questions, your AirPort hardware will be properly configured and ready to use.

Audio MIDI Setup

Maybe you've heard that Mac OS X comes with spectacular internal wiring for music, sound, and MIDI (Musical Instrument Digital Interface, a standard "language" for inter-synthesizer communication). It's available, that is, to music software companies that write their wares to capitalize on these new tools. (The big-name programs, including Digital Performer, are ready to go.)

This configuration program offers two tabs. The first, Audio Devices, is the master control panel for all your various sound inputs and outputs: microphones, line inputs, external speakers, and so on. Of course, for most people, this is all meaningless, because most Macs have only one input (the microphone) and one output (the speakers). But if you're sitting even now in your darkened music studio, humming with high-tech audio gear whose software has been designed to work with this little program, you're smiling.

The second tab, MIDI Devices, lets you click Add Device to create a new icon that represents one of your pieces of gear. Double-click the icon to specify its make and model. Finally, by dragging lines from the "in" and "out" arrows, you teach your Mac (and its MIDI software) how the various components are wired together.

Bluetooth File Exchange

One of the luxuries of owning a Bluetooth-equipped Mac is the ability to shoot files (to similarly forward-thinking colleagues) through the air, up to 30 feet away. Bluetooth File Exchange makes it possible, as described on page 354.

ColorSync Utility

This "bet-you'll-never-touch-it" utility performs a fairly esoteric task: repairing ColorSync profiles that may be "broken" because they don't strictly conform to the *ICC profile* specifications. (ICC [International Color Consortium] profiles are part of Apple's ColorSync color management system.)

Console

Console is a magic window that shows you what's happening under the hood of your Mac as you go about your business. Its function is to record a text log of all the internal status messages being passed between the Mac OS X and other applications as they interact with each other.

Opening the Console log is a bit like stepping into an operating room during a complex surgery; you're exposed to stuff the average person just isn't supposed to see. (Typical Console entries: "kCGErrorCannotComplete" or "doGetDisplayTransferByTable.") You can adjust the font and word wrapping using Console's Format menu, but the truth is that the phrase "CGXGetWindowType: Invalid window −1" looks ugly in just about *any* font.

Console isn't useless, however. These messages can be of value to programmers who are debugging software or troubleshooting a messy problem, or to tech-support helpers you call.

DigitalColor Meter

DigitalColor Meter can grab the exact color value of any pixel on your screen, which can be helpful when matching colors in Web page construction or other design work. After launching the DigitalColor Meter, just point to whichever pixel you want to measure, anywhere on your screen. A magnified view appears in the meter window, and the RGB color value of the pixels appears in the meter window. You can display the color values as RGB percentages or actual values, in Hex form (which is how colors are defined in HTML; white is represented as #FFFFFF, for example), and in several other formats.

Here are some tips for using the DigitalColor Meter to capture color information from your screen:

- To home in on the exact pixel (and color) you want to measure, drag the Aperture Size slider to the smallest size—one pixel. Then use the *arrow keys* to move the aperture to the precise location you want.

- Press Shift-⌘-C (Color→Copy Color) to put on the Clipboard the numeric value of the color you're pointing to.

- Press Shift-⌘-H (Color→Hold Color) to "freeze" the color meter on the color you're pointing to—a handy stunt when you're comparing two colors onscreen. You can point to one color, hold it using Shift-⌘-H, then move your mouse to the second color. Pressing Shift-⌘-H again releases the hold on the color.

- When the Aperture Size slider is set to view more than one pixel, DigitalColor Meter measures the *average* value of the pixels being examined.

Directory Access

If you use your Mac at home, or if it's not connected to a network, you'll never have to touch Directory Access. Even if you *are* connected to a network, there's only a remote chance you'll ever have to open Directory Access—unless you happen to be a network administrator, that is.

This utility controls the access that each individual Mac on a network has to Mac OS X's *directory services*—special databases that store information about users and servers. Directory Access also governs access to *LDAP directories* (Internet- or intranet-based "white pages" for Internet addresses).

A network administrator can use Directory Access to do things like select NetInfo domains, set up search policies, and define *attribute mappings*. If those terms don't mean anything to you, just pretend you never read this paragraph and get on with your life.

Disk Utility

This important program serves two key functions:

- It's Mac OS X's own little Norton Utilities, a powerful hard-drive administration tool that lets you repair, erase, format, and partition disks. If you make the proper sacrifices to the Technology Gods, you'll rarely need to run Disk Utility. But it's worth keeping in mind, just in case you ever find yourself facing a serious disk problem.

- Disk Utility also creates and manages *disk images,* electronic versions of disks or folders that you can send electronically to somebody else.

The following discussion tackles the program's two personalities one at a time.

Disk Utility, the hard drive-repair program

Here are some of the tasks you can perform with this half of Disk Utility:

- Repair folders, files, and program that don't work because you supposedly don't have sufficient "access privileges." This is by far the most common use of Disk Utility, not to mention the most reliable and satisfying. Using the Fix Permissions button fixes an *astonishing* range of bizarre Mac OS X problems, from programs that won't open to menulets that freeze.

- Get size and type information about any disks attached to your Mac.

- Fix disks that won't appear on your desktop or behave improperly.

- Completely erase disks—including rewritable CDs (CD-RW).

- Partition a disk into multiple *volumes* (that is, subdivide a drive so that its segments appear on the desktop with separate disk icons).

- Set up a *RAID array* (a cluster of separate disks that acts as a single volume).

Note: Disk Utility can check the startup disk for damage—the disk on which your system software is currently running. It can also fix the permissions of the disk it's on, thank goodness.

Any other operation, like reformatting, erasing, partitioning, or actually repairing the disk, requires the Mac to start up from a different disk (your Tiger DVD, for example). Otherwise, it'd be like a surgeon performing an appendectomy on himself—not a great idea.

The left Disk Utility panel lists your hard drive and any other disks in your Mac at the moment. When you click the name of your hard drive's mechanism, like "74.5 GB Hitachi iC25N0…" (not the "Macintosh HD" partition label below it), you see a panel with five tabs, one for each of the main Disk Utility functions:

- **First Aid.** This is the disk-repair part of Disk Utility, and it does a great job at fixing many disk problems. When you're troubleshooting, Disk Utility should always be your first resort. To use it, you click the icon of a disk and then click either Verify Disk (to get a report on the disk's health) or Repair Disk (which fixes whatever problems the program finds).

  If Disk First Aid reports that it's unable to fix the problem, *then* it's time to invest in a program like DiskWarrior (*www.alsoft.com*).

Tip: If Disk First Aid finds nothing wrong with a disk, it reports, "No repairs were necessary." That's the strongest vote of confidence Disk First Aid can give.

You may wind up using the Verify and Repair Disk *Permissions* buttons even more often. Their function is to straighten out problems with the invisible Unix file permissions that keep you from moving, changing, or deleting files or folders. (The occasional software installer can create problems like this.) You'd be surprised how often running one of these permission checks solves glitchy little Mac OS X problems.

- **Erase.** Select a disk, choose a format (almost always Mac OS Extended), give it a name, and click Erase to wipe the disk clean and apply the format you chose.

- **Partition.** With the Partition tools, you can erase a hard drive in such a way that you subdivide its surface. Each disk is represented on your screen by two (or more) different hard drive icons. (See Figure 14-37.)

  There are some very good reasons *not* to partition a drive these days, though: A partitioned hard drive is more difficult to resurrect after a serious crash, requires more navigation when you want to open a particular file, and offers no speed or safety benefits.

- **RAID.** RAID stands for Redundant Array of Independent Disks, and refers to a special formatting scheme in which a group of separate disks are configured to work together as one very large, very fast drive. In a RAID array, multiple disks share the job of storing data—a setup that can improve speed and reliability.

  Most Mac users don't use or set up RAID arrays, probably because most Mac users only have one hard drive (and Disk Utility can't make your startup disk part of a RAID array).

  If you're using multiple external hard disks, though, you can use a RAID to merge them into one giant disk. Just drag the icons of the relevant disks (or disk partitions) from the left-side list of disks into the main list (where it says, "Drag disks here to add to set"). Use the RAID Scheme pop-up menu to specify the RAID format you want to use (Stripe, for example, is a popular choice for maximizing disk speed), name your new mega-disk, and then click Create. The result is a single "disk" icon on your desktop that actually represents the combined capacity of all the RAID disks.

- **Restore.** This tab lets you make a *perfect copy* of a disk or a disk image, much like the popular shareware program CarbonCopy Cloner. You might find this useful when, for example, you want to make an exact copy of your old Mac's hard drive on your new one. (You can't do that just by copying your old files and folders manually via, say, a network. If you try, you won't get the thousands of *invisible* files that make up a Mac OS X installation. If you use the Restore function, they'll come along for the ride.)

Start by dragging the disk or disk image you want to copy *from* into the Source box. Then drag the icon of the disk you want to copy *to* into the Destination box.

Tip: If you want to copy an *online* disk image onto one of your disks, you don't have to download it first. Just type its Web address into the Source field. You might find this trick convenient if you keep disk images on your iDisk (page 147), for example.

Figure 14-37:
To partition your drive—which involves erasing it completely—launch Disk Utility, switch to the Partition pane, and select the hard drive you want to partition from the list on the left. From the Volume Scheme pop-up menu, choose the number of partitions you want (or, for two equal chunks, click Split below the map). Now drag the horizontal divider in the Volumes map to specify the relative sizes of the partitions you want to create. Assign a name and format for each partition in the Volume Information area, and then click Partition.

If you turn on Erase Destination, Disk Utility will obliterate all the data on your target disk before copying the data. If you leave this checkbox off, however, Disk Utility will simply copy everything onto your destination, preserving all your old data in the process. (The Skip Checksum checkbox is available only if you choose to erase your destination disk. If you're confident that all of the files on the source disk are 100% healthy and whole, turn on this checkbox to save time. Otherwise, leave it off for extra safety.)

Finally, click the Restore button. (You might need to type in an administrator password.) Restoring can take a long time for big disks, so go ahead and make yourself a cup of coffee while you're waiting.

Tip: Instead of clicking a disk icon and then clicking the appropriate Disk Utility tab, you can just Control-click a disk's name and choose Information, First Aid, Erase, Partition, or Restore from the shortcut menu.

Disk Utility, the disk-image program

The world's largest fan of *disk images* is Apple itself; the company often releases new software in disk-image form. A lot of Mac OS X add-on software arrives from your Web download in disk-image form, too.

Disk images are popular for software distribution for a simple reason: Each image file precisely duplicates the original master disk, complete with all the necessary files in all the right places. When a software company sends you a disk image, it ensures that you'll install the software from a disk that *exactly* matches the master disk.

It's important to understand the difference between a *disk-image file* and the *mounted disk* (the one that appears when you double-click the disk image). Figure 14-38 makes the distinction clear.

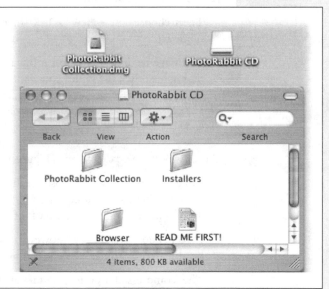

Figure 14-38:
The usual life cycle of a disk-image file: First, you download it from the Internet. The result is an icon whose name usually ends in .img or .dmg (upper left). (Files that end with .smi are also disk images, but self-mounting ones that don't require Disk Utility.) Second, when you double-click this icon, an invisible program called DiskImageMounter creates an icon that simulates a new disk (upper right). Finally, when you double-click this icon, you see exactly what the original creator of the image wanted you to see (bottom).

You can create disk images, too. Doing so can be very handy in situations like these:

- You want to create a backup of an important CD. By turning it into a disk-image file on your hard drive, you'll always have a safety copy, ready to burn back onto a *new* CD. (This is an essential practice for educational CDs that kids will be handling soon after eating peanut butter and jelly.)

- You want to replicate your entire hard drive—complete with all of its files, programs, folder setups, and so on—onto a new, bigger hard drive (or a new, better Mac), using the new Restore feature described earlier.

- You want to back up your entire hard drive, or maybe just a certain chunk of it, onto an iPod or another disk. (Again, you can later use the Restore function to complete the transaction.)

- You bought a game that requires its CD to be in the drive at all times. Many programs like these run equally well off of a mounted disk image that you made from the original CD.

- You want to send somebody else a copy of a disk via the Internet. You simply create a disk image, and then send *that*—preferably in compressed form.

Here's how you make a disk image.

- **To image-ize a disk or partition.** Click the name of the disk you want (in the left-panel list, where you see the disks currently in, or attached to, your Mac). (The topmost item is the name of your *drive,* like "484.0 MB MATSHITADVD-R" for a DVD drive or "74.5 GB Hitachi" for a hard drive. Beneath that entry, you generally see the name of the actual partition, like "Macintosh HD," or the CD's name as it appears on the screen.)

    Then choose File→New→Disk Image from [whatever the disk or partition's name is].

- **To image-ize a folder.** Choose Image→New→Image from Folder. In the Open dialog box, click the folder you want and then click Open.

Tip: Disk Utility can't turn an individual *file* into a disk image. But you can always put a single file into a folder, and then make a disk image of *that.*

Either way, the next dialog box (Figure 14-39) offers some fascinating options.

- **Image Format.** If you choose "read/write," your disk image file, when double-clicked, will turn into a superb imitation of a hard drive. You'll be able to drag files and folders onto it, drag them off of it, change icons' names on it, and so on.

    If you choose "read-only," however, the result will behave more like a CD. You'll be able to copy things off of it, but not make any changes to it.

    The "compressed" option is best if you intend to send the resulting file by email, for example, or if you'd like to preserve the disk image on some backup disk for a rainy day. It takes a little longer to create a simulated disk when you double-click the disk image file, but it takes up a lot less disk space than an uncompressed version.

    Finally, choose "DVD/CD master" if you're copying a CD or a DVD. The resulting file is a perfect mirror of the original disc, ready for copying onto a blank CD or DVD when the time comes.

- **Encryption.** Here's a great way to lock private files away into a vault that nobody else can open. If you choose "AES-128 (recommended)," you'll be asked to assign a password to your new image file. Nobody will be able to open it without the password—not even you. On the other hand, if you save it into your Keychain (page 345), it won't be such a disaster if you forget the password.

- **Save As.** Choose a name and location for your new image file. The name you choose here doesn't need to match the original disk or folder name.

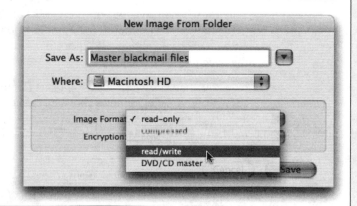

Figure 14-39:
These two pop-up menus let you specify (a) what kind of disk image you want, and (b) whether or not you want it password-protected. The latter option is great when you want to password-protect one folder, without bothering with your entire Home folder.

When you click Save (or press Enter), if you opted to create an encrypted image, you'll be asked to make up a password at this point.

Otherwise, Disk Utility now creates the image and then *mounts* it—that is, turns the image file into a simulated, yet fully functional, disk icon on your desktop.

When you're finished working with the disk, eject it as you would any disk (Control-click it and choose Eject, for example). Hang onto the .dmg disk image file itself, however. This is the file you'll need to double-click if you ever want to recreate your "simulated disk."

Turning an image into a CD

One of the other most common disk-image tasks is turning a disk image *back* into a CD or DVD—provided you have a CD or DVD burner on your Mac, of course.

All you have to do is drag the .dmg file into the Disk Utility window, select it, and click the Burn icon on the toolbar (or, alternatively, Control-click the .dmg icon and choose Burn from the shortcut menu). Insert a blank CD or DVD, and then click Burn.

Grab

Grab takes pictures of your Mac's screen, for use when you're writing up instructions, illustrating a computer book, or collecting proof of some secret screen you found buried in a game. You can take pictures of the entire screen (press ⌘-Z, which for once in its life does *not* mean Undo) or capture only the contents of a rectangular selection (press Shift-⌘-A). When you're finished, Grab displays your snapshot in a new window, which you can print, close without saving, or save as a TIFF file, ready for emailing, posting on a Web page, or inserting into a manuscript.

Tip: The Mac also has built-in screen-capture keystrokes, just as Windows does; see page 199 for details.

Grapher

This equation grapher is an *amazing* piece of work.

When you first open Grapher, you're asked to choose what kind of virtual "graph paper" you want: two-dimensional (standard, polar, logarithmic) or three-dimensional (cubic, spherical, cylindrical). Click a name to see a preview; when you're happy with the selection, click Open.

Now the main Grapher window appears (Figure 14-40). Do yourself a favor: Spend a few wow-inducing minutes choosing canned equations from the Examples menu, and watching how Grapher whips up gorgeous, colorful, sometimes animated graphs on the fly.

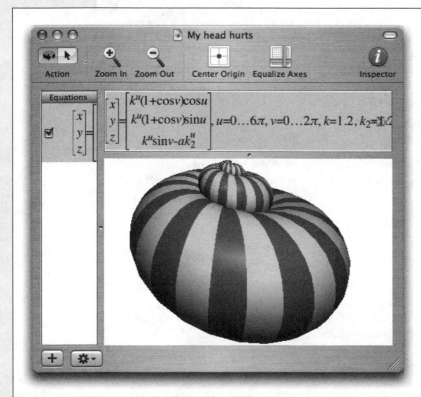

Figure 14-40:
In general, you type equations into Grapher just as you would on paper (like z=2xy). If in doubt, check the online help, which offers enough hints on functions, constants, differential equations, series, and periodic equations to keep the A Beautiful Mind guy busy for days.

When you're ready to plug in an equation of your own, type it into the text box at the top of the window. (If you're not such a math hotshot, or you're not sure of the equation format, work from the canned equations and mathematical building blocks that appear when you choose Equation→New Equation from Template or Window→Show Equation Palette.)

Once the graph is up on the screen, you can tailor it like this:

- To move a 2-D graph in the window, choose View→Move Tool and then drag; to move a 3-D graph, ⌘-drag it.

- To rotate a 3-D graph, drag it around.

- To change the colors, line thicknesses, 3-D "walls," and other graphic elements, click the ❶ button (or choose Window→Show Inspector) to open the formatting palette. The controls you find here vary by graph type, but rest assured that Grapher can accommodate your every visual whim.

- To change the fonts and sizes, choose Grapher→Preferences. On the Equations panel, the four sliders let you specify the relative sizes of the text elements. If you click the sample equation, the Font panel appears (page 121), so you can fiddle with the type.

- Add your own captions, arrows, ovals, or rectangles using the Object menu.

Installer

You'll never launch this. It's the engine that drives the Mac OS X installer program and other software installers. There's nothing for you to configure or set up.

Java Folder

Programmers generally use the Java programming language to create small programs that they sometimes embed into Web pages—animated effects, clocks, calculators, stock tickers, and so on. Your browser automatically downloads and runs such applets (assuming that you have "Enable Java" turned on in your browser), thanks to the Java-related tools in this folder.

Keychain Access

Keychain Access manages all your secret information—passwords for network access, file servers, FTP sites, Web pages, and other secure items. For instructions on using Keychain Access, see page 345.

Migration Assistant

This little cutie automates the transfer of all your stuff—your Home folder, network settings, programs, and more—from one Mac to another. It assumes that you've connected them using a FireWire cable, because it relies on Target Disk Mode (page 157) to get the copying done quickly. (It can also copy everything over from a secondary hard drive or partition.)

The instructions on the screen guide you through the setup process; then the Assistant automates the transfer.

NetInfo Manager

NetInfo is the central Mac OS X database that keeps track of user and group accounts, passwords, access privileges, email configurations, printers, computers, and just about anything else network related. NetInfo Manager is where a network administrator (or a technically inclined Mac guru) can go to view and edit these various settings.

To dive into NetInfo Manager, start by clicking the padlock button at the bottom of the main window and enter an administrator's password. Then examine the various parameters in the top-left Directory Browser list. As you'll quickly discover, most of these settings are written in Unix techno-speak.

Although most of NetInfo is of little use to a typical Mac fan, a few parts are easy enough to figure out. If you click *users* in the left-side list, you'll see, in the next column, a list of accounts you've created. Click one of the user names there, and you'll see, in the properties pane at the bottom of the screen, some parameters that may come in handy—such as each person's name, password, and password hint. By double-clicking one of these info items, you can edit it, which can come in genuinely handy if someone on your school or office network forgets their password.

Network Utility

The Network Utility gathers information about Web sites and network users. It offers a suite of advanced, industry-standard Internet tools like these:

- Use **Whois** ("who is") to gather an amazing amount of information about the owners of any particular domain (such as *www.apple.com*)—including name and address info, telephone numbers, and administrative contacts—using the technique shown in Figure 14-41.

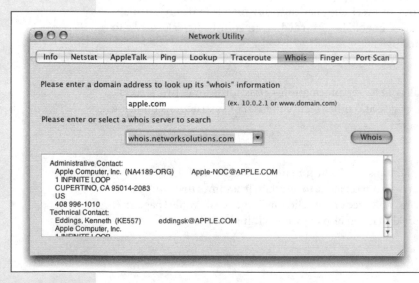

Figure 14-41:
The Whois tool is a powerful part of Network Utility. First enter a domain that you want information about, then choose a Whois server from the pop-up menu (you might try whois.networksolutions. com). When you click the Whois button, you'll get a surprisingly revealing report about the owner of the domain, including phone numbers, fax numbers, contact names, and so on.

- Use **Ping** to enter a Web address (such as *www.google.com*), and then "ping" (send out a "sonar" signal to) the server to see how long it takes for it to respond to your request. Network Utility reports the response time in milliseconds—a useful test when you're trying to see if a remote server (a Web site, for example) is up and running.

- **Traceroute** lets you track how many "hops" are required for your Mac to communicate with a certain Web server. Just type in the network address then click Trace. You'll see that your request actually jumps from one *trunk* of the Internet to another, from router to router, as it makes its way to its destination. You'll find that a message sometimes crisscrosses the entire country before it arrives at its destination. You can also see how long each leg of the journey took, in milliseconds.

ODBC Administrator

This program is designed to arbitrate of ODBC access requests. Any questions?

If you have no idea what that means, and no corporate system administrator has sat down with you to explain it to you, then your daily work probably doesn't involve working with corporate ODBC (Open Database Connectivity) databases. You can ignore this program or throw it away.

POWER USERS' CLINIC

The XCode Tools

The Tiger DVD includes a special batch of programs, known as the XCode Tools, just for developers (programmers) who write Mac OS X software. You'll need some of these programs if you want to get into some of the more esoteric (or, as some would say, fun) Mac OS X tricks and tips.

To install these tools, open Xcode Tools→XcodeTools.mpkg in the DVD window. After following the on-screen prompts, you wind up with a new folder called Developer on your hard drive. In its Applications→Utilities folder, you'll find a few programs that are user-friendly enough even for nonprogrammers.

If you visit Developer→Applications→Graphics Tools, for example, you'll find Quartz Composer. That program lets you build screen savers, animations, and tons of other graphical goodies without writing a single line of code.

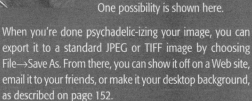

(Use File→New from Template to get started with some preassembled possibilities.)

Also, don't miss Core Image Fun House (also in Developer→Applications→Graphics Tools). With that single program, you can apply dozens of mind-blowing visual effects to your images and movies—distortions, color corrections, solar flares, and so on—with nothing more than a few clicks. (If your Mac is fast enough, you can even adjust filters in *real time*, so you can see the result of your modifications as you make them.) One possibility is shown here.

When you're done psychadelic-izing your image, you can export it to a standard JPEG or TIFF image by choosing File→Save As. From there, you can show it off on a Web site, email it to your friends, or make it your desktop background, as described on page 152.

Print Center

This is the hub of your Mac's printing operations. You can use the Print Center to set up and configure new printers, and to check on the status of print jobs, as described in Chapter 8.

System Profiler

System Profiler is a great tool for learning exactly what's installed on your Mac and what's not—in terms of both hardware and software. The people who answer the phones on Apple's tech-support line are particularly fond of System Profiler, since the detailed information it reports can be very useful for troubleshooting nasty problems.

Tip: Instead of burrowing into your Applications→Utilities folder to open System Profiler, it's sometimes faster to use this trick: Choose →About This Mac. In the resulting dialog box, click the More Info button. Boom—System Profiler opens. (And if you click your Mac OS X version number twice in the About box, you get to see your Mac's serial number!)

When you launch System Profiler, it reports information about your Mac in a list down the left side (Figure 14-42).

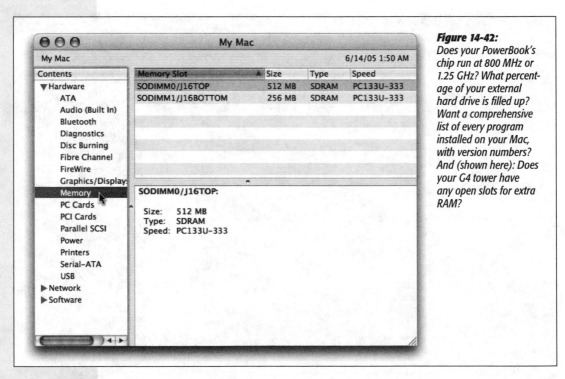

Figure 14-42:
Does your PowerBook's chip run at 800 MHz or 1.25 GHz? What percentage of your external hard drive is filled up? Want a comprehensive list of every program installed on your Mac, with version numbers? And (shown here): Does your G4 tower have any open slots for extra RAM?

Terminal

Mac OS X's resemblance to an attractive, mainstream operating system like Windows or the old Mac OS is just an optical illusion; the engine underneath the pretty skin is Unix, one of the oldest and most respected operating systems in use today. And Terminal is the rabbit hole that leads you—or, rather, the technically bold—straight down into the Mac's powerful Unix world.

The first time you see it, you'd swear that Unix has about as much in common with the Mac OS X illustrated in the other chapters of this book as a Jeep does with a watermelon (see Figure 14-43).

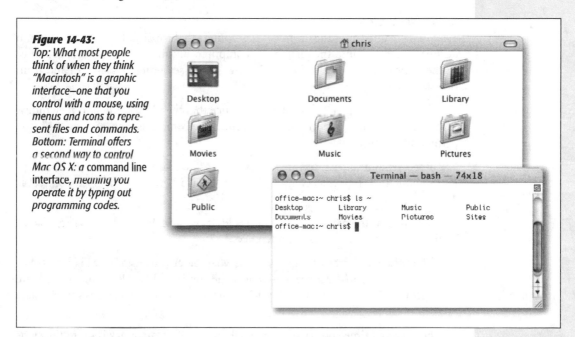

Figure 14-43:
Top: What most people think of when they think "Macintosh" is a graphic interface—one that you control with a mouse, using menus and icons to repre-sent files and commands. Bottom: Terminal offers a second way to control Mac OS X: a command line interface, meaning you operate it by typing out programming codes.

What the illustration at the bottom of Figure 14-43 shows, of course, is a *command line interface:* a place where you can type out instructions to the computer itself. This is a world without icons, menus, or dialog boxes; even the mouse is almost useless.

Surely you can appreciate the irony: The brilliance of the original 1984 Macintosh was that it *eliminated* the command line interface that was still the ruling party on the computers of the day (like Apple II and DOS machines). Most non-geeks sighed with relief, delighted that they'd never have to memorize commands again. Yet here's Mac OS X, Apple's supposedly ultramodern operating system, complete with a com-mand line! What's going on?

Actually, the command line never went away. At universities and corporations worldwide, professional computer nerds kept right on pounding away at the little *C:* or % prompts, appreciating the efficiency and power such direct computer control afforded them.

Now, you never *have* to use Mac OS X's command line. In fact, Apple has swept it far under the rug, obviously expecting that most people will use the beautiful icons and menus of the regular desktop.

For intermediate or advanced computer fans with a little time and curiosity, however, the command line opens up a world of possibilities. It lets you access corners of Mac OS X that you can't get to from the regular desktop. It lets you perform certain tasks with much greater speed and efficiency than you'd get by clicking and dragging icons. And it gives you a fascinating glimpse into the minds and moods of people who live and breathe computers.

A Terminal crash course

Terminal is named after the terminals (computers that consist of only a monitor and keyboard) that tap into the mainframe computers at universities and corporations. In the same way, Terminal is just a window that passes along messages to and from the Mac's brain.

The first time you open Terminal, you'll notice that there's not much in its window except the date and time of your last login, a welcome message, and the "$" (the command line prompt).

For user-friendliness fans, Terminal doesn't get off to a very good start—this prompt looks about as technical as computers get. It breaks down like this (see Figure 14-44):

- **office-mac:** is the name of your Mac (at least, as Unix thinks of it), as recorded in the Sharing panel of System Preferences.

- **~.** The next part of the prompt indicates what folder you're "in" (see Figure 14-44). It denotes the *working directory*—that is, the current folder. (Remember, there are no icons in Unix.) Essentially, this notation tells you where you are as you navigate your machine.

  The very first time you try out Terminal, the working directory is set to the symbol ~, which is shorthand for "your own Home folder." It's what you see the first time you start up Terminal, but you'll soon be seeing the names of other folders here—*[office-mac: /Users]* or *[office-mac: /System/Library]*, for example. (More on this slash notation on page 51.)

Note: Before Apple came up with the user-friendly term *folder* to represent an electronic holding tank for files, folders were called *directories*. (Yes, they mean the same thing.) But in any discussion of Unix, "directory" is the correct term.

- **chris$** begins with your short user name. It reflects whoever's logged into the *shell* (the current terminal "session"), which is usually whoever's logged into the *Mac* at the moment. As for the $ sign: Think of it as a colon. In fact, think of the whole prompt shown in Figure 14-44 as Unix's way of asking, "OK, Chris, I'm listening. What's your pleasure?"

The insertion point looks like a tall rectangle at the end of the command line. It trots along to the right as you type.

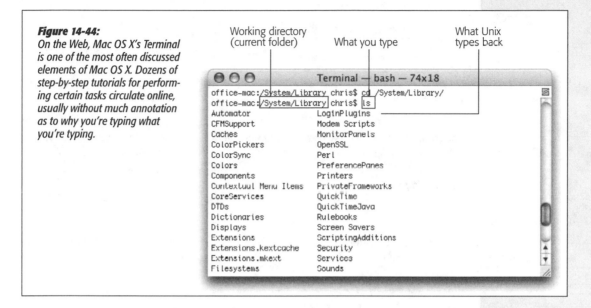

Figure 14-44:
On the Web, Mac OS X's Terminal is one of the most often discussed elements of Mac OS X. Dozens of step-by-step tutorials for performing certain tasks circulate online, usually without much annotation as to why you're typing what you're typing.

Working directory (current folder)

What you type

What Unix types back

As you read this section, remember that capitalization matters in Terminal, even though it doesn't in the Finder. As far as Unix commands are concerned, *Hello* and *hello* are two very different things.

Unix programs

Each Unix command generally calls up a single application (or *process*, as geeks call it) that launches, performs a task, and closes. Many of the best-known such applications come with Mac OS X.

Here's a fun one: Just type *uptime* and press Enter. (That's how you run a Unix program: just type its name and press Enter.) On the next line, Terminal shows you how long your Mac has been turned on continuously. It shows you something like: "6:00PM up 8 days, 15:04, 1 user, load averages: 1.24, 1.37, 1.45"—meaning your Mac has been running for 8 days, 15 hours nonstop.

You're finished running the *uptime* program. The $ prompt returns, suggesting that Terminal is ready for whatever you throw at it next.

Try this one: Type *cal* at the prompt, and then press Enter. Unix promptly spits out a calendar of the current month.

```
[office-mac:~] chris$ cal
      June 2003
 S  M Tu  W Th  F  S
 1  2  3  4  5  6  7
 8  9 10 11 12 13 14
15 16 17 18 19 20 21
22 23 24 25 26 27 28
29 30
[office-mac:~] chris$
```

As you can see, it wraps up the response with "[office-mac:~] chris$"—yet another prompt, meaning that Terminal is ready for your next command.

This time, try typing *cal 11 2005, cal -y,* or *cal -yj.* These three commands make Unix generate a calendar of November 2005, a calendar of the current year, and a *Julian* calendar of the current year, respectively.

Navigating in Unix

If you can't see any icons for your files and folders, how are you supposed to work with them?

You use Unix commands like *pwd* (tells you what folder you're looking at), *ls* (lists what's *in* the current folder), and *cd* (changes to a different folder).

Tip: As you can tell by these examples, Unix commands are very short. They're often just two-letter commands, and an impressive number of those use *alternate hands* (ls, cp, rm, and so on).

UP TO SPEED

Pathnames 101

In many ways, browsing the contents of your hard drive using Terminal is just like doing so with the Finder. You start with a folder, and move down into its subfolders, or up into its parent folders.

In Terminal, you're frequently required to specify a certain file or folder in this tree of folders. But you can't see their icons from the command line. So how are you supposed to identify the file or folder you want?

By typing its *pathname.* The pathname is a string of folder names, something like a map, that takes you from the *root*

level to the next nested folder, to the next, and so on. (The root level is, for learning-Unix purposes, the equivalent of your main hard drive window. It's represented in Unix by a single slash. The phrase */Users,* in other words, means "the Users folder in my hard drive window," or, in other terms, "the Users directory at the root level.")

To refer to the Documents folder in your own Home folder, for example, you could type */Users/chris/Documents* (if your name is Chris, that is). Or you could replace the path to your home folder with a tilde (~), and specify your Documents folder with nothing more than ~/*Documents.*

Getting help

Mac OS X comes with nearly 900 Unix programs. How are you supposed to learn what they all do? Fortunately, almost every Unix program comes with its own little help file. It may not appear within an elegant Mac OS X window—in fact, it's pretty darned plain—but it offers much more material than the regular Mac Help Center.

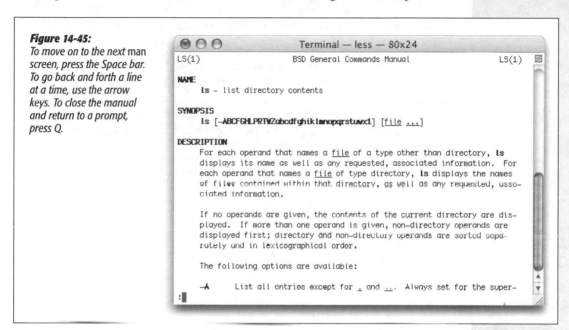

Figure 14-45:
To move on to the next man *screen, press the Space bar. To go back and forth a line at a time, use the arrow keys. To close the manual and return to a prompt, press Q.*

These help files are called user-manual pages, or *manpages*, which hold descriptions of virtually every command and program available. Mac OS X, in fact, comes with manpages on about 4,000 topics—about 9,000 printed pages' worth. Unfortunately, manpages rarely have the clarity of writing or the learner-focused approach you'll find in the Mac Help Center. They're generally terse, just-the-facts descriptions. In fact, you'll probably find yourself needing to reread certain sections again and again. The information they contain, however, is invaluable to new and experienced users alike, and the effort spent mining them is usually worthwhile.

To access the manpage for a given command, type *man* followed by the name of the command you're researching. For example, to view the manpage for the *ls* command, enter: *man ls*. Now the manual appears, one screen at a time, as shown in Figure 14-45.

For more information on using *man,* view its *own* manpage by entering—what else?—*man man.*

Tip: The free program ManOpen, available for download from the "Missing CD" page of *www.missing manuals.com,* is a Cocoa manual-pages reader that provides a nice-looking, easier-to-control window for reading manpages.

Learning more

Unix is, of course, an entire operating system unto itself. If you get bit by the bug, here are some sources of additional Unix info:

- *www.ee.surrey.ac.uk/Teaching/Unix.* A convenient, free Web-based course in Unix for beginners.

- *www.megazone.org/Computers/manual.shtml.* A fast-paced, more advanced introduction.

- *Learning Unix for Mac OS X Tiger,* by Dave Taylor & Brian Jepson (O'Reilly Media). A compact, relatively user-friendly tour of the Mac's Unix base.

Tip: Typing *unix for beginners* into a search page like Google.com nets dozens of superb help, tutorial, and reference Web sites. If possible, stick to those that feature the *bash shell.* That way, everything you learn online should be perfectly applicable to navigating Mac OS X via Terminal.

Installation and Troubleshooting

I f you're lucky, this is a wasted chapter. After all, you'll probably never have to install Mac OS X (assuming it came preinstalled on your Mac), and in the best of all technological worlds, you won't have to do much troubleshooting, either. But here's this chapter, anyway—just in case.

Installing Mac OS X 10.4

If your computer came with Mac OS X 10.4 already installed on it, you can skip this write-up—for now.

But if you're running an earlier version of the Mac OS and want to savor the X experience, this chapter describes how to install the new operating system on your Mac. It also prepares you for the inevitable arrival of Mac OS X 10.5, 10.6, or whatever else comes down the pike.

Four Kinds of Installation

Mac OS X requires a Mac with a G3, G4, G5, or Intel processor, 1.5 gigabytes of free disk space, and (for reasonable speed) 256 megabytes of memory or more. If all of that checks out, then read on.

The Mac OS X installer can perform a number of different installations. For example, it can put a copy of Mac OS X 10.4 onto a hard drive that currently has:

- **Nothing on it.** If you one day have to erase your hard drive completely—because it's completely hosed, or, less drastically, because you you've bought a new, empty external hard drive—see "The Basic Installation" on the next page.

- **Mac OS 9 on the hard drive.** See "The Basic Installation," below, for step-by-steps.

- **Mac OS X 10.0 through 10.3.** The 10.4 installer can turn your older copy of Mac OS X *into* the 10.4 version, in the process retaining all of your older preferences, fonts, documents, accounts, and so on. See "The Upgrade Installation" on the facing page.

  On the other hand, a substantial body of evidence (specifically, hundreds of moaning Mac fans online) points to the wisdom of performing a *clean install*, described next, rather than an upgrade installation. (Apple calls this the "Archive & Install" option.) A clean installation provides a healthier, more glitch-proof copy of 10.4. See "The Clean Install" on page 466.

- **Mac OS X 10.4.** In times of dire troubleshooting, you can actually give yourself a *fresh copy* of 10.4, even though 10.4 is already on the hard drive. This process is called a *clean install*, and it's an infinitely simpler procedure than the clean install in Windows. See "The Clean Install" on page 466.

The Basic Installation

The installation process takes about an hour, but for the sake of your own psyche, you'll probably want to set aside a whole afternoon. Once the installation is over, you'll want to play around, organize your files, and learn the lay of the land.

Here's how you install Tiger onto a drive that doesn't have any version of Mac OS X on it already:

1. **Insert the Mac OS X DVD (or CD). Double-click the Install Mac OS X icon. When the Restart button appears, click it.**

   The Mac starts up from the disc and takes you directly to the first Installer screen.

   The installer will soon fall into a pattern: Read the instructions, make a couple of choices, and click Continue to advance to the next screen. As you go, the list on the left side of the screen reveals where you are in the overall procedure.

Tip: You can back out of the installation at any time before step 6, just by choosing Installer→Quit Installer. When the Restart button appears, click it. Then eject the Mac OS X disc, either by holding down the mouse button while the computer restarts or, if you have a tray-loading CD drive, by pushing its eject button during the moment of darkness during the restart.

---

2. **Work your way through the Select Language screen, Welcome screen (scroll down for important information), and Software License Agreement screen, clicking Continue each time.**

   The Software License Agreement requires you to click a button confirming that you agree with whatever Apple's lawyers say.

3. **On the Select a Destination screen, click the disk or partition on which you want to install Mac OS X.**

Icons for all of your disks (or partitions) appear on the screen, but ones that are off-limits to Mac OS X (like CDs and USB hard drives) appear dimmed. Click the icon of the drive or partition that will be your new main startup drive.

Note: If a yellow exclamation-point triangle logo appears on a drive, it probably has a *newer* version of Mac OS X on it. (Click it and read the message at the bottom of the dialog box to find out.) That's the case if you're trying to install from the original 10.4 DVD, but you already have 10.4.2 on the hard drive, for example. No problem; you should be reading "The Clean Install" instructions on page 466 anyway.

---

4. **Click Continue.**

You arrive at the Easy Install screen. The easiest way to proceed here is to click Install. But you can save a few hundred megabytes of disk space if you take the time to click Customize.

The Installer shows you a list of the various chunks that constitute Mac OS X. A few of them are easily dispensable. For example, if you turn off Additional Fonts, Language Translations (for Japanese, German, French, and so on), and the printer models that you don't own, you save a staggering 3.8 *gigabytes*. It's like getting a whole mini–hard drive for free!

5. **Click Install.**

Now you're in for a 25-minute wait as the Installer copies software onto your hard drive. (If you're working from CDs that you ordered, you'll be asked to insert Disc 2, Disc 3, and so on.)

When the installer's finished, you see a message indicating that your Mac will restart in 30 seconds. If you haven't wandered off to watch TV, click the Restart button to end the countdown and get on with it.

Mac OS X is now installed on your Mac—but you're not quite ready to use it yet. See "The Setup Assistant" on page 467.

Note: Every kind of Tiger installation puts iCal, iTunes, Mail, Dictionary, Address Book, and Safari on your hard drive. But what if, in a fit of troubleshooting or carelessness, you find yourself wishing you could reinstall one of these programs? Or what if you declined to install the foreign-language fonts or printer drivers, and now change your mind?

To install these on demand, double-click the Optional Installs installer on your Tiger DVD. It lets you choose which individual programs or "additional install" options you want, without making you install all of Tiger.

The Upgrade Installation

If Mac OS X version 10.0 through 10.3-point-anything is on your hard drive, the Tiger installer can neatly nip and tuck its software code, turning it *into* version 10.4.

Everything remains just as you had it: your accounts, folders, files, email, network settings, everything-else settings, and so on.

As noted earlier, this sophisticated surgery *occasionally* leaves behind a minor glitch here and there: peculiar cosmetic glitches, a checkbox that doesn't seem to work, and so on. If that possibility concerns you, a clean install is a much safer way to go.

If you're still game to perform the upgrade installation, follow the preceding steps 1 through 3. On the Select Destination screen, however, click Options.

Now you're offered four variations of the basic installation. The one you want is Upgrade Mac OS X. Click it and then click OK. Proceed with the previous step 4. (The button described there now says Upgrade, though, instead of Install.)

The Clean Install

In Windows, the *clean install* is an essential last-ditch troubleshooting technique. It entails installing a second Windows folder—a fresh one, uncontaminated by the detritus left behind by you and your software programs.

But in general, you and your software *can't* invade the Mac OS X System folder. The kind of gradual corruption that could occur in other operating systems is theoretically impossible in Mac OS X, and therefore the need to perform a clean install is almost completely eliminated.

That's the theory, anyway. In fact, somehow or other, things do go wrong with your Mac OS X installation. Maybe you or somebody else has been fiddling around in Terminal and wound up deleting or changing some important underlying files. Certain shareware programs can perform deep-seated changes like this, too.

The point is that eventually, you may wish you could just start over with a new, perfect copy of Mac OS X. And now, thanks to the new clean install ("Archive and Install") option, you can—without having to erase the hard drive first.

Start by following the preceding steps 1 through 3. On the Select Destination screen, though, click Options. Now you're offered four kinds of installation. Turn on "Archive and Install." ("Preserve Users and Network Settings" should be on, too.)

This powerful option leaves all of your accounts (Home folders, documents, pictures, movies, Favorites, email, and so on) *untouched.* As the option's name implies, it also leaves your network and Internet settings alone. But it deactivates your old System folder (you'll find it, later, in a new folder called Previous System Folders) and puts a new one in its place. And that's exactly what you want.

Click OK and then continue with the previous step 4. When it's all over, you'll be confident that your Mac OS X installation is clean, fresh, and ready for action.

Erase & Install

The final installation option is called Erase & Install. As you can guess, it erases your entire hard drive and installs the ultimate clean, fresh, sparkling new copy of Tiger and its applications there. Use this "nuke-and-pave" option when you're about to sell your Mac and want to ensure that no trace of your former stuff is still there.

If you're absolutely certain that you won't regret *completely erasing the computer,* follow the preceding steps 1 through 3. On the Select Destination screen, though, click Options, and select Erase & Install. Continue with the previous step 4.

The Setup Assistant

When the Mac restarts after a basic installation, an Erase & Install installation, or an Archive and Install installation where you *didn't* also click "Preserve Users and Network Settings," the first thing you experience is some jazzy music and a fancy parade of 3-D, computer-generated translations of the word "Welcome." Once Apple is quite finished showing off its multimedia prowess, you arrive at a Welcome screen.

Once again, you're in for a click-through-the-screens experience, this time with the aim of setting up your Mac's various settings. After answering the questions on each screen, click Continue.

The number and sequence of information screens you'll encounter depend on whether you've upgraded an existing Mac or started fresh, but here are some possibilities:

- **Welcome.** Click the name of the country you're in.

  (At the bottom of this screen is a special message for visually impaired people: "Do you need to hear instructions for setting up the Mac? To learn how to use VoiceOver to set up your computer, press the Escape key now." If you do so, you're treated to a crash course in VoiceOver, the screen-control/screen-reading software described on page 381.)

- **Do you already own a Mac?** If you choose "Transfer my information from another Mac," the installer will assist you in sucking all of your old programs, files, folders, and settings from the old Mac to the new one. Of course, that won't help if you're switching from a Windows PC.

- **Select your Keyboard.** Different countries require different keyboard layouts. For example, if you choose the Canadian layout, pressing the] key on a U.S. keyboard produces the ç symbol. Click Continue.

- **Select a Wireless Service.** This is your chance to introduce the Mac to any wireless networks in the vicinity. Click the network name you want to join, if you see it. If you don't see it, click Rescan to make the Mac sniff again in an attempt to locate the network. Or if there's no wireless service at all—hey, it could happen—click Different Network Setup.

  In that event, you're offered choices like AirPort wireless, Telephone modem, Cable modem/DSL modem, Local network (Ethernet), and "My computer does not connect to the Internet." (Bummer!) When you click Continue, you may be asked for specific information—the local access number, account name, password, and so on—regarding your Internet account. See page 245 for information on where you can find these settings on your old PC.

- **Enter your Apple ID.** Here, you're offered the chance to type in, or create, an Apple ID—which is your email address. An Apple ID doesn't cost anything, but it makes life easier if you want to buy songs from the iTunes Music Store, order gift books or prints from iPhoto, and so on. (If you have a .Mac account—see page 147—put that account info here.)

- **Registration Information.** This is your chance to become a grain of sand on the great beach of the Apple database (and set up your own "card" in Mac OS X's Address Book program).

Tip: If you're not interested in providing your personal information to Apple, or if you've already done so during a previous install, press ⌘-Q. A message offers you Skip, Shut Down, and Cancel buttons. If you click Skip, you jump straight ahead to "Create Your Account," below.

- **A Few More Questions.** Where will you primarily use this computer? What best describes what you do? Do you want to get junk mail from Apple?

- **Create Your Account.** Most of the steps up to this point have been pretty inconsequential, but this is a big moment. You're about to create your *account*—your Administrator account, in fact (page 323).

  All you have to do is make up a name—usually a short variation of your name—and a password. Choose carefully, because you can't easily change your account name later. (If you're the only one who uses your Mac, it's perfectly OK to leave the password blank empty.)

  What you come up with here is extremely important, especially if several different people use this Mac at different times, or if other people connect to it on a network. See page 325 for details on creating a password and a hint that will help you remember it.

- **Select Time Zone, Set the Date and Time.** These screens help you set your Mac's built-in clock—a surprisingly important step, because it determines how the files you create will know whether they are older or newer than other versions. (To change the date, either click the appropriate date on the calendar, or click its digits and then type over them using your keyboard. To change the time, you can either drag the clock's hands—fun!—or, again, click the digits above it and then retype.)

- **Your .Mac Billing Information.** If you have a .Mac membership (page 147), Apple cheerfully lets you know when it will expire.

- **Thanks for being a .Mac member.** Aw, shucks.

- **Thank You.** This screen clues you in on some of the excitement you're about to have with Tiger. When you click Go, you wind up at the Mac OS X desktop, just as described in Chapter 1.

Troubleshooting

Mac OS X is far more resilient than its predecessors, but it's still a complex system with the potential for occasional glitches.

It's safe to say that you'll have to do *less* troubleshooting in Mac OS X than in Windows, especially considering that most freaky little glitches go away if you just try these two steps one at a time:

- Quit and restart the wayward program.
- Log out and log back in again.

It's the *other* problems that will drive you batty.

Problems That Aren't Problems

Before you panic, accept the possibility that whatever is frustrating you is a Mac OS X *difference,* not a Mac OS X *problem.* Plenty of "problems" turn out simply to be quirks of the way Mac OS X works. For example:

- **My System Preferences controls are dimmed.** As noted in Chapter 13, many of Mac OS X's control panels are off-limits to standard account holders. Even if you're an administrator, in fact, Tiger requires that you unlock System Preferences the first time you open it (by clicking the padlock icon at the lower-left corner of System Preferences and then entering your password).

- **I can't log in! I'm in an endless login loop!** If the standard Login screen never seems to appear—and you go straight to someone else's account every time—it's because somebody has turned on the automatic login feature described on page 334. You won't have a chance to sign in with your own account until somebody choose ⌘→Log Out.

- **I can't move or open a folder.** Like it or not, Mac OS X is Unix, and Unix has a very strict sense of who, among the people who share a Mac over time, *owns* certain files and folders. For starters, people who don't have Administrator accounts aren't allowed to move, or even open, certain important folders. Page 323 has much more on this topic.

If whatever problem you're having doesn't fall into one of those categories, then maybe something truly has gone wrong; read on.

Minor Eccentric Behavior

All kinds of glitches may befall you, occasionally, in Mac OS X. Your desktop picture doesn't change when you change it in System Preferences. A menulet doesn't open when you click it. A program won't open—it just bounces in the Dock a couple of times and then stops.

When a single program is acting up like this, but quitting and restarting it does no good, try the following steps, in the following sequence.

First resort: Repair permissions

An amazing number of mysterious glitches arise because the *permissions* of either that item or something in your System folder have become muddled—that is, the complex mesh of interconnected Unix permissions that govern what you and your programs are allowed to do with the files on your drive.

When something just doesn't seem to be working right, therefore, open your Applications→Utilities folder and open Disk Utility. Proceed as shown in Figure 15-1.

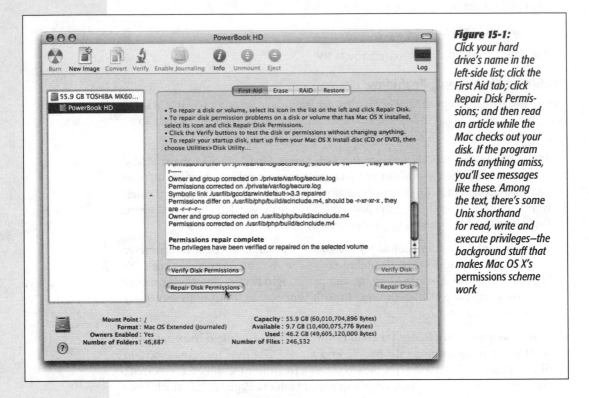

Figure 15-1:
Click your hard drive's name in the left-side list; click the First Aid tab; click Repair Disk Permissions; and then read an article while the Mac checks out your disk. If the program finds anything amiss, you'll see messages like these. Among the text, there's some Unix shorthand for read, write and execute privileges–the background stuff that makes Mac OS X's permissions scheme work

This is a really, *really* great trick to know.

Second resort: Look for an update

If a program starts acting up immediately after you've installed Mac OS 10.4, chances are good that it has some minor incompatibility. Chances are also good that you'll find an updated version on the company's Web site.

Third resort: Toss the Prefs file

Take this simple test: Log in using a different account (perhaps a dummy account that you create just for testing purposes). Run the problem program. Is the problem gone? If so, then the glitch exists only when *you* are logged in—which means it's a problem with *your* copy of the program's preferences.

Return to your own account. Open your Home folder→Library→Preferences folder, where you'll find neatly labeled preference files for all of the programs you use. Each ends with the file name suffix *.plist.* For example, com.apple.finder.plist is the Finder's preference file, com.apple.dock.plist is the Dock's, and so on.

Put the suspected preference file into the Trash, but don't empty it. The next time you run the recalcitrant program, it will build itself a brand new preference file that, if you're lucky, lacks whatever corruption was causing your problems.

If not, quit the program. You can reinstate its original .plist file from the Trash, if you'd find that helpful as you pursue your troubleshooting agenda.

Remember, however, that you actually have *three* Preferences folders. In addition to your own Home folder's stash, there's a second one in the Library folder in the main hard drive window (which administrators are allowed to trash), and a third in the System→Library folder in the main hard drive window (which nobody is allowed to trash).

The only way to throw away the .plist files from this most deep-seated source (inside the System folder) is to use one of the security-bypass methods described in the box on page 472.

In any case, the next time you log in, the Mac will create fresh, virginal preference files.

Fourth resort: Restart
Sometimes you can give Mac OS X or its programs a swift kick by restarting the Mac. It's an inconvenient step, but not nearly as time-consuming as what comes next. And it can fix problems that cropped up when you started up the computer.

Last resort: Trash and reinstall the program
Sometimes reinstalling the problem program clears up whatever the glitch was.

First, however, throw away all traces of it. Just open the Applications folder and drag the program's icon (or its folder) to the Trash. In most cases, the only remaining piece to discard is its .plist file (or files) in your Home→Library→Preferences folder, and any scraps bearing the program's name in your Library→Application Support folder. (You can do a quick Spotlight search [page 65] to round up any other pieces.)

Then reinstall the program from its original CD or installer—after first checking the company's Web site to see if there's an updated version, of course.

Frozen Programs (Force Quitting)
The occasional unresponsive application has become such a part of Mac OS X life that, among the Mac cognoscenti online, the dreaded, endless "please wait" cursor has been given its own acronym: SBOD (Spinning Beachball of Death). When the SBOD strikes, no amount of mouse clicking and keyboard pounding gets you out of the recalcitrant program.

Here are the different ways you can go about *force quitting* a stuck program (the equivalent of pressing Ctrl-Alt-Delete in Windows), in increasing order of desperation:

- **Use the Dock.** If you can't use the program's regularly scheduled File→Quit command, try Control-clicking its Dock icon and choosing Quit or (if the program *knows* it's dying) Force Quit from the pop-up menu.

- **Force quit the usual way.** Choose →Force Quit to terminate the stuck program, or use one of the other force-quit methods described on page 99.

- **Force quit the sneaky way.** Some programs, including the Dock, don't show up at all in the usual Force Quit dialog box. Your next attempt, therefore, should be to open the Activity Monitor program (in Applications→Utilities), which shows *everything* that's running. Double-click a program and then, in the resulting dialog box, click Quit to force quit it.

Tip: If all of this seems like a lot to remember, you can always force-restart the Mac. On desktop Macs, hold the power button in for six seconds; on laptops, press Control-⌘-power button.

The Wrong Program Opens

As noted in Chapter 4, the way documents are linked to the programs that can open them is very different in Mac OS X than it was before. Some documents have invisible, four-letter type and creator codes that tell them which programs they "belong to." Other documents lack these codes, and open up in whichever program recognizes its file name extension (.doc or .txt, for example).

WORKAROUND WORKSHOP

Fixing Permissions Problems

Sooner or later, when you try to move, rename, or delete a certain file or folder, you may get an error message like this—"The folder 'Junk' could not be opened because you do not have sufficient access privileges"—or this: "The operation could not be completed because this item is owned by Chris" (or by *root,* which means by Mac OS X itself).

What they're trying to say is, you've run into a permissions problem.

As noted in Chapter 12, Mac OS X is designed to accommodate a number of different people who share the same Mac over time. Nobody is allowed to meddle with other people's files or folders. But even if you're the solo operator of your Mac, you still share it with Mac OS X itself (which the error messages may refer to as *root* or *system*).

In any case, if you're confident that whatever you're trying to do isn't some kind of nihilistic, self-destructive act like trashing the Applications folder, it's easy enough to get past these limitations. Just highlight the recalcitrant file or folder and then choose File→Get Info. In its window, you'll find an Ownership & Permissions panel that lets you reassign ownership of any icon to, for example, yourself (if you have an Administrator account, that is). Make sure your permission is "Read & Write." (Just don't perform this surgery on files in the System folder.)

Now you *own* that folder or file, and you can do whatever you like with it.

Page 110 shows you how to choose which program opens a certain document (or kind of document). But that's not much help when you double-click a SimpleText document and have to sit there while SimpleText opens up—*in Classic,* mandating a 45-second wait.

The simple rule to remember here is that *creator codes override file name extensions.* In other words, a file called Contract.txt generally opens in Mac OS X's TextEdit—*if* it doesn't have a four-letter creator code behind the scenes. If that same file has SimpleText's creator code (ttxt), however, it opens in SimpleText (and Classic) no matter what its file name is.

In other cases, the quickest solution may be to *strip away* the type and creator codes. You can do that by dragging the troubled files' icons onto a program like Wipe Creator (available from the software page of *www.missingmanuals.com*). At that point, Mac OS X has only the document's file name extension to go on when choosing a program to open it.

Can't Empty the Trash

If you're having trouble emptying the Trash, start by holding down the mouse on *the Trash icon itself.* When you choose Empty Trash from the pop-up menu, Mac OS X empties the Trash without complaint, locked files and all.

If emptying the Trash gives you "Could not be completed because the item is owned by Marge," you're trying to move or delete another Mac account holder's stuff. As you know, that's a big no-no in Mac OS X.

In that case, just make yourself the new owner of the file or folder, as described in the box on the facing page.

Can't Move or Rename an Icon

If you're not allowed to drag an icon somewhere, the error message that appears almost always hits the nail on the head: You're trying to move a file or folder that *isn't yours.* Again, the box on the facing page explains the solutions to this problem.

Application Won't Open

If a program won't open (if its icon bounces merrily in the Dock for a few seconds, for instance, but then nothing happens), begin by trashing its preference file, as described on page 470. If that doesn't solve it, reinstalling the program usually does.

Startup Problems

Not every problem you encounter is related to running applications. Sometimes trouble strikes before you even get that far. The following are examples.

Kernel panic

When you see the dialog box shown in Figure 15-2, you've got yourself a *kernel panic*—a Unix nervous breakdown.

(In such situations, *user panic* might be the more applicable term, but that's programmers for you.)

Kernel panics are extremely rare. If you see one at all, it's almost always the result of a *hardware* glitch—most often a bad memory (RAM) board, but possibly an accelerator card, graphics card, SCSI gadget, or USB hub that Mac OS X doesn't like. A poorly seated AirPort card can bring on a kernel panic, too, and so can a bad USB or FireWire cable.

If simply restarting doesn't solve the problem, detach every shred of gear that didn't come from Apple. Restore these components to the Mac one at a time until you find out which one was causing Mac OS X's bad hair day. If you're able to pinpoint the culprit, seek its manufacturer (or its Web site) on a quest for updated drivers, or at least try to find out for sure whether the add-on is compatible with Mac OS X.

Tip: This advice goes for your Macintosh itself. Apple periodically updates the Mac's own "drivers" in the form of a *firmware update.* You download these updates from the Support area of Apple's Web site (if indeed Mac OS X's own Software Update mechanism doesn't alert you to its existence).

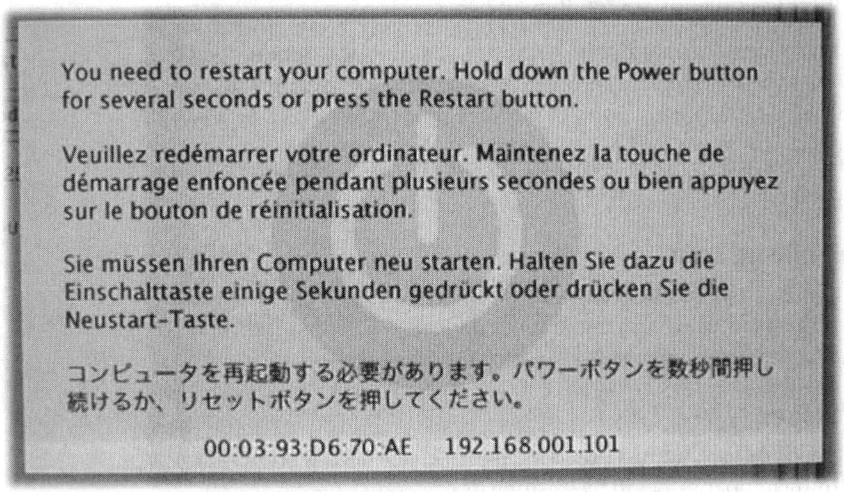

You need to restart your computer. Hold down the Power button for several seconds or press the Restart button.

Veuillez redémarrer votre ordinateur. Maintenez la touche de démarrage enfoncée pendant plusieurs secondes ou bien appuyez sur le bouton de réinitialisation.

Sie müssen Ihren Computer neu starten. Halten Sie dazu die Einschalttaste einige Sekunden gedrückt oder drücken Sie die Neustart-Taste.

コンピュータを再起動する必要があります。パワーボタンを数秒間押し続けるか、リセットボタンを押してください。

00:03:93:D6:70:AE   192.168.001.101

Figure 15-2:
A kernel panic is almost always related to some piece of add-on hardware. And look at the bright side: At least you get this handsome dialog box in Tiger. That's a lot better than the Mac OS X 10.0 and 10.1 effect–random text gibberish superimposing itself on your screen.

There's one other cause for kernel panics, by the way: moving, renaming, or changing the access permissions for Mac OS X's essential system files and folders—the Applications or System folder, for example. This cause isn't even worth mentioning, of course, because nobody would be that foolish.

Safe Mode (Safe Boot)

In times of troubleshooting, Windows fans turn to Safe Mode when starting up their computers. Although not one person in a hundred knows it, Mac OS X offers the same kind of emergency keystroke. It can come in handy when you've just installed some new piece of software and find that you can't even start up the machine, or when one of your fonts is corrupted, or when something you've designated as a Login Item turns out to be gumming up the works. With this trick, you can at least turn on the computer so that you can uninstall the cranky program.

The trick is to *press the Shift key* as the machine is starting up. Hold it down from the startup chime until you see the words "Safe Boot," in red lettering, on the login screen.

Welcome to Safe Mode.

What have you accomplished? You've checked your hard drive, for one thing, and brought up the login screen—even if you normally have Automatic Login turned on. You've also turned off your *kernel extensions* (chunks of software that add various features to the basic operating system), superfluous fonts, font cache, and login items. In other words, you've shed all the stuff Mac OS X doesn't need in order to run.

Once you reach the desktop, you'll find a long list of standard features inoperable. You can't use DVD Player, capture video in iMovie, use a wireless network, use certain microphones and speakers, or use your modem. (The next time you restart, all of this goodness will be restored, assuming you're no longer clutching the Shift key in a sweating panic.)

In any case, the beauty of Safe Mode is that it lets you get your Mac going. You have access to your files, so at least the emergency of crashing-on-startup is over. And you can start picking through your fonts and login items to see if you can spot the problem.

Gray screen during startup

Confirm that your Mac has the latest firmware, as described earlier. Detach and test all your non-Apple add-ons. Finally, perform a disk check, as described on the next page.

Blue screen during startup

Most of the troubleshooting steps for this problem (which is usually accompanied by the Spinning Beachball of Death cursor) are the same as those described under "Kernel panic" above. But there's one other cause to examine: a corrupted font file in your *Mac OS 9* System Folder.

To test for this problem, restart the Mac in Mac OS 9 (if your Mac can do that), open its System Folder (that's the folder called System Folder, not just System), and drag the Fonts folder to the desktop. Restart in Mac OS X. If the startup proceeds smoothly, you know you've got a damaged font file in that Fonts folder.

Forgotten password

If you or one of the other people who use your Mac have forgotten the corresponding account password, no worries: just read the box on page 336.

Fixing the Disk

The beauty of Mac OS X's design is that the operating system itself is frozen in its perfect, pristine state, impervious to conflicting system extensions, clueless Mac users, and other sources of disaster.

That's the theory, anyway. But what happens if something goes wrong with the complex software that operates the hard drive itself?

Fortunately, Mac OS X comes with its own disk-repair program. In the familiar Mac universe of icons and menus, it takes the form of a program in Applications→Utilities called Disk Utility. In the barren world of Terminal and the command line interface (akin in many ways to DOS), there's a utility that works just as well but bears a different name: *fsck* (for file system check).

In any case, running Disk Utility or its alter ego *fsck* is a powerful and useful trouble-shooting tool that can cure all kinds of strange ills, including these problems, among others:

- Your Mac freezes during startup, either before or after the Login screen.
- The startup process interrupts itself with the appearance of the text-only command line.
- You get the "applications showing up as folders" problem.

The easiest way to check your disk is to use the Disk Utility program. Use this method if your Mac can, indeed, start up. (See Method 2 if you can't even get that far.)

Disk Utility can't check the disk it's *on* (except for permission checks, described earlier). That's why you have to restart the computer from the Tiger installation disc (or another startup disk), and run Disk Utility from there. The process goes like this

1. **Start up the Mac from the Tiger DVD or CD.**

   The best way to do that is to insert the disc and then restart the Mac while holding down the C key.

   You wind up, after some time, at the Mac OS X Installer screen. Don't be fooled— installing Mac OS X is *not* what you want to do here. Don't click Continue!

2. **Choose Utilities→Disk Utility.**

   That's the unexpected step. After a moment, the Disk Utility screen appears.

3. **Click the disk or disk partition you want to fix, click the First Aid tab, and then click Repair Disk.**

   The Mac whirls into action, checking a list of very technical disk-formatting parameters.

If you see the message, "The volume 'Macintosh HD' appears to be OK," that's meant to be *good* news. Believe it or not, that cautious statement is as definitive an affirmation as Disk Utility is capable of making about the health of your disk.

Disk Utility may also tell you that the disk is damaged, but that it can't help you. In that case, you need a more heavy-duty disk-repair program like Drive 10 (*www. micromat.com*) or DiskWarrior (*www.alsoft.com*).

Where to Get Troubleshooting Help

If the basic steps described in this chapter haven't helped, the universe is crawling with additional help sources. You probably already know about the Mac's built-in help-screen system (choose Help→Mac Help), but you also probably know that in times of troubleshooting, it rarely describes exactly the symptom your machine is having.

Help Online

These Web sites contain nothing but troubleshooting discussions, tools, and help:

- **MacFixIt** (*www.macfixit.com*). The world's one-stop resource for troubleshooting advice.

- **Mac newsgroups** (such as *comp.system.mac*). A newsgroup is an Internet bulletin board, which you can access using a program like Microsoft Entourage or Unison (*www.panic.com*). If you're polite and concise, you can post questions to the multitudes here and get more replies to them than you'll know what to do with.

- **Apple's help site** (*www.apple.com/support*). Apple's help Web site also includes downloadable manuals, software updates, frequently asked questions, and many other resources.

  It also has a Search box, which may look mild-mannered but is actually the mother of all troubleshooting resources: the Knowledge Base. This is the collection of 50,000 individual technical articles, organized in a searchable database, that the Apple technicians themselves consult when you call for help. You can search it either by typing in keywords or using pop-up menus of question categories.

Help by telephone

Finally, consider contacting whoever sold you the component that's making your life miserable: the printer company, scanner company, software company, or whatever.

If it's a Mac OS problem, you can call Apple at 800-275-2273 (that's 800-APL-CARE). For the first 90 days following your purchase of Mac OS X (which, as far as Apple knows, is the date of your first call), the technicians will answer your questions for free.

After that, unless you've paid for AppleCare for your Mac (a three-year extended warranty program), Apple will charge you to answer your questions—unless the problem turns out to be Apple's fault, in which case they won't charge you.

Part Five:
Appendixes

5

The "Where'd It Go?" Dictionary

All the words and pictures so far in this book are just great for leisure reading. But in a crisis of helplessness on your new Mac, this appendix may be more useful. It's an alphabetical listing of every common Windows function and where to find it in Mac OS X. After all, an operating system is an operating system. The actual functions are pretty much the same—they're just in different places.

About [This Program]

To find out the version number of the program you're using, don't look in the Help menu. Instead, look in the *application* menu next to the menu—the one that bears the name of the program you're in. That's where you find the About command for Macintosh programs.

Accessibility Options Control Panel

The special features that let you operate the computer even with impaired vision, hearing, or motor control are called Universal Access in Mac OS X. It's in System Preferences (see Chapter 8).

Active Desktop

The Mac never displays Web pages directly on the desktop—and knowing Apple, that's probably a point of pride. But Dashboard (Chapter 5) keeps Internet information only a keystroke away.

Add Hardware Control Panel

The Mac requires no program for installing the driver for a new external gadget. The drivers for most printers, mice, keyboards, cameras, camcorders, and other accessories are preinstalled. If you plug something into the Mac and find that it doesn't work immediately, just install the driver from the included CD (or the manufacturer's Web site).

Add or Remove Programs Control Panel

Here's another one you just don't need on the Macintosh. Installing a program onto the Mac is described on page 128. Removing a program simply involves dragging its icon to the Trash. (For a clean sweep, inspect your Home→Library→Preferences and Library→Application Support folders to see if any preference files got left behind.)

All Programs

There's no Programs menu built into Mac OS X, like the one on the Windows Start menu. If you'd like one, drag your Applications folder into the end of the Dock. Now its icon is a tidy pop-up menu of every program on your machine.

Alt Key

On the Mac, it's the Option key. You can substitute Option for Alt in any keystroke in most popular programs. The Option key has a number of secondary features on the Mac, too: It hides the windows of one program when you click into another, for example. (As for operating the Mac's menus from the keyboard, see page 115.)

Automatic Update

The System Preferences→Software Update panel does exactly the same thing.

Backspace key

It's in the same place on the Macintosh keyboard, but it's called the Delete key.

Battery Level

The status of the battery in your PowerBook or iBook laptop now appears in the menu bar, rather than in the system tray. (If you don't see it, open System Preferences→ Energy Saver and turn it on.)

BIOS

You'll never have to update or even think about the ROM of your Macintosh (the approximate equivalent of the BIOS on the PC). It's permanent and unchanging. The very similar *firmware* of your Macintosh does occasionally have to be updated in order to work with a new version of the Mac operating system or some dramatic new feature—once every four years, perhaps. You'll be notified on the screen when the time comes.

Briefcase

Mac OS X doesn't have anything like the Briefcase, a Windows invention designed to help you keep your files in sync between a laptop and a desktop computer. On the other hand, if you sign up for a .Mac account (page 147), you get a program called Backup that is similarly designed to keep folders synchronized between two machines. And you can use iSync (Chapter 14) to keep your calendar, addresses, and other items synced among multiple computers.

Calculator

The calculator program in Mac OS X is almost identical to the one in Windows XP, except that it can also perform conversions (temperature, distance, currency, and so on) and features an editable "paper tape." It sits in your Applications folder and is described in Chapter 14. (There's a simpler Calculator in Dashboard [page 108], too).

Camera and Scanner Wizard

When you connect a digital camera or scanner to your Mac, either iPhoto or Image Capture opens automatically and prepares to download the pictures automatically. Details on Image Capture on page 407, and iPhoto on page 419.

CDs

If your Mac keyboard has an Eject or F12 key in the upper-right corner, you hold it down for a moment to open the CD/DVD drawer, or, if you have a slot-loading CD drive, to spit out the disc that's in it. If it's an older Mac keyboard without an Eject key, you can eject a CD (or any other disk) by Control-clicking its desktop icon and choosing Eject from the contextual menu. There are various other ways to eject a disk, but the point is that you never do so by pushing the Eject button on the disk drive itself.

Character Map

This Windows program helps you find out what keys you need to press to trigger trademark symbols, copyright symbols, and other special characters. The equivalent on the Mac is called Keyboard Viewer (page 369)—but the Character Palette (page 369) is even easier to use.

Clean Install

The Mac OS X installer can give you a fresh, virginal copy of the operating system, just as the Windows installer can. Instructions are in Chapter 15.

Clipboard

The Macintosh clipboard works almost exactly like the one in Windows. In the Finder, you can choose Edit→Show Clipboard to see whenever you have most recently copied or cut.

Command Line

In Mac OS X, the command line is alive and well—but it speaks Unix, not DOS. You get to it by opening Terminal (page 457).

Control Panel

The Control Panel in Mac OS X is called System Preferences, and it's represented on the Dock by a little light-switch icon. As in Windows XP, you can view these icons either by category or in a simple alphabetical list: Just choose either Organize by Categories or Organize Alphabetically from the View menu.

Copy, Cut, Paste

When you're editing in a word processor or graphics program, the Mac OS X Cut, Copy, and Paste commands work exactly as they do in Windows.

At the desktop, however, there are a few differences. You can indeed copy icons and paste them into a new window using the Copy and Paste commands—you just can't *cut* them out of a window, as you can in Windows. On the other hand, Mac OS X offers a handy secondary feature: If you paste into a word or text processor instead of into another desktop window, you get a tidy list of the names of the icons you copied.

Ctrl Key

On the Macintosh, you generally substitute the ⌘ key in keystrokes that would normally involve the Control key. In other words, the Save command is now ⌘-S instead of Ctrl-S, Open is ⌘-O instead of Ctrl-O, and so on.

Date and Time

You set your Mac's calendar and clock in the Date & Time pane of System Preferences.

Delete Key (Forward Delete)

Desktop Mac keyboards have a forward-delete key (labeled *Del*) exactly like the ones on PCs. On Mac laptops, you trigger the forward-delete function by pressing the regularly scheduled Delete key while pressing the Fn key in the lower-left corner of the keyboard.

Desktop

The Macintosh desktop is pretty much the same idea as the Windows desktop, with a few key differences:

- Disk icons show up on the Mac desktop as soon as they are inserted or connected. You don't have to open a window to see their icons.

- You change the desktop picture using the Desktop & Screen Saver pane of System Preferences.

- The Trash is an icon on the Dock, not loose on the desktop.

Directories

Most people call them *folders* on the Mac.

Disk Defragmenter

There's no such utility included with Mac OS X, although Norton Utilities for the Mac will do the job if you feel that it's essential to have your hard drive neatly defragmented. (A *defragmenting* program moves around the pieces of files on your hard drive in an effort to optimize their placement and speed of opening.)

Disks

Working with disks is very different on the Mac. Every disk inside, or attached to, a Macintosh is represented on the screen by an icon. Mac OS X does have something like the My Computer window (choose Go→Computer), but both the icons on the desktop and the icons in the Computer window reflect only the disks currently inserted in your Mac. You'll never see an icon for an empty drive, as you do on Windows, and there's no such thing as drive letters (because the Mac refers to *disks,* not to *drives*—and refers to them by name).

Display Control Panel

The functions of the Windows Display Control Panel lurk in the Mac OS X System Preferences program—just not all in one place. You set a desktop picture and choose a screen saver using the Desktop & Screen Saver pane, and adjust your monitor settings using the Displays pane. (Mac OS X offers no equivalent to the Appearance tab in Windows, for changing the system-wide look of your computer.)

DLL Files

The Macintosh equivalent of DLL files—shared libraries of programming code—are invisible and off-limits. As a result, no Macintosh user ever experiences DLL conflicts or out-of-date DLL files.

DOS Prompt

There's a command line in Mac OS X, but it's Unix, not DOS. See page 457.

Drivers

See "Add or Remove Programs."

End Task Dialog Box

If some Macintosh program is hung or frozen, you escape it pretty much the same way you would in Windows: by forcing it to quit. To bring up the Force Quit dialog box, you press Option-⌘-Esc.

Exiting Programs

You can quit a program either by choosing Quit from the menu bearing its name (next to the menu), or by right-clicking its Dock icon (or Control-clicking) and then choosing Quit from the pop-up menu.

Explorer

The Mac has its own "tree" view of the files and folders on your hard drive: list view. By expanding the "flippy triangles" of your folders, you build a hierarchy that shows you as much or as little detail as you like.

If you prefer the Explorer effect of clicking a folder in *one* pane to see its contents in the next, try column view instead. Both views are described in Chapter 1.

Favorites

In Mac OS X, there isn't one single Favorites menu that lists both favorite Web sites and favorite icons. The Bookmarks menu of Safari, the Web browser, lists only Web sites. In the Finder, you can use your Home→Favorites folder to keep favorite files.

Faxing

Faxing is built into Tiger; it's described on page 211. (Hint: Choose File→Print; from the PDF button at the bottom of the print dialog box, choose Fax PDF.)

File Sharing

See page 138 for an in-depth look at the Macintosh networking and file-sharing system.

Floppy Disks

Floppy drives on Macs disappeared in about 1998. According to Apple, it's much more efficient to transfer files between machines using an Ethernet cable, a CD that you burned, or email.

Of course, you can buy an external USB floppy drive for any Mac for about $45.

Folder Options

The Folder Options control panel in Windows is a crazy collection of unrelated settings that boil down to this:

- **General tab.** Exactly as in Windows, it's up to you whether or not double-clicking a folder opens up a second window—or just changes what's in the first one. On the Mac, you make these changes using the Finder→Preferences command. There you'll find the option called "Always open folders in a new window."

- **View tab.** Most of the options here don't exist on the Mac. For example, you can't opt to make all the invisible system files visible (at least not without add-on shareware). You can, however, choose whether or not you want to see the file name extensions in your desktop windows (like .doc and .html). Choose Finder→Preferences, and turn "Show all file extensions" on or off.

- **File Types tab.** Just as in Windows, you can reassign certain document types so that double-clicking opens them up in the program of your choice. But on the Mac, you can reassign either a whole class of files at once, as on Windows, *or* one file at a time. To do it, use the Get Info window as described on page 110.

- **Offline Files.** There's no equivalent feature on the Mac.

Fonts

The Mac and Windows both use TrueType, PostScript, and Open Type fonts. (In fact, your Mac can even use the exact font files you had on Windows.) A complete discussion is on page 217.

FTP (File Transfer Protocol)

You can pull up FTP servers right on your screen (just type their addresses into the Go→Connect to Server dialog box). To put files *onto* an FTP server, though, you need a shareware program like RBrowser or Fetch.

Help and Support

At the desktop, choose Help→Mac Help. In other programs, the Help command is generally at the right end of your menus, exactly as in Windows.

Hibernation

The Mac can't hibernate at all, as modern PCs do, cutting all power but remembering what programs and documents you had open for a faster restart later. Sleep mode is the closest it gets (see "Standby Mode" in this appendix).

Internet Explorer

Microsoft abandoned Internet Explorer for Mac several years ago—right after Apple introduced its own, better, faster browser called Safari. If you come across a site that *requires* Internet Explorer, you can still download the program from *www.mactopia. com*.

Internet Options

You find the options for your Web browser by choosing Safari→Preferences.

IRQs

They don't exist on the Mac.

Java

This interpreter of tiny programs written in the Java programming language is alive and well in Mac OS X. Java programs run fine in all Mac Web browsers.

Keyboard Control Panel

You can make exactly the same kinds of settings—and more—on the Keyboard Panel of System Preferences.

Logging In

As it turns out, the multiple-accounts feature of Mac OS X is extremely similar to that of Windows 2000 and Windows XP. In either case, you can, if you wish, create a requirement to login with a name and password before using the computer. This arrangement keeps separate the documents, email, and settings of each person who uses the computer. (Chapter 12 tells all.)

Mail Control Panel

Mac OS X comes with its own email program (see Chapter 10); all of its settings are contained within the program.

Maximize Button

On the Mac, clicking the Zoom button (the green button at the upper-left corner of a window) does something like the Maximize button in Windows: It makes your window larger. On the Mac, however, clicking the Zoom button rarely makes the window expand to fill the entire screen. Instead, the window grows—or *shrinks*—precisely enough to enclose its contents.

Menus

Here's one of the biggest differences between the Mac and Windows: On the Macintosh, there's only one menu bar, always at the very top of the screen. The menus change depending on the program and the window you're using, but the point is that the menu bar is no longer inside each window you open.

Tip: Just because you don't see the little underlines in the menus doesn't mean you can't operate all of the menus from the keyboard, as in Windows. See page 115 for details.

Minimize Button

You can minimize a Mac OS X window to the Dock, just the way you would minimize a Windows window to the taskbar. You do so by double-clicking its title bar, pressing ⌘-M, choosing Window→Minimize Window, or clicking the yellow Minimize button at the top left of a window. (Restore the window by clicking its icon on the Dock.)

Mouse Control Panel

The equivalent settings await you in the Keyboard & Mouse panel of system Preferences.

My Computer

The Mac's Computer window is very similar (choose Go→Computer), in that it shows the icons of all disks (hard drive, CD, and so on). On the other hand, it shows *only* the disks that are actually inserted or connected (see "Disks").

My Documents, My Pictures, My Music

The equivalent buckets for your everyday documents, music files, and pictures are the Documents, Pictures, and Music folders in your Home folder.

My Network Places

To see your "network neighborhood," click the Network icon in the Sidebar (the panel at the left side of every Finder window). Click My Network. All of the Macs and PCs on your network show up in the resulting list (see page 140).

Network Neighborhood

See the previous entry.

Notepad

There's no Mac OS X Notepad program. But give Stickies a try (page 433).

Personal Web Server

If you're technically proficient, you can turn your Mac into a Web site. On the Sharing pane of System Preferences, turn on Personal Web Sharing. Any HTML documents you put into your Home→Sites folder are now available on your network or the Web.

Phone and Modem Options Control Panel

To find the modem settings for your Mac, open System Preferences. Click Network, choose Internal Modem from the Show pop-up menu, and click the Modem tab.

Power Options

To control when your Mac goes to sleep and (if it's a laptop) how much power it uses, use the Energy Saver panel of System Preferences (Chapter 13).

Printer Sharing

To share a USB inkjet printer with other Macs on the network, open the Sharing panel of System Preferences on the Mac with the printer. Turn on Printer Sharing.

To use the shared printer from across the network, open the document you want to print, choose File→Print, and choose the name of the shared printer from the first pop-up menu.

Printers and Faxes

For a list of your printers, open the Printer Setup Utility in your Aplications→Utilities folder. For details on faxing, see "Faxing."

PrntScrn Key

You capture pictures of your Mac screen by pressing Shift-⌘-3 (for a full-screen grab) or Shift-⌘-4 (to grab a selected portion of the screen). Details on page 199.

Program Files Folder

The Applications folder (Go→Applications) is like the Program Files folder in Windows—except that you're not discouraged from opening it and double-clicking things. On the Macintosh, every program bears its true name. Microsoft Word is called Microsoft Word, not WINWORD.EXE.

Properties Dialog Box

You can call up something very similar for any *icon* (file, folder, program, disk, printer) by highlighting its icon and then choosing File→Get Info. But objects in Macintosh *programs* generally don't contain Properties dialog boxes.

Recycle Bin

Mac OS X has a Trash icon at the end of the Dock. In general, it works exactly like the Windows Recycle Bin—and why not, since the Macintosh Trash was Microsoft's inspiration?—but there are a couple of differences. The Macintosh never auto-empties it, for example. That job is up to you (the simplest way is to Control-click it, or right-click it, and choose Empty Trash from the shortcut menu).

The Mac never bothers you with an "Are you sure?" message when you throw something into the Trash, either. In fact, it doesn't even ask for confirmation when you *empty* the Trash (at least, not when you empty it by Control-clicking). The Mac interrupts you for permission only when you choose File→Empty Trash—and you can even turn that confirmation off, if you like (in Finder→Preferences).

To put icons into the Trash, drag them there, or just highlight them and then press ⌘-Delete.

Regional and Language Options Control Panel

The close equivalent is the International pane of System Preferences.

Registry

There is no registry. Let the celebration begin!

Run Command

The equivalent command line is Terminal (page 457).

Safe Mode

You can press the Shift key during startup to suppress the loading of certain software libraries, but Mac OS X's "safe mode" (page 474) isn't quite as stripped-down as Windows' Safe Mode.

ScanDisk

Just like Windows, the Mac automatically scans and, if necessary, repairs its hard drive every time your machine starts up. To run such a check on command, open Disk Utility (located in the Applications→Utilities folder), and then click the First Aid tab.

Scheduled Tasks

To schedule a task to take place unattended, use the *launchd* command in Terminal (geeks only), or one of the scheduling programs listed at *www.versiontracker.com*.

Scrap Files

On the Mac, they're called *clipping files,* and they're even more widely compatible. You create them the same way: Drag some highlighted text, or a graphic, out of a program's window and onto the desktop. There it becomes an independent clipping file that you can drag back in—to the same window, or a different one.

Screen Saver

The Mac's screen savers are impressive. Open System Preferences and click the Desktop & Screen Saver icon.

Search

In Mac OS X Tiger, you have the ultimate file-searching tool: Spotlight (page 65). Get psyched!

To find Web sites, use the Google Search box at the top of the Safari browser.

Shortcut Menus

They work exactly the same as they do in Windows. You produce a shortcut menu by Control-clicking things like icons, list items, and so on. (If you have a two-button mouse, feel free to right-click instead of using the Control key.)

Shortcuts

On the Mac, they're known as *aliases.* See page 57.

Sounds and Audio Devices

Open System Preferences; click the Sound icon. You may also want to explore the Audio MIDI Setup program in Applications→Utilities.

Speech Control Panel

The Mac's center for speech recognition and text-to-speech is the Speech pane of System Preferences. As Chapter 14 makes clear, the Mac can read aloud any text in any program, and it lets you operate all menus, buttons, and dialog boxes by voice alone.

Standby Mode

On the Mac, it's called Sleep, but it's the same idea. You make a Mac laptop sleep by closing the lid. You make a Mac desktop sleep by choosing →Sleep, or just walking away; the Mac will go to sleep on its own, according to the settings in the Energy Saver pane of System Preferences.

Start Menu

There's no Start menu in Mac OS X. Instead, you stash the icons of the programs, documents, and folders you use frequently onto the Dock at the edge of the screen, or into the Sidebar at the left edge of every Finder window.

Exactly as with the Start menu, you can rearrange these icons (drag them horizontally), or remove the ones you don't use often (drag them away from the Dock and then release). To add new icons of your own, just drag them into place (applications go to the left of the Dock's divider line, documents and folders to the right).

StartUp Folder

To make programs launch automatically at startup, include them in the list of Login Items in the System Preferences→Accounts pane.

System Control Panel

The Mac has no central equivalent of the System window on a Windows PC. But its functions have analogs here:

- **General tab.** To find out your Mac OS X version number and the amount of memory on your Mac, choose →About This Mac.

- **Computer Name tab.** Open System Preferences, click Sharing, and edit your computer's network names here.

- **Hardware tab.** The closest thing the Mac has to the Device Manager is System Profiler (in your Applications→Utilities folder). See page 456.

- **Advanced tab.** In Mac OS X, you can't easily adjust your virtual memory, processor scheduling, or user profile information.

- **System Restore tab.** This feature isn't available in Mac OS X.

- **Automatic Updates tab.** Open System Preferences and click Software Updates.

- **Remote tab.** These features are unavailable in Mac OS X.

System Tray

The perfect Mac OS X equivalent of the System Tray (also called the notification area) is the row of *menulets* at the upper-right corner of your screen; see page 18.

Taskbar

Mac OS X doesn't have a taskbar, but it does have something very close: the Dock (Chapter 3). Open programs are indicated by a small black triangle beneath their icons on the Dock. If you hold down your cursor on one of these icons (or Control-click it, or right-click it), you'll get a pop-up list of the open windows in that program, exactly as in Windows XP.

Control-clicking a folder or disk icon on the Dock is even more useful. It produces a pop-up menu of everything inside that disk or folder—a terrific form of X-ray vision that has no equivalent in Windows.

On the other hand, some conventions never die. Much as on Windows, you cycle through the various open programs on your Dock by holding down the ⌘ key and pressing Tab repeatedly.

Taskbar and Start Menu Control Panel

To configure your Dock (the equivalent of the taskbar and Start menu), choose ⌘→Dock→Dock Preferences, or click the Dock icon in System Preferences.

"Three-Fingered Salute"

Instead of pressing Ctrl-Alt-Delete to jettison a stuck program on the Mac, you press Option-⌘-Esc. A Force Quit dialog box appears. Click the program you want to toss, click Force Quit, confirm your choice, and then relaunch the program to get on with your day.

ToolTips

Small, yellow identifying balloons pop up on the Mac almost as often as they do in Windows. Just point to a toolbar icon or truncated file name without clicking. (There's no way to turn these labels off.)

TweakUI

The closest equivalent for this free, downloadable, but unsupported Microsoft utility for tweaking the look of your PC is TinkerTool for Mac OS X. You can find it at, and download it from, *www.versiontracker.com.*

User Accounts Control Panel

Like Windows 2000 and Windows XP, Mac OS X was designed from square one to be a multiuser operating system, keeping the files, mail, and settings of each person separate. You set up and manage these accounts in System Preferences→Accounts (Chapter 12).

Window Edges

You can enlarge or shrink a Mac OS X window only by dragging its lower-right corner—not its edges.

Windows (or WINNT) Folder

Mac OS X's operating system resides in a folder simply called System, which sits in your main hard drive window. Exactly as in recent Windows versions, you're forbidden to add, remove, or change anything inside. Also as in Windows, most of it is invisible anyway.

Windows Logo Key

The Mac has no equivalent for the ⊞ key on most PC keyboards.

Tip: If you hook up a USB Windows keyboard to your Mac, the ⊞ key behaves like the Mac's ⌘ key.

Windows Media Player

The Mac comes with individual programs for playing multimedia files:

- **QuickTime Player** (Chapter 14) to play back movies and sounds.

- **iTunes** (Chapter 8) to play CDs, Internet radio, MP3 files, and other audio files. (iTunes for Mac, like its Windows brother, can even *create* MP3 files.)

- **DVD Player** (Chapter 8) for playing DVDs. If your Mac does, in fact, have a DVD player built in, this program is in the Applications folder.

Windows Media Player *is,* however, available in a Macintosh version, paradoxical though that may sound. You can download it from *www.microsoft.com/mac.*

Windows Messenger

Mac OS X's voice and videoconferencing software is called iChat, and it's described on page 304.

WordPad

The TextEdit program (in the Applications folder) is a barebones word processor like WordPad. It can even open and save Word files, as WordPad can.

Zip Files

Zip files exist on the Mac, too, and you create them almost the same way: Control-click (or right-click) a file or folder and choose Create Archive from the shortcut menu. See page 128 for a discussion of software compression standards on the Mac.

Running Windows on Macintosh

Freaky, yes, but true: If your Mac model debuted in 2006 or later—a Mac Mini, iMac, MacBook or MacBook Pro laptop, or whatever—it contains an Intel processor (either a Core Solo or Core Duo, the successor to the Pentium). And that means that it can run Windows. And Unix and Linux, too, for that matter. You're the proud owner of the first computer that can run 100 percent of the world's desktop software.

Here's how it works.

Boot Camp: Your Mac as Windows PC

In April 2006, Apple shocked the Cult of Macintosh by releasing what seemed to be a heretical piece of software called Boot Camp. Its sole purpose: to let you install Windows XP on an Intel-based Mac, so that you can run any of the tens of thousands of Windows-only programs.

(It's supposedly a beta version—not quite finished—of a feature that will be built into Leopard, the upcoming 10.5 version of Mac OS X. But it works great.)

Some people hated the idea—and didn't see the point. Wouldn't Boot Camp open up the Mac to the nightmare world of viruses and spyware that PC owners confront every day? (The answer, by the way, is yes. If you install Windows on your Mac, you must also install Windows antivirus and antispyware software to protect that half of the computer. The Mac side is still unaffected by Windows viruses, however.)

But think of all the potential switchers who are tempted by the Mac's sleek looks, yet worry about leaving Windows behind entirely. Or the people who love Apple's iLife programs, but have jobs that rely on Microsoft Access, Outlook or some other piece of Windows corporate-ware. Even true-blue Mac fans occasionally look longingly at some of the Windows-only software (and Internet Explorer-only Web sites) they thought they'd never be able to use.

Boot Camp is a free download for Mac OS X Tiger (10.4.6 or later) from *www.apple. com/macosx/bootcamp*. It runs on any Mac containing an Intel chip.

It comes with a PDF document containing installation instructions. Follow them explicitly—don't skip any of the steps, including the part about backing up your Mac before you begin.

Double-click the icon called BootCampAssistant.pkg (on the downloaded "disk image") to open the Boot Camp assistant. Right up front, you're asked to insert a blank CD, which the Boot Camp installer fills with Windows-compatible drivers for your Mac's components. After the burn, set this CD aside.

Next, you're asked to *partition*—subdivide—your hard drive, setting aside a certain amount of space for Windows and all the PC software you'll install (Figure B-1).

Tip: This is technical, but important: If, at this point, you choose a size less than 32 gigabytes for the Windows partition, the Windows installer will, later in the installation, let you choose the unappetizingly named scheme called *FAT32* as the hard drive format for Windows. The advantage of doing so is that, when it's all over, you'll be able to drag files back and forth from the Windows partition to the Mac partition.

(This works only when you're in Mac OS X; when you're in Windows, you can't see the Mac side of the hard drive without a commercial program like MacDrive [macdrive.com].)

If you choose the NTFS scheme instead—a requirement if the size is over 32 gigabytes—you can see what's on the Windows partition, but can't add, remove, or change any files.

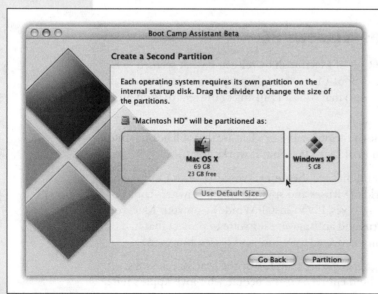

Figure B-1:
The partitioning process does not involve erasing your whole hard drive. In fact, if you ever tire of the Boot Camp experience, you can un-partition your hard drive using the same Boot Camp installer, once again without having to erase it.

Note, by the way, that Boot Camp requires a drive that hasn't already been partitioned.

The slider lets you control how much space you want to dedicate to the Windows side.

You'll also be prompted to install your own copy of Windows XP (Home or Pro edition), Service Pack 2. No other version of Windows, no multi-disk installation, and no "update CD" will work.

The installation process takes about an hour. Most of that time is spent running Windows's own installer (Figure B-2).

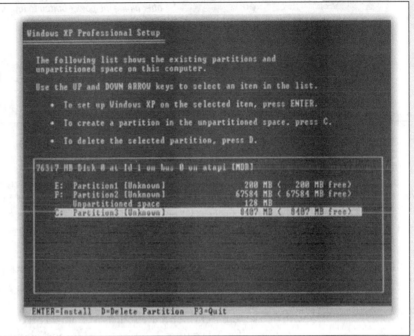

Figure 14-36:
The trickiest part of the Boot Camp installation takes place this Windows installer screen. Here, you're supposed to press your up- and down-arrow keys to highlight a partition's name—the one that you'll want to contain your copy of Windows.

Be sure to select the one labeled C:!

Once the computer restarts and you see—gasp—Windows on the screen, insert the CD you burned at the beginning of the process. (You may have to eject the Windows CD first, using the usual Windows method—that is, by visiting My Computer.)

Then insert the CD you burned at the beginning of the process. Apple's Macintosh-drivers installation should open automatically. When this wizard is complete, you'll have Windows-on-Macintosh drivers for things like networking, wireless, graphics card, and so on.

When it's all over, you can choose an operating system each time you start up the computer; just press Option key as the Mac is starting up. Proceed as described in Figure B-3.

Or, if you switch only rarely, here's a way to specify which OS you want to run *most* of the time: open the Startup Disk pane of System Preferences and select either Mac OS X or Windows as your "most of the time" operating system. Weirdly enough, an identical Startup Disk icon appears in the Windows XP Control Panel, too, so that you can switch systems from either "side."

Either way, if you choose Windows, then you really do start up in Windows. You can install and run Windows programs, utilities, and even games; you'll discover that they run really fast and well. Even games do well.

Figure B-3:
To turn your Mac into a PC (or vice versa), press the Option key just after hitting the power button to turn it on (or just after using the Restart command). When these two icons appear, click the one you want and press Enter.

Parallels: Windows in a Window

The problem with Boot Camp is that every time you switch to or from Windows, you have to close down everything you were working on and restart the computer—and reversing the process when you're done. You lose two or three minutes each way. And you can't copy and paste between Mac and Windows programs.

There is another way: an $80 utility called Parallels Workstation for Mac OS X (*www. parallels.com*). It lets you run Windows and Mac OS X simultaneously; Windows hangs out in a window of its own, while the Mac is running Mac OS X (Figure B-4). It's something like the old, dog-slow emulation software known as Microsoft VirtualPC, with one key difference: speed. Parallels is about 90 percent as fast as Boot Camp—not fast enough for 3-D games, but plenty fast for just about everything else.

FREQUENTLY ASKED QUESTION

Windows on Mac—Minus the Windows Keyboard

A reminder for anyone running Windows on a Mac:

First, the keyboard shortcuts aren't the same. Actually, they're *mostly* the same, but remember to substitute the Ctrl key for the ⌘ key. So in Windows programs, Copy, Save, and Print are Ctrl-C, Ctrl-S, and Ctrl-P. (Your Mac has both ⌘ and Ctrl keys.) Similarly, the Alt key is the Windows equivalent of the Option key.

If you're using a MacBook laptop, which has only one mouse-click button, you may wonder how you're supposed to "right-click" things on the screen.

Answer: once something is highlighted, press Shift-10 to open its shortcut menu.

If you're a Windows veteran, you may also wonder what to do about Ctrl-Alt-Delete, the time-honored Windows keystroke for force quitting a locked-up program.

Answer: assign it to a different key, like F8, using a program like Microsoft's ReMapKey (available from this book's "Missing CD" page at *www.missingmanuals.com*).

Once again, you have to supply your own copy of Windows for the installation process. This time, though, it doesn't have to be Windows XP. It can be *any* version of Windows, all the way back to Windows 3.1—or even Linux, FreeBSD, Solaris, OS/2 or MS-DOS.

Figure B-4:
The strangest sight you ever did see: Mac OS X and Windows XP.

On the same screen. At the same time.

Once Parallels is installed, you start it up as you would any other program: by double-clicking its icon in your Applications folder (or clicking its icon on your Dock). Your "virtual Windows" opens up in its own window. At this point, you can install Windows programs and do Windows work as usual—or even copy and paste text and graphics between Windows programs and Mac programs. You can be working on a design in iWork, duck into a Microsoft Access database (Windows only), look up an address, copy it, and paste it into Microsoft Word for the Mac.

And what if you can't decide whether to use Boot Camp (fast and feature-complete, but requires restarting) or Parallels (fast and no restarting, but no 3-D games)? No problem—install both. They coexist beautifully on a single Mac.

Index

Index

Colophon

This book was written and edited in Microsoft Word 2004 on various Macs.

The screenshots were captured with Ambrosia Software's Snapz Pro X *(www. ambrosiasw.com)*. Adobe Photoshop CS and Macromedia Freehand MX *(www.adobe. com)* were called in as required for touching them up.

The book was designed and laid out in Adobe InDesign 3.0 on a PowerBook G4 and Power Mac G5. The fonts used include Formata (as the sans-serif family) and Minion (as the serif body face). To provide the and ⌘ symbols, custom fonts were created using Macromedia Fontographer.

The book was then generated as an Adobe Acrobat PDF file for proofreading, indexing, and final transmission to the printing plant.